THE SEX OFFENDER

NEW INSIGHTS,

TREATMENT INNOVATIONS AND

LEGAL DEVELOPMENTS

VOLUME II

Edited by
Barbara K. Schwartz, Ph.D.
and
Henry R. Cellini, Ph.D.

CRI Civic Research Institute
4490 U.S. Route 27 • P.O. Box 585 • Kingston, NJ 08528

Copyright © 1997

By Civic Research Institute, Inc.
Kingston, New Jersey 08528

Printed in the United States of America

Library of Congress Cataloging in Publication Data
The sex offender: Volume II: New Insights, treatment innovations and legal practice/Barbara K. Schwartz, Henry R. Cellini

ISBN 1-887554-02-5

Library of Congress Catalog Card Number 95-70893

Acknowledgments

The editors wish to thank the publisher, Arthur Rosenfeld, for his support of numerous projects designed to support and upgrade correctional treatment. To Lori Jacobs whose timely and meticulous attention to the production of this book have greatly facilitated our efforts go our heartfelt thanks. We would also thank our family, friends and co-workers at Justice Resource Institute and TriCorp for their support and encouragement.

"To the loving memory of Henry and Joan Cellini and William and Edith Cellini and Anne Lenore Liser."

Preface

Sex offender treatment in the 1990s has been characterized by rapid growth in an atmosphere of increasingly reactionary and politically motivated public policies which, although they may be well intended, have little proven efficacy and may indeed increase the danger to the public. Most of these measures, such as public notification, are not part of a comprehensive systems approach. For example, although the public may feel comforted by the fact that they now know that their neighbor is a sex offender, few citizens realize that unless that individual is on community supervision, little can legally be done if that individual engages in high-risk behavior. Parole boards have become increasingly reluctant to release sex offenders under their jurisdiction, and yet this is clearly the safest way to return these individuals to society.

As an ultimate punishment, California recently passed mandatory physical or chemical castration for repeat child molesters. As conviction for a sex offense begins to carry more onerous implications and sanctions that punish the family as well as the offender, more sex offenders will plea bargain to other crimes and fewer intrafamilial offenders will be reported. Secrecy feeds the deviance of sex offenders and these new public policies encourage that secrecy.

While legislatures blithely enact these obviously controversial statutes — none of which have been well researched — controversy continues over the efficacy of treatment. Surely this is nothing new in the mental health community. There is very little agreement on the effectiveness of any mental health treatment other than psychopharmacological approaches. However, few voices are heard advocating for the elimination of the mental health professions. In fact, the federal government just mandated insurance companies to treat mental health care in the same way that they treat physical health care. Research in the field of mental health is difficult and often can be questioned on ethical grounds. Do you study a suicide prevention approach by denying half the patients care? How do you administer a psychological placebo?

Sex offender treatment is even more difficult to study because it is not a modality that is offered in settings which can afford or even value comprehensive research. Few corrections departments are able to devote funds necessary to carrying out the elaborate studies needed to make definitive comments about the efficacy of treatment. Furthermore, they would certainly be open to criticism if they undertook to systematically deny treatment to certain individuals who requested it while providing it to others in the name of sound research and then these individuals went out and reoffended. Most sex offender treatment is offered by private practitioners who are not in a position to conduct research and would not have access to a matched sample control group.

The issue is further complicated by the rapid growth and change in the field which seeks to refine treatment and increase its efficacy. However, good long-term follow-up research demands that a group is given treatment and then followed for a number of years. The study that is then generated will obviously be reporting on a methodology that is years behind the current treatment practices. Most other mental health research can study treatment effects which occur within a matter of weeks or months.

However, as long as recidivism within one's entire lifetime is the only criteria used to judge the effectiveness of treatment, research will be left with this quandary.

Another problem is one of double standards when it comes to judging sex offender treatment effectiveness. In a 1995 report by the National Institute of Justice, entitled " 'Boot Camp' Drug Treatment and Aftercare Intervention: An Evaluative Review," researchers reviewed studies from 11 states and found that only three programs showed lower recidivism rates for boot camp graduates. They stated, "The research just discussed leads to the conclusion that, at this point in time, there is no persuasive evidence that boot caps have a measurable or long-term impact on the recidivism of program participants" (p. 30). Yet the report goes on to support the concept using Canadian studies of effective correctional programs and making a number of constructive recommendations. Another National Institute of Justice study, "Evaluation of Drug Treatment in Local Corrections" (1996), concluded that despite the fact that two of the five programs showed no difference in recidivism, "these programs had a modest positive effect on the probability but not the timing of recidivism . . ." (xi). These studies are referenced not to question the efficacy of the methods but to point out how standards of "success" are highly subjective.

In contrast to these two reviews of research, the United States General Accounting Office published a report entitled "Sex Offender Treatment: Research Results Inconclusive About What Works to Reduce Recidivism" (1996), which reviewed reviews of research. This was an interesting though questionable approach as there was much duplication of studies in these reviews. The authors state that "only two reviews attempted to quantify the overall benefit of treatment programs" (p. 7), and both of these reported positive results. They quote the Canadian Solicitor General as reporting that treatment could reduce recidivism from 25% to 10–15%, they reference the "only known statistical aggregation" study's finding that treatment can result in 8 fewer sex offenders per 100. Given an average recidivism between 25% and 40%, which has been reported in a number of studies, this would reduce recidivism from one-third to one-fifth. In some states with the popular "one-two strikes, you're out," a reduction of eight recidivists would represent a dollar savings of $12 million plus possibly hundreds of victims. Yet the study concluded that the data was inconclusive, which is interesting in light of the conclusions of the two previously discussed studies.

The need for well-funded and planned research with realistic goals and an established criteria for judging success is well established. However, well-designed studies do exist which continue to be minimized in the minds of the public and among many mental health professionals not familiar with the field. This volume includes a number of chapters with valuable research which has been conducted to validate theoretical constructs. It is hoped that readers will be enlightened by new insights into the management and supervision of sex offenders through the work and research of the contributing authors who represent a wide range of backgrounds and special interests in this area.

About the Authors

Debra Baker, M.A.

Ms. Baker received her master's degree in counseling from Rider College. She has directed a sex offender treatment program for the New Jersey Department of Corrections and was a Unit Director for the Washington Department of Corrections Sex Offender Treatment Program. Later in her career she directed treatment at the Special Commitment Center for sexually violent predators in Monroe, Washington. Currently she is the Director of Justice Resource Institute's Intensive Treatment Program for the Massachusetts Department of Corrections Sex Offender Treatment Program. She is also a consultant for the National Institute of Corrections.

Larry L. Bench, M.A.

Mr. Bench is a research consultant for the Utah Department of Corrections. He holds degrees in philosophy, psychology, and sociology from the University of Utah, where he teaches classes in criminology and criminal justice. Mr. Bench is currently a Ph.D. candidate in the Department of Sociology at the University of Utah. His major research interests include sex offender recidivism, prison classification validation, and cognitive restructuring.

Stephen Brake, Ph.D.

Dr. Brake received his doctorate in psychology from the University of Texas in 1976. He is a licensed psychologist who has worked with sex offenders in private practice in Colorado since 1988. He also works as a psychologist for the State of Colorado Office of Youth Services and has served as a consultant for various agencies in working with sex offenders.

John Bergman, M.A., R.D.T.

Mr. Bergman is a registered drama therapist who specializes in working with sexual and violent offenders. He received his master's degree in theater from Humboldt State College and served as adjunct faculty at the University of Iowa. He is the founder and director of The Geese Theater, which operates in the United States and England. He conducts ongoing programs for Justice Resource Institute in Boston, the San Francisco Sheriff's Department, and the Vermont Department of Corrections. He has trained internationally, most recently in Rumania, Australia, and South America.

Kurt Bumby, Ph.D.

Dr. Bumby received his doctorate in clinical psychology from the University of Nebraska-Lincoln, as part of the Forensic Psychology Specialty Track of the Law and Psychology Program. At present, Dr. Bumby is employed by the Missouri Department of Mental Health at Fulton State Hospital and is a Clinical Assistant Professor of Psychiatry and Neurology at the University of Missouri-Columbia School of Medicine. In addition, he is the contracted psychologist for the Adolescent Sexual Offender Evaluation and Treatment Program for the Thirteenth Judicial Circuit in Boone County, Missouri. Dr. Bumby specializes in the assessment and treatment of sexual offenders and has worked in both state and federal correctional systems and in forensic hospital settings.

Nancy Halstenson Bumby, Ph.D.

Dr. Bumby received her doctorate in clinical psychology from the University of Nebraska-Lincoln. She is a Clinical Assistant Professor of Psychiatry and Neurology at the University of Missouri-Columbia School of Medicine and provides outpatient services to a wide range of clientele at the Green Meadows Psychiatry Clinic. She is also employed by the Missouri Department of Mental Health at Fulton State Hospital, where she is involved in the research and outcome evaluation project of a program which treats personality disordered and sexually offending patients. Dr. Bumby specializes in adolescent issues, as well as eating disorders. She has worked with sexual abuse victims as well as adolescent sexual offenders.

Nicolas Carrasco, Ph.D.

Dr. Carrasco is a clinical psychologist in private practice in Austin, Texas. He received his bachelor's degree in psychology from St. Edwards University in Austin and his Ph.D. in clinical psychology from the University of Texas, at Austin. He works primarily with low-income children and their families. Dr. Carrasco also works with Spanish-speaking adult sex-offenders and with adolescent sex offenders. He serves as consultant for a girls residential treatment center in Austin and for the Arizona Department of Juvenile Corrections. He recently open his own residential facility for treating delinquent adolescent boys.

Henry R. Cellini, Ph.D.

Dr. Cellini received his doctorate from Southern Illinois University in counseling psychology. He is on the faculty of the University of New Mexico and is the president of TriCorp, a consulting company that specializes in providing training and treatment materials related to corrections, drugs, gangs, violence, and sexual assault. He has written widely in the field and provided training and consultation throughout the country. He is the co-editor of The Sex Offender: Corrections, Treatment and Legal Practice, the author of Alcohol, Tobacco and Other Drugs of Abuse, and contributor to Managing Delinquency Programs That Work and is currently authoring a book for the American Correctional Association on managing juvenile offenders in adult corrections.

Fred Cohen, L.L.B., L.L.M.

Mr. Cohen received his undergraduate degree from Temple University and his law degree from Yale. He has served on the law school faculty of the University of Texas, New York University, and the universities of Iowa, Arizona, and Puerto Rico. Currently he is professor of Criminal Justice at the State University of New York at Albany. Mr. Cohen is also the editor-in-chief of the Criminal Law Bulletin and co-editor of the Correctional Law Report and the Community Corrections Report. He is the monitor of the federal consent decree for the Ohio Department of Corrections.

Emily Coleman, M.A.

Ms. Coleman has nearly 20 years of clinical and research experience in the assessment and treatment of sex offenders. She received her master's degree in behavior modification in 1975 from Southern Illinois University and then began work on the first major National Institute of Mental Health grant to research the treatment of sexual aggressives through the University of Tennessee. Subsequently, she developed and directed sex offender programs for the Colorado Department of Corrections and the Bronx-Lebanon Hospital Forensic Clinic in New York City. For the last eight years, Ms. Coleman has been the Director of the Sex Offender Program at Clinical & Support Options, Inc.,a community mental health center in Greenfield, Massachusetts. Ms. Coleman lives in the country with her two horses, Flying Rooster and Indian Summer; her therapy dog, Abra; and her cat, Wild Otto.

Cindy L.S. Crimmins

Ms. Crimmins received her master's degree from the University of Minnesota with an emphasis in criminology. She is currently a doctoral student in sociology and the research assistant for the Juvenile Sex Offender Evaluation Project at the Program in Human Sexuality, Department of Family Practice and Community Health, Medical, University of Minnesota.

Susan Erickson

Ms. Erickson has been involved in the assessment and treatment of adult and adolescent sex offenders in correctional and hospital settings. She is currently a Ph.D. candidate in the Department of Counseling Psychology at the University of Utah. Her current research focus is the development of a classification system for the cognitive factors of sexual assault.

Dewey Ertz, Ed.D.

Dr. Ertz is a licensed psychologist, school psychologist, and marriage and family therapist in private practice who specializes in the treatment of sexual deviance, substance abuse, and self-destructive behaviors in American Indians. He received his degrees from the University of South Dakota. He has taught a variety of courses at the college level and presented at numerous conferences.

Diana Garza-Louis, M.Ed.

Ms. Garza-Louis is a licensed professional counselor, a licensed marriage and family therapist, and a registered sex offender treatment provider. She received her master's in degree in education at Southwest Texas State University in San Marcos, Texas and established her private practice in Austin, Texas. She has worked with sexual offenders since 1984 and provides Spanish-language services to offenders, victims, and families. Ms. Garza-Louis is coauthor of Ventura: A Treatment Manual and its Spanish version, *Un Manual Para Tratamiento de Agresores Sexuales*. She has presented on treatment for sexual offenders both nationally and internationally.

Mark Gould, Ph.D.

Dr. Gould is the clinical director of Cliffs House Program of Justice Resource Institute in Meridan, CT. Cliffs House is a residential, adolescent sex offender program. Dr.

Gould has evaluated and treated sex offenders since 1973. He earned his Doctorate in Clinical Psychology from the Fielding Institute. He also received degrees in psychology from the University of Michigan and Duquesne University.

R. Karl Hanson, Ph.D.

Dr. Hanson received his doctorate in clinical psychology from the University of Waterloo in 1986. He has worked for the Ontario Ministry of Correctional Services, York University (Toronto), and the Clarke Institute of Psychiatry. Since 1991, he has been a Senior Research Officer with the Department of the Solicitor General of Canada, and an Adjunct Research Professor at Carleton University (Ottawa, Ontario). His research focuses on the psychological assessment of sexual offenders and male batterers.

Stephen M. Hudson, Ph.D., Dip. Clin. Psych.

Dr. Hudson is a senior lecturer in clinical psychology at the University of Canterbury, Christchurch, New Zealand, and is the consultant psychologist to the Kia Marama Sex Offender Treatment Program at Rolleston Prison. He has been treating sex offenders and carrying out research in the area of sexual aggression since 1983. He is co-editor of The Juvenile Sex Offender (with H. E. Barbaree and W. L. Marshall).

M. K. Johnson, Ph.D.

Dr. Johnson received her doctorate from Virginia Technological Institute. She did her internship with Dr. William Murphy at the Professional Psychology Internship Consortium. She has worked with adolescent sex offenders and sexually and physically abused juveniles at Project Trust. In 1991 she became staff psychologist at the Veterans Affairs Medical Center in Salem, Virginia, where she started the Comprehensive Abuse and Assault Program, which includes a program for sex offenders who are 70 years of age and older.

Scott Johnson, M.A.

Mr. Johnson received his master's degree in counseling and psychological services from St. Mary's College in Minneapolis, Minnesota. He has worked with sex offenders at Project Pathfinder and Alpha Services. In addition, he has worked in the area of domestic violence through several agencies. Currently he is a Sex Offender Assessor with the Minnesota Department of Corrections. He is the author of Man to Man: When Your Partner Says "No" and When "I Love You" Turns Violent and has presented throughout the country on issues of relationship violence and sexual assault.

Stephen P. Kramer, Ph.D.

Dr. Kramer received his Ph.D. in psychology in 1979 at the University of Utah. Since that time he has directed a prison-based sex offender for 5 years and a community-based sex offender program for 10 years and has served as Director of Clinical Services for the Utah Department of Corrections. He has also served as forensic consultant to several juvenile sex offender programs and has provided expert witness services in numerous cases. He is credited with pioneering the use of phallometric testing in the state of Utah.

Barb D. Kraemer, Ph.D.

Dr. Kraemer is a licensed psychologist who has worked in the social services field for approximately 10 years. She is currently employed as a clinical psychologist at Mille

Lacs Academy, a residential, not-for-profit, juvenile treatment center in Onamia, Minnesota.

Julie McCormack, B.Sc.(Hons.)

Ms. McCormack is a postgraduate clinical psychology student at the University of Canterbury, Christchurch, New Zealand. She is particularly interested in the application of social cognitive models to interpersonal functioning in sex offenders.

Michael Miner, Ph.D.

Dr. Miner received his Ph.D. from St. Louis University. He is currently assistant professor and psychologist in the Department of Family Practice and Community Health, Medical School, University of Minnesota. He has been involved in sex offender treatment and research since 1986, first serving as a research psychologist for California's Sex Offender Treatment and Evaluation Project and then moving to the program in human sexuality at the University of Minnesota in 1992. He has published numerous papers and book chapters on relapse prevention with sex offenders, sex offender treatment outcome, and forensic and sex offender assessment. His current research focuses on evaluation of juvenile sex offender treatment and the factors associated with sexual abuse and aggression in adolescence.

Rebecca Palmer, M.S.

Ms. Palmer is currently the Director of Programs and Administration at The Center for Contextual Change, Ltd. She did her postgraduate training in marriage and family therapy at the Institute for Juvenile Research at the University of Illinois, where she currently serves as adjunct faculty in the Family Systems Program. Ms. Palmer is also adjunct faculty at the Illinois School for Professional Psychology, where she teaches the Sex Offender and Couples and Family Therapy. She has trained nationally in the areas of marital therapy with survivors of sexual assault, parenting sexually abused and reactive children, working with abusive family systems, and sex offender evaluation and treatment. She has also consulted on sexual abuse by clergy.

Stephen Price, B.A.

Mr. Price is a therapist with the Massachusetts Department of Corrections Statewide Sex Offender Treatment Program operated by Justice Resource Institute. He interned as a pastoral counselor at the Worcester Pastoral Counseling Center and has worked with sex offenders and mentally ill offenders for the South Carolina Department of Corrections and the Massachusetts Treatment Center. Currently he doing graduate work at the University of Massachusetts.

Sandra B. Salisbury, B.A.

Ms. Salisbury is currently employed as a psychometrist and research analyst at Mille Lacs Academy. Her areas of specialty include data analysis and research design.

Sandra L. Schneider, Ph.D.

Ms. Schneider received her doctorate from the University of Wisconsin, Madison. She is a cognitive psychologist and associate professor of psychology at the University of

South Florida. Presently she is co-principal investigator on a National Institute of Mental Health grant to study of the cognitive representation of sex offenders.

Anita Schlank, Ph.D.

Dr. Schlank received her degrees in clinical psychology with an emphasis on forensic psychology from the University of Nebraska-Lincoln. She is currently the Clinical Director of the Minnesota Sexual Psychopathic Personality Treatment Center in Moose Lake, MN.

Barbara K. Schwartz, Ph.D.

Dr. Schwartz received her degrees from the University of New Mexico and the New School for Social Research in New York City. She is a licensed psychologist and certified mental health counselor who has specialized in the treatment of sex offenders since 1971. She has directed statewide treatment programs for corrections departments in New Mexico and Washington State. Currently she is the Clinical Director for Sex Offender Programs for Justice Resource Institute and directs programs for the Massachusetts Treatment Center and the Massachusetts Department of Corrections and is clinical consultant to Cliff's House, an adolescent sex offender program in Connecticut. She has edited major works in the field and authored numerous articles, conference presentations, and media products.

Lori Koester Scott, M.C.

Ms. Scott is currently the supervisor of the special sex offender unit in the Maricopa County Adult Probation Department in Phoenix, Arizona. She has been working with offenders for 15 years, beginning with an internship/therapist position in the Arizona State Prison. She has lectured both nationally and in Europe on the community management of sex offenders and has been a contributing author for several criminal justice textbooks.

Diann Shannon, Ph.D.

Dr. Shannon received her doctorate degree in clinical psychology from the University of Denver, School of Professional Psychology in 1992. Dr. Shannon began her private practice in 1984 and has extensive experience with individuals who exhibit personality disorders, behavioral disorders, depression, anxiety, and posttraumatic stress. She has been working with sex offenders since 1994 in association with Dr. Stephen Brake.

Ted Shaw, Ph.D.

Dr. Shaw received his degrees in psychology from the University of Florida. he is the former director of the sex offender treatment program at North Florida Evaluations and Treatment Center and currently directs the Adolescents Who Sexually Offend Program in Gainesville and Ocala, Florida.

Cindy R. Spielman, Ph.D.

Dr. Spielman, a licensed psychologist, is currently the Clinical Director of Mille Lacs Academy. Her job duties include ensuring quality clinical practice and promoting research activities.

Veronique N. Valliere, Psy.D.

Dr. Valliere is a licensed psychologist and Director of Outpatient Services at Forensic Treatment Services, an outpatient sex offender program and Confront, an outpatient drug and alcohol and mental health treatment program in Allentown, PA. She is also in private practice. She received her doctorate in clinical psychology from the Graduate School of Applied and Professional Psychology, Rutgers University in New Jersey. She did her dissertation research on alcohol expectancies and rape at the Adult Diagnostic and Treatment Center, Rahway, NJ. She has presented on this topic at both local and national conferences and has provided training on a number of related issues, including domestic and other interpersonal violence. Her experience includes working with victims, nonoffending parents, and perpetrators of sexual abuse in a number of settings.

Tony Ward, Ph.D., Dip. Clin. Psych.

Dr. Ward is currently Director of Clinical Training at the University of Canterbury, Christchurch, New Zealand, and is a research consultant to the Kia Marama Sex Offender Program at Rolleston Prison. His research interests include the areas of attachment and intimacy deficits in sexual offenders, cognitive distortions, and relapse prevention treatment models.

Mack E. Winn, M.S.W.

Mr. Winn, a graduate of the Loyola School of Social Work—Chicago, has been treating sexual offenders since 1980. He is currently in private practice specializing in the treatment of this population. He received postgraduate training in cognitive/behavioral treatment of the sexual offender. He has also been trained at the Loyola Sexual Dysfunction Training Program. In addition, he is on the adjunct faculty of the University of Illinois—Chicago Circle Family Systems Program. Previously, he was the assistant director at an agency specializing in sexual offender treatment and training. Also, he has lectured nationally and published on the topics of denial, resistance, and ritualistic interventions designed to enhance compliance in substance abuse and sexual abuse treatment.

Robert C. Wright, Ph.D.

Dr. Wright received his degrees from the University of Wisconsin at Whitewater and Madison. He has been treating sex offenders since 1985 and is the founder and current director of Personpectives Sexual Abuse Treatment Program in Tampa, Florida.. He is an assistant professor at the University of South Florida, Department of Psychiatry. Currently he is co-principal investigator on a National Institute of Mental Health grant to study the cognitive representations of sex offenders.

Introduction

Americans are scared! They are scared of muggers, stalkers, robbers, and murderers, but they are particularly scared of sex offenders. Despite the fact that violent crime is actually decreasing, a variety of factors have combined to make the average citizen afraid. Unfortunately, crime, and particularly sexual assault, has become a political issue. And unfortunately, when something becomes a political issue, a rational response is replaced by the "quick fix." Currently Americans are spending $3 billion on new prisons, and the 1995 crime bill allocated another $9 billion. Parole boards are refusing to parole offenders who need to make a supervised transition back into the community. Fewer individuals are receiving probation or alternative sanctions. Sex offenders are being registered, identified, and involuntarily committed. However, there is no evidence that any of these measures improves public safety.

Not only do they not improve public safety, these measures are devouring the funds that this society needs to feed its hungry children, provide medical care for its elderly, and educate its youth. Representative Robert C. Scott from Virginia illustrated that fact when he pointed out that the elimination of parole in his state cost $8.8 billion in construction and $800 million in operating funds, which could have paid to construct a Boys and Girls Club in 2,000 precincts and run them perpetually as well as double the funds for mental health programs and drug rehabilitation, hire 200 police for each congressional district, guarantee college tuition for poor students, provide summer recreation and jobs to every poor child, double Head Start programs, quadruple school dropout prevention programs, double the funds for prison education, and eliminate every building code violation in the state while wiping out unemployment in the building trades. While usurping all these funds, parole elimination also raises the risk to the average citizen by later having to release offenders without conditions or supervision.

Perry Smith, past president of the American Correctional Association, stated in his farewell address that society is following a universal tendency to scapegoat segments of its population by exaggerating statistics or distorting facts to justify internment, segregation, or banishment. He stated:

> [W]hen we believe that the primary threat to our well-being is the depredations of the convicted — and when we distort and exaggerate the extent of that danger, creating a false sense of peril to justify our treatment of these demonized few, we are scapegoating. And our immediate next instinct is to call for banishment of these demons to the fullest extent. Which today means calling for an almost unlimited use of prison — at great cost, and to little effect, since banishing scapegoats has about as much actual effect on crime as it did on flood and famine in Biblical times.

However, there is alternative way to approach the issue of crime in this society. Not by locking up more felons or announcing the presence of ex-offenders in neighborhoods, not even by adding a few programs here and there, but by totally rethinking the paradigm through which we view the whole issue of criminal justice. Currently we are locked into a retributive view of justice. Howard Zehr in *Changing Lenses*[1] summarizes retributive justice as follows:

Crime is a violation of the state, defined by lawbreaking and guilt. Justice determines blame and administers pain in a contest between the offender and the state directed by systemic rules. (p. 181)

We tend to believe that the way our justice system is now is the way it has always been. However, this system only dates back to the sixteenth century, when the state rather than the victim took center stage in the drama. The model of retributive justice did not really take hold in the United States until the nineteenth century. For those deeds defined as "crimes," the process of resolving a hurt or a wrong imposed by another became more and more mechanical and impersonal. Humans now began to take on roles—the offender, the victim, only two members of a very large and complex cast of characters. As Zehr states, the crime is "described and dealt with in symbolic and legal terms foreign to the people actually involved. The whole process [is] mystified and mythologized and thus [becomes] a useful tool in the service of the media and the political process" (p. 182).

Today, increasingly, the criminal justice system ignores the victim and his or her needs. The offender is removed from all responsibilities and isolated and exposed to an environment that aggravates his[2] problems. The community does not experience the healing process that occurs when wrongs are acknowledged and righted.

The alternative vision is that of restorative justice, which Zehr describes as follows: "Crime is a violation of people and relationships. It creates obligations to make things right. Justice involves the victim, the offender, and the community in a search for solutions which promote repair, reconciliation, and reassurance" (p. 181).

The two views contrast in a number of ways. Whereas retributive justice focuses on blame-fixing, the past, making victim's needs secondary, and balancing harm to the victim by inflicting harm on the offender, the restorative justice model focuses on problem solving, the future, making victim's needs primary, and balancing the harm done by the offender with making it right.

The field of sex offender treatment is an example of restorative justice. Not only does the field seek to restore the offender as a functioning member of society, but it does that by helping the offender acknowledge the pain of the victim, take responsibility for his or her actions, and in some way either materially or symbolically make reparations to that victim. By standing as an example of restorative justice in the middle of a system organized around retributive justice, the field is constantly being assailed. Critics accuse sex offender treatment programs of being "soft on crime," although anyone who has ever attended a sex offender group knows that it is much more difficult to be confronted with the implications of one's behavior than mopping a floor in a prison corridor. Other critics hold up the example of one relapsed offender to damn programs that may have had hundreds of success stories. However, fortunately, the field is continuing to grow. More corrections departments are realizing that "these men are going to get out and we must do something!"

A classic example of the difference between the retributive paradigm and the restorative paradigm is the question of reintegrating the sex offender back into the community after his incarceration. The recent popularity of public notification is a classic retributive justice response to the idea that a recently released sex offender might be moving into one's neighborhood. It is curious that the outraged public rarely considers that this is probably not some stranger from out of state. It is probably someone who left that neighborhood to serve his prison sentence. He may be moving home with his wife or his mother or returning to a home he owns. Regardless, his arrival is widely publicized, property values in the neighborhood may plummet, and even if he moves out later, the stigma may remain. His victims are often revictimized by the process as their identity may be impossible to hide, particularly if the offender has been convicted of "incest."

The neighborhood is victimized because the people who live there are frightened but not given any way to cope with the situation. In Washington State, citizens responded first by burning down the offender's house and the next time by burning down a neighbor's house, as the wrong address had been announced. Citizens believe that because they are aware of the identity of the sex offender, they can legally keep him from engaging in such high-risk behaviors as hanging out around parks or talking to children. However, a parallel policy is developing: there is movement away from paroling sex offenders, thus forcing them to finish their sentences and leave prison with no supervision whatsoever. Consequently, the state cannot exercise any control over the sex offender until he actually commits another crime. This is in sharp contrast to the paroled offender who may have dozens of strict stipulations on his conduct, the violation of which can result in immediate reincarceration.

Public notification interferes with offender's ability to readjust to the community. In all likelihood he will be shunned, but his family and relatives may become objects of derision as well. As a result, he may be unable to find housing or a job. He may have to drop out of a carefully arranged therapy program. He may try to hide his identity or hide his pain from himself by using drugs or alcohol. Perceiving rejection, isolating, withdrawing, and harboring secrets are four of the major high-risk situations for the sex offender, and public notification is a perfect setup for all of them. The sex offender's chances of relapsing skyrocket. Has the safety of the public been served?

Contrast this to a restorative justice approach. The main focus would be on making sure that the victim's needs have been addressed. It is hoped that the offender has either directly or indirectly contributed to that restitution. He may have placed part of his prison pay into a victim restitution fund. Furthermore, rather than having this sum mandated by the court and automatically withdrawn from his account, he has had some responsible input into the process. He is likely to have been part of a treatment program that has helped him to develop empathy and to appreciate the consequences of his actions. He may have met with victims to allow them to vent their anger and give them the chance to question an offender.

Upon his release on parole, he will hand his parole officer a carefully prepared relapse prevention plan which outlines his particular high-risk situations and what interventions he has developed and intends to use. His therapist will be fully aware of the plan as well as his support system, including his 12-step sponsor, family members, and employer. This team will work with the offender to provide assistance, support, and encouragement. However, in the event the offender fails to respond and begins to backslide, they will also be in a position to have him placed in a more structured situation up to and including prison prior to his committing another offense. Ideally, rather than a neighborhood vigilante task force, there might be a network of individuals from the neighborhood who could be part of that support team. This could be similar to the Community Sentencing Circles used in Native Canadian communities or Family Group Conferences developed by the Maori in New Zealand, both of which seek to bring reconciliation to the community as well as to the victim and offender. Working together the community would reintegrate the offender back into itself.

Does this country really care about public safety or is it such an alluring campaign topic or quick news story that citizens are willing to hand it over to those who would turn it into a 30-second bite? Fortunately, many people, politicians and journalist among them, are willing to take the time and expend the energy to try out different approaches and to push for programs that have proven successful. Some of those individuals are represented in this Yearbook, which updates *The Sex Offender: Corrections, Treatment and Legal Issues.*

There is extensive discussion of theoretical issues, including the development of empathy, bonding issues, and the effect of alcohol and stress in rapists and child molesters. This volume addresses new treatment techniques and refinements. In another section experts describe the adaptation of treatment to special age groups, including male and female juveniles as well as the geriatric offenders. Sex offender treatment modified for different ethnic groups is the focus of another section. One group that has long been described as "untreatable" is the offender in denial. In this volume, authors describe new techniques for working with this challenging population. Finally there is an update on the ever-changing legal issues in the field.

It is hoped that by integrating the information and the philosophical approach that has developed in the field of treating sex offenders to the overall criminal justice model, a new paradigm of restorative justice will be reinforced which will make us all feel safer.

Footnotes

---

[1] Zehr, H. (1990). *Changing Lenses: A New Focus on Crime and Justice.* Scottsdale, PA: Herald Press.

[2] We refer to offenders with male pronouns throughout this article. We recognize, of course, that offenders are of both sexes. However, because most reports of sexual offenses involve male perpetrators, we have chosen to simplify our writing by using male pronouns.

Table of Contents

PART 1: THEORETICAL ISSUES

Chapter 1: Invoking Sympathy—Assessment and Treatment of Empathy Deficits Among Sexual Offenders

Chapter 2: Attachment Style, Intimacy Deficits, and Sexual Offending

Chapter 3: Relationships Between Alcohol Use, Alcohol Expectancies, and Sexual Offenses in Convicted Offenders

Chapter 4: An Empirical Investigation of Floodgates Factors in Child Sexual Abusers

PART 2: TREATING RESISTANT SEX OFFENDERS

Chapter 5: Using Pretreatment to Increase Admission in Sex Offenders

Chapter 6: Treating Sexual Offenders Who Deny— A Review

Chapter 7: Using Strategic, Systemic, and Linguistic Principles to Enhance Treatment Compliance

Chapter 8: Deviant Sexual Fantasies as Motivated Self-Deception

PART 3: SPECIAL POPULATIONS

Chapter 11: Juvenile Sex Offender Psychometric Assessment

Chapter 16: Community Management of Sex Offenders

Chapter 17: Psychological Force in Sexual Abuse—Implications for Recovery

Chapter 18: Assessment and Treatment of Incest Families

Chapter 19: Developing Therapeutic Communities for Sex Offenders

PART 5: LEGAL ISSUES IN THE TREATMENT OF SEX OFFENDERS

Chapter 22: Sexually Dangerous Persons/Predators Legislation

Chapter 23: The Treatment and Supervised Release Relationship

Chapter 24: Megan's Laws—Sex Offender Registration and Notification Statutes and Constitutional Challenges

Appendices

Part 1

Theoretical Issues

In this section five theorists explore fundamental issues regarding sex offenders, including the development of empathy, the roles of alcohol and stress as disinhibitors, the need for intimacy, and the role of fantasies. Backed by research, all these authors have formulated theories regarding these factors.

In Chapter 1, R. Karl Hanson challenges the assumption that practitioners should help sex offenders develop empathy as if it were a unitary concept. Empathy, according to Dr. Hanson, is a complex phenomenon that involves at least three different skills. To empathize with another person, an individual initially must establish a caring or at least a benign relationship with that person. Next, an individual must be able to accurately perceive another's perspective. Finally, an individual must believe that he or she can cope constructively with the perceived distress of others. These different skills require very different cognitive and affective abilities. Empathy classes, groups, and exercises traditionally focus on exposing offenders to the pain and suffering that victims experience. If an offender does not have a benign or caring attitude toward that victim, the victim's suffering may only excite the offender. If the offender cannot understand or cognitively process depictions of the consequences to his victim, the offender will not be able to appreciate the repercussions of his own behavior. If the offender is shown the consequences to victims and if the offender can appreciate the victim's suffering but cannot perceive any way of coping constructively with that pain, he may flee into denial to defend against tremendous pain and frustration.

Research in this area has uncovered important differences in the types of deficits in empathy, which may have implications for treating and supervising different types of offenders. For example, violent offenders do not have deficits in perspective taking. They are angry at their victims and want them to suffer. It would be naive to believe that showing them that victims suffer will change their desire to hurt others. However, nonviolent offenders who are sober at the time of their offense often do have deficits in perspective taking. Therefore, prior to developing a program to enhance empathy, clinicians should assess the types of deficits each offender exhibits and then individualize the training accordingly.

Intimacy is another area that practitioners have viewed as a unitary concept but which has proven to be much more complicated. Theory has suggested that sex offenders, particularly child molesters, have trouble establishing intimate relationships with adults and thus turn to children to satisfy these needs. Rapists have been conceptualized as being highly sensitive to rejection and thus angry at females because they are perceived either individually or as a sex as deceitful and manipulating—taking a man's trust and then spurning him. However, just as empathy is not a unidimensional concept, intimacy also has many facets.

In Chapter 2, Tony Ward, Stephen M. Hudson, and Julie McCormack review the research on intimacy and discuss their adaptation of Bartholomew's two-dimensional model, which addresses one's view of oneself as well as one's view of others. This model identifies four types of attachments—secure, fearful, dismissing, and preoccupied. Secure attachments reflect a positive view of oneself and others. However, an individual with a negative view of himself and others develops a fearful attachment which in sex offenders is reflected by impersonal sexual contacts, a lack of empathy, and little compunction regarding the use of force. The person with a positive attitude toward himself but a negative attitude toward others develops dismissing attachments which may be actively hostile and aggressive. Those who have a positive view of others but a negative view of themselves develop preoccupied attachments which are insecure and are often seen in the child molester who perceives himself to be in love with his child victim. As a result of their research, Ward and associates propose that identifying sex offenders by their attachment styles may contribute significantly to appropriate treatment and supervision.

The use of alcohol has been a controversial issue simply because many sex offenders present their behavior as a by-product of alcohol intake. "I was drunk" becomes an easy excuse, which, unfortunately, therapists, judges, and juries sometimes buy into. Granted alcohol impairs judgment, disinhibits behavior, and increases aggression. However, research has shown that this is not a pharmacological effect but results from changes in perception. The intoxicated person attends more to the obvious cues in a situation rather than to the peripheral ones, including long-range implications. The effects of alcohol are also a function of one's expectations. Veronique N. Valliere's research, discussed in Chapter 3, explores the relationship between alcohol and violent sexual behavior. She found certain relationships between drinking and sexual aggression among the alcoholic rapists in the study. However, alcohol was not related to the degree of violence or the number of rapes. Insight into the expectancies these offenders had about alcohol would have been a valuable piece of information; however, the treatment these men underwent changed the expectancies, or at least the reported expectancies. Certainly, Dr. Valliere challenges the assumption that the "booze made me do it."

Mark A. Gould has also researched the effect of alcohol on sex offenders, in this case child molesters. In addition, he has studied stress, which offenders also blame for their sex offenses. His study, outlined in Chapter 4, tests the theoretical construct developed by Barbara K. Schwartz, which hypothesizes that motivators and disinhibitors combine to produce the plan to sexually offend. Like Dr. Valliere's study, this research explores whether alcohol and stress can be "blamed" for sexually aggressive behavior. Dr. Gould studied both incarcerated and nonincarcerated offenders who had offended both intrafamilially and extrafamilially. Of the incarcerated offenders, 66% reported significant problems with substance abuse. Moreover, the most serious offenders showed the most disinhibitors, including both alcohol and stress. However, Dr. Gould hypothesizes that alcohol may serve different roles for different types of offenders. Although the most entrenched offenders may use alcohol to facilitate their deviancy by reducing guilt and shame and providing false courage, situational offenders may have experienced disinhibition secondary to intoxication. As in Dr. Valliere's research with rapists, the data does not support a simple cause-and-effect relationship between sexual acting out and alcoholism.

This section explores four issues related to sexual assault. The research of these authors demonstrates the complex, multidimensional relationship between empathy, attachment, intimacy, and substance abuse and sexual deviancy. Each of these issues has interesting implications for treatment.

Chapter 1

Invoking Sympathy— Assessment and Treatment of Empathy Deficits Among Sexual Offenders

by R. Karl Hanson, Ph.D.

Overview

The goal of victim empathy treatment for sexual offenders is to develop caring, compassionate responses to victims. Such sympathetic responses are most likely to be elicited when the offender (1) can develop a caring or benign relationship with the victim, (2) can engage in accurate perspective taking, and (3) has the ability to cope constructively with the suffering of others. This chapter provides suggestions for the assessment and treatment of each of these components of empathy.

The Need for Empathy Training

Interviewer: So what were you thinking about when you first became sexually involved with your stepdaughter?
Offender: I knew I should not be doing it, but she seemed to really want it.
Interviewer: How could you tell?
Offender: Well, the way she kept coming on to me. Walking around the house in her nightgown, hugs and kisses, that sort of thing. You could tell what was on her mind.
Interviewer: How did she react when you started touching her?
Offender: She was really quiet at first, but she loosened up. I talked her through it and she was more than willing.
Interview: What effect has it had on her now
Offender: As far as I know, nothing much has changed. She was pretty upset when the police arrested me. I am not allowed to talk to her now. I guess she misses me.

Anybody working with sexual offenders has had similar conversations. Given that the offender's account is typically in sharp contrast to the feelings of shame, betrayal, and violation described by his victims, it is not surprising that most treatment programs for sexual offenders aim to address victim empathy deficits (Knopp, Freeman-Longo, & Stevenson, 1992; Wormith & Hanson, 1992). Victim empathy treatment frequently increases the salience of victim suffering. Sexual offenders are often asked to read victim accounts, review videos, and carefully document the negative impact of their assaults on their own victims (e.g., Hildebran & Pithers, 1989). The basic assumption is that the awareness of victim harm can be an important barrier to reoffending. Such an assumption, however, may not apply to all sexual offenders. Some offenders intended to hurt their victims, others do not care, and others are already overburdened by shame. I argue here that a careful understanding of the role of empathy in sexual offending is required to adequately assess and treat sexual offenders' empathy deficits.

The concept of "empathy" is relatively new and it continues to evolve (Allport, 1985; Davis, 1983; Eisenberg & Strayer, 1987; Hanson, in press; Marshall, Hudson, Jones, & Fernandez, 1995). "Sympathy," or concern for other people, has a long intellectual history, but the term "empathy" was rarely used in psychological or popular discourse prior to the 1940s. Originally used to explain how works of abstract art elicit viewers' emotions, it was subsequently used to describe how we sense the emotions of other people (Allport, 1985; Murphy, 1949). Most contemporary theories of empathy consider empathy to be multidimensional (Davis, 1983; Eisenberg & Strayer, 1987; Marshall et al., 1995). A fundamental distinction common to many of these models is that between the intellectual ability to understand other people (perspective taking) and the emotional responses to these perceptions. Those people concerned with sexual offenders' empathy deficits are typically concerned with the offender's ability to accurately perceive victim suffering and to respond in a caring, compassionate manner (Marshall et al., 1995; Pithers, 1994). Such caring, compassionate responses are often referred to as sympathy (Eisenberg & Miller, 1987). It is important to recognize, however, that sympathetic responses do not necessary follow from accurate perceptions of victim suffering. Children, for example, may react with fear or avoidance when presented with images of other children suffering (e.g., Strayer, 1993).

The Foundations of Empathy

As I have previously argued (Hanson, in press), there are most likely three pre-conditions for sympathetic responses: (1) a caring or benign relationship, (2) accurate perspective taking, and (3) an ability to cope constructively with the perceived distress of others. Offenders' overall capacity for sympathy is limited by their area of greatest weakness. Accurately understanding victim suffering will not lead to sympathy if offenders feel their victims deserve to suffer. Consequently, treatment for one area need not lead to overall improvement in sexual offenders' victim empathy. Each area should be separately assessed, and distinct interventions for each area may be necessary.

Offender-Victim Relationships

The offenders' relationship with their victims is the primary determinant of sympathetic or nonsympathetic reactions to victims. These relationships can be roughly classed into those that are caring (e.g., parent-child, friends), adversarial, and detached/indifferent (e.g., complete strangers). In caring relationships, the other's happiness is considered a value in itself, and evidence of suffering is distressing. By contrast, in adversarial relationships, the other's distress is considered desirable. Taking delight in another's suffering is not a response reserved for sadists. Almost all of us have at times welcomed the misfortune of our adversaries: the reprimand of a difficult coworker, the bankruptcy of a store manager who does not honor guarantees, the pain of the thief who breaks his finger while trying to steal your car.

Similarly, there are probably many types of relationships in which offenders may feel motivated to inflict sexual harm. A common theme to these relationships would likely be a perception of the victim as sexually threatening or hostile. Some sexual offenders, for example, may believe that sexual relationships are inherently adversarial. These offenders may perceive that the woman's goal is to get as much as possible from the man before submitting to his sexual advances, whereas the man's goal is to obtain sexual access at the lowest possible cost. Once the man has contributed more than he thinks the woman is worth, he may feel that she has reneged on their bargain and has been playing with him. The man may then feel entitled to force the woman into sexual activity, fully realizing, and desiring, that she will find it degrading ("she needs to be put in her place"). Such feelings of sexual entitlement can be further supported by both individual and cultural values in which men's sexual needs take priority over the potential consequences for women and children (Hanson, Gizzarelli, & Scott, 1994; Herman, 1990).

The most common detached/indifferent relationships are between those with whom we have had no real contact. Some sexual offenders, however, are indifferent to their victims' reactions even though they may have had numerous interactions, not all of which were assaultive. This lack of concern may apply to a particular individual or to groups of individuals (e.g., minorities or prostitutes), or it may be part of a more general personality style (e.g., schizoid personality disorder or psychopathy).

Attention to the relationship between the offenders and their victims is important because a minimal level of caring is necessary before victim suffering can act as a deterrent. Just because offenders may have wanted their victims to suffer does not mean that these offenders cannot benefit from treatment. All relationships are rooted in certain beliefs, desires, habits, and conflicts. For many offenders, it is necessary to begin victim empathy treatment by identifying and addressing the factors that contribute to adversarial or uncaring relationships with potential victims. Before such factors are addressed, there is little reason to believe that interventions based on increasing the salience of victim suffering should have any positive impact.

Assessing Empathy Deficits

There are several methods for assessing the extent to which sexual offenders' empathy deficits are based on relationship problems. One of the most useful indicators is the sexual offense history. For offenders who used overt force (e.g., weapons, injured victim, or abduction), it is implausible to believe that the offender mistakenly thought the victim enjoyed the activity. Overt force signals an intent to harm, or an indifference to victim suffering. In contrast, the least problematic relationships are likely to be found in those cases in which the abuse occurs within the context of a previously caring or intimate relationship (e.g., date rapists, incest offenders, or clergy).

The offenders' own accounts of their crimes can often be used to identify their relationship with their victims. Although denial and fabrications are common, offender accounts can nonetheless provide clues to the implicit assumptions and motivations guiding their interactions with their victims (Pollock & Hashmall, 1991; Ward, Hudson, & France, 1993). Some of these deviant attitudes can be assessed directly through questionnaire measures (Abel et al., 1989; Bumby, 1996; Hanson et al., 1994); in general, however, there has been surprisingly little empirical evidence for the validity of attitude questionnaires for sexual offenders (Hanson, Cox, & Woszczyna, 1991a, 1991b).

Detailed social histories can also be useful for determining the generality of the relationship deficits. Evidence of a lifestyle characterized by shallow, uncaring relationships can be reliably assessed by Factor I of the Psychopathy Checklist (Hare, 1991; Hare et al., 1990). The Psychopathy Checklist is a standardized assessment procedure based on a semistructured interview, a file review, and an explicit scoring system.

Whatever methods are used, it is important to identify and address relationship problems before attempting to treat the other components of empathy.

Perspective-Taking Ability

The second major component of empathy, perspective-taking ability, is the cognitive understanding of another person's thoughts and feelings. Perspective-taking ability itself is built on various subcomponent skills. These skills include the ability to decode facial expressions, body language, and tone of voice. In addition, perspective taking requires a general understanding of social situations and the likely effect of various events on particular individuals. Consequently, perspective-taking ability is considered an important element of general social competence (Hogan, 1969; McFall, 1990).

One way in which perspective-taking deficits contribute to sexual offending is through a failure to recognize victim suffering in the context of a caring or benign relationship. Sexual offenders may sincerely believe that their victims liked or enjoyed the abuse because they were unable to fully appreciate the victim's point of view. For example, some child molesters may honestly interpret children's natural warmth as sexual interest, their compliance as consent, and their silence as a desire for the abuse to continue. Similarly, a sexual offender may recognize signs of victim's distress but minimize such signs in the context of other factors (e.g., the victim continuing to desire the nonsexual support of the offender).

The available research suggests that perspective-taking deficits may be a clinically relevant problem for at least some sexual offenders. Hudson et al. (1993) found that sexual offenders were less able than nonviolent criminals to identify the emotions in brief presentations of faces. Moreover, they found that the child molesters in their study had difficulty identifying emotions in drawings of both adults and children (Hudson et al., 1993). The nonsexual violent offenders in Hudson et al.'s (1993) study had the least difficulty with emotional recognition skills. This finding is consistent with the position that violent offenses are more likely to be motivated by adversarial relationships than by perspective-taking deficits.

Hanson and Scott (1995) also found that perspective-taking deficits were most common among the least violent offenders. In their study, Hanson and Scott (1995) used written vignettes to assess perspective taking among child molesters and rapists. Two series of vignettes were used. The first series described interactions between adults and children (the Child Empathy Test, or CET) and the second series described heterosexual interactions between adults (the Empathy for Women Test, or EWT). The vignettes were created to range from socially acceptable interactions to explicit examples of sexual abuse and rape. Most of the vignettes, however, were ambiguous. The respondent's task was to rate how the child or woman would likely feel at the end of the interaction. Respondents could make errors either by underestimating or by overestimating the level of distress. The correct answers were based on samples of community women (the EWT) or on the responses of a panel of experts on child sexual abuse (for the CET).

The sexual offenders in treatment made fewer errors on the CET than did the untreated sexual offenders. In addition, the incest offenders made more errors on the incest item of the CET than did the other groups. There were no overall group differences between the sexual offenders, the nonsexual criminals, and community comparison groups on the CET. In contrast, the sexual offenders made more errors on the EWT than did the community comparison group. More important, however, were the differences among the sexual offenders. As predicted, those offenders who used overt force during their offenses made significantly fewer errors than those offenders who did not use force. Moreover, those offenders who were intoxicated at the time of the offense made fewer errors than those nonviolent offenders who had committed all their offenses while sober. It is possible for some offenders to lose their perspective-taking ability when intoxicated but to maintain reasonable social judgment when sober. In contrast, those offenders who were never intoxicated and never overtly violent were the most likely to have stable perspective-taking deficits (Hanson & Scott, 1995).

Studies using videotaped vignettes have found that men who report sexual aggression against women often have difficulties interpreting heterosocial interactions. Lipton, McDonel, and McFall (1987) found that convicted rapists tended to underestimate women's negative signals when viewing videotaped vignettes depicting dating situations. Errors in the interpretation of women's reactions to men's sexual advances have also been associated with self-reported sexual aggression (Malamuth & Brown, 1994; Murphy, Coleman, & Haynes, 1986) and self-reported likelihood of raping

(McDonel & McFall, 1991). Malamuth and Brown (1994) interpreted their findings as supporting a "suspicious schema" among sexually aggressive men. They argued that the sexually aggressive men were able to recognize the outward signs of female hostility, but the men's generalized expectation about women (their "schema") made them discount the honesty of the women's emotional displays.

Malamuth and Brown's (1994) study points to an important interaction between the offender-victim relationship and perspective taking. Not only can faulty perspective taking lead to adversarial relationships, but the expectation of adversarial sexual relationships can corrupt accurate interpretations of women. Even when women are responding honestly and cooperatively, sexually aggressive men may interpret the women's actions as masking malicious intent.

Assessing Perspective Taking

In principle, perspective taking is the easiest component of empathy to assess. Because perspective taking is a skill, it is possible to construct objective perspective-taking tests that are immune to deliberate faking. The basic format of these tests would be to ask sexual offenders to interpret examples of social interactions. The offender's responses would then be compared to the correct answers, as determined by community norms. By varying the stimuli, it would be possible to identify areas of strength and weakness, for example, whether the offender has specific problems with emotional voice tone, children's affection, women's rejection in dating situations, or any complex social situation.

There are no available measures of perspective taking, however, that meet acceptable psychometric standards. Hanson and Scott (1995) and Beckett and Fisher (1994) have both proposed questionnaire measures, but the reliability and validity of these measures have yet to be established. The internal consistencies of Hanson and Scott's (1995) measures were unacceptably low (alphas less than 0.50). A pilot test ($n = 42$) of a revised version of the EWT has shown improved reliability (alpha = 0.82) and promising validity (Hanson, 1996); however, additional testing is required before the measure can be recommended for general use.

Questionnaire measures are inexpensive to create and administer, but there would be advantages to developing standardized videotaped measures of perspective taking. Video vignettes can have high levels of realism, can address many of the subcomponent skills (body language, tone of voice, etc.), do not require literacy, and can be constructed to monitor the speed as well as the accuracy of responding. Various sets of videotapes have been used in the studies mentioned previously, but the need remains to develop a standardized video-based test that could be appropriate for various offender groups.

Even if offenders do have perspective-taking skills, they may not be able to use them. Perspective-taking ability can be impaired in certain crucial situations (e.g., when an individual is intoxicated, angry, or sexually aroused). However, McClelland (1981) cautioned that behaviors assessed under demand situations (e.g., "drink as much as you can") should not be confused with the typical pattern of such behaviors (e.g., "How much do you usually drink?"). Consequently, it is not clear that those offenders who demonstrate good perspective-taking skills in clinical assessments can necessarily be expected to use them in high-risk situations. Because the use of perspective-taking skills in high-risk situations is difficult to monitor, assessments about whether offenders actually use perspective-taking skills rely on self-report measures. The Perspective-Taking subscale from the Interpersonal Reaction Inventory (IRI) is one potentially useful self-report measure (Davis, 1980, 1983). This questionnaire addresses the extent to which respondents believe that they habitually consider the perspective of others (e.g., "Before criticizing somebody, I try to imagine how I would feel if I were in that person's place."). The Perspective-Taking scale appears to have acceptable psychometric properties, although sexual offender assessments may benefit from more sex-specific questions (e.g., "Before having sex, I carefully consider how the other person would feel about it."). In support of its validity, Hudson et al. (1993) found that the Perspective-Taking subscale correlated with the ability of sexual offenders to identify emotions from facial drawings.

Perspective-Taking Training

The treatment of perspective-taking deficits can follow many of the same procedures used for teaching any cognitive skill. Offenders can be taught general principles concerning victims' reactions to sexual assault, and they can then practice their knowledge through the interpretation of specific cases including their own. Treatment progress can be monitored by the accuracy of their interpretations of complex social situations. The major challenge of treating perspective-taking deficits is generalization. It is important to provide help for sexual offenders in applying the skills learned in treatment to high-risk situations. The extent to which offenders genuinely "feel" for others, instead of only intellectually understanding them, would be more closely related to the offenders' relationships with others than to the offenders' perspective-taking ability. Consequently, the best route to encouraging the use of perspective-taking skills may be to improve the relationship between the offender and potential victims.

Coping With the Distress of Others

Fully appreciating the impact of sexual assault can be highly distressing to those sexual offenders who have even a minimal level of caring for their victims. A common assumption is that the experience of such intense negative affect should inhibit sexual offenders from reoffending. There are reasons to believe, however, that the experience of intense distress may have no effect on recidivism or may even lead to behavioral deterioration.

Coping with the distress of others can be a difficult task, particularly when compounded by a sense of responsibility for the other's distress. As with any stressful event, there are different ways of responding to the perception of another's suffering. It is not uncommon for children to become anxious or angry when exposed to the suffering of other children (Eisenberg & Miller, 1987). Many "normal," nonoffending adults blame victims for their misfortunes (Janoff-Bulman, 1979; Shaver, 1970). There is some experimental evidence suggesting that victim blaming increases with the intensity of the negative affect associated with witnessing another's suffering (Thornton, 1984).

Coping with one's own transgressions is more difficult than simply witnessing distress caused by others. Emotion researchers make a useful distinction between guilt and shame (Lewis, 1971; Tangney, 1991). Guilt refers to the capacity to recognize certain of one's own behaviors as reprehensible yet maintain a general sense of positive self-esteem. In shame reactions, individuals deplore themselves, not just their specif-ic problematic behavior. Guilt-prone individuals tend to make attempts at restitution and reconciliation. In contrast, shame-prone individuals are more likely to withdraw, and, paradoxically, they become hostile and angry (Tangney, Wagner, Fletcher, & Gramzow, 1992). Much earlier, Baruk (1945) similarly observed that the greatest hatred and violence were perpetrated by those psychiatric patients who experienced the most profound sense of guilt (culpability).

There is a risk that exposure to salient victim suffering can increase the extent of vic-tim blaming and cognitive distortions among sexual offenders (Beckett, Beech, Fisher, & Fordham, 1994). In their review of community-based sexual offender treatment pro-grams, Beckett et al. (1994) found that cognitive distortions increased in some programs following the victim empathy module. Qualitative analysis suggested that the programs showing this deterioration tended to have harsh, confrontational therapists. Not being provided with models on how to integrate their transgressions into an acceptable self-concept, it is likely that the offenders in these problematic programs simply relied on their habitual methods for maintaining their self-esteem (e.g., externalization and denial).

There has been little research on the assessment of how sexual offenders cope with their own transgressions. Some authors have considered the offenders' cognitive dis-tortions to be attempts to justify their crimes to themselves and to others (Abel et al., 1989; Hanson & Slater, 1993; Pollock & Hashmall, 1991). Such cognitive distortions have been considered problematic, but rarely has there been any discussion of alternate forms of coping. One way to identify cognitive distortions as coping mechanisms is by their fixed, irrational quality. Simple errors in perspective taking change with new evi-dence, but defensive beliefs persist despite overwhelming evidence to the contrary.

One questionnaire that has been used to assess reactions to social transgressions is the Test of Self-Conscious Affect (TOSCA) developed by Tangney, Wagner, and Gramzow (1989). The questionnaire presents brief vignettes (e.g., "You break some-thing at work and then hide it.") followed by four or five response options. The options are intended to assess (1) guilt, (2) shame, (3) detachment, (4) externalization, and, for the potentially positive scenarios, (5) pride. The TOSCA appears to have rea-sonable psychometric properties with nonoffender community populations. Many items, however, would not be appropriate to typical offender populations (e.g., diet-ing and examinations). Consequently, an alternative version of the TOSCA was writ-ten that was intended to be appropriate for both offender and nonoffender populations (TOSCA-SD; Hanson & Tangney, 1996). However, psychometric information on the new TOSCA-SD is not currently available.

Sexual offender treatment programs often devote little attention to training offenders to cope with their transgressions, although it is reasonable to expect many offenders to have problems in this area. Social skills training is common, but most social skills programs (e.g., Alberti & Emmons, 1982) focus on coping with the offen-sive behavior of others, not on one's own offensive behavior. Socially competent responses to minor transgressions often involve some form of apology and restitution (e.g., "Sorry about spilling your beer. Say, can I buy you another one?"). It is much more difficult to cope with serious transgressions (e.g., sexual victimization). In most cases of sexual assault, apologies are inappropriate and restitution impossible. Offenders can respond constructively to their guilt, however, by affirming their com-mitment never to reoffend and by taking all the steps necessary to obtain that goal (e.g., attending treatment, avoiding high-risk situations, and developing prosocial friends). Hildebran and Pithers (1989) expressed a similar idea when they said that victim empathy training can be used to enhance motivation for treatment. I have argued in this chapter that awareness of victim suffering leads to prosocial goals only when the offenders have at least a minimally positive relationship with the victim and the capacity to cope constructively with their own guilt.

Assessing Sympathy

The goal of victim empathy training for sexual offenders is to promote caring, compassionate responses. Offenders should understand and feel for their victims and be motivated toward constructive actions (Marshall et al., 1995; Pithers, 1994). Such sympathetic responses imply a capacity to give to others and to temporarily renounce self-interest. The chronic dysfunction of many offenders has left them with few resources to give, making the induction of sympathy a significant therapeutic challenge.

The assessment of sympathy is best accomplished through a combination of self-report and direct observation. The Empathic Concern subscale for the IRI (Davis, 1980, 1983) is a potentially useful self-report measure. It is short and internally consistent, and it targets a general concern for others (e.g., "I often have tender, concerned feelings for people less fortunate than me."). As with all self-report measures, the offenders' responses are limited by their candor and self-awareness, characteristics for which sexual offenders are not known to excel. Consequently, it would be useful to supplement self-report measures with direct observations of offenders in relevant situations. Observations in the most relevant situations are both impractical and unethical (e.g., private access to victims). It would be possible, nonetheless, to obtain useful information by observing sexual offenders' reactions in group and institutional settings and by examining their reactions to victims' accounts.

Sympathy Training

Training for sympathy should begin by addressing the other three components of empathy. Sympathetic responses are most likely given when the offender has a positive or benign relationship, accurate perspective-taking abilities, and the ability to cope with and perceive victim suffering. Each of these components of empathy can be separately assessed and treated. It is important to remember that an intervention tailored for one type of empathy deficit may have no influence on other types of empathy deficits. Moreover, deficits in one area can undermine strengths in other areas. It is quite possible that no special attention to sympathy is required once the other three components are addressed. Like good health, sympathy is based on a well-functioning system.

Conclusion

Many treatment programs aim to increase sexual offenders' victim empathy by increasing the salience of victim suffering (Hildebran & Pithers, 1989; Pithers, 1994). An image guiding these programs is that sexual offenders do not really want to hurt their victims and would stop committing sexual offenses if they were fully aware of the damage they were causing. Given that this image does not fit many offenders, there are several possible reasons for the popularity of this approach. Those who are well socialized and caring about others (e.g., therapists) may have difficulty empathizing with those who are cruel. It is much easier for therapists to sympathize with offenders who unwittingly hurt their victims than with those who intentionally inflict harm. Those who intentionally harm others are often perceived as candidates for punishment rather than for treatment. Punishing sexual offenders may be morally and socially justified, but there is no reason to believe that punishment should teach sexual offenders that hurting others is wrong. Addressing offenders' desire to hurt others requires addressing the factors that contribute to their adversarial relationships with potential victims. Changing relationships from adversarial to benign may be more difficult than teaching perspective taking, but it is a treatment goal well worth pursuing. It is only when offenders adopt a minimally positive stance toward victims that other aspects of victim empathy training can be effective.

References

Abel, G. G., Gore, D. K., Holland, C. L., Camp, N., Becker, J. V., & Rathner, J. (1989). The measurement of cognitive distortions in child molesters. *Annals of Sex Research, 2,* 135–153.

Alberti, R. I., & Emmons, M. L. (1982). *Your perfect right: A guide to assertive living*. San Luis Obispo, CA: Impact.

Allport, G. W. (1985). The historical background of social psychology. In G. Lindzey & E. Aronson (Eds.), *Handbook of social psychology* (3rd. ed., pp. 1–46). New York: Random House.

Baruk, H. (1945). *Psychiatrie morale expérimentale, individuelle et sociale: Haines et réactions de culpabilité* [Moral experimental, individual and social psychiatry: Hatred and guilt reactions]. Paris: Presses Universitaires de France.

Beckett, R., Beech, A., Fisher, D., & Fordham, A. S. (1994). *Community-based treatment for sex offenders: An evaluation of seven treatment programmes* [Home Office Occasional Paper]. London: Home Office.

Beckett, R., & Fisher, D. (1994, November). *Assessing victim empathy: A new measure*. Paper presented at the 13th Annual Conference of the Association for the Treatment of Sexual Abusers, San Francisco.

Bumby, K. M. (1996). Assessing the cognitive distortions of child molesters and rapists: Development and validation of the MOLEST and RAPE scales. *Sexual Abuse: A Journal of Research and Treatment, 8,* 37–54.

Davis, M. H. (1980). A multidimensional approach to individual differences in empathy. *JSAS Catalog of Selected Documents in Psychology, 10*(4), 85.

Davis, M. H. (1983). Measuring individual differences in empathy: Evidence for a multidimensional approach. *Journal of Personality and Social Psychology, 44,* 113–126.

Eisenberg, N., & Miller, P. A. (1987). Empathy, sympathy, and altruism: Empirical and conceptual links. In N. Eisenberg & J. Strayer (Eds.), *Empathy and its development* (pp. 292–316). Cambridge, MA: Cambridge University Press.

Eisenberg, N., & Strayer, J. (Eds.). (1987). *Empathy and its development*. Cambridge, MA: Cambridge University Press.

Hanson, R. K. (in press). Assessing sexual offenders' capacity for empathy. *Psychology, Crime and Law*.

Hanson, R. K. (1996). *Assessing sexual offenders' perspective taking ability: The Empathy for Women Test — Revised version*. Manuscript submitted for publication.

Hanson, R. K., Cox, B., & Woszczyna, C. (1991a). *Sexuality, personality and attitude questionnaires for sexual offenders: A review* (User Report No. 1991-13). Ottawa: Corrections Branch, Ministry of the Solicitor General of Canada.

Hanson, R. K., Cox, B., & Woszczyna, C. (1991b). Assessing treatment outcome for sexual offend-ers. *Annals of Sex Research, 4,* 177–208.

Hanson, R. K., Gizzarelli, R., & Scott, H. (1994). The attitudes of incest offenders: Sexual entitle-ment and acceptance of sex with children. *Criminal Justice and Behavior, 21,* 187–202.

Hanson, R. K., & Scott, H. (1995). Assessing perspective taking among sexual offenders, nonsexu-al criminals and nonoffenders. *Sexual Abuse: A Journal of Research and Treatment, 7,* 259–277.

Hanson, R. K., & Slater, S. (1993). Reactions to motivational accounts of child molesters. *Journal of Child Sexual Abuse, 2*(4), 43–59.

Hanson, R. K., & Tangney, J. P. (1996). *The Test of Self-Conscious Affect—Social Deviance (TOSCA-SD) version.* [Unpublished test]. (Available from R. K. Hanson, Department of the Solicitor General of Canada, 340 Laurier Ave., West, Ottawa, K1A 0P8)

Hare, R. D. (1991). Manual for the revised Psychopathy Checklist. Toronto: Multi-Health Systems.

Hare, R. D., Harpur, T. J., Hakstian, A. R., Forth, A. E., Hart, S. D., & Newman, J. P. (1990). The Revised Psychopathy Checklist: Reliability and factor structure. *Psychological Assessment, 2,* 338–341.

Herman, J. L. (1990). Sex offenders: A feminist perspective. In W. L. Marshall, D. R. Laws, & H. E. Barbaree (Eds.), *Handbook of sexual assault: Issues, theories and the treatment of the offender* (pp. 177–190). New York: Plenum Press.

Hildebran, D., & Pithers, W. D. (1989). Enhancing offender empathy for sexual-abuse victims. In D. R. Laws (Ed.), *Relapse prevention with sex offenders* (pp. 236–243). New York: Guilford Press.

Hogan, R. (1969). Development of an empathy scale. *Journal of Consulting and Clinical Psychology, 33,* 307–316.

Hudson, S. M., Marshall, W. L., Wales, D., McDonald, E., Bakker, L. W., & McLean, A. (1993). Emotional recognition skills of sex offenders. *Annals of Sex Research, 6,* 199–211.

Janoff-Bulman, R. (1979). Characterological versus behavioral self- blame: Inquiries into depression and rape. *Journal of Personality and Social Psychology, 37,* 1798–1809.

Knopp, F. H., Freeman-Longo, R. E., & Stevenson, W. (1992). *Nationwide survey of juvenile and adult sex-offender treatment programs.* Orwell, VT: Safer Society Press.

Lewis, H. B. (1971). *Shame and guilt in neurosis.* New York: International Universities Press.

Lipton, D. N., McDonel, E. C., & McFall, R. M. (1987). Heterosocial perception in rapists. *Journal of Consulting and Clinical Psychology, 55,* 17–21.

Malamuth, N. M., & Brown, L. M. (1994). Sexually aggressive men's perception of women's com-munications: Testing three explanations. *Journal of Personality and Social Psychology, 67,* 699–712.

Marshall, W. L., Hudson, S. M., Jones, R., & Fernandez, Y. M. (1995). Empathy in sex offenders. *Clinical Psychology Review, 15*(2), 99–113.

McClelland, D. C. (1981). Is personality consistent? In A. I. Rabin, J. Aronoff, A. M. Barclay, & R. A. Zucker (Eds.), *Further explorations in personality* (pp. 87–113). New York: Wiley.

McDonel, E. C., & McFall, R. M. (1991). Construct validity of two heterosocial perception skill measures for assessing rape proclivity. *Violence and Victims, 6,* 17–30.

McFall, R. M. (1990). The enhancement of social skills: An information-processing analysis. In W. L. Marshall, D. R. Laws, & H. E. Barbaree (Eds.), *Handbook of sexual assault* (pp. 311–330). New York: Plenum Press.

Murphy, G. (1949). *Historical introduction to modern psychology.* New York: Harcourt, Brace.

Murphy, W. D., Coleman, E. M., & Haynes, M. R. (1986). Factors related to coercive sexual behav-ior in a nonclinical sample of males. *Violence and Victims, 1,* 255–278.

Pithers, W. D. (1994). Process evaluation of a group therapy component designed to enhance sex offenders' empathy for sexual abuse survivors. *Behavior Research and Therapy, 32,* 565–570.

Pollock, N. L., & Hashmall, J. M. (1991). The excuses of child molesters. *Behavioral Sciences and the Law, 9,* 53–59.

Shaver, K. G. (1970). Defensive attribution: Effects of severity and relevance on the responsibility assigned for an accident. *Journal of Personality and Social Psychology, 14,* 101–113.

Strayer, J. (1993). Children's concordant emotions and cognitions in response to observed emotions. *Child Development, 64,* 188–201.

Tangney, J. P. (1991). Moral affect: The good, the bad, and the ugly. *Journal of Personality and Social Psychology, 61,* 598–607.

Tangney, J. P., Wagner, P., Fletcher, C., & Gramzow, R. (1992). Shamed into anger? The relation of shame and guilt to anger and self-reported aggression. *Journal of Personality and Social Psychology, 62,* 669–675.

Tangney, J. P., Wagner, P., & Gramzow, R. (1989). *The Test of Self-Conscious Affect.* Fairfax, VA: George Mason University Press.

Thornton, B. (1984). Defensive attribution of responsibility: Evidence for an arousal-based motivational bias. *Journal of Personality and Social Psychology, 46,* 721–734.

Ward, T., Hudson, S. M., & France, K. G. (1993). Self-reported reasons for offending behavior in child molesters. *Annals of Sex Research, 6,* 139–148.

Wormith, J. S., & Hanson, R. K. (1992). The treatment of sexual offenders in Canada: An update. *Canadian Psychology/Psychologie Canadienne, 33*(2), 180–198.

Chapter 2

Attachment Style, Intimacy Deficits, and Sexual Offending

by Tony Ward, Ph.D., Stephen M. Hudson, Ph.D., and Julie McCormack, B.Sc.

Overview

Recent theoretical and empirical research suggests that sexual offenders have intimacy skill deficits that may play a significant role in the etiology and maintenance of their dysfunctional sexual behavior. In this chapter we argue that attachment theory can provide a useful theoretical framework for the investigation of intimacy deficits in sexual offenders.

The Need for Intimacy

The need to belong and to be intimate with someone is arguably as fundamental a human motive as the need for food and sex (Baumeister & Leary, 1995). Satisfaction of this need requires frequent, affectively pleasant interactions with another person in the context of a stable and enduring relationship. Intimacy is viewed as an enduring motive that reflects an individual's preference or readiness to experience closeness, warmth, and communication. Although the definition of intimacy is the subject of some controversy, most researchers agree that it involves mutual self-disclosure in relationships, warmth and affection, and closeness and interdependence between partners (Fehr & Perlman, 1985; Weiss, 1973). Bass and Davis (1988) defined it as the "bonding between two people based on trust, respect, love and the ability to share deeply" (p. 223). Intimate relationships and the consequent sense of security and emotional comfort benefit individuals in a number of ways. For example, individuals with satisfactory close relationships appear to be more resilient to stress, feel better about themselves, and enjoy better physical and mental health (Fehr & Perlman, 1985).

Early interpersonal relationships are believed to play an important role in the development of sexually inappropriate behavior. This may be partly a result of their influence on adult attachment styles and subsequent fulfillment of intimacy needs in adult relationships (Marshall, 1989, 1993; Ward, Hudson, Marshall, & Siegert, 1995; Ward, Hudson, & Marshall, in press). The quality of a person's early interpersonal relationships has been found to be an important predictor of sexually inappropriate behavior in later life (Prentky, Knight, Rosenberg, & Lee, 1989). Similarly, an insecure attachment style has been found to be a vulnerability factor for criminal offending in general, with the various attachment styles being associated with different types of sexual offending (Ward, Hudson, & Marshall, 1995). Our most recent findings point to attachment style, as opposed to offense type, as a categorizing variable, because of its greater ability to predict the individual's experience of interpersonal relationships and general interpersonal style, which are thought to determine offense style (Hudson & Ward, in press-a, in press-b; Ward, Hudson, & Marshall, in press).

In this chapter we argue that attachment theory can provide a useful theoretical framework for the investigation of intimacy deficits in sexual offenders. Before considering the application of this perspective we review the available literature on intimacy deficits and sexual offending.

Intimacy Deficits in Sex Offenders

A number of researchers have consistently observed that sexual offenders are often socially isolated, lonely individuals who appear to have few intimate relationships (Fagan & Wexler, 1988; Marshall, 1989; Tingle, Barnard, Robbin, Newman, & Hutchinson, 1986). Those sexual offenders who have numerous social contacts paradoxically described these relationships as superficial and lacking intimacy (Marshall, 1989). These observations have led researchers to investigate intimacy in sexual offenders by isolating variables believed to be critical to the formation and maintenance of close adult relationships. Early research was based on the hypothesis that sexual offenders possess deficits in the skills necessary for normal sexual and social relationships. Some studies found sexual offenders to be less socially competent than control groups (Overholser & Beck, 1986), whereas others found no evidence for social skills deficits specific to this group (Marshall, Barbaree, & Fernandez, 1995; Stermac & Quinsey, 1986). These inconsistent findings and a general failure to replicate studies may in part be a function of such methodological weaknesses as inadequate control groups, the tendency to rely on behavioral observation and self-report, and the failure to measure social competence adequately. Alternatively, they may reflect a failure to ask the right questions concerning the relationship between interpersonal functioning and sexual crimes.

Failure to attain intimacy may lead to the experience of loneliness, which indeed appears to be a common experience for sexual offenders compared to other offending groups and controls (Awad, Saunders, & Levene, 1984; Fagan & Wexler, 1988; Saunders, Awad, & White, 1986; Seidman, Marshall, Hudson, & Robertson, 1994; Tingle et al., 1986). Although sexual offenders may desire or need intimacy, the fear of rejection may prevent its attainment. Two recent studies have provided some evidence for the association among loneliness, intimacy deficits, and sexual offending. Seidman et al. (1994) compared rapists, child molesters, violent non-sexual offenders, and a community control group on a number of measures of loneliness and intimacy. Their sexual offender groups included both incarcerated and nonincarcerated individuals. Based on the results, the authors suggested that sexual offenders were more deficient in intimacy and more lonely than the other groups. These findings were replicated by Bumby and Marshall (1994) with incarcerated sexual offenders. However, there were additional interesting findings in this study. Intrafamilial child molesters were more fearful of intimacy in relationships than were rapists or the non-sexual-offending control group. Rapists also reported less intimacy in their relationships with males and family members than did child molesters.

Fear of intimacy may be the result of certain beliefs and expectations about the accessibility and reliability of potential partners. A recent study examined beliefs associated with empathy deficits in sexual offenders. Lisak and Ivan (1995) tested the hypothesis that sexually aggressive (rapists) men would hold more gender stereotypes and be more deficient in intimacy and empathy skills than controls. In this study, rapists and control subjects completed a modified version of the Thematic Apperception Test depicting interactions between men and women. They also examined the relationships between empathy, sexual aggression, emotional recognition, sex-role attitudes, and rape myth acceptance in a large sample of undergraduate students using questionnaires. In addition to their finding that rapists had significantly lower intimacy scores than did control subjects, they found that sexually coercive men (in the college sample) were more likely to endorse rape myths, rated themselves as less "feminine," and were less empathic.

This preliminary research has provided some intriguing insights into the nature and extent of intimacy deficits in sexual offenders. However, overall it has suffered from the lack of a theory to organize and guide the research. In a number of theoretical and empirical papers we have suggested that attachment theory can provide a useful theoretical framework to approach the study of interpersonal deficits in sexual offenders (Marshall, 1989, 1993; Ward, Hudson et al., 1995; Ward, Hudson, & Marshall, 1995; Ward, McCormack, & Hudson, in press). In the remainder of this chapter we review this work.

Attachment Style and Intimacy Deficits

Marshall was the first theorist to explicitly make the link between attachment theory and sexual offending (Marshall, 1989, 1993). He argued that the failure of sexual offenders to develop secure attachment bonds in childhood results in a failure to learn the interpersonal skills and self-confidence necessary to achieve intimacy with other adults.

Marshall (1989) suggested that one consequence of a lack of intimacy skills and the subsequent experience of emotional loneliness is that sexual offenders may indirectly seek emotional intimacy through sex, even if they have to force a partner to participate. Individuals who are emotionally lonely may be superficially involved with other people, perhaps even in a long-term relationship; however, their inability to engage in intimate behaviors means that these relationships are ultimately emotionally unfulfilling. Emotional loneliness is said to lead to hostile attitudes and interpersonally aggressive behavior (Diamant & Windholz, 1981; Zilboorg, 1938). In addition, loneliness is related to the acceptance of violence and hostility toward women (Check, Perlman, & Malamuth, 1985).

The fusion of the need for emotional closeness with the drive for sex, together with the often dim awareness that they remain unfulfilled, can lead to persistent promiscuity and increasing sexual deviancy as offenders escalate their attempts to achieve emotional intimacy through sexual contact (e.g., "a more powerful orgasm will make me feel better"). Marshall stressed that social and cultural factors also have a major influence on an individual's capacity to form intimate relationships. The promotion of emotionally inadequate models in the media, for example, the "lonely hero," incapable of expressing his feelings or relating effectively with women, can convey inappropriate messages to vulnerable young men.

Recently we have extended Marshall's theory and proposed a more comprehensive model of the relationship between attachment style, intimacy deficits, and sexual offending. To provide the theoretical context for our work, we first briefly review attachment theory and research.

Attachment Theory

Attachment theory was originally developed by Bowlby (1969, 1973, 1980) and refined by Ainsworth (Ainsworth, 1989; Ainsworth, Blehar, Waters, & Walls, 1978; Ainsworth & Bowlby, 1991). Bowlby's key construct was the attachment system, which was originally developed as an explanatory system for aspects of emotional regulation in infants. The goal of this system was to regulate behaviors designed to obtain and maintain proximity to a preferred individual, the attachment figure, and so ensure that the infant is protected (Alexander, 1992). Attachments are thought to lead to positive emotional states such as joy (when attachments are renewed) and security (when the attachment bond is maintained). Negative emotional states can occur when attachments are threatened (anxiety and/or anger) or lost (sorrow and grief). These styles of emotional regulation persist into adulthood, as do the internal working models of self and significant others. Bowlby was careful, however, to stress that the attachment system is only one of several behavioral systems that regulate an infant's behavior.

It is the putative significance of early attachment experiences for later adult relationships that has recently engendered considerable research attention in clinical psychology and social cognition. According to Bowlby, the development of bonds to a caretaker during a child's early years constitutes the first stage of the attachment process. Whether positive or negative, attachment relationships in childhood are considered to provide growing children with a template for the construction of their future relationships (Bowlby, 1973; Hartup, 1986). In addition, infants develop expectations about the roles of themselves and others in their relationships. For example, they may see themselves as worthy and deserving of others' attention or conversely as worthless and undeserving of attention. It is Bowlby's thesis that the individual thus develops an internal working model about relationships, built around expectations, beliefs, and attitudes resulting from those early attachment experiences.

Ainsworth's work with infants (Ainsworth, 1989; Ainsworth & Bowlby, 1991) suggested three types of attachment: secure, anxious/ambivalent, and avoidant. Secure attachments develop when the parent is sensitive to the needs of the child and responds in a warm and affectionate manner (Paterson & Moran, 1988). Anxious/ambivalent attachment develops when caregivers respond inconsistently to infants. This inconsistency results in such children becoming attention seeking, impulsive, tense, passive, and helpless (Alexander, 1992). Avoidant attachments develop when the caregiver is typically detached, lacking in emotional expression, and unresponsive to the child's needs. These children are characterized by emotional detachment, lack of empathy, and hostile, antisocial behavior.

Recently, researchers have applied attachment theory to the study of adult romantic relationships. These relationships are thought to fulfill the requirements for attachment bonds and are moderately stable (Scharfe & Bartholomew, 1994; Weiss, 1982). For example, changes in personal circumstances, such as losing a partner or experiencing a supportive and loving relationship, may change the attachment style of individuals (Hazan & Shaver, 1994). Typically, researchers have found a correspondence between attachment styles observed in infants and those observed in adults, with between 55% and 65% of adults being classified as securely attached in most studies (e.g., Bartholomew, 1990; Bartholomew & Horowitz, 1991; Hazan & Shaver, 1987).

Bartholomew and her colleagues (Bartholomew, 1990; Bartholomew & Horowitz, 1991; Griffen & Bartholomew, 1991) have extended this early work using a two-dimensional model (of self and of others) that results in four attachment styles depending on whether the views of self and others are positive or negative. In this typology a secure attachment style reflects a positive view of both the self and others, and the preoccupied style, which corresponds to Ainsworth and Bowlby's anxious/ambivalent type, negative views of the self but positive views of others. The original avoidant style has been separated into a fearful type, where both models of the self and others are negative, and a dismissing type, where the model of the self is positive but others are viewed negatively. (See Table 2.1.)

Table 2.1
Attachment Model (Bartholomew, 1990)

		View of Self	
		Positive	Negative
	Positive	Secure	Preoccupied
View of Others	Negative	Dismissing	Fearful

These internal working models of the self, others, and relationships influence subsequent information processing (i.e., attention, appraisal, and interpretation) and the selection and evaluation of interpersonal strategies. Activation of internal working models may occur automatically or consciously in response to attachment-related stimuli (Shaver, Collins, & Clark, 1996). Information that is consistent with internal working models receives more attention than inconsistent information, leading to preferential processing of such data and the perpetuation of existing beliefs. In addition, internal working models direct people to search for attachment information consistent with their expectancies and beliefs.

Attachment Style and Sexual Offenders

Our model is based on Bartholomew's classification of attachment into four fundamental styles. We suggest that the three separate styles of insecure attachment (fearful, dismissive, and preoccupied) are determined by early interpersonal relationships and result in a failure to achieve intimacy within adult relationships (Ward, Hudson et al., 1995; Ward, Hudson, & Marshall, in press). Attachment styles are thought to be a function of different internal working models of the self and others, which develop as a result of cumulative experiences with interpersonal relationships over time. Each style is associated with different interpersonal goals, strategies, and relationship problems. Each style of insecure attachment, in combination with other factors, may lead offenders to pursue intimacy in sexually inappropriate ways.

People who are securely attached (positive self/positive others) have high self-esteem and view other people as generally warm and accepting (Bartholomew & Horowitz, 1991). Their interpersonal strategies and associated internal working models frequently result in high levels of intimacy in close adult relationships. Preoccupied individuals (negative self/positive others) have a sense of personal unworthiness, which, in conjunction with their positive evaluation of other people, leads them to seek the approval of valued others. This style is unlikely to lead to satisfactory relationships, may leave both partners feeling unhappy, or may lead to high levels of loneliness. They are typically sexually preoccupied and attempt to meet their strong needs for security and affection through sexual interactions (Shaver & Hazan, 1988). If a preoccupied man crosses the boundaries with a child and begins to fantasize about a sexual relationship because his attachment style involves a desire for intimacy, he will initiate grooming behavior. Such an offender typically can be expected to view the child as a lover, and the sexual involvement will most likely occur only after some period of courtship-like behavior. Also, he typically believes that the child enjoys the sexual involvement and considers the relationship to be mutual. Because these offenders are concerned about the victim's pleasure, we would not expect them to be aggressive or to use coercion. These expectations fit with the more general nonsexual findings concerning the anxious/ambivalent type (Alexander, 1992).

A major innovation in Bartholomew's work is her distinction between two types of avoidant attachment: fearful and dismissive. Fearful individuals (negative self/negative others) desire social contact and intimacy but experience pervasive interpersonal distrust and fear of rejection (Collins & Read, 1990; Hazan & Shaver, 1987). Because they desire intimacy, such individuals seek to establish close relationships, but their fear of rejection leads them to keep their partners at a distance. These fearful individuals are not likely to be actively hostile in their interactions with others but may express aggression indirectly. The fear of rejection and avoidance of closeness in relationships leads fearfully attached men to seek impersonal contacts with others. Because sex appears to be one way in which they (inadequately) attempt to meet their needs for intimacy, their lives should be characterized by impersonal sex. We can also expect fearfully attached men to be unconcerned about their victims' feelings, so they feel little empathy toward their victims and experience little in the way of guilt about their offending. Similarly, fearful men are self-focused during their offenses and are not inhibited about using force, if necessary, to achieve their goals.

Finally, dismissive individuals (positive self/negative others) are skeptical about the value of close relationships and place a great deal of value on remaining independent and invulnerable to negative feelings. They are more likely to be actively hostile in their interpersonal style. Dismissive individuals are viewed by others as emotionally aloof and cold, and the level of intimacy obtained in close relationships by this group is typically low. Their overriding goal is to maintain a sense of autonomy and independence, and therefore they are likely to seek relationships or social contacts that involve minimal levels of emotional or personal disclosure. Thus, they may, like fearfully attached men, seek impersonal contacts, but these contacts should be characterized by a degree of hostility. Because they blame others for their lack of intimacy, their hostility should be primarily directed toward the gender of their preferred adult partners. Their lack of experience in close relationships, in association with their hostility and lack of interest in the feelings of others, is likely to result in profound empathy deficits. When these men offend, they are likely to do so aggressively. Indeed, the expression of noninstrumental aggression may be as primary as, or more so than, the achievement of sexual goals. Some of these dismissively attached offenders may be so hostile, and may so frequently associate the expression of hostility with deep satisfaction, that they develop sadistic tendencies.

In summary, we identify three separate styles of insecure attachment in our model, each of which leads to a failure to achieve intimacy within adult relationships. These different styles have different internal working models of the self and others and are likely to be associated with different interpersonal goals, strategies, and relationship problems. We propose that intimacy deficits, combined with other factors, may lead offenders to pursue intimacy in sexually inappropriate ways. As a result of their diverse interpersonal styles and intimacy deficits, such individuals are likely to offend sexually in different ways and against different types of individuals. A more comprehensive attachment perspective has the potential to provide a fuller account of the complexity of intimacy deficits in sexual offenders. We suggest that intimacy deficits, combined with disinhibiting factors (e.g., deviant sexual fantasies, alcohol abuse, and cognitive distortions), may lead some men to pursue intimacy in maladaptive ways.

Research Into Attachment Style in Sex Offenders

There has been little research specifically into attachment style and sexual offending. In this section we examine some of our preliminary studies on the romantic attachment style of sexual offenders and other incarcerated offenders. However, first we review the literature on offenders' early interpersonal experiences as it can provide indirect support for the hypothesis that sexual offenders typically suffer disruptions to early attachment relationships.

The Early Interpersonal Relationships of Sexual Offenders. A survey of the empirical literature indicates that many sexual offenders have experienced some form of disruption to their early interpersonal relationships. There is evidence that family variables, specifically the quality of early interpersonal relationships and the experience of sexual deviation and abuse, play a major role in the development and severity of later sexual aggression (Prentky, Knight, Sims-Knight et al., 1989). These two factors are consistent with, and anticipated by, our attachment model. One of the foremost predictions of attachment theory is that the quality of a person's attachment to a primary caregiver is crucial to the development of interpersonal attachment style. In view of this, it seems judicious to review the literature on what is known about sexual offenders' early relationships with their parents

Relationships With Parents. The literature suggests that sexual offenders typically perceive their mothers more positively than their fathers (Hazelwood & Warren, 1989; Tingle et al., 1986). However, this difference appears only to be one of degree. For example, in one study, 36% of sexual offenders described their relationship with their mothers as warm and close and a further 31% described their mothers as cold, distant, uncaring, indifferent, hostile, and aggressive (Hazelwood & Warren, 1989). Apparently, sexual offenders' perceptions of their mother range the full continuum from positive to negative, a finding that provides us with little predictive utility.

One study has provided further information on this issue (Tingle et al., 1986). These researchers found that although the majority of child molesters (83%) reported that their relationships with their mothers were close, only a quarter of these described their mother as someone to whom they could turn with a problem. These authors suggested that the closeness of child molesters to their mothers may be of a more dependent nature rather than a reciprocal one.

Specifically, a number of difficulties have been noted in the relationships between sexual offenders and their mothers. Blaske, Borduin, Henggeler, and Mann (1989) compared adolescents who had committed a sexual offense with other nondelinquent adolescents and found lower rates of positive mother-son communication in the sexual offender group. With respect to differences across sexual offender types, rapists were found to have significantly more arguments with their mothers than were child molesters (Tingle et al., 1986). There is also evidence that sexual offenders identify less with their mothers than with members of other offender groups (Levant & Bass, 1991).

In the sexual offending literature it has traditionally been suggested that the role of the father in the etiology of an individual's sexual offending is insignificant (Tingle et al., 1986). This perspective may have originated from the father's relative lack of involvement in the childhood of many sexual offenders. However, the picture appears to be more complex. Of those sexual offenders who had a father present in their childhood, the relationship is typically described as more problematic and negative than that between mother and son (Lisak & Roth, 1990). This negative perception may be related to the reported high rates of childhood physical abuse inflicted by both biological fathers and stepfathers on sexual offenders (Kahn & Chambers, 1991).

An interesting finding was that rapists' relationship with their fathers was perceived as more distant than child molesters' (Tingle et al., 1986). Rapists' negative view of their fathers was also associated with hostility toward women and issues of anger and power (Hazelwood & Warren, 1989; Lisak & Roth, 1990). Moreover, sexual offenders appear to identify less with their fathers than do other offender groups (Levant & Bass, 1991).

Overall, these findings suggest that fathers may have a significant role in the development of an individual's sexual offending. This may be a function of a lack of involvement in the upbringing of their sons or violence inflicted on them. Arguably, such experiences will have an impact on sexual offenders in their ability to develop working models of relationships.

Loss of Relationship with Caregivers. Another important source of developmental disruption resides in the experience of loss of caregivers. The relationship between parents and their children is necessarily related to the parents' presence or absence in the family home. In a study by Ryan and Lane (1991), a large number (57%) of juvenile sexual offenders were found to have experienced some form of parental loss through death, divorce or separation.

Physical Abuse. A number of researchers have reported high rates of physical abuse in the histories of sexual offenders (e.g., Ryan & Lane, 1991; Seidman et al., 1994). This abuse is most often carried out by biological fathers (44%) and stepfathers (20%) (Kahn & Chambers, 1991). The presence of physical abuse is unlikely to be specific to sexual offenders as rates are high for nonsexual offenders (Lewis, Shanock, & Pincus, 1981). Physical abuse also tends to be more predictive of nonsexual aggression than of sexual offenses (Prentky, Knight, Sims-Knight et al., 1989). The experience of physical violence is likely to result in the development of insecure attachment and the associated belief that relationships are inherently dangerous.

Sexual Abuse. The occurrence of sexual abuse as a child may occur in parallel with physical violence or exist as a separate problem. Estimates of the prevalence of sexual abuse in offenders range from 9% (Fagan & Wexler, 1988) to 47% (Longo, 1982). Milner and Robertson (1990) noted that family sexual deviation is more common in the family backgrounds of sexual offenders than that of other offenders. Across subtypes of sexual offenders, child molesters were around twice as likely to have been sexually abused than rapists (Seghorn, Prentky, & Boucher, 1987). However, rapists were more likely to have been abused by a family member, whereas child molesters were more likely to have been abused by nonfamily members (Seghorn et al., 1987). Such abuse is likely to disrupt attachment in a number of ways (Alexander, 1992), for example, by adversely affecting the development of the self and the capacity to effectively regulate negative affective states. Another possible mechanism is the learning of an association between sexually abusive behavior and close relationships.

Caregiver Inconstancy. The consistency of caregiver availability and response also has important implications for attachment style. The only study to specifically examine this variable used the term "caregiver inconstancy" to describe the stability of the primary caregiver relationship, as measured by the length of time spent with a single caregiver (Prentky, Knight, Rosenberg et al., 1989). They found that this variable was highly predictive of the severity of future sexual aggression.

Peer Relationships. A major factor associated with the development of insecure attachment in childhood is the quality of individuals' peer relationships. Those who have insecure attachments with their caregivers are also likely to have dysfunctional relationships in other areas. Blaske et al. (1989) concluded that sexual offenders typically have lower levels of emotional bonding with peers. Similarly, Tingle et al. (1986) reported that 86% of adult rapists and 74% of their sample of child molesters had few or no friends when young. The importance of peer groups for the development of adult attachment patterns, particularly in adolescence, is currently the focus of theoretical and empirical research in the attachment area (Hazan & Shaver, 1994).

In summary, there is ample evidence that sexual offenders' early interpersonal experiences are characterized by a number of problems. Many of the variables present in their histories have the potential to disrupt their interpersonal relationships and lead to the development of insecure attachment styles. Sexual offenders typically have negative relationships with both parents, identify with their parents less than other offender groups, experience high rates of physical and sexual abuse, are more likely to experience loss of caregivers, are less likely to have a stable and constant relationship with caregivers, and communicate less with parents. In theory, the internal working models of these men reflect these cumulative experiences with relationships and lead to problematic interpersonal expectancies, goals, and strategies.

Romantic Attachment. In a recent study we tested our model of attachment style and intimacy deficits in sexual offenders (Ward, Hudson, & Marshall, in press). In brief, we investigated romantic attachment style in an incarcerated group of child molesters, rapists, violent nonsexual offenders, and nonviolent, nonsexual offenders. The majority of the participants reported an insecure attachment style. This led us to conclude that insecure attachment was likely to be a general vulnerability factor for offending behavior, rather being specific to sexual offenders. As predicted by our model, child molesters were more likely to have a preoccupied or fearful attachment style than were rapists and were less likely to be dismissive. Rapists were indistinguishable from violent offenders in that both groups tended to be dismissive in style. Finally, the nonviolent nonsexual offenders were comparatively the most frequently securely attached. These encouraging results suggested that romantic attachment style is associated with different offending patterns and may underlie the interpersonal difficulties of sexual offenders.

Offender Characteristics and Attachment Style. The focus of a another recent research project was to see how characteristics of offenders such as their level and style of dealing with anger, attitudes toward women and sexual assault, loneliness, and fear of intimacy would relate both to the predominant type of criminal activity they had committed and to the attachment style they reported as most closely resembling theirs. This study indicated that attachment style provided more utility than offense type as a categorizing variable. This was because of its greater ability to predict the individual's experience of interpersonal relationships and general interpersonal style, from which offense style is thought to be determined (Hudson & Ward, in press-a). This suggests that attachment style may be more useful clinically for determining an individual's motivations for offending and offending style than the offense itself.

Offenders' Perceptions of Their Intimate Relations. In a third study (Ward, McCormack, & Hudson, in press) we attempted to obtain more information concerning sexual offenders' perceptions of their intimate relationships. The participants were interviewed and a set of categories was developed from the data using a grounded theory analysis. In the second part of the study these categories were used to identify differences in the perceptions of adult romantic relationships between sexual offenders and the comparison groups. Relationship commitment, evaluation of the partner, self-disclosure, trust, expression of affection, sexual satisfaction, the giving and receiving of support, empathy, conflict resolution, autonomy, and sensitivity to rejection all emerged as significant aspects of sexual offenders' perceptions of their intimate relationships. Our findings also suggested that sexual offenders have a number of intimacy deficits that create difficulties in their romantic relationships. These deficits were to a large extent shared by the violent offenders and, therefore, were not specific to sexual offenders. They represent a general vulnerability factor leading to the development of a variety of offenses and life problems.

This study also attempted to fill in some of the gaps in our knowledge about various aspects of internal working models. In general we found that sexual and violent offenders described relationships with greater impairment of features of intimacy than did nonviolent offenders. Both rapists and child molesters were not very self-disclosing, were reluctant to express physical affection, were not very supportive or empathic, and had poor conflict resolution skills. These features of intimacy correspond with the behavioral plans and strategies of internal working models.

With respect to the differences between sexual offender types, child molesters were more sensitive to rejection, more committed to their relationship and more positive about their partners, and less satisfied with their sexual relationship than were other offender groups. The child molesters' greater sensitivity to rejection arguably reflects their negative beliefs about themselves and contrasts with the tendency to view their partners more favorably. On the other hand, rapists and violent offenders perceived themselves as receiving less support from their partner and tended to evaluate their partners more negatively than did nonviolent offenders. These findings provide some evidence for the existence of more negative internal working models of others and close relationships in these offenders.

Conclusion

The primary aim of this chapter has been to outline our theoretical framework for understanding the intimacy deficits of sexual offenders and to review its direct and indirect empirical support. Our attachment model provides a detailed account of how intimacy deficits may, in conjunction with other factors (e.g., disinhibition), lead to a sexual offense. We suggest that different attachment styles are a result of different internal working models, which develop as a result of cumulative interpersonal experiences. These internal working models are associated with very different emotions and interpersonal beliefs, goals, and strategies. They influence information processing by virtue of their effect on attention, selection, interpretation, encoding, retrieval, enactment, and evaluation. Ultimately, they determine the goal that is salient within an interpersonal context.

We have spelled out the clinical implications of our attachment model in a number of recent publications. In brief, the assessment of each man's attachment style and the associated interpersonal goals and strategies can better inform the process and delivery of treatment. In fact, attachment style has been found to have more predictive utility with respect to interpersonal variables than does category of offense. Different offenders have quite unique interpersonal problems and intimacy deficits, arguably related to their internal working models. For example, the intimacy problems faced by a man whose offending is characterized by fears of rejection and the attempt to cultivate "safe" relationships are very different from those of a man who is dismissive of the value of emotional intimacy. Unless appropriate goals related to overcoming the problematic relationship style are clearly specified, relationship or social skills interventions may be less than optimally effective.

As a final thought, we suggest that the study of intimacy deficits will provide both clinicians and researchers with a more complete understanding of sexually deviant behavior. Our hope is that the framework described in this chapter will facilitate this process and lead to more effective treatment.

References

Ainsworth, M. D. S. (1989). Attachments beyond infancy. *American Psychologist, 44,* 709–716.

Ainsworth, M. D. S., Blehar, M. C., Waters, E., & Walls, S. (1978). *Patterns of attachment: A psychological study of the strange situation.* Hillsdale, NJ: Erlbaum.

Ainsworth, M. D. S., & Bowlby, J. (1991). An ethological approach to personality development. *American Psychologist, 46,* 333–341.

Alexander. P. C. (1992). Application of attachment theory to the study of sexual abuse. *Journal of Consulting and Clinical Psychology, 60,* 185–195.

Awad, G., Saunders, E., & Levene, J. (1984). A clinical study of male sex offenders, International *Journal of Offender Therapy and Comparative Criminology, 28,* 105–115.

Bartholomew, K. (1990). Avoidance of intimacy: An attachment perspective. *Journal of Social and Personal Relationships, 7,* 147–178.

Bartholomew, K., & Horowitz, L. M. (1991). Attachment styles among adults: A test of a four category model. *Journal of Personality and Social Psychology, 61,* 226–244.

Bass, E., & Davis, L. (1988). *The courage to heal.* New York: Harper & Row.

Baumeister, R. F., & Leary, M. R. (1995). The need to belong: Desire for interpersonal attachments as a fundamental human motivation. *Psychological Bulletin, 117,* 497–529.

Blaske, D. M., Borduin, C. M., Henggeler, S., & Mann, B. (1989). Individual, family and peer characteristics of adolescent sexual offenders and assaultive offenders. *Developmental Psychology, 25,* 846-855.

Bowlby, J. (1969). *Attachment and loss: Attachment* (vol. 1). New York: Basic Books.

Bowlby, J. (1973). *Attachment and loss: Separation* (vol. 2). New York: Basic Books.

Bowlby, J. (1980). *Attachment and loss: Loss, sadness and depression* (vol. 3). New York: Basic Books.

Bumby, K. M., & Marshall, W. L. (1994, October). *Loneliness and intimacy deficits among incarcerated rapists and child molesters.* Paper presented at the 13th Annual Research and Treatment Conference of the Association for the Treatment of Sexual Abusers, San Francisco.

Check, J. V. P., Perlman, D., & Malamuth, N.M. (1985). Loneliness and aggressive behavior. *Journal of Social and Personal Relationships, 2,* 243–252.

Collins, N. L., & Read, S. J. (1990). Adult attachment, working models and relationship quality in dating couples. *Journal of Personality and Social Psychology, 58,* 644–663.

Diamant, L., & Windholz, G. (1981). Loneliness in college students: Some theoretical, empirical and therapeutic considerations. *Journal of College Students Personality, 22,* 515–252.

Fagan, J. & Wexler, S. (1988). Explanations of sexual assault among violent delinquents. *Journal of Adolescent Research, 3,* 363–385.

Fehr, B., & Perlman, D. (1985). The family as a social network and support system. In L. L'Abate (Ed.), *Handbook of family psychology and therapy* (vol. 1, pp. 323–356). Champaign, IL: Dow.

Griffen, D. W., & Bartholomew, K. (1991). The metaphysics of measurement: The case of adult attachment. In K. Bartholomew & D. Perlman (Eds.), *Attachment processes in adulthood* (pp. 17–52). London: Jessica Kingsley.

Hartup, W. W. (1986). On relationships and development. In W. W. Hartup & Z. Zubin (Eds.), *Relationships and development* (pp. 1–26). Hillsdale, NJ: Erlbaum.

Hazan, C., & Shaver, P. (1987). Romantic love conceptualised as an attachment process. *Journal of Personality and Social Psychology, 52,* 511–524.

Hazan, C., & Shaver, P. (1994). Attachment as an organisational framework for research on close relationships. *Psychological Inquiry, 5,* 1–22.

Hazelwood, R. R., & Warren, J. (1989). The serial rapist: His characteristics and victims (conclusion). *FBI Law Enforcement Bulletin, 58,* 18–25.

Hudson, S. M., & Ward, T. (in press-a). Attachment, anger, and intimacy in sexual offenders. *Journal of Interpersonal Violence.*

Hudson, S. M., & Ward, T. (in press-b). Rape: Psychopathology and theory. In D. R. Laws & W. T. O'Donohue (Eds.), *Handbook of sexual deviance: Theory and application.* New York: Guilford Press.

Kahn, T. J., & Chambers, H. J. (1991). Assessing reoffence risk with juvenile sexual offenders. *Child Welfare, 70,* 333–345.

Levant, M. D., & Bass, B. A. (1991). Parental identification of rapists and pedophiles. *Psychological Reports, 69,* 463–466.

Lewis, D. O., Shanock, S. S., & Pincus, J. H. (1981). Juvenile male sexual assaulters. *American Journal of Psychiatry, 136,* 1194–1196.

Lisak, D., & Ivan, C. (1995). Deficits in intimacy and empathy in sexually aggressive men. *Journal of Interpersonal Violence, 10*(3), 296–308.

Lisak, D., & Roth, S. (1990). Motives and psychodynamics of self-reported, unincarcerated rapists. *American Journal of Orthopsychiatry, 60,* 268–280.

Longo, R. F. (1982). Sexual learning and experience among adolescent sexual offenders. International *Journal of Offender Therapy and Comparative Criminology, 26,* 235–241.

Marshall, W. L. (1989). Invited essay: Intimacy, loneliness & sexual offenders. *Behavior Research and Therapy, 27,* 491–503.

Marshall, W. L. (1993). The role of attachment, intimacy, and loneliness in the etiology and maintenance of sexual offending. *Sexual and Marital Therapy, 8,* 109–121.

Marshall, W. L., Barbaree, H. E., & Fernandez, Y. M. (1995). Some aspects of social competence in sexual offenders. *Sexual Abuse: A Journal of Research and Treatment, 7,* 113–127.

Milner, R. P., & Robertson, D. S. (1990). Comparison of physical child abusers, intrafamilial sexual child abusers and child neglecters. *Journal of Interpersonal Violence, 5,* 37–48.

Neubeck, G. (1974). The myriad of motives for sex. In L. Gross (Ed.), *Sexual aggression: Current issues* (pp. 56-87). Flushing, NY: Spectrum.

Overholser, C., & Beck, S. (1986). Multimethod assessment of rapists, child molesters, and three control groups on behavioral and psychological measures. *Journal of Consulting and Clinical Psychology, 53,* 55–63.

Paterson, R. J., & Moran, G. (1988). Attachment theory, personality development, and psychotherapy. *Clinical Psychology Review, 8,* 611–636.

Prentky, R. A., Knight, R. A., Rosenberg, R., & Lee, A. (1989). A path analytic approach to the validation of a taxonomic system for child molesters. *Journal of Quantitative Criminology, 6,* 231–259.

Prentky, R. A., Knight, R. A., Sims-Knight, J. E., Straus, H., Rokous, F., & Cerce, D. (1989). Developmental antecedents of sexual aggression. *Development and Psychopathology, 1,* 153-169.

Ryan, G., & Lane, S. (1991). *Juvenile sexual offending: Causes, consequences and correction.* Lexington, MA: Lexington Books.

Saunders, E., Awad, G. A., & White, G. (1986). Male adolescent sexual offenders: The offender and the offence. *Canadian Journal of Psychiatry, 31,* 542–549.

Scharfe, E., & Bartholomew, K. (1994). Reliability and stability of adult attachment patterns. *Personal Relationships, 1,* 23–43.

Seghorn, T. K. Prentky, R. A., & Boucher, R. J. (1987). Child abuse in the lives of sexually aggressive offenders, *Journal of the American Academy of Child and Adolescent Psychiatry, 26,* 262–267.

Seidman, B., Marshall, W. L., Hudson, S. M., & Robertson, P. J. (1994). An examination of intimacy and loneliness in sex offenders. *Journal of Interpersonal Violence, 9,* 518–534.

Shaver, P. R., Collins, N., & Clark, C. L. (1996). Attachment styles and internal working models of self and relationship partners. In G. O. Fletcher & J. Fitness (Eds.), *Knowledge structures in close relationships: A social psychological approach* (pp. 25–61). Hillsdale, NJ: Erlbaum.

Shaver, P. R., & Hazen, C. (1988). A biased overview of the study of love. *Journal of Social and Personal Relationships, 5,* 473–501.

Stermac, L. E., & Quinsey, V. L. (1986). Social competence among rapists. *Behavioral Assessment, 8,* 171–185.

Tingle, D., Barnard, G. W., Robbin, L., Newman., G., & Hutchinson, D. (1986). Childhood and adolescent characteristics of pedophiles and rapists. *International Journal of Law and Psychiatry, 9,* 103–116.

Ward, T., Hudson, S. M., & Marshall, W. L. (1995). Attachment style in sex offenders: A preliminary study. *Journal of Sex Research.*

Ward, T., Hudson, S. M., Marshall, W. L., & Siegert, R. (1995). Attachment style and intimacy deficits in sex offenders: A theoretical framework. *Sexual Abuse: A Journal of Research and Treatment, 7,* 317–335.

Ward, T., Louden, K., Hudson, S. M., & Marshall, W. L. (1995). A descriptive model of the offense chain for child molesters. *Journal of Interpersonal Violence, 10,* 453–473.

Ward, T., McCormack, J., & Hudson, S. M. (in press). Sexual offenders perceptions' of their intimate relationships. *Sexual Abuse: A Journal of Research and Treatment.*

Weiss, R. S. (1973). *Loneliness: The experience of emotional and social isolation.* Cambridge, MA: MIT Press.

Weiss, R. S. (1982). Attachment in adult life. In C. M. Parkes & I. Stevenson-Hinde (Eds.), *The place of attachment in human behavior* (pp. 171-185). New York: Basic Books.

Zilboorg, G. (1938). Loneliness. *Atlantic Monthly,* pp. 14–19.

Chapter 3

Relationships Between Alcohol Use, Alcohol Expectancies, and Sexual Offenses in Convicted Offenders

by Veronique N. Valliere, Psy.D.

Overview

The United States is number one in the world in number of reported rapes (Gelman et al., 1990), and alcohol use has been frequently cited as a, if not the, significant causal factor in criminal behavior of all types, including sexual offenses. The relationship between alcohol and rape is complicated, yet very important with regard to implications for treatment and risk assessment of sex. Should rape be treated as a crime of alcohol or a crime of an aggressive, sexually troubled individual? Is "beer to blame"?

Blaming Alcohol

Offenders will state, indeed, that beer is to blame. In fact, the belief that alcohol may cause criminal behavior permeates our culture often to the extent that alcohol, and not the individual, is held responsible for crime. Determining guilt or innocence or sentencing is often influenced by arguments involving the perpetrator's (or victim's) use of alcohol (Critchlow, 1983). For example, "normal" subjects held a rapist less responsible for a rape in case scenarios in which the rapist was drinking. But the same subjects attributed more responsibility and blame to the victim if the scenario said she had been drinking (Richardson & Campbell, 1982)! A review by Critchlow (1983) summarizes the extreme ambivalence and inconsistency Americans demonstrates toward drinking. Alcohol is used as an acceptable excuse for disinhibited behavior. However, as common as these beliefs are, research has not determined whether it is the effects of alcohol as a drug or the drinker's expectations of the effects of alcohol that contribute to criminal behavior.

Alcohol as a Pharmacological Agent

Alcohol is well-known as a central nervous system depressant. At different levels in the blood, it may produce mild to significant sedation, impaired judgment, poor concentration, euphoria, disinhibition, impaired sexual functioning, and increased aggression (Swonger & Constantine, 1983). Although the physical effects of alcohol are known, clear or causal relationships between alcohol and behavior are undetermined (Carpenter & Armenti, 1972; Marlatt & Rohsenow, 1980). Studies show many contradictory effects of alcohol on different people, suggesting that the effect of alcohol is not consistent or predictable (Lindman, 1982; Rohsenow & Bachorowski, 1984; Steele & Josephs, 1990). Even the pharmacological, or drug, effects of alcohol that seem consistently produced can be influenced by other factors or not produced at all (e.g., Sayette, Contrada, & Wilson, 1990).

Alcohol and Cognitive Processes

Alcohol seems to have some pharmacological effect on cognitive functioning, specifically in information processing, perception, and attention (Medina, 1970; Josephs & Steele, 1990; Steele & Josephs, 1990; Steele & Southwick, 1985). One effect alcohol may have is to produce what some researchers call alcohol myopia.

Alcohol Myopia. Alcohol seems to narrow one's attention, concentration, and perception to only the most immediate cues. Consequently, the drinker's responses to the environment are simplified and only to the most direct stimuli without typical regard to other peripheral cues or internal prohibitions, especially if the stimuli are strong (Josephs & Steele, 1990; Steele & Josephs, 1990; Steele & Southwick, 1985). These researchers argue that alcohol does not directly affect mood by relieving tension, producing euphoria, or increasing aggression. Instead, these effects are secondary to a decreased attention to the stimuli that produce tension or stress and increased attention to stronger stimuli such as positive social interaction, sexual stimulation, or provocation. Apparently, "alcohol myopia" helps to block out stressful things when other, more immediate stimuli are present (Steele & Josephs, 1988; Steele, Southwick, & Pagano, 1986).

These findings may explain why going out with friends to "drink and have a good time" is effective at reducing stress. What is foremost is the music, the friends, and the lively atmosphere rather than the boss, the spouse, or the overdue bills. On the other hand, alcohol alone, or with a negative stressor, would have the effect of increasing stress and increasing a reaction to stress. For example, a drinker, drinking alone, may ruminate on the impending divorce and end up "crying in his beer." In other words, alcohol myopia may cause a worsening of stress, anger, and anxiety if stronger pleasant cues or demands on attention are absent (Josephs & Steele, 1990).

Inhibitory Conflict. The effect of alcohol on information processing ("alcohol myopia") has implications for explaining why drinkers find themselves doing things they believe they would not do if they were not drinking. People usually experience inhibitory conflict" when faced with choosing behaviors against personal or social rules or values, such as indiscriminate sex or aggression. Most people consider consequences, either external or internal, or other factors that help them choose against the action. As alcohol narrows attention to only the most powerful stimuli, the drinker pays less and less attention to the internal and external inhibitions and barriers to the behavior, increasing the chances that the behavior will occur. Basically, alcohol does not cause behaviors or impulses but may influence behavior by increasing the likelihood that the drinker will act on an urge. Alcohol will not have a great effect on weakening very strong inhibitions (Steele & Josephs, 1990; Steele & Southwick, 1985). In other words, drinking probably increases the chances a person will act on something he or she is ambivalent about rather something he or she feels strongly against doing. Alternatively, the person may act out on strong internal impulses (e.g., the urge to offend) that are only controlled by fear of reprisal or such external factors as probation or getting caught. Behaviors would be determined by social, contextual, and psychological factors of the person and the drinking situation, not by the drug effects of alcohol itself.

Alcohol's effect on information processing and inhibitory conflict may be important in explaining rape. Many interviewed rapists claimed that drinking "gave them the courage" to do what they already had impulses to do (Loza & Clements, 1991). It appears that the men presumably are potential rapists with or without alcohol. Studies of arousal to tapes of forced sex support this supposition; rapists showed greater arousal than normals to violent sexual stimuli (Barbaree, Marshall, & Lanthier, 1979). Drinking, for these men, gives greater focus to their impulse to rape while decreasing their attention to the social, personal, or environmental cues that would lead to prohibition of the rape. Drinking cannot make men rape who have no preexisting impulse to rape. This is important information to use in the treatment and assessment of sexual offenders who say that the "beer is to blame."

Alcohol and Aggression/Violence

Reviews of studies by Pernanen (1976) and Evans (1980) demonstrate a relationship between alcohol use of victims and perpetrators and violence. In rape cases, the use of more brutal physical force and violence is associated with the presence of alcohol during the rape (Amir, 1967; Johnson, Gibsen, & Linden, 1978).

Despite the co-occurrence of alcohol use and violence in many studies (see Pernanen, 1976; Evans, 1980), researchers have not demonstrated a clear causal relationship between alcohol and aggression, even in animal studies (Evans, 1980; Pernanen, 1976; Rohsenow & Bachorowski, 1984). A review of animal studies by Evans (1980) shows that animals react to things more or less aggressively depending on other variables (e.g., territory, newness of the environment, and competition) rather than through the effect of alcohol. Although alcohol may affect displays of aggression, as explored previously, alcohol seems to be only one of a number of factors that influence aggressive behavior.

Alcohol and Sexual Behavior

Alcohol and sex go together almost unchallenged in popular "mythology." Yet physiologically alcohol is known to be related to sexual dysfunction, including loss of libido and impotence in heavy users or at higher levels (Carpenter & Armenti, 1972; Wright, Gavaler, & Van Thiel, 1991). Even at lower levels, alcohol increases the time needed to become physiologically prepared for sex by delaying the time of erection and vaginal lubrication, as well as increasing the time needed to achieve orgasm in men and women (George & Norris, 1991; Goldman & Roehrich, 1991). Chronic use of alcohol creates even more profound sexual dysfunction (Crowe & George, 1989).

Some subjects in research use "alcohol as an excuse" for deviant sexual behavior. For instance, sexual deviants (e.g., rapists) and those who experience a high degree of guilt over their sexuality may find more use in blaming alcohol for their sexual behaviors than those who feel less guilty or show less deviance. Scully and Marolla (cited in George & Norris, 1991) found that rapists in their study did a great deal of "excuse seeking" to justify their crimes, naming their use of alcohol as one of the factors that contributed to the rape. Another study found that men who had a great degree of sexual guilt were able to view sexual material for longer periods when they thought they had been drinking. In other words, when these men expected "alcohol as an excuse" for disinhibition, they felt less guilty about indulging in enjoying pornographic material, whether or not they had actually consumed alcohol (Lang, Searles, Lauerman, & Adesso, 1980).

Alcohol and Sexual Crimes

Although there is a long history of studying alcohol's relationship to violent (Pernanen, 1976), sexual (Carpenter & Armenti, 1972), and criminal (Pernanen, 1976) behavior, there has been little adequate research on alcohol and sexual offenses, which typically comprise all of the above. In general, research has found that a significant number of sexual offenders are intoxicated or have been drinking at the time of the offense (Amir, 1967; Johnson et al., 1978; Rada, 1975, 1976; Pernanen, 1976). What Amir (1967) termed "sexual humiliation" (e.g., oral sex) occurred more frequently in rapes in which alcohol was present.

Alcohol Expectancies and Behavior

Alcohol expectancies are anticipatory thoughts or beliefs about the expected relationship between alcohol use and subsequent behavior, a type of "if-then" process used to structure and define relationships (Goldman, Brown, & Christiansen, 1987). Examples might be, "If I go out and drink, then I'll have a good time," or "I'll have a drink and then I'll be relaxed."

Expectancy theory is useful in explaining how alcohol affects people in different ways or why people blame alcohol for things that alcohol does not create (see Goldman et al., 1987, for review). In addition, society, media, or other sources influence the development of alcohol expectancies. Alcohol expectancies can affect drinking behavior even before drinking has begun (George, Derman, & Nochajski, 1989; Maisto, Connors, & Sachs, 1981). Expectancies can enhance, counteract, or otherwise affect the effects of alcohol (e.g. Marlatt & Rohsenow, 1980; Sutker, Allain, Brantley, & Randall, 1982).

Alcohol Abuse and Dependence and Alcohol Expectancies

Alcohol expectancies can help professionals understand problem drinking. Problem drinking or alcohol abuse/dependence has a great many serious and negative consequences, including job loss, family conflict, and social undesirability, as well as significant physical deterioration (American Psychiatric Association, 1987). Yet, if problem drinkers have high positive alcohol expectancies, they may give less regard to negative consequences and reinforce their own drinking through their positive expectations of alcohol (Critchlow, 1983). Leigh (1987) found that people who drink more often and more heavily reported greater positive effects of alcohol than lighter, less frequent users. Moreover, heavier drinkers reported fewer negative effects or minimized negative effects whereas lighter drinkers did not. Southwick, Steele, Marlatt, and Lindell (1981) found, too, that heavier drinkers had greater positive expectancies of alcohol than did moderate or lighter drinkers.

Changes in expectancies seem to be related to a decrease in problem drinking. Connors, Tarbox, and Faillace (1993) studied alcohol expectancies of both male and female problem drinkers being treated on an outpatient basis. Decreased positive expectancies were significantly correlated with decreased drinking behavior.

Alcohol expectancies and their effect on problem drinking have implications for other behavior as well. If heavy drinkers continue to believe that drinking is more positive than negative, despite the negative consequences of problem drinking, positive expectancies may influence and possibly promote other socially undesirable behaviors, such as aggression, violence, deviance, and sex. If people continue to believe behavior is "worth it" despite negative consequences, the behavior may continue.

Alcohol Expectancies and Aggressive Behavior

Alcohol use is strongly associated with aggression and violence. However, most studies on humans of the relationship between alcohol and aggression have failed to control for alcohol expectancies (Marlatt & Rohsenow, 1980). Brown, Goldman, Inn, and Anderson (1980) found that subjects believed or expected alcohol to increase aggression and sexual arousal in people who have been drinking. Placebo studies have shown mixed support for Brown et al.'s (1980) findings.

Mixed results may be confounded by other alcohol expectancies, namely, that alcohol reduces tension and elevates mood (Rohsenow & Bachorowski, 1984). Studies (e.g. Loza & Clements, 1991; Steele & Josephs, 1988) may support a coping process hypothesis for offenders. In this hypothesis, offenders may drink prior to the commission of a crime with the expectation that alcohol will calm them or give them the courage to proceed with the crime. In any event, research supports the idea that alcohol's relationship to aggression is moderated by expectancies that have a far greater effect on behavior than the alcohol itself.

Alcohol Expectancies and Sexual Behavior

There are a number of myths about alcohol and sexual behavior — that alcohol enhances sex, decreases inhibition, makes others more sexually available, among others (Brown et al., 1980). In testing alcohol expectancies related to sexual arousal, research has focused on the expected disinhibiting qualities of alcohol. Namely, researchers presume that sober subjects will not spend time viewing erotica, whether or not they are deviant (e.g., violent), or reporting arousal to the erotica (especially the deviant) as they are more likely to inhibit their sexual expressions.

Numerous studies (using a blind placebo design) demonstrate that male subjects believing they had consumed alcohol, whether or not they had, demonstrated more sexual arousal to both nondeviant and deviant stimuli (Briddell et al., 1978; George et al., 1989; George & Marlatt, 1986; Lang et al., 1980; Lansky & Wilson, 1981). It appears that alcohol expectancies provide some acceptable release of inhibition to sexual arousal, whereas alcohol itself has little to do with sexual arousal. The effects of alcohol expectancies were greater in some subjects as the deviance of the material was increased.

George and Marlatt (1986) found that the impact of alcohol expectancies was greater for subjects viewing slides of violent erotica, a more deviant stimulus than erotic or violent slides. Measurements of penile tumescence demonstrated that subjects who believed they had consumed alcohol both demonstrated and reported greater arousal to sadistic and forcible rape stimuli (Briddell et al., 1978; see Roehrich & Kinder, 1991, for a review of some of this literature).

Based on a review of previous research, it seems clear that people seem to attribute behavior to effects of alcohol that are not definitively pharmacological. Likewise, genuine physical effects of alcohol are exaggerated or used to provide justifications for behaviors and emotions when no clear evidence of causality exists. Expectancies, and their relationship to violent sexual crimes, deserve examination and clarification, especially for issues of criminal defense, treatment, and education.

Purpose of Research

To help clarify some issues regarding alcohol, alcohol expectancies, and rape, I performed a preliminary study with 31 sexual offenders convicted of rape and incarcerated in a treatment center for compulsive sex offenders. Clinically, this research may help shed light on issues in treatment of sexual offenders for alcohol abuse/dependence and demonstrate relationships between alcohol use, alcohol expectancies, and sexual offenses. First, the research explored the relationships between alcohol use and sexual offenses. Previous research suggests that alcohol use in offenders at the time of the crime would be present the majority of the time (Bennett & Wright, 1984; Evans, 1980; Johnson et al., 1978; Mayfield, 1976; Rada, 1975). The rate of alcohol dependence or abuse would be expected to be more prevalent in the surveyed population than in the general population (Rada, 1975). In addition, one would expect higher rates of violence in those offenses in which the perpetrator had been drinking (see Pernanen, 1976, for a review). Offenders who are alcohol dependent or abuse alcohol will be more likely than nonabusing offenders to be drinking at the time of the offense, be drinking during every offense, and offend during their life period of heaviest drinking.

The relationship between alcohol ingestion and rape was examined. Subjects were not expected to attribute the rape solely to the ingestion of alcohol or demonstrate high expectancies that alcohol will lead to their deviant sexual behavior (Henderson & Hewstone, 1984). In other words, they will not say alcohol made them rapists. However, they may reveal that alcohol was a factor in the commission ("It gave me the courage to do what was in my mind"), as described in the study by Henderson and Hewstone (1984) and Loza and Clements (1991), supporting the notion that subjects may use alcohol to decrease inhibitory conflict (Steele & Josephs, 1988; Steele & Southwick, 1985) or to cope with the emotions or situations that contribute to the subjects' decision to offend (Cooper, Russell, & George, 1988). Drinking subjects believe alcohol will calm them or that alcohol gives them "the nerve" to complete an offense they had already planned to commit. Alcohol abusers/dependents are more likely than nonabusing offenders to cite alcohol as a factor in the commission of the crime (Loza & Clements, 1991).

Differences in alcohol expectancies should be found between subjects who meet criteria for alcohol dependence according to the third edition, revised, of the *Diagnostic and Statistical Manual for Mental Disorders* (DSM-III-R; American Psychiatric Association, 1987) and those who do not. Previous research suggests that alcohol-dependent subjects would have higher positive alcohol expectancies and lower negative expectancies than nondependent subjects (Brown et al., 1980; Leigh, 1987; Mann, Chassin, & Sher, 1987; Oei, Hokin, & Young, 1990).

Finally, given the research findings on acquaintance rape (Abbey, 1991) and responses to erotic rape stimuli in nonincarcerated male subjects (e.g., George et al., 1989), it was hypothesized that there would be no significant differences in alcohol expectancies between incarcerated sexual offenders and nonincarcerated subjects (normative data developed on a nonincarcerated population).

Method

Thirty-one adult male sexual offenders were surveyed from a population of offenders imprisoned in a treatment center for compulsive sexual offenders. Admission to the treatment center requires inmates to have a history of repetitive and compulsive sexual offenses. Only offenders who were convicted for sexual crimes against adults (versus children) were interviewed, because of the legal and ethical issues involved in the revelation of crimes against children. Subjects were informed that participation was entirely voluntary and confidential and included no compensation for participation.

Measures were administered in a fixed order. Data was collected for the three most recent offenses of each subject. Only offenses known to the court were reported, to protect the rights of each subject. Information about alcohol environment, violence, and victim use were collected as some research has suggested that these factors are influenced by or influence alcohol use and expectancies (Lindman, 1982; Pernanen, 1976; Richardson & Campbell, 1982).

Structured Clinical Interview for DSM-III-R (SCID). The SCID Section E questionnaire (Spitzer, Williams, & Gibbon, 1985) assisted clinicians in establishing the presence/absence of a DSM-III-R diagnosis of lifetime substance abuse/dependence. Subjects, depending on the outcome of this interview, received substance abuse and/or dependence diagnoses, according to the criteria established by DSM-III-R (American Psychiatric Association, 1987).

Alcohol Expectancy Questionnaire—III (Adult) (AEQ). The AEQ measures alcohol expectancies on six subscales: positive global changes, enhanced sexual performance and experience, physical and social pleasure, increased social assertiveness, relaxation and tension reduction, and arousal and power (Brown, Christiansen, & Goldman, 1987; Brown et al., 1980). It is a self-administered, true-false questionnaire. Higher scores on the scales indicate stronger beliefs or expectancies.

Results

Demographics and Descriptive Data. Subject demographics of this sample differed in some ways from samples of other studies. For example, Henn, Herjanic, and Vanderpearl (1976), in a sample of 69 rapists, found 75% under the age of 30. Hodgins and Lightfoot's (1989) sample had a mean age of 28.6 years. The mean age of this sample was 37 years. The age difference could be explained in part by this sample's long treatment and incarceration history. Also, MacDonald's (cited in Henn et al., 1976) and Amir's (1967) samples of rapists were predominantly black males, whereas this sample consisted mainly of white males. Race, previous psychiatric history, age of first sexual intercourse, age of first arrest, and age of first offense were not significantly related to a diagnosis of alcohol dependence.

Characteristics of Alcohol Use. More than 61% of the sample reported drinking immediately prior to the commission of the rape. Alcohol dependence diagnoses were given to 45.2% ($n = 14$) of this subject population. Drug dependence was found in 38.7% ($n = 12$) of the subjects.

Chi-square analyses of the data revealed a number of significant relationships. Surprisingly, an alcohol dependence diagnosis was only somewhat related to citing alcohol as a factor in the commission of the rape with the corrected value [c2 (1) = 3.7, 5.24, $p < .10$, $p < .05$. Subjects who met criteria for alcohol abuse or dependence diagnoses were significantly more likely to be drinking during every offense than those who did not meet criteria for any alcohol abuse or dependence diagnoses [c2 (1) = 13.33, 16.36, $p < .001, p < .001$]. Subjects who were likely to abuse alcohol were also more likely to use it during the crime, as predicted. Finally, as predicted, alcohol dependence diagnoses were significantly related to whether or not the offense occurred during the subjects life-time period of heaviest drinking [c2 (1) = 9.14, 11.52, $p < .01, p < .001$]. The alcohol-dependent subjects raped during the time in their life they were exhibiting the most severe symptoms of alcohol dependence or when they were drinking more heavily than they had at any other time of their life. This finding implies that these alcohol-dependent men had uncontrolled sexual, aggressive, and drinking behavior during this period.

Characteristics of Sexual Offenses. Data on 61 rapes was analyzed. Subjects were asked whether they had planned the rape prior to commission or whether they used physical violence other than the rape itself, such as battering, choking,, or punching the victim, or had a weapon the victim saw during the rape. Data related to the offense was corroborated with victim accounts of the crime.

Chi-square analyses were used to analyze the data. Alcohol dependence was not significantly related to rape characteristics of violence, premeditation, occurrence in a drug or alcohol environment, or victim use of drugs or alcohol prior to the rape. Drinking during the offense was not significantly related to the presence of violence during the rape.

Subjects were generally consistent in their rape behavior. When an offender was violent during any rape, he was significantly more likely to be violent in all his rapes [c2 (1) = 13.28, 16.12, $p < .001, p < .001$]. If the subject planned or premeditated one rape, he was significantly more likely to premeditate others, or not to premeditate any [c2 (1) = 9.71, 12.47, $p < .01, p < .001$]. Premeditation and violence were not related significantly to substance use and may represent behaviors not resultant from alcohol or drug use or severe character pathology but specific to certain subtypes of rapists.

Alcohol Expectancy Data and Analyses. Independent t-tests were used to compare scores from the six subscales of the AEQ. Within the sample, AEQ scores of alcohol-dependent subjects were compared to the AEQ scores of nondependent subjects, to explore whether the alcohol-dependent subjects had significantly higher positive alcohol expectancies or lower negative expectancies than the nondependent group, as data from Leigh (1987) and Southwick et al. (1981) would suggest. None of analyses revealed significant differences in expectancies between the alcohol-dependent and the nondependent group. Although these findings are not consistent with the hypotheses, they may be consistent with the fact that alcohol dependence did not show a strong relationship to identifying alcohol as a factor in commission of the offense.

Independent t-tests were performed to compare this sample's AEQ scores on the five subscales with the norms of the AEQ. As predicted, this sample's alcohol expectancies were not significantly higher than the normative sample for any of the five scales (excluding the scale measuring increased power and arousal). These subjects did not feel that alcohol caused behavior any more than "normal" subjects do. In general, alcohol expectancies did not differentiate these repetitive and significantly alcohol abusing subjects from other populations. However, these subjects had significantly lower expectancies of enhanced sex than did the normative sample [t (469) = 2.18, $p < .05$]. These findings suggest that these subjects may have been educated about the relationship, or lack thereof, between alcohol use and sexual behavior.

The sample was divided into alcohol-dependent and nondependent subgroups and each subgroup compared to the AEQ norms. Findings were consistent with those of comparisons of the total sample with AEQ norms. Using independent t-tests, there was no difference between the alcohol-dependent subjects and the normative sample on all five scales.

Discussion

This exploratory study has supported the finding of other researchers (e.g., Rada, 1975) who have found that the incidence of alcohol use and dependence in sex offenders exceeds that expected in a normal population. More than 61% of this sample had been drinking prior to every offense, similar to findings by Johnson et al. (1978) who found that 63.1% of their sample had been drinking prior to a rape. More than 45% of this sample met diagnostic criteria for alcohol dependence. Alcohol dependence was not correlated with race, age, or education. From this data, no profile of a typical rapist or drinking rapist appeared.

However, there was some evidence for consistency in the rapists' behavior. If an offender was likely to abuse alcohol, he was likely to be drinking at the time of every offense. If an offender was likely to be violent during one offense, he was likely to have been violent in all his offenses. Again, if he premeditated one rape, he was likely to have premeditated all his rapes. These factors were not significantly interrelated.

The hypotheses that alcohol would be present in the rape situation a majority of the time and that the prevalence of alcohol dependence would be greater in this population than expected in the general population were supported by this data. Alcohol-dependent subjects were significantly more likely to be drinking at the time of the offense and to commit the offense in their lifetime heaviest period of drinking, as hypothesized. Alcohol-dependent subjects were only slightly more likely to cite alcohol as a factor in the commission of the rape, supporting the hypothesis only weakly.

As predicted, this sample had no significantly different alcohol expectancies than did the normative sample in Brown et al.'s (1980) study of 440 male subjects from a variety of settings. Intuitively, as rape is a sexually violent crime, one might expect a rapist to use alcohol because he expects it to increase his arousal, aggressiveness, or social assertiveness or expects it to increase the woman's sexual permissiveness or even expects alcohol to enhance the sexual experience for both himself and the victim. These beliefs about alcohol give the perfect excuse, as in acquaintance rape, to act in a sexually disinhibited manner. This evidence is supported by numerous studies on expectancies and sexual and aggressive behavior (e.g., Briddell et al., 1978; Henderson & Hewstone, 1984; Lang et al., 1980).

The lower alcohol expectancies of this sample may reflect the effect of treatment for alcohol-related disorders. In the interviews, subjects revealed to this examiner that they had been taught about the "true" effects of alcohol and confronted for their "blame" of alcohol for their behavior. Education and treatment may have modified alcohol expectancies of this group. Or, these men may never have differed in their expectancies from a nonrapist, nonincarcerated population. Thus, the beliefs of the alcohol-dependent subjects differed from those that were predicted.

Study of this limited subject pool limits the generalizability of the results. Any significant relationships, or lack of relationships, found between alcohol use, alcohol expectancies, and rape may be true only for severe and repetitive rapists. However, if the results in this study are similar to those relationships between alcohol and rape found in presumably less severe offenses (e.g., acquaintance rape) and more typical subjects (e.g., college or nonincarcerated males), they may validate those relationships and imply that relationships found are consistent throughout the continuum of male sexual behavior. In other words, alcohol and rape may be related in consistent, predictable ways and the decision to rape or severity of a rape results from differences in the offender and not the use of alcohol.

In this study, that appears true. Drinking at the time of the offense was not significantly related to violence or premeditation. Alcohol dependence did not correlate significantly with number of rapes or violence. The use of alcohol appears to be a relatively discrete variable that may have been a factor in the crime but was not a significant element determining any characteristics of the crime or in identifying the rapist.

Given theses results, it would appear that alcohol expectancies are not the most useful measures to identify rapists or alcohol abuse by rapists. For example, measuring alcohol expectancies of college students to determine the effect alcohol may have on their decision to rape may not provide predictive information, perhaps, to target for education. However, one must not lose track of the fact that the men in this study had been in prolonged treatment in a therapeutic environment; moreover, many of the alcohol-dependent subjects had had prior alcohol treatment and it is possible that treatment may have successfully challenged and modified the subjects' expectancies prior to this study.

The exact relationship between rape and alcohol use or alcohol dependence in these subjects continues to be unclear. What is clear, and what was predicted, is that alcohol did not cause these men to rape, to be violent in the rapes, or to premeditate rape. Many of the subjects interviewed commented that alcohol was not the cause of their behavior. Some anecdotally attributed their behavior to their own sexual abuse history; their problems with anger, women, or authority; or other severe trauma in their lives. "Alcohol gave me the courage to do it," was frequently stated in one way or another by many of the subjects who had been drinking. These statements, plus the findings, support the idea that rape is a by-product of internal states, thoughts, and emotions in conjunction with environmental and social variables.

As a result of the evidence in both this and other research, I support the theory that alcohol provides a "myopic" view or perception of internal and external prohibitions to crime, specifically rape. As Steele and Josephs (1988, 1990) and Steele and Southwick (1985) suggest, alcohol affects information processing in such a way as to decrease the conflict that enforces social rules and produces socially acceptable behavior, if only through awareness of the consequences of inappropriate behavior. When some people drink, alcohol's effect of decreasing attention to only the most demanding and salient stimuli may free them from the only moderate inhibitions against their impulses to fight, steal, or rape. People with demanding impulses to rape may cope with these impulses by decreasing their conflicts about them through drinking. Alcohol provides an acceptable excuse, as well as the "courage" for the behavior. The impulse exists, and for some is acted out, without alcohol.

The implications of this theory in regard to treatment are significant. Addressing and combatting alcohol myopia in sex offenders is twofold. Treatment professionals should be reluctant to adopt an "alcohol is to blame" explanation of sex offending. Sex offending starts with preexisting impulses and arousal. First, abstinence from alcohol should be a lifetime goal for offenders. It is important to encourage offenders to avoid stimuli that would increase their reoffense risk. Although alcohol does not cause offending, it may increase the chance that an offender will act on an urge he may otherwise be too conflicted to carry out. Of course, not drinking will not prevent offenses, either. Second, a segment of treatment should focus on increasing an offender's conflict about offending. The stronger the inhibitory conflict, the less likely it will be diminished easily.

All levels of media, from newspapers to posters, promote that belief that there is a direct causal relationship between alcohol and rape. Yet, research is not as clear on this conclusion. Education as to the "real" effect, or lack of effect, of alcohol on behavior should be provided to the public. Successful education would promote greater awareness throughout the criminal justice system, as well as in the general public, thereby, perhaps, modifying decision making in the areas of guilt or innocence of offenders, the blame of victims, or treatment and sentencing.

Conclusion

Rape is a serious issue in this country for both men and women. Factors affecting rape should continue to be explored in research. Alcohol use, especially if it serves to decrease offenders' conflicts regarding rape, should be a subject in treatment and research.

Research on factors leading to recidivism of rapists should continue. Education of rapists on their own and other's drinking behavior should continue to be a component in treatment. Methods of treatment to increase the cues against rape, and thus the inhibitory conflict, may be successful in combatting rape impulses. This would be useful for both the rapists who drink and those who do not. A greater study of the individual and the environmental factors that produce rape behavior should continue.

To be able to say that "rape starts here" or that "beer is to blame" for rape would incredibly simplify two highly complex and somehow interwoven behaviors: drinking behavior and rape behavior. Both men and women suffer from the stereotypes and myths about rape, from the act to derisive and abusive treatment in court to useless and improper treatment and sentencing. To effectively address rape as an issue, research and education must focus on uncovering the variables that combine to produce rape, with alcohol being one, not cited as *the* one.

References

Abbey, A. (1991). Acquaintance rape and alcohol consumption on college campuses: How are they linked? *Journal of American College Health, 39,* 165–169.

American Psychiatric Association. (1987). *Diagnostic and statistical manual of mental disorders* (3rd ed., rev.). Washington, DC: Author.

Amir, M. (1967). Alcohol and forcible rape. *British Journal of Addictions, 62,* 219–232.

Barbaree, H., Marshall, W., & Lanthier, R. (1979). Deviant sexual arousal in rapists. *Behavior Research and Therapy, 17,* 215–222.

Bennett, T., & Wright, R. (1984). The relationship between alcohol use and burglary. *British Journal of Addiction, 79,* 431–437.

Briddell, D. W., Rimm, D. C., Caddy, G. R., Krawitz, G., Sholis, D., & Wunderlin, R. (1978). Effects of alcohol and cognitive set on sexual arousal to deviant stimuli. *Journal of Abnormal Psychology, 87,* 418–430.

Brown, S. A., Christiansen, B. A., & Goldman, M. S. (1987). The Alcohol Expectancy Questionnaire: An instrument for the assessment of adolescent and adult alcohol expectancies. *Journal of Studies on Alcohol, 48,* 483–491.

Brown, S. A., Goldman, M. S., Inn, A., & Anderson, L. R. (1980). Expectations of reinforcement from alcohol: Their domain and relation to drinking patterns. *Journal of Clinical and Consulting Psychology, 48,* 419–426.

Carpenter, J., & Armenti, N. (1972). Some effects of ethanol on human sexual and aggressive behavior. In B. Kissin & H. Begleiter (Eds.), *The biology of alcoholism: Physiology and behavior* (vol. 2, pp. 509–543). New York: Plenum Press.

Connors, G. J., Tarbox, A. R., & Faillace, L. A. (1993). Changes in alcohol expectancies and drinking behavior among treated problem drinkers. *Journal of Studies on Alcohol, 53,* 676–683.

Cooper, M. L., Russell, M., & George, W. H. (1988). Coping, expectancies, and alcohol abuse: A test of social learning formulations. *Journal of Abnormal Psychology, 97,* 218–230.

Critchlow, B. (1983). Blaming the booze: The attribution of responsibility for drunken behavior. *Personality and Social Psychology Bulletin, 9,* 451–473.

Crowe, L. C., & George, W. H. (1989). Alcohol and human sexuality: Review and integration. *Psychological Bulletin, 105,* 374-386.

Evans, C. M. (1980). Alcohol, violence, and aggression. *British Journal on Alcohol and Alcoholism, 15*(3), 104-117.

Gelman, D., Springen, K., Elam, R., Joseph, N., Robins, K., & Hager, M. (1990, July 23). The mind of the rapist. *Newsweek,* pp. 46–52.

George, W., Dermen, K. H., & Nochajski, T. H. (1989). Expectancy set, self-reported expectancies, and predispositional traits: Predicting interest in violence and erotica. *Journal of Studies on Alcohol, 50,* 541–551.

George, W., & Marlatt, G. A. (1986). The effects of alcohol and anger on interest in violence, erotica, and deviance. *Journal of Abnormal Psychology, 95,* 150–158.

George, W., & Norris, J. (1991). Alcohol, disinhibition, sexual arousal, and deviant sexual behavior. *Alcohol Health and Research World, 15,* 133–138.

Goldman, M. S., Brown, S. A., & Christiansen, B. A. (1987). Expectancy theory: Thinking about drinking. In H. T. Blane & K. E. Leonard (Eds.), *Psychological theories about drinking and alcoholism* (pp. 181–226). New York: Guilford Press.

Goldman, M. S., & Roehrich, L. (1991). Alcohol expectancies and sexuality. *Alcohol Health and Research World, 15,* 126–132.

Henderson, M., & Hewstone, M. (1984). Prison inmates' explanations for interpersonal violence: Accounts and attributions. *Journal of Consulting and Clinical Psychology, 52,* 789–794.

Henn, F. A., Herjanic, M., & Vanderpearl, R. H. (1976). Forensic psychiatry: Profiles of two types of sex offenders. *American Journal of Psychiatry, 133,* 694–696.

Hodgins, D. C., & Lightfoot, L. O. (1989). The use of the Alcohol Dependence Scale with incarcerated male offenders. *International Journal of Offender Therapy and Comparative Criminology, 33,* 59–67.

Johnson, S. D., Gibson, L., & Linden, R. (1978). Alcohol and rape in Winnipeg: 1966–1975. *Journal of Studies of Alcohol, 39,* 1887–1894.

Josephs, R. A., & Steele, C. M. (1990). The two faces of alcohol myopia: Attentional mediation of psychological stress. *Journal of Abnormal Psychology, 99,* 115–126.

Lang, A. R., Searles, J., Lauerman, R., & Adesso, V. (1980). Expectancy, alcohol, and sex guilt as determinants of interest in and reaction to sexual stimuli. *Journal of Abnormal Psychology, 89,* 644–653.

Lansky, D., & Wilson, G. T. (1981). Alcohol, expectations, and sexual arousal in males: An information processing analysis. *Journal of Abnormal Psychology, 90,* 35–45.

Leigh, B. C. (1987). Evaluation of alcohol expectancies: Do they add to the predictability of drinking patterns? *Psychology of Addictive Behavior, 1,* 135–139.

Lindman, R. (1982). Social and solitary drinking: Effects on consumption and mood in male social drinkers. *Physiology and Behavior, 28,* 1093–1095.

Loza, W., & Clements, P. (1991). Incarcerated alcoholics' and rapists' attributions of blame for criminal acts. *Canadian Journal of Behavioural Science, 23,* 76–83.

Maisto, S. A., Connors, G. J., & Sachs, P. R. (1981). Expectation as a mediator in alcohol intoxication: A reference level model. *Cognitive Therapy and Research, 5,* 1–18.

Mann, L. M., Chassin, L., & Sher, K. J. (1987). Alcohol expectancies and the risk for alcoholism. *Journal of Consulting and Clinical Psychology, 55,* 411–417.

Marlatt, G. A., & Rohsenow, D. J. (1980). Cognitive processes in alcohol use: Expectancy and balanced placebo design. *Advances in Substance Use, 1,* 159–199.

Mayfield, D. (1976). Alcoholism, alcohol, intoxication and assaultive behavior. *Diseases of the Nervous System, 37,* 228–231.

Medina, E. L. (1970). The role of alcohol in accidents and violence. In R. Popham (Ed.), *Alcohol and alcoholism* (pp. 351–355). Toronto: University of Toronto Press.

Oei, T. P. S., Hokin, D., & Young, R. (1990). Differences between personal and general alcohol-related beliefs. *International Journal of Addictions, 25,* 641–651.

Pernanen, K. (1976). Alcohol and crimes of violence. In B. Kissin & H. Begleiter (Eds.), *Social aspects of alcoholism* (pp. 351-443). New York: Plenum Press.

Rada, R. T. (1975). Alcoholism and forcible rape. *American Journal of Psychiatry, 132,* 444–446.

Rada, R. T. (1976). Alcoholism and the child molester. *Annals of the New York Academy of Sciences, 273,* 492–496.

Richardson, D., & Campbell, J. L. (1982). Alcohol and rape: The effect of alcohol on attributions of blame for rape. *Personality and Social Psychology Bulletin, 8,* 468–476.

Roehrich, L., & Kinder, B. N. (1991). Alcohol expectancies and male sexuality: Review and implications for sex therapy. *Journal of Sex and Marital Therapy, 17*(1), 45–54.

Rohsenow, D. J. & Bachorowski, J. (1984). Effects of alcohol and expectancies on verbal aggression in men and women. *Journal of Abnormal Psychology, 93,* 418–432.

Sayette, M. A., Contrada, R. J., & Wilson, G. T. (1990). Alcohol and correspondence between self-report and physiological measures of anxiety. *Behavior Research and Therapy, 28,* 351–354.

Southwick, L., Steele, C., Marlatt, A., & Lindell, M. (1981). Alcohol-related expectancies: Defined by phase of intoxication and drinking experience. *Journal of Consulting and Clinical Psychology, 49,* 713–721.

Spitzer, R. L., Williams, J. B. W., & Gibbon, M. (1985, July 1). *Instruction manual for the Structural Clinical Interview for DSM-III-R (SCID)* (rev.). New York: Research Department, New York State Psychiatric Institute.

Steele, C. M., & Josephs, R. A. (1988). Drinking your troubles away II: An attention allocation model of alcohol's effect on psychological stress. *Journal of Abnormal Psychology, 97,* 196–205.

Steele, C. M., & Josephs, R. A. (1990). Alcohol myopia: Its prized and dangerous effects. *American Psychologist , 45,* 921–933.

Steele, C. M., & Southwick, L. (1985). Alcohol and social behavior I: The psychology of drunken excess. *Journal of Personality and Social Psychology, 48,* 18–34.

Steele, C. M., Southwick, L., & Pagano, R. (1986). Drinking your troubles away: The role of activity in mediating alcohol's reduction of psychological stress. *Journal of Abnormal Psychology, 95,* 173–180.

Sutker, P. B., Allain, A. N., Brantley, P. J., & Randall, C. L. (1982). Acute alcohol intoxication, negative affect, and autonomic arousal in women and men. *Addictive Behaviors, 7,* 17–25.

Swonger, A. K., & Constantine, L. L. (1983). *Drugs and therapy: A handbook of psychotropic drugs.* Boston: Little, Brown.

Wright, H. I., Gavaler, J. S., & Van Theil, D. (1991). Effects of alcohol on the male reproductive system. *Alcohol Health and Research World, 15,* 110–114.

Chapter 4

An Empirical Investigation of Floodgates Factors in Child Sexual Abusers

by Mark A. Gould, Ph.D.

Overview

In the last 100 years, since the pioneering work of Krafft-Ebing (1882/1965) concerning pedophilia, many theories have been proposed to understand perpetrators of child sexual abuse. The first theories developed from clinical practice and were based on the theoretical orientation of the researcher. Models and theories of child sexual abuse were developed from medical classification systems (Krafft-Ebing, 1882/1965), from psychodynamic theory (Bell & Hall, 1971; Fenichel, 1945; Freud, 1905/1962; Groth, Hobson, & Gary, 1982; Peters, 1976; Stoller, 1975), behavioral approaches (Abel, Becker, Murphy, & Flanagan, 1981; LoPiccolo, 1992; Maletzky, 1991; Quinsey, 1977), relapse prevention (Pithers, 1988), and family therapy interventions (Faller, 1988; Giarretto, 1982; Justice & Justice, 1979; Madanes, 1990). Recently, a trend has developed for more integrated theories of child sexual abusers from a psychodynamic perspective (Knight & Prentky, 1990; Schwartz & Masters, 1993), from a cognitive-behavioral approach (Marshall & Barbaree, 1990), and from social psychology (Finkelhor, 1984). These attempts at integration of the research and knowledge about child sexual abusers have been very useful in furthering understanding and interventions with child sexual abusers, but they have continued to be somewhat biased as they are based on one theory or another. What is needed is a comprehensive model that allows for the integration of all the other approaches, motivational and disinhibition factors, and offense dynamics.

The Dynamics of Sexual Assault

Schwartz (1988, 1995) developed the "dynamics of sexual assault" model to incorporate all the previous models and research involving perpetrators of sexual assault. This model facilitates knowledge concerning all types of sexual offending. It integrates and provides a framework to understand the significance and levels of motivational factors in the commission of sexual assaults. Disinhibition factors are specified and their variable functions in sexual assaults can be assessed. External factors of environmental opportunities and attributes of the victims are also part of this model. Finally, the specific offense dynamics of the sexual assault are included. The dynamics-of-sexual-assault model serves as a framework for an integrated, holistic, and individualized approach to the understanding and treatment of people who sexually assault, including child sexual abusers (Schwartz, 1995).

The dynamics-of-sexual-assault model (Schwartz, 1988, 1995) has five basic components:

- The reservoir of motivation
- The floodgates of inhibition
- Environmental opportunities
- Attributes of the victim
- The sexual assault

These components are presented in a dynamic model that functions like a dam. The motivation to sexually assault builds in the reservoir and then runs against the floodgates, which may restrain it if they are intact and the energy level is low or may allow its expression if the floodgates are impaired or if the level of motivation is high enough to overcome them. Once the motivation to sexually abuse goes beyond the internal control of the person, he or she begins to examine the environment for opportunities to satisfy this drive. Depending on the specific offender pattern, the individual may initiate a search for an acceptable victim. If he or she finds any potential victim, has an opportunity for sexual assault, and has the motivation, a sexual assault may occur.

Each of these five basic components is inclusive of previous models and research and incorporates a wide range of offender dynamics. The reservoir of motivation can include any of the previous models or theories of offender motivational factors. The variability and buildup of motivation to sexually abuse can be examined in this model, as well as differentiating the situational from the chronicity of the motivation. In the Schwartz (1988, 1995) model, the reservoir of motivation includes the emotional, sexual arousal, and blockage factors (beliefs, values, thoughts, feelings, and behaviors). It can also incorporate such other models of sex-offending behavior as sexual addictions (Carnes, 1983), relapse prevention (Pithers, 1988), and the more traditional models of motivation to sexually offend. In fact, what is perceived as comprising the reservoir of motivation is based on the theoretical orientation of the therapist (Schwartz, 1988). The motivational factors are not bound to any specific theoretical orientation in the Schwartz (1988, 1995) model, which makes this a comprehensive and integrated model.

The general function of the floodgates can be assessed and their involvement in allowing the expression of the motivation to sexually abuse can be evaluated. Because the floodgates factors are delineated, each can be evaluated for specific offenders and their functioning can be monitored over time. Some offenders may have occasional dysfunction in these floodgates, whereas other offenders may have chronic impairment in one or more of these factors. There may also be an additive function in the impairment of these factors. The degree and chronicity of impairment of these factors can be used to differentiate risk assessment for offenders. There is always a ratio between the motivational and floodgates factors for every case of sexual assault (Schwartz, 1988). Floodgates factors also may vary within an offender over time. There is considerable variance in the ratio and interaction of the motivational and disinhibition factors.

The environmental opportunities factor can be used to establish high-risk situations for each offender and to develop relapse prevention strategies. In determining the specific environmental opportunities for offenders, their cruising behaviors (looking for potential victims) can be identified and disrupted. How each offender manipulates his or her environment and how these actions affect their offense cycle can also be useful in understanding and treating sex offenders.

The attributes of the victim can differentiate how specific in victim selection each offender is, how much access and availability he or she has to potential victims, how grooming behaviors (selecting a potential victim and gaining his or her trust and confidence) have been used, and how they interact in the perpetrator's offense cycle. By examining attributes of the victim, researchers can make a differential assessment of the offender's sexual preferences and identify arousal patterns (Barbaree & Marshall, 1989; Dougher, 1988; Quinsey, 1977). Some offenders have specific preferences, whereas others may respond to a wide range of potential targets.

The sexual assault illustrates each offender's modus operandi, offender profiling, level of experience in sexual assaults, offense history, specific dynamics of offending, level of violence, premeditation, and additional information concerning his or her offense cycle. Strategies and coping skills can be developed to address offenders' assault patterns in a relapse prevention plan. Based on the dynamics of the sexual assault, practitioners can identify specific thoughts, feelings, behaviors, and offense cycle for each offender.

All the dynamics-of-sexual-assault stages (Schwartz, 1995) can be used to understand, evaluate, classify, and treat offenders. The five-step model suggests that there are numerous places for intervention and treatment, and that a more comprehensive understanding of the offender's patterns and sequences of behaviors can be used in evaluation and treatment. Overall, the model developed by Schwartz (1988, 1995) is comprehensive, integrating current research and theories on sexual offenders and serving as a basis for further research in the field. The motivational factors are central to sexually assaultive behavior, but they are highly individualized and variable among offenders, so that they do not lend themselves to empirical validation. The floodgates factors are more specific and identifiable. These factors lend themselves well to empirical study. Environmental opportunities, characteristics of victims, and the sexual assaults are specific and unique to each offender, so they are also difficult to study. Therefore, given the current state of knowledge concerning sex offenders, the best place for research to begin is with the floodgates-of-inhibition factors.

In the Schwartz (1988, 1995) model, the floodgates factor presumably functions to restrain the impulse to sexually abuse. Factors that can open the so-called floodgates include stress, substance abuse, mental retardation, psychosis, brain damage, criminal thought processes, lack of empathy, and peer pressure (Schwartz, 1988). Pornography has recently been added as a factor. However, its addition occurred subsequent to this research being conducted. The floodgates are specific and central to allowing the expression of motivational energy to sexually abuse that is required but not sufficient for sexual abuse to occur. Further, the floodgates play a variable role for different types of offenders (Schwartz, 1988, 1995). Situational offenders are theorized to "have a problem primarily with the floodgates portion of this system" (Schwartz, 1995, p. 2-27). The importance of the floodgates for inhibition of motivational energy is greatest when the motivational levels are low or moderate. At such times, if the floodgates are intact, no motivation to abuse is expressed. If the floodgates are impeded though, even low levels of motivation are released and the risk of an offense occurring increases. When motivation to sexually abuse is high, the floodgates are generally unable to inhibit it; thus it is assumed that they are not a significant factor at such times. Patterned offenders, as a result of their high levels of motivation, may quickly overcome the floodgates. The most predatory types of offenders may have a severe disruption of these factors: "[T]he control system is almost totally destroyed so that the offender is always either committing a sexually deviant act or in the process of preparing to commit one" (Schwartz, 1995, p. 2-27). Impairment in the floodgates may also be additive. "The lack of control may be enhanced in an additive manner by failures at many separate points (stress + intoxication + a momentary lack of empathy), or by the continual influence of one's disinhibitors (e.g., chronic alcoholism)" (Schwartz, 1995, p. 2-27). It is this differential influence of the floodgates that is useful in separating persons who have high motivation to sexually abuse children from those who have much lower interest.

What is needed is an empirically based study on the impact of the involvement of the floodgates factors in sexually assaultive behavior for an identified offender population. This study was an investigation of floodgates factors for child sexual abusers. A close examination of inhibition/floodgates factors highlights the similarities and differences between intrafamilial and extrafamilial child sexual abusers. The floodgates of inhibition (Schwartz, 1988) can be divided into three categories: situational (stress, alcohol), characterological (criminal thought processes, lack of empathy, peer pressure), and neurological impairment factors (mental retardation, psychosis, and brain damage). The situational factors stand out as the most variable of the categories. Because they have the highest variability in the situational floodgates, and they are postulated to be involved in situational child sexual abuse (Schwartz, 1988), they are marked as a good candidate for exploring differences between extrafamilial and intrafamilial offenders.

Stress has been cited as an important factor, particularly in the occurrence of intrafamilial sexual abuse (Justice & Justice, 1979; Mayer, 1983; Ingersoll & Patton, 1990). Justice and Justice (1979) described stress as involving excessive life changes in the family. They used the Schedule of Recent Experiences (SRE) developed by Holmes (1981) to measure these life changes in incestuous families. Justice and Justice (1979) hypothesized that excessive change in families puts demands on each member of the family. These demands may result in stress, and too much stress may result in child sexual abuse (Justice & Justice, 1979) and other problems (Justice & Justice, 1976). However, Justice and Justice (1979) did not statistically evaluate the level of stress in the families with which they worked but rather simply presented anecdotal information. Given such weak evidence, an empirical study of the role of stress in intrafamilial sexual abuse appears warranted.

The second situational floodgates factor, alcohol abuse, has been identified as important in classification systems since Krafft-Ebing (1882/1965). Estimates of alcohol abuse rates for sex offenders have ranged from 20% (Shaken, 1939) to 66% (Owen & Steele, 1991). Incarcerated intrafamilial child sexual abusers have been found to have the highest rates of alcohol abuse of all sex offenders (Aarens et al., 1978). The limitations of this study were that all the offenders Aarens et al. (1978) studied were institutionalized, and the sample of incest offenders was disproportionately low in comparison to the number of child molesters. Therefore, the observed differences may be the result of biased samples.

In her statewide study in Michigan, Faller (1988) found that 52.7% of a community-based sample of intrafamilial offenders had a serious problem with addiction to drugs or alcohol. Her study is limited in that all her data was predicated on a community-based sample of persons reported to a human services department for child sexual abuse. Faller's sample consisted of primarily intrafamilial child sexual abusers, and she lacked significant numbers of both extrafamilial abusers and the more serious type of offenders, who usually end up incarcerated. Groth et al. (1982) also noted the importance of alcohol abuse for some child sexual abusers. As a whole, these studies support the idea that measuring alcohol abuse in a systematic manner would be useful in exploring differences and similarities between incarcerated and community-based intrafamilial and extrafamilial child sexual abusers. Unfortunately, such systematic collection of data has not yet been carried out. Although these studies are flawed, they do point to the potentially important role of alcohol as a floodgates factor.

Given that offenders are found both in prison and in the community, and that these populations may differ in critical ways, my study drew from both of these populations. The current study was designed to systematically explore differences in situational floodgates factors for incarcerated and community-based samples of intrafamilial and extrafamilial child sexual abusers. Stress and alcohol were expected to exert a greater effect on the occurrence of situational child sexual abuse (Schwartz, 1988). Intrafamilial offenders have been hypothesized to be situational offenders (Quinsey, Chaplin, & Carrigan, 1979; Quinsey, 1977; A. N. Groth, personal communication, May 15, 1987). Therefore, the situational factors of stress and alcohol were expected to have a greater impact on the occurrence of abuse with intrafamilial child sexual abusers than with extrafamilial abusers.

With regard to population, independent of familial type, prison-based subjects were hypothesized to have higher motivation to sexually abuse and thus be less influenced by these same floodgates factors than community-based subjects, who were expected to have a lower motivation to abuse. One reason is that child sexual abusers who are incarcerated are more serious offenders in that they may have a greater number of victims, more violent crimes, or a longer history of offenses. Therefore, it is likely that there was a higher percentage of patterned, chronic child sexual abusers in the prison-based populations than in the community-based populations. The chronic, patterned-type offenders may be less likely to be influenced by situational floodgates factors, or they may have such a profound lack of impulse control that they would act on even a small amount of deviant motivation (Schwartz, 1988).

Additional moderator variables, which in past studies have been variously related to intrafamilial and extrafamilial child sexual abusers, were included in this study. These variables are as follows: age of the offender at time of first offense (Groth et al., 1982), gender of the victim(s) (Abel, Becker, Cunningham-Rathner, Mittelman, & Rouleau, 1988; Groth et al., 1982), and number of prior arrests or convictions for sex offenses (Marshall, Jones, Ward, Johnson, & Barbaree, 1991; Quinsey, 1977). The present study also examined whether variation in these variables was related to type of sexual abuse and custody status. Data obtained provided a better understanding of the similarities and differences between intrafamilial and extrafamilial child sexual abusers sampled from two different populations.

Methods

Participants. All 139 participants in this study were men ages 21 to 72 years old who had been arrested for sexual involvement with children and who were in treatment programs in the same northwestern state. The participants were all volunteers and they were divided into four groups based on custody status (outpatient vs. incarcerated) and familial status with the victim (intrafamilial vs. extrafamilial). The distribution of the participants is indicated in Table 4.1.

For the purposes of this study, intrafamilial child sexual abuse includes adult child sexual interactions within the same household where both parties are related by heredity (parent, grandparent, uncle, etc.) or where the perpetrator was in a caregiving or parental role with authority and power over the child(ren), such as a live-in boyfriend (Faller, 1988). The participants were designated "intrafamilial" based on self-report to a question in the survey that asked: "Were the victim(s) in your present offense related to you and/or members of your immediate household?" If they answered in the

Table 4.1
Number of Volunteers Representing Each of the Factors of
Familial and Custody Status

Custody Status	Extrafamilial	Intrafamilial	Totals
Outpatient	$N = 31$	$N = 55$	$N = 86$
Incarcerated	$N = 22$	$N = 31$	$N = 53$
Totals	$N = 53$	$N = 86$	$N = 139$

affirmative, the participants were classified as intrafamilial. If they answered "no," they were considered extrafamilial. No efforts were made to verify status through official records, questions to therapists, or any other external means of verification.

Inclusion criteria were that participants were adult men who had been sexually involved with children under 18 years of age and at least five years younger than themselves, that they were in sex offender treatment programs, and that they completed and returned the survey packet, particularly providing data on the instruments and the demographic and floodgates factors.

Instruments. The Michigan Alcohol Screening Test (MAST) is a 24-item yes/no instrument that has been validated for the evaluation of alcohol abuse and dependence in wide array of populations (Miller & Marlatt, 1984; Seltzer, 1971; Skinner, 1979; Zung, 1979). The MAST is considered the standard instrument for measuring these disorders (Aarens et al., 1978). It has been used to assess problems with alcohol abuse for sex offenders (Faller, 1988; Rada, 1976). The MAST was scored according to the standard criteria established by Seltzer (1971).

The SRE (Holmes, 1981) is a 42-item yes/no survey scale that includes statements concerning changes in family, economic, or social status occurring over the previous year. The reliability ($r = .062$) of the SRE for offenders was found to be consistent for the period prior to and during incarceration (Masuda, Cutler, Hein, & Holmes, 1978), and it is useful for measuring life change events (Holmes & Rahe, 1967).The SRE has been used in various anecdotal studies with sex offenders against children (Gould, 1986; Justice & Justice, 1979) and is based on theories (Mayer, 1983; Schwartz, 1988) that include stress as an important factor for child sexual abusers.

A brief, 29-question demographic and floodgates factor questionnaire was also included in the survey and was used to obtain information concerning current age, age at time of present offense, relationship to victim(s), year of present offense, history of prior offenses, number and gender of victims, and ethnicity of the offenders. There were also other questions concerning the Schwartz (1988) floodgates factors of a history of psychiatric disorders, serious head trauma, developmental disabilities, previous sexual and nonsexual felonies, alcohol and illegal drug use, and prior incarcerations. These questions required either a yes/no or brief answer (e.g., a date or number).

Procedures

Incarcerated Sample. A formal written request to conduct research was made to the corrections department in a northwestern state which had specialized units for sex offender treatment. Once permission was granted to do research, the researcher contacted the acting director of the sex offender program was contacted to make the necessary arrangements for data collection. Prospective participants were informed by the staff at the correctional center that a researcher would be conducting a survey.

The researcher recruited volunteers within the day rooms of their living units for two days by distributing a letter of invitation and by inquiring if they would be interested in participating in the survey. Men who expressed an interest in the study were given an informed consent form to read and sign. Once the men signed it, they were given a survey to fill out at their leisure, which they were asked to return to the researcher. No incentive for participation was provided or given. The completed questionnaires were collected and the participants thanked. All data was anonymous.

Outpatient Sample. Outpatient sex offender treatment providers were identified in the same state as the correctional center program through their membership in a national organization, the Association for Treatment of Sexual Abuses. The researcher contacted these treatment providers by phone. The researcher discussed the goals and objectives of the research with the providers and requested their cooperation in distributing survey packets. If the providers agreed, they were asked how many potential participants they had in the their programs. Survey packets (including a letter of invitation, consent form, survey form, and a return, self-addressed, stamped envelope) were sent to the outpatient sex offender therapists to distribute to prospective volunteers. The participants completed the consent form and survey at their leisure and mailed them back to the researcher. Approximately two months were allocated for data collection. The outpatient therapists were reminded and advised prior to the end of data collection to ask their clients who wished to participate to return the completed consent forms and surveys to the researcher.

All data collection with both the incarcerated and outpatient samples was anonymous. The consent form stated that participation was voluntary, that participants could withdraw at any time, that there were no incentives or any repercussions for completing or failing to complete the survey, and that only aggregate summaries of the data would be shared with the treatment staff. Debriefing procedures were explained and if participants wanted a copy of the findings, all they had to do was put their name and address on the consent form. If they had any questions, the researcher's name and phone number were noted. All data was coded, entered, and scored in a mainframe computer for analysis.

Results

Sample Description. Table 4.2 shows the profile of the typical participant. As illustrated in Table 4.2, this sample is composed of white, middle-aged men (average age 39.3 years) who are facing their first arrest for sexual involvement with girls (79.9%). Although for the majority of the participants this was their first arrest, two-thirds of them acknowledge prior sexual involvement with children. Statistically they averaged 19.9 prior victims, but the median was 4 victims, which suggests that a small minority of offenders had a large number of prior victims. Only a small number of participants (19.4%) had a previous arrest for a sex offense. An additional 14.4% of participants had convictions for other nonsexual prior felonies. More than a quarter of the sample had been previously incarcerated. The majority acknowledged use of alcohol for many years.

Floodgates Factors Data

As Table 4.3 demonstrates, the most frequently endorsed floodgates factors were alcohol (61.2%) and drug (64.7%) use. Among drug users, marijuana was the most frequently used substance. A considerable number of men reported that they had sustained a serious head injury in the brain damage factor (mean = 28.8%) or had been diagnosed as developmentally disabled or been in special education classes in school (mean = 23%). Almost one-fifth of the offenders (19.4%) reported previous convic-

Table 4.2
Profile of a Typical Survey Participant

Factor	Mean	S.D.	Range
Demographics			
Age	39.3	10.56 years	21–72 years of age
S.O. Tx.	26.32 months	26.29	1–132 months
Ethnicity	82% white (7.2% Hispanic, 4.3% Native American, 2.9% African American)		
Gender orientation	80% hetero (9.6.% bisexual, 4.4% homosexual)		
Education	12.75 years	2.77	4–20 years of schooling
Income	$22,010.57	$15,681.31	$0–$100,000
Present Offense			
First conviction	80.6%		
Yr. of offense	1987.76	3.99 yrs.	1973 to 1993
Age at crime	34.2 yrs	11.21	15–68 years old
# of victims	1.46	0.82	0–6 victims
Gender of victims	79.7% girls (13.8% boys,6.5% both)		
Prior Offense History			
Did you have prior involvement?	67% yes		
Age of first offense	24.28	13.33	6–64 years
# of prior victims	19.90	43.33	1–300 victims, median = 4
Prior S.O. arrests	19.4%		
# of prior S.O. arrest	2.22	1.87	1–8 arrests
Gender of victim	63% girls, 23% both, 14% boys		1
Prior non-S.O. felonies	14.4%'		
# prior felonies	1.89	1.33	1–6 felonies
Prior incarcerations	26% yes		
# of incarcerations	1.97	1.30	1–6 priors
ETOH use	59%	1.30	
Years ETOH	20.41	11.65	2–60 years
# daily drinks	8.71	9.20	0–48 drinks per day

$N = 139$

Table 4.3
Distribution of Floodgates Factors in Total Sample

Item No.	Focus	N	% Acknowledge	Comments
1	Psych. Dx.	16	11.5	schiz = 1; dep = 4; unk = 3; man dDep = 1; PTSD = 3; sex psycho = 2; dual personality = 1; MR = 1; brain damage = 1
2	Brain damage	40	28.8	
3	Senility	2	1.4	
4	DD/MR	32	23	
5	Codefendant	0	0	
6	Lack of empathy	19	13.7	
7	Prior S.O.	27	19.4	M = 2.22 prior sex offenses
8	Prior felonies	20	14.4	M = 2.55 prior non-sex felonies
9	Alcohol use	85	61.2	
10	Drug use	90	64.7	pot 77%; coke, 24%; hallucinogen, 11%, speed, 10%; heroin, 4%; sedative/downer, 4%; crack, 2%; crank, 2%; inhalant, 1%

$n = 139$

tions for sexual offenses (mean = 2.22 sex offenses) and 14.4% had prior nonsexual felonies (mean = 2.55% felonies). Although 11.5% stated they had a prior psychiatric diagnosis, most were for depression (four cases), posttraumatic stress syndrome (three cases), unknown (three cases), and sexual psychopath (two cases). Only 1.4% had had a psychiatric disturbance (one case each of schizophrenia and manic depression). Senility occurred only in two cases and no one reported having a codefendant who might have exerted peer pressure in the commission of the present offense.

Clearly, the reported rates of several factors (brain injury, developmental disability, psychiatric diagnosis) are higher than was expected from previous research. The rates of substance abuse clearly are much higher than most of the previous research concerning sexual abusers found. The vast majority (64.7%) of offenders in the current sample acknowledged it as a problem. This is an area that might profit from more systematic, empirical research.

Table 4.4 presents a comparison of similarities and differences of floodgates-of-inhibition factors for child sexual abuses. The factors in the chart are based on the information obtained in the survey and on self-report by the men who participated in the study. Significant results are discussed by main effect categories.

Table 4.4
Analysis of Similarities and Differences on Floodgates Factors Among Child Sexual Abusers

Floodgates Factor	Type of Test	Type of Score	Community Based		Incarcerated		Interaction Effect (p level)	Total Community Based	Total Incarcerated	Main Effect (p level)	Total Extra-	Total Intra-	Main Effect (p. level)
			Extra	Intra	Extra	Intra							
Dx	Chi Square	%	13.8	18.2	7.1	16.1	N.S.	10.5	17	N.S.	15.1	10.3	N.S.
Head injury	chi sq.	%	24.1	25	36.4	38.7	N.S.	25.6	37.7	N.S.	29.4	29.9	N.S.
Senility	chi sq.	%	0	0	4.5	3.2	N.S.	0	3.8	N.S. (p = .069)	2	1.1	N.S.
MR/DD	chi sq.	%	17.2	18.2	50*	25.8	p = .012 (E)	18.8	35.8*	p = .025	31.4	20.9	N.S.
Codefendants	chi sq.	%	0	0	0	0	N.S.	0	0	N.S.	0	0	N.S.
Victim suffer	chi sq	% no	27.6*	5.5	4.5	1.3	p = .032 (E)	13.3	9.4	N.S.	17.6	8.2	N.S.
Prior S.O.	chi sq.	%	24.1	3.6	59.1*	16.1*	p = .011 (E) p = .039 (I)	10.5	34***	p = .0007	39.2***	8	p = .0001
# of S.O.	ANOVA	Mean	.35	0.04	1.55	0.45	N.S. (p = .050)	0.14	.91***	p = .000	.86**	0.18	p = .001
Prior felonies	chi sq.	%	6.9	10.70	33.3*	16.10	p = .016 (E)	9.3	23.1*	p = .026	18	12.6	N.S.
# of prior	ANOVA	Mean	1.00	2.67	1.57	1.75	N.S.	2.25	1.64	N.S.	1.44	2.3	N.S.
Use of alcohol	chi sq.	% yes	41.4	56.4	72.7	71.0	N.S.	50.60	71.70	p = .010	54.9	63.1	N.S.
# of years	ANOVA	Mean	9.54 (yrs.)	11.09	13.43	13.52	N.S.	10.56	13.48	N.S.	11.20	11.95	N.S.
Passed out	chi sq.	% yes	21.4	47.3	61.9	43.3	p = .014	38.5	51.0	p = .043	38.8	45.9	N.S.
Offense ETOH	chi sq.	% yes	17.9	29.6	47.6	26.7	N.S. (p = .052)	25.6	38.3	N.S.	30.1	28.6	N.S.
Daily drinks	ANOVA	Mean drinks	1.89	1.39	9.5	6	N.S.	1.6	7.54**	p = .000	4.72	3.11	N.S.
Use of drugs	chi sq.	% yes	55.2	69.6	81.8	66.7	N.S. (p = .082)	64.7	73.1	N.S.	66.7	68.6	N.S.
N =		n =	31	55	22	31		86	53		53	86	139
MAST	ANOVA	Mean	10.04	14.48	21.96*	13.71	p = .019	12.96	17.34*	p = .039	15.39	14.21	N.S.
SRE	ANOVA	Mean	236.65	322.33	420.27*	354.03	p = .017	293.7	381.53**	p = .001	320.81	334.17	N.S.

* p < .05, ** p < .01, ***p < .001

Extrafamilial child sexual abusers scored significantly higher on having previous sex offenses and on the number of convictions for previous sex offenses. All the other variables showed no significant differences when participants were classified based on intrafamilial versus extrafamilial present offenses.

The other main effect was based on custody status. Incarcerated participants scored significantly higher on six factors directly related to their offense history and five other factors connected to impairment of their impulse control. The offense history factors included significantly lower age for first sex offense, a higher number of prior sex offense convictions, having prior sexual involvement with children, prior convictions for nonsexual felonies, and previously being incarcerated. These factors (longer offense history, higher rates of convictions for past sexual offenses and nonsexual felonies, and a greater number of offenses per offender) indicate that these men may be higher-risk offenders, which may increase their likelihood of being incarcerated. The other factors that were also significantly higher for incarcerated participants were having a history of being placed in special education classes and alcohol use/abuse issues (having used alcohol, MAST scores, amount drank daily, and having passed out while drinking). Being in special education classes may have been the result of behavioral problems and/or developmental disabilities and may reflect higher impulsivity. In addition, the sex offender treatment program surveyed had a special unit for developmentally disabled sex offenders, so some of the increase in numbers reflects the composition of the correctional center program, where approximately 20% of the residents were in the developmental disability unit. Higher levels of alcohol abuse could also contribute to impairment in impulse control.

Extrafamilial outpatient child sexual abusers showed significantly less empathy for their victims than did other offender groups. The incarcerated extrafamilial offenders showed significantly higher levels of having been in special education classes, of previous convictions for sexual offenses and nonsexual felonies, and a higher number of prior sex offenses. These arrest history risk factors for incarcerated, extrafamilial child sexual abusers are considerably higher than those for incarcerated, intrafamilial child sexual abusers and serve as much of the basis for the higher rates indicated for incarcerated participants.

Addictive Aspects of Floodgates Factors

The incarcerated, extrafamilial child sexual abusers had the highest rates on six of the floodgates factors, as Table 4.5 shows. They had the highest situational factor scores (for stress and alcohol abuse), the highest characterological scores (for prior sexual offenses and nonsexual felonies), the highest ranking in two of three neurological impairment factors (mental retardation/developmental disability and senility) and the highest ranking for prior diagnosis of psychosis. Only peer pressure could not be ranked due to lack of response to this item by all the participants.

This group also exhibited the longest criminal involvement and arrest history. The incarcerated extrafamilial child sexual abusers were the youngest of the offender groups (30 years old) at the time of their current offenses and they had the lowest annual income ($14,044). They had the highest percentage of boys as their victims (22.7%) and a higher incidence of both boys and girls as victims in their current offenses (13.6%). They had significantly higher rates of conviction for both sexual

Table 4.5
Rank Order of Floodgates Factors X Custody X Familial Status

		Custody Status			
Floodgates Factor		**Outpatient**		**Incarcerated**	
		Extra	**Intra**	**Extra**	**Intra**
I	Stress (SRE)	4	3	1	2
II	Substance abuse				
	Alcohol (MAST)	4	2	1	3
	Drugs	4	2	1	3
III	Criminal thought process				
	Prior sex offenses	2	4	1	3
	Prior felonies	4	3	1	2
IV	Lack of empathy	1	2	3	4
V	Peer pressure (Codef't)	0	0	0	0
VI	MR/DD	4	3	1	2
VII	Brain damage				
	Head injury	4	3	2	1
	Senility	0	0	1	2
VIII	Psychosis	2	0	1	0

(59%) and nonsexual felonies (33%), a higher number of past sexual crimes (1.55 offenses), more frequent past incarcerations (0.74), and a greater average number of past victims (30.81). Overall, the incarcerated, extrafamilial child sexual abusers are the most chronic of the offender groups.

Schwartz (1988, 1995) considered the floodgates factors to be additive and the data for the incarcerated, extrafamilial child sexual abusers is consistent with her conceptualization of the functions of the floodgates of inhibition. The incarcerated extrafamilial offenders have high rates of impairment in six of the eight floodgates factors. They also have the highest rates of offense behavior (number of convictions, number of victims, and length of offense history). The incarcerated, extrafamilial child sexual abusers seem to be a high-risk group with significant impairment in three-quarters of the Schwartz (1988, 1995) floodgates-of-inhibition factors.

Discussion

Honesty and self-disclosure appeared to be good in this study based on the admission of two-thirds of the subjects that they had prior, largely undetected sexual contact with children before their present offense. Less than 20% had been previously arrested for another sexual offense. Had participants doubted the confidentiality of the study, they would not have disclosed prior undetected sexual involvement because they resided in a state in which they could have been prosecuted for acknowledging prior, undisclosed sex offenses against children. The cooperation, candor, and self-disclosure of participants in this study was facilitated by their participation in treatment and their willingness to volunteer.

The rates of substance abuse (65% moderate to severe alcohol dependency) in this study were higher than those found in many of the previous studies (Faller, 1988; Gebhard, Gagnon, Pomeroy, & Christenson, 1965; Hucker et al., 1986; Justice & Justice, 1979; Pithers, Kashima, Cumming, Beal, & Buell, 1988; Rada, 1976; Stokes, 1964). Only Owen and Steele (1991) reported a comparable rate of 66% for incarcerated incest offenders. The rate of alcohol dependency for incarcerated child sexual abusers in the present study was 66.1%. Clearly, alcohol abuse and dependency are severe problems for most child sexual abusers.

The lack of separate data for drug use in prior studies is a serious oversight based on the current findings. The data from this study indicates that 64.7% of the participants acknowledged use of illegal drugs. This is clearly an area that might benefit from further investigation.

The high rates of substance abuse found in the present study may be the result of an increase in substance abuse in recent years, or the fact that few investigators have used a standardized instrument to measure substance abuse, or that they have failed to ask about illegal drug use, or that the participants were more forthright in their answers in the current study. Whatever the reason, substance abuse seems to be an important factor for child sexual abusers. Substance abuse may serve a disinhibitory function for first-time, situational offenders and then may be used to address issues of shame and guilt in chronic offenders (Schwartz, 1988).

The floodgates factors of brain injury (28.8%) and developmental disabilities (23%) also were much higher than expected from the general sex offender literature (Faller, 1988; Mohr, Turner, & Jerry, 1964; Murphy, Coleman, & Haynes, 1983). Only Peters (1976) found a comparable rate of developmental disabilities (33%) in an outpatient sample of pedophiles, using a Revised Beta Examination cutoff rate of IQ of < 85. The higher incidence of these factors in the present study may reflect that the specific sex offender treatment program utilized for data collection had a specialized unit for developmentally disabled and brain injured residents. The community rate of 18.8% for developmental disabilities is closer to the average in the general sex offender population as reported by Murphy et al. (1983) of all sex offenders. The rates of serious head injury were not significantly different among the groups in this study. It may be that the current findings are the result of a too general question or that other studies have looked at brain damage based only on test results (Rubenstein, 1992). The present data may have cast a broader net. It may also be that other researchers have not asked questions about brain or head injury because they lacked a theoretical model (Schwartz, 1988, 1995) that specified it as an important disinhibition factor. Further research might compare rates of minor brain injury for child molesters with that of the normal population and in the context with other floodgates factors. Prentky and Burgess (1991) have postulated a multifactoral mechanism that includes brain lesions (which would be the result of head trauma) in combination with other factors as a basis for repetitive sexual aggression. Research in this area may be more complex than investigators have typically undertaken.

Theoretical models (Schwartz, 1995; Prentky & Burgess, 1991) may help guide further inquiry in this area.

The floodgates aspect of the Schwartz (1988, 1995) model has proven to be empirically validated by my study. Her floodgates factors can differentiate between offenders, identify higher-risk offenders, and serve as a basis for further research. The only factor that did not generate a response was the peer pressure question. It may be that this is not a significant factor for child sexual abusers (as they generally act alone in secrecy) or that better questions were not offered to validate this factor for child sexual abusers. Peer pressure was included to help explain gang rape.

Second, Schwartz's (1988, 1995) hypothesis that the effect of the floodgates factors may be additive was clearly shown for the incarcerated, extrafamilial child sexual abusers. They led the other groups in 75% of the floodgates factors and they are the most chronic and serious offenders (highest number of victims, highest number of prior convictions for sex offenses, longest history of offending behavior, etc.)

The incarcerated, extrafamilial child sexual abusers had the highest scores on both the MAST (mean = 21.96) and the SRE (mean = 420.27). This group also had the highest levels of impairment in six of the eight floodgates factors. Half reported attending special education classes. More than one–third reported a history of serious head injury. Just under 5% reported diagnosis either for senility or psychosis (schizophrenia), which was the highest rate for all offender groups. They reported a history of alcohol use for more than 13 years with daily alcohol consumption averaging 9.5 drinks. The incarcerated, extrafamilial sex offender group seems to have poor impulse control, as is evident in their leading the observed offender groups in the vast majority of floodgates factor categories and in their highest rates of acting out sexually and criminally.

The additive effect of the floodgates factors can be seen in the offense histories of this group. They have the highest rates of previous sex offenses (59.1%) and the largest number of prior victims (mean = 30.81 prior victims). The data supports Schwartz's (1988, 1995) additive effect of the floodgates factors, but it also questions her assumption that floodgates factors are only significant for situational offenders (Schwartz, 1988). The results are more in line with her current view (Schwartz, 1995) that severe and chronic impairment in the floodgates factors along with high motivational energy may result in an offender who is always either committing or planning a new sexual offense.

Conclusion

The current data lends some empirical support for the Schwartz (1988, 1995) dynamics-of-sexual-assault model, particularly for the floodgates of inhibition. Several of the floodgates factors were present for a large part of the sample. Substance abuse (including drugs and alcohol) was a factor for about two-thirds of the sample. Developmental disabilities and brain injury were present in a large number of the cases, particularly for the incarcerated sample. High levels of stress for the year prior to the most recent offense were present for the vast majority of the child sexual abusers. Finally, the additive function of the floodgates factors was evident in the chronicity and offense histories of the incarcerated, extrafamilial child sexual abusers. As a result of impairment in the majority of floodgates factors and their offense histories, this group tends to have poor impulse control.

The floodgates factors of alcohol abuse and stress may serve different functions for various groups of child sexual abusers. For the incarcerated, extrafamilial group, alcohol use may be part of their chronic offending cycles in that it may reduce the guilt and shame after offending and assist them in tolerating their abusive behavior. For the outpatient, intrafamilial sample, the floodgates factors of stress and alcohol may reflect a situational disturbance that contributed to the lowering of inhibitions in the initiation of their offense (Justice & Justice, 1979; Mayer, 1983).

The theory supported from the current data depends on the population studied. If only the outpatient population is studied, the data appear to level support for the family-based theories that see intrafamilial child sexual abusers as being different from other sex offenders (Giarretto, 1982; Giarretto, Giarretto, & Sgroi 1978; Madanes, 1990) and more highly influenced by the situational variables of stress (Justice & Justice, 1979; Mayer, 1983) and alcohol (Aarens et al., 1978).

If only the incarcerated sample is examined, the data supports various sex offender theories that consider intrafamilial and extrafamilial child sexual abusers to represent an overlapping heterogeneous continuum of sex offenders where offenders abuse children both within and outside the family (Abel, Becker, Mittelman, Cunningham-Rathner, & Murphy, 1987; Finkelhor, 1984, 1986; Marshall & Barbaree, 1990; Quinsey, 1977; Pithers, 1988; Salter, 1988; Schwartz, 1988). If both the incarcerated and outpatient samples are combined, they are seen as a heterogeneous population that is differentiated by custody status and not relationship status. The northwestern state in which this study was undertaken does appear from this data to have clearly differentiated child sexual abusers into appropriate custody statuses. The most impulsive and chronic offenders are incarcerated and the most situational-type offenders are in the community.

This study suggests further research in such areas as a closer examination of the floodgates factors (Schwartz, 1988, 1995). The usefulness of the role of the floodgates factors in finding differences and similarities among child sexual abusers was partially supported by this study. These floodgates factors may be of value in understanding and evaluating child sexual abusers. A more thorough and systematic evaluation of these factors in differing offender groups is needed. Many of the floodgates factors have been understood individually but have not been studied collectively and in combination. The present study found that the additive function of the floodgates factors was present in the most chronic group of child sexual abusers.

Given the larger than expected percentage of developmentally disabled offenders in the incarcerated sample and the high incidence of a past history of serious head injury, further research on the significance of neurological impairment of this population might be warranted.

Substance abuse focusing on both alcohol and illegal drug use of child sexual abusers could benefit from further research. Drug use has not been systematically studied for this population. As two-thirds of the participants acknowledged use of illegal drugs and often use of several drugs, it may be beneficial to explore drug use and involvement in child sexual abuse. The multiple roles of substance abuse and dependency for child sexual abusers might also be further studied. The function and meaning of substance abuse may differ between first-time and chronic offenders and should be further evaluated. As previously mentioned, pornography has been added as a floodgates factor and should be studied in this context.

This model was developed to explain all types of sexual assault. Therefore, research should be conducted with other types of sex offenders.

Finally, researchers should analyze the relationship between motivation and inhibition. This could be done with child molesters by obtaining a measure of deviant arousal and examining its relation to floodgates factors. Offenders with high levels of deviant arousal would be expected to offend because they are highly motivated to do so, not because they spontaneously lose control of a situational impulse. The highest rate of offending would be found in individuals with high motivation coupled with susceptibility to numerous floodgates factors or the chronic presence of one or more of them. Low rates of offending would be associated with susceptibility on only a few of the factors and low motivation. Moderate levels would be associated with higher motivation coupled with fewer factors or more factors and lower motivation. The interaction of motivation and floodgates should be the next phase of investigation of this theory.

References

Aarens, M., Cameron, T., Roizen, J., Roizen, R., Room, R., Schneberk, D., & Wingard, D. (1978). *Alcohol, casualties and crime.* Berkeley, CA: Social Research Group.

Abel, G. G., Becker, J. V., Cunningham–Rathner, J. Mittelman, M., & Rouleau, J. L. (1988). Multiple paraphilic diagnoses among sex offenders. Bulletin of the American Academy of *Psychiatry and the Law, 16*(2), 153–168.

Abel, G. G., Becker, J. V. Mittelman, M., Cunningham–Rathner, J., & Murphy, W. D. (1987). Self–reported sex crimes of incarcerated paraphilics. *Journal of Interpersonal Violence, 2*(1), 3–25.

Abel, G. G., Becker, J. V., Murphy, W. D., & Flanagan, B. (1981). Identifying dangerous child molesters. In R. B. Short (Ed.), *Violent behavior: Social learning approaches to prediction, management and treatment* (pp. 116–137). New York: Brunner/Mazel.

Barbaree, H. E., & Marshall, W. L. (1989). Erectile responses among heterosexual child molesters, father–daughter incest offenders, and matched non–offenders: Five distinct age preference profiles. *Canadian Journal of Behavioral Science, 21*(1), 70–82.

Bell, A. P., & Hall, C. S. (1971). *The personality of a child molester.* Chicago: Aldine–Atherton.

Carnes, P. J. (1983). *The sexual addiction.* Minneapolis, MN: CompCare Press.

Dougher, M. J. (1988). Clinical assessment of sex offenders. In B. K. Schwartz (Ed.), *A practitioner's guide to treating the incarcerated male sex offender: Breaking the cycle of sexual abuse* (pp. 77–84). Washington, DC: Department of Justice, National Institute of Corrections.

Faller, K. C. (1988). *Child sexual abuse: An interdisciplinary manual for diagnosis, case management, and treatment.* New York: Columbia University Press.

Fenichel, D. (1945). *The psychoanalytic theory of neurosis.* New York: Norton.

Finkelhor, D. (1984). *Child sexual abuse: New theory and research.* New York: Free Press.

Finkelhor, D. (1986). *A sourcebook on child sexual abuse.* Newbury Park, CA: Sage.

Freud, S. (1962). *Three essays on the theory of sexuality* (J. Strachey, Trans.). New York: Basic Books. (Original work published 1905)

Gebhard, P., Gagnon, J., Pomeroy, W., & Christenson, C. (1965). *Sex offenders: An analysis of types.* New York: Harper & Row.

Giarretto, H. (1982). *Integrated treatment of child sexual abuse: A treatment and training manual.* Palo Alto, CA: Science and Behavior Books.

Giarretto, H., Giarretto, A., & Sgroi, S. M. (1978). Coordinated community treatment of incest. In A. W. Burgess, A. N. Groth, L. L. Holmstrom, & S. M. Sgroi (Eds.), *Sexual assault of children and adolescents* (pp. 42–68). Lexington, MA: Lexington Books.

Gould, M. A. (1986, February). *Treatment of incest offenders in a correctional facility.* Paper presented at the annual meeting of the New Mexico Association for Counseling and Development, Las Cruces, NM.

Groth, A. N., Hobson, W. F., & Gary, T. S. (1982). The child molester: Clinical observations. In *Social work and child sexual abuse* (pp. 129–144). New York: Haworth Press.

Holmes, T. H. (1981). *Schedule of Recent Experiences (SRE).* Seattle: University of Washington Press.

Holmes, T. H., & Rahe, R. H. (1967). Social readjustment rating scale. *Journal of Psychosomatic Research, 11,* 213.

Hucker, S., Langevin, G., Wortzman, G., Bain, J., Handy, L., Chambers, J., & Wright, S. (1986). Neuropsychological impairment in pedophiles. *Canadian Journal of Behavioral Science, 18,* 440–448.

Ingersoll, S. L., & Patton, S. O. (1990). *Treating perpetrators of sexual abuse.* Lexington, MA: Lexington Books.

Justice, B., & Justice R. (1976). *The abusing family.* New York: Human Science Press.

Justice, B., & Justice, R. (1979). *The broken taboo: Sex in the family.* New York: Human Sciences Press.

Knight, R. A., & Prentky, R. A. (1990). Classifying sexual offenders: The development and corroboration of taxonomic models. In W. L. Marshall, D. R. Laws, & H. E. Barbaree (Eds.), *Handbook of sexual assault: Issues, theories, and treatment of the offender* (pp. 23–52). New York: Plenum Press.

Krafft–Ebing, R. (1965). *Psychopathia sexualis with especial reference to the antipathic sexual instinct: A medico–forensic study* (F. S. Klaf, Trans.). New York: Stein & Day, Scarborough Books Edition. (Original work published 1882)

LoPiccolo, J. (1992). *Handbook for assessment and treatment of sexual deviance.* St. Louis, MO: Author.

Madanes, C. (1990). *Sex, love, and violence: Strategies for transformation.* New York: Norton.

Maletzky, B. M. (1991). *Treating the sexual offender.* Newbury Park, CA: Sage.

Marshall, W. L., & Barbaree, H. E. (1990). An integrated theory of the etiology of sexual offending. In W. L. Marshall, D. R. Laws, & H. E. Barbaree (Eds.), *Handbook of sexual assault: Issues, theories, and treatment of the offender* (pp. 257–275). New York: Plenum Press.

Marshall, W. L., Jones, R., Ward, T., Johnson, P., & Barbaree, H. E. (1991). Treatment outcome with sex offenders. *Clinical Psychology Review, 11,* 465–485.

Mayer, A. (1983). *Incest: A treatment manual for therapy with victims, spouses and offenders.* Holmes Beach, FL: Learning Publications.

Miller, W. R., & Marlatt, G. A. (1984). *Manual for the comprehensive drinker profile.* Odessa, FL: Psychological Assessment Resources.

Mohr, I. W., Turner, R. E., & Jerry, M. B. (1964). *Pedophilia and exhibitionism.* Toronto: University of Toronto Press.

Murphy, W. D., Coleman, E. M., & Haynes, M. R. (1983). Treatment and evaluation issues with the mentally retarded sex offender. In J. G. Greer & I. R. Stuart (Eds.), *The sexual aggressor: Current perspectives on treatment* (pp. 22–42). New York: Van Nostrand Reinhold.

Owen, G., & Steele, N. (1991). Incest offenders after treatment. In M. Q. Patton (Ed.), *Family sexual abuse: Frontline research and evaluation* (pp. 178–198). Newbury Park, CA: Sage.

Peters, J. J. (1976). Children who are victims of sexual assault and the psychology of offenders. *American Journal of Psychotherapy, 30,* 398–421.

Pithers, W. D. (1988). Relapse prevention. In B. K. Schwartz (Ed.), *A practitioner's guide to treating the incarcerated male sex offender: Breaking the cycle of sexual abuse* (pp. 123–140). Washington, DC: Department of Justice, National Institute of Corrections.

Pithers, W. D., Kashima, K., Cumming, G. F., Beal L. S., & Buell, M. (1988). Relapse prevention of sexual aggression. In R. Prentky & V. Quinsey (Eds.), *Human sexual aggression: Current perspectives* (pp. 43–78). New York: New York Academy of Sciences.

Prentky, R. A., & Burgess, A. W. (1991). Hypothetical biological substrates of a fantasy–based drive mechanism for repetitive sexual aggression. In A. W. Burgess (Ed.), *Rape and sexual assault III: A research handbook* (pp. 235–256). New York: Garland.

Quinsey, V. L. (1977). The assessment and treatment of child molesters: A review. *Canadian Psychological Review, 18*(3), 204–220.

Quinsey, V. L., Chaplin, T. C., & Carrigan, W. F. (1979). Sexual preferences among incestuous and non–incestuous child molesters. *Behavior Therapy, 10,* 562–565.

Rada, R. T. (1976). *Alcoholism and the child molester.* Annals of New York Academy of Sciences, 273, 492–496.

Rubenstein, J. R. (1992). *Neuropsychological and personality differences between controls and pedophiles.* Doctoral dissertation, University of New Mexico, Albuquerque.

Salter, A. C. (1988). *Treating child sex offenders and victims: A practical guide.* Newbury Park, CA: Sage.

Schwartz, B. K. (1988). *A practitioner's guide to treating the incarcerated male sex offender: Breaking the cycle of sexual abuse.* Washington, DC: Department of Justice, National Institute of Corrections.

Schwartz, B. K. (1995). Theories of sex offenders. In B. K. Schwartz & H. R. Cellini (Eds.), *The sex offender: Corrections, treatment, and legal practice* (pp. 2-1–2-32). Kingston, NJ: Civic Research Institute.

Schwartz, M. F., & Masters, W. H. (1993). Investigation of trauma–based, cognitive behavioral, systematic and addiction approaches for treatment of hypersexual pair–bonding disorder. In P. J. Carnes (Ed.), *Sexual addiction and compulsivity* (vol. 1, pp. 153-189). New York: Brunner/Mazel.

Seltzer, M. L. (1971). The Michigan Alcoholism Screening Test: The quest for a new diagnostic instrument. *American Journal of Psychiatry, 127,* 89–94.

Shaken, D. (1939). 100 sex offenders. *American Journal of Orthopsychiatry, 9,* 565–569.

Skinner, H. A. (1979). Multivariate evaluation of MAST. *Journal of Studies on Alcohol, 40,* 831–844.

Stokes, R. E. (1964). A research approach to sexual offenses involving children. *Canadian Journal of Corrections, 6,* 87–94.

Stoller, R. J. (1975). *Perversion: The erotic form of hatred.* New York: Random House.

Zung, B. J. (1979). Psychometric properties of the MAST and two brief versions. *Journal of Studies on Alcohol, 40,* 845–859.

Part 2

Treating Resistant Sex Offenders

Few topics in the treatment of sex offenders engender more controversy than whether to treat sex offenders who are in denial. "Denial" is a term with many definitions and numerous categories. An offender might claim that he is absolutely innocent, that it was a case of mistaken identity, that he was out of the country when the crime was committed. This is clearly a case of denial. However, the offender might claim that he did indeed have sex with his accuser but the sex was voluntary or even that he was seduced. He may claim that he did certain acts but not the ones he is charged with. On an even subtler level, the offender may claim that his behavior was the result of alcohol or stress or various psychological dynamics. Different therapists have different definitions of what constitutes denial. However, the definition of denial might dictate whether a sex offender is placed on probation with a stipulation to go to treatment or whether he receives a prison sentence.

There has been a variety of lawsuits surrounding the issue of denial within the context of sex offender treatment and the granting of various privileges within the criminal justice system. For example, some judges sentence offenders to complete a treatment program, but the offender who refuses to admit his guilt might later be removed from the program. This was the case in *Mace v. Amestoy*,[1] where it was determined that it was unconstitutional to force someone to relinquish his right to avoid self-incrimination by forcing him to admit his guilt as a condition of remaining out of prison. However, disagreement remains as to whether a parole board can mandate completion of a treatment program or whether a corrections department can insist that a sex offender complete a treatment program that requires an admission of guilt to earn certain privileges.

The issue has been raised in cases such as *State v. Imlay*,[2] *McMorrow v. Little*,[3] and *Morstad v. State*.[4] In the latter case, the federal district court found that denial of parole hearings based on an offender's refusal to admit guilt and consequent failure to complete a sex offender treatment program violated the defendant's constitutional rights. Furthermore the court ruled that because the unlawfulness of the sexual offender program was apparent in light of preexisting law,[5] the penitentiary staff was not entitled to qualified immunity. Therapists remain confused about the implication of these cases.

On the other hand, various professional Codes of Ethics suggest that it is not ethical to treat someone for a condition he maintains that he does not have. No one would suggest that a physician treat an individual for cancer unless both the doctor and the patient agree that cancer treatment is appropriate. It can also be extremely disruptive to a sex offender treatment to have to deal with participants who maintain their innocence. Some therapists insist that it is misleading to the courts to suggest that sex offenders who deny their guilt can be treated; however, in some jurisdictions judges have ordered those who treat sex offender to treat individuals in denial.

In the following chapters, the authors present a number of ways of dealing with denial. All the authors agree that denial comes in variety of guises. Furthermore, they agree that denial has a purpose and that the therapist must understand the purpose to successfully challenge the denial. Chapter 5, by Dr. Stephen C. Brake and Dr. Diann Shannon, outlines a pretreatment group program that addresses the different stages of denial, as well as appropriate interventions for each stage. Their chapter is repliant with specific suggestions for addressing the various types of denial and minimization.

Chapter 6 reviews a treatment program developed by Dr. Anita Schlank and Dr. Ted Shaw. Their denier's program offers, among other techniques, monetary incentives to encourage the abandonment of denial within a supportive group therapy program. The group explores the dynamics of denial as well as the development of victim empathy.

Mack E. Winn, In Chapter 7, presents a variety of approaches to resistant clients based on a systemic and strategic therapies developed for family therapy. He points out the uses of denial, which often functions to protect the family. The therapist must then help the offender explore his fears about what would happen if the offender and his family admitted that the allegations of sexual assault were true. He explores how the therapist can best build a therapeutic alliance which can tolerate confrontation. In addition to maintaining denial, the offender can also resist therapy by refusing to cooperate with various treatment modalities, particularly behavioral techniques which may require homework and may be aversive and intrusive as well. Mr. Winn presents approaches to encouraging cooperation by framing assignments in language that the offender can identify with to utilizing paradoxical prescriptions and predictions. He also describes various therapeutic ordeals, rituals, and rites of passage which evoke emotional commitment.

Chapter 8, by Dr. Robert C. Wright and Sandra L. Schneider develops an elaborate theory which examines the role of fantasies in helping sex offenders distort their thinking so that they can simultaneously sexually assault others while maintaining a positive view of themselves as "good people." Their fantasies slowly change their realities and their view of the behavior of victims so that each step in the grooming process is justified. The authors point out that expecting offenders to immediately see through these distortions and accept full responsibility is therefore unrealistic. It is vital that offenders carefully examine their fantasies so that they can see what needs they are fulfilling. This is viewed as a much more positive way of dealing with fantasies than just immediately eliminating them.

Almost all sex offenders come into therapy in some form of denial. Indeed it may be that the healthier (relatively speaking) sex offender shows more denial because he is more embarrassed by his behavior and it is more ego dystonic. Much of the therapist's time is spent in confronting denial and minimization in its many forms. As soon as one type of denial is overcome, another type may crop up to replace it. Consequently, it is not a question of whether therapists will treat sex offenders in denial but how long they will treat a sex offender in a certain stage of denial or in complete denial.

Some offenders stay in basic denial forever. Some therapists may choose to continue their treatment and others will not. Either way, the more ways the treatment provider has to confront this problem, the more effective the therapy will be and the more public safety will be enhanced.

Footnotes

[1]765 F. Supp. 847 (D. Vt. 1991).
[2]249 Mont. 82, 813 P.2d 979 (1991).
[3]No. A1-94-95 (D.N.D. Sept. 29, 1995).
[4]518 N.W.2d 191 (N.D. 1994).
[5]Ibid.

Chapter 5

Using Pretreatment to Increase Admission in Sex Offenders

by Stephen C. Brake, Ph.D. and Diann Shannon, Psy.D.

Overview

Methods for the management and treatment of sexual offenders are still evolving. A cognitive-behavioral and/or relapse prevention model of treatment may be the most effective therapy for many offenders (Hall, 1995; Marshall & Barbaree, 1990; Pithers & Cumming, 1995; Steele, 1995), but no one model seems ideally suited for all offenders. Offenders in denial pose particularly difficult problems for those involved in their treatment and management. In this chapter, we review some of the problems and describe a treatment approach we have recently begun to use with at least some success.

Should We Attempt to Treat Sex Offenders in Denial?

Many believe that probation and community-based treatment is a privilege which should be offered to moderately low risk offenders who are willing to meet certain conditions. One reasonable criterion is that the offender must admit that he committed the offense for which he was adjudicated. A community may accept a perpetrator who has accepted responsibility for his behavior and expressed a desire to change. The same community, however, may feel reluctant to extend such a privilege to an offender whose denial contributes to the continuing emotional harm to victims as well as their family, friends, and associates. Thus, one problem in treating deniers is that the community may not wish to accept them.

There are other problems associated with treating deniers. Some believe that it is unethical to attempt to treat individuals who do not wish it, or who may choose treatment reluctantly under "coercive" conditions. The *Ethical Principles* of the American Psychological Association, for example, direct that psychologists "obtain appropriate informed consent to therapy" which means that the potential client "has freely and without undue influence expressed consent" (American Psychological Association, 1992). This is an issue that is legally and ethically complicated (e.g., Cohen, 1995; Committee on Government Policy, 1994; Maletsky, 1996). Some believe that it is indeed ethical to offer treatment to resistant clients, but the difficulty of resolving this issue could argue against offering treatment to deniers.

Problems may also arise after an offender in denial has been accepted into a treatment program. Despite his decision to participate, he is often resistant to the process. He can be highly disruptive in a group that consists largely of motivated offenders. Many offense-specific therapy groups do not admit deniers for this reason, or they choose to discharge them after a relatively short period.

Another problem is that the offender in denial may be at higher risk for recidivism than an "admitting" offender, all other things being equal. Certainly many guidelines for estimating an offender's risk to the community include factors relating to "denial," "accountability," or "locus of control." Thus, a treatment program that works with clients in denial may have accepted a client who is an unacceptably high risk to the community.

Still another problem with offering treatment to offenders in denial is that the treatment provider runs the risk of simply enabling or strengthening the denial if it is allowed to continue "unchecked" for a long period of time (we address this issue later).

Prison probably offers the best environment for working with deniers. Containment is high, the general public is safe, and the time available for therapy is usually plentiful. Even in prison, however, some of the same problems can exist. For example, deniers can slow and severely disrupt otherwise effective therapy groups, and treatment providers run the risk of enabling denial.

Finally, the offender "in denial" may be innocent. The usual solution to this problem is to accept the justice system's determination (the verdict at trial) or the offender's plea ("guilty") as truth, even if the offender later claims that he was "railroaded" or "had" to accept a plea bargain or no-contest plea to stay out of jail or avoid a longer sentence. Still, it is sometimes difficult to dismiss completely the thought that the legal system may have made an error and that as a therapist you are offering a service that is not warranted.

Clearly, there are good arguments to be made for not attempting to treat offenders in denial. However, there are also a number of strong arguments in favor of making such an attempt. Perhaps the most compelling among these is that deniers who do not receive treatment are likely to reoffend and cause continued harm to others and themselves. This is an even more persuasive point when a practitioner considers that there *are* treatment approaches that can be effective with at least some offenders in denial.

It could also be argued that it is unethical to refuse to offer treatment to an offender who, for the moment, denies his crime. Many clients enter psychotherapy with great reluctance and resistance, yet it is a goal of therapy to assist them in understanding resistance and taking new perspectives. In this regard, we may benefit from the experience of those who provide treatment for substance abusers. Court-ordered treatment is a common occurrence for those convicted of substance-related offenses, even though many of these offenders enter treatment with reluctance and resentment. In this case, we honor both our ethical responsibility to the community and our responsibility to care for the offender by mandating counseling as a condition of remaining in the community. Another reason to offer community-based treatment to offenders in denial is that it isn't feasible to incarcerate all offenders who initially deny their crime. Further, it is probably less expensive to manage offenders in the community than it is to manage them in prison (Prentky & Burgess, 1992; Steele, 1995).

Finally, offering some type of ongoing community-based therapy to offenders in denial has the advantage of being "reality-based." Almost all offenders are in some stage of denial at one time or another. Denial is not dichotomous or static; it is continuous and fluid. Trying to determine who is a "denier" and who isn't on the basis of a "snapshot" assessment is problematic. Should the police make the assessment of denial at the time of their investigation, the judge at the time of the trial or at sentencing, or the treatment provider at the time therapy might begin? What do treatment providers do with offenders who recant their admission once therapy has begun; do they remove them from the group immediately? After a week? A month? How severe must denial be before treatment providers judge the offender to be inappropriate for offense-specific treatment? A program for treating "deniers" offers the advantage of being able to evaluate the offender over time and deal with the range of his oppositional behavior in an authentic and constructive fashion.

How Do We Define Denial?

Few offenders are wholly "admitters" or "deniers." Denial is part of most offenders' pathology to a greater or lesser extent. Denial is dynamic. It waxes and wanes depending on a variety of internal and external events. An accurate assessment of denial should take into account the full range of the offender's resistance and defensiveness, both conscious and subconscious. A description of this process is beyond the scope of this chapter. Instead, we focus on the first step, which is to characterize the offender's denial based on statements about the instant offense. Following are descriptions of different types of denial based on such statements (see Table 5.1). We group types of denial according to four different levels. We hypothesize that level 1 types of denial are weak and least resistant to change, level 4 types of denial are severe and most resistant to change, and levels 2 and 3 types

Table 5.1
Levels and Types of Denial

Level 1: Weak Avoidance
Type 1: Minimize denial
Type 2: Denial of future behavior
Type 3: History-specific denial

Level 2: Projections/Moderate Avoidance
Type 4: Partial denial—justifications
Type 5: Partial denial—minimizations
Type 6: Denial of arousal

Level 3: Projections/Strong Avoidance
Type 7: Denial "screen"
Type 8: False dissociation

Level 4: Primitive Denial/Severe Avoidance
Type 9: Current-incident-specific denial
Type 10: "Plausible denial
Type 11: Full denial
Type 12: Pathological denial

of denial are in between. Others have described many of the types of denial discussed here (Barbaree & Cortoni, 1993; Green, 1995; Laflen & Sturm, 1993; Salter, 1988; Winn, 1996).

Level 1: Weak Avoidance. This level consists of three types of denial which are statements reflecting weak avoidance of responsibility. Offenders presenting with level 1 denial are usually considered to be "admitters of fact" and are often not considered to be "deniers."

- *Type 1: Minimal denial.* The offender admits committing the instant sexual offense with little minimization or justification.
- *Type 2: Denial of future behavior.* The offender admits committing the instant offense but denies the possibility of committing similar offense in the future.
- *Type 3: History-specific denial.* The offender admits committing the instant offense but denies committing any other offense at any other time even though collateral information indicates otherwise.

Level 2: Projections/Moderate Avoidance. This level consists of three types of moderate avoidance. Offenders at this level admit to some of the behavior involved in the instant offense, but justify its occurrence or minimize its importance. In some cases offenders presenting with level 2 denial are considered "admitters of fact," in other cases they may be considered "deniers."

- *Type 4: Partial denial—justifications.* The offender admits committing the instant offense but justifies his behavior. For example, he might say "I did it, but she wanted to do it, too," or "I was provoked," or "It wasn't really sexual because I touched her while rubbing lotion on a rash," or "I would not have done it if I had not been drunk."
- *Type 5: Partial denial—minimizations.* The offender admits committing the instant offense but minimizes its harm. For example, he might say that the victim didn't behave as if any harm was done, or that they were "just playing."
- *Type 6: Denial of arousal.* The offender admits committing the instant offense but denies that he was sexually aroused during the offense.

Level 3: Splitting/Strong Avoidance. This level consists of two types of stronger avoidance. Offenders at this level do not admit committing the instant sexual offense but may admit to engaging in "less harmful" behaviors, or they may simply say they cannot recall the behavior in question. Offenders presenting with level 3 denial are usually considered "deniers of fact."

- *Type 7: Denial "screen."* The offender denies committing the instant sexual offense but admits that other aspects of his behavior (usually more "acceptable" or "nonsexual" aspects) were somehow harmful to the victim. For example, he might say, "I hit the victim, but I did not rape her."
- *Type 8: False dissociation.* The offender claims that he does not remember the offense and therefore cannot admit to committing it. For example, he might state that he was drunk at the time.

Level 4: Primitive Denial/Severe Avoidance. This level consists of four types of denial which reflect severe statements of avoidance. Offenders at this level deny committing the current sexual offense and may refuse to acknowledge responsibility for even remotely similar behaviors.

- *Type 9: Current-incident-specific denial.* The offender admits committing past sexual offenses, but not the instant offense.
- *Type 10: "Plausible" denial.* The offender denies committing the instant offense but is able and willing to accurately describe the harm resulting to a victim of such an offense.
- *Type 11: Full denial.* The offender denies committing any offense and does not seem willing to acknowledge the harm of such offenses.
- *Type 12: Pathological denial.* The offender denies committing any offense and is excessively hostile, delusional, or defensive.

What Kinds of Treatment Might Lessen Denial?

Offenders who consistently maintain level 3 or 4 denial are different from offenders who are more easily able to admit their offenses. They respond to continuing confrontation with increased resistance. Treating these steadfast deniers in the same way as other offenders may not be the most productive approach to their therapy. Indeed, immediate and consistent confrontation of denial may do more harm than good (e.g., Scalia, 1994).

This has been recognized in the treatment of substance abuse and addiction. DiClemente and Prochaska and their colleagues (DiClemente & Hughes, 1990; Prochaska & DiClemente, 1992; Prochaska, DiClemente, & Norcross, 1992) introduced the concept of "stage matching" in their work with resistant substance users. Their approach is to match therapeutic interventions to the level of the offender's denial, thus confronting resistance gradually through the use of successive approximation. Miller and his colleagues (Miller, Benefield, & Tonigan, 1993; Miller & Rollnick, 1991) have employed somewhat similar methods. They call their approach motivational interviewing. Others (e.g., Howard, Lueger, Maling, & Martinovich, 1993) have also proposed a phase model of treatment in working with substance abusers.

Therapists working with sexual offenders have employed similar approaches too. Jenkins (1990) and Blanchard (1995) have written extensively about the importance of a gradual, respectful treatment approach with offenders while employing cognitive-behavioral techniques. Groth (1982, 1992), Maletsky (1996), Puffer and Sawyer (1993), and Steen (1992, 1995) have discussed ways of confronting deniers gradually and systematically. Winn and his colleagues (Hoke, Sykes, & Winn, 1989; Winn, 1995; 1996) employ family therapy strategies in helping to explain the function of denial and then in assisting the offender to work with his family in more productive ways. Shaw and Schlank (Shaw & Schlank, 1995; Schlank & Shaw, 1996) offer treatment modules (empathy videos, relapse prevention exercises) to deniers without any explicit attempt to work through denial. Others have now used this approach (Murphy & Barry, 1995; Norris, 1993)—in one case in conjunction with a motivational interviewing model (Burditt, 1995). Polygraph tests have also been effective in eliciting disclosures from offenders in treatment (Abrams, Hoyt, & Jewell, 1991; Emerick & Dutton, 1993; Janes, 1993). In most of these cases, however, the offender has already made admissions about the current offense; the polygraph was most useful in encouraging admissions about undisclosed past offenses. It is unclear whether the use of a polygraph test early in treatment with highly resistant (type 3 or 4) offenders encourages disclosures about the current offense or, instead, heightens the offender's resistance. We believe that it may do either, depending on the offender's level of denial and when the test is introduced in therapy.

A Pretreatment Program for Deniers

We have developed a program of therapy for offenders in denial which is similar in many ways to the models described previously. We call our approach pretreatment to differentiate it from subsequent offense-specific treatment. We believe that it is important to make a distinction between therapy that has a limited goal of lessening denial and therapy intended to provide a broad range of treatment techniques designed to lessen the risk of recidivism. The latter is what we usually refer to as offense-specific treatment. The goal of pretreatment is to lessen denial about the instant offense. Once this has been accomplished, the offender is referred to an offense-specific treatment program. In other words, pretreatment is intended to prepare a client for offense-specific therapy, not to replace offense-specific therapy.

The pretreatment program consists of six stages (see Table 5.2). Each stage consists of a series of strategies or interventions designed to lessen denial. We attempt to

Table 5.2
Stages of Pretreatment

<u>**Pretreatment Stage 1: Containment**</u>
　　　　Intervention 1: Respect the offender as an individual
　　　　Intervention 2: Honor the denial
　　　　Intervention 3: Allow the offender to save face

<u>**Pretreatment Stage 2: Symptom Relief**</u>
　　　　Intervention 4: Acknowledge the offender's discomfort
　　　　Intervention 5: Describe hope ("treatment works")
　　　　Intervention 6: Offer to stand by the offender
　　　　Intervention 7: Establish a contingency disclosure/treatment

<u>**Pretreatment Stage 3: Reframe Denial**</u>
　　　　Intervention 8: Explain denial
　　　　Intervention 9: Reframe sexual arousal
　　　　Intervention 10: Deemphasize stigmatization

<u>**Pretreatment Stage 4: Reframe Accountability**</u>
　　　　Intervention 11: Decline the invitation to blame others
　　　　Intervention 12: Invite personal choice and accountability
　　　　Intervention 13: Reinforce positive change

<u>**Pretreatment Stage 5: Model Empathy**</u>
　　　　Intervention 14: Talk about the family
　　　　Intervention 15: Model empathy
　　　　Intervention 16: Acknowledge the offender's victimization
　　　　Intervention 17: Use hypothetical examples or questions
　　　　Intervention 18: Use role reversal

<u>**Pretreatment Stage 6: Successive Approximation of Confrontation**</u>
　　　　Intervention 19: Request permission for confrontation
　　　　Intervention 20: Confrontation by successive approximation
　　　　Intervention 21: Suggest a polygraph test

match the stages of pretreatment to the offender's level of denial. Interventions are offered in weekly, individual (one-on-one) counseling sessions rather than in therapy groups. We employ this approach to more carefully match treatment intervention to each offender's level of denial.

Offenders in more severe denial (level 4) usually encounter basic treatment interventions designed to contain fears and provide immediate symptom relief (pretreatment stages 1 and 2) before moving on to more advanced stages of pretreatment. Offenders whose denial is less severe (levels 3 and 2) might be more immediately amenable to more advanced interventions designed to reframe thought patterns (pretreatment stages 3 and 4). Some offenders presenting with level 2 denial might even be amenable to gradual confrontation (pretreatment stage 6) soon after entering the program. Simply put, offenders presenting the severe denial need to begin pretreatment at stage 1, whereas less resistant offenders may begin at more advanced stages.

Of course, working through denial is rarely such a straightforward process. Offenders may move forward and backward among the levels of denial throughout the course of pretreatment.

Pretreatment Stage 1: Containment. The first step is to deescalate and contain power struggles. The therapist must not accept the offender's projections of helplessness and hostility (Scalia, 1994).

- *Intervention 1: Respect the individual.* The therapist should express an interest in the offender as an individual and recognize his strengths. The offender should be treated with respect. For example, the therapist can say, "Like all of us, you have done both good things and bad things. Your present situation should not take away what is good about you."
- *Intervention 2: Honor the denial.* Initially, the therapist must work with whatever the offender is willing to disclose rather than discounting what he has to say (e.g., Groth, 1992). It is helpful to acknowledge that denial has served a useful purpose in the past but that its usefulness may now be diminishing. (For example, the therapist might say, "I know that you do not admit committing this offense. I think there are many understandable reasons that a person may have for not admitting things.")
- *Intervention 3: Allow the offender to save face.* Sometimes the most effective strategy in dealing with resistance is simply to let it pass by (Jenkins, 1990; Schwartz, 1995). If the offender finds it too difficult to discuss an issue, the therapist may find it helpful to let the offender save face by not challenging him on the issue. The therapist can return to the issue at a later time. (For example, he might say, "Okay, let's talk about something else, for now.")

Pretreatment Stage 2: Symptom Relief. The offender's defensive maneuvers are designed to protect him from perceived harm or loss. The maneuvers, however, are only partially successful, resulting in continued despair and helplessness. Effective therapy should provide relief from these symptoms. Once the offender has become accustomed to the new boundaries of pretreatment (stage 1), this process of symptom relief can begin.

- *Intervention 4: Acknowledge the offender's discomfort.* The therapist can provide an important initial reduction in the offender's discomfort by simply acknowledging it. It is helpful to explain that a goal of treatment is to lessen discomfort. This, in turn, gives him a reason to continue in treatment. The resistant offender will need such acknowledgement before he can begin to empathize with others. (For example, the therapist might say, "I know you are in a really bad situation right now. It must feel confusing and frightening.")
- *Intervention 5: Describe hope ("treatment works").* The offender needs to know that there is a good chance for positive change and that the therapist can help him achieve it. He needs to know that the therapist might be able to help him reunite with family and friends, avoid being in trouble with the law again,

or even avoid being accused again. (For example, the therapist might say, "It may take some time, but the work we do here can help get you out of this bad situation and possibly begin to restore you to your family.")

- *Intervention 6: Offer to stand by the offender.* It is helpful for the therapist to tell the offender that he will stand by him as much as possible. This is a crucial step in alleviating fears about loss and abandonment. This does not negate the therapist's responsibility to hold the offender accountable. The offender should understand that future incidents of inappropriate behavior will not be excused and that rules of treatment and probation must be followed. However, the offender should also understand that the therapist will support him as long as he is working to the best of his ability in therapy. The therapist might also ask the offender how therapy can be made safer for him. (For example, "If you can work with me in this program, I will do my best to keep you safe and help represent your position to others.")

- *Intervention 7: Establish a contingency between disclosure and duration of treatment.* Pretreatment can lengthen the amount of time that offenders will be in treatment. The offender may feel additional motivation to disclose whether this contingency is explained (Happel & Auffrey, 1995). It should be made clear that the contingency is not designed to be punitive. It can be explained that the community and the judicial system ask that offenders in denial remain in treatment longer to give them ample opportunity to be accountable. The therapist can reassert that he or she can be most helpful if the offender is honest.(For example, the therapist might say, "You can move on to helpful treatment more quickly if you are honest." Or, "I can better help you if you are honest.")

Pretreatment Stage 3: Reframe Denial. It is helpful to assist the offender to understand the protective function of his denial. The therapist can reframe the offender's defensive maneuvers as understandable attempts to lessen his fears. Once the offender has experienced hope and symptom relief (stage 2), this process may begin.

- *Intervention 8: Explain denial.* Denial is common and serves a purpose. It may be harmful to attempt to challenge denial without first understanding and illustrating its protective function (Hoke et al., 1989; Steen, 1992; Winn, 1996;). Offenders need to understand that it is not abnormal to experience denial and resistance, particularly when faced with fears of loss, criticism, and legal sanction. Blocking memories, for example, can help protect us from our fears. The therapist can acknowledge that it is not unusual to block memories, but that they usually return when the time is right. Or, the therapist might reframe the denial by saying that denial is often an understandable expression of anger or frustration, or that it is an understandable attempt to maintain the structure of the family, or to keep a job. The therapist can explain that excessive denial usually leads to more pain and despair and that there are other ways to maintain positive control. The therapist might ask the offender to consider that the truth is usually a combination of all the different stories and that there can be at least some truth to the accusations. The therapist can assist the offender to realize that it is not so important to "hang on to" a particular version of events. (For example, the therapist might say, "People do forget sometimes but often remember later when it is safe to do so." Or, "I can imagine that you are angry for having to be here and maybe that's why you would rather not say anything." Or, "I have found that truth is usually some combination of what everybody is saying. Perhaps there is at least some truth to these charges." Or, "People usually have pretty good reasons to keep things secret, but sometimes it can be more trouble than it is worth.")

- *Intervention 9: Reframe sexual arousal.* It is important to help the offender understand that other people have inappropriate sexual feelings like his. Later, the therapist can show the offender that he does not have to act on these feelings and that he can make more appropriate choices about his behavior when faced with these urges. (For example, the therapist might say, "You know, many men have some sexual arousal to children. You are not alone in this." Or, "It must be confusing and frustrating to be aroused like this. Did you know others feel this way, too?" And later, "You have the power not to act on these feelings") (see intervention 13).

- *Intervention 10: Deemphasize stigmatization.* Sometimes good people act on sexual feelings when they shouldn't. We all make mistakes, and the resistant offender needs to know that making a mistake is not tantamount to being a "monster" or "pervert" who will never have a place in society. Although many offenders face a lifelong process of learning how to redirect sexual behavior, resistant offenders also need to know that they can be forgiven and that they are not forever outcasts if they take steps to change their behavior (Schwartz, 1995). (For example, the therapist might say, "We all make mistakes, and we benefit by learning from them." Or, "People aren't monsters; most people don't wish to hurt anybody.")

Pretreatment Stage 4: Reframe Accountability. The offender may now be ready to risk abandoning old defensive maneuvers and accept increasing accountability and prosocial behavior.

- *Intervention 11: Decline the invitation to fix blame on others.* It is not helpful to engage in arguments with the offender about how others may be to blame because it draws attention away from the offender's responsibility. As Jenkins (1990) has said, it is better to decline invitations to argue the facts of the case and instead invite the offender to begin to accept responsibility for his predicament. (For example, the therapist might say, "You know, we have already spoken about what others had to do with this; lets move on.")

- *Intervention 12: Invite thoughts and actions that emphasize personal choice and accountability.* The therapist can encourage speech and behavior that reflect the client's attempts to take responsibility for his life. The therapist can *invite* offenders to participate in accepting responsibility by encouraging discussion of their behavior (Jenkins, 1990). The therapist can do this by embracing discussions that focus on how the offender's behavior contributed to his current predicament. The therapist can also illustrate how to be accountable by highlighting choices that a person makes on a daily basis. The therapist can model accountability by explaining some of the choices that he or she makes. It is helpful to acknowledge that satisfaction comes from making proactive decisions and taking responsibility for one's actions. (For example, the therapist might say, "Instead of talking about how others are to blame, let's talk about your part in all of this." Or , "Let me tell you about some decisions I made yesterday.")

- *Intervention 13: Reinforce positive change.* It is important to underscore the positive changes that the offender has made because this encourages further changes. Encouragement can include reinforcing the fact that the offender has chosen to continue with therapy. (For example, the therapist might say, "I think that was a really good comment that you made about being responsible." Or, "I'm glad you've chosen to stay in therapy.")

Pretreatment Stage 5: Enhance Empathy. As the offender begins to accept increasing personal responsibility for his behavior (stage 4), he can begin to recognize the pain of others and identify it as his own. A danger exists that the offender could reinvoke old defensive maneuvers such as projection (blaming others) to avoid experiencing his own guilt, but if earlier stages of pretreatment have been successful, he will be more likely to engage in appropriate grieving.

- *Intervention 14: Talk about the family.* It may now be helpful to acknowledge that many of the problems experienced by the offender are problems that involve the entire family (Hoke et al., 1989; Winn, 1996). It is not helpful to blame others for his behavior, but it could be helpful to acknowledge that the offender is not behaving in a vacuum. He can then begin to develop a more comprehensive perspective of the problem. As this happens, the offender begins to realize that his behavior can cause harm to those he loves and needs. This can motivate him to take more responsibility for his behavior. (For example, the therapist might say, "Do you think some of your problems come from feeling disconnected from your family?" Or, "Have you ever made mistakes that can hurt your family?")

- *Intervention 15: Model empathy.* Empathy is a difficult concept to teach, but it can be modeled. The therapist can do this by showing that he or she cares that the offender is in discomfort. The therapist can also model empathy by referring to events that concern others. (For example, the therapist might say, "I feel badly that you are hurting so much.")

- *Intervention 16: Strengthen victim empathy by acknowledging the offender's victimization.* One key to lessening resistance is to acknowledge the offender's own victimization. It is helpful to request permission to address this subject. The therapist may need to approach the offender's victimization through a process of successive approximations, beginning with less damaging incidents. This strategy should be employed with caution as the therapist wishes to acknowledge the client's history but does not wish to excuse the client's offending behavior by "explaining it away." We introduce this strategy after the offender has begun to accept more responsibility for his behavior. (For example, the therapist might say, "It must feel really awful to remember being abused.")

- *Intervention 17: Use "hypothetical" examples or questions.* It is often helpful to request that the offender do an exercise or assignment "as if" he had committed the offense (see Hoke et al., 1989; Shaw & Schlank, 1995). The therapist might ask the offender to imagine how he could have "groomed" the victim, as if he had committed the offense. Or, the therapist might guide the offender toward reexamining his fears by asking him what life would be like if he were to admit the offense. (For example, the therapist might say, "I would like for you to assume that you committed the offense just as the victim says and then tell me what kinds of triggers or warning signals could have led to it." Or, "How would you convince your victim that you understand the harm of the offense?" or, "Why do people lie or deny things?" Or, "Who believes you about this? What would they say if you admitted the offense? I can imagine that would be really hard.")

- *Intervention 18: Use role reversal.* The therapist might illustrate the value of honesty by asking the offender to assume another's role or position (Hoke et al., 1989). The therapist might remind him that the victim continues to believe that he committed the offense and that it is important for him to begin to appreciate that others do not see things the same way that he does and that he will have to deal with this sooner or later. The therapist might then ask the offender to take the victim's role. (For example, the therapist might say, "I will pretend that I am the offender while you pretend that you are the victim. What do you have to say to me?")

Pretreatment Stage 6: Successive Approximation of Confrontation. The offender may now be ready to accept gradual confrontation of his behavior.

- *Intervention 19: Request permission for confrontation.* The therapist should make clear to the offender that he or she would like permission to talk about a potentially difficult subject (e.g., Jenkins, 1990). (For example, the therapist might say, "May I say something you may not like?")
- *Intervention 20: Confrontation by successive approximation.* The offender may now be ready to allow confrontation about past behaviors that were similar to the instant offense. This can be done through a series of successive approximations (Happel & Auffrey, 1995). Minor incidents should be discussed first. Then, the offender may be willing to disclose facts about the current offense. It is helpful first to ask about the least "damaging" aspects of the offense. (For example, the therapist might say, "I see that you were once charged with verbally harassing a woman. May we talk about that? It seems pretty clear that you did something like that." Or, "You have been accused of touching the victim's private parts. May I ask you about that? Could we agree that you touched her in some way which was uncomfortable to her?" And then, "May I ask you something directly? It actually seems clear that you did touch her private parts. Could you say that?")In difficult cases, the first attempt at successive approximation may be to confront the offender about his denial of casual and appropriate sexual interests. (For example, the therapist might say, "May I say something to you? I don't really believe that you aren't interested in sexy women, like you say.")
- *Intervention 21: Suggest a polygraph test.* Highly resistant offenders often react to the suggestion that they take a polygraph test by becoming more defensive. Thus, it may be unwise to use a polygraph during the early stages of pretreatment. Later, however, a polygraph test can be an effective tool in lessening denial. Many offenders volunteer to take the test, particularly if they have some control over

when the test will be scheduled, and many choose to make disclosures preceding or following the test. The test may also be used as a last resort when the therapist has tried repeatedly but unsuccessfully to reframe denial and invite discussion of personal accountability. In such cases, it can be explained that the test may be a way to help determine whether accusations made against the client are in error. (For example, the therapist might say, "You have admitted quite a lot here, but some questions remain. Do you think a polygraph test could be helpful to us in clarifying these questions?" Or, "We seem to be at an impasse here. What would you think about taking a polygraph test to clear this up a little bit?")

Effectiveness of Pretreatment in Reducing Denial

To date, we have seen a significant reduction of denial in 58% of offenders (64% child molesters; 36% rapists) who have received pretreatment. Specifically, 44% of offenders initially presenting with level 3 or 4 denial finished the program presenting with level 1 or 2 denial. Of these, 34% made full admissions of the instant offense (moved to level 1). All offenders initially presenting with level 2 denial finished the program presenting with level 1 denial: 51% of those in the program were referred to offense-specific therapy programs after completion of pretreatment; 50% of offenders entering at level 4 and 37% entering at level 3 made no progress in the program and were terminated unsuccessfully.

How Long Should We Work With Sex Offenders in Denial?

The potential benefit in working with "deniers" is that they will admit their offense and go on to participate in offense-specific therapy. When progress in lessening denial is slow, however, it may be difficult to decide when to quit. Some have suggested that the best course of action is to keep trying indefinitely. They argue that months or years could be necessary to successfully reduce denial in some offenders, and that some treatment is better than no treatment and staying in treatment (and/or staying on probation) offers the offender at least some structure and deterrence that he would not otherwise have.

On the other hand, the probability of significant disclosure most likely diminishes after a certain point, whereas the probability of enabling the offender's denial increases. In other words, the longer treatment continues without any progress, the more likely it becomes that the offender believes he has simply "gotten away with it" again. In such a situation, his risk to recidivate may actually increase while in treatment. In addition, the risk for emotional revictimization of his past victims and victims' families increases the longer the denying offender remains in the community.

We have chosen to work with offenders in denial for six months. If the offender shows little change in his denial or resistance after that amount of time, we terminate him with the opinion that he does not appear to be amenable to treatment at this time. We believe, based on our results and the results of others (Burditt, 1995; Murphy & Barry, 1995; Schlank & Shaw, 1995), that this amount of time is sufficient for many offenders to relinquish denial. It would be helpful to know whether longer periods might result in greater success; further research may address this issue. However, even if longer-duration pretreatment were to result in slightly greater disclosure, the potential harm of a longer "denier's program" may outweigh the benefits.

Termination of Treatment With Deniers

An offender's disclosure of the current offense results in successful completion of the pretreatment program and referral to offense-specific therapy. Terminating an offender from a denier's program because of lack of disclosure, however, can cause problems. One of these problems is that the treatment provider may be called on to explain why he or she has terminated a client who attended every session, paid his bill on time, was not openly oppositional, obeyed all rules and conditions of treatment and probation, and in most respects was a "model" client. Another problem arises in considering subsequent disposition. Should the court send the offender to another program and try again or should it revoke his probation and incarcerate him? If he is to be incarcerated, should this be for the remaining time on his sentence, or should he be reevaluated for amenability to treatment after a relatively short time with the hope that incarceration will allow him time to reevaluate his position? The court may find it difficult or inappropriate to revoke the probation of the offender who has followed all of the rules but simply does not admit the offense, particularly if the offender has professed his innocence from the start (e.g., State v. Imlay, 1991).

There are no easy solutions to these problems. A partial solution may be to ensure that the offender is aware that nonparticipation, uncompleted homework, and unpaid fees can be grounds for termination and subsequent revocation. An alternative approach would be to initiate treatment during a period of extended evaluation *prior* to sentencing. If an offender makes progress (e.g., moving from level 3 to level 2) during this time, it might be reasonable to sentence him to community-based treatment while on probation. If an offender does not make progress, it might be more reasonable to consider other options (incarceration). This might help avoid problems associated with trying to revoke deniers on probation. Creative thinking would be required to build a containment field with offenders not yet adjudicated, but, if this can be done, a number of offenders "in denial" might receive helpful treatment who might otherwise not be given the opportunity.

Conclusion

Some offenders are more resistant to treatment than others and do not relinquish their denial quickly enough to be accepted into standard offense-specific group treatment programs. Specialized programs can decrease resistance and denial in a significant number of these offenders who can then be referred to offense-specific group programs. This ultimately maximizes the effect of offense-specific treatment programs and lowers the number of offenders who otherwise might not receive any treatment at all.

References

Abrams, S. A., Hoyt, D., & Jewell, C. (1991). The effectiveness of the disclosure test with sex abusers of children. *Polygraph, 20,* 197–203.

American Psychological Association. (1992). Ethical principles of psychologists and code of conduct. *American Psychologist, 47*(12), 1597–1611.

Barbaree, H. E., & Cortoni, F. A. (1993). Treatment of the juvenile sex offender within the criminal justice and mental health systems. In H. E. Barbaree (Ed.), *The juvenile sex offender* (pp. 57–76). New York: Guilford Press.

Blanchard, G. T. (1995). *The difficult connection: The therapeutic relationship in sex offender treatment.* Brandon, VT: Safer Society Press.

Burditt, T. (1995). *The application of motivational interviewing to the denier's pilot study.* Paper presented at the 14th Annual Meeting of the Association for the Treatment of Sexual Abusers, New Orleans.

Cohen, F. (1995). Right to treatment. In B. K. Schwartz & H. R. Cellini (Eds.), *The sexual offender: Corrections, treatment, and legal practice* (pp . 24-1-24-18). Kingston, NJ: Civic Research Institute.

Committee on Government Policy, Group for the Advancement of Psychiatry. (1994). *Forced into treatment: The role of coercion in clinical practice.* Washington, DC: American Psychiatric Press.

DiClemente, C. C., & Hughes, S. O. (1990). Stages of change profiles in outpatient alcoholism treatment. *Journal of Substance Abuse, 2,* 217–235.

Emerick, R. L., & Dutton, W. A. (1993). The effect of polygraphy on the self report of adolescent sex offenders: Implications for risk assessment. *Annals of Sex Research, 6,* 83–103.

Green, R. (1995). Comprehensive treatment planning for sex offenders. In B. K. Schwartz & H. R. Cellini (Eds.), *The sexual offender: Corrections, treatment, and legal practice* (pp. 10-1–10-9). Kingston, NJ: Civic Research Institute.

Groth, N. A. (1982). The incest offender. In S. M. Sgroi (Ed.), *Handbook of clinical intervention in child sexual abuse* (pp. 34–56). Lexington, MA: Lexington Books.

Groth, N. A. (1992). *Understanding sexual assault: The offense and the offender.* Paper presented at Restorative Justice for Juvenile Sex Offenders, Lake Tahoe, NV.

Hall, G. C. (1995). Sexual offender recidivism revisited: A meta-analysis of recent treatment studies. *Journal of Consulting and Clinical Psychology, 63*(5), 802–809.

Happel, R. M., & Auffrey, J. J. (1995). Sex offender assessment: Interrupting the dance of denial. *American Journal of Forensic Psychology, 13*(2), 5–22.

Hoke, S. L., Sykes, C., & Winn, M. (1989). Systemic/strategic interventions targeting denial in the incestuous family. *Journal of Strategic and Systemic Therapies, 8*(4), 44–51.

Howard, K. I., Lueger, R. J., Maling, M. S., & Martinovich, Z. (1993). A phase model of psychotherapy outcome: Causal mediation of change. *Journal of Consulting and Clinical Psychology, 61*(4), 678–685.

Janes, M. S. (1993, June). Polygraph: A current perspective. *Interchange—Cooperative Newsletter of the National Adolescent Perpetrator Network,* p. 1.

Jenkins, A. J. (1990). *Invitations to responsibility.* Adelaide, South Australia: Dulwich Centre Publications.

Laflen, B., & Sturm, W. R. (1993). *Understanding and working with denial in sexual offenders and their families.* Paper presented at the 12th Annual Meeting of the Association for the Treatment of Sexual Abusers, Boston.

Maletsky, B. M. (1996). Denial of treatment or treatment of denial? *Sexual Abuse: A Journal of Research and Treatment, 8*(1), 1–5.

Marshall, W. L., & Barbaree, H. E. (1990). Outcome of comprehensive cognitive-behavioral treatment programs. In W. L. Marshall, D. R. Laws, & H. E. Barbaree (Eds.), *Handbook of sexual assault* (pp. 24–56). New York: Plenum Press.

Miller, W. R., Benefield, R. G., & Tonigan, J. S. (1993). Enhancing motivation for change in problem drinking: A controlled comparison of two therapist styles. *Journal of Consulting and Clinical Psychology, 61*(3), 455–461.

Miller, W. R., & Rollnick, S. (1991). *Motivational interviewing: Preparing people to change addictive behavior.* New York: Guilford Press.

Murphy, J. J., & Barry, D. J. (1995). *A six-month adapted version of the denier's pilot study.* Paper presented at the 14th Annual Meeting of the Association for the Treatment of Sexual Abusers, New Orleans.

Norris, C. (1993). *An approach to treating incarcerated sex offenders who are resistant to treatment involvement.* Paper presented at the 12th Annual Meeting of the Association for the Treatment of Sexual Abusers, Boston.

Pithers, W. D., & Cumming, G. F. (1995). Relapse prevention: A method for enhancing behavioral self-management and external supervision of the sexual aggressor. In B. K. Schwartz & H. R. Cellini (Eds.), *The sexual offender: Corrections, treatment, and legal practice* (pp. 20-1–20-32). Kingston, NJ: Civic Research Institute.

Prentky, R., & Burgess, A. W. (1992). Rehabilitation of child molesters: A cost-benefit analysis. *American Journal of Orthopsychiatry, 60,* 108–117.

Prochaska, J. O., & DiClemente, C. C. (1992). Stages of change in the modification of problem behaviors. In M. Hersen, R. M. Eisler, & P. M. Miller (Eds.), *Progress in behavior modification* (pp. 84–97). Sycamore, IL: Sycamore Publishing.

Prochaska, J. O., DiClemente, C. C., & Norcross, J. C. (1992). In search of how people change: Applications to addictive behaviors. *American Psychologist, 47*(9), 1102–1114.

Puffer, P., & Sawyer, S. (1993). *Treatment model for treating the resistant client.* Paper presented at the 12th Annual Meeting of the Association for the Treatment of Sexual Abusers, Boston.

Salter, A. C. (1988). *Treating child sex offenders and victims.* Newbury Park, CA: Sage.

Scalia, J. (1994). Psychoanalytic insights and prevention of pseudosuccess in the cognitive-behavioral treatment of batterers. *Journal of Interpersonal Violence, 9*(4), 548–555.

Schlank, A. M., & Shaw, T. (1996). Treating sexual offenders who deny their guilt: A pilot study. *Sexual Abuse: A Journal of Research and Treatment, 8*(1), 17–23.

Schwartz, B. K. (1995). Group therapy. In B. K. Schwartz & H. R. Cellini (Eds.), *The sexual offender: Corrections, treatment, and legal practice* (pp. 14-1–14-15). Kingston, NJ: Civic Research Institute.

Shaw, T., & Schlank, A. M. (1995). *An update on a denier's pilot study.* Paper presented at the 14th annual meeting of the Association for the Treatment of Sexual Abusers, New Orleans.

State v. Imlay, 249 Mont. 82, 813 P.2d 979 (1991).

Steele, N. (1995). Cost effectiveness of treatment. In B. K. Schwartz & H. R. Cellini (Eds.), *The sexual offender: Corrections, treatment, and legal practice* (pp. 4-1–4-19). Kingston, NJ: Civic Research Institute.

Steen, C. (1992). *Treating the denying juvenile sex offender.* Paper presented at Restorative Justice for Juvenile Sex Offenders, Lake Tahoe, NV.

Steen, C. (1995). Treating denying sex offenders. *California Coalition on Sexual Offending Newsletter,* pp. 2, 2–3.

Winn, M. (1995). *Advances in the management of denial in the cognitive/behavioral treatment of sexual offenders.* Paper presented at the 14th Annual Meeting of the Association for the Treatment of Sexual Abusers, New Orleans.

Winn, M. (1996). The strategic and systemic management of denial in the cognitive/behavioral treatment of sexual offenders. *Sexual Abuse: A Journal of Research and Treatment, 8*(1), 25–36.

Chapter 6

Treating Sexual Offenders Who Deny—A Review

by Anita M. Schlank, Ph.D. and Ted Shaw, Ph.D.

Overview

Most sexual offenders deny or greatly minimize their deviant behavior at some point following their arrest. Because treatment of other issues often cannot begin until an offender admits to having committed the sexual offense(s), many offenders are denied admission to treatment programs if they continue to deny committing their crimes.

This chapter discusses the varying levels of denial and the impact denial has on the treatment process. In addition, it discusses various strategies for modifying an offender's denial.

Denial and Minimization

It is quite rare to find a sexual offender who is completely honest about his history of deviant behavior. Even after their legal battles have ended and they are presented with rewards for being honest (e.g., being placed on probation), many sexual offenders continue to deny having committed any offenses. For example, Maletzky (1991) noted that over a 17-year period, 87% of offenders referred to the Sexual Abuse Clinic in Oregon denied all or part of their crime when first interviewed. Barbaree (1991) found that 54% of incarcerated rapists and 66% of incarcerated child molesters denied that they had committed an offense. When minimization was included as a form of denial, these numbers increased to include approximately 98% of all offenders.

The reasons for offender denial are many. Salter (1988) suggests that sexual offenders may engage in a type of "magical thinking" in which "if they say it isn't so, it isn't so." She suggests that for many offenders "sexual deviance does not occur when they commit the act, it occurs when they admit it" (p. 186). Happel and Auffrey (1995) suggest that sexual offenders use denial "to avoid feelings of shame, confusion, embarrassment, inadequacy, responsibility, and guilt. . . . The thought of being a sexual deviate can be so frightening or repugnant to them that they hide from themselves for years" (p. 6). In addition, they suggest that sexual offenders are also afraid of the subsequent disapproval and rejection, assuming that they will lose their families, friends, and jobs and suffer mental and emotional breakdown, as well as retaliation. "Even when not intentionally deceitful, sex offenders will deny their deviance to avoid others believing that there is something wrong with their sexuality" (p. 6).

Families and Denial

In work with family systems, denial appears to be a natural defense, where it is seemingly in everyone's best interests to minimize and deny. When offenses are denied or minimized, family members can imagine that the nonoffending family members have not failed to recognize the problem, the offender has not committed heinous acts, and victims have not been badly hurt. One researcher has suggested that when denial occurs among adolescent sexual offenders, family dynamics are often involved. In her 1990 study, Sefarbi noted that approximately half the adolescent offenders at the Philadelphia Child Guidance Clinic denied their offenses, and their families invariably supported the adolescent's denial. This contrasted with the usual response of families to other types of delinquent behavior, such as substance abuse or theft. Sefarbi also observed the relationship between family dynamics and denial. Adolescents who denied their offenses tended to be in an "enmeshed" family organization, whereas those who admitted tended to be in a "disengaged family system." By admitting, the adolescent in the disengaged family system called attention to the dysfunction in family members who were otherwise distant and unavailable. Adolescents in the enmeshed family system were likely to have been "parentified" by a mother who was overwhelmed and needed the adolescent to provide child care. This type of family frequently maintained the denial, even after the perpetrator admitted, claiming that the boy "had been pressured into admission by the psychotherapy peer group" (p. 464).

Types of Denial

Many researchers consider denial to occur on a continuum, beginning with some form of minimization. There are a wide variety of ways in which offenders minimize their sexually deviant behavior. For example, Barbaree (1991) noted three forms of minimization: (1) minimizing the harm to the victim, (2) minimizing the extent of previous offenses, and (3) minimizing individual responsibility for the offenses.

Happel and Auffrey (1995) suggested that denial has at least 12 steps, including (1) denial of the crime itself, (2) denial of responsibility for the crime, (3) denial of intent and premeditation, (4) denial of deviant arousal and fantasies, (5) denial of the frequency of the deviant acts, (6) denial of the intrusiveness of the offense behavior, (7) denial of injury to victims, (8) denial of sexual gratification from the offense behaviors, (9) denial of various types of grooming behavior, (10) denial of risk management activities, (11) denial of the difficulty of change and need for help, and (12) denial of relapse potential and possible recidivism. With the exception of the first, these are all minimizations of an admitted behavior and are often successfully challenged during the early phase of treatment groups. Schlank and Shaw (1996) have described "absolute denial" as the continuation of denial of the sexual offense after the process of confrontation in a traditional sex offender treatment setting.

Treating Minimization and Absolute Denial

Because it is expected that most sexual offenders minimize or deny their charges, experienced clinicians have developed numerous strategies for confronting these defenses and assisting clients in fully participating in their treatment. Routinely, offenders who have denied their charges in court and even in court-ordered sexual offender specific psychological evaluations admit their guilt and subsequently take responsibility for their offenses once they have been exposed to the safety of a well-facilitated sexual offender treatment program. Thus, most programs allot a specific amount of time and sometimes specific procedures for confronting denial during the early phase of treatment. In recognition of this process, most programs have already allowed offenders in complete denial to participate in treatment for a limited period of time, during which the offender is expected to respond to the support and the peer pressure of the group by admitting culpability. Schwartz (1995) noted that denial seems to disappear once the "individual understands that the therapist will not reject him and brand him as a sex-crazed pervert" (p. 14-6). She discusses other techniques, including deliberately ignoring the denier until he begins to bond with the other group members, using paradoxical interventions, and using hypnosis (either to retrieve memories that were actually suppressed or to allow an offender an opportunity to admit while "saving face").

For many years now, clinicians have incorporated erectile measures and polygraphy to interfere with minimization and denial. Barnard, Fuller, Robbins, and Shaw (1989) described a computerized lab as a component of the sex offender treatment program where penile plethysmograph evaluations were routinely utilized to confront the minimization and denial of treatment participants. Numerous treatment programs utilize routine polygraph assessments where offenders' minimization and denial are confronted in the context of community management of the offenders. Adolescent offenders in the Fuller's community-based treatment program, "Adolescents Who Sexually Offend," are administered polygraphs which question the details of their offense descriptions as well as reviewing their overall honesty in group and their exposure to high-risk factors that might jeopardize their relapse prevention plans. Recent court decisions have supported the therapeutic use of polygraphs as long as they do not cause the client to self-incriminate.

Marshall (1994) routinely includes offenders who totally deny any deviant behavior in his treatment groups. During group sessions, each offender is asked to disclose to the group the nature of his offenses in detail, including not only the assaults but also the surrounding preceding circumstances, his thoughts and feelings at the time, his emotional and mental state, his level of intoxication (if relevant) and how this was induced, and his interpretation of the victim's behaviors and emotional reaction.

Therapists are provided with detailed court reports of the offenses and challenge each offender's version while also providing a supportive environment for change. Each offender is asked to repeat his version of the offenses until it closely matches the court report. In Marshall's study, only 2 deniers remained out of 25 who began the treatment groups.

Marshall's technique appears highly effective with incarcerated populations, where treatment staff have some leverage (e.g., being able to recommend an offender for early release if he benefits from treatment). However, this technique is less powerful with offenders in community-based programs with limited incentives to offer or with offenders who are incarcerated with no possibility of early release.

Dealing With Continued Denial

However, the most difficult task seems to be the treatment of offenders who are in complete and resistant denial. Many programs point to the limited number of treatment beds available and refuse to accept offenders who will not admit to committing their crimes. Happel and Auffrey (1995) presented further justification for excluding denying offenders, stressing the importance of both limiting the time and money spent on offenders "who are unwilling to admit their deviance and work in group" and also avoiding the difficulties involved in accepting "sex offenders who threaten cohesion and confidentiality through their denial and intimidation of others" (p. 17). A recent court case (State v. Imlay, 1991) suggests that these reasons may not be adequate anymore. In this Montana case, a sexual offender on probation was found not to be in violation of his probation after being terminated from his sex offender group for failure to admit to his offense. The court stressed that this man was only "asserting his constitutional right against self-incrimination." However, it continues to be routine to eject denying sexual offenders from treatment programs after several weeks or months in the treatment program.

On the other hand, some clinicians have maintained deniers in treatment without requiring admission. As mentioned earlier, Maletzky (1991, 1993) has reported on his experience treating offenders who deny and has begun follow-up studies of their recidivism rates. Steen (1992) also described a treatment program that included offenders who completely denied their charges. In her program, offenders were considered to have successfully completed treatment without admitting, and she has described an apology letter written by a denier to his victim at the time of reunification. In this letter, the denier refers to vague ways in which the victim may have felt hurt and apologizes for this rather than for the specific offenses. In addition, O'Donohue and Letourneau (1993) reported some success in a community-based treatment group in which offenders who denied their guilt were provided with an overview of victim empathy training, cognitive restructuring, sex education, assertiveness and social skills training, and education about sexual offender therapy.

A Program for Treating Deniers

In an effort to treat resistant deniers outside the traditional ongoing group setting, Shaw and Schlank (1992) described some early data that provided support for introducing victim empathy and relapse prevention elements in a nonthreatening manner to prepare denying offenders (who were court-ordered to community-based treatment) for entrance into a sexual offender treatment program. Their early data was supported by continued success using this method (Shaw & Schlank, 1993; Schlank & Shaw, 1996). Specifically, this procedure provided for accepting referrals for sexual offenders who had maintained their denial in a traditional treatment setting. A screening interview was scheduled during which the clients were told that the upcoming group was not considered sexual offender treatment but was a module aimed at reducing a person's denial and possibly preparing him to participate in a regular treatment program. Each client was asked to sign a contract that stated that he would attend each of the 16 sessions, would pay a sliding-scale fee for the session, and would also pay one-sixteenth of the fee for an evaluation using the penile plethysmograph and a polygraph. This evaluation would take place at the end of the module if he still denied guilt. Clients were informed that if they were no longer in denial by the end of the module, they would not be required to undertake the evaluations and would be refunded the money they contributed toward the evaluations.

During the initial sessions, the therapists discussed the reasons many offenders deny their offenses and the various functions denial serves. This discussion provided for the possibility of a client later admitting to his offense without having necessarily to admit that he had been deliberately lying prior to his admissions. Examples were also provided of offenders who initially denied, but later admitted to their offenses, including their explanations about why they held onto denial for so long and how it felt to finally admit their problem.

Group members were then informed that during the next 10 sessions, they would participate in a victim empathy exercise and would learn about the effects of crimes similar to those they had been accused of committing. Each client was given an outline for a victim empathy project they would be expected to present to the group after learning about the effects on victims. The next 10 sessions were spent viewing videotapes about the effects of sexual abuse on victims, discussing these videos, and reading articles on the same topic. Group members were then required to present a written report to the group discussing the short-and long-term effects on a victim of a crime similar to the one they had been accused of committing. In addition, they were asked to discuss how it would affect such a victim to have his or her perpetrator deny that he had committed the offense.

During the remainder of this time-limited group, members were introduced to basic concepts of relapse prevention, including a discussion of the terms "external high-risk factor," "internal high-risk factor," "seemingly unimportant decision," "lapse," and "relapse." They were first asked to apply these concepts to a behavior they were willing to change, such as smoking marijuana or becoming verbally abusive toward a partner. Once they were able to demonstrate some ability to apply this model to a chosen behavior, each client was asked to apply the model to his charges, imagining the relapse prevention issues for a person who was guilty of the offense for which the denier had been accused. For example, each participant was asked to imagine what a perpetrator of such crimes might identify as high-risk factors.

At the end of the group, a written report summarizing each client's progress during group sessions, and the results of the evaluations (if necessary), was sent to each client's probation officer. By the end of this module, 50% of the denying offenders had admitted their offenses and were ready for treatment.

Burditt (1995) used a modified version of the denier's pilot study with his outpatient population of court-ordered sex offenders in Texas. Basically following the same format, he added visits from admitting sex offenders to the group and also introduced concepts from "motivational interviewing." At the end of Burditt's first group module, he also had a 50% success rate. He offered the pretreatment group a second time and obtained a 66% success rate.

While Burditt was conducting his study in Texas, Murphy and Berry (1995) were conducting a similar study in Colorado. They modified Shaw and Schlank's format by extending the number of weeks for the module, allowing open-ended groups in which clients were admitted immediately after their intake and using more written assignments. In addition, they added two individual therapy sessions and a full disclosure polygraph to be completed during the time the denier was in the program. During the initial project, 24 clients were terminated for violation of the treatment contract, 2 transferred to other programs, 2 completed parole, and 1 was released from treatment by the judge. Of the remaining 23 clients, 16 admitted to their offenses and progressed to the first phase of the traditional sex offender treatment program.

The cited studies suggest that there are some methods for altering an offender's denial, even when the peer pressure of being in a group of admitters has been unsuccessful. Interestingly, Maletzky (1991, 1993) suggests that there also may be some hope for those who never admit. In his studies, he found that the majority of men who completed a behavior/cognitive group and also participated in individual therapy sessions were successful at avoiding relapse even when they never did admit their guilt. In fact, those who completed a treatment program but remained in denial were actually more successful than those who admitted their guilt but did not complete treatment (Maletzky & McFarland, 1995).

Conclusion

Most sexual offenders initially deny committing their offenses, and many continue to minimize their behavior in a number of ways. Increasingly, therapists may be requested to treat offenders who deny their offenses, particularly given recent court decisions that protect the right of an individual not to testify against him- or herself.

Although initially many practitioners required admission of some part of the crime before beginning treatment, many are now asserting that some forms of treatment can be successful in assisting offenders to admit their guilt. In addition, it appears that even those who never admit receive some benefit from sex offender treatment. Concomitantly, new efforts are under way to more efficiently confront the minimization and denial of offenders with the hope of making complete treatment available to previously "untreatable" offenders.

References

Barbaree, H. E. (1991). Denial and minimization among sex offenders: Assessment and treatment outcome. *Forum on Corrections Research, 3*, 30–33.

Barnard, G. W., Fuller, A. K., Robbins, L., & Shaw, T. (1989). *The child molester: An integrated approach to evaluation and treatment*. New York: Brunner/Mazel.

Burditt, T. (1995, October). *Treating sex offenders who deny their guilt: The application of motivational interviewing to the denier's pilot study*. Paper presented at the Annual Research and Treatment Conference of the Association for the Treatment of Sexual Abusers, New Orleans.

Happel, R. M. & Auffrey, J. J. (1995). Sex offender assessment: Interrupting the dance of denial. *American Journal of Forensic Psychology, 13*(2), 5–22.

Haywood, T. W. & Grossman, L. S. (1994). Denial of deviant sexual arousal and psychopathology in child molesters. *Behavior Therapy, 25,* 327–340.

Maletzky, B .M. (1991). *Treating the sexual offender.* Newbury Park, CA: Sage.

Maletzky, B. M. (1993). Factors associated with success and failure in the behavior and cognitive treatment of sexual offenders. *Annals of Sex Research, 6,* 241–258.

Maletzky, B. M., & McFarland, B. (1995). *Treatment results in offenders who deny their crimes.* Manuscript submitted for publication.

Marshall, W. L. (1994). Treatment effects on denial and minimization in incarcerated sex offenders. *Behavior Research and Therapy, 32*(5), 559–564.

Murphy, J. J., & Berry, D. J. (1995, October). *Treating sex offenders who deny their guilt: A six month adapted version of the denier's pilot study.* Paper presented at the Annual Research and Treatment Conference of the Association for the Treatment of Sexual Abusers, New Orleans.

O'Donohue, W., & Letourneau, E. (1993). A brief group treatment for the modification of denial in child sexual abusers: outcome and follow-up. *Child Abuse & Neglect, 17,* 299–304.

Salter, A. (1988). *Treating child sex offenders and victims.* Newbury Park, CA: Sage.

Schlank, A .M., & Shaw, T. (1996). Treating sexual offenders who deny their guilt: A pilot study. *Sexual Abuse: A Journal of Research and Treatment 8*(1), 17–23.

Schwartz, B. (1995). Group therapy. In B. K. Schwartz & H. R. Cellini (Eds.), *The sex offender: Corrections, treatment and legal practice* (pp. 14-1–14-15). Kingston, NJ: Civic Research Institute.

Sefarbi, R. (1990). Admitters and deniers among adolescent sex offenders and their families: A preliminary study. *American Journal of Orthopsychiatry, 60*(3), 460–465.

Shaw, T., & Schlank, A. M. (1992, October). *Treating sexual offenders who deny their guilt.* Paper presented at the Annual Research and Treatment Conference of the Association for the Treatment of Sexual Abusers, Portland, OR.

Shaw, T., & Schlank, A. M. (1993, November). *Update: Treating sex offenders who deny their guilt.* Paper presented at the Annual Research and Treatment Conference of the Association for the Treatment of Sexual Abusers, Boston.

State v. Imlay, 249 Mont. 82, 813 P.2d 979 (1991).

Steen, C. (1992, October). *Treating sexual offenders who deny their guilt.* Paper presented at the Annual Research and Treatment Conference of the Association for the Treatment of Sexual Abusers, Portland, OR.

Chapter 7

Using Strategic, Systemic, and Linguistic Principles to Enhance Treatment Compliance

by Mack E. Winn, L.C.S.W.

Overview

Cognitive-behavioral treatment of sexual offenders is a process that is dependent on securing the client's compliance in following through with stressful, vulnerable therapeutic processes. The strategic, systemic, and linguistic models, most recognized for their ability to manage resistance, have been presented to reduce denial and increase motivation by providing concepts and techniques designed to enhance compliance. It is hoped that this integration will make cognitive behavioral therapy of sex

offenders more available to those offenders who could benefit from this treatment but
are resistive to doing so.

Dealing With Denial

In working with sex offenders the first task is always to deal with the varied forms
of denial. This is such a challenging task that many treatment providers refuse even
to consider working with offenders who are "in denial." The definition varies from "If
he'll admit he was in the country when the crime occurs, I'll try to deal with him." to
"He must admit and take responsibility for all charges." Denial is seen as a negative,
oppositional response. However, it could be interpreted as a necessary adaptation to
what the offender and his family perceive as the destruction of life as they have known
it. It can be viewed as an automatic response to maintaining the homeostasis of the
system (Barrett, Sykes, & Byrnes, 1986).

Offenders can maintain denial in a variety of ways. First, the offender may use a
variety of cognitive distortions to protect himself from facing the shame and responsibility connected with acknowledging his deviance. He may claim that he does not
remember the situation because he was drunk or on drugs or in a blackout of undetermined origin or even asleep when the crime allegedly occurred. He may use a variety of cognitive distortions to minimize, justify, or blame. Second, he may regulate his
emotions to protect himself from vulnerability. He may have a predisposition to numb
his emotions that may date from traumatic early experiences. He may have been
socialized so that the only emotion he can feel is anger. This serves him well if he can
replace guilt and shame with self-righteous indignation. Third, he can encourage the
natural response of the family system to deny such traumatic information. Those close
to the offender may attempt to protect the family from humiliation by denying or minimizing the charge. This becomes particularly destructive when the victim is also a
family member. The sum totals of these cognitive, emotional, and systemic processes
constitute the offender's denial system.

When denial is viewed as a whole systems phenomenon, it becomes possible to
intervene at a variety of levels because influencing one part of the system affects the
other parts. Therefore, changing the offender's cognitive distortions will affect the
way he feels about his behavior. Changing his feelings about his behavior may influence the family's level of denial.

Although many sex offender treatment providers rely on direct confrontation of
denial, many clients may be too vulnerable or dependent on this defense to react well
to this approach. It may only result in the denial becoming more rigid and entrenched.
Meta-confrontation is a method of dealing with the function of denial. It is a way of
pulling the offender to accept responsibility for his behavior rather than pushing him
(Winn, 1996). It also provides a way of dealing with the offender's perception of the
threat of confrontation.

Meta-Confrontation and the Negative Consequences of Denial

The basic question that this model addresses is, "What bad things would happen
if the offender or family began thinking, feeling or behaving differently about the sex-

ual abuse?" If the therapist can acknowledge the self-protective function of denial, there is a chance that it can be empathetically reframed. It is vital that the therapist acknowledge the negative consequences of change (Fisch, Weaklund, & Spiegel, 1982; Watzlawick, Weaklund, & Fisch, 1974; Haley, 1973; Haley, 1976; Hoke, Sykes, & Winn, 1989; Winn, 1996). For example, in dealing with an offender whose cognitive distortion is that his sexual assault was actually a well-intended form of sex education, the therapist might pose the question, "I wonder what bad things would happen if you began thinking differently about your behavior?" Or, "How would you feel if it were impossible to think about your actions as educational?" As the offender is repeatedly challenged in this way within an empathetic relationship, he may eventually admit, "I'll feel like a freak." Or, "I can't live with myself." The therapist can then use paradoxical agreeing and restraining by encouraging the offender to remain in denial so it becomes a challenge. "Bob, I would suggest that you continue that form of thinking so that you can protect yourself from experiencing the harm that may have occurred to your daughter because you may not be strong enough to deal with it." This must not be done in a cynical manner but must be offered with real concern for the offender as it reflects his real fear. Yet it frequently prompts the offender to meet the challenge to redefine his behavior.

When this approach is successful, it is because there is a level of congruence between the therapist's challenge to change and his or her respect for the offender's need to stay the same. This approach can be used anytime denial is resurrected to protect the offender from renewed shame or disclosure, such as admitting to fantasizing or planning or preparing to take a polygraph.

Partialization of Denial

It is important to help the client realize when denial is being activated. The internal family systems (IFS) model (Schwartz, 1992) can be adapted to increase an offender's recognition and self-confrontation of denial. IFS therapy theorizes that there is a rational "self" in all individuals but "parts" that once served a useful function can become too powerful and function to defeat the self. Parts may operate to protect the offender or to carry his anger. Therefore, there can be parts that undermine the recovery that the self is pursuing. Consequently, it is important to learn to identify when these parts are beginning to take over. This theoretical construct allows the offender to distance his more distasteful parts from his basic personhood.

By identifying with the strengths of the client and aligning with the powerful self that craves recovery, the therapist can position himself between the self that is healthy and parts that want to protect and deny. The offender can then learn to identify when the parts are trying to take control. This can be framed in terms of relapse prevention. This is similar to the ideas of the "new self" and "old self" developed by Jim Haaven in dealing with developmentally disabled sex offenders (Haaven, Little, & Petre-Miller, 1990).

Preparing for Confrontation

Many clients respond rebelliously to the mechanistic application of confrontation. They act as if they had been attacked, meeting it with rebellion. This is often the case in new groups where a culture of responsibility has not yet been established. When the client experiences confrontation as unwelcome advice or as an attack, he may mobilize well-established defenses. For example, he may automatically assume the role of the victim or the offender (Trepper & Barrett, 1989). It is, however, possible for the therapist to elicit the offender's permission to be confronted.

Hypnotherapists frequently elicit cooperation to go along with a hypnotic suggestion by using "ideomotor signaling." For example, the client is told that he will nonverbally inform the clinician when he is ready to successfully incorporate the suggestion and comply. The therapist states, "The index finger on your right hand will twitch automatically when you are ready to accept the suggestion."

This concept can be incorporated into sex offender treatment. Although it seems unrealistic that an offender would overtly grant his therapist or his group the right to confront him, there are a variety of ways in which this can be accomplished. There can be an overt request for permission which increases feelings of autonomy or cooperation. Scott (1993) proposed constructing a prototypical sex offender as the standard of deviance against which the group members' behavior can be measured. Comparing the client's behavior to how "Sam" might act can lead into a request for permission to confront. Group members may join in encouraging the offender to accept the "challenge to be challenged." Therapists can also explain to the client how sex offenders routinely deal with denial or have them read books on the subject. If the offender refuses to grant permission for confrontation, that decision should be respected but the motivation behind his refusal can be explored through a megaconfrontational use of therapist positioning.

Using an indirect strategy, the therapist can preempt or predict the offender's defensive response to confrontation. The therapist suggests that there is something that he would like to state to the offender that could prove very useful to his recovery. However, he fears that the offender cannot tolerate hearing it. Alternatively, the therapist might predict that the client will react to a confrontation with denial or rebellion. Should the client accept the challenge to accept the confrontation without responding in the predicted way, the therapist can then ask the client to predict how he will react if he begins to become uncomfortable. Group members can be asked the same question to increase the universality for the offender on center stage. Again, if he remains resistant to confrontation, that decision should be respected but the resistance should be explored in terms of its function to himself and family.

Empathy, Consistency, and Flexibility

Offenders in denial may respond better if they can be made to feel less vulnerable and less in need of this defense. Therefore, the relationship should contain empathy and nurturance. This is not to be confused with collusion. However, it has been observed that offenders are more willing to accept confrontation when they know that it comes from someone who has the client's best interest at heart. To do that, the therapist needs to keep in mind how denial is operating in the offender's life—not as a personal affront to the treatment provider but as a natural method of self-protection.

The sex offender also needs to be able to rely on his therapist to consistently challenge his parts when he is unable to that by himself. The therapist's responses become internalized over time and the offender begins to apply his therapy in his daily life (Tarragona & Orlinsky, 1988).

The therapeutic relationship also needs to be flexible. At times the therapist, being first a human being and therefore prone to make mistakes, may need to apologize, reposition, and negotiate with the client. Experiencing this can provide the offender with healthy feelings of empowerment and a memorable role model.

Empathy, consistency, and flexibility allow a multifaceted relationship to support the client in new experiences where he can challenge and expand his sense of responsibility and empathy for others.

Often these individuals may be socially underdeveloped and experiencing shame and vulnerability. They may consequently be in need of a "curative relationship" with the therapist. However, this must be balanced by an appreciation that sex offenders may also try to manipulate a therapist into collusion or derail the therapy process so that only those issues the offender feels comfortable with are pursued. An experienced therapist should be able to shift along the continuum between support and confrontation according to the needs of the client—not the needs of the therapist.

Denial in its many forms will continue to be an issue throughout the course of therapy. However, once the offender's denial becomes less important, he begins to accept responsibility for his actions and will be more amenable to cooperating in cognitive and behavioral techniques that will be difficult to perform and make him feel vulnerable in the process.

Reducing Resistance to Cognitive-Behavioral Procedures

Cognitive-behavioral interventions have become a standard component of the sex offender's treatment regimen (Abel, Blanchard, & Becker, 1978; Maletzky, 1991; Salter, 1988). These techniques and principles, primarily designed to recondition the offender's deviant sexual arousal, have evolved out of the knowledge base of behaviorism. They are procedures which demand compliance of the offender in executing what is necessary to manage his deviancies effectively. Treatment failures using behavioral methods may be attributed to problems with the offender completely following through with the homework assignments (Maletzky, 1991). However, it is possible to expand the responsibility for change beyond the individual client and adapt a cocreative orientation. Compliance with behavioral treatment may be enhanced by improving therapist-client communication to motivate the offender to comply with aversive, time-consuming, vulnerability-engendering practices. In addition, compliance may be improved by attaching a therapeutic meaning or frame of reference to these practices that is powerful enough to influence the offender to cooperate with treatment. The therapist-client interaction may be the causal factor in the offender's compliance with these necessary interventions. The behavioral literature, however, offers little in the way of enhancing compliance to perform these practices, other than informing the offender that research says they are helpful or threatening him with incarceration should he refuse to participate.

The strategic literature is most often cited for its focus on managing resistance (Fisch et al., 1982; Haley, 1973, 1976, 1984; Watzlawick et al., 1974). This school of thought approaches resistance and denial as an understandable, adaptive reactions to the demands required to change a long practiced behavior. It acknowledges that symptoms and behaviors serve functions to detour broader levels of individual or ecological pathology from being experienced (Bergman, 1985; Haley, 1973; Selvini-

Palazzoli, Boscolo, Cecchin, & Prata, 1978; Tomm, 1986). Consequently, homeostatic forces are seen as maintaining problem behavior to avoid the anxiety of encountering change (Minuchin, 1981). Resistance is not viewed as a situation to be confronted but an opportunity to manage cooperation between therapist and client (de Shazer, 1985). Characteristics such as the client's need for autonomy are deliberately integrated into the therapist's position and directives. This maximizes opportunities for the client to follow through with what is expected of him (Hoke et al., 1989; Rohrbaugh, Tennen, Press, & White, 1981; Winn, 1996).

Systemic philosophy focuses on how individuals or families create their own unique version of reality (Anderson & Goolishian, 1988; Hoyt, 1994; Jenkins, 1990; White 1986). Behavioral therapy assumes that acting differently will change the meaning of an unwanted symptom. However, the systemic/constructivist orientation focuses on the meaning of a behavior as defined between therapist and client. It assumes that a change in that context will increase the chances of internalizing therapy and behaving differently. The demands of behavioral therapy require the client to comply with interventions that are action oriented and often painstaking to do. Asking the client to engage in minimal arousal conditioning or boredom aversion, for example, requires the client to manage his resistance to comply. Therefore, a focus on helping a client shift how he views his problem and his therapy can be helpful in managing compliance and enhancing motivation. Systemic and constructivist philosophy offers the therapist working with offenders the option of introducing changes at the level of meaning in influencing the offender to engage in treatment.

In the strategic/systemic/linguistic theory resistance is viewed as self-protection the offender accesses in the face of experiencing therapeutic exercises that are aversive and will activate his sense of vulnerability (Barrett et al., 1986; Trepper & Barrett, 1989; Hoke et al., 1989; Winn, 1996). The therapist's use of direct and indirect positioning shall be discussed as means of positively maximizing the use of the client's defensive reactivity (Fisch et al., 1982; Haley, 1976; Watzlawick et al., 1974). The purposeful use of language (Fisch et al., 1982; Anderson & Goolishian, 1988; Grinder & Bandler, 1976; Haley, 1973, 1976) can provide a non confrontational means of influence in shaping the client's view of therapy. Interventions that promote changes can be created by reshaping meaning with paradoxical prediction and prescription (Selvini-Palazzoli et al., 1978; Watzlawick et al., 1974; Weeks & L'Abate, 1982). Finally, ordeal theory, rituals, and rites of passage can create a context from which to reframe complying with behavioral treatment through creating a change in perception (Imber-Black, 1989).

Direct and Indirect Positioning

Therapists attempt to influence clients from two basic positions: direct and indirect. Direct efforts may include advice giving, psychoeducational exchange, confrontation, instruction, and interpretation. Clinicians operating from this position assume a role of leadership and authority. This means of influence is often employed by the therapist working with sexual offenders. Behavioral therapy is a direct form of treatment. It requires the therapist to give instructions to the client in a straightforward manner, and the offender is expected to follow through with the task assigned to him. When the client shows resistance to the nature of the task, many therapists respond with confrontation or by using safeguards to ensure compliance (e.g., the audiotaping of masturbatory exercises).

Indirect positioning requires the therapist to take more of a "one down" posture in relation to the offender. It more resembles a "Columbo" image as opposed to a "Rambo" image. From this position, the therapist may also employ interventions that manipulate metaphors and analogies used by the offender to enhance compliance with behavioral treatment. The therapist may incorporate paradoxical intention to purposefully redirect the offender's reactivity so that he can rebel against the therapist's directives to "stay the same or go slow" (Fisch et al., 1982; Watzlawick et al., 1974). Indirect efforts also take into account the function of resistance. They can mobilize the client's need to rebel against the therapist's position that the client may be too emotionally vulnerable to succeed in mastering the therapeutic intervention (Hoke et al., 1989). Indirect efforts may be particularly helpful with offenders who do not respond well to direct confrontation. This position is helpful when the therapist requests the client to participate in behavioral interventions that are aversive and time-consuming or will engender vulnerability in the client. In addition, this position is especially powerful when working with autonomy-driven adolescents. This developmental position can be used to challenge adolescent clients by getting them to disagree with the therapist's pessimistic position.

The Purposeful Use of Language

Therapists generally interact with their clients in three ways. They ask questions, make statements, and give directives (Breunlin, Schwartz, & MacKune Karrer, 1992). Language is the medium that delivers these forms of communications to its recipients. However, the message intended to be sent is not always the one received (Satir, 1964). Therapeutic communication is a process that requires both therapist and offender to enter a mutual feedback loop. This loop is a series of interactions in which the therapist and client create a mutual reality from which the nature of therapy is defined. The therapist must take great care in presenting treatment to the client in a way that minimizes the possibility of engendering the client's resistance. Using the client's language, metaphors, and world view can accomplish this goal.

The therapist should listen carefully to the offender's language so that his words and concepts can be incorporated into the therapeutic dialogue. People may feel more secure in a conversation that is presented in a language they are used to. Slang expressions, analogies, and metaphors contain powerful opportunities for the therapist to join the offender's world view and increase the possibility of influencing him to engage in treatment. Metaphors contain occasions for the therapist to talk with the client at conscious and unconscious levels simultaneously (Haley 1973, 1976). The clinician can develop metaphors that are congruent with the values and interests of the offender or he can amplify metaphorical communication that is initiated by the client.

Using the client's world view involves the therapist's purposeful integration of the offender's interests, values, and beliefs in defining treatment or influencing him to comply with a directive. Any information the therapist has about the offender, which the client strongly identifies with, can be creatively used as a context to frame the importance or nature of therapy. Metaphors involving computer technology, religion, the work ethic, 12-step programs, or even sports can be employed in enhancing compliance with behavioral treatments. For example, a therapist working with a man who had sexually abused his 4-year-old granddaughter was in need of the covert sensitization procedure. However, his cognitive distortions were so entrenched that he could not generate any scenes that did not put the child in the role of the aggressor. During a session, the therapist learned that the offender was a Christian Scientist. Inquisitively, the therapist asked the client to teach him about his religion. The client went on to describe the fundamental spiritual struggle of the Christian scientist: the conflict between the "mortal mind" and the "divine mind." This dichotomy describes a common spiritual theme of overcoming inappropriate thoughts or desires in exchange for the internal tranquility offered through spiritual means. The client's religious belief related to mental processes created a language for the therapist to introduce his theme of thinking errors into a frame of reference with which the client was familiar. As a result, the therapist began to postulate to the client that perhaps his mortal mind was interfering with his desire to engage in treatment. As a result, they developed a framework through which the client's cognitive distortions could be presented in an acceptable context. Even if the offender were to seek out the services of a Christian Scientist practitioner (a person authorized to perform healing), he would still have to return to the therapist and demonstrate that he is more in control of his mortal mind by thinking differently about the child's level of initiation of the abuse. In addition, the conflict between the two minds, metaphorically depicts the theme of impulse control and the problem of immediate gratification (Marlatt, 1989). Consequently, it contains analogic material to the principals of covert sensitization, which the therapist was later able to introduce as a frame to enhance compliance with the procedure. That is, covert sensitization was framed as a tool to help the client tame his mortal mind, therefore, addressing his deviances in a more Christian Science manner. Consequently, the concept of cognitive distortions was transformed into a framework that was more congruent with the offender's values and world view. As the client began to think differently about the child's level of initiation in the abuse, he could produce meaningful scenes for his covert sensitization. Interestingly, the trigger phrase for his thought stopping in the escape/reward sequence of the tape involved a spiritual command.

The preceding example illustrates how the clinician can sensitively scan the client for information that can help the therapist enhance compliance. All too often, therapists working with offenders are tempted to confront the offender with what they define as "the truth." However, often, direct, aggressive confrontation only irritates the offender and maintains his resistance to treatment and his vulnerability to cognitive distortions (Hoke et al., 1989; Ward, Hudson, & Marshall, 1995; Winn, 1996). Creative use of the offender's language allows the therapist a nonconfrontational means to influence the offender's participation in a therapeutic task. This meta-confrontation (Winn, 1996) is accomplished by changing the meaning of the task to one with which the client can more strongly identify. For example, offenders with an interest in computers may have their behavioral work framed as "reprogramming." Visualization exercises that use computer imagery can be employed to enhance self-monitoring skills. Men who are also involved in 12-step programs can see apology sessions or victim empathy exercises as 8th-step work (the step where the alcoholic should make amends for his actions). Men who have a history of gambling can discuss the "odds" of reoffense if certain behavioral measures are not taken. Offenders who enjoy gardening can be encouraged to use behavioral techniques in an attempt to make sure "the soil is not fertile" for reoffense and discuss the "nutrients" necessary for prevention. All these descriptions can be amplified and integrated into treatment as the need to manage compliance arises.

Paradoxical Prescription and Prediction

Strategic and systemic therapists have long employed strategies that respect the homeostatic forces operating in families and individuals whose purpose is to preserve the status quo. Offender treatment with its emphasis on measurable behavioral and cognitive changes often activates these forces quickly and powerfully. This is often seen when the subject of behavioral treatment is broached with the offender. The techniques of paradoxical prediction and prescription are two strategic interventions (Bergman, 1985; Haley, 1976; Selvini-Palazzoli et al., 1978).

Paradoxical predictions and prescriptions are forecasts or sometimes directives given by the therapist to indirectly encourage change by requesting or predicting that the offender stays the same. A prediction is most often used to preempt a resistive response. It is employed to block an offender's maladaptive reaction to a suggestion about to be given by the therapist or group. This intervention follows the format, "I would like to tell you something important but I'm afraid you won't hear us . . . will become defensive . . . will go into your victim role . . . will get aggressive . . . etc." It can be combined with a one down posture by stating, "You will probably think I'm crazy when I say this or I'd like to say something that would powerfully affect your treatment but I'm afraid you will become angry and close up if I do." Predictions can be used to interrupt undesirable responses or a return to prior thinking, feeling, or behavior that the therapist fears will reappear between sessions when the influence of the therapist and group is not immediately present.

A *prescription* is a less subtle variation of the aforementioned. The undesirable behavior is directed to be performed, coupled with a statement concerning why it is important to behave, think, or feel in the manner the client does despite the consequences. This means of influence, for example, follows the following format: "Between this session and next I would consider continuing to believe that covert sensitization is the same as the movie *Clockwork Orange* because if the procedure worked and your deviances were better managed you would end up wanting to sexually approach your wife and that would start up that old couple's conflict about sex."Prescriptions are most valuable as a tool to dislodge a belief or feeling that confrontation has been unsuccessful in ameliorating. In such instances, the therapist can suggest the continuance of the client's resistance to performing boredom aversion during the session or can suggest that the self-protective belief be maintained between sessions. When this technique is used, it is important that the offender or family understand the purpose of this seemingly bizarre antitherapeutic directive.

Empathy must be conveyed concerning the *function* of the resistance such that the offender and/or his family can see that their behavior, feelings, and thoughts serve a protective purpose to avoid having to face some painful aspect of himself or family life (Hoke et al., 1989; Trepper & Barrett, 1989, 1992; Ward et al., 1995; Winn, 1996). Should the therapist fail in delivering these directives with purpose, empathy, and compassion, the offender will dismiss them as sarcastic and continue his unwanted resistance.

The implications of using paradoxical predictions and prescriptions in behavioral work with sexual offenders are extensive. This is often a highly resistive population. The behavioral techniques used in treatment require the offender's compliance to benefit from them. However, Maletzky's follow-up study (1991) indicated that many offenders did not completely comply with what was expected of them. These techniques provide a means of redirecting the offender's resistance to performing behavioral work by using that and the client's sense of autonomy to enhance his compliance. They are also particularly powerful with adolescent offenders whose issues of autonomy are often paramount. When the adolescent's autonomy is challenged in this manner, a change in meaning often occurs which helps compliance. What was once perceived as someone "tellin me what to do" is now perceived as "I can handle it," "I'll show them," or "I can tolerate the negative consequences that would occur if I profited from treatment."

Therapeutic Ordeals, Rituals, and Rites of Passage

Ordeals, rituals, and rites of passage have been used in cultures throughout civilization to help move people from one stage of life to another. Often these practices take several years of preparation and there is great emotional intensity before the ordeal is executed. The participant also experiences exhilaration and healing when the ritual has been accomplished. The successful execution of a rite of passage also brings with it celebration and new acceptance from others. Rituals and ordeals have been used for a long time to dramatically and powerfully elevate individuals into new stages of life that are seen as important or difficult to accomplish.

In the last decade, the strategic and systemic models of therapy have implemented more aesthetic concepts by utilizing rituals and ordeals (Bergman, 1985; Haley, 1976; Imber-Black, 1989; Selvini-Palazzoli et al., 1978). These exercises have been used to highlight and intensify moments in treatment, enabling the family to surpass the homeostatic forces that engender resistance. They have also been implemented to explain the importance of following through with a therapeutic directive that the client system sees as difficult to accomplish. Similarly, ordeals have been utilized to engender support from the environment in completing painful or arduous tasks.

Ritualistic themes can be woven into the treatment of sexual offenders, enhancing the compliance and attribution of meaning with the directives in behavioral treatment. In fact, many ritualistic elements in treatment programs go on without notice. For example, we can explain the use of beginning group sessions from a behavioral language perspective by describing a "layout" as a way of reinforcing the offender's thinking in a more responsible manner by repetition. Often treatment is described in only cognitive or behavioral terms. In so doing, the opportunity to more richly engage the client in investing himself is lost as the ritualistic element is ignored. It requires a powerful ordeal to signify a rite of passage into another culture—the culture of recovery. The therapist can also build group cohesion by creating a culture that respects the importance of ritual and ordeal.

Aversive behavior rehearsal is another technique that can be viewed as a ritualistic ordeal. If framed as something the client must do to comply with treatment, he will comply but may not internalize its meaning enough to truly help him change.

However, if the framing of the process is explained as a rite of passage that is part of making amends for his abusive actions, challenging himself to be courageous enough to encounter the deviant side of himself, or as a ritual he wants to complete to prove his determination in remaining abstinent, compliance and integration can be enhanced.

Evan Imber-Black (1989) has described four rituals that exist in families, cultures, and other systems: membership, healing, identity definition, and celebration. I have introduced a fifth: commitment rituals. Use of these techniques may enhance a client's motivation by helping him attach more significant meanings to the practices employed in treatment.

Membership. According to Imber-Black (1989), "All human systems must deal with questions of who is in or who is out, who belongs to the system, who defines membership, and how one gains or loses it" (p. 66). Similarly, offender treatment often reflects similar questions. This is particularly relevant in group treatment as the newer group members are enculturated into this foreign, confusing context. The forces operating in a group that facilitates members' desire for inclusion can be amplified by overt rituals. When the offender can attach a personal meaning to being a full member of the group, he will be more inclined to participate in behavioral or cognitive treatment that is often aversive in nature. The client's devotion to the tasks required of him will then be partially defined by his desire for membership. Rituals such as framing the completion of a rich layout as a contingency of full membership into the group can be one such strategy. The ritual of awarding a symbolic object upon full acceptance can also enhance desire for membership. Having a new group member formally convince the group that he is ready to be a full member and the group's membership reaching consensus on his acceptance can be a powerful ritual. The ritual of full disclosure can be complemented by helping the offender realize that passing his polygraph examination is an important "stepping-stone" in managing his deviancies.

Healing. Rituals involving healing can be incorporated into the sexual offender's treatment. We rarely even hear the language of healing in sexual offender treatment. Rather, we explain the techniques and processes of therapy as described as "conditioning" or "restructuring" some aspect of the client's behavior or thinking. However, sexual offenders are often people who have had painful life experiences and are in great need of healing. Helping offenders realize that they need some form of healing can often help them attach a more significant level of meaning to the demands of treatment.

Victim empathy role plays or aversive behavior rehearsal can be greatly enhanced by introducing the process as a healing ritual. When the technique is framed in this manner, offenders can more effectively integrate the process by realizing that the powerful catharsis that usually follows is a purging that is necessary to heal themselves from the guilt and shame that have been carried around for many years. Viewing the video of an aversive behavior rehearsal (ABR) with family, friends, or the group can be ritualized as a healing ceremony by helping the family realize that exposing the secretive, deviant side of the offender is a rite of passage that takes courage and determination for all. Even deciding who will attend the viewing can be a ritual that intensifies the meaning and importance of the task. When the family can have the emotional experience of viewing the ABR session, another healing ritual takes place for all members. They are able to look at the offender's deviance directly in a ceremony designed to heal them from the painful secrets of the client's harmful behavior.

Identity Definition. Rituals can also be used to help an individual define a new identity. Bar mitzvahs, weddings, and the like are examples of how certain cultures highlight a person's entrance into a new stage of life. In a wedding, when the parents of the bride walk their daughter down the aisle and offer her to the future spouse, a symbolic ritual takes place that metaphorically shifts the intergenerational relationship. This practice, which is often intertwined with much emotion, signifies a difficult passage for all involved.

Rituals of identity definition can be integrated into the treatment of the sexual offender as part of the goal of treatment to redefine the offender's identity into a more responsible, empathic, and less sexually driven individual. For example, one offender who was preparing to begin masturbatory satiation decided to rid himself of a secret box of pornographic material as a commitment to the process of change. When consulting with his therapist about the matter, the therapist suggested that he write a eulogy that would address his sacrifice of his pornography and highlight his new identity as an offender in recovery. The therapist encouraged the offender to invite some friends and relatives who had been supportive of him during the process of disclosure and home confinement. The therapist also instructed him to burn the box of material in the presence of these people and allow himself to experience whatever feelings of grief and mourning arose. The client invited his son and a longtime colleague to the event. He cried intensely throughout the ritual but the next week began to feel better. The client later stated that the ritual helped him to feel that he had moved on in his commitment to avoid deviant thinking and helped him to feel a new part of him be born. He also said that the public nature of the ritual intensified his commitment to be viewed by others as a nondeviant person. This mourning ritual allowed the client to emotionally move on in his development and grieve the loss of his deviances. This process of healing and identity redefinition appeared to allow the client to more fully follow his satiation regimen.

Celebration. Rarely in offender treatment do we hear of celebration beyond the concept of graduation from a program. Celebration rituals, however, can be used intermittently throughout treatment to punctuate successes along the way. According to Imber-Black (1989), "while the term 'celebration' generally conjures up festivities, it also may refer to more solemn and sacred rituals. . . . These expected and familiar processes function as abbreviated metaphors for personal connections symbolizing warmth, comfort, support and cultural affiliation" (p. 62). Rituals of celebration can be used to highlight completion of behavioral interventions. When the culture of treatment programs can include periodic celebration rituals as the client goes throughout treatment, a new level of meaning can be internalized by the client, increasing his motivation to comply with the directives expected of him. These rituals can be as simple as beginning each group with personal congratulations from each member upon a fellow offender's completion of an aversive task. It can involve the presentation of symbolic objects that signify the commitment and determination necessary to take a new step in managing one's deviancies. Celebration rituals can also be used to punctuate the forward progress in the offender's treatment by breaking treatment into stages and publicly acknowledging the passage of each client as he moves from one stage to another. In any event, these processes are designed to enhance the level of meaning the client ascribes to therapy by creating a context in which his accomplishments are highlighted and he can receive the warmth, comfort, support, and cultural affiliation previously described.

Commitment. I believe that there is, yet, another ritual beyond Imber-Black's framework that is helpful in changing the meaning of treatment for sexual offenders. This rite of passage is known as the commitment ritual. Rites of this nature have been used throughout history to help individuals increase their determination to accomplish a difficult but meaningful task. In the movie *A Man Called Horse*, Richard Harris, an Anglo male, desires entrance into a Native American Indian tribe in order to marry one of the clan's members. He is put through a series of painful ordeals (e.g., being bitten by snakes) to prove his commitment to becoming a member of the new culture. Fraternities and sororities also have ritualistic procedures in which new members are asked to perform a variety of aversive tasks to prove their commitment to the organization.

Cognitive-behavioral interventions are often aversive and intrusive. However, they can also provide opportunities for the sexual offender to ritualize and *prove his determination* to lead a deviancy-free lifestyle. If clinicians can purposefully present the meaning of the interventions in a ritualistic framework, it appears as if compliance and integration can be enhanced. This can be accomplished by presenting the procedures as "rites of passage." This level of commitment cannot be achieved intellectually. Rather, it must be experienced by doing something that challenges the offender in a profound manner. When the client can accept this challenge, he can ascribe a new meaning to participating in behavioral treatment and better internalize its contribution to his well-being.

Conclusion

The purpose of this chapter has been to present a strategic, systemic, and linguistic philosophy for reducing denial and enhancing sexual offenders" compliance with behavioral treatment. Because compliance is a prerequisite for successful outcome, I have presented in this chapter three models that are known for their effectiveness in addressing resistance for enhancing compliance with treatment. These models have been used to enhance the offender's level of meaning attached to the importance of participating in the difficult job of therapy. They have also been employed to reduce the amount of coercion or confrontation used by therapists to engage offenders in this type of therapy.

This chapter describes meta-confrontation, partialization, direct and indirect therapist positioning, the purposeful use of language and utilization of the client's world view, paradoxical prediction and prescription and therapeutic rituals, and ordeals and rites of passage. These concepts and practices have been employed as alternative means of effecting compliance as opposed to the traditional direct approach, which may instill a negative attitude regarding participation in cognitive-behavioral sex offender treatment. It is hoped that the integration of this body of knowledge will avail more clients to more richly invest themselves in treatment and further humanize treatment for sexual offenders.

References

Abel, G. G., Blanchard, E. B., & Becker, J. V. (1978). An integrated treatment program for rapists. In R. Rada (Ed.), *Clinical aspects of the rapist.* New York: Grune & Stratton.

Anderson, A., & Goolishian, H., (1988). Human systems as linguistic systems: Preliminary and evolving ideas about the implications of clinical theory. *Family Process, 27,* 371–394.

Barrett, M. J., Sykes, C., & Byrnes, W. (1986). A systemic model for the treatment of intra-family child sexual abuse. In T. Trepper & M. J. Barrett (Eds.), *Treating incest: A multiple systems perspective* (pp. 67-82). New York: Haworth Press.

Bergman, J. (1985). *Fishing for barracuda: Pragmatics of brief systemic therapy.* New York: Norton.

Breunlin, D., Schwartz, R., & MacKune Karrer, B. (1992). A blueprint for family therapy. In D. Breunlin, R. Schwartz, & B. MacKune Karrer (Eds.), *Metaworks: A new blueprint for family therapy.* San Francisco: Jossey-Bass.

de Shazer, S. (1985). *Keys to solution in brief therapy.* New York: Norton.

Erickson, M. H., & Rossi, S. L. (1976). *Hypnotic realities: The induction of clinical hypnosis and forms of indirect suggestion.* New York: Irvington.

Fisch, R., Weaklund, J. H., & Spiegel, L. (1982). *The tactics of change: Doing therapy briefly.* San Francisco: Jossey-Bass.

Grinder, R., & Bandler, R., (1976). *The structure of magic II: A book about communication and change.* Palo Alto, CA: Science and Behavior Books.

Haaven,J., Little, R., & Petre-Miller, D. (1990). *Treating intellectually disabled sex offenders: A model residential program.* Orwell, VT: Safer Society.

Haley, J. (1973). *Uncommon therapy: The psychiatric techniques of Milton Erickson, M.D.* New York: Norton.

Haley J. (1976). *Problem solving therapy: New strategies for effective family therapy.* San Francisco: Jossey-Bass.

Haley, J. (1984). *Ordeal therapy.* San Francisco: Jossey-Bass.

Hoke, S., Sykes, C., & Winn, M. (1989). Strategic/systemic interventions targeting denial in the incestuous family. *Journal of Strategic and Systemic Therapies, 8,* 44–51.

Hoyt, M. F. (1994). Constructive therapies: Introduction. In M. F. Hoyt (Ed.), *Constructive therapies* (pp. 2–10). New York: Guilford Press.

Imber-Black, E. (1989). Creating rituals in therapy. *Family Therapy Network, 13*(4), 38–44.

Jenkins, A. (1990). *Invitations to responsibility: The therapeutic engagement of men who are violent and abusive.* Adelaide, Australia: Dulwich Centre.

Maletzky, B. (1991). *Treating the sexual offender.* Newbury Park, CA: Sage.

Marlatt, G.A. (1989). Feeding the pig: The problem of immediate gratification. In D. R. Laws (Ed.), *Relapse prevention with sex offenders* (pp. 56–62). New York: Guilford Press.

Minuchin, S. (1981). *Family therapy techniques.* Cambridge, MA: Harvard University Press.

Rohrbaugh, M., Tennen, H., Press, S., & White, L. (1981). Compliance, defiance, and therapeutic paradox: Guidelines for strategic use of therapeutic interventions. *American Journal of Orthopsychiatry, 51,* 581–599.

Salter, A. (1988). *Treating child sex offenders and victims: A practical guide.* Newbury Park, CA: Sage.

Satir, V. (1964). *Conjoint family therapy.* Palo Alto, CA: Science and Behavior Books.

Scott, W. (1993). Group psychotherapy for male sex offenders: Strategic interventions. *Journal of Family Psychotherapy, 5,* 1–20.

Selvini-Palazzoli, M., Boscolo, L., Cecchin, G., & Prata, G. (1978). *Paradox and counterparadox.* New York: Jason Aronson.

Tarragona, M., & Orlinsky, D. E. (1988). *Beyond the therapeutic hour: An exploration of the relationship between patients' experiences of therapy within and between sessions.* Paper presented at the annual meeting of the Society of Psychotherapy Research, Santa Fe, NM.

Trepper, T., & Barrett, M. J. (1989). *Systemic treatment of incest: A therapeutic handbook.* New York: Brunner/Mazel.

Tomm, K. (1986). Interventive interviewing: Part I, strategizing as a fourth guideline for the therapist. *Family Process, 26,* 3–13.

Ward, T., Hudson, S. M., & Marshall, W. (1995). Cognitive distortions and affective deficits in sex offenders: A cognitive deconstructionist interpretation. *Sexual Abuse: A Journal of Research and Treatment, 7,* 67–83.

Watzlawick, P., Weaklund, J., & Fisch, R. (1974). *Change: Principles of problem formation and problem resolution.* New York: Norton.

Weeks, G., & L'Abate, L., (1982). *Paradoxical psychotherapy: Theory and practice with individuals, couples and families.* New York: Brunner/ Mazel.

White, M. (1986). Negative explanation, restraint & double description: A template for therapy. *Family Process, 22,* 255–273.

Winn, M. (1996). The strategic and systemic management of denial in the cognitive behavioral treatment of sexual offenders. *Sexual Abuse: A Journal of Research and Treatment, 8*(1), 25–36.

Wolf, S., Conte, J., & Meung, M. (1988). Assessment and treatment of the sex offender in a community setting. In L. Walker (Ed.), *Handbook on sexual abuse of children* (pp. 365–383). New York: Springer.

Chapter 8

Deviant Sexual Fantasies as Motivated Self-Deception

by Robert C. Wright, Ph.D. and Sandra L. Schneider, Ph.D.

Overview

This chapter provides a framework for conceptualizing the sexual fantasies of child sexual offenders from a broader perspective, one that includes a wider variety of motivational and functional components of sexual fantasies. We start by summarizing the results of a study investigating several factors that have been described as nonsexual motivations underlying sexual offenses. We report evidence of when and which of these factors seem to play a role in the sexual fantasies of offenders. We also identify how offenders differ from nonoffenders in their cognitive representations of the relationships between sexual fantasies and motivational factors. This analysis leads to a discussion of the role of self-deceptive strategies in sexual fantasy and the process by which self-deception leads to cognitive distortions precipitating abuse.

History of Research

In their review of the role of sexual fantasies in human sexuality, Leitenberg and Henning (1995) summarize the power of sexual fantasies as follows: "Certainly, it is by now a truism that one's brain is at least as important a sexual organ as one's genitals. What humans think about can either enhance or inhibit sexual responsiveness to any form of sensory stimulation, and, in the absence of any physical stimulation, sexual fantasy alone is arousing" (p. 469).

The power of the mind, as exhibited in sexual fantasy, plays a key role in both normal and deviant sexual behavior. Sexual behavior is influenced by sexual fantasies, as well as the reverse, in both normal and deviant populations. Sexual fantasies can be defined as intentional patterns of thought that serve one or more goals (Leitenberg & Henning, 1995). One obvious goal is the generation or enhancement of sexual arousal and pleasurable sexual feelings. Contrary to what one might suppose, having sexual fantasies is associated with healthy sexual relationships. It is estimated that approximately 95% of adults with no known sexual pathology report having sexual fantasies (Leitenberg & Henning, 1995). In fact, the absence of sexual fantasies often contributes to problems of sexual dysfunction (Zimmer, Borchardt, & Fischle, 1983).

Nevertheless, sexual fantasy is also assumed to play an important role in the chain of events leading to sexually abusive behavior (Abel & Blanchard, 1974; Laws & Marshall, 1990), and deviant sexual fantasies are common among sexual offenders (Marshall, Barbaree, & Eccles, 1991). The primary emphasis in the literature on sexual offenders to date has been limited to the role of sexual fantasies in increasing sexual arousal and maintaining deviant sexual interests (Abel & Blanchard, 1974; Laws & Marshall, 1990). The hypothesis underlying this emphasis is that deviant arousal both increases and is increased by deviant sexual fantasies, which in turn increases the likelihood of deviant sexual behavior. Within this context, the focus primarily has been on deviant imagery elicited around the time of the offense. In particular, significant attention has been given to intrusive deviant sexual fantasies and masturbatory fantasies as direct precursors to sexual offenses. As a result, treatment has emphasized the use of behavioral interventions (e.g., masturbatory satiation, orgasmic reconditioning, and covert simulation) to directly alter deviant fantasies for the purpose of reducing arousal to inappropriate sexual outlets (Maletzky, 1991). Recently, the presence of deviant fantasies has also been identified as a factor that increases the risk of a reoffense and conceptualized as a lapse requiring direct and immediate intervention (Pithers, Kashima, Cumming, & Beal, 1988; Pithers, 1990).

In the current treatment of child sexual offenders, attention to sexual fantasies has been limited to the fantasy's content and its role in maintaining deviant sexual interests or increasing deviant arousal. In addition, attention has been focused almost exclusively on those fantasies that are proximal to the offense. However, deviant sexual fantasies serve a variety of other functions besides increasing arousal at the time of the offense. Specifically, fantasies are a medium within which the offender can shape his ideas, organize his perceptions, increase the certainty of his distorted beliefs, plan activities, and, in so doing, increase his motivation to engage in offense behavior. An examination of these added dimensions of an offender's sexual fantasies is likely to shed light on the role of nonsexual motivations in sexual deviancy, more clearly specify cognitive processes resulting in cognitive distortions (cf. Abel, Becker, & Cunningham-Rathner, 1984; Murphy, 1990; Segal & Stermac, 1990), and suggest additional treatment interventions to address them directly.

Emotions, Ego, and Power as Motivators of Abuse

The sexual and nonsexual motivations of child sexual offenders can be more clearly understood by identifying the specific goals of offenders in sexual situations. This is true because the goals pursued by individuals create the framework within which they interpret and react to events (Dweck & Elliott, 1983; Dweck & Leggett, 1988). In other words, goals shape the way individuals see the world, or they shape an individual's cognitive representations of the world. These representations are responsible for allowing individuals to anticipate what they can expect to happen in different types of situations.

By examining cognitive representations of child sexual offenders, we can gain insights into when deviant sexual arousal patterns are likely to be activated and what types of internal and external cues are likely to elicit and maintain these deviant patterns. Given the substantial role of fantasies in the commission of sexual offenses, we were especially interested in examining cognitive representations surrounding fantasies for evidence of the goals that offenders try to achieve in sexual situations.

A review of the literature indicates that the primary nonsexual goals motivating offenders to commit child sexual abuse are that offenders (1) use sex to achieve desired emotional states (Finkelhor, 1984; Groth & Burgess, 1979; Pithers, Buell, Kashima, Cumming, & Beal, 1987), (2) use sex to acquire a sense of power and control (Herman, 1990; Howells, 1978, 1981; Sgroi, 1982), and (3) use sex to enhance their view of themselves (Finkelhor & Araji, 1986; Langevin, 1983; Loss & Glancy, 1983). We concentrated on each of these three areas in our investigation of contributors to sexual fantasy.

Research

Subjects. Our study included 119 men on probation for a felony sexual offense involving abuse of a victim under 16 years of age. Eighteen of these men were eliminated from the analysis because our denial scale indicated that they were not admitting to one or more critical aspects of their abuse. On our substantive measures, these men tended to report having little or no sexual drive or sexual arousal in general. They reported reduced levels of feelings of any sort on most questions, with considerable evidence of responses motivated largely by social desirability. By leaving these respondents out, we limited responses to those who were more likely to reflect accurate appraisals of the items of interest. Our control subjects were 89 men on probation for felony offenses that were not sexual in nature. Any potential control subject who reported having committed or having been accused of a sexual offense was not included in our analysis.

Questionnaire. Our questionnaire focused on several aspects of respondents' experience with various emotions, ego-related feelings, and power-related feelings that previously had been linked to sexual offenses. We collected data on the frequency of these feelings in general, as well as the degree to which these feelings are associated with sexual situations and with sexual fantasies, in particular.

Examining the Roles of Emotional, Ego-Related, and Power-Related Feelings

When responding to general questions about the frequency of various feelings, sex offenders, like non-sex offenders, generally report feeling good emotionally, having a positive self-view, and maintaining a sense of control without focusing on domination. On the other hand, sex offenders seem more vulnerable than non-sex offenders, being more susceptible to feeling sorry for themselves, feeling criticized or inadequate, and feeling powerless. Hence, our general portrait of the sex offender is one of a person with a relatively positive but fragile outlook.

Study participants also responded to specific questions regarding how goals were involved in initiating sexual fantasies. Here, the results showed that none of our items seemed especially likely to prompt sexual fantasies in either group; however, positive emotions and ego-related goals were most often associated with having a sexual fantasy than were other items. Most power-related items were not associated with initiating a fantasy, with the exception that "feeling someone is all mine" and "feeling in control" were reported to be present occasionally. Although members of neither group were likely to fantasize in response to putting someone in their place, offenders reported virtually never fantasizing under these conditions. However, sex offenders reported that they would be more likely than non-sex offenders to feel sorry for themselves or jealous when initiating a fantasy.

We also evaluated the expectations that sex offenders and non-sex offenders have of sexual fantasies. Both groups clearly expect fantasies to provide positive moods and make them feel good about themselves. Even more than non-sex offenders, sex offenders expect fantasies to make them feel wanted. To a lesser extent, members of both groups expect fantasies to leave them feeling in control and as if someone is all theirs. Members in neither group expect a sexual fantasy to promote negative emotions or a negative self-view. Sex offenders, in particular, emphasize that they never feel inadequate, criticized, or like a failure in any of their sexual fantasies.

Overall, then, sexual fantasies are clearly associated with positive emotions and a positive self-view, with power issues being secondary and then typically involving personal control rather than domination issues. Sex offenders have a stronger expectation that their fantasies will make them feel wanted and will not threaten their self-view in any way. Hence, for members of both groups, sexual fantasies appear to play a role in maintaining and increasing positive emotions and a positive self-view. For sex offenders, fantasies are especially important in bolstering the self-view and avoiding any threat to the self-view. Although fantasies do reinforce a sense of control for both groups, there is little self-report evidence that power-related motives play a substantial role in fantasizing.

Sexual Abuse and the Theory of Motivated Self-Deception

The study just described shows that child sexual offenders differ from controls in two important ways. First, sex offenders appear to have a more fragile self-view than nonoffenders. Although they report feeling positive about themselves as often as non-sex offenders, they spend more time than non-sex offenders questioning and doubting their self-view. Second, sex offenders are more focused on ego-related motivations in their sexual fantasies than are nonoffenders. Sex offenders are more likely to use fantasies as a tool to reinforce their positive self-view and to minimize any potential threats to their positive self-view.

The sex offender's intense concern over his self-view, particularly in the context of real or imagined sex, seems consistent with a desire to eliminate any impression formed by others or himself that his sexual behavior is deviant or inappropriate. Instead, the sex offender, like anyone else, wants to think of himself in a positive light and to believe that others who know him well will also see him in a positive light. However, he may have more difficulty accomplishing this goal given his deviant motivations and behavior.

In our theory of motivated self-deception (Wright & Schneider, 1996), we suggest that sex offenders use the same types of ego-protecting and ego-enhancing strategies that non-sex offenders use to maintain their positive self-view. Nevertheless, because of their deviant motivations, sex offenders use these strategies to excess in an attempt to convince themselves that their deviant behavior is acceptable and that their actions should not threaten their self-view. Because normal self-deceptive strategies tend to be very effective, the result is that the sex offender comes to believe that his actions are not reprehensible given his interpretation of the situations surrounding his abusive acts. As we discuss later, the sexual fantasies of sex offenders are likely to incorporate very powerful self-deceptive strategies that play a key role in developing and maintaining the distorted belief system that enables the offender to abuse without recognizing the harm he is causing.

The desire to think positively about ourselves is a strong and fundamental motivation driving many aspects of human behavior. Indeed, Taylor and Brown (1988) argue that maintaining good mental health may depend on the use of a variety of strategies that are aimed at reinforcing a positive self-view, cultivating a healthy optimism about ourselves, and sustaining the perception of control over our environment. Nevertheless, Taylor and Brown provide numerous examples of how these strategies lead to biases in thinking and ultimately allow us to deceive ourselves about our positive qualities. For instance, most people tend to believe that they have more desirable qualities than others, that their views are shared by most others, that their futures are brighter than others, and that they have some control over random events. In addition, people are biased toward taking credit for their successes but blaming failure on some aspect of the situation.

The Theory of Confirmation Bias

One of the most common and powerful of biased thinking strategies is confirmation bias. People typically seek out evidence that is likely to confirm their beliefs or suspicions while ignoring information that might disconfirm their beliefs or bring doubt on their suspicions (Harris, 1991; Klayman & Ha, 1989; Stangor & Ford, 1992). For instance, if an individual believes that someone is unfriendly, he is likely to focus on the person's actions that seem consistent with the unfriendly interpretation. Even neutral information may be interpreted as evidence of the person's unfriendly demeanor. A neutral "hello," for instance, may be seen as sarcastic or insincere. Even if the person does do something friendly, we may ignore the evidence or discount it as reflecting some ulterior motive. In this way, people tend to confirm what they are predisposed to believe, rather than continually questioning and analyzing whether their impressions are as accurate as they assume.

Although the confirmation bias may bolster the self-view by reinforcing already-held beliefs, the bias also serves the function of reducing the amount of thinking we need to do in everyday situations. The confirmation strategy represents one of a number of short-cut rules of thumb that we regularly use to cut down on the amount of information we need to attend to. Given that we have so much to deal with in our lives, these rules of thumb, or heuristics, are essential for going about our business efficiently. Nevertheless, these heuristics do sometimes lead to inaccuracies in our thinking, which may result in poor decisions or the development of erroneous beliefs. With respect to the confirmation strategy, we can expect to be both efficient and accurate whenever our original beliefs are correct. However, if our beliefs are not accurate, we tend to discount or ignore evidence that would help us learn that our beliefs need to be changed.

Generating Expectation Outcomes

Another more subtle bias that helps us make efficient decisions occurs when we try to explain or imagine how something might happen. When we generate an explanation for some event, we typically come to believe that the event is more likely to occur (e.g., Koehler, 1991). In one study, for instance, people were asked to imagine winning a contest or being arrested for a crime. Afterward, the people actually came to believe that these things were more likely to happen to them (Gregory, Cialdini, & Carpenter, 1982). The reason they came to believe that they were more susceptible to such an event is that the imagination task made them think up scenarios in their mind that would have to occur for the event to happen. When asked later to judge the likelihood of the event, those scenarios were easily brought to mind, making such an event seem more likely. There is also evidence to suggest that once such impressions are formed, they tend to persevere even when contradictory information is presented (Ross, Greene, & House, 1977; Ross, Lepper, & Hubbard, 1975).

Creating Mental Simulations

Kahneman and Tversky (1982) have pointed out that people frequently decide on the likelihood of an event based on the ease with which they can picture the event occurring. "Picturing an event" can be thought of as a mental simulation. Technically, a mental simulation is described by Kahneman and Tversky (1982) as a mental operation that brings things to mind by constructing examples or scenarios. They argue that people commonly use a simulation heuristic in which these mental simulations are relied on to determine the likelihood of events. These simulations may be used to predict future events, to assess the likelihood of particular events, or to assess the likely causes of different events. All these judgments are subject to bias in that those simulations that can be brought to mind easily are judged to be likely to occur, independent of whether the events really are likely.

In small doses, self-deceptive strategies and heuristics in reasoning may serve useful functions by reinforcing a positive self-view or allowing us to be efficient thinkers. But if these strategies and heuristics are used too often, their results are exaggerated, leading to serious cognitive distortions that result in errors of judgment and reasoning, unresponsiveness to feedback, and an overestimation of personal control. Based on the theory of motivated self-deception, we argue that sexual offenders have fallen into just this kind of trap. As described earlier, evidence suggests that offenders have a fragile self-view and excessive concern with protecting their self-image especially in the sexual arena. As a result, offenders are likely to have developed an over-reliance on normal self-deceptive strategies and heuristics to protect or enhance their self-view. Over time, they become proficient in the use of self-deceptive strategies to legitimize their deviant sexual goals and facilitate the abuse without compromising their positive view of themselves.

Motivated Self-Deception in the Offenders' Sexual Fantasies

The theory of motivated self-deception suggests that sexual offenders become adept in the use of self-deceptive strategies so that over time they are able to convince themselves that their deviant behavior is acceptable. One way they accomplish this is by incorporating self-deception in their fantasies to bypass their own standards of judgment and to create a context conducive to abuse. Self-deception provides the offender a means of shaping or gradually distorting his perceptions so that he can dismiss the implications of his behavior. By employing these strategies he can justify his deviant behavior, downplay its consequences, and avoid blame by gradually creating the illusion that everything about the abusive incident(s) is normal, understandable, and, in fact, followed an inevitable progression.

Sexual fantasies are the perfect medium to carry out self-deception. Fantasies are private. They are not subject to social sanctions or to interpersonal pressures. They do not need to reflect reality, but they can (Leitenberg & Henning, 1995). It is within this context that offenders, through self-deceptive strategies and heuristics, can shape their ideas until they seem to fit reality. By strategically applying these cognitive processes, the offender essentially becomes a "con man" of his own mind (see Wright & Schneider, 1996). From this broader perspective, deviant sexual fantasies can be seen as serving multiple functions that facilitate abuse. They are used not only to increase arousal but also (1) to sustain and intensify a desire for the victim, (2) to increase the offender's subjective certainty that the victim holds similar sexual interests or desires, (3) to cultivate and legitimize deviant sexual goals and ideas, (4) to make the offensive act appear ordinary, reasonable, and plausible, and (5) to covertly plan the details of the offense.

The Function of Fantasies

Fantasy is not simply a matter of imagining something pleasurable or arousing. Instead, it serves a variety of other functions that allow the offender to deceive himself and to create illusions that make the offensive behavior appear to be something other than what it is. To accomplish these things, the offender makes use of the same types of self-deceptive strategies and heuristics described earlier. Within any fantasy, for instance, the offender always maintains a positive self-view. This requires that the offender engage in biased thinking that emphasizes his positive characteristics or abilities while minimizing or omitting any details suggestive of wrongdoing. Hence, the entire climate within the fantasy is one that reinforces the offender's belief that he is a good person who does not do harmful things to innocent others.

On a more subtle level, the offender uses confirmation and simulation strategies to bias his thinking even further. These biases often occur in the absence of conscious awareness on the part of the offender. In their fantasies, for instance, offenders eroticize their view of the victim by picturing arousing behaviors and features of the victim while omitting nonsexual components of behavior. Outside the fantasy, offenders then seek to confirm this impression of the victim as a sexualized being. They may even use neutral information as evidence of seductive intentions. Many offenders describe actions such as crossing legs, playing with legs apart, and smiling shyly as evidence suggesting that the victim is sexually attracted to them. In this way, imagined actions invented within a fantasy may serve as the foundation for an erroneous belief that the offender seeks to confirm in real life through observation of subtle and ambiguous behaviors.

Perhaps the most pervasive effect of fantasies, however, is due to the simulation heuristic. Most deviant sexual fantasies involve the unfolding of a sexual scenario. As the offender repeatedly constructs and refines a scenario about a particular victim in his mind, it becomes increasingly easier to imagine the scenario actually occurring. Just as in any other mental simulation, imagining how the event could happen makes that event seem more likely. Through the simulation in fantasy, there is a movement in the mind of the offender from possible to probable. Over time, there is a gradual shift from how the offense could happen to how it is likely to happen. In this way, the offender not only can come to believe that specific offense behavior is bound to happen sooner or later but can also refine the details of just how it might come about.

Together, confirmation and simulation biases related to fantasies are likely to be primary forces in the development of the cognitive distortions that convince the offender that there is nothing wrong with his behavior. The offender's construction of scenarios typically strengthens the subjective certainty of his deviant impressions of the victim and allows the offender to reinterpret her behavior in a manner consistent with his sexual desires. Furthermore, these biases and resulting distortions direct or automatically guide the offender's behavior toward securing responses from the victim consistent with the premise that the victim shares similar sexual interests. By elaborating, rehearsing, and fine-tuning the details of the desired scenario, the offender can increase his certainty of the validity of his perceptions.

The offender's construction of scenarios involving the victim also establish causal explanations of his perception of the victim's behavior as erotic, consensual, or seductive. In other words, if the offender's fantasies begin to include scenarios in which the victim either desires, consents, or seeks sexual contact with him, such images are likely to form the basis of later interpretations of the victim's actual behavior.

Moreover, the offender is likely to forget over time which of his impressions of the victim were generated in his fantasies and which were based on actual observations (biased though they may be). To the extent that this occurs, offenders are likely to become convinced that the victim actually desires to become sexually involved with him. In addition, these processes distract the offender's attention away from inconsistent information displayed by the victim, disguise the source of the case being built by him, and provide a cohesive logic that strengthens the perceived reasonableness of his perceptions and sexually abusive behaviors.

Examples of Motivated Self-Deception in Deviant Sexual Fantasies

Fantasies typically do not occur to the offender as a finished product. Instead, they evolve over time as the offender progressively incorporates additional details until the scenario fits with his deviant desires. A case in point includes an offender who, after extensive treatment, was describing how he developed his fantasies about his 7-year-old victim. "At first I fantasized about the fact that she was innocent and not slutty like everybody else that I've always known. And then it progressed to the point where I'd start turning her into a trashy person in my mind. I fantasized about her doing numerous things like being with other women, and other men while I watched, and stuff like that. It's weird. I picked her because she was innocent and not slutty, and then I turned her into that in my head."

By gradually adding details to the fantasy, the offender can transform innocent or playful behaviors into plausible depictions of those sexual interests and desires he wishes to see in the victim. "When I first started fantasizing about her, it was more like innocent love. Then I started thinking about teaching her about the sexual side to love. There could be nice slow music in the background or whatever. I mean, it was like a Disney fantasy or something. But then it got to be more where she was like the aggressor, and it got to be where she would start doing things to me." Yet another offender reported, "In my fantasy I would eventually bring her around to having sex, and she would think of it as a good thing. It was like waking her sexual drive and that sort of thing. But toward the end, I fantasized about her masturbating, and I would walk in on her masturbating and help her, and then she'd have sex with me."

These fantasies not only sustain and intensify the offender's arousal for the victim but also progressively accentuate features of the victim's behavior which would suggest that she is both interested in sexual activity and desires the perpetrator as a sexual partner. In the latter case, not only did the victim respond in a positive manner to the perpetrator, but "she [thought] of it as a good thing." In his mind, the offender had constructed a scenario in which the victim not only behaved sexually but did so intentionally due to her sexual desire for him. In addition, the victim not only is sexually responsive in this scenario but eventually becomes the initiator while the offender becomes the passive recipient of her desires.

The construction of such a scene allows the offender to view himself, even in his own fantasies, as an object acted upon by the force of the victim's desire. Once this occurs, it is that much easier to attribute not only this but any future interactions to this same factor. In this way, the offender is able to gradually emphasize features of his sexual interaction with the victim that creates an impression that he is not really victimizing someone. Instead, such features suggest that his behavior is not really of his own design and does not have negative repercussions for the victim because his sexual behavior is merely a response to her initiative and desire.

Replaying such scenes in the offender's mind also increases his ability to selectively attend to only those features that suggest the victim's sexual desire and sexual interest in him. As his familiarity with these features increases through his repeated construction of such scenarios, it is also likely to affect his subsequent expectations and observations of the victim. In other words, his repetitive construction of such a detailed scenario is likely to distort his actual perceptions of the victim, and increase his subjective certainty that her behavior actually reflects these inclinations.

This process is accelerated as the offender begins to incorporate his actual inter- actions with the victim into his fantasies and introduces pieces of fantasy material into his actual interactions with the victim. An offender who had advanced substantially in treatment described his fantasies as follows: "First I just fantasized about her talking dirty. And then I would lead up to actually doing it. That's how it always worked for me. I always fantasized about something for awhile before I would get up enough nerve to try it. Fantasy was really part of the grooming. After fantasizing about it for awhile I started making her talk dirty to me about sexual stuff too. Which she was to young to know about. That way it was easier for me to abuse her. Because the more she talked about sexual stuff, the easier it was for me to believe that she really liked it and wanted it." As an offender begins to blend deviant fantasy material with his actual interactions with the victim, the distinctions between the two are reduced and become blurred, so that it becomes easier to believe that his observations are ground- ed in fact.

Sexual fantasies are also frequently used by the offender to plan an offense and work out the arrangements to assure that it will occur. "A lot of times while I was at work, I would think about setting all this straight in my mind. I would picture her mother going to work, and imagine her getting home from school about 4:30 P.M. So, if I'm home about that time then, I could be there when she's there and get all this set up. We could have supper, or I could take her out to eat. Then once we get back home we could start."

Through repetitions of the fantasy, the offender is able to rehearse his specific engagement strategy and progressively increase the ease with which he can imagine the compliance of the victim as well as a desirable outcome to the scenario that he imagines. "I'd fantasize about what I was going to do, and how I was going to do this, that, and the other. I'd picture how she liked to have her back massaged and her legs massaged, and I would start that way. Then the massage would kinda put her to sleep. Then I would pick her up and carry her to the bedroom and take her clothes off. . . ." The rehearsal of this scenario is not isolated to the confines of the offender's mind. Instead, it gradually affects the offender's subsequent expectations of the victim. It is likely to alter both his interpretations of her future behavior under similar conditions as well as his estimate of the likelihood that she would respond in such a fashion if she had the opportunity. It is not difficult to imagine how such fantasies could pro- gressively form the basis of a framework that predisposes the offender to distort his perceptions and interpretations of the victim and her behavior until it conforms with his imagined scenarios.

It is also easier to believe something if others can be induced to act as if it is true too. It is for this reason that offenders sometimes integrate their fantasies into their relationship with a partner or spouse. In this way, they essentially enlist them into their fantasies and further reduce the distinction between their fantasies and real life. "I'd start talking to my wife when we started making love about things that I saw during the day that turned me on. I might ask her something like, have you seen anything that looks nice lately? Or, if I saw some woman at work or on TV who looked real nice, I'd tell her about her and how she'd probably like to have these kinds of things done to her. I'd tell her these things in a real soothing voice so she'd respond as much to my voice as what I was saying. Then eventually I'd start saying things about what her sister (i.e., victim) would probably like until we both got off on what we were doing and what I was saying." By introducing these fantasies into his relationship with his wife, he was able to convert her into an unknowing accomplice. Her responsiveness in effect became a tacit approval of his own deviant interests, indirectly supporting the validity of his own perceptions, and further diminishing the distinction between fantasy and reality.

Treatment Implications

An understanding of the role of self-deception in deviant sexual fantasies and sexual offenses suggests that these factors must be given serious consideration in treatment. For instance, given the cognitive distortions that result from these processes, it is not reasonable to expect the offender to immediately admit to some set of "objective" facts or to immediately accept responsibility for the abuse. From the offender's point of view, it may not be clear that he is responsible for everything that occurred. Hence, an approach that forces him to unwillingly assume responsibility at the outset is likely to increase resistance or, at best, produce only compliant behavior that is not likely to be maintained once treatment is discontinued.

It is not just that most offenders choose to deny responsibility for their offense or are inherently oppositional. Rather, they often continue to deny because they have developed an elaborate network of distorted ideas, grounded in evidence accrued through biased processes, that are incompatible with a view of their own responsibility for the offense. If someone is confident in their understandings of an event, they are not likely to be open to alternative explanations that appear to be incompatible with their own perceptions. With this understanding, it becomes more difficult to hold to the notion that offenders in denial have the ability immediately to admit to their offense but simply choose not to disclose that information. The presence of self-deception in sexual offenses suggests that there is more to admitting to an offense than simply choosing or not choosing to do so. The use of self-deceptive strategies is likely to have progressively distorted the offender's beliefs and increased his subjective certainty in both his perceptions of the situation and his explanations as to how it evolved.

Before the offender will be willing to discuss his offense openly or to truly consider other ideas about what occurred, he must address the distortions that he has developed through fantasy and other means. To accomplish this, it is helpful to use the offender's subjective view of his offense as an anchor point from which to add new understandings that will eventually modify the understandings he initially holds. This approach has significant advantages over direct attempts to dispute or abolish the offender's distortions or behavior in that it bypasses much of the resistance contributing to the offender's continued denial of responsibility and assists the offender in establishing gradual control over his behavior.

The current formulation also suggests that sexual fantasies play a much broader role in the commission of sexual offenses than has typically been described in the literature. Currently, deviant sexual fantasies are primarily viewed as precursors to offense behavior and indicative of deviant sexual interests (Abel & Blanchard, 1974; Laws & Marshall, 1990). As such, their presence suggests an increased level of risk of relapse to the offender (see, e.g., Pithers et al., 1988; Pithers, 1990). Treatment interventions have therefore focused on the development of skills to monitor and immediately extinguish deviant fantasies as they occur.

Another factor that has been described as moving offenders toward a relapse is the presence of covert planning composed of a series of apparently irrelevant decisions (Jenkins-Hall & Marlatt, 1989). These decisions allow the offender to place himself in circumstances conducive to abuse without disclosing his intentions even to himself. In this way, he can attribute responsibility to situational contingencies and continue to view himself as victimized by circumstances. We hypothesize that the covert planning that takes place during fantasy may be responsible for the production of many of these apparently irrelevant decisions that move the offender closer to committing an offense.

It is important to recognize that fantasies are not just immediate precursors to offending but are also a primary vehicle used routinely by offenders to shape their distorted beliefs. We propose that offenders progressively incorporate deviant material into imagined scenarios until, by means of heuristics such as simulation and confirmation, their view of the victim becomes eroticized and a sexual encounter seems plausible or even inevitable. This, in turn, influences their subsequent interactions with the victim, shaping the situation to become increasingly consistent with their cognitive distortions.

Conclusion

Given this expanded role of deviant sexual fantasies in sexual offenses, additional interventions are needed to directly address the functions served by fantasies. Deviant fantasies hold considerable information about the strategies offenders employ and the methods they use to convince themselves of the legitimacy of their deviant behavior. As a result, interventions that do not attempt to immediately extinguish fantasies but instead examine the functions served by them are likely to provide important information that can be used by the clinician to help the offender better understand how fantasies contribute to his abusive behavior. By expanding the focus of treatment to include fantasies that have occurred across the entire chain of abuse, the content of an offender's fantasies can be used to teach him how to recognize, monitor, and control his input into those fantasies, thereby minimizing fantasies' impact on his behavior.

This focus on the functional components of deviant fantasies also introduces the notion of "deliberateness" and "choice" into an event that is frequently experienced by the offender to be automatic and outside his control. This functional perspective highlights the offender's ability to organize and establish conditions necessary for abuse to occur, which in itself draws attention to the strategic choices that set particular fantasies in motion or continue to maintain them. As a result, an approach that examines the functions served by fantasies makes it more difficult for the offender to use self-handicapping strategies in which he comes to view himself as a victim of forces outside his control. This, in turn, is likely to increase the offender's sense of personal responsibility for his behavior by emphasizing that fantasies do not simply occur to him but are constructed by him to accomplish deviant goals and by highlighting those choices he would have to actively make to reoffend.

It is not surprising that offenders would rather not realize the consequences of what they are doing. They would rather not even think about the effects of their behavior because such thoughts are disturbing and would spoil everything. Instead, they want to believe that what they are doing is reasonable without having to think about it or question it. They would rather just let things unfold "naturally" because it is within this context that there is room to maneuver and shape things to their liking through biased thinking strategies. Addressing the functions served by deviant fantasies throughout the entire chain of abuse does not by itself stop offenders from reoffending. However, it does hold the potential to make it more difficult for them to ignore how they create the latitude they need to interpret things as they wish, and how they are ultimately responsible for their choices to act.

Acknowledgments

Preparation of this article was supported by National Institute of Mental Health Grant MH 52273. We would like to thank Christine Caffray, Eric Sellers, and David Styers for their assistance in data collection. Portions of this work were presented at the 1995 NOTA/ATSA International Conference, Cambridge University, Cambridge, England.

References

Abel, G. G., Becker, J. V., & Cunningham-Rathner, J. (1984). Complications, consent and cognitions in sex between children and adults. *International Journal of Law and Psychiatry, 7,* 89–103.

Abel, G. G., & Blanchard, E. E. (1974). The role of fantasy in the treatment of sexual deviation. *Archives of General Psychiatry, 30,* 467–475.

Dweck, C. S., & Elliott, E. S. (1983). Achievement motivation. In P. H. Mussen (Gen. Ed.) & E. M. Hetherington (Vol. Ed.), *Handbook of child psychology: Social and personality development* (vol. 4, pp. 643–691). New York: Wiley.

Dweck, C. S., & Leggett. E. L. (1988). A social-cognitive approach to motivation and personality. *Psychological Review, 95,* 256–273.

Finkelhor, D. (1984). *Child sexual abuse: New theory and research.* New York: Free Press.

Finkelhor, D., & Araji, S. (1986). Explanations of pedophilia: A four factor model. *Journal of Sex Research, 22,* 145–161.

Gregory, W. L., Cialdini, R. B., & Carpenter, K. M. (1982). Self-relevant scenarios as mediators of likelihood estimates and compliance: Does imagining make it so? *Journal of Personality and Social Psychology, 43,* 89–99.

Groth, N. A., & Burgess, A. W. (1979). Sexual trauma in the life histories of rapists and child molesters. *Victimology, 4,* 10–16.

Harris, M. J. (1991). Controversy and culmination: Meta-analysis and research on interpersonal expectancy effects. *Personality and Social Psychology Bulletin, 17,* 316–322.

Herman, J. L. (1990). Sexual offenders: A feminist perspective. In W. L. Marshall, D. R. Laws, & H. E. Barbaree (Eds.), *Handbook of sexual assault* (pp. 177–193). New York: Plenum Press.

Howells, K. (1978). Some meanings of children for pedophiles. In Cook, M., & Wilson, G. (Eds.), *Love and attraction* (pp. 57–82). London: Pergamon Press.

Howells, K. (1981). Adult sexual interest in children: Considerations relevant to theories of aetiology. In M. Cook, & K. Howells (Eds.), *Adult sexual interest in children* (pp. 55–94). New York: Academic Press.

Jenkins-Hall, K. D., & Marlatt, G. A. (1989). Apparently irrelevant decisions in the relapse process. In D. R. Laws (Ed.), *Relapse prevention with sex offenders* (pp. 47–55). New York: Guilford Press.

Kahneman, D., & Tversky, A. (1982). The simulation heuristic. In D. Kahneman, P. Slovic, & A. Tversky, (Eds.), *Judgment under uncertainty: Heuristics and biases* (pp. 201–208). New York: Cambridge University Press.

Klayman, J., & Ha, Y-W. (1989). Confirmation, disconfirmation, and information on hypothesis testing. *Psychological Review, 94,* 211–228.

Koehler, D. J. (1991). Explanation, imagination, and confidence in judgment. *Psychological Bulletin, 110,* 499–519.

Langevin, R. (1983). *Sexual strands: Understanding and treating sexual anomalies in men.* Hillsdale, NJ: Erlbaum.

Laws, D. R., & Marshall, W. L. (1990). A conditioning theory of the etiology and maintenance of deviant sexual preference and behavior. In W. L. Marshall, D. R. Laws, & H. E. Barbaree, (Eds.), *Handbook of sexual assault* (pp. 209–229). New York: Plenum Press.

Leitenberg, H., & Henning, K. (1995). Sexual fantasy. *Psychological Bulletin, 117,* 469-496.

Loss, P., & Glancy, E. (1983). Men who sexually abuse their children. *Medical Aspects of Human Sexuality, 17,* 328–329.

Maletzky, B. M. (1991). *Treating the sexual offender.* Newbury Park, CA: Sage.

Marshall, W. L., Barbaree, H. E., & Eccles, A. (1991). Early onset and deviant sexuality in child molesters. *Journal of Interpersonal Violence, 6,* 323–336.

Murphy, W. D. (1990). Assessment and modification of cognitive distortions in sex offenders. In W. L. Marshall, D. R. Laws, & H. E. Barbaree, (Eds.), *Handbook of sexual assault* (pp. 331–342). New York: Plenum Press.

Pithers, W. D. (1990). Relapse prevention with sexual aggressors: A method for maintaining therapeutic gain and enhancing external supervision. In W. L. Marshall, D. R. Laws, & H. E. Barbaree (Eds.), *Handbook of sexual assault* (pp. 343–362). New York: Plenum Press.

Pithers, W. D., Buell, M. M., Kashima, K. M., Cumming, G. F., & Beal, L. S. (1987). *Precursors to sexual offenses.* Proceedings of the first annual meeting of the Association for the Behavioral Treatment of Sexual Aggressors, Newport, OR.

Pithers, W. D., Kashima, K. M., Cumming, G. F., & Beal, L. S. (1988). Relapse prevention: A method of enhancing maintenance of change in sex offenders. In A. C. Salter (Ed.), *Treating child sex offenders and victims: A practical guide* (pp. 131–170). Newbury Park, CA: Sage.

Ross, L., Greene, D., & House, P. (1977). The "false consensus effect": An egocentric bias in social perception and attribution processes. *Journal of Experimental Social Psychology, 13,* 279–301.

Ross, L., Lepper, M. R., & Hubbard, M. (1975). Perseverance in self-perception and social perception: Biased attributional processes in the debriefing paradigm. *Journal of Personality and Social Psychology, 32,* 880–892.

Segal, Z. V., & Stermac, L. E. (1990). The role of cognition in sexual assault. In Marshall, W. L., Laws, D. R., & Barbaree, H. E. (Eds.), *Handbook of sexual assault* (pp. 161–174). New York: Plenum Press.

Sgroi, S. (1982). *Handbook of clinical intervention in child sexual abuse.* Lexington, MA: Lexington Books.

Stangor, C., & Ford, T. E. (1992). Accuracy and expectancy-confirming processing orientations and the development of stereotypes and prejudice. *European Review of Social Psychology, 3,* 57–89.

Taylor, S. E., & Brown, J. D. (1988). Illusion and well-being: A social psychological perspective on mental health. *Psychological Bulletin, 103,* 193–210.

Wright, R. C., & Schneider, S. L. (1996). *A theory of motivated self-deception in child sexual offenders.* Manuscript submitted for publication.

Zimmer, D., Borchardt, E., & Fischle, C. (1983). Sexual fantasies of sexually distressed and non-distressed men and women: An empirical comparison. *Journal of Sex and Marital Therapy, 9,* 38–50.

Part 3

Special Populations

Although most people think of sex offenders as adult males, this population is spread over both genders, all ages, and every subculture and minority group. Diversity is one of the factors that makes sex offenders an interesting population to study and treat. Within prison populations, sex offenders tend to be the most heterogeneous group, with individuals who are developmentally disabled and mentally ill as well as those who are highly educated and overly represented in the class of inmates with graduate degrees and professional careers. They include individuals who are all ages, from sexually reactive children as young as 3 or 4 to geriatric offenders who have life-long histories of sex offending or whose behavior may be a by-product of neurological impairment.

Female offenders are a group largely ignored in the glare of publicity on sex offenders. Although this group, conservatively speaking, represents at least 10% of all sex offenders, they often go unreported. Furthermore, there are at least two significantly different types of female offenders—those who offend under the influence of a male sex offender and those who offend independently. The specialty of treating female sex offenders is just being developed but will undoubtedly identify special needs and treatment techniques.

Sex offenders of different ages present different developmental issues. Adolescent offenders are not just smaller or more impulsive adults. They think, feel, and perceive the world in a manner different from their middle-age counterparts. Likewise, a 70-year-old offender has different issues, needs, and challenges. Treatment must respect these differences and respond with special techniques.

Any type of treatment program should be sensitive to the cultural, racial, and ethnic origins of its clients. To impose a program developed for an urban, white, middle-class population on an inner-city black or rural Hispanic population is not only bound to alienate the client but could do additional damage. It also misses the potential strengths of that culture which can be recruited in support of the patient. Such statements apply to any therapy program, no less to sex offender treatment.

In Chapter 9, Michael H. Miner and Cindy L. S. Crimmins present an overview of the major sociological theories used to explain juvenile delinquency. They follow this overview with research exploring which theories are most applicable. They begin by contrasting differential association theory with social control theories. The first explanation of delinquency is that individuals become socialized into a deviant society. Their antisocial peers then reinforce their antisocial attitudes. Social control assumes that individuals would naturally act in self-serving and antisocial ways but their attachment to others and desire for acceptance by these others modify their behavior. The behavior of adolescent sex offenders, with the exception of gang rapists, would be difficult to explain through differential association as rarely do these youthful offenders act out with their peers. However, clinical intuition from the earliest beginnings of sex offender treatment has led therapists to look at the disrupted interpersonal relations of this group. Disruption of parental relations and expectations of rejection by significant others support the social control theories. The authors researched adolescent male sex offenders and non-sex offending delinquents and contrasted their characteristics. Their findings show an interesting divergence between the attitudes and behaviors of adolescent sex offenders. They then apply their findings to treatment and prevention.

Kurt M. Bumby and Nancy Halstenson Bumby have empirically researched a group of adolescent female offenders. Chapter 10 initially presents descriptive information on this population and then contrasts them to non-sex offending adolescent females and sex offending and non-sex offending adolescent males. Their patient population, from a residential treatment program, showed a significant history of aggressive and delinquent behavior. They appeared to be the most pathological of the groups on several dimensions. One of the most dramatic characteristics of this group was that all of them had been sexually assaulted as younger children. The Bumbys explore how the "information processing of trauma" model could be applied to adolescent female offenders to understand the interaction of their backgrounds with their abuse.

B. D. Kraemer, C. R. Spielman, and S. B. Salisbury, working in a private residential treatment facility for adolescent sex offenders, have developed a comprehensive psychological assessment known as the Mille Lacs Academy/Nexus Test Battery. This assessment technique, described in Chapter 11, combines instruments designed to measure intellectual/neurological functioning, personality/psychopathology, behavioral characteristics, and sexual deviance. Using the psychological tests suggested by the authors, the psychologist assessing adolescent sex offenders should be able to gather a great deal of information regarding psychopathology, specific problem areas, openness to treatment, clients' beliefs regarding their offending behavior, barriers to treatment, and specific interventions that might be useful. Based on this battery, the authors developed the Nexus Predictive Treatment Index. This index helps to identify those patients who are most likely to respond to treatment. This information should be very valuable to professionals seeking to maximize resources either by selecting the most amenable candidates for treatment or by devising individualized treatment plans to maximize motivation.

The geriatric sex offender is an almost ignored population. Treatment providers tend to be prejudiced against taking the mental health needs of the elderly seriously. Some mental health providers tend to view all emotional problems of seniors as by-products of physical illnesses or the aging process. Others adhere to the belief that they "can't teach an old dog new tricks." Just as the elderly need specialized mental health treatment for their issues, the older sex offender needs a treatment program that responds to his developmental issues.

In Chapter 12, M. K. Johnson outlines such a program. Older clients may have a variety of problems associated with their age which complicate their treatment. For example, they may have difficulty establishing a social network. Many sex offenders become estranged from their families when their sexual deviance is revealed. This is difficult enough for younger offenders but may be a major challenge to the older adult whose social network may have been decimated by illness and death. These individuals may have numerous health problems themselves. They may have problems with reading as a result of either limited education or impaired vision. These offenders often have difficulty with alcoholism. For this age group, specialized treatment in this problem area also may be difficult to find. Another major difficulty is in the area of assessment. It may be a challenge to assess as older offenders with phallometry. Dr. Johnson's program copes with such issues as the following: "What is the appropriate age of a partner for a 60-year-old?" He offers a number of other specific suggestions.

Sex offenders who are members of minority groups are another group that demands special attention. Therapists who wish to ensure that their treatment is individualized must take into account issues associated with culture and ethnicity. In Chapter 13, Nicolas Carrasco and Diane Garza-Louis explore the difference between machismo, macho, and machista and the meaning of these concepts in treating Hispanic sex offenders. These concepts are particularly related to sex offenders because a stereotyped view of the Hispanic male suggests that this person may typecast women into subservient roles and demonstrate false bravado and chauvinism—traits that might be associated with individuals who would act out sexually. The Federal Bureau of Investigation, in researching the traits that predicted that a rapist would escalate, used the term "macho" to describe those offenders who behaved in an unempathetic, domineering manner. If a culture values behavior that contributes to sexual assault, we might conclude that the members are at risk. Carrasco and Garza-Louis carefully outline the meaning of the three concepts for the Hispanic male. Their theory is backed by research contrasting Anglos, African Americans, and Hispanics on their values and beliefs about the relations between males and females. The authors point out how Hispanic sex offenders have violated their own cultural values by distorting the role of the male. These offenders cling to power in relationships while ignoring the cultural emphasis on responsibility, respect, and love. They demonstrate chauvinistic attitudes toward females without acknowledging the reverence in which women are held in the Hispanic culture. By understanding what is meant by macho to the Hispanic, the therapist working with these offenders can use the cultural values to reinforce a different view of the role of men in relation to women.

In Chapter 14, Dewey J. Ertz discusses American Indian sex offenders and how their history, present socioeconomic situation, and concomitant problems can be addressed using culturally sensitive methods. When dealing with a sex offender who is defined as an American Indian, the first task is find out what that definition means to the offender. The manner in and degree to which an individual can balance remaining culturally aligned and moving toward assimilation are highly individualized. Also, American Indians are divided into tribes, each of which is unique. Therefore, the therapist must learn the specific values and customs of a specific tribe. However, American Indians do share a common history of oppression, poverty, prejudice, and subservience. Many American Indian sex offenders were raised in boarding schools, an experience that produced its own trauma even in the most benign situations. The fact that American Indians as a group have in actuality been traumatized and passed this trauma on to the individuals makes dealing with issues of victimization important. Dr. Ertz has developed a life graph technique for exploring such traumas. He also makes recommendations for incorporating traditional healing approaches (e.g., American Indian healers and rituals) as well as culturally sensitive addictions treatment models such as the "red road" approach. Dr. Ertz outlines how basic assumptions of the Anglo culture on such issues as consequences and locus of control can be misapplied to this population.

In following the history of the development of the field of sex offender treatment, we see that sex offenders were first thought of as mental patients if they were institutionalized in hospitals or prisoners if they were placed in prisons. Gradually specialized programs began to develop which recognized that sex offenders had special treatment, supervision, and policy needs. Currently therapists are beginning to look at subgroups of sex offenders and analyze their special needs. This section offers suggestions for understanding and treating sex offenders of different genders, ages, and ethnic backgrounds.

## Chapter 9

Adolescent Sex Offenders—Issues of Etiology and Risk Factors

by Michael H. Miner, Ph.D. and Cindy L. S. Crimmins, M.A.

Overview

    This chapter addresses the factors associated with sexual aggression in adolescents. Research on the etiology of sex offending in adolescence is relatively young and has not yet benefited from much theoretical consideration. Therefore, in this chapter, we put the work on adolescent sex offending within the context of the more mature body of literature on juvenile delinquency. Specifically, we look at two theories: social control theory (Hirschi, 1969) and differential association theory (Sutherland & Cressey, 1978), which appear to have some validity in explaining juvenile delinquency. They also appear to fit the current concepts of adolescent sexual perpetration, at least if we can extrapolate a prevailing conceptualization of etiology from the overwhelming use of treatment modalities based on social cognitive theory (Bandura, 1986). In addition to reviewing the literature on juvenile sex offending, we present data from a preliminary study we have recently completed. Using this data, we explore the applications of social control and differential association theories and provide thoughts on the implications of our findings for treatment and prevention interventions.

Theories of Delinquency

Social control theory (Hirschi, 1969) and differential association theory (Sutherland & Cressey, 1978) can be classified as "process" or "socialization" theories. They both argue that delinquency is somehow tied to the quality of socialization and that relationships with family, peers, and school (the primary agents of socialization) are instrumental in forging behavior patterns that are at odds with the conventional society.

Differential Association Theory. Differential association theory in the tradition of social learning theories assumes that deviant behavior is the product of successful socialization into a deviant lifestyle. Criminal behavior is learned in the same way that all other behaviors are learned—in interaction with other persons through the process of face-to-face communication within intimate interpersonal groups. The learning includes techniques for committing the crime as well as motives, drives, rationalizations, and attitudes. Deviants learn how to react properly to their criminal acts (when to defend, rationalize, show remorse, etc.). Deviance occurs when the ratio of definitions favorable to violation of the law outweighs definitions unfavorable to violation of the law. Exposure to definitions favorable to deviance vary by frequency of exposure, duration of exposure, priority (early age) of exposure, and intensity of the relationship to the person conveying favorable attitudes toward deviant acts.

Social Control Theory. Social control theory assumes people are born with the propensity to commit hedonistic acts but are "controlled" by close associations with others and institutions that exert pressure to behave in socially acceptable ways. Deviance results when bonds to the major social institutions (family, school, peers) are severed and people feel free to exercise antisocial choices. In short, deviance occurs as the result of a failed process in which low self-control results from parental failure to socialize children into appropriate patterns of conventional behavior. Self-control is exercised via the efficacy of the "social bond," which consists of attachments to conventional others, commitment to conventional activities, involvement in conventional activities, and belief in the moral validity of conventional norms and values.

Hirschi (1969) found that delinquency is negatively related to the degree of attachment between parents and child, a relationship that has been supported in other research (Brownfield & Sorenson, 1993; Gove & Crutchfield, 1982; Loeber & Stouthamer-Loeber, 1986). Other family variables that may have an impact on the parent-child bond include parents' mental or physical health (Gove & Crutchfield, 1982; Loeber & Stouthamer-Loeber, 1986), parents' marital status (Gove &

Crutchfield, 1982) or marital relationship, and lack of parental supervision, parental rejection, and parental absence (Loeber & Stouthamer-Loeber, 1986). Although Mak (1990) did not find an association between the parental bond and delinquency, he found that the interaction of parental bond and expressions of empathy was related to low levels of delinquent behavior.

Gove and Crutchfield (1982) conclude that the way the parent experiences the child (the authors' measure of parent-child bond) is by far the strongest predictor of delinquency, but the direction of the relationship is unable to be determined. Negative variables are associated with delinquency, but positive variables are not associated with nondelinquency. This raises a critical point of contention between differential association theory and social control theory, a point clarified by Menard and Huizinga (1994), who hypothesize that conventional beliefs are not conceptually the same as delinquent values.

Negative Parenting Theories. That parental use of physical punishment is strongly associated with delinquency (Gove & Crutchfield, 1982; Loeber & Stouthamer-Loeber, 1986) appears to suggest that negative parental actions may negate the positive effects of the parental bond, acting as a high-priority, high-intensity positive definition of deviance. Strauss (1991) hypothesizes that the use of physical punishment by authority figures for morally correct reasons may teach children that violence can and should be used when other methods fail. Furthermore, parental criminality predicts delinquency (Loeber & Stouthamer-Loeber, 1986), suggesting that the parent-child bond may deter delinquency only insofar as the child is bonded to a relatively "conventional" parent. However, there does not appear to be much empirical evidence suggesting that children learn to be criminal from their criminal parents, nor does there appear to be literature testing whether a parental attachment to a criminal parent is associated with low belief in the moral validity of conventional norms and values. In short, it is not clear whether the association between parental criminality and delinquency is a result of the youth's being socialized into a deviant lifestyle or the lack of a supportive parent-child bond.

Peer Theories. Most peer theories, including both differential association and control theories, point to the bodies of psychological literature hypothesizing that beliefs follow (not precede) behaviors. Hypothesizing just the opposite, Menard and Huizinga (1994) selected respondents to the National Youth Survey (NYS) age 11 and above who demonstrated a strong "belief" bond with conventional society. They rejected subjects for whom prior or concurrent delinquent activity was indicated. Their analysis, across five panels of NYS data, suggests that there is no significant direct negative effect of "belief" on illegal behavior; however, there is an indirect negative effect of belief on delinquent behavior through exposure to delinquent peers. Furthermore, illegal behavior had a direct, negative, and significant impact on belief. Apparently, exposure to delinquent peers influenced the development of a belief system compatible with illegal behavior. Furthermore, a cycle of mutual influence was found in which minor offending appears to weaken prosocial beliefs, which appears to precede more serious offending, which is followed by further weakened beliefs.

Junger-Tas (1992) tested the social control model with delinquents and nondelinquents in two cities in Holland. Most of the juveniles in Junger-Tas's sample espoused commitment to conventional norms (belief) regarding delinquent behavior with the exception of a small group of very frequent offenders. The sample became significantly more conventional in their beliefs as they aged over a two-year follow-up period. Furthermore, Junger-Tas's findings suggest that school integration (conventional activities) is a better predictor of delinquent behavior than family integration (attachment) and school functioning (involvement) is more important than the school bond (commitment). Research further indicates that high grade point averages are related to lower levels of criminal behavior at all ages (Menard, Elliott, & Wofford, 1993) and that time spent on homework was more negatively correlated with delinquency than with parental attachment (Brownfield & Sorenson, 1993). This data appears to indicate that involvement in conventional activities, particularly in academic activities, is related to low levels of delinquent behavior.

Junger-Tas (1988, 1992) found a relationship between delinquency and peer affiliations that supports social control theory as well as elements of differential association theory. Junger-Tas found that delinquents were less committed to their friends than were nondelinquents, although most reported spending time with peers. In addition, high-frequency offenders were significantly more likely than low-frequency offenders to have friends who approved and supported their behavior and to have friends who had been picked up by police. Short (1960) found a consistent relationship between number of delinquent friends and delinquent behavior in a group of institutionalized youths who had committed serious delinquent acts.

Differential association theory suggests that exposure to delinquent peers increases the likelihood of deviant behavior by increasing exposure to positive definitions regarding deviance; however, Hirschi (cited in Agnew, 1991) believes that a strong attachment to peers negatively affects deviance regardless of peer delinquency. Brownfield and Thompson (1991) do not seem to support Hirschi's contention. These authors found that attachment to peers had no inhibiting effect on self-reported delinquency but association with delinquent peers was strongly related to self-reported delinquency. According to Agnew (1991), most adolescents have at least one friend who has committed at least one delinquent act they know of. When the attachment to delinquent peers, time spent with delinquent friends, peer approval of delinquent acts, and pressure to commit delinquent acts are low to moderate, association with delinquent peers has no effect or a negative effect on delinquency. When these variables are high, the effect of association with delinquent peers on delinquency is positive.

There appears to be support for both a social control and a differential association theory of delinquency. Association with delinquent peers has consistently been found to relate to higher levels of delinquent behavior, apparently supporting the hypothesis that delinquency is learned from others. However, the direction of this association is unclear; that is, it is not clear whether association with delinquent peers leads to delinquent beliefs and then behavior or whether delinquent beliefs and behavior lead to a tendency to associate with delinquent peers. In addition, the data on the association of delinquent behavior with parental involvement and the parent-child bond is equivocal. Also, the literature has found some evidence to indicate that involvement in conventional activities, at least with respect to academic achievement and school involvement, influences the level of delinquent behavior. Thus, it would appear that elements of both social control and differential association theories are related to the development of delinquent behavior, and it may be that different types of delinquency develop in different ways.

Research on Juvenile Sex Offending

Udry (1988) observes that Hirschi's social control model does not specifically deal with sexual behavior. However, he cites a review by Jessor and Jessor (1977) which finds sexual behavior among a class of crimes whose occurrence is intercorrelated and predicted by the same models. Although Hirschi's social bonds are not specifically invoked by adolescent sex researchers, sex researchers frequently apply similar concepts of social control, including parental attitudes, family structure, religiosity and church attendance, other family and neighborhood variables, and peer effects (Udry, 1988).

Psychological literature tells us a lot about the characteristics of sex offenders but appears somewhat devoid of theoretical guidance. Lakey (1994) observes that there have been several "theories" of sexually aggressive behavior but describes none of them and dismisses them as a group because none has received "unequivocal empirical support." Hunter and Becker (1994) suggest that the exploration of "etiologic factors" such as history of maltreatment, exposure to pornography, and exposure to aggressive models of behavior may help "explain" juvenile sexual offending as the result of inappropriate sexual arousal learned by pairing sexual arousal with inappropriate stimuli. This conceptualization, which appears consistent with differential association theory, has not received much empirical validation.

Much of the work in this area focuses on typologies of sexual offenders (Skinner, Carroll, & Berry, 1995; Barbaree, Seto, Serin, Amos, & Preston, 1994; Knight & Prentky, 1987; Becker, Kaplan, & Tenke, 1992) or offender characteristics (Becker, Cunningham-Rathner, & Kaplan, 1987; Fehrenbach, Smith, Monastersky, & Deisher, 1986; Davis & Leitenberg, 1987; Groth & Loredo, 1981; Van Ness, 1984) compared to "normals" (Lakey, 1994; Cotten-Hustan, 1984) or compared to nonsexual criminals (Hanson, Scott, & Steffy, 1995; Awad, Saunders, & Levine, 1984). Lakey (1994) identified only two studies (both more than a decade old) that compared juvenile sex offenders to other juvenile violent offenders (Lewis, Shankok, & Pincus, 1979; Tartar, Hegedus, Alterman, & Katz-Garris, 1983), both of which found "no differences" in descriptive characteristics among the two groups.

Most other work focuses on treatment paradigms (Sapp & Vaughn, 1990; Margolin, 1984; Brannon & Troyer, 1991; Becker, 1990; Smets & Cebula, 1987; Saunders & Awad, 1988; Stenson & Anderson, 1987; Borduin, Henggeler, Blaske, & Stein, 1990) and/or measures of recidivism and reoffending (Camp & Thyer, 1993; Kahn & Chambers, 1991; Smith & Monastersky, 1986; Furby, Weinrott, & Blackshaw, 1989).

Several factors have been explored to explain the onset of sexual aggression in the teenage years. These characteristics include a lack of social and assertiveness skills (Awad & Saunders, 1989; Fagan & Wexler, 1986; Katz, 1990; Shoor, Speed, & Bartlett, 1986), a history of nonsexual delinquency (Fehrenbach et al., 1986), low academic performance (Awad & Saunders, 1989, 1991; Fagan & Wexler, 1986), and lack of impulse control (Becker, Kaplan, Tenke, & Tartaglini, 1991; Smith,

Monastersky, & Deisher, 1987). Studies of adolescent sex offenders have also identified an unstable home environment, which may include having distant relationships or no relation at all with siblings and parents as well as such unhealthy home
situations as parents having a sexual pathology or the child viewing sexual interactions between parental figures (Smith & Israel, 1987). Evidence also suggests that
adolescent sex offending is related to the youth experiencing sexual or physical
abuse (Johnson, 1988) and witnessing violence in the family (Davis & Leitenberg,
1987). Although not guided by any theoretical models, these factors suggest that
elements from both social control and differential association theories might explain
sex offending.

Problems With the Research

The previous studies have a number of methodological flaws. First, most of the
research on the characteristics of adolescent sex offenders has not compared sex
offenders with either nonsex delinquents or nondelinquent adolescents. In fact,
Becker, Harris, and Sales (1993) found only five articles that studied sex offender
and offense characteristics by comparing a sample of sex offenders with a random
sample of either juvenile offenders who had not committed sexual offenses or juveniles from the general population. Shaw et al. (1993) explored a sample of youths
ages 9 to 14 who were admitted to a residential treatment program. They compared
this sample of identified sex offenders with a sample drawn from the *Diagnostic and
Statistical Manual of Mental Disorders (DSM-IV) Field Trials for Disruptive
Behavior Disorders* (American Psychiatric Association, 1994), which included boys
from a variety of psychiatric, psychological, and pediatric clinics and from one correctional facility. Controls were matched to sex offenders on presence of a DSM-III-
R (American Psychiatric Association, 1987) diagnosis of conduct disorder, age, and
ethnicity. This study found that there were no differences between sex offenders and
conduct-disordered youth on psychiatric symptoms, nor did the groups differ in
terms of aggressive behavior.

A study using Cattell's High School Personality Questionnaire (Cattell, Cattell, &
Johns, 1984) found no significant differences between a sample of sex offenders and
oppositional defiant adolescents drawn from an adolescent residential treatment center (Moody, Brissie, & Kim, 1994). However, the researchers did find that the sex
offenders scored more than one standard deviation lower than oppositional subjects
on the measure of conformity, whereas the oppositional subjects scored more than one
standard deviation below the sex offenders on the Withdrawal subscale. Using the
Child Behavior Checklist, Kempton and Forehand (1992) found that sex offenders
were viewed as being less aggressive than nonsex offenders but also found that those
youths who had committed sex crimes only scored lower on measures of
Social/Withdrawal, Anxiety, and Inattentiveness than did either confrontational only
or sex and confrontational youth. Kempton and Forehand (1992) further subdivided
the sex offender sample into those who had been arrested for rape or sodomy and not
child molestation and those who had been arrested for child molestation but not rape
or sodomy. They found no differences between these groups on any of the measures
from the Child Behavior Checklist.

In a study that compared sexual assaulters with matched samples of nonsex juvenile delinquents and child molesters, Awad and Saunders (1991) found no differences between the groups in terms of parental psychiatric disturbances, rates of being physically abused, and histories of nonsexual assaultive behavior. Child molesters did show significantly poorer social adjustment than the other two groups and were likely to have an earlier onset of school problems. The two sex offender groups were significantly less likely than nonsex delinquents to have a history of alcohol or drug abuse (Awad & Saunders, 1991). Not only did Benoit and Kennedy (1992) find that the incidence of physical and sexual victimization did not differ across sex and nonsex delinquent, or between aggressive sex offenders and child molesters, but they also found that the majority of child molesters had not been sexually abused.

Although research suggests that the previous descriptions are characteristic of adolescent sex offenders, there is no empirical evidence for a definite set of characteristics that would lead to sexual offending, nor is there empirical evidence to describe how the factors interact to explain the etiology of juvenile sex offending (Becker et al., 1993). All the previously cited studies involved small samples. In fact, the largest cell size included in any of the previously discussed studies was 45 subjects, which was compared with two samples of 24 subjects. Thus, this body of literature has a severe limitation due to lack of statistical power.

Malamuth (1986) found that the presence of any single predictor is unlikely to result in high levels of sexual aggression. In fact, this study indicates that various factors such as those discussed earlier combine in an interactive model to predict sexual aggression. Using samples of heterosexual and bisexual college students, Malamuth and his colleagues found that sexual aggression can be explained by the interaction of two independent paths: hostile masculinity and sexual promiscuity (Malamuth, Sockloski, Koss, & Tanaka, 1991). Data indicates that these paths are not uniquely related to sexual aggression. Specifically, the hostile masculinity path, which involves beliefs that masculine identity involves power, risk taking, toughness, dominance, aggressiveness, honor defending, and competitiveness, is associated with coercion of both a sexual and nonsexual nature. The sexual promiscuity path, which involves the age of first intercourse experience and the number of sexual partners since age 14, was directly related to the common variance between sexual and nonsexual aggression and was inversely related to nonsexual aggression. The interaction between these two paths significantly predicted sexual aggression against women, indicating that high levels of sexual aggression were related to high scores on both the hostile masculinity measures and the sexual promiscuity measures. Low scores on either of these measures lead to lower levels of sexual aggression (Malamuth, Heavey, & Linz, 1993; Malamuth et al., 1991).

The research cited in this section indicates that juvenile sex offenders share many characteristics with other juvenile delinquents. When differences have been found, they appear to be in the areas of interpersonal attachment and social interactions. Only Malamuth's work appears to directly address the ways that factors may combine to lead to sexual aggression. However, his work has focused on young adults and thus implicates already developed belief systems. It provides little insight into how these belief systems develop. Moreover, the research on sex offender characteristics has not drawn on the already better developed studies of juvenile delinquency even though the literature cited here indicates that sex offenders are very much like other delinquents in almost all the suspected causes of deviant behavior.

Minnesota Survey of Adolescent Sex Offenders

The previously described studies fail to provide much insight into factors that might lead to sexually aggressive behavior, as opposed to other types of criminal behavior. The research on juvenile delinquency has, for the most part, not differentiated violent from nonviolent crimes and a differentiation of sexual from nonsexual crimes is nonexistent. The sex offender literature has focused primarily on describing the characteristics of youths who have committed sexual crimes. Those few studies that have attempted to determine differences between sex and nonsex offenders have found few, if any, differences. In this section we describe a preliminary study designed to explore the early indicators of sexual aggression and abuse. The study involves the application of a structured interview with identified juvenile sex offenders which is being used by others to explore juvenile delinquency. This interview, based on instrumentation used by the NYS (Elliott & Huizinga, 1987), was used to collect data from 78 youths in sex offender treatment programs in Minnesota. Two comparison groups were then constructed using data from the third nationwide survey of the longitudinal sample of the NYS (Elliott, 1994). These comparison groups included violent youth (i.e., those who self-reported attacking someone with intent to seriously hurt or kill them), who had been involved in gang fights or had used force or strong-arm methods to get money or things and who indicated no behaviors that would be considered a sex offense, and nondelinquent youth. Stratified samples of violent and nondelinquent youth were then drawn to ensure comparable ethnic distributions across all three samples. The three samples were comparable with respect to age and residence in urban or rural settings.

Results

The data was analyzed using univariate analysis of variance to explore differences in group means across the three groups. Significant univariate F's were then explored using Scheffe's tests to make pairwise comparisons. We present the differences between groups on variables important for social control and differential association theories as well as delinquent attitudes, delinquent behaviors, indications of social isolation, attachment and involvement in peer groups and the characteristics of those peer groups, and school achievement.

Delinquent Attitudes. The relevant attitudes explored in this study include the degree to which subjects believe that delinquent behaviors, that is both minor activities such as truancy and cheating on tests and more serious behavior such as drug use, violence and theft, are wrong and a series of three scales that measure normlessness. Conceptually, normlessness refers to the belief that one must violate social norms to achieve personal goals or aspirations (Elliott, Huizinga, & Ageton, 1985). This concept is measured for family, school, and peers. We found few differences between sex offenders and other delinquents with respect to delinquent attitudes. That is, sex offenders are similar to other delinquents and differ from nondelinquents with respect to their attitudes toward the appropriateness of the use of alcohol and drugs and their normless beliefs with respect to attaining and keeping friends and achieving in school. They do differ from both delinquents and nondelinquents in two very telling areas: overall attitude toward delinquency and family normlessness. Sex offenders hold very negative attitudes toward delinquent behavior, even more extreme than nondelinquent youths, and also are more normless in their beliefs about family interactions than either of the other two groups.

Delinquent Behaviors. With respect to delinquent behaviors, sex offenders appear to behave in ways similar to nonsex delinquents, or in some cases they are even more extreme. Only with respect to cheating on tests and hitchhiking where it is illegal are the sex offenders less likely to engage in deviant behavior than are other delinquent youth.

Substance Use. Sex offenders behave very much like other adolescents with respect to substance use. The three groups did not differ with respect to alcohol use, but this appeared to be due to the wide range in usage patterns within all three groups. Frequency of alcohol use showed very high variances across all the groups, indicating that a subset of youths are regular users of alcohol whereas others use no alcoholic beverages or very little. Sex offenders showed patterns of illicit drug use similar to nonoffending youth, with the violent delinquent youth reporting significantly more use of such drugs as marijuana, barbiturates, hallucinogens, and cocaine. Because of the temporal difference between the interviews of the sex offenders and the other two samples, it was not possible to look at crack cocaine usage patterns.

Social Isolation. Indicators of social isolation suggest that those youths committing sex offenses were much more likely to be isolated from peers and families than either nondelinquent or violent youth. In addition, they tended to put much more emphasis on conforming to the expectations of their peers than did either of the other two groups. Although the sex offenders in this sample tended to have school achievement levels comparable to nondelinquent youth, they perceived their teachers as having negative views of them similar to the violent youth, who had significantly poorer school achievement than the other two groups. Interestingly, the association between school achievement and teacher labeling, a measure of whether subjects perceived their teachers as thinking of them as disturbed or bad, was significant and substantial for violent and nondelinquent youth but virtually zero for sex offenders.

Summary of Results. In general, this study appears to lend some support for a social control theory of sex offending. Sex offenders resemble violent, nonsex delinquents in terms of certain attitudes and certain nonserious deviant behavior. Sex offenders' general beliefs about delinquent behavior are extremely negative. However, when tied directly to their goals, they appear to moderate this negative attitude and allow themselves to lie, cheat, and behave in other antisocial ways to achieve success and status. The sex offenders in this sample were quite isolated, especially from peers and family. This lack of ties to family was not only indicated by measures of involvement but also in their willingness to behave in antisocial ways with family members, an attitude they did not share with the violent youth. Sex offenders appeared to expect rejection from their teachers to an extent similar to violent youth, but their expectations were not tied to academic performance, which was the case for both violent and nondelinquent youth.

Implications for Intervention

Our data appears to indicate that a social control theory of etiology may explain the development of sex offending, independent from other forms of juvenile delinquency. The sex offenders in our sample differed from other delinquents primarily in their isolation from both peers and their families. This isolation appears to lead them to a willingness to violate their generally prosocial belief structure and engage in whatever behavior would be necessary to attract and keep friends. Although we have no empirical evidence of this belief, it may include turning to inappropriate partners and behaviors to meet sexual and affiliative needs. Sex offenders appear to be less attached to primary supports such as their families than are other delinquent youth, further supporting the hypothesis that sex offending is related to an isolation from possible sources of emotional support and an inability to form appropriate attachments (Prentky et al., 1989; Ryan, Lane, Davis, & Isaac, 1987).

Social control theory postulates that sex offenders develop inappropriate behavior as a result of the lack of bonds to conventional social structures, in this case an isolation from peers and family. In keeping with Ryan et al.'s (1987) concept that the sex offender's expectation of rejection from others leads to isolation, we can probably assume that if we break the process of social isolation, we can have some impact on the development of sexually inappropriate behavior. That is what most treatment programs using group therapy and social-cognitive intervention strategies attempt to do. This data further suggests that family interventions would be appropriate for treatment programs serving sexually abusive youth. Their normlessness with respect to family interactions is likely to further alienate them from parents and siblings. These youths have few peer attachments and do not feel a positive attachment to school. Support of more prosocial behavior would likely be enhanced by the youths' integration into the family structure. The data indicated that a lack of emotional attachments rather than an attachment to deviant peers is related to sexually inappropriate behavior. Furthermore, the finding that youths who commit sex offenses hold generally prosocial beliefs suggests that integrating sex offending youth into a peer structure would be an appropriate therapeutic milieu

Implications for Prevention

Our findings have a number of interesting implications for prevention programs. Sex offending does appear to be a subset of other delinquent behavior, and those youths who have committed sex crimes also appear to have been involved in other minor criminal behavior and acting out in school. Thus, those programs aimed at ameliorating conduct-disordered and other delinquent behavior may have some implications for preventing sex offending. However, generalized attitudes against being delinquent and participating in delinquent acts does not appear related to sex offending. In fact, sex offenders appear to be extremely prosocial with respect to their beliefs about the inappropriateness of committing crimes and acting in deviant ways. However, when directly related to the youths' achievement of their goals, they do allow for the use of antisocial behavior and, in fact, value it. Thus, behavior with respect to goal achievement, and especially affiliative goal achievement, appears to be most important in the development of sexually abusive behavior. Finally, the most distinguishing factor about the sex offenders we have studied is that they are very isolated from both age-appropriate peers and their families. They appear to be youth who expect to be seen negatively, regardless of the quality of their performance or achievements, and thus would not respond to social messages intended to improve their self-esteem. These findings, consistent with earlier studies of the characteristics of sex offenders, point to the primacy of isolation and poor social adjustment as distinguishing characteristics of adolescent sex offenders, indicating that interventions that maximize the ability to build interpersonal attachments potentially affect the propensity to engage in sexually abusive and aggressive behaviors.

Conclusion

The data from our study indicated that sex offenders differed in their interpretation of available environmental data, at least with respect to school achievement and their expectations of rejection by adults. Specifically, although school achievement and perceived teacher rejection were related in the violent and nondelinquent youth, this association did not exist in sex offending youth. This finding may indicate that those youth at risk for committing sex crimes cognitively process evaluative information very differently than do other youth. One possible avenue of exploration may be the cognitive model of helpless depression initially proposed by Abramson, Seligman, and Teasdale (1978).

As noted earlier, the literature on the causes of sexual abuse and aggression has a number of methodological weaknesses. Although the study described in this chapter advances the previous research, it has a number of methodological flaws that temper our enthusiasm for the conclusions we have drawn. Specifically, the three groups were defined quite differently, with sex offenders being defined as participants in sex offender-specific treatment programs and the other two groups being defined by self-reported behavior; data collection on the three groups took place 16 years apart, with the sex offender survey being conducted in 1994-1995 and the other two groups being part of a national probability sample surveyed in 1979; and finally, although the two survey instruments used were substantially the same, there were some differences between the survey used with the sex offender sample and the one used in 1979 with the other two groups. This limited the number of available variables for exploration. Most important, we were unable to compare the groups with respect to experiences of sexual abuse, the acceptance of rape myths, or sexual behavior other than heterosexual intercourse and obscene phone calls.

In general, our data and the available information from the literature indicate that future studies of the causes of sexual abuse and aggression should focus on affiliation and attachment variables and would benefit from theoretical guidance, mainly from social control and strain theories. Our study also leads us to the assumption that further investigation is needed to explore the primacy of family isolation in the etiology of sex offending, as well as the factors associated with the observed isolation and normlessness.

Acknowledgments

The data reported in this paper was collected with funding and assistance from the Institute for Child and Adolescent Sexual Health. We also acknowledge funding from the Minnesota Department of Corrections (Contract No. 085388011). The opinions expressed here are those of the authors and do not reflect the official positions of either the Institute for Child and Adolescent Sexual Health or the Minnesota Department of Corrections.

References

Abramson, L. Y., Seligman, M. E. P., & Teasdale, J. D. (1978). Learned helplessness in humans: Critique and reformulation. *Journal of Abnormal Psychology, 87*, 49–74.

Agnew, R. (1991). The interactive effects of peer variables on delinquency. *Criminology, 29*, 47–72.

American Psychiatric Association. (1987). *Diagnostic and statistical manual for mental disorders* (3rd ed., rev.). Washington, DC: Author.

American Psychiatric Association. (1994). *Diagnostic and statistical manual for mental disorders* (4th ed.). Washington, DC: Author.

Awad, G. A., & Saunders, E. B. (1989). Adolescent child molesters: Clinical observations. Child *Psychiatry and Human Development, 19*, 195–206.

Awad, G. A., & Saunders, E. B. (1991). Male adolescent sexual assaulters: Clinical observations. *Journal of Interpersonal Violence, 6*, 446–460.

Awad, G. A., Saunders, E. B., & Levine, J. (1984). A clinical study of male adolescent sexual offenders. *International Journal of Offender Therapy and Comparative Criminology, 20*, 105–116.

Bandura, A. (1986). *Social foundations of thought and action: A social cognitive theory.* Englewood Cliffs, NJ: Prentice Hall.

Barbaree, H. E., Seto, M. C., Serin, R. C., Amos, N. L., & Preston, D. L. (1994). Comparisons between sexual and nonsexual rapist subtypes: Sexual arousal to rape, offense precursors, and offense characteristics. *Criminal Justice and Behavior, 21*, 95–114.

Becker, J. V. (1990). Treating adolescent sexual offenders. *Professional Psychology: Research and Practice, 21*, 362–365.

Becker, J. V., Cunningham-Rathner, J., & Kaplan, M. S. (1987). Adolescent sexual offenders: demographics, criminal and sexual histories, and recommendations for reducing future offenses. *Journal of Interpersonal Violence, 1*, 431–445.

Becker, J. V., Harris, C. D., & Sales, B. D. (1993). Juveniles who commit sexual offenses: A critical review of research. In G. C. N. Hall & R. Hirschman (Eds.), *Sexual aggression: Issues in etiology and assessment, treatment and policy* (pp. 215–228). Washington, DC: Taylor & Francis.

Becker, J. V., Kaplan, M. S., & Tenke, C. E. (1992). The relationship of abuse history, denial, and erectile response profiles of adolescent sexual perpetrators. *Behavior Therapy, 23*, 87–97.

Becker, J. V., Kaplan, M. S., Tenke, C. E., & Tartaglini, A. (1991). The incidence of depressive symptomology in juvenile sex offenders with a history of abuse. *Child Abuse and Neglect, 15*, 531–536.

Benoit, J. L., & Kennedy, W. A. (1992). The abuse history of male adolescent sex offenders. *Journal of Interpersonal Violence, 7*, 543–548.

Borduin, C. M., Henggeler, S. W., Blaske, D. M., & Stein, R. J. (1990). Multisystemic treatment of adolescent sexual offenders. *International Journal of Offender Therapy and Comparative Criminology, 34*, 105–113.

Brannon, J. M., & Troyer, R. (1991). Peer group counseling: A normalized residential alternative to the specialized treatment of adolescent sexual offenders. *International Journal of Offender Therapy and Comparative Criminology, 35*, 225–234.

Brownfield, D., & Sorenson, A. M. (1993). Self-control and juvenile delinquency: Theoretical issues and an empirical assessment of selected elements of a general theory of crime. *Deviant Behavior, 14*, 243–264.

Brownfield, D., & Thompson, K. (1991). Attachment to peers and delinquent behavior. *Canadian Journal of Criminology, 33*, 45–60.

Camp, B. H., & Thyer, B. A. (1993). Treatment of adolescent sex offenders: A review of empirical research. *Journal of Applied Social Sciences, 17*, 191–206.

Cattell, R. B., Cattell, M. D. L., & Johns, E. P. (1984). *Manual and norms for the High School Personality Questionnaire.* Champaign, IL: Institute for Personality and Ability Testing.

Cotten-Hustan, A. L. (1984). Comparisons of sex offenders with non-offenders on attitudes toward masturbation and female fantasy as related to participation in human sexuality sessions. *Journal of Offender Counseling, Services, and Rehabilitation, 8*, 13–26.

Davis, G. E., & Leitenberg, H. (1987). Adolescent sex offenders. *Psychological Bulletin, 101*, 417–427.

Elliott, D. S. (1994). *National Youth Survey: Wave III, 1978.* Ann Arbor, MI: Inter-university Consortium of Political and Social Research.

Elliott, D. S., & Huizinga, D. (1987, March). *Scales from the National Youth Survey: Progress report* (Project report no. 38). Boulder, CO: Institute for Behavioral Science.

Elliott, D. S., Huizinga, D., & Ageton, S. S. (1985). *Explaining delinquency and drug use.* Beverly Hills, CA: Sage.

Fagan, J., & Wexler, S. (1986). Explanations of sexual assault among violent delinquents. *Journal of Adolescent Research, 3*, 363–385.

Fehrenbach, P. A., Smith, W., Monastersky, C., & Deisher, R. W. (1986). Adolescent sexual offenders: Offender and offense characteristics. *American Journal of Orthopsychiatry, 56*, 225–233.

Furby, L., Weinrott, M. R., & Blackshaw, L. (1989). Sex offender recidivism: A review. *Psychological Bulletin, 105*, 3–30.

Gove, W. R., & Crutchfield, R. D. (1982). The family and juvenile delinquency. *Sociological Quarterly, 23*, 301–319.

Groth, A. N., & Loredo, C. M. (1981). Juvenile sexual offenders: Guidelines for assessment. *International Journal of Offender Therapy and Comparative Criminology, 25*, 31–39.

Hanson, R. K., Scott, H., & Steffy, R. A. (1995). A comparison of child molesters and nonsexual criminals: Risk predictors and long-term recidivism. *Journal of Research in Crime and Delinquency, 32*, 325–337.

Hirschi, T. (1969). *Causes of delinquency.* Berkeley: University of California Press.

Hunter, J. A. Jr., & Becker, J. V. (1994). The role of deviant sexual arousal in juvenile sexual offending. *Criminal Justice and Behavior, 21*, 132–149.

Jessor, R., & Jessor, S. L. (1977). *Problem behavior and psychological development.* New York: Academic Press.

Johnson, T. C. (1988). Child perpetrators—children who molest other children: Preliminary findings. *Child Abuse and Neglect, 12*, 219–229.

Junger-Tas, J. (1992). An empirical test of social control theory [Special issue]. *Journal of Quantitative Criminology, 8*, 9–28.

Kahn, T. J., & Chambers, H. J. (1991). Assessing reoffense risk with juvenile sexual Offenders. *Child Welfare, 70*, 333–345.

Katz, R. C. (1990). Psychological adjustment in adolescent child molesters. *Child Abuse and Neglect, 14*, 567–575.

Kempton, T., & Forehand, R. (1992). Juvenile sex offenders: Similar to, or different from, other incarcerated delinquent offenders? *Behavior Research and Therapy, 30*, 533–536.

Knight, R. A., & Prentky, R. A. (1987). The developmental antecedents and adult adaptations of rapist subtypes. *Criminal Justice and Behavior, 14*, 403–426.

Lakey, J. F. (1994). The profile and treatment of male adolescent sex offenders. *Adolescence, 29*, 755–761.

Lewis, D. O., Shankok, S. S., & Pincus, J. H. (1979). Juvenile male sexual assaulters. *American Journal of Psychiatry, 136,* 1194–1196.

Loeber, R., & Stouthamer-Loeber, M. (1986). Family factors and correlates and predictors of juvenile conduct problems and delinquency. In M. Tonry & N. Morris (Eds.), *Crime and justice: An annual review of research* (vol. 7, pp. 29–149). Chicago: University of Chicago Press.

Mak, A. S. (1990). Testing a psychosocial control theory of delinquency. *Criminal Justice and Behavior, 17,* 215–230.

Malamuth, N. M. (1986). Predictors of naturalistic sexual aggression. *Journal of Personality and Social Psychology, 50,* 953–962.

Malamuth, N. M., Heavey, C. L., & Linz, D. (1993). Predicting men's antisocial behavior against women: The interaction model of sexual aggression. In G. N. Hall, R. Hirschman, J. Graham, & M. Zaragosa (Eds.), *Sexual aggression: Issues in etiology, assessment, and treatment* (pp. 63–97). Washington, DC: Hemisphere.

Malamuth, N. M., Sockloski, R. J., Koss, M. P., & Tanaka, J. S. (1991). Characteristics of aggressors against women: Testing a model using a national sample of college students. *Journal of Consulting and Clinical Psychology, 59,* 670–681.

Margolin, L. (1984). A treatment model for the adolescent sex offender. *Journal of Offender Counseling, Services and Rehabilitation, 8,* 1–11.

Menard, S., Elliott, D. S., & Wofford, S. (1993). Social control theories in developmental perspective. *Studies on Crime and Crime Prevention, 2,* 69–87.

Menard, S., & Huizinga, D. (1994). Changes in conventional attitudes and delinquent behavior in adolescence. *Youth and Society, 26,* 23–53.

Moody, E. E., Brissie, J., & Kim, J. (1994). Personality and background characteristics of adolescent sexual offenders. *Journal of Addictions and Offender Counseling, 14,* 30–48.

Prentky, R. A., Knight, R. A., Sims-Knight, J. E., Strauss, H., Rokous, F., & Cerce, D. (1989). Developmental antecedents of sexual aggression. *Development and Psychopathology, 1,* 153–169.

Ryan, G., Lane, S., Davis, J., & Isaac, C. (1987). Juvenile sex offenders: Development and correction. *Child Abuse and Neglect, 11,* 385–395.

Sapp, A. D., & Vaughn, M. S. (1990). Juvenile sex offender treatment at state-operated correctional institutions. International *Journal of Offender Therapy and Comparative Criminology, 21,* 131–143.

Saunders, E. B., & Awad, G. A. (1988). Assessment, management, and treatment for male adolescent sexual offenders. *American Journal of Orthopsychiatry, 58,* 571–579.

Shaw, J. A., Campo-Bowen, A. E., Applegate, B., Perez, D., Antoine, L. B., Hart, E. L., Lahey, B. B., Testa, R. J., & Devaney, A. (1993). Young boys who commit serious sexual offenses: Demographics, psychometrics, and phenomenology. *Bulletin of the American Academy of Psychiatry and Law, 21,* 399–408.

Shoor, M., Speed, H. H., & Bartlett, C. (1986). Syndrome of the adolescent child molester. *American Journal of Psychiatry, 122,* 783–798.

Short, J. F. Jr. (1960). Differential association as a hypothesis: Problems of empirical testing. *Social Problems, 8,* 14–25.

Skinner, L. J., Carroll, K. A., & Berry, K. K. (1995). A typology for sexually aggressive males in dating relationships. *Journal of Offender Rehabilitation, 22,* 29–45.

Smets, A. C., & Cebula, C. M. (1987). A group treatment program for adolescent sex offenders: Five steps toward resolution. *Child Abuse and Neglect, 11,* 247–254.

Smith, H., & Israel, E. (1987). Sibling incest: A study of dynamics of 25 cases. *Child Abuse and Neglect, 11,* 101–108.

Smith, W. R., & Monastersky, C. (1986). Assessing juvenile sexual offenders' risk for reoffending. *Criminal Justice and Behavior, 13,* 115–140.

Smith, W. R., Monastersky, C., & Deisher, R. M. (1987). MMPI-based personality types among juvenile sexual offenders. *Journal of Clinical Psychology, 43,* 422–430.

Stenson, P., & Anderson, C. (1987). Treating juvenile sex offenders and preventing the cycle of abuse. *Journal of Child Care, 3,* 91–102.

Strauss, M. A. (1991). Discipline and deviance: physical punishment of children and violence and other crime in adulthood. *Social Problems, 38*, 133–154.

Sutherland, E. H., & Cressey, D. R. (1978). *Criminology.* Philadelphia: J.B. Lippincott.

Tarter, R. E., Hegedus, A. M., Alterman, A. I., & Katz-Garris, L. (1983). Cognitive capacities of juvenile, violent, nonviolent, and sexual offenders. *Journal of Nervous and Mental Disease, 171*, 564–567.

Udry, J. R. (1988). Biological predispositions and social control in adolescent sexual behavior. *American Sociological Review, 53*, 709–722.

Van Ness, S. R. (1984). Rape and instrumental violence: A study of youth offenders. *Journal of Offender Counseling Services and Rehabilitation, 9*, 161–170.

Chapter 10

Adolescent Female Sexual Offenders

by Kurt M. Bumby, Ph.D. and Nancy Halstenson Bumby, Ph.D.

Overview

Of all the general types of sex offenders, the adolescent female sex offender has received the least attention. In this chapter, we present both descriptive and comparative studies of the characteristics of this population. Our research compares adolescent female sex offenders to adolescent female nonoffenders to adolescent male sex offenders and finally to adolescent male nonoffenders. Perhaps the most significant finding is that the adolescent female sex offenders were all sexually abused at a significantly greater rate than the other groups. We then use the information processing of trauma model to explain some of the dynamics of the adolescent female sex offenders.

Review of Research

Recent crime statistics reveal that although females comprise less than 10% of all persons arrested for sexual offenses, this seemingly small statistic actually represents nearly 7,000 reported cases of sexual offenses per year (Federal Bureau of Investigation, 1991). Researchers have suggested that approximately 20% of male victims and 5% of female victims of sexual abuse have been victimized by women (Finkelhor & Russell, 1984). Retrospective surveys of college students, incarcerated males, and other specialized samples have yielded a much wider range of findings, with as few as 2% and as many as 78% of those having been sexually abused reporting that the perpetrator was a female (Finkelhor, Williams, & Burns, 1988; Fromuth & Burkhart, 1987; Risin & Koss, 1987).

Despite the significance of female sexual offending, empirical studies on female sexual offenders remain scarce. Existing research has focused largely on adult female sexual offenders, with the following characteristics being most commonly reported: (1) the perpetration often occurs in caregiving situations and may occur independently or as a result of coercion by, or in conjunction with, a male offender (Chasnoff et al., 1986; Finkelhor et al., 1988; Kaplan & Green, 1995; Margolin, 1991; McCarty, 1986; O'Connor, 1987; Rowan, Rowan, & Langelier, 1990); (2) a history of perpetrator alcohol and drug abuse, with the onset of the chemical abuse beginning during adolescence (Faller, 1987; Kaplan & Green, 1995; Matthews, Mathews, & Speltz, 1991; McCarty, 1986; O'Connor, 1987; Rowan et al., 1990); (3) emotional disturbance and previous psychiatric treatment for nonpsychotic difficulties such as major depression and posttraumatic stress disorder (PTSD) (Faller, 1987; Green & Kaplan, 1994; Kaplan & Green, 1995; McCarty, 1986; O'Connor, 1987; Rowan et al., 1990; Travin, Cullin, & Protter, 1990; Wakefield & Underwager, 1991); (4) a history of poor school performance (Matthews et al., 1991; McCarty, 1986); (5) social isolation, with few to no friends and no sense of attachment or belonging (McCarty, 1986; Travin et al., 1990); and (6) a history of sexual abuse during childhood and/or adolescence, with a large percentage also having experienced physical abuse (Green & Kaplan, 1994; Kaplan & Green, 1995; Matthews et al., 1991; McCarty, 1986; Rowan et al., 1990; Travin et al., 1990). In contrast to incarcerated non-sex offending females, female sexual offenders were sexually abused during childhood at almost twice the rate and were more likely to have been sexually abused by a family member (Green & Kaplan, 1994; Kaplan & Green, 1995).

Although there is a paucity of research on adult female sexual offenders, it appears that adolescent females who sexually perpetrate have been afforded the least attention in the sexual offending literature, despite the fact that the arrest rate for sexual offenses committed by adolescent females rose 31.5% between 1980 and 1990 (Federal Bureau of Investigation, 1991). According to the Office of Juvenile Justice and Prevention (1992), statistics indicate that females accounted for 2% of the forcible rapes perpetrated by juveniles and 7% of other sexual offenses committed by juveniles; these percentages represent approximately 1,500 juvenile female sexual offenders. Interestingly, there has been an explosion of literature on adolescent male perpetrators, perhaps because males are believed to represent more than 90% of the perpetrators of sexual offenses committed by persons under the age of 18 (Fehrenbach, Smith, Monastersky, & Deisher, 1986; Federal Bureau of Investigation, 1991).

The lack of a parallel trend in the identification and examination of adolescent female sexual offenders is troubling. It has been suggested that adolescent female sexual offenders may be either underrepresented or underreported in the literature for several reasons, including the following: (1) adolescent females may be less insecure or fearful about their sexuality than adolescent males and thus commit fewer offenses; (2) adolescent females may be better able to separate emotional, power, and control needs from the sexual realm; and (3) a double standard may exist whereby sexual contact between an adolescent female and a young boy is seen as less problematic than similar contact between an adolescent male and a young girl (Davis & Leitenberg, 1987). Further, Allen (1991) has suggested that there may be a lack of recognition of female sexual offending as a result of an overextension of feminist explanations that categorize sexual offending as a male-only crime. In addition, an overgeneralization and overemphasis on the reported statistics exist, suggesting that female sexual offending is uncommon. Finally, one explanation for the scarcity of research on adolescent female sexual offenders may be the difficulty in accessing samples of these offenders. Currently, the limited literature consists of single case studies, brief descriptions of these perpetrators as small subsets of adult female offender samples or adolescent male offender samples, and reported characteristics of the offenses and victims, with minimal descriptions of the adolescent female perpetrators themselves.

Descriptive Studies of Adolescent Female Sex Offenders

One of the first substantive investigations of adolescent female sex offenders was reported by Fehrenbach and Monastersky (1988), who examined 28 female adolescents treated at the Juvenile Sexual Offender Program at the University of Washington between 1978 and 1985. The victims of these female offenders were 12 years old or younger, with the sole exception of one female who perpetrated against an adult. Ten of the females (35.7%) sexually perpetrated exclusively against males, 16 of the females (57.1%) exclusively assaulted females, and 2 (7.1%) perpetrated against both male and female victims. The victims were either family members or acquaintances. The most common relationship of the victim to the juvenile female sexual offender was acquaintance (57.1%), followed by sibling/stepsibling (28.6%) and other relative (14.3%). More than two-thirds of these sexual offenses occurred during a caregiving activity (i.e., babysitting). Four of the females (14.3%) committed more than one sexual offense. Other delinquency was uncommon. Half the female sample reported a history of sexual abuse, and 21.4% reported a history of physical abuse. The type of offense committed by these females included oral, anal, or vaginal intercourse or other penetration (53.6%) or fondling (46.4%).

The Fehrenbach and Monastersky (1988) study was a significant contribution to the dearth of literature on adolescent female sexual offenders. However, the investigators essentially limited the examination of these females to descriptions of their victims and offense characteristics. Little data was reported that provided insight into the psychological characteristics and dynamics of females themselves. It was not until Hunter, Lexier, Goodwin, Browne, and Dennis (1993) published detailed findings from an inpatient sample of 10 adolescent female offenders that a considerable amount of descriptive characteristics of adolescent female offenders was revealed.

Each of the 10 females in the Hunter et al. (1993) study was involved in a residential treatment program for juveniles with emotional and behavioral difficulties. The females were identified as sexual offenders as a result of acknowledged and documented histories of sexual offenses against children. The mean age of the female offenders was 15 years (range 13–17 years), and the sample was primarily Caucasian (80% Caucasian, 20% African American). The investigators examined data regarding developmental history, including intellectual ability and psychiatric diagnosis. In addition, they explored the females' histories of maltreatment (e.g., physical abuse and sexual abuse), as well as their perceptions of sexual victimization experiences. Finally, the authors examined offenders' histories of perpetration and other sexual deviancy.

In terms of psychiatric history, the majority (80%) of the females had received previous mental health treatment. No history of psychosis was reported in the group. Sixty percent had a history of suicidal ideation/attempts, while another 60% had evidenced runaway behaviors. Alcohol/drug abuse was found in half the females and 40% had difficulties with enuresis. The mean IQ of the females was 94.1 (range 73 to 119), with 40% evidencing a history of learning disabilities.

Of particular interest was the fact that all the females reported a history of sexual victimization. These females reported having been sexually abused by more than one offender (mean number of molesters was 5, range 2–7), beginning at an early age (median age 4.5, range 1–8 years of age). All the females reported having been molested by a male, and 60% reported having been molested by a female as well. The most common relationship between the female and her perpetrator was that of a known acquaintance (43.8%), followed by a relative other than a parent or sibling (27.1%), father/stepfather (12.5%), stranger (10.4%), mother/stepmother (4.2%), and finally sibling (2.1%). Ninety percent of the females indicated that they had been subjected to attempted or actual vaginal penetration, while 60% reported that actual or attempted anal intercourse had occurred. Sixty percent reported that they had performed oral sex on their perpetrator, and 70% indicated that oral sex had been performed on them. All the females reported being subjected to fondling; the use of force occurred in 90% of the cases. The majority (80%) of the females indicated that they experienced some degree of sexual arousal during at least one of their own experiences of victimization. Of those experiencing arousal, 100% of those victimized by a male perpetrator indicated that they experienced some degree of arousal, compared to 66.6% reporting arousal from victimization by a female.

The median age at which the females reportedly first committed a sexual offense was 9.5 years (range, 5–14 years). They tended to have molested more than one victim (median 2.5 victims, range 1–12) and perpetrated numerous acts per victim (median 15 acts, range 1–47). Their victims tended to be young children (median age 5.5 years, range 1–13 years); 60.6% of the victims were male. More than half the females (60%) offended against both male and female victims, 30% had exclusively perpetrated against males, and 10% had exclusively victimized a female. Interestingly, the most common relationship between the females and their victims was that of a stranger (39.4%), followed by an older sibling (30.3%), other relative (18.2%), and acquaintance (12.1%). However, when combining the categories to reflect intrafamilial, stranger, and extrafamilial/acquaintance offenses, it is clear that the offenders tended to perpetrate against family members (48.5%). Each of the female offenders engaged in fondling; 70% engaged in oral sex, 70% engaged in vaginal intercourse, and only 10% engaged in anal intercourse with their victims. Fewer than half (40%) the females indicated that they had used force during the commission of at least one of their sexual offenses. The majority of the females (80%) reported having fantasized about the deviant sexual behavior; 60% reported that they had fantasized about the behavior prior to the first act of perpetration. Only two of the females (20%) acknowledged having masturbated to such fantasies. Additional deviant sexual behavior was relatively uncommon among these females. Only one female reported exhibitionism, one reported obscene phone calling, two reported bestiality, and two reported frottage.

Hunter et al. (1993) reported that the majority of the females in the study had difficulties with nonsexual behaviors as well, such as stealing and physical aggression, although most had not been arrested for such behavior. In addition, attention was called to the apparent deliberateness of these acts of sexual perpetration by the females (e.g., fantasizing about the victimization), challenging the "curiosity" or "experimentation" theories and offering evidence for the females' development of deviant arousal patterns.

In addition, Hunter et al. (1993) emphasized the need to examine the relationship between juvenile females' own substantial histories of sexual and other victimization and their commission of sexual offenses, particularly in light of their reported experiences of sexual arousal during their victimization.

Findings

Recently, we (Bumby & Bumby, 1993) reported detailed findings from an inpatient sample of 12 adolescent female perpetrators, describing demographic and family information; victimization and perpetration history; and school, peer, and psychological adjustment of these female sexual offenders. These females were involved in treatment at an inpatient psychiatric facility for emotionally and behaviorally disordered children and adolescents. Each of these females was known to have perpetrated, or disclosed having committed, sexual offenses against another individual. The histories of sexually perpetrating behaviors were further substantiated by examining existing records and reports from family members and treatment providers. Sexual perpetration was defined as falling into one or both of the following categories: (1) using force or coercion to have sexual contact with another individual or (2) having sexual contact with persons too young to give valid consent or understand that they were being violated.

Types of Victims. The mean number of victims of the female perpetrators was two (range 1 to 5), with the victims generally being young children. Five perpetrated only against female victims (42%), three exclusively against male victims (25%), and four perpetrated against both females and males (33%). Nine of the adolescent females (75%) perpetrated only against family members (e.g., siblings, cousins, nephews, and nieces), and two females (16%) perpetrated exclusively against nonfamily members (e.g., neighbor children, same-age peers). Only one of the females perpetrated against both a family member and a nonfamily member. None of the victims were strangers to the female perpetrators. Finally, all but one of the female offenders perpetrated while in a caregiving situation; the remaining offender perpetrated against a same-age peer during a sleepover.

Cognitive Functioning. With the exception of three of the perpetrators, the adolescent females fell within the average range of intellectual functioning (mean Full Scale IQ [FSIQ] = 95.3, Standard Deviation [*SD*] = 9.7, range 81 to 108). However, the clear majority (83%) evidenced academic difficulties (i.e., failing grades). One-third of the offenders had been retained a grade on at least one occasion. Only one of the female offenders was classified as learning disabled. All but one had significant problems with peers at school (e.g., physical altercations). Two-thirds of the females (67%) had been suspended or expelled from school at least once for incidents such as smoking and aggression toward teachers and/or peers.

Delinquency. The adolescent females were found to have engaged in a variety of delinquent behaviors as well. Nine of the female perpetrators (75%) had histories of alcohol abuse, and seven of the females (58%) had a history of drug use. More than half the offenders (58%) had run away from home, and one-third (33%) had been arrested for stealing. In addition, seven of the females (58%) had a history of truancy.

Psychiatric Diagnoses. Axis I diagnoses of the females at the time of their admissions included the following: conduct disorder, oppositional-defiant disorder, major depression, PTSD, adjustment disorder, and chemical dependency (American Psychiatric Association, 1994). Four of the females (33%) had previous inpatient hospitalizations, and 10 (83%) had received prior psychological services on an outpatient basis. One-third of the perpetrators (33%) had a history of such self-mutilative behaviors as carving; more than half (58%) had made prior suicide attempts. Ten (83%) had a history of depression. Two-thirds of the offenders (67%) were seen by their families, teachers, and/or prior mental health professionals as having anger control problems, and all participants reported low self-concept.

Social Relations. Nine of the perpetrators (75%) were described as significantly socially isolated, which may in part be due to the fact that two-thirds of the females (67%) had a history of aggressive behaviors toward peers. Over half (58%) were viewed as being sexually promiscuous, having had numerous sexual relations with older males.

Family Backgrounds. Dysfunctional and chaotic families of origin were common among the perpetrators. Fifty percent of the females came from homes in which domestic violence had occurred. The majority (83%) had at least one parent who abused alcohol or drugs, and nearly all came from divorced families. Each of the families reported a history of significant behavioral problems with their adolescent daughters (e.g., aggression, running away, incorrigibility, lying, and stealing).

Three-fourths of the adolescent females had been physically abused, either by parents/stepparents, grandparents, or foster parents. Furthermore, physical and emotional neglect were common among this group of adolescent females (42%).

Sexual Victimization. Of particular significance, all the adolescent female perpetrators had been sexually abused during childhood and/or adolescence. The mean age at the onset of their own sexual victimization was 7.5 years of age ($SD = 4.1$), with a range from 1 to 12 years of age. They tended to have been sexually abused by more than one person (mean = 2.6, mode = 2). Two (16%) had been abused only by nonfamily members; three (25%) were abused only by family members. Seven (58%) had been sexually abused by both a family member and a nonfamily member. It is important to note that the sexually abusive nonfamily members were either adult male friends of the family or boyfriends of the girls' mothers. The sexually abusive family members were generally fathers or stepfathers.

Continuing Questions

Although the findings of the aforementioned studies (Bumby & Bumby, 1993; Fehrenbach & Monastersky, 1988; Hunter et al., 1993) shed some light on the previously unexplored area of the adolescent female sexual offender, several questions remain unanswered. Most notably, it is unclear whether the adolescent female sexual offender is significantly different from nonoffending delinquent females or from adolescent male sexual offenders. Therefore, future research specifically including comparison samples of adolescent male sexual offenders and adolescent female and male nonsexual offenders is needed. Indeed, as Davis and Leitenberg (1987) reported, "We were not able to locate a single published study that systematically compared female and male adolescent sex offenders" (p. 421). In an attempt to address this concern, Bumby and Bumby (1995) identified additional female offenders for inclusion in their initial sample of females and utilized comparison samples of nonoffending females adolescents, as well as sex offending and non-sex offending adolescent males.

A Comparison Study

As was the case with the original sample, participants were juveniles in an inpatient psychiatric facility for emotionally and behaviorally disordered children and adolescents. Data was collected from the following four groups of juveniles: female sexual offenders ($n = 18$, mean age 14.9 years), female nonoffenders ($n = 36$, mean age 15.8 years), male sexual offenders ($n = 18$, mean age 13.2 years), and male nonoffenders (n = 24, mean age 14.7 years). Juveniles were classified as sexual offenders based on documented histories of sexual perpetration, which generally involved the victimization of younger family members.

Comprehensive record reviews were utilized to obtain the following: (1) standard clinical interviews focusing on family, school, criminal, and sexual histories; (2) standard psychological assessment batteries, which included the Minnesota Multiphasic Personality Inventory—Adolescent version (MMPI-A), Reynolds Adolescent Depression Scale, Suicidal Ideation Questionnaire, Revised Children's Manifest Anxiety Scale, and Piers Harris Self-Concept Scale; and (3) supplementary records consisting of individual and group therapy notes, school reports, court documents, and prior mental health records.

Psychological Test Results. On the MMPI-A, the mean t-scores of adolescent female sexual offenders suggested the presence of a variety of pathological symptoms and traits, including clinically significant elevations on the Depression, Psychopathic Deviate, Paranoia, Psychasthenia, Schizophrenia, and Mania subscales. In contrast to the female controls, only the Psychopathic Deviate, Paranoia, and Psychasthenia elevations were significantly higher for the female sexual offenders. No significant differences were found among the female sexual offenders, male sexual offenders, or male controls on these elevations.

The female sexual offenders reported significantly more anxiety than the female controls across the three subscales (physiological, worry/oversensitivity, social concerns) of the Revised—Children's Manifest Anxiety Scale (RCMAS). In addition, the female sexual offenders were significantly more anxious than the female controls based on their total RCMAS score. However, no significant differences were found on any of the RCMAS subscales or the total RCMAS score between the female sexual offenders and the male sexual offenders. Similarly, on the Piers-Harris Self Concept Scale, the total mean score revealed that the female sexual offenders had reported significantly lower overall self-concepts than did the female controls, but they did not report significantly lower self-concept than did the male sexual offenders. On the Reynolds Adolescent Depression Scale and Suicidal Ideation Questionnaire, the female sexual offenders respectively reported significantly more depressive symptoms and suicidal thoughts/behaviors than did the female controls. Again, no significant differences were revealed between the adolescent female sexual offenders and the adolescent male sexual offenders in depressive symptoms and suicidal thoughts/behaviors.

School Histories. An examination of school histories revealed the following: (1) female sexual offenders were retained at least one grade in school at a significantly higher rate than the male sexual offenders, but at no different rate from other controls, and (2) female sexual offenders had a higher truancy rate than the male sexual offenders but were not significantly different from the other controls. There were no significant differences between the proportion of female sexual offenders enrolled in special education classes and any of the control groups.

History of Delinquency. Delinquent behaviors (running away, stealing, alcohol abuse, drug abuse) were common among the female sexual offenders. However, there was not a significantly higher prevalence of delinquent behaviors within the female offenders group in comparison to the other control groups, with the exception of drug abuse. Female sexual offenders abused drugs at a higher rate than did the male sexual offenders, and no differences were found between female offenders and the other control groups. More than half the female offenders engaged in such self-destructive behaviors as promiscuity, suicidal gestures, and self-mutilation, although the only category in which the female sexual offenders were found to exhibit more difficulty was sexual promiscuity. In this instance, the female offenders were found to have more problems with promiscuity than were the male sexual offenders.

Abuse Histories. Finally, abuse histories of the samples were examined. High rates of physical and sexual victimization were revealed across the samples. Although the rates of physical abuse were not significantly different across the groups, a greater proportion of the female sexual offenders were sexually abused than in the female control, male sexual offender, and male control groups. Indeed, all the female offenders were found to have been sexually abused, compared to approximately 78% of the female controls, 63% of the male sexual offenders, and 55% of the male controls.

Summary of Findings

The data suggested that the adolescent female sexual offenders (1) were emotionally disturbed, reporting a variety of anxiety-related, depressive, and suicidal symptomatology; (2) evidenced pathological personality traits; (3) had low self-concepts; (4) engaged in a variety of self-destructive and delinquent behaviors; and (5) experienced physical and sexual abuse. The female sexual offenders were similar to the male sexual offenders on measures of depression, anxiety, suicidal ideation, self-concept, and personality characteristics, often evidencing more maladjustment than the non-sex offending juveniles. Variables such as school history, delinquent behaviors, and self-destructive behaviors, which were generally comparable among the female and male sex offenders, did not clearly distinguish them from the control groups. However, particularly noteworthy was the rate of sexual victimization, which clearly differentiated the female sex offenders from the male sex offender and nonoffending samples.

Identification of Risk Factors

It is important to note that the aforementioned studies are limited by sample size and subpopulation of juveniles (i.e., emotionally/behaviorally disordered juveniles). Nevertheless, in combination with previous research, the current findings suggest several risk factors to be considered in the assessment and treatment of adolescent female sexual offenders, such as depression, suicidal ideation, anxiety, and poor self-concept. Perhaps the most salient risk factor is related to the high proportion of sexual abuse found among the sample of adolescent female perpetrators, implying the existence of an association between victims and victimizers.

The Information Processing of Trauma Model

Understanding the relationship between childhood sexual victimization and later sexual perpetration is certainly a challenging endeavor. Indeed, it is virtually impossible to determine causality from such examinations. It is important to consider that sexual victimization should not be used as an "excuse" for committing sexual offenses, especially as most victims who are abused do not go on to victimize others. However, given the comorbidity of childhood sexual victimization among adolescent female sexual offenders, exploring the potential relationship between the two may be beneficial in developing etiological hypotheses when considering the adolescent female sexual offender.

In recent years, various frameworks for conceptualizing the effects of and responses to child sexual abuse have been postulated. Such frameworks may be particularly useful when attempting to understand the sexually aggressive behaviors of young children and adolescents with histories of sexual victimization. It has been suggested that sexually abused youth may perpetuate or reenact their own victimization on younger children, creating new victims and the potential for new, younger perpetrators (Cantwell, 1988; Friedrich & Luecke, 1988; Johnson, 1988, 1989).

One framework that may have utility in undertaking this challenge is the information processing of trauma model (IPTM), proposed by Burgess and her colleagues (Burgess, Hartman, McCausland, & Powers, 1984; Burgess, Hartman, & McCormack, 1987; Burgess, Johnson, & van der Kolk, 1993; Hartman & Burgess, 1988, 1993). The four contextual phases of this comprehensive approach take into account a variety of factors prior to, during, and following a traumatic event such as sexual abuse, which may mediate the manner in which an individual responds to, or deals with, the abusive experience.

Pretrauma Phase. The pretrauma phase considers a variety of individual and social variables (e.g., age, development, emotional adjustment, family dynamics, parental attitudes, and behaviors) prior to the abuse.

Trauma Encapsulation Phase. Next, the trauma encapsulation phase takes into account the complex factors affecting the child and focuses on the abusive experience and the defense mechanisms used to cope with the resultant anxiety from the abusive experience. Trauma learning and trauma replay (e.g., reenactment, repetition, and displacement of the abuse) may occur during this phase.

Disclosure Phase. The disclosure phase occurs when the victim reveals that abuse has occurred. At this point, the potential for the family and social context to influence the manner in which the child responds to the trauma is acknowledged. The responses of significant others may either resolve the trauma or intensify it through further stressful encounters.

Posttrauma Phase. Finally, the posttrauma phase delineates a continuum of response patterns to the abuse and subsequent disclosure. The respective ends of the continuum are the integrated response, whereby the child masters the anxiety and is generally asymptomatic, and the aggressive response, whereby the child experiences considerable anxiety-related symptoms and masters the anxiety surrounding the abuse by exploiting others (typically younger persons) and adopting an isolative, antisocial, and aggressive position toward peers, family, and school.

Studying the IPTM With Adolescent Abuse Victims

In an attempt to explore the association between victimization and posttrauma outcomes in adolescents by utilizing the IPT framework, Bumby, Burgess, and colleagues examined the records of 56 randomly selected adolescents (36 females and 20 males) from a larger sample of adolescents, all of whom had a history of both physical and sexual abuse (Bumby et al., 1994). The mean age of the sample was 14.4 years ($SD = 2.2$), with a range of 9 to 18 years. The mean educational level of the adolescents was 8.8 years ($SD = 1.9$), range 4 to 12 years. Axis I diagnoses of the adolescents included the following: depressive disorders (59.3%), PTSD (53.7%), oppositional-defiant disorder (32.7%), conduct disorder (30.2%), adjustment disorder (30.2%), and chemical dependency (26.4%) (American Psychiatric Association, 1994). Statistical analyses revealed virtually no significant differences between the males and females on the variables of interest, and, consequently, the findings are presented for males and females combined.

Phase 1: Pretrauma. The mean age of the onset of sexual abuse was 9.5 years. The majority of these youth came from chaotic and unstable homes where considerable violence and substance abuse occurred; approximately 40% witnessed domestic violence. The majority of these adolescents had at least one alcoholic parent. The intellectual functioning of these youth was generally within the average range (mean Wechsler FSIQ = 95.8) (Wechsler, 1981).

Phase 2: Trauma Encapsulation. Both the physical abuse and sexual abuse were typically perpetrated by a family member, generally the parent or stepparent. The adolescents tended to have been sexually assaulted by more than one abuser on numerous occasions. Trauma replay, in the form of reenactment and repetition, was evident. For example, 42.9% of the adolescents went on to sexually offend. Of those adolescents who committed sexual offenses, 87% perpetrated against younger family members (e.g., siblings, cousins, and nieces/nephews), and 31.6% perpetrated against younger nonfamily members or peers. The clear majority of these adolescents were also physically aggressive toward family members (89.1%) and more than two-thirds (67.9%) were physically aggressive toward peers. More than half the adolescent males and females were diagnosed with PTSD, suggesting that these adolescents were experiencing considerable anxiety and difficulties associated with the abuse.

Phase 3: Disclosure. In many of the cases, even following disclosure of their own victimization, the adult perpetrators continued to abuse these youth. In part, this was a result of (1) the parent's lack of belief in the allegations, (2) complete denial of the allegations, and (3) blaming the child victim. When social services intervened, several of the mothers failed to protect the child by choosing to allow the adult perpetrator (often a spouse or boyfriend) to remain in the home over keeping the child; hence, several of these victims were considered "throwaway" children. Twenty percent of the adolescents were subsequently placed in foster care.

Phase 4: Posttrauma Outcome. In general, the adolescents were found to manifest academic and peer difficulties, depressive and anxiety-related symptomatology, delinquency, and substance abuse. Moreover, these adolescents tended to manifest isolative and antisocial behaviors toward school, peers, and family. The majority of the adolescents acted out in a physically aggressive manner, and a large proportion were sexually aggressive as well. Consistent with the proposed IPTM, the findings suggested that myriad contextual factors may affect responses to abuse. Specifically, the impact of multiple traumas (i.e., both physical and sexual abuse), chaotic family environments, and negative familial reactions on disclosure of abuse appeared to be related to aggressive responses of adolescent victims of physical and sexual abuse.

Studying the IPTM With Sexually Aggressive Adolescent Females

In another investigation, the IPT framework was applied specifically to an inpatient sample of 18 sexually aggressive females, all of whom had been sexually victimized themselves (Bumby, Bumby, Burgess, & Hartman, 1996). The data indicated that the adolescent female offenders came from extremely chaotic and dysfunctional homes where domestic violence, parental drug and alcohol abuse, emotionally disturbed parents, and polyabuse of children occurred (pretrauma phase). As the IPTM suggests, the combination of these factors increases the likelihood of a more negative impact of and/or aggressive outcome/reaction to the trauma of having been victimized. Second, the females were often sexually abused by more than one perpetrator, with the abuse typically beginning at an early age and lasting for extended periods (trauma phase).

They evidenced considerable depressive and anxiety-related symptoms; fragmentation and trauma replay, reenactment, and displacement were shown by the females, who universally utilized reenactment and displacement of sexual aggression against younger children within their families (trauma encapsulation phase). As these females came from unstable, chaotic, and abusive households, the likelihood of successfully "mastering" the anxiety related to the abuse following disclosure of the abuse was already low. The adult perpetrators were typically the mother's boyfriend or the adolescent female's father/stepfather. When disclosing their sexual victimization, many of the adolescent females were rejected, ignored, discounted, and/or blamed by the mother or other family members and were often held "responsible" for their own victimization (e.g., "She is promiscuous/seductive," "She asked for it," and "She walked around looking for trouble") (disclosure phase). The aggressive posttrauma outcome was clearly evidenced by the female perpetrators, given their propensity for repetition of sexually aggressive behaviors on younger children, physical aggression toward peers, social isolation, and numerous emotional and behavioral difficulties (posttrauma phase).

In summary, previous investigators, supported by the aforementioned findings utilizing the IPTM, suggest an association between childhood sexual abuse and the development of sexually aggressive behaviors in adolescence for some at-risk females (Bumby et al., 1996; Burgess et al., 1987; Burgess et al., 1993; Cantwell, 1988; Friedrich & Luecke, 1988; Higgs, Canavan & Meyer, 1992; Hunter et al., 1993; Knopp & Lackey, 1989; Matthews et al., 1991). Specifically, sexually aggressive posttrauma outcomes appear to be associated with various factors (e.g., individual and family/social variables and reaction to disclosure) surrounding the abusive experience. Implications for therapeutic interventions include the following: (1) identifying and interrupting child sexual abuse; (2) understanding the organization of the victim's defensive structure and its relationship to abuse; (3) modifying the psychological defenses so that the victim can tolerate discussing abuse; (4) unlinking the trauma at sensory, perceptual, and cognitive levels from dysfunctional behaviors; (5) processing the integrated trauma to past memory; and (6) rebuilding coping behaviors that provide for a positive interaction with the future (Burgess et al., 1987; Hartman & Burgess, 1988, 1993).

Conclusion

Female sexual offenders have received very little attention in empirical studies of sexual offenders—adolescent females have received the least attention. The current state of the literature is plagued by small sample sizes and samples of populations which may not necessarily represent female sexual offenders in general. Nonetheless, the present review of the current findings regarding adolescent female sexual offenders suggests the following:

1. Adolescent female offenders tend to commit multiple acts of sexual abuse against younger family members, often in caregiving situations. This is consistent with the previous research on adolescent female and male sexual offenders as well as adult female sexual offenders (Fehrenbach et al., 1986; Margolin, 1991; Finkelhor et al., 1988; Margolin, 1991; McCarty, 1986; Chasnoff et al., 1986).
2. Adolescent female offenders tend to be of average intelligence but manifest academic difficulties. Earlier research on both adult and youthful female and male sexual offenders (Awad, Saunders, & Levene, 1984; Fehrenbach et al., 1986; Davis & Leitenberg, 1987; Matthews et al., 1991; Friedrich & Luecke, 1988; Faller, 1987) has revealed histories of academic and behavioral difficulties in school.
3. Adolescent female offenders may engage in a variety of delinquent behaviors, including substance abuse. Substance abuse has been found to be common among adult female offenders (Faller, 1987; Matthews et al., 1991; McCarty, 1986; O'Connor, 1987; Rowan et al., 1990) and adult and adolescent male offenders (Awad et al., 1984; Ballard et al., 1990; Becker, Kaplan, Cunningham-Rathner, & Kavoussi, 1986; Fehrenbach et al., 1986).
4. Adolescent female offenders suffer from emotional and psychological difficulties, most often evidenced by suicide attempts, anxiety, depression, and PTSD, similar to the emotional disturbances found among adult female offenders (Faller, 1987; McCarty, 1986; O'Connor, 1987; Rowan et al., 1990; Travin et al., 1990). Similarly, psychiatric and emotional disturbance have been reported among samples of adolescent male sexual offenders (Awad et al., 1984; Becker, Kaplan et al., 1986; Davis & Leitenberg, 1987).
5. Adolescent female offenders come from chaotic households where parental instability, domestic violence, substance abuse, and numerous forms of maltreatment occur. Such familial chaos is commonly reported in studies of adult and adolescent female and male sexual offenders (Awad et al., 1984; Ballard et al., 1990; Becker, Cunningham-Rathner, & Kaplan, 1986; Davis & Leitenberg, 1987; Fehrenbach et al., 1986; Johnson, 1988, 1989; Longo, 1982; Matthews et al., 1991; Pithers & Cummings, 1989).

6. Adolescent female offenders tend to have been victims of sexual abuse themselves, often at the hands of more than one offender. In addition, this abuse typically begins at an early age and happens on multiple occasions. Female offenders may report sexual arousal to their own victimization and may reenact their own histories of victimization. This is one of the most significant considerations when examining female sexual offenders. In the existing studies of female sexual offenders, nearly 100% of the female offenders reported having been sexually victimized (Cantwell, 1988; Friedrich & Luecke, 1988; Johnson, 1989; Knopp & Lackey, 1987; Matthews et al., 1991; McCarty, 1986; Rowan et al., 1990; Travin et al., 1990; Wakefield & Underwager, 1991).

Histories of childhood sexual victimization have been reported in samples of adolescent male perpetrators as well, although the victimization rates for the female offenders are considerably higher than those found among adult and adolescent male sexual offenders (Awad et al., 1984; Ballard et al., 1990; Becker, Kaplan et al., 1986; Davis & Leitenberg, 1987; Fehrenbach et al., 1986; Longo, 1982; Pithers & Cummings, 1989). Hence, it is possible that a history of sexual victimization may be more etiologically influential in the case of the adolescent female offender.

Juvenile female sexual offenders have often been overlooked in the literature with respect to appropriate comparison samples. The current review suggests that whereas juvenile female sexual offenders resemble juvenile male sexual offenders on a variety of dimensions (e.g., emotional disturbance such as depression, anxiety, and suicidal ideation; low-self-concept; and maladaptive personality characteristics), they may not differ from other emotionally and behaviorally disturbed juveniles on other characteristics (e.g., delinquency, alcohol abuse, academic difficulties, and physical abuse history). However, a history of sexual victimization may be more etiologically significant for juvenile female sexual offenders.

Clearly, considerable room remains for growth in the study of this significant but relatively unexamined group of offenders. Although the research on females perpetrators is gradually increasing, there is room for much more. Optimistically, some of the existing professional and societal biases that have inhibited the reporting and recognition of sexual offending by females may be lessening. Hence, the assumed low rates of female sexual offending need not remain a barrier to further research on this smaller, yet very significant group of sexual offenders.

References

Allen, C. M. (1991). Women as perpetrators of child sexual abuse: Recognition barriers. In A. L. Horton, B. L. Johnson, L. M. Roundy, & D. Williams (Eds.), *The incest perpetrator: A family member no one wants to treat* (pp. 108–125). Newbury Park, CA: Sage.

American Psychiatric Association. (1994). *Diagnostic and statistical manual of mental disorders* (4th ed.). Washington, DC: Author.

Awad, G., Saunders, E., & Levene, J. (1984). A clinical study of male adolescent sexual offenders. *International Journal of Offender Therapy and Comparative Criminology, 28,* 105–116.

Ballard, D. T., Blair, G. D., Devereaux, S., Valentine, L. K., Horton, A. L., & Johnson, B. L. (1990). A comparative profile of the incest perpetrator: Background characteristics, abuse history, and use of social skills. In A. L. Horton, B. L. Johnson, L. M. Roundy, & D. Williams (Eds.), *The incest perpetrator: A family member no one wants to treat* (pp. 43–64). Newbury Park, CA: Sage.

Becker, J. V., Cunningham-Rathner, J., & Kaplan, M. S. (1986). Adolescent sexual offenders: Demographics, criminal and sexual histories, and recommendations for reducing future offenses. *Journal of Interpersonal Violence, 1*, 431–445.

Becker, J. V., Kaplan, M. S., Cunningham-Rathner, J., & Kavoussi, R. (1986). Characteristics of adolescent incest perpetrators: Preliminary findings. *Journal of Family Violence, 1*, 85–97.

Bumby, K. M., & Bumby, N. H. (1993, November). *Adolescent females who sexually perpetrate: Preliminary findings.* Paper presented at the 12th annual Research and Treatment Conference of the Association for the Treatment of Sexual Abusers, Boston.

Bumby, K. M., & Bumby, N. H. (1995, October). *Emotional, behavioral, and developmental comparisons between juvenile female sexual offenders and nonoffenders.* Paper presented at the 14th annual Research and Treatment Conference of the Association for the Treatment of Sexual Abusers, New Orleans.

Bumby, K. M., Bumby, N. H., Burgess, A. W., & Hartman, C. R. (1996). *From victims to victimizers: Sexually aggressive post-traumatic responses of sexually abused adolescent females.* Manuscript in preparation.

Bumby, K. M., Burgess, A. W., Hartman, C. R., Bumby, N. H., Raney, T. J., & McAuliff, B. D. (1994, July). *The information processing of trauma model and adolescent aggressive response patterns to physical and sexual abuse.* Paper presented at the 1994 National Conference on Family Violence: Research and Practice, Omaha, NE.

Burgess, A. W., Hartman, C. R., McCausland, M. P., & Powers, P. (1984). Response patterns in children and adolescents exploited through sex rings and pornography. *American Journal of Psychiatry, 141*, 656–662.

Burgess, A. W., Hartman, C. R., & McCormack, A. (1987). Abused to abuser: Antecedents of socially deviant behaviors. *American Journal of Psychiatry, 144*, 1431–1436.

Burgess, A. W., Johnson, T. C., & van der Kolk, B. (1993, November). *Childhood trauma and aggressive outcome.* Paper presented at the 12th annual Research and Treatment Conference of the Association for the Treatment of Sexual Abusers, Boston.

Cantwell, H. B. (1988). Child sexual abuse: Very young perpetrators. *Child Abuse and Neglect, 12*, 579–582.

Chasnoff, I. J., Burns, W. J., Schnoll, S. H., Burns, K., Chisum, G., Kyle-Sproe, L. (1986). Maternal-neonatal incest. *American Journal of Orthopsychiatry, 56*, 577–580.

Davis, G., & Leitenberg, H. (1987). *Adolescent sex offenders. Psychological Bulletin, 101*, 417–427.

Faller, K. (1987). Women who sexually abuse children. *Violence and Victims, 2*, 263–276.

Federal Bureau of Investigation. (1991). *Uniform crime reports for the United States, 1990.* Washington, DC: Author.

Fehrenbach, P. A., & Monastersky, C. (1988). Characteristics of female sexual offenders. *American Journal of Orthopsychiatry, 58*, 148–151.

Fehrenbach, P. A., Smith, W., Monastersky, C., & Deisher, R. W. (1986). Adolescent sexual offenders: Offender and offense characteristics. *American Journal of Orthopsychiatry, 56*, 225–233.

Finkelhor, D., & Russell, D. (1984). Women as perpetrators: Review of the evidence. In D. Finkelhor (Ed.), *Child sexual abuse: New theory and research* (pp. 171–187). New York: Free Press.

Finkelhor, D., Williams, L. M., & Burns, N. (1988). *Nursery crimes: Sexual abuse in day care.* Newbury Park, CA: Sage.

Friedrich, W. N., & Luecke, W. J. (1988). Young school-age sexually aggressive children. *Professional Psychology: Research and Practice, 19*, 155–164.

Fromuth, M. E., & Burkhart, B. R. (1987). Childhood sexual victimization among college men: Definitional and methodological issues. *Violence and Victims, 2*, 241–253.

Green, A., & Kaplan, M. (1994). Psychiatric impairment and childhood victimization experiences in female child molesters. *Journal of the American Academy of Child and Adolescent Psychiatry, 33*, 954–961.

Hartman, C. R., & Burgess, A. W. (1988). Information processing of trauma: Case application of a model. *Journal of Interpersonal Violence, 3*, 443–457.

Hartman, C. R., & Burgess, A. W. (1993). Information processing of trauma. *Child Abuse and Neglect, 17,* 47–58.

Higgs, D. C., Canavan, M. M., & Meyer, W. J. (1992). Moving from defense to offense: The development of an adolescent female sex offender. *Journal of Sex Research, 29,* 131–139.

Hunter, J. A., Lexier, L. J., Goodwin, D. W., Browne, P. A., & Dennis, C. (1993). Psychosexual, attitudinal, and developmental characteristics of juvenile female sexual perpetrators in a residential treatment setting. *Journal of Child and Family Studies, 2,* 317–326.

Johnson, T. C. (1988). Child perpetrators: Children who molest other children: Preliminary findings. *Child Abuse and Neglect, 12,* 219–229.

Johnson, T. C. (1989). Female child perpetrators: Children who molest other children. *Child Abuse and Neglect, 13,* 571–585.

Kaplan, M. S., & Green, A. (1995). Incarcerated female sexual offenders: A comparison of sexual histories with eleven female nonsexual offenders. *Sexual Abuse: A Journal of Research and Treatment, 7,* 287–300.

Knopp, F., & Lackey, L. (1989). *Female sexual abusers: A summary of data from 44 treatment providers.* Orwell, VT: Safer Society Press.

Longo, R. E. (1982). Sexual learning and experience among adolescent sexual offenders. *International Journal of Offender Therapy and Comparative Criminology, 26,* 235–241.

Margolin, L. (1991). Child sexual abuse by nonrelated caregivers. *Child Abuse and Neglect, 15,* 213–221.

Matthews, J. K., Mathews, R., & Speltz, K. (1991). Female sexual offenders: A typology. In M. K. Patton (Ed.), *Family sexual abuse: Frontline research and evaluation* (pp. 199–219). Newbury Park, CA: Sage.

McCarty, L. (1986). Mother-child incest: Characteristics of the offender. Child Welfare, 65, 447–458.

O'Connor, A. A. (1987). Female sex offenders. *British Journal of Psychiatry, 150,* 615–620.

Office of Juvenile Justice and Prevention. (1992). *Juvenile offending and victimization: A national report.* Washington, DC: Author.

Pithers, W. D., & Cummings, G. F. (1989). Can relapse be prevented? Initial outcome data from the Vermont Treatment Program for sexual aggressors. In D. Lewis (Ed.), *Relapse prevention with sex offenders* (pp. 313–325). New York: Guilford Press.

Risin, L. I., & Koss, M. P. (1987). The sexual abuse of boys: Prevalence and descriptive characteristics of childhood victimizations. *Journal of Interpersonal Violence, 2,* 309–323.

Rowan, E. L., Rowan, J. B., & Langelier, P. (1990). Women who molest children. Bulletin of the *American Academy of Psychiatry and Law, 18,* 79–83.

Travin, S., & Cullin, K., & Protter, B. (1990). Female sex offenders: Severe victims and victimizers. *Journal of Forensic Sciences, 35,* 140–150.

Wakefield, H., & Underwager, R. (1991). Female child sexual abusers: A critical review of the literature. *American Journal of Forensic Psychology, 9,* 43–69.

Wechsler, D. W. (1981). *Wechsler Adult Intelligence Scale—Revised.* New York: Psychological Corporation.

Chapter 11

Juvenile Sex Offender Psychometric Assessment

by B. D. Kraemer, Ph.D., C. R. Spielman, M.A., and S. B. Salisbury, B.S

Overview

Psychological tests add a critical dimension to the comprehensive assessment of juvenile sex offenders. Clinical interviews and historical information provide a foundation from which an adolescent's offense behavior can be interpreted. Psychometric assessment adds a norm-based reference that can assist in determining placement in an appropriate treatment modality, developing a viable treatment plan, and assessing treatment progress.

A comprehensive test battery used to assess juvenile sex offenders needs to be cost- and time-efficient; demonstrate reliability, validity, and utility; and be age appropriate. To increase predictive power, testers prefer a battery of tests over a single instrument. A basic test battery should assess all clients and can be supplemented with more specialized testing when additional information is needed.

This chapter provides a sample test battery. This battery is currently being used at Mille Lacs Academy, a Nexus treatment program located in Onamia, Minnesota. Mille Lacs Academy/Nexus is a private, not-for-profit inpatient facility that treats juvenile males ages 11 to 18 who have committed sexual offenses or engaged in harmful sexual behaviors. Referrals are received from the court system, social services, mental health agencies, other treatment programs, and private parties. Mille Lacs Academy/Nexus residents typically have a history of unsuccessful prior placements and treatment failures. The average length of treatment is 12 to 18 months. To ensure a smooth transition from residential living back into the community, relapse prevention and discharge planning are critical components of every resident's treatment plan.

Domains of Functioning

The Mille Lacs Academy/Nexus test battery is a group of psychometric tests designed to provide a comprehensive psychological assessment of the juvenile male sex offender. This assessment is used not only to provide an objective picture of the current psychological functioning of the juvenile but also to identify relevant treatment issues, develop a treatment plan, and monitor progress throughout treatment. The following test domains are included in the assessment battery:

- Intellectual/neurological assessment
- Personality functioning/psychopathology
- Behavioral assessment
- Sexual deviance

Intellectual/Neurological Assessment. Testers assess intelligence to screen for mental retardation or borderline intelligence. They also use intellectual assessment to screen for information processing problems associated with neurological problems, brain injury, attention-deficit disorder, or learning disabilities. This information helps determine the juvenile's ability to understand abstract treatment concepts and gauge the likelihood of benefiting from insight-oriented psychotherapy.

The Slosson Intelligence Test—Revised (SIT-R) (Slosson, 1991) is used in the Mille Lacs Academy/Nexus basic test battery to measure intelligence. The Bender-Gestalt and the Test of Variables of Attention (TOVA) are used as supplemental tests for possible neurological impairment and attention-deficit hyperactivity disorder.

Personality Functioning/Psychopathology. The domain of personality functioning/psychopathology is used to identify personality characteristics and patterns, assess current personality functioning, and suggest possible psychiatric diagnoses. Identifying depressive symptomatology is of particular importance because of the pervasive nature of the mood disorder in the juvenile population.

The Millon Adolescent Clinical Inventory (MACI) is used in the Mille Lacs Academy/Nexus basic test battery to assess personality functioning in adolescents ages 13 to 19. The Roberts Apperception Test for Children (RATC) is used for clients 6 to 12 years old. The Minnesota Multiphasic Personality Inventory—Adolescent (MMPI-A) is used as a supplemental test when indicated. The Reynolds Adolescent Depression Scale (RADS) or the Reynolds Child Adolescent Depression Scale (RCDS) is used in the Mille Lacs Academy/Nexus basic test battery to screen for depressive symptomatology.

Behavioral Assessment. The behavioral domain is assessed through the classification system of I-level theory. I-level theory identifies personal characteristics, behaviors, and the meaning of behaviors (particularly delinquent behaviors), as well as the type of intervention most appropriate for a particular client. I-level theory also predicts the interaction between client type and therapeutic intervention, which increases the likelihood for successful therapeutic intervention. Determining the limits of a client's perceptual differentiation facilitates the task of identifying treatment issues and interventions.

I-level theory is a cognitive and social developmental theory that proposes a normal (not pathology-based) childhood developmental progression, starting with a level characterized by minimal perceptual differentiation between self and others, culminating at the highest level with a maximal level of differentiation of the environment and consequent integration of perception. This perceptual framework is consistent, ordered, and predictable. The initial theory outlines seven successive levels of development of integration. In short, I-level theory is a social/perceptual frame of reference through which individuals view themselves, the world, and the interaction between them.

Because the model is developmental, the individual incorporates gradually expanding experiences, expectations, and perceptions, cognitively restructuring these new experiences into higher levels of integration. Higher levels represent less distortion, finer and more discriminations among persons, greater self-awareness, and increased understanding of the motivations of both self and others. Greater reliance on internalized values as behavioral guides, increased autonomy and increased integration of perceptions into a unified, more accurate understanding of the world are also noted at higher levels of interpersonal maturity. Although I-level theory identifies levels of I-1 through I-7, virtually all juvenile offenders fall into the I-2, I-3, and I-4 categories. I-levels are based on an individual's way of perceiving the world; subtypes within each I-level category characterize the individual's typical mode of response to his or her view of the world. The Jesness Inventory (JI) is used in the Mille Lacs Academy/Nexus basic test battery to assess the behavioral domain and identify I-level and subtype.

Sexual Deviance. Areas identified as important in understanding the domain of sexual deviance are sexual behavior for which there are legal concerns (child molestation, rape, exhibitionism, etc.), sexual behavior for which there are cultural or clinical concerns but which may not be illegal (transvestism, bondage and discipline, fetish behaviors, gender identity, sexual orientation, etc.), and behavioral and cognitive progressions of sex offenders, justifications, cognitive distortions and other defenses used, and treatment attitudes.

The Multiphasic Sex Inventory—Juvenile—Revised (MSI-J-R) is the instrument used to assess the domain of sexual deviance.

Test Battery

Tests chosen to measure the aforementioned psychometric domains thought to be important in the assessment of adolescent sex offenders include the JI, RADS, MACI, and MSI-J-R. These instruments were chosen as a primary test battery; other more specialized tests, including the TOVA, Bender-Gestalt, and MMPI-A, are given when required.

The core tests were chosen for inclusion in a basic test battery because of their pervasive use with juvenile populations and their high published levels of reliability and validity. A more detailed description of each test follows.

The Jesness Inventory. The JI is the test instrument currently used at Mille Lacs Academy/Nexus to identify I-level and differential intervention for each juvenile. The JI consists of 155 true-false personality items used to classify offenders. The JI predicts delinquency and monitors a juvenile's psychological change over time. The original Jesness norming sample consisted of 970 adjudicated offenders and 1,075 nonoffenders drawn from 10 public schools in California. These scales were derived with cluster analysis, regression, or multiple discriminant analysis.

Of the 11 personality characteristics measured by the Jesness, 5 measure the aforementioned factors shown in the literature as being useful in predictors of treatment outcome (Saunders & Davies 1976; Shark & Handel, 1977). These scales include Social Maladjustment, which is a measure of self-esteem; Autism, a measure of impulsivity; Manifest Aggression, a measure of aggressive tendencies; Alienation, which is a measure of social coping; and I-level, a composite measure of social maturity. The JI is computer-scored with software available from Multi-Health Systems, the test manufacturer. When the classification of I-level appears to fit an I-4 category but the Jesness Denial subscale is above two standard deviations from the mean, Mille Lacs Academy classifies profiles at the next highest I-3 t-score elevation. Further ambiguities are resolved using scoring criteria outlined by Jesness (1966, 1991).

Reynolds Depression Scales—Adolescent and Child Forms. The RADS is composed of 30 items selected based on criteria for depression and dysthymia according to the third edition of the Diagnostic and Statistical Manual for Mental Disorders (DSM-III; American Psychiatric Association, 1980), as well as symptoms specified by other measures of both adult and childhood depression. Reynolds reports acceptable reliability and validity. Some 8,000 adolescents were included in the original standardization sample. Norms are provided for male and female juveniles in grades 7 to 12. A cumulative raw score is converted to a percentile based on these published norms.

The RCDS also uses 30 items and is a downward revision of the original RADS. The RCDS is used for male and female children in grades 1 through 6. The author reports acceptable reliability and validity. A total sample of 1,547 was used to develop norms for the RCDS. This sample included both girls and boys and was composed of 1,121 Caucasians, 291 blacks, 76 Hispanics, and 59 Asians. Like the RADS, a single raw score is computed, transformed into a percentile based on these normative subgroups. The RADS is scored using templates available from the author.

Millon Adolescent Clinical Inventory. The MACI is a measure of personality similar in appearance to the MMPI-A. The MACI is based on Millon's theories of personality, including domains of personality such as pleasure-deficient, interpersonally imbalanced, intrapsychically conflicted, and structurally defective. Within these overall personality types, subcategories of personality disorders are classified.

Multiphasic Sex Inventory—Juvenile—Revised. One of the few sex offender-specific measures of thought and behavior that has been used to predict treatment outcome is the MSI (Simkins, Ward, Bowman, & Rinck, 1989). Nichols and Molinder (1984) developed the MSI as a self-report questionnaire designed to assess a wide range of psychosexual characteristics of individuals with a history of sexually abusive behaviors. The juvenile version of the MSI, the MSI-J-R, is an experimental form of the test as empirical scales and juvenile norms are still being developed. Two highly utilized MSI-J-R subscales are the Sexual Obsessions subscale (SOS), a measure of preoccupation with sexual thought, and the Sexual Assault Behavior subscale (SAB), a measure of the number of sexually inappropriate behaviors in which an adolescent has engaged. The MSI-J-R is scored using templates available from the authors.

Clinical Uses of Test Battery Information

A good psychological test battery provides much useful information during the evaluation phase of treatment. Facets of interest include the following:

- Psychopathology, if present, type, and severity
- Problem areas in need of focus
- Resistance/openness to treatment
- Client beliefs regarding offending behaviors
- Potential barriers to treatment success
- Interventions most likely to be useful

Together, these factors give the clinician an estimate of a particular client's likelihood of success, a method of maximizing a client's potential to succeed, and a means of delivering the highest-quality services in an economically feasible time period. The sample test battery provided in this chapter gives the clinician an estimate of each of the aforementioned factors.

Client Psychopathology

Very high scores (above 70) on the JI Autism (Au) subscale often characterize individuals with egocentric perceptions, markedly differing at times from reality.

These youths tend to display very hostile-aggressive behaviors, are emotionally labile, and have poor relationships with staff members (Jesness, 1991).

The Clinical Syndromes subscales on the MACI are also useful in this regard in identifying psychopathology. Both the Paranoid and the Schizoid personality patterns on the MACI typically characterize individuals who have problems relating to others, are emotionally labile, and are reclusive (Millon, 1996).

High scores on the RADS portend extreme emotional distress in need of immediate attention (Reynolds, 1987). Of special concern are "critical item" responses that signify disturbance in eating patterns, thoughts of self-harm, feelings of hopelessness, and feelings of alienation.

MSI-J-R responses that signify high levels of distortion and justification of sexually inappropriate behaviors are cause for concern. The reverse side of the MSI-J-R protocol form highlights questions for discussion (Nichols & Molinder, 1984).

Client psychopathology, when present, is also frequently manifested in the form of bizarre responses or unusual written comments in the margins of test materials. Such comments are often useful means to explore a client's way of thinking.

Problem Areas

Clients identify areas of significant concern when taking psychological test batteries. Of these areas, particular attention should be paid to profile scatter. Relatively high profile elevations in most areas tested tend to indicate psychological instability, lack of behavioral predictability, and deficits in treatment readiness. By contrast, relatively low profiles in most test areas other than denial usually indicate reluctance to engage in treatment, lack of awareness of problem areas, repression of problem areas, or denial of interpersonal crisis. These types of client may engage in physically aggressive behaviors when pressed to discuss treatment issues they are unwilling to examine. A good psychological profile serves as a road map for treatment, plotting both detours that should be taken and access to the most direct means of problem resolution.

Resistance/Openness to Treatment. A tendency to deny problem areas on psychological tests is as significant clinically as is high item endorsement. Systematically low scores in any one area signify areas of potential impasse in therapy. Significantly low scores on the Jesness Ma (Manifest Aggression) subscale, combined with a significant elevation on the conforming subscale of the MACI, for example, may signify a juvenile sex offender who is reluctant to voice disagreement with others. When pressed, he may resort to passive-aggressive means of anger expression, sabotage of further treatment efforts by regression to more primitive behavioral patterns, or, in extreme cases, overtly aggressive actions.

Client Beliefs Regarding Offending Behaviors. The MSI-J-R and the Jesness Imm (immaturity) scale will give the clinician a good idea how to access the client's sexual thought patterns and beliefs. Test materials serve as a way to gather much information in a single session, with each area being fully explored during treatment. High elevations on the MSI-J-R Cognitive Distortion subscales and high Jesness Imm (immaturity) elevation, for example, may signify an offender who justifies involvement with younger children. Elevations on MSI-J-R Physical Disabilities or

Impotence subscales may signify an offender who believes himself to be deviant either psychologically or physically, unable to become fully aroused without sexually deviant materials.

Psychological testing with juvenile sex offenders should identify areas the juvenile is open to examining in treatment. Successful resolution of these areas may decrease client resistance to examining more intrusive problem areas.

Potential Barriers to Treatment Success

Once potential areas of impasse are delineated, the clinician can forge plans to bolster a client's chance of success. The adolescent who is reluctant to express anger openly, for example, may be encouraged to role-play generic expressions of anger before concentrating on sex-specific areas. Once the client becomes comfortable with expressing anger about neutral topic areas, he or she can begin to express anger appropriately about more volatile areas.

Approaches Most Likely to Be Successful

Psychological test profiles outline approaches most likely to be successful with juvenile offenders. The I-level typology, as discussed earlier, assesses an individual's social maturity level (Jesness, 1991). Behavioral approaches tend to be most successful with I-2s, who are rather egocentric and externally oriented. Cognitive therapies, such as reality therapy and rational emotive therapy, work well with I-3s who tend to get lost in faulty thought process and logic. Such insight-oriented approaches as psychoanalytic, Rogerian, and Adlerian therapies tend to work best with those at the I-4 level of interpersonal maturity. At this level, adolescents appear to think more like adults, can evaluate the reasons for their behavior, and have mature conceptions of guilt and empathy. By using the approach most suited for a juvenile's maturity level, the clinician maximizes treatment success.

Taken together, a good psychological profile provides the material for clinical interview. Test results should not be interpreted on the basis of profile data alone. An examination of the thought processes leading to the conclusions reached is as useful therapeutically as the conclusions themselves. The I-level typology, for example, outlines supplemental test questions to be used during the interview process. These questions help clinicians understand the mechanics of a particular client's view of the world.

Understanding the client from a phenomenological point of view is important in establishing rapport, which is the building block of treatment success. A well-designed and adroitly used psychological test battery helps to accomplish these goals.

Developing a Predictive Index of Treatment Outcome

Although careful examination of a test battery provides much useful information about treatment prognosis with juvenile sex offenders, prediction of treatment prognosis is still largely subjective in nature. An objective instrument predicts treatment outcome at a rate significantly higher than what would be derived by chance or subjective examination alone.

It is difficult to measure personality characteristics of potentially chronic offenders by mere observation. Rubin, LeMare, and Lollis (1990) epitomize this problem in their research of withdrawn children, noting that sociometric assessments of peer neglect, peer assessments of withdrawal, teacher assessments of withdrawal, and behavioral observations appear to be unreliable means of identifying withdrawn children. Durkin and Durkin (1975) also acknowledge this difficulty, suggesting that psychometric measures of personality be used to measure treatment efficacy.

Psychometric measures of personality are useful in systematically identifying offenders likely to be unsuccessful treatment candidates. Juvenile sex offenders with abnormal psychometric subscale deviations on measures of aggression, depression, self-esteem, impulsivity, and social skills will most likely be unsuccessful in their treatment endeavors. Although an adolescent's prior history of offenses should significantly predict treatment success/failure, the role of sexually deviant thought patterns is unclear.

A review of the literature suggests that it is easier to treat less maladjusted offenders than more severely impaired offenders (Cowden, Peterson, & Pacht, 1969; Durkin & Durkin, 1975; Kunce & Hemphill, 1983; Munson & Blincoe, 1984). Among this group of highly maladjusted offenders, recidivism is common (Davis & Leitenberg, 1987). Indeed, adaptability at admission appears significantly related to cultural role fulfillment five years later (Durkin & Durkin, 1975).

Identifying those aspects of personality that predict chronic offending behaviors would allow treatment providers to vigorously target potentially unsuccessful treatment candidates. Incarcerated juveniles appear to have more deviant profiles than do first-time offenders, probationers, or nonoffenders (Graham, 1981; Kunce & Hemphill, 1983). Identifying potentially chronic offenders at an early stage is therefore emotionally, practically, and fiscally economical.

Aggression/Impulsivity. Among possible predictors of treatment failure, aggression appears most powerful (Waters, Revella, & Baltrusaitis, 1990). Combative children seem to become offenders more frequently than do passive children (Coie, Lochman, Terry, & Hyman, 1992; Jesness, 1966; Moskowitz & Schwartzman, 1989; Rubin et al., 1990; Stattin & Magnusson, 1989; Windle, 1993). Underneath this aggressive demeanor, offending adolescents appear plagued with a host of other interpersonal difficulties. Childhood impulsivity has been negatively correlated with treatment outcome (Jesness, 1966; Knight & Prentky, 1993; Kunce & Hemphill, 1983; Walters & Chlumsky, 1993). Even when rated in kindergarten by teachers, impulsivity was the best predictor of which boys would have the highest self-reported ratings of delinquency at ages 10 to 13 (Tremblay, Pihl, Vitaro, & Dobkin, 1994).

Given their impulsivity, offending boys do not appear as socially mature as their nonoffending counterparts (Jesness, 1966; Kunce & Hemphill, 1983; Rubin et al., 1990). Chronic offenders may be less likely to cope with the tasks of daily living than their less offender counterparts (Graham, 1991; Jesness, 1966; Kunce & Hemphill, 1983; Martin, 1981; Munson & LaPaille, 1984; Moskowitz & Schwartzman, 1989). Given these myriad factors, it seems probable that peers will reject these troubled youths.

Withdrawal/Depression. Although aggressive adolescents may not appear especially sensitive to rejection, they are actually quite withdrawn and sometimes depressed.

This combination of aggressiveness and interpersonal pessimism appears to predict treatment failure (Blatt, Hart, Quinlan, Leadbeater, & Auerbach, 1993; Rubin et al., 1990). Interaction with others is likely to be guarded, given aggressive adolescents' lack of faith in their own skills.

Unsuccessful adolescents seem to lack self-esteem and are more frequently classified by both themselves and others as socially inferior to successful adolescents (Blatt et al., 1993; Tremblay et al., 1994; Jesness, 1966). They do not see themselves as performing satisfactorily on even routine tasks and may make decisions impulsively because of their lack of faith in their own judgment.

Application to Juvenile Sex Offenders

Although research on juvenile sex offenders is considerably more sparse than research on non-sex offenders, some evidence suggests that juvenile sex offenders share many characteristics with other types of offenders. Oliver, Nagayama Hall, and Neuhaus (1993) found that juvenile sex offenders did not differ from non-sex offenders when compared in terms of IQ, highest grade level completed, number of siblings, or offense history.

Juvenile sex offenders also tend to be aggressive (Fehrenbach, Smith, Monastersky, & Deisher, 1986; Nichols & Molinder, 1984; Oliver et al., 1993), withdrawn/depressed (Davis & Leitenberg, 1987), self-critical (Blatt et al., 1993; Fehrenbach et al., 1986; Davis & Leitenberg, 1987), and impulsive (Knight & Prentky, 1993). They are often rejected by peers (Davis & Leitenberg, 1987; Knight, & Prentky, 1993; Oliver, Nagayama Hall, & Neuhaus, 1993) and socially immature (Davis & Leitenberg, 1987; Fehrenbach et al., 1986; Nichols & Molinder, 1984; Oliver et al., 1993), and they display poor coping skills (Nichols & Molinder, 1984).

Among juvenile sex offenders who continue to commit sexual crimes into adulthood, poor self-esteem, impulsivity, alienation, social maladjustment, and lack of coping skills (Knight & Prentky, 1993) appear to be critical factors.

There is some debate in the literature regarding the predictive power of juvenile deviant sexual fantasies and treatment outcome. Nichols and Molinder (1984) found that deviant sexual fantasies play an integral part in understanding the juvenile sex offender. No differences, however, were found among adult onset sex offenders and adult sex offenders with a history of juvenile sex crimes in terms of deviant fantasy (Knight & Prentky, 1993). These authors conclude that all sex offenders share deviant sexual fantasies and that deviant fantasies per se do not predict the onset of later sexually abusive behavior.

Nexus Predictive Treatment Index

The Nexus Predictive Treatment Index (NPTI) is a prognostic instrument developed to supplement more subjective means of predicting treatment prognosis. The NPTI is a means of predicting at intake which clients are most likely to drop out of treatment. The NPTI is thus an attempt to factor out which subscales are the best predictors of treatment success on entrance into a treatment facility.

Logistic regression, a technique used in predictive models of this sort, was used to develop a model based on the current test battery. Factors from the battery were selected based on review of the literature. Factors found to be influential in the final model included the Jesness Au subscale, a measure of impulsivity; the RADS raw score, a measure of depressive symptomatology; the MSI-J-R SAB subscale, a measure of a client's history of sexually inappropriate behaviors; and the MSI-J-R SOS subscale, a measure of preoccupation with sexual thoughts and fantasies.

The JI Au scale is a measure of the length to which individuals will distort reality to accommodate their personal desires. Individuals who score high on the Au subscale of the JI are egocentric. They fail to consider another's point of view before fulfilling their desires. Such a paradigm describes the stereotypical sexual offender, who displays a conspicuous lack of empathy for his victims and appears to have the ability to negate feedback from others during an assault.

The RADS/RCDS utilizes a cutoff score to determine the severity of depressive symptomatology. This score can then be used to delineate level of clinical depression. The NPTI utilized the overall total score from the RADS/RCDS as one of the factors in the prediction of treatment outcome.

The two MSI-J-R subscales used in this study were the SOS, a measure of preoccupation with sexual thought, and the SAB, a measure of the number of sexually inappropriate behaviors in which an adolescent has engaged. The SOS subscale not only assesses the individual's obsession with sex but also the tendency to exaggerate problems. The low and high scores for this subscale identify individuals attempting to either "fake good" or "fake bad." The midrange of scoring provides an idea of the degree to which the individual is honest about and driven by sexual thoughts. The SAB subscale is a quick reference tool used to determine the history of an individual's sexually assaultive behavior. The responses can be compared to a victim's statement to determine whether the offender is portraying accurate details of the assault.

Demographics characterizing the unsuccessful group are likely typical of individuals who score high on the SAB subscale. That is, individuals who have chronic offending histories are likely to be older and to have been in more placements and are more likely to be involved with the probation system. Similarly, individuals who endorse many sexually assaultive behaviors in their past are more prone to continue to engage in these behaviors.

Thus, four psychometric variables measured were found to predict treatment outcome. These include the Jesness Au scale, the RADS raw score, the SOS scale from the MSI-J-R, and the SAB scale from the MSI-J-R. It may be that individuals who are experiencing denial or repression of problem areas are not as amenable to treatment as are individuals experiencing acute psychological distress. This hypothesis may account for the tendency of successful candidates to have higher SOS and RADS scores than their unsuccessful counterparts.

By contrast, individuals who are highly impulsive, egocentric, and hedonistic are less likely to be successful in an inpatient setting than are their more compliant counterparts. In addition, individuals who are impulsive, egocentric, and hedonistic appear even more likely to be unsuccessful in an inpatient treatment setting if they also have committed multiple offenses and are preoccupied with sexual thought and behavior patterns.

The aforementioned tests and subscales are the factors that make up the NPTI. The interaction of these factors constitutes the prediction of an individual's treatment outcome. When the scores of the four factors, weighted by the respective coefficients and the constant, are calculated, the resulting calculation is a predictive value between 0 and 1. This value reflects the hypothesized treatment outcome. If the predictive value is less than 0.50, the prediction is for treatment termination. Conversely, if the predictive value is equal to or greater than 0.50, the predicted outcome is treatment completion.

For any particular individual's test scores, the regression formula can be used to calculate the predicted probability of its membership in either the successful group or the unsuccessful group. Using this equation, 70.2% of all clients entering Mille Lacs Academy over a two-year period were correctly classified. Because results of 51.2% or below would be attributable to chance alone, the present model offers a significant predicative improvement.

Conclusion

Although a prognostic index increases the chances of maximizing success, such an instrument should not be used solely to determine who is accepted for treatment and who is rejected. The treatment index should supplement a more subjective inspection of the test battery as described earlier; this index should also be considered along with behavioral observations and statements of treatment intent uttered by the client in question.

Should a client appear to have a poor prognosis of treatment success given all these factors, a number of options are feasible. Although the evaluating agency can opt not to treat this juvenile, research suggests that untreated juveniles have a high risk of again perpetrating inappropriate sexual behaviors.

Murphy (1996) discussed these issues in a recent edition of the newsletter for the Association for the Treatment of Sexual Abusers. Murphy suggests that a perpetrator resistant to therapy is actually more in need of treatment than one who is open to the experience. He adds that intensive treatment settings may be more common in the future as fiscal restraint narrows the scope of referrals to inpatient treatment settings.

By using a psychological testing battery in the ways outlined in this chapter, clinicians can plan intensive treatment to remediate deficits that typically suggest a client is unmotivated for treatment. In these cases, "pretreatment" may be advisable, where the focus is on building trust and rapport with the therapist, acclimating a client to psychological interpretations of problem areas, and addressing issues of denial and repression of problem areas. Intensive pretreatment of this type is typically thought to yield results within the first six months. Murphy (1996) suggests that a client who maintains denial beyond this time frame should be considered for termination from further treatment programming. Termination typically involves a return to court as this type of juvenile is at very high risk to reoffend.

Beyond the issue of whether to treat the denying, resistant juvenile is the more basic question of why we, as clinicians, typically do not want to treat this type of offender. Designing effective treatment for the resistant juvenile involves reassessing our own methods of therapy and possibly a reexamining the essentials of therapy.

A common source of countertransference may be our tendency to rely heavily on having the juvenile adopt our thinking patterns before treatment can proceed effectively. Some clients will not process information in this manner. Instead, they need the comfort of reaching their own conclusions about what was appropriate or inappropriate about their behavior. The masochistic client, for example, may have to discern what it was about harming others that is arousing for him before he can ascertain the moral turpitude of his actions. This course of therapy is particularly difficult for the therapist who believes that failure to confront cognitive distortion immediately, forcibly, and without discussion is to reinforce and sanction that behavior for the client.

Resistant juveniles may see this type of therapy as a re-creation of a parental environment they viewed as overly controlling and authoritarian. Their denial and resistance may be a means of asserting independence in a manner similar to what they deemed essential to their psychological survival at home.

A better route with resistant juveniles may be to target therapeutic interventions toward their developmental maturity level, helping them to resolve the conflict on their own. This strategy may strengthen the juveniles' trust of authority figures and, consequently, their ability to function in a sex offender-specific group. Once resistant juveniles have, of their own accord, adjusted their perceptions to a level where they are comfortable examining issues within a group setting, they can be moved into a more mainstream type of program.

By using the NPTI to ascertain which clients are at high risk for later treatment dropout, clinicians can focus treatment interventions toward maximizing success for this resistant group. These interventions not only involve refining client approaches but also a thorough examination of our own countertransference toward these resistant clients.

References

American Psychiatric Association. (1980). *Diagnostic and statistical manual for mental disorders* (3rd ed.). Washington, DC: Author.

Blatt, S. J., Hart, B., Quinlan, D. M., Leadbeater, B., & Auerbach, J. (1993). Interpersonal and self-critical dysphoria and behavioral problems in adolescents. *Journal of Youth and Adolescence, 22,* 253–267.

Coie, J. D., Lochman, J. E., Terry, R., & Hyman, C. (1992). Predicting early adolescent disorder from childhood aggression and peer rejection. *Journal of Consulting and Clinical Psychology, 60*(8), 783–792.

Cowden, J. E., Peterson, W. M., & Pacht, A. R. (1969). The MCI vs. the Jesness Inventory as a screening and classification instrument at a juvenile correctional institution. *Journal of Clinical Psychology, 25,* 57–60.

Davis, G. E., & Leitenberg, H. (1987). Adolescent sex offenders. *Psychological Bulletin, 101*(3), 417–427.

Durkin, R. P., & Durkin, A. B. (1975). Evaluating residential programs for disturbed children. In M. Guttentag & E. Strevening (Eds.), *Handbook of evaluation research* (vol. 2, pp. 275–339). Newbury Park, CA: Sage.

Fehrenbach, P. A., Smith, W., Monastersky, C., & Deisher, R. W. (1986). Adolescent sexual offenders: Offender and offense characteristics. *American Journal of Orthopsychiatry, 56*(2), 225–233.

Graham, S. A. (1981). Predictive and concurrent validity of the Jesness Inventory Asocial Index: When does a offender become a offender? *Journal of Consulting and Clinical Psychology, 49*(5), 740–742.

Jesness, C. F. (1966). *The Jesness Inventory* (rev. ed.). North Tonawanda, NY: Multi-Health Systems.

Jesness, C. F. (1991). *Classifying juvenile offenders.* North Tonawanda, NY: Multi-Health Systems.

Knight, R. A., & Prentky, R. A. (1993). Exploring characteristics for classifying juvenile sex offenders. In H. E. Barbaree, W. L. Marshall, & S. M. Hudson (Eds.), *The juvenile sex offender* (pp. 45–83). New York: Guilford Press.

Kunce, J. T., & Hemphill, H. (1983). Delinquency and Jesness Inventory scores. *Journal of Personality Assessment, 47*, 632-634.

Martin, R. D. (1981). Cross-validation of the Jesness Inventory with offenders and nonoffenders. *Journal of Consulting and Clinical Psychology, 49*(1), 10–14.

Millon, T. (1996). *Disorders of personality: DSM-IV and beyond.* New York: Wiley.

Moskowitz, D. S., & Schwartzman, A. E. (1989). Life paths of aggressive and withdrawn children. In D. M. Boss, & N. Cantor (Eds.), *Personality psychology: Recent trends and emerging directions* (pp. 99–114). New York: Springer-Verlag.

Munson, R. F., & Blincoe, M. M. (1984). Evaluation of a residential treatment center for emotionally disturbed adolescents. *Adolescence, 14*(74), 253–261.

Munson, R. F., & LaPaille, K. (1984). Personality tests as a predictor of success in a residential treatment center. *Adolescence, 19*(75), 697–701.

Nichols, H. R., & Molinder, I. (1984). *Multiphasic sex inventory manual.* Tacoma, WA: Authors.

Oliver, L., Nagayama Hall, G. C., & Neuhaus, S. M. (1993). A comparison of the personality and background characteristics of adolescent sex offenders and other adolescent offenders. *Criminal Justice and Behavior, 20*(4), 359–370.

Reynolds, W. M. (1987). *Reynolds Adolescent Depression Scale.* Odessa, FL: Psychological Assessment Resources.

Reynolds, W. M. (1989). *Reynolds Child Depression Scale.* Odessa, FL: Psychological Assessment Resources.

Rubin, K. H., LeMare, L. J., & Lollis, S. (1990). Social withdrawal in childhood: Developmental pathways to peer rejection. In S. R. Asher & J. D. Coie (Eds.), *Rejection in childhood* (pp. 17–59). Cambridge, England: Cambridge University Press.

Saunders, G. R., & Davies, M. B. (1976). The validity of the Jesness Inventory with British offenders. *British Journal of Social and Clinical Psychology, 15*, 33–39.

Shark, M. L., & Handel, P. J. (1977). Reliability and validity of the Jesness Inventory: A caution. *Journal of Consulting Psychology, 45*(4), 692–695.

Simkins, L., Ward, W., Bowman, S., & Rinck, C. M. (1989). The Multiphasic Sex Inventory: Diagnostic and prediction of treatment response in child sexual abusers. *Annals of Sex Research, 2*, 205–226.

Slosson, R. L. (1991). *Slosson Intelligence Test SIT-R* (rev. ed.). East Aurora, NY: Slosson Educational Publications.

Stattin, H., & Magnusson, D. (1989). The role of early aggressive behavior in the frequency, seriousness, and types of later crime. *Journal of Consulting and Clinical Psychology, 57*(6), 710–718.

Tremblay, R. E., Pihl, R. O., Vitaro, F., & Dobkin, P. L. (1994). Predicting early onset of male antisocial behavior from preschool behavior. *Archives of General Psychiatry, 51*(9), 732–739.

Walters, G. D., & Chlumsky, M. L. (1993). The Lifestyle Criminality Screening Form and antisocial personality disorder: Predicting release outcome in a state prison sample. *Behavioral Sciences and the Law, 11*, 111–115.

Walters G. D., Revella, & Baltrusaitis II, W. J. (1990). Predicting parole/probation outcome with the aid of the lifestyle criminality screening form. *Psychological Assessment: A Journal of Consulting and Clinical Psychology, 2*(3), 313–316.

Windle, M. (1993). A retrospective measure of childhood behavior problems and its use in predicting adolescent problem behavior. *Journal of Studies on Alcohol, 54*(4), 422–431.

Chapter 12

Clinical Issues in the Treatment of Geriatric Sex Offenders

by M. K. Johnson, Ph.D.

Sitting on the Park Bench,
Eyeing Little Girls with Bad Intent.
Snot is Running Down his Nose.
Greasy Fingers Smearing Shabby Clothes.
Hey Aqualung . . .
Drying in the Cold Sun,
Watching as the Frilly Panties Run.

—Jennie Anderson (1973)

Overview

The "dirty old man" stereotype, as exemplified by these lyrics from the 1970s popular rock song "Aqualung," by the English group Jethro Tull, contains both elements of truth and exaggerations. A review of the online database of psychiatric liter-

ature from 1979 reveals only two articles (Hucker, 1984; Watson, 1989) that specifically addressing issues pertinent to geriatric sex offenders. However, a small body of
literature studies the general issue of aged criminals, with a particular focus on their
experience during incarceration. This chapter combines information derived from
several sources: the literature on aging male sexuality, depression and suicide in the
elderly, and geriatric criminals, along with anecdotal clinical observations from my
work with a group of geriatric sex offenders.

The information provided in this chapter covers the following aspects of treatment of geriatric sex offenders:

- Legal issues and the criminal justice system
- Social functioning
- Emotional health including anxiety, depression, substance abuse, and suicide
- Physical health concerns, including sexuality and sexual dysfunction, the
  impact of the dementias, and general health care needs
- Treatment issues specific to working with this population.

Prevalence

For the purposes of this chapter, geriatric sex offenders are defined as "those sex
offenders age 60 years and above." The 1993 Uniform Crime Reports (Department
of Justice, 1993) contain the following pertinent statistics regarding elderly criminals: 1.3% of all reported crime committed in the United States in 1993 was committed by persons 60 years of age or older. For sex offenders, geriatric offenders
accounted for 1.7% of all reported "forcible rapes" and 3.79% of all reported "other
sex offenses," for a total of 5.5% of all reported sex crimes. In Virginia, the statistics
for elderly sex offenders are somewhat higher: 2.28% of all reported "forcible rapes"
and 4.64% of all reported "other sex offenses," for a total of 6.92% of all reported
sex crimes (Virginia Department of State Police, 1993). Clearly, geriatric sex offenders account for a small yet significant number of the sex crimes being committed in
the United States.

Legal Issues

When senior citizens are charged with a sexual crime, what is likely to happen to
them in the criminal justice system? The popular stereotype is that older offenders
"get off easy" because of their age. This is both true and false. Wilbanks (1988), in a
study of both sex offenders and non-sex offenders, found that they are treated more
harshly at the "front end" of the criminal justice system than are younger offenders.
That is, they are more likely to be arrested and have their cases sent on to the prosecutor and less likely to have their cases dropped or "nolle prossed." When it comes to
sentencing, however, elderly non-sex offending criminals generally receive more
lenient treatment. They are more likely to be charged with a misdemeanor as opposed
to a felony and are less likely to be incarcerated. Elderly sex offenders, however, are
less likely to receive leniency in sentencing, resulting in an increased likelihood of
incarceration and/or probation as opposed to a suspended sentence (Turner &
Champion, 1989; Wilbanks, 1988).

Studies of elderly probationers have found between 21% and 30% of male probationers have been convicted of sex crimes. Of those probationers, 25% to more than 50% have prior criminal records with up to 25% having prior sex offense records including periods of probationary or parole supervision (Ellsworth & Helle, 1994; Hucker, 1984; Schichor, 1988). They present their probation officers with a wide range of problems, including substance abuse (primarily alcohol), chronically poor physical health, low rates of education, poverty, and limited social support networks which tend to inhibit rehabilitative efforts (Aday, 1994a; Ellsworth & Helle, 1994; Hucker, 1984; Schichor, 1988).

Incarcerated Geriatric Offenders

The limitation in social support is frequently exacerbated by the conditions under which elderly criminals are incarcerated. Elderly criminals bring their wide range of physical health problems and resulting medical and environmental needs with them to jail or to prison. They require greater access to physicians and dentists; physical space adjustments to accommodate canes, walkers, and wheelchairs; and, frequently, nursing home-type care (Aday, 1994a, 1994b). These particular needs have led many states to create separate geriatric facilities for all their elderly criminals, often resulting in increased geographical distance from families and friends, their usual source of social support. This distance presents a hardship to aging friends and families; one study found that 57% of elderly inmates had no family visits while incarcerated. The vast majority, however, do maintain some contact with families and friends through phone calls and letters (Vega & Silverman, 1988).

Although this isolation from families and friends can be stressful, there are other equally distressing aspects of prison life for older convicts. Vega and Silverman (1988) found that 78% of their elderly convict sample experienced some type of problem with other inmates, while 27% experienced "disturbing incidents" with other inmates, 55% of these occurring on a daily basis. The physical frailties associated with aging and chronic illness make elderly convicts easy targets for healthy, aggressive, more youthful offenders in age-mixed correctional environments. The high noise levels, rapid and regimented pace in prisons, and relative lack of physical comfort can be especially threatening and upsetting to first-time elderly incarcerees (Aday, 1994a; Vega & Silverman, 1988).

Social Support Issues

Being convicted of a sex crime can lead to the disruption of family and friendship networks for sex offenders of all ages, but it is particularly difficult for elderly offenders. Unlike offenders in their 30s to 50s, 60- and 70-year-old offenders do not have a reasonable assurance of 20-plus years to rebuild their lives. They face end-of-life issues in which their peers are naturally dying off, leaving them with few options for replacing them.

An offender now in our program remained in denial for more than a year, until he was faced with possible revocation of his probation due to nonparticipation in mandatory sex offender treatment. When he finally became accountable for his crimes, his wife of 30-plus years divorced him. He moved into his own apartment and was doing quite well except for loneliness. After several months he suffered a series of strokes which left him significantly weakened and cognitively slowed. He would like to live with relatives in another state. However, they are reluctant to take him in due to his offending history and appropriate concern over their ability to provide adequate supervision.

This problem of appropriate placement is common for older offenders, particularly as their physical health deteriorates. Watson (1989) and Aday (1994a) note that geriatric institutions are unlikely to take residents with known sexual problems, and family placement may be impossible or imprudent due to inadequate supervision or the existence of generational patterns of abuse.

In addition to factors related to the crime itself, social support may also be limited by the experience of aging. Mobility can be severely hampered by illness or poverty, leaving elderly sex offenders reliant on senior citizen transit or increasingly limited public transportation systems. Lack of transportation is particularly hard on offenders in rural environments and may prevent them from accessing much needed treatment for sexual offending problems as well as for physical and mental health needs.

Lack of social support can lead to increased vulnerability to exploitation by others. A lonely, chronic alcoholic (in remission) elderly man in our program whose wife died while he was incarcerated for his most recent sexual offense repeatedly "befriended" younger alcoholics who would use him to obtain significant amounts of money. When he was inevitably dropped by these people, he became depressed and attempted suicide. Following his hospitalization, a close examination of his life revealed a pattern of "buying friendships." At 72, he faces the difficult task of changing this behavior in the face of a diminishing pool of potential peers.

When devising a treatment program, it is important to take into consideration the social situation and developmental issues facing the geriatric population. We encountered problems in our program when our therapy groups were age-mixed. Originally, due to work schedule constraints, two of our most verbally aggressive younger offenders were in our afternoon group with the geriatric offenders. Their loud, argumentative style, occasional stomping around the room and slamming doors and chairs, severely frightened the older group members. As a consequence, the older offenders' verbal participation decreased, resulting in a group that worked neither for them nor for the younger members. When we transferred the younger men to a better age-matched group they benefited from peers willing to confront them, while the older group members felt safe enough to once again talk in group. They are willing to challenge and confront each other they just choose to do so at a lower decibel level.

Emotional Health

Poor limited social support networks can lead to a variety of emotional problems for aging offenders. Studies of aging populations indicate that the presence of social support networks can have a significant impact on depression, suicide, and mortality rates (Bowling, Edelmann, Leaver, & Hoekel, 1989; Bryant & Rakowski, 1992; Kivela & Pahkala, 1989; Pritchard, 1992). A study of elderly African Americans found that those with few social involvements, particularly those alienated from their families, had an increased likelihood of suicide. The risk of death from all causes was 2.1 times greater for those without family contact. An increased mortality risk was also associated with those who participated in only one or no outside activities, those without church involvement, and those who did not talk to or visit with friends (Bryant & Rakowski, 1992). A Finnish study (Kivela & Pahkala, 1989) found that men previously undiagnosed with depression had a poorer prognosis for the disorder if they experienced feelings of guilt, had decreased social participation, and experienced social stress prior to the onset of the depression, a profile which fits many elderly sex offenders.

Depression in the elderly can have extremely serious consequences. During the period 1974 to 1987, there was a 35% increase in elderly suicides in the United States, whereas the suicide rate for 35- to 64-year-olds either stayed the same or decreased. This pattern of increasing suicide by the elderly, primarily elderly men, is seen in the majority of developed countries (Pritchard, 1992). Elderly male suicide is most likely to occur in late spring and peaks on the fifth day of the month and then declines the rest of the month (McCleary, Chew, Hellsten, & Flynn-Bransford, 1991). Unfortunately, the statistics on elderly suicide do not distinguish between depression-driven versus physical health-driven suicides.

Depressed and lonely aged sex offenders may also experience concomitant problems of alcohol abuse. Rates of alcoholism in all elderly criminals range from 21% to 31%, with one study finding 55% of their elderly criminals experiencing occasional to frequent alcohol abuse (Ellsworth & Helle, 1994; Hucker, 1984; Taylor & Parrott, 1988). By extrapolation, alcohol abuse then becomes a significant risk factor in the offending relapse cycle of elderly sex offenders, requiring yet another area of treatment intervention. In addition, chronic alcohol abuse exacerbates the poor physical condition frequently seen in this population.

Although alcohol is perhaps the most common substance abused by the elderly convict population, the abuse of other drugs, whether deliberate or inadvertent, particularly prescription medications, can also be problematic. In addition, the problem of medication-synergistic interactions is especially acute given the prevalence of multiple chronic health problems, including chronic pain, among the elderly population, which require treatment with multiple medications. Coordinated medical care is especially necessary for this population, including elderly sex offenders, to monitor medication usage.

Sexual Functioning

As noted previously, treating the multiple health problems of elderly offenders with numerous medications can create problems. Decreased sexual desire and impotence are common side effects of many medications taken by the elderly. Normal aging in men is associated with an increased time to achieve full erection, an increased need for physical stimulation to achieve erection, an increased time required to achieve ejaculation, a decrease in the force of ejaculation, and an increase in the duration of the refractory phase (Cogen & Steinman, 1990; Kaplan, 1990; Libman et al., 1990; Mulligan & Moss, 1991; Schiavi, Mandeli, & Schreiner-Engel, 1994; Schiavi, Schreiner-Engel, Mandeli, Schanzer, & Cohen, 1990; Spence, 1992). These normal alterations in sexual functioning can be hastened or worsened by the effects of many medications, as well as by the medical disorders themselves. The potential impact on treatment of elderly sex offenders is varied. Elderly offenders may not be able to achieve an erection sufficient for penile plethysmography. Although a decrease in sexual desire may be viewed as positive when the object of that desire is children, the absence of desire makes sexual activity with consensual, age-appropriate partners difficult at best. Further, limited or absent erectile functioning is no guarantee against offending behavior. Hucker (1984) notes that 79% of his sample of elderly male sexual offenders did not attempt penetration during their sexual offenses. The crimes of elderly sex offenders tend to follow the sexual behaviors engaged in by their nonoffending peers, namely, touching and caressing, and to a lesser extent, masturbation, mutual masturbation, and oral-genital sex (Cogen & Steinman, 1990; Mulligan & Moss, 1991; Spence, 1992).

The following classes of medications are possible sources of impotence and/or decreased sexual desire in elderly males: antihypertensives (thiazide diuretics are worse than beta blockers), phenothiazines, tricyclic antidepressants, selective serotonin reuptake inhibitors, antihistamines, and cardiovascular medications, including heparin. Paradoxically, treatment of Parkinson's disorder with L-Dopa has been associated with hypersexual behavior. The following physical conditions are potential sources of sexual dysfunction: diabetes, strokes, multiple sclerosis, hypothalamic-pituitary problems, spinal cord injury, spinal cord tumors, alcoholism, sensory neuropathy, vascular problems such as atherosclerosis, primary hypogonadism, corpus cavernosa problems such as venous leakage and Peyronie's disease, hyperthyroidism, testicular cancer, prostate cancer and effects of prostate surgery, nutrient deficiencies, particularly zinc, and Parkinson's and Alzheimer's disorders (Brown, Jahanshahi, Quinn, & Marsden, 1990; Garrison, 1989; Mishra & Shulka, 1988; Morley, Korenman, Mooradian, & Kaiser, 1987; Zeiss, Davies, Wood, & Tinklenberg, 1990).

In addition to problems of impotence, Parkinson's, Alzheimer's, and other dementias can involve problems associated with sexually inappropriate acting-out behavior. The belief that elderly crime can be traced to dementia is prevalent but inaccurate. Hucker (1984) notes "Our data do not suggest that elderly sex offenders suffer from organic brain syndrome to any greater extent than the elderly population in general" (p. 71). In a study of the impact of dementia on families, which interviewed caregivers of demented patients living at home, only 2% of the families reported inappropriate sexual behavior. None of them considered it to be a significant problem (Rabins, Mace, & Lucas, 1982). However, other studies have found somewhat higher rates of inappropriate sexual behavior ranging from 6% (Burns, Jacoby, & Levy, 1990) to 17% (Sourander & Sjogren, cited in Burns et al., 1990). This behavior appears to be more common in those with more severe clinical dementia (Burns et al., 1990). Kellett (1993) hypothesized that people suffering from the subcortical dementias, such as Huntington's chorea or frontal lobe syndrome, "retain their drive without having the skills to attract a suitable partner. They may seek other methods of release including child abuse, voyeurism, exposure and frotteurism" (p. 312), though no data is presented to bear out these assertions.

Treatment Implications

Treatment interventions for elderly sex offenders are not necessarily the same as those for younger offenders. Although elderly offenders may present issues similar to those of younger offenders, such as depression, loneliness, and substance abuse, they frequently have fewer internal resources with which to address those problems. In addition, elderly offenders also have to cope with many physical problems and develop strategies to cope with death and dying.

Our program has the resources of the entire Veteran Administration Medical Center at its disposal. This has meant increased coordination of care for all our veteran offenders, and in particular for our elderly offenders. All medical, psychiatric, and substance abuse treatment is offered in-house, allowing for a great ease of communication (most frequently via electronic mail) among all treatment providers. When medical emergencies occur, the emergency room is only a short distance away. Perhaps most significant for our elderly offenders is the existence of the day treatment center (DTC), a program originally intended for the chronically mentally ill but increasingly used by high-functioning geriatric patients. Several of our group members participate in DTC on a part- or full-time basis, going on trips, participating in a variety of supportive therapy groups, and simply hanging out with new friends playing pool. Because the DTC staff are aware of their status as sex offenders, we are assured that appropriate supervision will be provided when they are away from the medical center. Group members who participate in DTC report feeling better about themselves because they can be a source of support and help to more impaired program participants. They also report decreased loneliness as a result of making new friends and participating in new and interesting activities.

Supplementary Treatment Activities. For those sex offender treatment providers without the resources of a medical center, coordinated, multifaceted care for elderly offenders remains necessary and possible, albeit more difficult. Ancillary treatment, such as that for substance abuse and medical issues, may be coordinated through the offender's probation or parole officer, perhaps utilizing programs offered through the local social services department or senior citizen's centers. Senior centers can be sources of assistance for a wide range of issues, including social support, food and housing, transportation, health care, and recreational activities. Given the roles that substance abuse, depression, anxiety and loneliness can play in precipitating or maintaining sex offenders' relapse cycles, attention to these problems in the form of referrals to programs and agencies outside the sex offender treatment program, when necessary, is essential.

Finding Appropriate Treatment Material. Within the sex offender treatment program, elderly offenders present unique problems as well as opportunities. Their general lack of much formal education (Schichor, 1988) can lead to difficulty in comprehending the rather complex information offered in a cognitive-behavioral relapse prevention-oriented program. We have found that some of our older offenders have difficulty with reading comprehension and writing ability. Although we continue to require written homework assignments for those who can write, we increasingly emphasize the offender's verbal explanation of his homework. We use the Pathways (Kahn, 1990) workbook in our program because of its simpler language. Our program members have not reported significant problems in "translating" the adolescent-focused material.

Problems Modifying Deviant Arousal. Elderly offenders present increased challenges in programs including behavioral modification of sexual arousal patterns. Use of the penile plethysmograph to document sexual arousal patterns may be difficult, if not impossible, for men with aging-, health-, or medication-related difficulties. Altering sexual arousal patterns in middle-age sex offenders is difficult; the problem is only magnified when dealing with geriatric offenders with 50 or 60 years' duration of deviant fantasies and behavior. The selection of appropriate partners and fantasy objects can also present more of a dilemma. One of our elderly offenders reported that the women to whom he was attracted and about whom he fantasized were generally in their early to mid-30s. He felt this was appropriate because they were adults; however, the treatment team felt somewhat uneasy with the 40-year age difference. An examination of the literature on sexuality in aging men revealed that men over the age of 60 generally preferred women their own age as ideal sexual partners (Starr & Weiner, 1982, cited in Spence, 1992).

American society's ageist attitude, viewing the elderly as "sexless" (Kaplan, 1990; Mulligan & Moss, 1991; Spence, 1992), can inhibit appropriate treatment of elderly offenders. Everyone involved in the care of an elderly offender, from judges and probation officers to physicians and family members, may discount the seriousness of their crimes and minimize the possibility of reoffending because of their advanced age. My colleagues in a variety of medical and mental health disciplines frequently astound me by their incredulity when they discover we have a group specifically focused on sex offenders over 65. Within the treatment program, ignorance of the natural course of sexuality across the lifespan can leave therapists vulnerable to being misled about the extent of offenders' fantasies and behaviors.

Using Geriatric Sex Offenders as Mentors. Working with geriatric sex offenders gives the therapist a new view of the pattern of offending behaviors across the lifespan. We plan to use our geriatric offenders as resource people, both for the treatment team and for the younger offenders. A combined group of both our older and younger offenders is conducted six times a year. During those groups, older offenders may recount their offending histories, providing information on the impact (or lack thereof) of prior arrests, convictions, and incarcerations on their subsequent offending behavior and their patterns of hiatus from offending and their inevitable resumption of sexual crimes. We hope that this will affect/change younger offenders' attitudes that offending is all in the past and will instead instill in them the conviction that if they are not vigilant, they could find themselves reoffending and back in prison and/or treatment well into their 60s and 70s. For the older offenders, this "mentoring" of their younger colleagues usually provides them with a sense of usefulness, that their experience may help to change and better other lives.

Differences in Treating the Geriatric Sex Offender. For the therapists in our program, working with geriatric offenders has both necessitated an alteration in therapeutic stance and challenged our belief systems and patterns of relating to others. Pacing of treatment is necessarily slower and requires more didactic teaching and coaching. Increased patience is required to cope with the slowness of treatment and the sometimes interminable and convoluted stories from the past. That patience, however, is rewarded by fascinating glimpses of Depression-era life and sexual offending behaviors during supposedly more "innocent" times. We find that we take an increased caretaker role with these men largely as a result of their medical problems and social isolation. Our confrontational stance, although intact, is clearly mitigated by their age. These men are very easily intimidated by younger people and authority figures; thus we confront gently and offer more support and praise for accomplishments in treatment than we would to younger offenders, always keeping in mind, however, the inherent manipulativeness of sex offenders. The need for confrontation has frequently clashed with our enculturated injunctions to "respect your elders." These generational issues are particularly keen for our female therapists, while the elderly offenders report increased difficulty in discussing sexuality with women as that violates the social norms with which they were raised. Emotionally, working with offenders who remind us of our grandfathers has been both disconcerting and sobering. For all of us, some of the time, it is a challenge to see past the grandfather image to the old man who hurts children. At those times, the words of one of our sex offenders are enormously helpful, "I used to be Santa Claus, then I turned into the Grinch who stole Christmas." Working with men who have been offending longer than we have been alive is humbling when we think in terms of treatment effectiveness.

Conclusion

Elderly sex offenders, although they account for a very small proportion of sex offenders in general, present the sex offender treatment provider with unique challenges, problems, and resources. A multitude of medical problems, poor education, minimal financial resources, and limited social support combine to produce a patient who requires multifaceted coordinated care while having limited resources of his own to draw on. Medical problems (and their solutions) can further complicate already complex sexuality. Some 50 to 60 years of offending behavior and its accompanying cognitive distortions and deviant fantasies present an inordinate challenge for those engaging in sexual arousal reconditioning. The physical, and, sometimes emotional, fragility of elderly offenders requires therapists to alter treatment practices to better suit the pace and abilities of these clients. Nevertheless, working with this population can be extremely rewarding, enriching, and enlightening for the therapist. It requires challenging our prior beliefs about aging and end-of-life issues. The reward is, as always, preventing reoffenses from occurring. Moreover, we have the satisfaction of watching and helping someone at the end of his life become a more honest and law-abiding, less manipulative and destructive person than he was for the majority of his life.

References

Aday, R. H. (1994a). Aging in prison: A case study of new elderly offenders. *International Journal of Offender Therapy and Comparative Criminology, 38*(1), 79–91.

Aday, R. H. (1994b). Golden years behind bars: Special programs and facilities for elderly inmates. *Federal Probation, 58*(2), 47–54.

Anderson, J. (1973). "Aqualung." On *Jethro Tull: Aqualung.* New York: Chrysalis Records.

Bowling, A. P., Edelmann, R. J., Leaver, J., & Hoekel, T. (1989). Loneliness, mobility, well-being and social support in a sample of over 85 year olds. *Personality and Individual Differences, 10*(11), 1189–1192.

Brown, R. G., Jahanshahi, M., Quinn, N., & Marsden, C. D. (1990). Sexual function in patients with Parkinson's disease and their partners. *Journal of Neurological and Neurosurgical Psychiatry, 53*, 480–486.

Bryant, S., & Rakowski, W. (1992). Predictors of mortality among elderly African-Americans. *Research on Aging, 14*(1), 50–67.

Burns, A., Jacoby, R., & Levy, R. (1990). Psychiatric phenomena in Alzheimer's disease. IV: Disorders of behaviour. *British Journal of Psychiatry, 157*, 86–94.

Cogen, R., & Steinman, W. (1990). Sexual function and practice in elderly men of lower socioeconomic status. *Journal of Family Practice, 31*(2), 162–166.

Ellsworth, T., & Helle, K. A. (1994). Older offenders on probation. *Federal Probation, 58*(4), 43–50.

Garrison Jr., J. E. (1989). Sexual dysfunction in the elderly: Causes and effects. Journal of *Psychotherapy and the Family, 5*(1-2), 149–162.

Hucker, S. J. (1984). Psychiatric aspects of crime in old age. In E. S. Newman, D. J. Newman, & M. L. Gewirtz (Eds.), *Elderly criminals* (pp. 57–71). Cambridge, MA: Oelgeschlager, Gunn & Hain.

Kahn, T. J. (1990). *Pathways: A guided workbook for youth beginning treatment.* Brandon, VT: Safer Society Press.

Kaplan, H. S. (1990). Sex, intimacy and the aging process. *Journal of the American Academy of Psychoanalysis, 18*(2), 185–205.

Kellett, J. M. (1993). Sexuality in later life. *Reviews in Clinical Gerontology, 3*, 309–314.

Kivela, S., & Pahkala, K. (1989). The prognosis of depression in old age. *International Psychogeriatrics, 1*(2), 119–133.

Libman, E., Creti, L., Amsel, R., Fichten, C. S., Weinstein, N., & Brender, W. (1989). Sleeping and waking-state measurement of erectile function in an aging male population. *Psychological Assessment, 1*(4), 284–291.

McCleary, R., Chew, K. S. Y., Hellsten, J. J., & Flynn-Bransford, M. (1991). Age- and sex- specific cycles in United States suicides, 1973–1985. *American Journal of Public Health, 81*, 1494–1497.

Mishra, D. N., & Shulka, G. D. (1988). Sexual disturbances in male diabetics: Phenomenological and clinical aspects. *Indian Journal of Psychiatry, 30*(2), 135–143.

Morley, J. E., Korenman, S. G., Mooradian, A. D., & Kaiser, F. E. (1987). UCLA geriatric grand rounds: Sexual dysfunction in the elderly male. *Journal of the American Geriatrics Society, 35*, 1014–1022.

Mulligan, T., & Moss, C. R. (1991). Sexuality and aging in male veterans: A cross-sectional study of interest, ability and activity. *Archives of Sexual Behavior, 20*(1), 17–25.

Pritchard, C. (1992). Changes in elderly suicides in the USA and the developed world 1974–87: Comparison with current homicide. *International Journal of Geriatric Psychiatry, 7*, 125–134.

Rabins, P. V., Mace, N. L., & Lucas, M. J. (1982). The impact of dementia on the family. *Journal of the American Medical Association, 248*(3), 333–335.

Schiavi, R. C., Mandeli, J., & Schreiner-Engel, P. (1994). Sexual satisfaction in healthy aging men. *Journal of Sex and Marital Therapy, 20*(1), 3–13.

Schiavi, R. C., Schreiner-Engel, P., Mandeli, J., Schanzer, H., & Cohen, E. (1990). Healthy aging and male sexual function. *American Journal of Psychiatry, 147*(6), 766–771.

Schichor, D. (1988). An exploratory study of elderly probationers. *International Journal of Offender Therapy and Comparative Criminology, 32*(2), 163–174.

Spence, S. H. (1992). Psychosexual dysfunction in the elderly. *Behavior Change, 9*(2), 55–64.

Taylor, P. J., & Parrott, J. M. (1988). Elderly offenders: A study of age-related factors among custodially remanded prisoners. *British Journal of Psychiatry, 152*, 340–346.

Turner, G. S., & Champion, D. J. (1989). The elderly offender and sentencing leniency. *Journal of Offender Counseling Services and Rehabilitation, 13*(2), 125–140

Vega, M., & Silverman, M. (1988). Stress and the elderly convict. *International Journal of Offender Therapy and Comparative Criminology, 32*(2), 153–162.

Watson, J. M. (1989). Legal and social alternatives in treating older child sexual offenders. *Journal of Offender Counseling Services and Rehabilitation, 13*(2), 141–147.

Wilbanks, W. (1988). Are elderly felons treated more leniently by the criminal justice system? *International Journal of Aging and Human Development, 26*(4), 275–288.

Zeiss, A. M., Davies, H. D., Wood, M., & Tinklenberg, J. (1990). The incidence and correlates of erectile problems in patients with Alzheimer's disease. *Archives of Sexual Behavior, 19*(4), 325–330.

Chapter 13

Hispanic Sex Offenders— Cultural Characteristics and Implications for Treatment

by Nicolas Carrasco, Ph.D. and Diane Garza-Louis, M.Ed.

Overview

To treat sex offenders who are members of different ethnic and cultural groups, clinicians must recognize special issues which may require treatment to be adapted and modified. For example, among Hispanics *macho* and *machismo* are important cultural concepts relating to the abuse of power and stereotypical attitudes toward women—traits common among sex offenders. Because machismo is thought to be particularly characteristic of Hispanics, treatment providers must understand these concepts to provide appropriate intervention for Hispanic sex offenders. In this chapter, we examine the relationship between cultural values and macho/machismo and discuss treatment interventions.

Selecting Appropriate Treatment

Traditional methods of treatment, such as individual insight-oriented or supportive psychotherapy in which the therapist seeks to establish a therapeutic alliance with a client to evoke positive change, have proven effective in treating many disorders. However, traditional treatment modalities have proven ineffective in diminishing sexually abusive behaviors. Because of their denial of guilt, lack of motivation for treatment, and generally uncooperative attitudes, sex offenders have been considered poor candidates for traditional types of treatment (Crawford, 1981). Yet studies have proven that cognitive-behavioral therapy and its derivatives can have a significant impact on sex offenders, helping them to control deviant sexuality and reducing recidivism rates (Abel, Osborn, Anthony, & Gardos, 1982). The effective community-based treatment programs require offenders to attend weekly group meetings and emphasize acceptance of responsibility for the offense and the development of victim empathy and relapse prevention strategies. Treatment is confrontational in nature, especially in the beginning stages, and offenders are asked to make drastic changes in cognitions, values, attitudes about women, nature of family relationships, and gender identity.

As in most areas of mental health, theories about deviant sexuality and its treatment have been developed, first and foremost, with the help of Anglo-American research participants and for implementation with Anglo-American populations. A literature search yielded no studies in which Hispanic samples were included. Our study will not fill the existing void in Hispanic sex offender literature, but it is a first step in the right direction. In this chapter, we use the concepts of macho and machismo to demonstrate the need for cultural sensitivity. We also present preliminary results of an investigation that included African-American, Mexican-American, Anglo-American, and Hispanic (the majority being Mexican immigrants) sex offenders. The results we present here focus primarily on cross-cultural differences in attitudes and values regarding women and male/female roles, although we also discuss relationship to the victim.

Macho and Machismo

There is ample literature on machismo (De La Cancela, 1986; DeYoung & Zigler, 1994; Lara-Cantu, 1989; Neff, Prihoda, & Hoppe, 1991; Villemez & Touhey, 1977). Machismo has been the subject of interest and investigation since early anthropological and sociological studies of Mexican and Mexican-American families were conducted (e.g., Lewis, 1959; Madsen, 1964). Vigil (1980) suggests that machismo evolved as a "native reaction" to the political and social oppression that occurred during the Spanish conquest.

> Because of the misfortune that befell the natives at the time, there was a need for this male attitude and behavior, especially to defend the honor of women . . . that is, as a defense against the Spaniards. On the other hand, the macho syndrome included some negative traits, such as masculine tyranny in the home. . . . Another legacy linked to machismo was an increase in drinking and fighting. (pp. 79–80)

In short, the concepts of macho and machismo are viewed as having originated in Mexican and/or Hispanic culture and play an important part in the Hispanic male's self-concept.

Through the process of acculturation, the concepts macho and machismo are now a part of American culture. In the vernacular, such terms as "Mr. Macho" and "Macho man" are commonly used. In general, these terms are uncomplimentary and refer to the negative traits of the macho/machismo concepts. The terms are used to describe chauvinistic or exaggerated male attitudes and/or behaviors. In the United States, macho is used to describe a man who is aggressive, a womanizer, alcoholic, and arrogant. In addition, dominance over others, authoritarian attitudes, belief in strict adherence to sex roles, and nonnurturing tendencies are reported to be common traits of machismo (DeYoung & Zigler, 1994). In *Merriam Webster's Tenth Collegiate Dictionary*, macho is defined as "characterized by machismo: aggressively virile" (p. 697).

In Hispanic cultures, the term "machismo" also has negative connotations and refers to behavior that manifests machista, or "chauvinistic," attitudes. The word "macho," on the other hand, has positive connotations and is used to describe a male of any age who behaves in a "manly" manner; that is, a man who manifests courage, dignity, respect for others, pride and honor, protection of women, and love and affection for family and children (Valdez, Baron, & Ponce, 1987). In Hispanic culture, all males, regardless of age, are expected to be *hombres* (men) and to manifest macho attitudes and behaviors. But men who exhibit machismo are not considered truly macho. They are described as *se cree muy macho*; that is, "he believes he is very manly." This characterization connotes a false sense of manhood, a self-deception on the part of the man.

In sum, there is a lack of "conceptual equivalence" across cultures with respect to macho and machismo; that is, the words mean one thing in Hispanic culture and quite another in Anglo-American culture. In Anglo-American culture, macho and machismo are synonymous and both words have negative connotations. In Hispanic cultures, macho and machismo are distinct and (as illustrated in Table 13.1) antithetical concepts. Macho refers to being "manly"; machismo, on the other hand, refers to behavior that manifests machista (chauvinistic) attitudes and a false sense of manhood.

Table 13.1
Differences Between Macho and Machismo in Hispanic Culture

Macho	*Machismo*
True pride	False pride
Dignity	Arrogance
Honor women	Dishonor women
Authoritative	Authoritarian
Benevolent	Neglectful
Protective	Antagonistic
Respectful	Disrespectful
Just	Unjust
Faithful	Unfaithful
Responsible	Irresponsible
Brave	Bravado

Machismo and the Sex Offender

Behavior and attitudes associated with machismo are also associated with sex-offending behavior (e.g., arrogance, abuse of power, abuse of authority in the family, double standards, degradation of women, promiscuity, and alcoholism) (Garza-Louis & Peralta, 1993). As machismo is thought to be particularly characteristic of Hispanic males, it is essential that professionals working with Hispanic sex offenders understand the relationship between culture and machismo and how these factors may relate to a sex offense. In our study, we collected data to clarify and understand cultural differences regarding machismo and cultural values. Results of data analyses are used to draw conclusions regarding appropriate interventions for Hispanic offenders.

Research Into Machismo

Data was collected from a cross-cultural sample of sex offenders, including 66 Anglo Americans, 21 African Americans, 51 Mexican Americans (Hispanics born in the United States), and 42 Hispanics (Hispanics born in Latin American countries, the majority from Mexico). We used the Family Attitude Scale (FAS; Ramirez, 1967; Carrasco, 1990) to measure value orientation. Carrasco (1990) tested the cross-cultural equivalence of the FAS using the Statistical Package for the Social Sciences-X version of LISREL VI, which allows for the use of confirmatory factor analysis (CFA) to test an a priori or theoretical factor structure. The CFA was used to derive an "invariant model" (i.e., a cross-culturally equivalent model) from the FAS, with alpha coefficients of .77 for Anglo Americans and .74 for Mexicans and Mexican Americans. The Attitude Toward Women (ATW) scale (Spence & Helmreich, 1978), the Attitude Toward Male Roles (ATMR) scale (Neff et al., 1991), and the Sex Stereotyping and Sex Discrimination (SSSD) scale (Villemez & Touhey, 1977) were used as measures of machismo.

Analyses were conducted using the statistical program StatView. Although still preliminary, we believe that the results we present here are reliable and valid. Some findings appear contradictory, including the common (from a U.S. perspective) notion of traditional values and concordant attitudes. But, we were encouraged by conversations with a Mexican psychologist, who confirmed that the findings are in keeping with Mexican cultural patterns.

Results Regarding Family Values

In general, it is accepted that Hispanics hold more traditional values than do Anglo Americans. Thus, we hypothesized that Hispanics and Mexican Americans would manifest stronger adherence to traditional values than would Anglos and African Americans. Results of an analysis of variance (ANOVA) yielded support for this hypothesis. On the FAS, Hispanics and Mexican Americans reported significantly greater adherence to traditional values than did the two control groups ($F = 15.12$; $df = 3,176$; $p < .0001$). Results of our study are relatively consistent with results of Carrasco (1990) (see Table 13.2). In that study, mean scores for Anglo-American, Mexican-American, and Mexican parents were 83, 77, and 74, respectively.

Table 13.2
FAS Mean Scores

Cultural Group	N	Mean	SD
Anglo American	66	81.4	6.9
African American	21	77.6	6.3
Mexican American	51	74.5	6.8
Hispanic	42	72.1	9.8

Results Regarding Machismo

Although differences in values were expected, as this is a study of sex offenders, we hypothesized that there would be no difference in machista (chauvinistic) attitudes across cultures. Our hypothesis received only partial support. Consistent with the stated hypothesis, no significant difference was found across cultures on the SSSD scale ($F = 1.99$; df = 3,176; $p < .12$), but significant results were obtained on the ATMR scale ($F = 3.15$; df = 3,176; $p < .03$) and on the ATW scale ($F = 6.11$; df = 3,176; $p < .0006$). Post hoc analysis (using Bonferroni\Dunn, p x .0083) indicated significant differences between Anglo Americans and Hispanics on the ATMR scale, and significant differences on the ATW between Hispanics and Anglo Americans and Hispanics and African Americans (see Table 13.3). To better understand the obtained results, we conducted subsequent analyses of the ATMR and ATW scales. According to Neff et al. (1990) the ATMR is composed of two factors—a Machismo factor and an Egalitarianism factor. Consequently, for further analyses, the ATW was also subdivided into two factors, which were similar to the ATMR factors. A series of ANOVAs was then conducted. Results of these analyses indicated no significant differences across cultures on the Egalitarianism factor. On the Machismo factor, however, there was a significant difference on the ATMR ($F = 5.04$; df = 3,176; $p < 002$), and on the ATW ($F = 7.07$; df = 3,176; $p < .0002$). Post hoc analysis on the Machismo factor (using Bonferroni\Dunn, $p < .0083$) indicated significant differences between Hispanics and Anglo Americans and Hispanics and African Americans on the ATMR and significant difference between Hispanics and all other groups on the ATW (see Table 13.4).

Table 13.3
Mean Scores on Machismo Scales

Cultural Group	*SSD*		*ATMR*		*ATW*	
	Mean	*SD*	*Mean*	*SD*	*Mean*	*SD*
Anglo American	87.7	12.6	35.5	4.0	45.9	6.5
African American	88.7	11.2	35.8	5.2	46.2	6.0
Mexican American	85.4	10.2	34.2	5.2	43.8	5.4
Hispanic	83.3	11.0	32.7	5.9	41.3	5.2

Table 13.4
Mean Scores on Machismo Factor

Cultural Group	*ATMR*		*ATW*	
	Mean	*SD*	*Mean*	*SD*
Anglo American	22.1	2.8	24.7	4.0
African American	22.5	3.6	24.5	5.7
Mexican American	21.3	3.6	23.5	4.0
Hispanic American	19.7	4.0	20.8	5.0

The final hypothesis addressed the issue of relationship among the variables across culture. We hypothesized that the relationship between values and machismo would be different across cultures. To examine the relationship among the variables across cultures we conducted a series of correlational analyses. As illustrated in Table 13.5, in all groups correlations were high across scales on the similar dimensions. The ATW Machismo factor correlated highly with the ATMR Machismo factor and the ATMR Egalitarianism factor correlated highly with the ATW Egalitarian factor. Within scales, however, the relationship between the factors is less consistent. For Anglo Americans and to some extent for Mexican Americans, the Machismo and Egalitarianism factors correlate strongly within scales. For African Americans and for Hispanics, however, there is a weak (and sometimes negative) correlation between the Machismo and Egalitarianism factors within the same scale. The Machismo and Egalitarianism factors were also correlated with the FAS. These results are presented in Table 13.6. In all groups there is a strong correlation between traditional values and machista attitudes, but a significant correlation between traditional family values and attitudes about egalitarianism is evinced only within the Anglo-American sample.

Table 13.5
Correlation of Factors Across and Within Scales

	Ang. Am.	Af. Am.	Mex. Am.	Hispanic
Machismo				
ATW x ATMR	.485	.658	.679	.685
Egalitarianism				
ATW x ATMR	.590	.381	.542	.658
ATW Scale				
Mach. x Egal.	.573	-.091	.276	-.240
ATMR Scale				
Mach. x Egal.	.458	.146	.481	.204

Table 13.6
FAS Correlations with Machismo and Egalitarianism

	Ang. Am	Af. Am	Mex. Am.	Hispanic
ATW-Egal.	.337	-.114	.131	-.297
ATMR-Egal.	.328	-.061	.039	.076
ATW-Machismo	.586	.503	.292	.378
ATMR-Machismo	.436	.504	.356	.315

Discussion and Treatment Implications

Results of our study support the contention that Hispanic and Mexican-American sex offenders espouse more traditional values than do Anglo- and African-American offenders. The results also suggest that Hispanic sex offenders have stronger machista or chauvinistic attitudes than do other sex offender populations. Results of the correlational analysis suggest that adherence to traditional values is associated with degree of machista attitudes in all samples. In the Anglo-American sample, both these factors are positively correlated with degree of adherence to egalitarian/nonegalitarian attitudes. That is, Anglo-American sex offenders who believe in traditional values also believe in the strict division of sex roles and hold less egalitarian attitudes. Hispanics and Mexican Americans adhere more strongly to more traditional family values than do Anglo Americans, and Hispanics manifested stronger machista attitudes, but degree of adherence to these factors was not associated with attitudes about egalitarianism. That is, although Hispanics may hold more strongly to traditional values and to machista attitudes, they do not necessarily hold nonegalitarian attitudes. These results are contrary to what is seen in Anglo-American populations. Although they seem contradictory, the results are consistent with Hispanic cultural premises (R. Diaz-Loving, personal communication, 1996). Diaz-Loving suggested that the concept of *obedienca afiliativa* together with the cultural premise of mother-love may help explain the obtained results.

Obedienca Afiliativa. The concept of *obedienca afiliativa,* or filial obedience (as it has been translated by the authors), is a Mexican cultural premise which prescribes to the father unquestioned obedience from his children. Thus, in family relationships the father has a significant amount of power. However, in healthy Hispanic families the father's power is tempered by "love/responsibility." This love/responsibility is very much a part of the self-concept of the macho. The father who accepts the power granted to the male role by cultural prescription also accepts the love/responsibility that comes with that power. The macho male views power as a privilege which is safeguarded through his own actions through love, responsibility, and protection of family.

Hispanic offenders have distorted the concept of filial obedience. They demand the power granted through this cultural premise but negate the love/responsibility which balances that power. The distortion of the filial obedience premise is most clearly observed with respect to stepdaughter victims. A significantly greater proportion of Hispanic offenders (as compared to other cultural groups) have molested stepdaughters. Hispanic offenders intentionally distance the relationship with their stepdaughters, referring to them as *entenadas* (i.e., foster children) rather than hijastras (stepdaughters). The distancing of this particular family relationship gives the offending stepfather the power and control associated with filial obedience but none of the love/responsibility, thus, facilitating abuse. With Hispanic offenders, treatment providers should discuss and explain the concept of filial obedience within family relationships. Subsequently, they should address cognitive distortions regarding the father's culturally prescribed power. The offender's desire for power within the family does not need to be denied; rather the offender should be expected to accept the love/responsibility which legitimizes that power. Furthermore, offenders who attempt to distance the stepfather-stepdaughter relationship by using *entenada* rather than *hijastra* should be confronted regarding their minimization of the relationship and therefore the severity of their crime and harm to the victim. In working on this issue, the positive element found within the macho self-concept can be used to replace distorted or machista views. One of the elements of the macho concept is love and affection for children, and there is a strong Mexican value that promotes accepting all children as your own. These two elements of Hispanic culture can be used in combating the cognitive distortions of offenders who minimize the relationship with their stepdaughters.

Mother-Love. The concept of mother-love is also a strong cultural premise in Hispanic culture. For Hispanics, the mother is considered precious above all things. In healthy families, although the mother does not have the unquestioned authority of the father, she is revered, and she is granted absolute love by her children and respect and honor by her husband. The mother in turn proffers absolute devotion to her family. Diaz-Loving (personal communication, 1996) suggests that it is because of this cultural premise that egalitarian attitudes regarding women are associated with traditional Hispanic values. In this area of family relations, as we saw with filial obedience, Hispanic offenders frequently distort the cultural premise. The offender expects his spouse to be a completely devoted wife and mother, but he shuns his responsibility to honor and respect, resulting in extramarital affairs and at times bigamous relationships. In treatment, and especially in couple's therapy, discussing the *lugar* or special status that women/mothers hold in Hispanic culture can help an offender accept that his dishonor and disrespect of his wife is culturally proscribed. Presenting this information within the framework of cultural premises and the macho (vs. machismo) concept can help Hispanic offenders accept greater responsibility for changing their negative attitudes and behaviors. This information can also be used as a basis for helping the couple increase communication between themselves. By giving the wife permission to question her husband's behavior, secrecy is reduced and the spouse is allowed to seek outside support for herself. All this, together with the wife's role in the family as "devoted mother," can greatly reduce recidivism and make necessary changes in the family system to protect children.

Finally, if as treatment providers we can clarify for ourselves the concept of macho and machismo, we can use these concepts in treatment of our clients, encouraging positive change in offenders and their families through culturally appropriate interventions. Based on cultural prescriptions for Hispanics, male self-concept (i.e., being macho) is a positive set of attitudes and behaviors which can be delineated for the Hispanic offender. We can help him change from being a machista and having a false sense of manhood to being a macho and gaining a positive self-concept and self-esteem.

Conclusion

Cultural diversity is an integral part of our society and developing cultural awareness and competence should be a priority for all mental health professionals. But given the nature of sex offender treatment, which influences and demands changes at the core of personality structure and requires some degree of cross-cultural competence, it is imperative for sex offender treatment providers to acquire cross-cultural competence. Being macho is at the core of Hispanic male self-concept, but in the United States, macho and machismo are viewed as synonymous, negative concepts. Because sexual offenders frequently manifest the negative characteristics and attitudes associated with machismo, a lack of understanding on the part of the therapist regarding cultural differences in definition can result not only in cultural insensitivity but also in the stripping away of an offender's much-needed, positive elements of identity and self-esteem.

The results of this study provided information regarding family values and attitudes about women in four cultural groups of sex offenders. In all groups, there is a strong association between adherence to more traditional values and machista attitudes. However, an association between these two factors and attitudes regarding egalitarianism was observed in Anglo-American but not Hispanic populations. We contend that this difference is related to the distinction between macho and machismo/machista attitudes that is made in Hispanic cultures. This distinction helps clarify the nature of Hispanic family relationships and has implications for treatment of Hispanic sex offenders. Hispanic sex offenders have confused or distorted the elements of macho/machista concepts. Through cognitive distortion, the offender views himself as macho when in fact he is demonstrating machismo. We must confront this distortion in treatment. As indicated earlier, in Hispanic culture, all males are expected to be macho. It is a positive part of the male self-concept and self-esteem. We should encourage and foster macho attitudes associated with healthy, traditional values, which include love of family, respect for others, and egalitarian values. On the other hand, we need to confront and clarify machismo and machista attitudes, related to a false sense of manhood, arrogance, and irresponsible and abusive behaviors, and we need to encourage offenders to replace machista attitudes and behavior with those that are truly macho.

Acknowledgments

The authors would like to thank all the participants of this research project and Vivian Lewis-Hiene and Richard King for coordinating the project at their treatment sites. A special note of gratitude is extended to Sonia Carrillo and German Gutierrez for their invaluable assistance in data analyses.

References

Abel, G., Osborn C., Anthony, D., & Gardos, P. (Eds.). (1982). Current treatment of paraphiliacs. *Annual Review of Sex Offender Research: An Integrative and Interdisciplinary Review, 3.*

Bemm, S. L. (1985). Androgyny and gender schema theory: A conceptual and empirical integration. In T. B. Sonderegger (Ed.), *Psychology and gender* (pp. 179–226). Lincoln: University of Nebraska Press.

Carrasco, N. (1990). *The relationship between parental support and control and adolescent self-esteem in Mexican, Mexican- American and Anglo-American families.* Unpublished doctoral dissertation. University of Texas, Austin.

Carrasco, N., King, R., & Garza-Louis, D. (1996). The Hispanic sex offender: Machismo and cultural values. *Forum,* 4–5.

Crawford, D. A. (1981). Treatment approaches with pedophiles. In M. Cook & K. Howells (Eds.), *Adult sexual interest in children* (pp. 181–217). New York: Academic Press.

De La Cancela, V. (1986). A critical analysis of Puerto Rico machismo: Implications for clinical practice. *Psychotherapy, 23*(2), 291–296.

DeYoung, Y., & Zigler, E. F. (1994). Machismo in two cultures: Relation to punitive child-rearing practices. *American Journal of Orthopsychiatry, 64*(3), 386–394.

Garza-Louis, D., & Peralta, F. (1993). *The macho syndrome: Myths and and realities of the Hispanic sex offender.* Paper presented at the 1993 Annual Conference of Sex Offender Treatment, Huntsville, TX.

Lara-Cantu, M. A. (1989). A sex-role inventory with scales for "machismo" and "self-sacrificing women." *Journal of Cross-Cultural Psychology, 20*(4), 386–398.

Lewis, O. (1959). *Five families.* New York: Basic Books.

Madsen, W. (1964). *The Mexican American in south Texas.* New York: Holt, Rinehart & Winston.

Neff, J. A., Prihoda, T. J., Hoppe, S. (1991). "Machismo," self-esteem, education and high maximum drinking among Anglo, black and Mexican-American male drinkers. *Journal of Studies on Alcohol, 52,* 458–463.

Ramirez III, M. (1967). Identification with Mexican family values and authoritarianism in Mexican-*American Journal of Social Psychology, 73,* 3–11.

Spence, J. T., & Helmreich, R. L. (1978). *Masculinity and femininity: Their psychological dimensions, correlates and antecedents.* Austin: University of Texas Press.

Valdez, L. F., Baron, A., & Ponce F. Q. (1987). Counseling Hispanic men. In M. Scher, M. Stevens, G. Good, & G. A. Eichenfield (Eds.), *Handbook of counseling and psychotherapy* (pp. 126-147). Newbury Park, CA: Sage.

Vigil, J. D. (1980). *From Indian to Chicanos: A sociocultural history.* St. Louis, MO: Mosby.

Villemez, W. J., & Touhey, J. C. (1977). A measure of individual differences in sex stereotyping and sex discrimination: The macho scale. *Psychological Reports, 41,* 411–415.

Chapter 14

The American Indian Sexual Offender

by Dewey J. Ertz, Ed.D.

Overview

To be effective, the treatment of sex offenders must be individualized to consider the crucial dynamics of the individual offender. When that offender is a member of a minority group, the values, customs, and traditions of that group should be incorporated into the treatment. In this chapter, I discuss the dynamic of the American Indian and how to adapt treatment for this population.

Who Is the American Indian?

My initial task in this chapter is to provide an operational definition of an American Indian. Both racial and ethnic issues exist when defining a person in this manner. Race is biological or genetic, and it has been found to be a generally poor predictor of an individual's behavior. An individual's ethnic background determines his or her cultural beliefs, and it has a direct impact or bearing on behavior. Race represents our physical features and it derives directly from our biological parents. Our ethnic background determines much of our behavior because it is modeled from individuals from our environment as we grow and develop. Further, it includes specific expectations from the societal context of our environment, which is an important consideration for purposes of this chapter because appropriate sexual behaviors for individuals are defined as part of the societal boundaries.

American Indian people also identify under several different labels. Some prefer to be identified as Native American or Alaskan Natives. The term "American Indian" has come into more general use recently because other groups have begun to consider themselves native to America if it was their place of birth. Many individuals confuse race and ethnic issues (Wyatt, Michael, & Riederle, 1994), and such confusion can lead to inappropriate definitions and stereotypes. The concept of "Indian identification" is important in defining an individual as an American Indian. This concept refers to the way in which individuals with American Indian ancestry view themselves in relationship to their history and their family's past.

Indian identification can be viewed as a continuum from traditional beliefs and behaviors to full assimilation. Traditional Indian persons would be expected to practice many of the rituals and activities of their tribal group and to be fluent in their native language. They would identify with values from their tribal ancestry, and their systems of social control would be viewed and practiced within this context. On the other hand, a contemporary Indian person would be expected to identify with the values and social responsibilities of the dominant society and to display conduct consistent with these standards. Some Indian people have been found to identify with neither system of social control, and they are referred as being marginally identified. These individuals also display considerably more difficulty with alcohol or substance abuse (May, 1989), and they appear to have a greater frequency of emotional and behavioral difficulties. Presently, there are more than 500 recognized American Indian tribal groups within the United States, and each of these groups has a different cultural belief system. As a result, factors of cultural identity become highly important in the assessment and treatment of American Indian sexual offenders.

This chapter advocates a method of understanding these factors by gaining information on how an individual grew up and by identifying the adults in the environment who helped shape the person's current behaviors and belief patterns. Based on this overview, it is important to recognize that the labeling of a person as American Indian represents four different dimensions: race, ethnic background, personal identification, and the general family history of the individual. Additional dimensions may also be highly important for specific individuals, and no two individuals with exactly the same background would be expected to have the same behaviors and/or belief patterns. A further understanding regarding family history relates to the trauma or upheaval that the family and individuals have experienced and how they reacted to these disturbances.

The Context of Trauma

Trauma is usually some type of physical or emotional injury which causes a person to feel shock. Trauma may have short- or long-term consequences, and it implies that the individual or group has experienced some type of violence. All individuals experience trauma or violence in some form during their life. The context of these experiences is often detailed in family stories or myths. Bunk (1994) presented information that families vary in the coping styles they adopt to address trauma issues. Further, negative or inappropriate coping styles can become more problematic for subsequent generations than the actual trauma experiences.

A major historical trauma for most Indian people were government- and church-run boarding school systems. The boarding schools were conceived as places where Indians could learn to value and behave according to the expectancies of the dominant society. The boarding schools also presented expectations of lower academic achievement. Children were often taken from their parents at a young age and spent most of their formative years in such an environment. Many individuals lost their sense of personal identity in this process; at the same time they failed to adopt alternative social structures to address the loss. These institutions contributed to the problem of marginal personal identity, and they had a major effect on reducing the level of parenting skills of many American Indian people. In addition, many tribal groups have a specific history of death and violence at the hands of members of the dominant society, which contributes to the historical trauma tribal members experience.

The violence encountered by American Indian people today has at least four different expressions: racial prejudice, horizontal violence from their own family and community members, poverty, and systems of dependence.

Racial Prejudice. Allport (1954) defined prejudice as having two components: hostility and lack of knowledge. Prejudice is often described by those who experience it as a difference they cannot see but one they can "feel." Assessing whether an individual is prejudiced becomes rather complicated as several factors must be considered regarding both hostility and knowledge or lack thereof. Another major issue regarding prejudice is that hostility directed toward a person's family or an individual with whom the person identifies becomes hostility directed toward the person. It is beyond the scope of this chapter to discuss the effects of prejudice, but it is appropriate to note that prejudice results in a cycle of violence, distrust, and isolation that divides communities and leads to greater levels of turmoil.

Horizontal Violence. Horizontal violence is a concept that implies that individuals act out their aggressive impulses on targets who are immediately available to them, and whom they would protect under usual circumstances. This concept accounts for the reason parents employ harsh discipline with their children after having difficult experiences in the workplace or with their spouse. Domestic, family, and community violence can be classified as having a horizontal nature—as anger resulting in one setting can be acted out in another. Traditional Indian social interactions generally placed a high value on family as well as an inhibition on harming family or other tribal members. The experiences of trauma have weakened this prohibition and many Indian communities and families experience aggressive actions because of this displacement process. Mental health and other providers should heed a caution regarding family violence: When families are violent toward the members, family therapy or couple's therapy must be approached with care because it may increase the potential for further violent actions.

Poverty. Poverty usually represents a lack of resources which leads to deprivation or deficiencies in a person's daily lifestyle. The poorest county in the United States has been repeatedly found on an Indian Reservation in South Dakota, and high levels of dependency and depression have been associated with individuals who are unable to meet life's basic needs.

Dependency Systems. Added to poverty are systems of dependence which seek to provide minimal standards for an individual's lifestyle. These systems have been considered inadequate by the majority of Americans, but few alternatives have been considered to alleviate the problems with the systems. Tribal groups often replicate these same types of dependency systems from the dominant society. Issues such as housing and related subsidies become very complex when someone is living on assistance or in a supported housing project. Many American Indian families are currently coping with losing their self-sufficiency and becoming more and more dependent on such systems. Their cultural identity is being lost in this process as well.

Trauma During Childhood

We are beginning to understand that trauma and danger present special complications for children (Garbarino, Kostelny, & Dubrow, 1991; Garbarino, Dubrow, Kostelny, & Pardo, 1992). Children may develop intellectual impairments in response to danger, and they certainly can develop emotional responses that they carry on to adulthood. Three responses are common in this situation: predator/prey life views, the choice of feeling anxiety and loneliness, and a need to numb emotional responses.

Predator/Prey Life View. Individuals with a predator/prey life view consider themselves potential prey until they reach a point where they can become predators. Such a life view is supported by an assumption that the only safe way to exist is to be a head predator or the dominant member of the group. This view allows for violent actions and victimization, and such behaviors often become expectancies among entire families and communities.

Impaired Social Relations. A second coping process relates to the need all humans have to be bonded and to identify within social groups. Human beings are often referred to as social animals because of this need. Having this need means that we involve ourselves in social groupings and require the company of others to feel complete. However, social activities in a traumatic environment produce anxiety, and human beings respond to anxiety either by removing themselves from the situation or by somehow fighting what is making them anxious. It is difficult for children and individuals with a history of victimization to fight, so they begin a process of emotional isolation or withdrawal. The process presents another emotional complication in that once isolated, the person begins to feel lonely. The person is then presented with the choice of being either social and anxious or isolated and lonely. Many individuals employ addictive behaviors negatively to cope with this choice; as a result, they do not form trusting relationships.

Emotional Numbing. Choosing between anxiety and loneliness presents overwhelming emotional complications beginning early in life, and emotional numbing becomes a third coping mechanism. Children quickly become hypervigilant in response to their environment to predict danger and anticipate ways they can be safe. Substance use, anger, and sex often become a way of numbing. The use of substances, anger, and sex in the environment adds to the overall trauma and perpetuates the atmosphere of violence.

In summary, trauma has become the context and life experience for many American Indian people. This trauma has a past that includes boarding schools and several other losses which vary between tribal groups. Many individuals currently face further violence from prejudice, angry and aggressive family or community members, poverty, and systems of dependency. This trauma is compounded because efforts that Indian people employ to cope often produce more traumatic reactions and greater levels of victimization. The individual and cumulative effect of these traumas has been loss of traditional values and behavior, and these factors continue to increase for many American Indian people.

Assessing American Indian Offenders

In this chapter, I also outline five major issues in the assessment and treatment of American Indian sexual offenders.

Assessment of Indian Identity. First it is necessary to assess the Indian identification of the individual and his or her family. We can complete this assessment by obtaining genealogy information and reviewing the person's usual daily routines. It is important both to describe how the individual sees his or her identification area and to evaluate and compare this description with the person's actual behavioral routines. During the treatment process, treatment providers should expect and address inconsistency and conflicts.

Cultural Issues Around Aggression. The second issue involves cultural differences among the concepts of assertive, passive, and aggressive. Sexual offending is generally considered an aggressive response. However, definitions of aggressive behaviors vary widely between families and cultural groups. The most helpful technique involves defining each of these concepts and then asking the offender and his family to provide their own definitions from those established as a baseline.

Nonverbal Communication. Over the past several years, different information has been documented regarding nonverbal behavior among American Indian people. There is a danger of overgeneralizing about communication patterns without consideration of the specific intent, experiential background, and tribal affiliation of the individual. Clinicians must be careful to learn all they can about the background of the patient to avoid stereotypes.

Value Differences. The fourth issue involves value differences between the dominant society's methods of social control and American Indian methods of social control. Again, clinicians are cautioned to understand these differences in the context of the offender and his or her family. Sometimes there are only minor value differences; at other times major differences exist. Members of the same family or tribal group may also have different values or may express them differently. Therefore, it is important not to assume or to attribute a certain value stance but to question and clarify value areas in detail. Families are generally extended in the Indian world, which results in several unique value patterns that treatment providers need to understand and address.

The Role of Shame. Many American Indian people believe that shame is shared among family and tribal groups. This sharing of shame reflects a much different variable from the blaming of the individual that occurs in the dominant society. Further, the concept of sharing shame has a great impact on family members when a behavior such as sexual offending is present.

Assessing American Indian Victims

Two areas of special concern exist when assessing the American Indian victim of sexual assault. First, most clinicians are trained to gather information in victim assessments and to compare them to descriptions of the same incidents given by alleged offenders. The clinician must ensure that false memories have not somehow been established and reinforced within the victim. This becomes a concern when a member of the dominant society interviews alleged victims using methods developed for a different cultural group. The second concern is the use of anatomically correct dolls to help elicit information from victims who are American Indians. The use of such dolls has not been validated among American Indian children, which means that there is no expected baseline for comparing victim statements or reactions.

Multimodal Treatment

The most important issue to keep in mind when treating the American Indian sexual offender is that American Indian people are victims by nature of their history and life experience, and they are offenders with respect to inappropriate behavioral patterns. As a result, team participation is often necessary when assessing and treating such individuals. Treatment often covers four therapy areas:

- Cognitive-behavioral therapy and relapse prevention
- Substance use, abuse, and dependency treatment needs
- Attention deficit, conduct, and impulsive control concerns
- Affective disorders such as depression.

It is best to establish treatment methods that address all these issues in a single setting as opposed to involving several different settings and providers across programs.

Recommended Cognitive-Behavioral Techniques

Seven cognitive-behavioral techniques are recommended. These components can be offered to all sex offenders. They include satiation, covert sensitization, cognitive restructuring, anger control, social skills, sex education, and relapse prevention.

1. Verbal satiation is a process of tape recording thoughts about inappropriate sexual behavior to the point of extreme boredom to reduce the level of arousal.
2. Covert sensitization pairs deviant fantasies with disgusting or frightening ones.
3. Cognitive restructuring includes evaluating beliefs about sexual behavior to correct ideas that could justify inappropriate sexual acting out.
4. Anger control is defined as learning ways to address anger which do not lead to hurting oneself or others.
5. Offenders are trained in social skills to develop appropriate social relations.
6. Sex education is defined as learning about sexuality and how sexuality and emotions work together.
7. Relapse prevention is aimed at reviewing what was learned and developing a plan to stop the person from getting into trouble again.

Implementation of these components involves modification because of cultural differences. The actual modifications need to be based on information gained during the assessment process for each offender, and it is not uncommon to identify further modifications because of details learned while patients are in treatment. The treatment setting may be individual or group or a combination.

The Life Graph. In addition to the standard cognitive-behavioral techniques, many offenders present their own victim issues, which require still other techniques. One such technique is the life graph. This graph is completed in a booklet form, usually some type of bound notebook. Each offender is instructed to arrange the notebook by years starting with his year of birth. Two pages are used for each year and these pages should be opposite each other in the notebook. The left-hand page is used to list trauma associated with each year; the right-hand page is used to list healing experiences. Important anniversary dates such as births, deaths, marriages, and divorces need to be considered; offenders are encouraged to consult their family and friends regarding past issues. Sometimes records such as report cards or school data are also helpful. The life graph needs to be completed during the offender treatment process. During group therapy sessions, time should be allotted to address the various issues individual patients must deal with in their life graph.

Offenders should also be required to complete their own sexual history while they are working on the life graph. It is often interesting to compare the history from the life graph to assessment information completed before the offender was accepted into treatment. Offenders should list items in the life graph as topics only and use a pencil so that they can move items if they find that they have listed them incorrectly. Pictures, poems, and other methods of documentation can be employed in this process as well. Once completed, offenders can use the life graph as a reference point for alternative actions or behaviors in developing a nonoffending lifestyle. Moreover, it is a source of information when patients are developing their relapse prevention program.

Substance Abuse Treatment. Substance use has been acknowledged as a major problem among American Indians. Several reports of alcohol and other substance use in this population are available which indicate epidemic patterns of use (Herring, 1994). Many American Indian offenders have histories of both personal and family alcohol or substance use. To assess this history adequately requires a family history including the kinship and relationship patterns of the extended family group.

American Indian people have recognized the issues with substance use, and they have developed intervention methods that follow traditional beliefs and teachings. The "red road" approach (Arbogast, 1995) uses a holistic philosophy common to the traditional lifestyle of American Indian people. Providers working with American Indian patients need to be aware of this philosophy and integrate these concepts into the assessment and treatment processes. Discussion with community or tribal elders is the usual starting place in this process regarding values, concerns, and priorities for intervention. Elders are generally the keepers of knowledge in Indian ways, and their approval becomes necessary before the community at large accepts intervention efforts. Thus, non-Indian providers must become acculturated to the life views and behaviors of the Indian world.

Substances have a disinhibiting effect on behavior that leads to an increased potential for offending or reoffending. The objective for American Indian offenders is to remain substance free throughout the entire processes of treatment and aftercare.

Impulse Control. Impulse control is another major concern in offender assessment and treatment. Exposure to alcohol during gestation is an issue in the American Indian population that affects impulse control, but differences are present between tribal groups. Prevalence rates for alcohol-related birth defects among American Indians have been estimated as equal to or several times higher than the rates found in non-Indian populations (May, Hymbaugh, Aase, & Samet, 1983). Extensive information regarding the patient's pregnancy and birth history should be collected as part of the assessment process. This information may affect the treatment plan or methods employed during treatment. Care must be taken to avoid a stereotype that most Indian women consume alcohol while they are pregnant as the available information does not support this conclusion.

Affective Disorders. The final area of treatment I address in this chapter is depression and other affective disorders. The Swinomish Tribal Community (1993) has documented a triad of depression, alcohol abuse, and destructive acting out among American Indian patients seen for mental health services, and the prevalence of affective disorders may be significantly higher in the American Indian population as compared to the members of the dominant society. Depression and other affective disorders are also an associated feature of traumatic experiences and depressant drug use. As a result, the assessment and treatment of affective disorders are a high priority with American Indian sexual offenders.

Special Issues in Programming

Employing Traditional Indian Resources. Unique issues exist in the treatment setting for American Indian sexual offenders. A major concern is the ability to integrate traditional tribal or family beliefs and helping practices into sexual offender programming areas. This can be accomplished by using traditional healers and asking them to provide ceremonies or rituals for specific purposes. A sweat lodge ceremony is often used in this context, but clinicians should consult with traditional healers before they undertake any of these processes.

Socialization Patterns. Social interaction or socialization patterns are an important consideration. Socialization comprises five specific areas: daily routines, the ability of people to assist each other in task completion, offering and accepting emotional support, expressing and allowing others to express emotions, and emphasizing ownership. Values and cultural beliefs influence social activities. Major differences can exist in these five areas between cultures, and the therapy setting comes to represent a specific cultural environment. Those who are receiving treatment need to perceive the setting as being safe, and providers need to evaluate patients' progress and model each of these five areas. If treatment providers are unsuccessful in modeling any of these areas, they need to develop a specific plan to correct the situation.

Consequences vs. Antecedents. Another issue is the differences in approaches to behavioral management. Cultural differences exist in the concept and methods employed for behavioral management between traditional American Indian cultures and the dominant society. The dominant society generally considers behavioral management from the viewpoint of consequences. Consequences occur after a behavior in such a way that acceptable behavior is reinforced while unacceptable behavior is punished or becomes a criterion for the individual to be removed from positive social environments. Much of the life view of traditional American Indian ways did not rely on consequences to maintain social control.

Erickson (1950) recognized that American Indian people employed specific methods consistently when completing activities. One of these methods was to use antecedents as a behavioral management process. Antecedents were generally seen as positive adult role models and as a process of making it easy to follow an expected routine and difficult to deviate from this routine in some manner. Efforts were made to prepare children or other individuals to display the desired behavior. Antecedental methods appear to be very helpful when dealing with children or individuals from traumatic environments, as these methods fit well with hypervigilance and tendencies to compulsively survey the environment to ensure safety. These methods also foster internal control methods and recognize the need individuals have to make appropriate choices.

Locus of Control. Another issue relates to developing an internal locus of control. Four general objectives need to be considered:

- Developing knowledge and acceptance of each person's culture and family
- Obtaining a balance between the physical and spiritual parts of the self
- Developing a balance between cognitive and emotional functioning
- Developing the ability to make appropriate choices without the influence of cognitive distortions

Completing these tasks is based on understanding the cultural background of each offender and the input of traditional cultural leaders and healers.

Responsibilities of the Treatment Provider. Therapists have a responsibility to provide their patients with relevant treatment options; for American Indian offenders, relevant treatment includes traditional methods based on assessment data but also requires that their history as victims be addressed and considered as potential triggers that lead to their offending behavior and dysfunctional responses. Therapists need to realize that their patients are often struggling with belonging and psychological security issues. The main implication for therapy concerning this difference is that the therapist must ensure that the offender has established a level of bonding with the treatment process as therapy is being provided.

Conclusion

This chapter has discussed the assessment and treatment of the American Indian sexual offender based on three principles. These principles involve viewing each offender from an ethnic rather than a social or racial stance, considering identification issues for both offenders and their families, and understanding the context of historical and personal trauma. Current sources of trauma include prejudice, violence from family and community members, poverty, and systems of dependency.

Trauma has been generational and it begins early in childhood, as today's traumatized adults were yesterday's traumatized children. A process begins in which children accept being preyed on until they reach the point of being the predator or the dominant group member. The process results in individuals choosing between two undesired emotional states—either being anxious or being lonely. Ineffective addictive processes develop as coping methods to avoid making this choice, and such coping methods produce further trauma. Several areas of cultural differences were highlighted that included assessing Indian identification areas; differences between assertive, passive, and aggressive; avoiding stereotypes of nonverbal communication; value differences; and the role of shame in the two systems of social control.

Clinicians must be careful in the assessment process to question methods that may result in false memories and overconcerns regarding the use of anatomically correct dolls to gain or verify victim statements from American Indians, because such methods have not been sufficiently researched. Treatment of American Indian sexual offenders requires the introduction of cultural and ethnic issues in the cognitive-behavioral programming. Additional methods are also required to treat the victim issues that many American Indian offenders present. The treatment setting must be made safe on a social level, and a knowledge must be present regarding differences in behavioral management methods between American Indian societies and the dominant society. Indian people have been subjected to many traumatic events and life experiences. They have come to distrust other individuals who come from the dominant society as well as many individuals within their own community and tribal groups. It is difficult for them to accept supportive efforts from other individuals as a result, and they often resist bonding with therapists and other helping professionals. They have a greater ability to bond with systems that offer guidance and support. Providing such systems is the definition of safety at a societal level.

To be successful in treatment, American Indian offenders must address several personal adjustment areas so that they can make appropriate future choices. These personal adjustment issues include validating and resolving victim issues, coming to accept their family's history of traumatic events, and developing an identity with a societal structure that can provide a model of prosocial behaviors. They also include resolving any spiritual issues that may be present and adopting a belief structure that avoids conflicts between values and behaviors.

This chapter has highlighted the need for clinicians working with this population to commit to understanding cultural and ethnic issues. In addition, clinicians need to understand that their social functioning is at a higher level than that of the offenders they are treating and thus they must take extra care in creating a supportive, therapeutic environment. Understanding and integrating concepts from the traditions of the Indian offender's tribal and family background enhance the potential for positive outcomes from treatment.

Note

The opinions expressed in this chapter are those of the author and do not necessarily reflect the views of the Indian Health Service.

References

Allport, G. (1954). *The nature of prejudice*. Cambridge: Addison-Wesley.

Arbogast, D. (1995). *Wounded warriors—A time for healing*. Omaha, NE: Little Turtle.

Bunk, P. D. (1994). *Influence of parental coping on the psychological development of children following severe traumatization*. Paper presented at the 13th International Congress of the International Association for Child and Adolescent Psychiatry and Allied Professionals, San Francisco.

Erickson, E. H. (1950). *Childhood and society*. New York: Norton.

Garbarino, J., Dubrow, N., Kostelny, K., & Pardo, C. (1992). *Children in danger: Coping with the consequences of community violence*. San Francisco: Jossey-Bass.

Garbarino, J., Kostelny, K., & Dubrow, N. (1991). What children can tell us about living in danger. *American Psychologist, 46*, 376–383.

Herring, R. D. (1994). Substance use among Native American Indian youth: A selected review of causality. *Journal of Counseling and Development, 72*, 578–584.

May, P. A. (1989). Alcohol abuse and alcoholism among American Indians: An overview. In T. D. Watts & R. Wright (Eds.), *Alcoholism in minority populations* (pp. 96–119). Springfield, IL: Charles C. Thomas.

May, P. A., Hymbaugh, K. J., Aase, J. M., & Samet, J. M. (1983). Epidemiology of Fetal Alcohol Syndrome among American Indians of the southwest. *Social Biology, 30*, 374–387.

Swinomish Tribal Community. (1993). *A gathering of wisdoms.* LaConner, WA: Swinomish Tribal Mental Health Project.

Wyatt, G., Michael, N. & Riederle, M. H. (1994). *Sexual abuse and consensual sex.* Newbury Park, CA: Sage.

Part 4

Treatment and Supervision Issues

This section presents a number of different treatment issues. Some of the chapters deal with techniques that can be applied to any population of sex offenders; others focus on approaches to dealing with such special subgroups as incest offenders and date rapists. Currently sex offender treatment is moving in a multimodal direction, skirting a reliance on just one approach. This movement follows a developmental trend toward becoming more and more specialized and individualized.

We can see this trend evolving across the history of sex offender treatment. Originally sex offenders were either incarcerated in prisons, where there was no treatment for anyone, or they were hospitalized possibly under a sexually dangerous person statute in mental hospitals where they received generic treatment. The first specialized treatment began at Western State Hospital in Washington State where a group of sex offenders petitioned to be allowed to run their own groups. The late 1970s and 1980s saw the emergence of a specialized field of treatment for these individuals. Literally thousands of programs and specialized practices emerged, a national organization was founded, and specialized certification began in at least one state. The 1990s may be the age of specialization, when treatment becomes tailor-made to the individual.

In Chapter 15, L. L. Bench, Stephen P. Kramer, and Susan Erickson present a study conducted by the Utah Department of Corrections of the recidivism patterns of 408 sex offenders who were released over a 10-year period with an average "at risk" time of 4 years. The group included offenders who had successfully completed treatment, a group who actively failed to complete therapy, and a third group who failed treatment due to a cause beyond their control, such as illness or transfer. The researchers separately studied the group whose parole was revoked for violation of a condition, the group that committed new non-sex crimes, and the group that committed new sex crimes. Then they applied multivariate techniques to identify the variables that predicted each one of these conditions. Interestingly enough, in each of these cases different variables were predictive. This study, with its large sample, long follow-up period, and different therapy response groups, represents one of the best studies in the area of sex offender recidivism. Its conclusions can be directly applied in a variety of criminal justice settings to enhance public safety.

In Chapter 16, Lori Koester Scott outlines a model supervision program for sex offenders which has been developed in the Phoenix area. In an increasing number of states, parole has been eliminated or parole boards have become reluctant to parole any felons, particularly sex offenders. Understandably, these individuals and the elected officials who appoint them are concerned with what happens when a paroled offenders reoffends. In a number of states where this has happened, the press has had a field day—blaming the Board and the Governor for what is an inevitable occurrence. Probation and parole are not liberal, naive programs that release dangerous felons from jails or prisons, oblivious to the possibility of reoffense. They have been developed in the cause of public safety to attempt to at least partially control the behavior of criminals who will inevitably return to the community. To deny parole to offenders is simply to postpone their release until such time as they can walk out of the prison with no controls on them whatsoever, free to live anywhere they want, pursue any job they can get, and engage in any high-risk behaviors they choose. Furthermore, both probation and parole conserve resources. Maricopa County in Arizona has recognized the need for long-range supervision of sex offenders and has instituted lifetime probation. This allows trained officers to monitor these individuals for years and to incarcerate them should they begin to show warning signs of reoffending. These officers work very closely with therapists, even providing psychoeducational classes to offenders and their families. They utilize the most modern technologies, including both polygraphy and phallometric assessment. Their efforts to effectively supervise this population has resulted in decreases in reoffense rates.

Scott Johnson has written widely on date rape, an area in which many of the old rape myths still predominate. The criminal justice system in many states remains reluctant to prosecute these cases as they are not as clear-cut as the violent stranger rapist. The survey presented in Chapter 17 demonstrates that men and women still have different beliefs regarding sexual behavior. The chapter also stresses the importance of carefully evaluating the types of pressure, intimidation, and force that have been used in date rape situations.

In Chapter 18, Rebecca Palmer presents an approach to dealing with incest offenders which focuses on working with the families. Reuniting incest offenders with their families remains a controversial issue. Many programs, as well as probation and parole departments, mandate that incest offenders have no contact whatsoever with their families. However, in many instances offenders are under supervision or have finished with it. Their actions cannot be controlled by the state. They are free to rejoin their families if they wish. The question then becomes whether it is better to have worked with these families or to forbid contact until this mandate expires. Palmer's program works in conjunction with specialized treatment for the offender, the spouse, the victim and in some cases the siblings. Her program focuses on bringing the families out of denial. It focuses on three stages in which the therapy begins with assessment and creating a context for change that includes helping the family develop metaphors for change. The second stage includes practicing interventions; the third stage involves consolidating the changes that the family has made and anticipating and preparing for difficulties which the family may face.

In Chapter 19, Debra Baker and Stephen Price present an extensive review of the history and management of therapeutic communities. Basic models are available for treating sex offenders in institutions. The offenders can either live in the general population and come together for periodic treatment sessions or they can live together in a special housing unit. The latter model has numerous advantages, including the ability for the sex offenders to be open about who they are 24 hours a day rather than attempting to hide their identity to protect themselves from other criminals who are angered by the nature of their crimes. They can discuss and practice what they learn in treatment on an ongoing basis. In addition, their behavior can be closely monitored 24 hours a day. Unlike drug abusers, who have access to illegal substances in prison, thus their response to drug abuse treatment can be gauged, sex offenders are usually in high-risk situations while incarcerated. Most sex offenders do not assault other inmates. Small children do not roam around inside prisons. And, relatively speaking, women employees are rarely sexually assaulted. However, sex offenders do show offending patterns in a variety of social interactions. Pedophiles may groom and extract sexual favors from youthful-looking inmates. Rapists may attempt to manipulate female staff members. Treatment providers can observe and treat these patterns in therapeutic communities. This chapter presents numerous practical suggestions from how to establish the community in a prison to maintaining its integrity.

Treating a sex offender's own victimization is another controversial issue. Some therapists suggest that allowing a sex offender to discuss himself as a victim provides a ready-made excuse for his offending. He may shift the blame for his own crimes to his offender. However, many other therapists feel that a comprehensive sex offender treatment program must address past victimization if they are to obtain a complete picture of the offender's motivation. Whole schools of sex offender treatment, including the addictions model, make this a key facet of treatment. Research on the effects of early trauma offer many insights into sexual deviance. In Chapter 20, Barbara K. Schwartz and John Bergman review the literature on dealing with the effects of childhood sexual victimization. They then relate this to the field of drama therapy and present a theoretical justification for incorporating drama therapy into an integrated treatment program.

In Chapter 21, Emily Coleman presents a program for incorporating animal-facilitated therapy into the treatment of sex offenders. Some practitioners may perceive this effort as frivolous; however, animal-facilitated treatment has been used successfully with a variety of populations for hundreds of years. It is particularly effective with populations who have issues with trust, which certainly describes sex offenders. Moreover, many sex offenders have sexualized all touch. This may have occurred when as children the only times they were touched was when they were being sexually abused. Work with animals can help the offender desexualize physical contact. Coleman has used the technique primarily with developmentally disabled offenders in an outpatient clinic where it has facilitated social relations and helped the men to understand learning principles as well as developing metaphors for comprehending their own behavior. Other programs have successfully used this technique with a variety of offenders within an institutional settings. Each sex offender is a unique individual with specific needs which requires that programs develop a variety of techniques for responding to the differing emotional, cognitive and social needs of their clients. Animal facilitated therapy can be a valuable tool in dealing with this difficult population.

Sex offender therapy is an evolving and developing profession. Because it deals with basic components of the personality such as sexuality and social relations, it may require a large arsenal of techniques to address the problem's complexity. This section presents suggestions for both supervision and treatment of sex offenders.

Chapter 15

A Discriminant Analysis of Predictive Factors in Sex Offender Recidivism

by L. L. Bench, M.A., Stephen P. Kramer, Ph.D., and Susan Erickson, M.A.

Overview

The ability to predict with any degree of accuracy the outcome of a decision to release or to incarcerate a sex offender, or, stated another way, the ability to "screen for risk," is one many people seek for a variety of reasons. Public policymakers, judges, parole boards, and therapists are some of the individuals whose decision-making powers could be improved given some probabilistic ability to predict which offenders might reoffend or what type of recidivism could be expected. This ability has become even more interesting to researchers of late because (1) there has been an alarming increase in the frequency of sexual assaults to which the officials must respond in the most parsimonious way, (2) the impact of these assaults on the public has been devastating and must be reduced, and (3) the financial burden associated with these offenses has devastated public budgets because of the resulting prison overcrowding, judicial costs, costs of supervision and treatment, and victim expenses.

Current Statistics

Specifically, recent data reported by the Bureau of Justice Statistics indicates that forcible rape increased by over 600% per 100,000 residents from 1960 to 1993 (Bureau of Justice Statistics [BJS], 1994). A comparison of arrest data from 1984 to 1993 for sex offenses shows an alarming increase of 14% for offenders under 18 years of age (BJS, 1994). The number of sex offenders in state prisons across the nation has increased by 68% since 1986 during a period in which the generic inmate population increased by 57% (Snell, 1991). The emotional, physical, financial, vocational, behavioral, and social impacts of these crimes on the victims are only a few of the devastations documented by Conte (1988).

The rapid growth of sex offender treatment programs nationally has only recently reversed itself (Freeman-Longo & Knopp, 1992). Only the most effective programs have survived because of limited treatment dollars. The successful treatment providers have demanded information on treatment components and statistical and clinical variables which may help to predict the eventual outcome with their clientele. The cost of sex offender treatment in an intensive residential community setting for five years has been estimated at $27,500; the cost of incarceration without treatment for a similar period has been estimated at $132,268 to $152,618 (Pithers, 1987). These cost differences demonstrate without question the need for effective predictive instruments.

A swell of violent crime by young offenders generally fuels a periodic reactionary "get tough" penological philosophy. This has bestowed upon the United States the dubious distinction of incarcerating more citizens per capita than any country in the world. Ironically, severe prison overcrowding conditions inevitably lead to more lenient policies that are necessary to (1) free up space for incoming offenders and (2) protect institutions from lawsuits filed by inmates claiming protection under the eighth amendment (Ellis, 1991; Anson & Hancock, 1992).

At the root of the controversy over the effectiveness of treatment is an ongoing debate over the frequency and type of recidivistic activity for sex offenders (Marques, Day, Nelson, & Miner, 1990). This debate is further complicated by the fact that recidivistic activity can assume a variety of forms. For example, recidivism may refer to reconviction for the same type of sexual offense, arrest or investigation for the same type of offense without conviction, recommission of any type of sexual offense, or recommission of any non-sex criminal offense. Recidivism may also refer to parole and probation violations where a breach of agreement has occurred but no law has been violated (e.g., violation of curfew).

In a review of the literature on recidivism studies for offenders involved in a variety of criminal offenses, Boone (1994) found wide disparity in the definition of recidivism. For example, Boone found nine studies that used technical violations as the definition of recidivism (Petersilia & Turner, 1993; Commonwealth of Virginia, 1991; Hairston, 1988; Jamison, 1981; Murphy, 1981; Fox, 1980). Boone (1994) noted that a number of studies use new arrest as the defining criterion for recidivism (Petersilia & Turner, 1993; Chavaria, 1992; Jones, 1991; Cadigan, 1991; Schumacker, Anderson, & Anderson, 1990; Glaser & Gordon, 1991; Irish,

1989; Corbo, 1988; Greenwood & Turner, 1987; Erwin & Bennett, 1987; Vito, 1986; Walsh, 1985; Arriessohn, 1981; Byles, 1981; Jamison, 1981; Fox, 1981). Other studies restrict the definition of recidivism to new arrests resulting in conviction (Jones, 1991; Hairston, 1988; Erwin & Bennett, 1987; Corbo, 1988; Vito, 1986; Lichtman & Smock, 1982). The absence of any clear-cut standard for the definition of recidivism makes comparison of study results and the development of valid predictive instruments difficult if not impossible (Furby, Weinrott, & Blackshaw, 1989). Less than systematic methodological practices have left a somewhat muddled perspective as to the extent and type of recidivistic involvement of sex offenders, and they have confused and postponed the development of even a rudimentary ability to begin to statistically discriminate recidivists from nonrecidivists.

As prison populations continue to increase, who to release becomes a much more critical issue. For the reasons noted earlier, the ability to accurately predict which sex offenders will recidivate would be of tremendous value. Regrettably, attempts at predicting the success or failure of sex offenders have been disappointing.

Prior Research

Only a few studies have been conducted that focused on identifying factors associated with recidivistic activity for sex offenders. A study conducted by Abel, Mittelman, Becker, Rathner, and Rouleau (1988) evaluated the effectiveness of an outpatient cognitive-behavioral treatment program for 192 pedophiles. All clients who were willing to participate were allowed into the program except those clients who were severely psychotic or brain damaged. The clients included violent offenders with long offense histories and a great range of paraphilias. Treatment included masturbatory satiation and covert sensitization, sex education/sex dysfunction, cognitive restructuring, social skills training, and assertiveness training. Reoffense data was based on the information provided by the patient. All participants were interviewed with the understanding that all information would be kept confidential. Recidivism was evaluated using structured clinical interviews at 6- and 12-month intervals. The lack of a minimum two-year posttreatment follow-up makes it difficult to assess an actual success rate for the program.

At the end of the one-year follow-up period, 12.2% of the 98 pedophiles who were evaluated had recidivated. The results of a discriminant function analysis indicated that molestation of both boys and girls, as well as children and adolescents (expressed as a dichotomous variable), correctly classified 83.7% of all subjects. Abel et al. (1988) reported that in decreasing order of statistical power the following five pretreatment factors correctly classified 85.7% of the offenders as successes or failures: (1) molested both males and females, as well as children and adolescents, (2) failure to list increased communication with adults as a treatment goal, (3) committed both "hands on" and "hands off" offense behaviors, (4) divorced, and (5) molested familial and nonfamilial victims. Age, race, education, socioeconomic status, religious preference, motivation for seeking treatment, frequency of pedophilic acts before treatment, number of prior offenses, number of victims, and patient's sense of control over his pedophilic behavior were not significant factors in predicting recidivism. Treatment dropout rate was 34%.

Marshall, Jones, Ward, Johnston, and Barbaree (1988) evaluated the effectiveness of a cognitive-behavioral treatment program for child molesters. Subjects were 68 treated child molesters and 58 untreated child molesters. Only those clients who were actively psychotic or severely brain damaged were excluded from treatment. Clients who had IQ scores below 68 were not accepted into the program. The child molesters were further categorized into incest offenders, molesters of nonfamilial female children, or molesters of nonfamilial male children. The control group consisted of matched untreated child molesters who had admitted their crimes and expressed a desire to enter treatment. All the molesters were assessed at the same time.

The treatment program included electrical aversion, self-administration of smelling salts to decrease deviant arousal patterns, masturbatory reconditioning, skills training, conflict resolution, and the constructive use of leisure time. The clients were also administered pre- and post-plethysmograph tests.

Data sources for recidivism included offender self-reports, official police records which included charges (not just convictions) in the United States and Canada, and unofficial reports from child protection and police agencies. Recidivism results were based on the unofficial records which yielded higher rates of recidivism than did the official reports. Higher rates of recidivism for the unofficial reports are to be expected as they may have contained reports of reoffenses that may not have resulted in convictions in the legal system. The follow-up period was from 1 to 11 years. The recidivism rate for the treated molesters was 13.2% compared to a rate of 34.5% for untreated molesters.

Marshall and Barbaree (1990) reported that age of the offender and type of sexual contact predicted recidivism. However, these factors were not consistent across offense categories. Being under age 40 was a powerful predictor of recidivism between the two groups of nonfamilial child molesters, but age did not differentiate between incest offenders who reoffended and those who did not. Offenders that had genital-genital or genital-anal contact with their victims and, had molested female children (familial or nonfamilial females), were more likely to reoffend. Socioeconomic status, number or prior offenses, age of victim, intelligence level, and pre- and posttreatment indices of deviant sexual interests were not related to treatment outcome.

Rice, Quinsey, and Harris (1991) examined the recidivism of 136 nonfamilial child molesters who participated in a behavioral treatment program in a maximum security psychiatric institution. Treatment consisted of a laboratory-based aversion therapy designed to alter sexual age preference. Penile plethysmography measurements were obtained pre- and posttreatment.

Recidivism was defined as a new sexual offense conviction, being arrested or returned to the facility for any violent offense, an arrest or conviction for any offense, or the return to the institution for any reason. The average follow-up time was 6.3 years. Recidivistic activity was verified from various official correctional facilities (Lieutenant Governor's Board of Review, the Royal Canadian Mounted Police, and the National Parole Service of Canada) and institutional files.

Results indicated that 31% of the clients were convicted of a new sex offense, 43% committed a violent offense, and 56% were arrested for a new criminal offense. Factors associated with recidivism included number or prior sexual offenses, previous property convictions, the selection of male victims, diagnosis of a personality disor-

Table 15.3
Variables Associated With Predicting Technical Violations

Variable	Estimate	T for Ho	Significance
Finished	-.3231	-.678	.0001
Numparv1	0.1037	3.47	.0006
Lencust1	0.0266	3.15	.0018
Force1	-.1303	-2.17	.0306
Convnsxx	0.5314	3.89	.0001
Misconv	-.0614	-3.44	.0007
Drgtime	-.1662	-2.20	.0286
Abusekid	0.0900	1.98	.0485
R2 = .3002			

Table 15.4
Results of Classification Analysis for Technical Violations

	No Recidivism	Recidivism	Total
No recidivism	163 (77.25%)	48 (22.75%)	211 (100%)
Recidivism	19 (19.39%)	79 (80.61)	98 (100%)
Total	182 (58.90%)	127 (41.10%)	309 (100%)

and parameter values for individual variables. Discriminant analysis was then conducted for each model to determine classification accuracy based on the derived discriminant coefficients. Parameter estimates, R2 coefficients, and classification results are reported for each model. Variables are listed in the tables in accordance with their power to discriminate between recidivism and nonrecidivism.

Model 1: Technical Violations. This model was created to evaluate the likelihood of an offender committing a probation or parole violation after release. For purposes of this analysis, recidivism was defined as number of probation and parole violations. Tables 15.3 and 15.4 present the results of this analysis.

As indicated in Table 15.3, Finished was the variable with the most discriminating value between offenders who recidivated and offenders who did not. This variable indicates whether offenders completed treatment, passively failed treatment, or failed treatment outright. The negative sign associated with the parameter estimate indicates that recidivism is more likely to occur for those offenders who did not complete treatment. The results also indicate that the probability for recidivism increased for offenders who had a greater number of parole violations, served longer prison sentences, used physical forms of force on their victims (as opposed to verbal and nonphysical coercive forces), had a greater number of convictions for sex offenses, had a fewer number of misdemeanor convictions, reported that they did not use drugs, and were abused as children. Table 15.4 represents the results of the classification analysis. The model correctly predicted that no recidivism would occur in approximately 77% of cases and that recidivism could be accurately predicted for approximately 81% of the cases. The model had an overall error rate of approximately 21%. Classification results suggest that it is slightly more difficult to predict nonrecidivistic behavior as opposed to recidivistic behavior and that moderate improvement is gained in prediction as a result of using the model as specified.

Model 2: Recidivism for Non-Sex Offenses. Analysis was conducted to determine to what extent recidivism for non-sex offenses could be predicted. Recidivism was defined as any warrant, arrest, or conviction for any misdemeanor or felony that was not a sex offense and included the following definitions: warrant issued non-sex offense, rearrested misdemeanor non-sex offense, convicted misdemeanor non-sex offense, rearrested felony non-sex offense, convicted felony non-sex offense. Tables 15.5 and 15.6 represent the results of this analysis.

Table 15.5
Variables Associated With Predicting Recidivism for Non-Sex Offenses

Variable	Estimate	T for Ho	Significance
Misdarr	0.0639	6.44	.0001
Agefirst	-.0068	-3.42	.0007
Arsttt	-.0688	-3.80	.0002
Numparv1	0.0926	3.78	.0002
Numinst1	0.1393	2.73	.0168
Relmths1	0.0016	2.67	.0082
Arstnsx	0.0470	2.54	.0115
Force1	0.1157	2.44	.0474
Marital1	-.0522	-2.29	.0225

R2 = .3298

Table 15.6
Results of Classification Analysis for Non-Sex Offenses

	No Recidivism	Recidivism	Total
No recidivism	179 (84.83%)	32 (15.17%)	211 (100%)
Recidivism	6 (26.09) 71%)	17 (73.91)	54 (100%)
Total	194 (73.21%)	71 (26.79%)	265 (100%)

Table 15.7
Variables Associated With Predicting Recidivism for Sex Offenses

Variable	Estimate	T for Ho	Significance
Felconv	0.0868	3.48	.0006
Arstsx	0.1275	3.65	.0003
Arsttt	-.0633	-2.75	.0064
Arstnsx	.0515	2.25	.0256
Felarrst	.0396	2.04	.0423
Finished	-.1001	-2.27	.0244

R2 = .1902

Table 15.8
Results of Classification Analysis for Sex Offenses

	No Recidivism	Recidivism	Total
No recidivism	175 (82.94%)	36 (17.06%)	211 (100%)
Recidivism	18 (40.00%)	27 (60.00%)	45 (100%)
Total	193 (75.39%)	63 (24.61%)	256 (100%)

Number of misdemeanor arrests was the most powerful discriminator between recidivists and nonrecidivists. Following this variable, offenders who recidivated had the following characteristics: were younger when first arrested, had fewer total arrests, had a greater number of parole revocations, had an increased number of institutionalizations, were out on release for a greater period of time (time at risk), had a greater number of arrests for non-sex offenses, used physical forms of force on their victims, and were more likely to be single, separated, or divorced at time of arrest.

Model 2 correctly predicted nonrecidivism approximately 85% of the time and recidivism approximately 72% of the time. The overall error rate for model 2 was approximately 21.5%. Results of this analysis indicated that it is somewhat more difficult to predict recidivistic activity than nonrecidivistic activity. The model as specified showed moderate gains in prediction accuracy over chance.

Model 3: Recidivism for Sex Offenses. Model 3 was limited to recidivistic activity involving sex offenses, including warrant issued sex offense, rearrested misdemeanor sex offense, convicted misdemeanor sex offense, rearrested felony sex offense, convicted felony sex offense. The results are detailed in Tables 15.7 and 15.8.

The total number of felony convictions was the strongest predictor of recidivism involving sex-related offenses. In order of magnitude, characteristics that followed this variable were greater number of arrests for sex offenses, fewer number of total arrests, increased number of arrests for non-sex offenses, greater number of felony arrests, and failure to complete a treatment

Results of the classification analysis indicated that the model correctly predicted

Table 15.9
Variables Associated With Predicting Recidivism (All Definitions)

Variable	Estimate	T for Ho	Significance
Finished	-.2461	-5.04	.0001
Numparv1	0.0867	3.62	.0003
Convsxx	0.0276	2.34	.0195
R2 = .13333			

Table 15.10
Results of Classification Analysis Using All Definitions of Recidivism

	No Recidivism	Recidivism	Total
No recidivism	116 (54.98%)	95 (45.02%)	211 (100%)
Recidivism	50 (25.38%)	147 (74.62%)	197 (100%)
Total	166 (40.69%)	147 (74.62%)	408 (100%)

no recidivism approximately 83% of the time and recidivism approximately 60% of the time. The combined overall error rate for model 3 was approximately 29%. The model as specified resulted in moderate gains over chance for predicting nonrecidivism but only marginal gains in accuracy in predicting recidivism.

Model 4: All Definitions of Recidivism. All definitions of recidivism were combined and compared against offenders who did not recidivate for the construction of model 4. Tables 15.9 and 15.10 depict the results of this analysis.

Only three variables proved to be significant discriminators between recidivists and nonrecidivists when all definitions of recidivism were considered. The strongest factor associated with recidivists was failure to complete treatment (Finished) followed by an increased number of parole revocations and a greater total of convictions for non-sex offenses.

The model predicted nonrecidivism only slightly better than chance in accurately classifying only 55% of the cases. Prediction of recidivistic activity as compared to nonrecidivistic activity showed noticeable improved with an accuracy rate of approximately 75%. The model had an overall combined error rate of approximately 35%.

Conclusion

Until now, the business of how and when to release offenders convicted of sex offenses has been based predominantly on guesswork. The need for a valid and reliable instrument that clarifies this enigma is obvious. Our results suggest that the accuracy of predicting recidivistic activity of sex offenders can be moderately improved over chance by relying on certain variables and the specification of certain models.

The results on predicting recidivism as compared to no recidivism are mixed. Results indicate that it is easier to predict recidivism for offenders who are involved in both sex-related and non-sex-related offenses (models 2 and 3). However, nonrecidivism is more successfully predicted for offenders arrested for technical violations and when all recidivistic activity is compared with all nonrecidivistic activity (models 1 and 4).

Variables indicative of past criminal involvement such as number of parole revocations, amount of time in prison, number of misdemeanor arrests, age at first arrest, and total number of arrests are valuable indicators of future recidivistic activity. One variable that stands out that is not grouped under the traditional legal category of variables is "completion of treatment." This variable was the most influential factor in discriminating between recidivistic and nonrecidivistic activity for all definitions considered as a whole and, specifically, technical violations. This finding should gratify some clinicians, who have suspected, but have never been able to prove, that offenders who complete treatment are much better risks for release than candidates who never entered treatment or dropped out prematurely.

Some of our findings are supported by previous investigations. Studies conducted by Abel et. al (1988) and McGrath (1991) point to importance of marital status of the offender. Our results, as well as theirs, suggest that offenders who are single, divorced, or separated are at an increased risk of recidivism as compared to offenders who are married. The importance of prior number of sex convictions and total number of convictions as confirmed by our study is also supported by findings of other studies (Rice et al., 1991; McGrath, 1992). This finding is also bolstered by the importance of similar variables such as number of misdemeanor arrests, number of misdemeanor convictions, number of felony arrests, number of felony convictions, number of arrests for non-sex offenses, and number of arrests for sex offenses. However, this is contrary to findings of Abel et al. (1988) and Marshall et al. (1988), which failed to identify number of prior offenses as a significant factor in predicting recidivism. Our results also suggest that type of force used on the victim is a significant factor in predicting recidivism, as similarly identified by McGrath (1991).

Perhaps the most startling observation of our research is that only about 50% of sex offenders engaged in any recidivistic activity of any form, as can be clearly seen from Table 15.10. Our findings do not support the all-too-common presupposition that recidivism for sex offenders has a high probability of occurring. An analysis of this same data set (Kramer, Bench, & Erickson, 1996) indicates that only 6% of the offenders went on to commit felony sex offenses for which they were convicted.

In comparison to other offenders, sex offenders appear to be better than average candidates for release. In general these offenders are older, better educated, come from higher socioeconomic backgrounds, and are more compliant. Given the rather low recidivism rate of sex offenders in general and certain subgroups of offenders, most of these offenders could be placed on probation or parole with only minimal risk for reoffending. As noted earlier, the cost of treatment pales in comparison to the exorbitant costs associated with the vicious cycle of offending-release-reoffending.

Research on the development of risk assessment instruments remains limited. Development in this area has been hampered by adherence to rigorous methodological designs, small samples, inadequate data, and a lack of prioritization. The increasing population pressures on prisons, coupled with the predicted increased in criminal activity in all areas, mandate that prison space only be reserved for those for whom there is no other solution. Continued research in the areas of sex offender recidivism and the development of risk assessment instruments is mandatory if behavior by sex offenders is to be treated, rather than simply scorned, and that costly prison space is used judiciously.

References

Abel, G. G., Mittelman, M. S., Becker, J. V., Rathner, J., & Rouleau, J. L. (1988). Predicting child molesters' response to treatment. *Annals of the New York Academy of Sciences, 528*, 223–234.

Anson, R. H. & Hancock, B. W. (1992). Crowding, proximity, inmate violence, and the eighth amendment. *Journal of Offender Rehabilitation, 17*(3/4), 123–132.

Arriessohn, R. M. (1981). Recidivism revisited. *Juvenile and Family Court Journal, 32*(4), 59–68.

Boone Jr., H. N. (1994). An examination of recidivism and other outcome measures: A review of literature. *Perspectives, American Probation and Parole Association*, pp. 12–18.

Bureau of Justice Statistics. (1994). *Sourcebook of criminal justice statistics.* Washington, DC: U.S. Department of Justice, Office of Justice Programs.

Byles, J. A. (1981). Evaluation of an attendance center program for male juvenile probationers. *Canadian Journal of Criminology, 23*(3), 343–355.

Cadigan, T. P. (1991). Electronic monitoring in federal pretrial release. *Federal Probation, 55*(1), 26–30.

Chavaria, F.R. (1992). Successful drug treatment in a criminal justice setting: A case study. *Federal Probation, 56*(1), 48–52.

Commonwealth of Virginia. (1991). *Drugs in Virginia: A criminal justice perspective.* Richmond: Commonwealth of Virginia, Department of Justice Services.

Conte, J. R. (1988). The effects of sexual abuse on children: Results of a research project. In R. A. Prentky & V. I. Quinsey (Eds.), *Human sexual aggression: Current perspectives* (pp. 67–87). New York: New York Academy of Sciences.

Corbo, C. A. (1988). *Release outcome in New Jersey 1982 release cohort: A 36-month follow-up study.* Trenton: New Jersey Department of Corrections. (NCJRS Document No. 117207).

Ellis, K. (1991). Overcrowding, inmate violence and cruel and unusual punishment. *Criminal Justice Journal, 13*(1), 81–99.

Erwin, B. S., & Bennett, L. A. (1987). *New dimensions in probation: Georgia's experience with intensive probation supervision.* Washington, DC: U.S. Department of Justice, National Institute of Justice.

Fox, J. W. (1980). *Development of predictive factors for recidivism risk levels (Kentucky, 1979).* Richmond, KY: Eastern Kentucky University Department of Corrections. (NCJRS Document No. 076179).

Freeman-Longo, R. E., & Knopp, F. H. (1992). *State-of-the-art sex offender treatment: Outcome and issues.* Orwell, VT: Safer Society Press.

Furby, L., Weinrott, M. R., & Blackshaw, L. (1989). Sex offender recidivism: A review. *Psychological Bulletin, 105*, 3–30.

Glaser, D., & Gordon, M. A. (1991). Profitable penalties for lower level courts. *Judicature, 73*(5).

Gottfredson, S. D., & Gottfredson, D. M. (1979). *Screening for risk, a comparison of methods.* Washington, DC: U.S. Department of Justice National Institute of Corrections.

Greenwood, P. W., & Turner, S. (1987). *The VisionQuest Program: An evaluation.* Los Angeles: RAND Corporation.

Hairston, C. F. (1988). Family ties during imprisonment: Do the influence criminal activity? *Federal Probation, 52*(1), 48–52.

Hanson, R. K. (1991). *Assessing risk for sexual offending: A review of questionnaire measures.* Paper presented at the 10th Annual Research and Treatment Conference of the Association for the Treatment of Sexual Abusers, Portland, OR.

Irish, J. F. (1989). *Probation and recidivism: A study of probation adjustment and its relationship to pst-probation outcome for adult criminal offenders in Nassau County.* New York. Mineola, NY: Nassau County Probation Department. (NCJRS Document No. 124663).

Jamison, M. (1981). *Serious 602 offender project of the Contra Costa probation Department-Final Evaluation report.* San Francisco, CA: Urban and Rural Systems Associates. (NCJRS Document No. 085006).

Jones P. R. (1991). The risk of recidivism: Evaluating the public-safety implications of a community corrections program. *Journal of Criminal Justice, 19,* 49–66.

Kramer, S. P., Bench, L. L., Erickson, S. (1996). *A study of twelve different measures of recidivism on 450 sex offenders released since 1980.* Manuscript in preparation.

Lichtman, C. M., & Smock, S. M. (1982). Effects of social services on probationer recidivism—A field experiment. *Journal of Research in Crime and Delinquency, 19*(2), 277–298.

Marques, J. K., Day, D. M., Nelson, C., & Minor, M. H. (1990). The sex offender treatment and evaluation project: California's relapse prevention program. In D. R. Laws (Eds.), *Relapse prevention with sex offenders.* New York: Guilford Press.

Marshall, W. L., & Barbaree, H. E. (1990). An integrated theory of the etiology of sexual offending. In W. L. Marshall, D. R. Lewis, & H. E. Barbaree (Eds.), *Handbook of sexual assault: Issues, theories, and the treatment of the offender* (165–193). New York: Plenum Press.

Marshall, W. L., Jones, R., Ward, T., Johnston, P., & Barbaree, H. E. (1988). The long-term evaluation of a behavioral treatment program for child molesters. *Behavior Research and the Law, 26,* 499–511

McGrath, R. J. (1991). Sex offender risk assessment and disposition planning: A review of empirical and clinical findings. *International Journal of Offender Therapy and Comparative Criminology, 35*(4).

McGrath, R. J. (1992). Assessing sex offender risk. *American Probation and Parole Association: Perspectives, 16*(3).

Murphy, T. H. (1981). *Michigan risk prediction—A replication study—Final report.* Lansing, MI: Michigan Department of Corrections. (NCJRS Document No. 079872).

Petersilia, J., & Turner, S. (1993). *Evaluating intensive supervision probation/parole: Results of a nationwide experiment.* Washington DC: U.S. Department of Justice, National Institute of Justice.

Pithers, W. D. (1987). *Estimated cost savings of sex offender treatment in Vermont in 1987.* Waterbury, VT: Vermont Center for the Prevention and Treatment of Sexual Abuse.

Rice, M., Quinsey, V. L., & Harris, G. T. (1991). Sexual recidivism among child molesters released from a maximum security psychiatric institution. *Journal of Consulting and Clinical Psychology, 59*(3), 381–386.

Schumacker, R. E., Anderson, D. B., & Anderson, S. L. (1990). Vocational and academic indicators of parole success. *Journal of Correctional Education, 41*(1), 8–13.

Snell, T. L. (1991). *Correctional populations in the United States. Bureau of Justice Statistics, 1993* (NCJ-142729). Washington, DC: Bureau of Justice.

Vito, G. F. (1986). *Felony probation and recidivism in Kentucky.* Frankfort, KY: Kentucky Criminal Justice Statistical Analysis Center. (NCJRS Document No. 112566).

Walsh, A. (1985). An evaluation of the effects of adult basic education on rearrest rates among probationers. *Journal of Offender Counseling, Services, and Rehabilitation, 9*(4), 53–61.

Wormith, J. S., & Goldstone, C. S. (1984). The clinical and statistical prediction of recidivism. *Criminal Justice and Behavior, 11*(1), 52–65.

Chapter 16

Community Management of Sex Offenders

by Lori Koester Scott, M. C.

Overview

Lifetime probation. Polygraph testing. Surveillance officers. Specialized case-loads. Curfews. Community notification laws. These and other tools are available to Maricopa County probation officers in the Phoenix, Arizona metropolitan area for effectively managing sex offenders in the community. The National Institute of Justice has highlighted it as a model program because of the department's progressive and comprehensive components. This program and several others are used as key guidelines in this discussion of the community supervision of sex offenders on probation or parole.

Aggressive Community Supervision

Much of the research and data on sex offenders has been gathered from an incarcerated population. Yet the majority of sex offenders are living among us, especially incest offenders and those formerly considered more "harmless," such as exhibitionists. For these offenders, aggressively intervening as early as possible in their behavior patterns while keeping them under appropriate supervision can often be an effective way of community protection. One only has to look at the well-publicized case of Wesley Dodd, a Washington state sex offender who began his behavior as an exhibitionist and who subsequently murdered three children after numerous and ineffective contacts with the criminal justice system, to realize that the system unless effectively organized can fail.

Dodd's first police contact was in Richland, Washington at age 15, after two years of exhibitionist behavior. He admitted that "after a while it wasn't any fun," and he needed to touch his victims and have them touch him. At age 17 he confessed to six or seven crimes, and involvement with 20 victims, but he remained in the community. Ordered into counseling, he attended only briefly. He had been discharged from the Navy for similar behavior. By his early 20s he was convicted of child molestation in Idaho and given a 10-year prison sentence. He served four months because he made a good impression on the judge, who did not know that he was a repeated offender. When he was arrested in Seattle in 1987 for kidnapping a little boy, he received a minimal sanction and no treatment or supervision. He admitted that the "prospect of murder became exciting, an obsession," which he fantasized about continuously. Finally, as everyone in the state of Washington knows, he kidnapped, molested, and killed three young boys.

In community supervision, the key word should be "aggressive," both in the evaluation process and in subsequent monitoring and treatment. Numerous questions about the offense, the victim(s), the defendant, and his environment must be asked in detail. What are the factors contributing to the risk of a particular defendant? Can those factors be controlled in the defendant's environment? How can they be reduced? The philosophy of a specialized sex offender unit is to impose as many external controls as possible on defendants while giving them every opportunity to develop the inner controls necessary to keep from reoffending.

The Continuum of Control

A continuum of control can be developed in which community risk is minimized but rehabilitation can occur. In Arizona, as a result of the passage of the lifetime probation law in 1987, the development of an intensive and creative approach to the short- and long-term management of sex offenders became necessary. Explosive growth was occurring in the state's population, particularly in the Phoenix and Tucson areas, together with studies showing that as the numbers of sex offender convictions were increasing, more than two-thirds were being given probation. As in other jurisdictions around the country, reoffenses were occurring all too often. Sex offender probation in both metropolitan areas now includes the following elements which seem to encompass much more effective community management with this difficult population.

Specialized Conditions

Specialized conditions should be a primary component in the management of sex offenders. Such conditions have been developed by studying the patterns of sex offenders sentenced to probation who subsequently reoffended (Scott, 1994) and from research in studies of recidivism and rates of reoffending (McGrath, 1991; Marshall, Jones, Ward, Johnston, & Barbaree, 1991; Quinsey, Harris, Rice, & LaLumiere,

1995). In Maricopa County, every sex offender sentenced to probation is given 17 specialized sex offender terms in addition to the regular terms. The most important of these is the ban on any contact with children without prior approval of the probation officer. It would seem a sensible and logical restriction for an individual who has already crossed prohibited sexual boundaries, yet approximately 20% of U.S. jurisdictions still do not impose even this condition (English, Colling-Chadwick, Pullen, & Jones, 1996).

Judges sometimes give the defendant permission to live with his own children. Probation officers maintain that to do this may create a potential threat to those children. Because sex offenders are notoriously poor self-reporters (Abel, Mittelman, & Becker, 1985), no contact with any children should be allowed without a thorough assessment of the defendant's risk. The term "no contact" with children must be explained thoroughly. A written definition signed by the offender is preferable.

Regular probation conditions in most jurisdictions prohibit the use of alcohol either totally or to excess. A study of 89 Arizona sex offenders who failed on probation during a 30-month period showed that substance abuse was a significant factor in 91% of the cases (Scott, 1994). In Vermont, a study of 200 sex offenders revealed that alcohol and other substances were precursors to sexual aggression in 56% of the rapists and 30% of the pedophiles sampled (Pithers, Buell, Kashima, Cumming, & Beal, 1987). Substance abuse reduces clear thinking, lowers inhibitions, and provides an opportunity for cognitive distortions to become overwhelming. Therefore, it is highly recommended that such use be prohibited entirely. Little tolerance should be allowed for continued use, and offenders should be ordered into intensive drug/alcohol treatment or jailed.

The use of pornographic or sexually stimulating materials is also banned. Because sex offenders are highly dependent on fantasy to support their cycles of deviancy, such material continues to encourage the objectification of women or children, again supporting their cognitive distortions. Many offenders have used pornography as a means of gaining access to or stimulating their victims. Probation officers also confirm that sex offenders often lead isolated lives, lacking in social skills. Pornography impedes the process of learning to develop interpersonal relationships before moving to sexual intimacy. In Maricopa County, officers are allowed to search an offender's home with reasonable cause, and they often find large collections of pornography. One night, after spotting the car of probationer "Ron" parked in front of a video store, his surveillance officer entered the store, then realized that the defendant was in the "back room" selecting from the X-rated videos. When he followed Ron home, he searched Ron's apartment, where he found not only an extensive collection of such videos but also six guns and other assorted weapons.

Forbidden materials might also include collections of pictures of children or videos that appeal to children. Pedophiles have no business owning books and videos they can use for fantasy material or for grooming children.

Other special conditions include the restriction of the offender's movements in the community, specifically parks, playgrounds, swimming pools, arcades, schoolyards, and other areas determined by the probation officer. An offender who had a pattern of grabbing women in shopping malls was forbidden to patronize such areas without special permission. Every effort is also made to prohibit the offender from entering into new relationships with women who have children. Limitations can be placed on the offender's driving, depending on his known grooming patterns, or a curfew can be imposed if the offender is continually absent when field visits are attempted. Some jurisdictions have the option of electronic monitoring, as well as further restrictions on the possession of cameras, videorecorders, and movie cameras. Many departments are now struggling with ways of monitoring the use and abuse of computers and on-line services.

Specialized Officers and Surveillance

For larger departments the advantages of specialized officers are obvious. Whether it's 1 officer or 10, that officer can obtain the training, skills, and insight that can make community supervision much more effective and meaningful. Specialization means that no longer will the sex offender slip in the door just before 5:00 P.M., spend five minutes in the office talking about his job and last night's basketball game, pay his money, and leave. In the past the probation officer was no more eager to address the issues of sexual deviancy than the probationer was. Effective sex offender officers ask to see written homework from the offender's therapy group; discuss the offender's progress in learning to control his deviant fantasies, his understanding, and his use of the principles of relapse prevention; check up on his family contacts and the status of the victim and any other children who might be part of the offender's immediate or extended family and discuss his contacts in the community, the stability of his employment, and any positive achievements.

In the field, officers should know the description and license number of every vehicle the offender might be driving. Every person living at his residence must be told of his offense and the terms of probation. Extended family members should also be informed. The residence should be observed for toys, children's articles of clothing, children's videos or pornographic material, pictures of children, Nintendo games, and computer equipment, in addition to any signs of drug or alcohol use.

In Maricopa County, the use of surveillance officers allows for larger caseloads and more meaningful fieldwork. Surveillance officers will check out an apartment building or house, for example, to assess nearby schools and parks or the numbers of children who reside in the complex. The location of the apartment is scrutinized. Does it overlook the pool or a park? Are there children nearby? Can the complex only be accessed by a locked gate, prohibiting surprise visits? Officers are equipped with radios and emergency connections; they work evenings and weekends so that they may truly monitor how offenders are spending their leisure time, and if they are indeed residing with approved companions and avoiding contact with children.

But surveillance officers do much more. They gradually develop a rapport with the defendant's family and often spend time just talking. Sometimes they have the luxury of monitoring a residence for an hour or two to check on their hunches about an offender's behavior or to verify a tip from an acquaintance or relative. They learn to recognize various vehicles, neighbors, and unusual situations. Occasionally they might help with homework or discuss issues of relapse prevention. Both probation and surveillance officers attend therapy groups on a random basis so that they may also be familiar with the defendant's progress or lack thereof. Surveillance officers must be totally familiar with the specifics of the offense, circumstances, testing results, age and description of victims, use of alcohol or drugs, and other issues concerning the offender's environment.

Treatment and Teamwork

Special conditions should also include the order to participate in sex-offense-specific treatment and to remain in such treatment at the direction of the probation office. In Maricopa and Pima counties in Arizona and in 17 other states, the polygraph is also mandated as a component of probation (English, Pullen, & Jones, 1996). Because most sex offender program utilize some form of cognitive-behavioral therapy, probation officers need an in-depth understanding of this type of treatment to be effective in monitoring the defendant's application of the principles he is learning week by week. Officers are encouraged to attend groups from time to time on a random basis; contracted providers must agree to allow this. At sentencing, probationers must sign a release allowing therapists to divulge confidential information. This does not mean that officers want to know every detail of every session. It does means that information can be shared freely within the network that the probationer must set up to help keep him from reoffending.

In Tarrant County, Texas, incest offenders are still often allowed to return home immediately after sentencing. Probation officers have developed a program in which the defendant's spouse is immediately assigned the role of learning about her partner's sexual deviancy and how to monitor him and keep her children safe. Officers must rely on the partner to help them do the job. With the imposition of the "no contact" term, however, probation departments can make sure that the offender and partner both complete a substantial portion of treatment before such recontact occurs; indeed, they can use the goal of reunification to motivate both partners into completing appropriate treatment for them and their children.

In Maricopa County, every offender is expected to begin treatment by attending a series of classes on sexuality and sexual deviancy. Forty-five hours are devoted to such topics as basic human sexuality, society's attitudes and the development of stereotypes, understanding the offense cycle, victim trauma and its effects, and expectations surrounding treatment. Such an introduction provides a chance for offenders and their partners to begin discussing a subject that has always been taboo and a secret from everyone else. Officers discovered early on that the probationers were learning so much from the classes that they requested their spouses or partners also be allowed to attend.

New probation officers assigned to the specialized unit must also attend the class. This begins their specialized training and helps them to understand how to communicate with the sex offender therapists. Staffings are scheduled on a regular basis with therapists and problem probationers. Contracted therapists attend meetings of the specialized unit from time to time to stay in touch with changing personnel, court requirements, legal problems, therapy issues, and other concerns. In incest reunification cases or other situations in which an offender is working toward eventual contact with children, open communication and teamwork with treatment providers are vital.

Many past difficulties have been overcome by not allowing the offender to manipulate his therapist into taking his side against the probation officer. Time and again, officers have realized that if an offender is allowed to sit in a one-on-one session with a traditional therapist, he will most likely work on as many issues as he can without dealing directly with his sexual deviancy. Traditionally, probation officers have been unwilling and untrained in confronting the offender about his sexual behavior, even though they have no hesitation confronting other offenders about their drug usage, alcohol consumption, or other behaviors that have caused them to break the law. Specialized officers focus on anything they believe necessary to monitor change in the defendant's sexual views, attitudes, and actions.

The Polygraph

A recent survey of probation and parole departments by the National Institute of Justice revealed that 11% required sex offenders under their supervision to take the polygraph (English, Colling-Chadwick et al., 1996). Washington and Oregon pioneered the use of the polygraph in the 1980s. Those jurisdictions that now use it report that they could not get along without it.

Sex offenders live a life of secrecy. Unlike other criminal activities, they do not share their exploits with others and they are unlikely to brag about their conquests. Many of them have been committing numerous types of sex crimes for years and have never been caught. Often the victim is the only other person who is aware of the offender's behavior. Traditional therapy requires a lengthy, painstaking, and expensive process of self-disclosure, and still one can never be sure that the offender is telling the truth. The research of Abel and his colleagues and subsequent reports from treatment programs that use the polygraph reveal that sex offenders rarely tell the truth about the extent and type of their paraphilias. According to Sam Olsen, probation-parole officer in Jackson County, Oregon, a state which was one of the first to use the polygraph, "an offender is rarely caught and convicted for what later is determined to be an isolated incident of sexual contact with a child" (English, Pullen, & Jones, 1996, p. 47).

The polygraph is used in two ways in the supervision of sex offenders. Initially, as soon after sentencing as possible, a disclosure polygraph is required. In this session, the defendant first goes over all the questions to be asked with the polygrapher. These questions examine in detail the offender's sexual history and history of sexually deviant behavior.

"John" was assigned to a Phoenix probation officer for the crime of indecent exposure to a 12-year-old girl. In spite of recommended restrictions, he had been given special permission by the judge to live with his family: his wife and 3-year-old daughter. The concerned probation officer requested a polygraph as soon as possible to determine John's level of risk toward his child. John's paraphilic history was extensive: He admitted to at least 17 victims of "hands-on" offenses since he was 15 years old, one against a 3-year-old, and several against his sister's friends at various slumber parties. He also disclosed a history of obscene phone calls. The probation officer was able to convince the judge to order the defendant to live apart from his daughter until both he and his wife attended intensive treatment. Such disclosures give the probation officer and therapist a much more complete understanding of the offender's history, the range of behaviors that the offender needs to change, and an idea of the offender's risk to potential victims.

Jurisdictions should consult with legal counsel to ensure that their use of the polygraph is within legal limits. There may be problem in having offenders admit to further offenses without granting immunity from prosecution.

Further on in treatment, the polygraph is used not only to monitor the offender's compliance with the restrictions placed on him but to measure how he is managing his inappropriate thoughts and fantasies. This is usually referred to as a maintenance polygraph.

"Donald," age 40, had a fairly extensive history of molesting young girls, usually relatives. He was doing mediocre work in therapy, and his probation officer was concerned. He had been allowed to attend his church on Sundays, provided his wife was there to chaperon him and make sure that he did not associate with any children. When his polygraph was completed, it was discovered, among other things, that one of the reasons he liked attending church was that the little girls were usually wearing dresses, which was a high source of arousal to him.

Examples such as this can give a much clearer picture of situations that might never arise through self-disclosure. Also, because many offenders have a problem with substance abuse and it is difficult to test for alcohol, the polygraph is a good way to monitor suspected use of mind-altering substances.

Recently, in Phoenix, "George," an incest offender, was transferred to the specialized unit because his regular probation officer was uncomfortable with the fact that he had had only brief therapy before being allowed to move back into the home with the victim, "Lisa," his stepdaughter. George was immediately ordered to take a polygraph, but he began a lengthy program of resisting it, claiming that he had already gone through treatment and he was being harassed by the probation department. Just when the probation officer was preparing to take him back to court on the issue, Lisa came forward and notified authorities that George had been molesting her throughout his entire period of probation, even after she moved out to live with other relatives. He would "grab her any time he had the chance."

Records showed that the therapist had convinced the probation officer that the defendant was cured, that the victim had forgiven him, and that even though Lisa was still causing some problems at home, it was just taking her a little longer to get over things than the rest of the family.

It is precisely cases such as this which caused a change in the method in which sex offender cases are handled within the department. Now, all newly sentenced sex offenders are assigned to the specialized unit where they are assessed, sent through the class, polygraphed, ordered into treatment, and not transferred to regular probation until the officer and therapist believe that good progress is being made and the offender's risk level is low.

The Plethysmograph

Many programs use the penile plethysmograph as one of several components of testing and to help offenders in the behavioral reductions of deviant fantasies. Because of extensive controversy in recent years, in Arizona the plethysmograph can only be given with a doctor's prescription, and only audiotapes may be used for testing. Because visual stimuli are not being used at this time, many therapists believe that more offenders "flat-line" the assessment, resulting in less significant data.

Families and Reunification

In community supervision, especially probation, the percentage of family offenders is usually higher than in a prison population. If the offender's family wishes any type of recontact or reunification, the probation officer often becomes a case-worker and manager of the whole family's therapy and their connections with the offender. The philosophy of the Maricopa County unit is that it is a high-risk decision to put a convicted child molester back into an intimate living situation with vulnerable children who may be his victims until the offender, his partner, and the children have all been through considerable treatment. It is true that many recidivism studies show that incest offenders have a low risk of recidivism. However, the reasons for this may be complicated. As in the case of George and Lisa, for example, the fact that George's therapist and probation officer had both sanctioned his return to the family made the victim feel trapped by the system. George had been arrested, convicted, and then quickly allowed to return to a situation in which he continued to molest Lisa. Lisa's mother was extremely codependent and anxious to put things back together. She also had a young son who was a difficult behavior problem. Lisa knew her mother depended on her father to control the boy. Thus she kept silent about any further abuse.

Therefore, it appears more appropriate to say that incest offenders pose a lower risk if they can be kept from any future intimate living situations with children, or if their spouse and children receive intensive, knowledgeable, and preventive treatment. Although incest offenders may never get to a point where they are no longer aroused by children, many may be less likely to offend outside the home. Just as victim therapists have shown that one of the key elements in victim recovery and minimal trauma is the support of the nonoffending spouse (Hindman, 1990), so the victim may only feel safe again if she (or he) is assured that she will always be believed should the offending behavior ever reoccur.

"Wendy," age 13, told a friend at school that her father, "Nick," had been coming into her bedroom at night and putting his hands under her pajamas and molesting her. She pretended to be asleep. She also related that her father had drilled a hole into the bathroom from the kitchen, and when she was in the bathroom, she could feel him looking at her. By the time the prosecutor accepted the case, Wendy and her mother went back to the police and retracted her story. The most the prosecutor could get was a plea bargain to aggravated assault and three years' probation.

The next three years were a probation officer's nightmare, beginning with the fact that the judge allowed Nick to move back into the home immediately, a home in which there were four more daughters, all younger than the victim. It took five months of court appearances before the judge finally agreed to reconsider his decision based on a polygraph and other testing. In the polygraph Nick admitted that his father had molested all his sisters when he was younger, that he (Nick) had also molested one of his sisters, had tried to rape his wife's 13-year-old sister when she lived with them for a short time, had indeed been guilty of all the behaviors his daughter had disclosed, and was beginning to feel aroused by his next two daughters as they approached puberty. He had victimized a total of 15 females.

Nick actually did fairly well in treatment after he was able to admit that he had a problem, but no amount of persuasion on the part of probation staff could get his wife to participate. She could never bring herself to admit that her husband had actually committed the offenses on either her daughter or her sister, who wrote a letter confirming Nick's aggression toward her. Nick and his wife decided that they would live apart for the three years, just waiting until his probation was over. The victim never received any counseling. She dropped out of school when she was 16. Nick and his wife moved to a different city in a different state as soon as his probation was over.

Why is Nick's story so important? Because, again, it tells of all the things that can go wrong, and its details describe a very serious sex offender, highly aroused by females entering puberty, who, especially without a polygraph, would be labeled a "one-time incest offender." Worse yet, in this case, he was not convicted of a sex offense and not forced to register as a sex offender; thus, a new arrest or background check would not reveal the seriousness of his deviancy. We can only hope that he learned enough in treatment to keep his younger daughters safe.

In Maricopa County, the sex offender unit approaches each incest offender with a commitment to the safety of the child. But it absolutely requires as much of a commitment by the nonoffending parent, which is not always easy to obtain. In most cases, contracted therapists follow the guidelines of the model reunification procedure developed in Seattle by Meining and Bonner (1990), in which specific tasks and procedures are expected of all participants before reunification can be considered. The offender must be separated from the children, and all must go through lengthy and structured therapy. Many times the family members, including the victim, just want to "forgive and forget."

It is common for parents to demand that offenders be allowed contact with the victim's siblings, especially boys, who "need their father." But the offender's cognitive distortions, belief systems, views about females and sexuality, rationalization, minimizations, and justifications, which allowed him to be sexual with his daughter in the first place, are messages that should not covertly or overtly be passed along to another generation. The family can never go back to equal parenting. The family dynamic is forever changed by the offender's transgressions. Commonly, because most offenders are male, the wife needs to develop the emotional strength and parenting skills to make the major decisions and to be the disciplinarian.

It is extremely important that family members understand the patterns of the offender's abusive behavior. The family must address such issues as how the offender arranged time alone with the victim, how the secretiveness was maintained, and how the family members were controlled and manipulated by the offender. Family members should be able to recognize possible warning signs in the offender's behavior and know how to respond. Victims should be well prepared for recontact and should have confidence in their mother's ability to protect. Spouses should regularly attend partners' groups and couples' groups to continually process communication and reunification issues. This is extremely difficult for offenders who have a tremendous need to control the behavior of others, and who are often used to a patriarchal view of marriage and family.

The role of probation in this process is crucial. Officers are empowered to enforce what the therapist recommends, but at the same time probation officers who are trained to ask the right questions can demand accountability from those family therapists who want to reunify prematurely. The teamwork between therapist and the court in a reunification case can make the difference between mere survival for victims or emotional health, recovery, and growth. Well-designed guidelines for reunification should be a part of sex offender supervision. Of course, a systemwide coordinated approach is ideal, beginning with the initial investigation by police or social services. If the offend-

er is allowed to return to the home during the investigation and subsequent court proceedings, which could easily take a year or more, he is much less likely to do the hard
honest work his offense demands. Moreover, the victim and spouse will have no time
and space to address their own issues without pressure from the offender.

Lifetime Probation

One of the advantages of lifetime probation, even in "incest only" cases, is that
the offender can be assessed during different phases of his life. Case files on sex
offenders are filled with examples of the multigenerational offender who might have
molested his siblings as a teenager, his children as a parent, and his grandchildren 20
years later. A Phoenix offender who was sentenced to lifetime probation in 1988 petitioned the court in 1995 for an early termination, claiming that he had been in treatment, made excellent progress, and had been transferred out of the specialized case-
load. A review of his case showed that although he had indeed successfully completed a treatment program, he had subsequently remarried and fathered two children, and
his new wife had never been involved in any type of spousal support group or chaperon class. Early termination was denied.

Obviously, lifetime probation can be extremely effective in monitoring and managing pedophiles who might never be able to change their primary arousal by children. A key element in Arizona's law allows offenders convicted on multiple counts
to be incarcerated in prison on one and subsequently monitored on lifetime probation
on another. Even if an offender is sent to prison for 5 or 15 or 25 years, he can still be
released to the intensive program of the specialized unit to begin the difficult task of
trying to live in the community. In Arizona and many other states, the abysmal lack
of treatment for sex offenders while in prison makes it doubly important that treatment
occur upon release. Potential victimization can be minimized because of the expert
knowledge and supervisory techniques of specialized staff.

Certainly total safety can never be guaranteed. An interesting and unfortunate fact
is that in the three years that the specialized unit has been keeping statistics, half the
reoffenses for sexual crimes occurred because family members allowed their children
to be in contact with offenders, even though they had been appropriately informed. No
amount of supervision or number of special terms could have prevented that. The statistics are still overwhelmingly positive, however. Reoffenses have amounted to only
1% of the total number of the 850 sex offenders supervised so far in the three-year
period. Another 10% have been revoked and sent to prison before they reoffended.
Such technical violations were almost always for these three reasons: unauthorized
contact with children, repeated use of alcohol or other drugs, and failure to cooperate
in a sex offender treatment program. In one sense, the unit considers even those revocations positive, as they believe a part of their job is to further sort out those offenders who can make it in the community from those who, given every opportunity to
change, still choose to continue in their old patterns of behavior.

Lifetime probation gives the probation officer the time to work with difficult cases
without being rushed to monitor reunification or to see the terms of probation expire
for compulsive exhibitionists or pedophiles, knowing that they will reoffend. For some
offenders, their own childhood victimization has been so severe and traumatizing that
several years of work are needed before they can work through issues blocking their

progress. The department is now in the process of designing a more systematic method of long-term monitoring of these offenders. For some, it may mean a write-in report combined with an annual polygraph and one or two random field visits. For others, continued active supervision may be the only method of insuring community safety.

Cost

The cost of such supervision is an issue facing every department. Yet even fairly intensive supervision is much less costly than prison. Recent statistics from the National Institute of Justice show that there are presently more than 65,000 sex offenders now in prison; in some states they constitute the majority of the prison population. Although the length of prison terms varies widely from state to state, most sex offenders will at some point be released. Prentky and Burgess (1992) investigated and estimated the cost to the system of one sex crime and a subsequent five-year prison term to be $168,000. The Arizona program of treatment and specialized supervision would total $13,600 in five years, and with the offender paying all or partial costs of treatment, the amount would be further reduced.

Lifetime probation after 5 or 10 years could be a maintenance program with the offender paying nearly all costs of supervision by that time. Of course, no amount of money can measure the cost of sexual abuse on just one more victim, one more child. By the time today's offenders are released from jail or prison, Arizona will have one more tool at its disposal: community notification.

Community Notification and Registration

In 1995, 40 states had passed laws requiring convicted sex offenders to register (Thomas & Lieb, 1995). Only a few states have gone further to require that certain segments of the community must be notified when a sex offender is released from jail or prison. In Arizona, each offender will be evaluated according to the risk he presents, and therefore law enforcement will take a more active part in assisting the probation and parole departments in tracking released sex offenders.

Major questions have yet to be answered about the constitutionality of these laws, which vary in their applicability and population affected. Some probation officers hope that the prospect of public notification will serve as a deterrent to their sex offenders, improving their rate of compliance with specialized terms. However, public notification laws in some states have resulted in vigilante activities, including burning homes. From a public policy perspective, registration laws need to be computerized, similar in all 50 states, and linked to a central database that is easily accessible for investigators. As the Arizona experience reveals, often the people closest to the sex offender are the ones who give him most access to their children. Education and awareness of this problem will eventually go further than any legislation to combat the growing problem of sexual abuse in our society.

Conclusion

At the 1994 and 1995 national conferences for the Association for the Treatment of Sexual Abusers, several speakers commented on past and current research and treatment issues surrounding this difficult population. Most of its members have been treating sex offenders for many years. Many speakers mentioned the growing conclusion that sex offenders need a combination of both treatment and supervision so that they do not present a threat in the community; that treatment alone, effective though it is for many, may not be enough to lower the recidivism numbers among this population. Prolonged imprisonment without postrelease supervision is also short-sighted as it prevents the state from mandating any type of behavior on the part of the released sex offender. Strict monitoring by educated and specialized probation and parole agents can significantly reduce the recidivism rate.

References

Abel, G. G., Mittelman, M. S., & Becker, J. V. (1985). Sexual offenders: Results of assessment and recommendations for treatment. In M. H. Ben-Aron, S. J. Hucker, & C. D. Webster (Eds.), *Clinical criminology: The assessment and treatment of criminal behavior* (pp. 191–205). Toronto: University of Toronto.

English, K., Colling-Chadwick, S., Pullen, S., & Jones, L. (1996). *How are sex offenders managed on probation and parole? A national survey.* Washington, DC: National Institute of Justice and Colorado Division of Criminal Justice.

English, K., Pullen, S., & Jones, L. (1996). *Managing adult sex offenders: A containment approach.* Colorado Division of Criminal Justice & American Probation and Parole Association.

Hindman, J. (1990). *Just before dawn.* Ontario, OR: Alexandria.

Marshall, W. L., Jones, R., Ward, T., Johnston, P., & Barbaree, H. E. (1991). Treatment outcome with sex offenders, *Clinical Psychology Review, 11,* 465–485.

McGrath, R. (1991). Sex offender risk assessment and disposition planning: A review of empirical and clinical findings. *International Journal of Offender Therapy and Comparative Criminology, 35,* 329–351.

Meining, M., & Bonner, B. (1990, October). Returning the treated sex offender to the family. *Violence Update,* pp. 3–11.

Pithers, W. D., Buell, M. M., Kashima, K., Cumming, G. F., & Beal, L. S. (1987). *Precursors to sexual aggression.* Paper presented at the Association for the Behavioral Treatment of Sexual Abusers, Newport, OR.

Prentky, R., & Burgess, A. (1992). Rehabilitation of child molesters: A cost-benefit analysis. *American Journal of Orthopsychiatry, 60,* 108–117.

Quinsey, V. L., Harris, G. R., Rice, M. E., & LaLumiere, M. L. (1995). Predicting sexual offenses. In J. C. Campbell (Ed.), *Assessing dangerousness: Violence by sexual offenders, batterers, and child abusers* (pp. 114–137). Thousand Oaks, CA: Sage.

Scott, L. (1994). *An overview of sex offenders who failed on probation.* Paper presented at the Association for the Behavioral Treatment of Sexual Abusers, San Francisco.

Thomas, A., & Lieb, R. (1995). *Sex offender registration: A review of state laws.* Olympia, WA: Washington State Institute for Public Policy.

Chapter 17

Psychological Force in Sexual Abuse— Implications for Recovery

by Scott Johnson, M.A.

Overview

Anyone who has worked with sexual perpetrators or their victims knows that psychological force always accompanies the physical force of a sexual assault (Johnson, 1992, 1993). Sexual assault refers to any forced sexual contact. Examples would include being forced/coerced to be fondled on the genitals; being forced to fondle another's genitals; any forced penetration, oral, anal, or vaginal; being forced to have your clothing removed; being forced to look at someone else nude; being forced to watch pornography together; or being forced to watch the perpetrator have sex with another person. Again, force may involve psychological and/or physical force.

This chapter presents data from two studies concerning the prevalence and types of psychological force used to gain sexual contact. The first study, an attitudinal survey, contains responses from high school students about situations in which they could justify using psychological or physical force to obtain sexual contact from their partner. The second study contains responses from sex offenders identifying the types of psychological and physical force they used when committing their sexual offense.

Types of Force

Physical Force. The two types of force discussed in this chapter are physical and psychological. Physical force is often easier to understand and prove, as there are often bruises, scratches, or other types of physical evidence present. During date rapes, some common and often overlooked types of physical force occur. One example includes restraining a victim. Restraint may occur by physically holding the victim down or by immobilizing the victim's hands or feet, either with a rope or with the perpetrator's hands.

The body weight of the perpetrator may also serve to restrain the victim when the perpetrator uses a part of his body to pin down the victim. This may also include the perpetrator's leg being placed over the victim's leg or rolling onto the victim using the weight of one's body to restrain the victim. Any part of the body used to hold the victim down constitutes restraint that is a form of physical force.

When working with perpetrators who have used physical force to restrain their victim, I often get the impression that the criminal justice system overlooks and/or minimizes the impact of the physical restraint method uses. For example, it is rare to read a criminal complaint that expresses an accurate representation of the impact of the restraint used to subdue the victim. Further, the impression is often that the victim should have continued to fight back despite the perpetrator's strength and/or physical advantage. In addition, many perpetrators misinterpret the victim's lack of resistance as consent.

When the perpetrator begins to touch his victim against that person's will, this also constitutes physical force. The victim now has to deal with the fact that the perpetrator is unlikely to listen to her saying no. At this point, the victim may believe that any type of resistance may result in greater physical harm in addition to being sexually assaulted.

Another type of physical force that therapists often overlook is a kiss during which the victim is not able to refuse or to scream for help verbally because of the strength or duration of the kiss. The perpetrator's mouth becomes no different from the hand or gag that prevents the victim from sounding her plea for help. These forms of physical force are significant because they suggest that the perpetrator is aware that he is forcing the victim to be sexual and is also preventing the victim from vocally resisting the assault.

Psychological Force. The most overlooked force in sexual abuse is psychological force. Identifying the types of psychological force perpetrators used during their sexual offenses is important for the therapist. Constructing an offense cycle or reoffense prevention plan without understanding the types of force used by the perpetrator would be nearly impossible.

Psychological force occurs throughout sex offenses in many forms. However, this type of force is often difficult to prove because there may be no physical evidence that an individual was forced into sexual activity. In addition, it often comes down to the victim's word against the perpetrator's. Often, whoever has the better attorney or the more accepted reputation is likely to win the case. There are seven forms of psychological force, and I believe it is imperative for anyone who works with perpetrators or victims of any type of sexual abuse to be aware of and closely assess the type of psychological force that has occurred during the offense. The seven types are:

- Emotional blackmail
- Game playing
- Pressuring
- Boundary violations

- Lying
- Intimidation
- Threats

Emotional blackmail involves using emotions to pressure and trick the victim into being sexual. Common examples include, "If you love me, prove it"; "We have been dating so long and I spent so much money on you, now you owe me sex"; and "Show me how much you care for me." Emotional blackmail plays on the emotions of care, love, respect, and obligation. It also implies that unless sex is forthcoming, the relationship will be affected negatively.

Game playing involves manipulating situations that place the perpetrator at a distinct advantage. A common example is the initiation of a game, such as strip poker, tickling, or wrestling. When the time is right, the perpetrator takes advantage of the situation and begins to sexualize the touch or pressure the victim into being sexual. Game playing and manipulation can include misusing a hug or back rub or laying or sitting next to someone and taking advantage of the closeness to make unwanted sexual advances.

Pressuring involves repeated demands or requests for sexual contact that the victim has already refused. As children, we were all experts at begging and pressuring. Repeating requests was common: "Oh, please, please can't I stay up late," or "Can I have just another cookie, just one." Pressuring in that type of situation was innocent enough. However, when pressuring and begging are used to get sexual contact from one's partner, it becomes abusive and dangerous. Often, the message heard by the victim is that the perpetrator is going to continue to make requests until the victim submits. Furthermore, the perpetrator may do whatever is necessary to isolate the victim, thereby decreasing the likelihood of escaping the situation without being sexual.

Boundary violation involves crossing into someone else's space, making unwanted physical advances, and/or taking advantage of situations to observe someone's body without his or her knowledge or consent. Common examples would include watching someone dress/undress through a window or open doorway and looking down someone's shirt or up their shorts or skirt and may include making repeated requests or gestures of a sexual nature that are unwanted. Boundary violations are typical of sexual harassment. Continuing to ask someone out on a date or for sex when they have already refused constitutes a boundary violation and/or sexual harassment. In addition, it may include being in the victim's bedroom or other personal space and not allowing the victim privacy. Boundary violations also include making requests for sexual contact from someone with whom sexual contact would be inappropriate, such as a friend or coworker, or someone over whom you exercise power or authority.

Lying involves not keeping one's word. It is often used in a date rape situation. Common examples include getting the victim to agree to limited sexual contact but then pressuring her into intercourse. Other forms of lying may include deliberately misrepresenting the degree of emotional commitment in the relationship. The perpetrator may promise a long-term association or even marriage. In the Victorian age, it was a common practice to bring a civil suit against another person for "alienation of affection."

The five types of psychological force discussed above are known as psychological strategies on the continuum of force. These are the most subtle forms of force and we easily overlook and underestimate their powerful effects. Perpetrators use the above five methods of psychological force because they are aware that proving that psychological force was used is difficult. In addition, the perpetrator is aware that the victim will experience confusion and be easily manipulated.

The last two types of psychological manipulation are much more invasive and more believable. The sixth type of psychological force is intimidation. The goal of intimidation is to cause the victim to experience fear; fear not only for her physical and sexual safety but also fear for her life. Examples of intimidation include making statements such as "You'll do this or else," or "If you don't do this, then you'll be sorry." Intimidation can be behavioral, such as clenching of fists, attempts to remove the victim's clothing, or gestures and/or comments that indicate that it will not be acceptable for the victim to refuse the perpetrator in any way. If the victim is aware that the perpetrator has a history of engaging in physically abusive or assaultive behavior or has seen the perpetrator become abusive, the intimidation alone may force the victim to submit.

The last type of psychological force is threat. Threats are direct statements of impending harm. Common examples would include: "If you don't give in, I will take it from you"; "If you don't do this for me, then I will do even more to you later or to your friend." Threats take intimidation one step further by giving an ultimatum. Both threats and intimidation suggest more severe violence; perpetrators who use intimidation and threats are more dangerous and pathological than those who do not. These perpetrators are more comfortable with causing physical and sexual pain and are more likely to become physically assaultive during the sexual assault especially if the victim does not meet their demands.

In evaluating the offender or the offense, therapists should understand the seven types of psychological force and address the consequences of each type. It is imperative that we not minimize force we cannot see, that we hold perpetrators accountable for any type of force whether it is physical or psychological. Most of the perpetrators I have worked with have denied using psychological force when initially questioned about their offense behaviors. However, through the treatment process, they could identify the specific types of psychological force they used in their offense. They became sensitized to how they were using force in a variety of situations: in a harmless mode of force or coercion, such as talking friends or family into going to a movie other than the one they originally wanted, or a dangerous type of force, such as talking someone into going further sexually than she wishes.

On the continuum of force (see Table 17.1), we can see that perpetrators begin offending by using psychological force. The perpetrator gains power and control over his victim from the first six psychological strategies. However, when the psychological strategies no longer allow the perpetrator to feel empowered and satisfied, he will gradually move on to using threats, the seventh strategy. From there, it is a short step to using physical force. It does not matter whether the type of threat was simply to spread rumors or to end the relationship or cause physical harm. A threat is a threat; no matter where it is placed on the continuum of threats, it is dangerous. It is my experience that perpetrators who use threats are far more likely to progress to using physical force. Physical force may be used when threats no longer give the perpetrator the sense of control, empowerment, and satisfaction he needs. This physical abuse may result in the victim's being hit, slapped or restrained, or forced into sexual contact.

Table 17.1
Survey Results

1. a. If a guy spends a lot of money on a date, does the woman owe him sex in return?

Yes: M: 7%   F: 1%
No: M: 92%   F: 99%

b. How much pressure is okay for him to use to get sex in this situation?

	No Force	Psychological Force	Physical Force
M:	69%	28%	1%
F:	89%	9%	1%

2. If a guy is "so turned on" that he cannot stop, how much pressure is okay for him to use on his partner to get sex?

	No Force	Psychological Force	Physical Force
M:	48%	48%	2%
F:	73%	25%	2%

3. a. Is it okay to get anyone drunk or stoned so they will have sex?

Yes: M: 28%   F: 1%
No: M: 71%   F: 99%

b. If someone is drunk or stoned, how much pressure is okay to use to get sex from them?

	No Force	Psychological Force	Physical Force
M:	68%	29%	2%
F:	85%	12%	2%

4. If a female has a reputation for having sex with a lot of different guys but she says no to one guy, how much pressure is okay for him to use to get sex from her?

	No Force	Psychological Force	Physical Force
M:	55%	42%	3%
F:	76%	22%	2%

5. a. If a woman enjoys kissing and touching, does this mean she wants to have intercourse?

Yes: M: 14%   F: 2%
No: M: 84%   F: 98%

b. How much pressure is okay for him to use to get sex from her if she let him kiss and touch her but not want intercourse?

	No Force	Psychological Force	Physical Force
M:	55%	42%	2%
F:	75%	24%	1%

6. A couple has had sex before, but one of them does not want to be sexual this time. How much pressure is okay to use to get sex in this situation?

	No Force	Psychological Force	Physical Force
M:	57%	40%	2%
F:	74%	25%	1%

7. A couple had agreed earlier to have intercourse, but then one of them changes their mind and says no in the middle of being sexual:

a. Can a woman say no to sex in this situation?

Yes: M: 91%   F: 98%
No: M: 9% F: 2%

b. Can a man say no to sex in this situation?

Yes: M: 85%   F: 95%
No: M: 13%   F: 4%

c. How much pressure is okay to use to get sex in this situation?

	No Force	Psychological Force	Physical Force
M:	46%	52%	1%
F:	68%	32%	1%

8. A guy feels like his partner is just saying no to "tease" him or as a "get-back." How much pressure is okay for him to use to get sex in this example?

	No Force	Psychological Force	Physical Force
M:	41%	57%	2%
F:	65%	33%	1%

9. A couple who were living or going together have separated or broken up. How much pressure is okay to use to get sex from the ex-partner?

	No Force	Psychological Force	Physical Force
M:	70%	26%	4%
F:	85%	14%	1%

10. Two people are married. The wife does not want to have sex when her husband wants to. How much pressure is okay for him to use to get her to have sex with him?

	No Force	Psychological Force	Physical Force
M:	38%	58%	2%
F:	61%	38%	1%

11. How much pressure do teenagers feel from their peer groups to be sexual when they don't want to be?

	No Force	Psychological Force	Physical Force
M:	24%	71%	4%
F:	24%	74%	2%

12. If a female is wearing revealing clothing or acting seductively, is she asking to be raped?

Yes:	M: 17%	F: 9%
No:	M: 81%	F: 90%

13. If a hitchhiker gets raped, is it her own fault?

Yes:	M: 29%	F: 18%
No:	M: 68%	F: 80%

14. Does a woman out walking alone at night deserve to be raped?

Yes:	M: 5% F: 2%	
No:	M: 94%	F: 97%

15. Are males ever pressured or forced into unwanted sexual contact?

Yes:	M: 79%	F: 88%
No:	M: 20%	F: 11%

16. a. Have you or anyone you know ever been tricked, pressured, or forced into unwanted sexual contact?

Yes:	M: 29%	F: 58%
No:	M: 70%	F: 42%

b. Did you or your friend(s) ever tell anyone who could help? Or would you tell if this ever happened to you?

Yes:	M: 48%	F: 64%
No:	M: 48%	F: 31%

Evaluating Grooming Patterns

Language, verbal connotations, certain phrases, gestures, and eye movements may all play a role in the grooming process or during the actual offense. Most offenders are not even aware of how they groomed their victim until they have thoroughly examined their precursor and offense behavior. Examining the grooming process in depth and the behaviors that occurred as part of the offense to identify the type of psychological force is therefore crucial. The data presented offers support that most sex offenders use psychological rather than physical force in the commission of their offense.

In examining grooming patterns, we find that psychological force plays a significant role. Perpetrators attempt to build both a trusting and fear-based relationship with their victim, with an end goal of being able to get sexual contact without significant resistance. For example, when examining incest situations in which the father has sexually abused his daughter, it is common to find that the father increased physical activities with the daughter. Playing sports, tickling, wrestling, spending more time alone with and giving more attention to his daughter, giving hugs and kisses—all seem appropriate activities between father and daughter. However, the sex offender has another agenda: to establish a trusting relationship in which the victim will be accustomed to physical touch and he could easily explain the sexual behavior as an accident. For example, if a father is wrestling with his daughter and decides to slip his hand down her pants and fondle her vagina, he will already have an excuse to justify his actions. In his mind, it may appear easy to explain that while wrestling his hand went to push her off and his hand accidentally slipped down her pants. He did not mean to do it and says it will not happen again.

This type of situation occurs frequently, and it is imperative that professionals are aware of the different types of psychological strategies involved in the grooming process. Otherwise, it would be next to impossible to hold a perpetrator accountable. Grooming behaviors occur so often and go unnoticed. In fact, a perpetrator can be grooming his victim even during a therapy session, and if the therapist is unaware of the behavior, both the perpetrator and victim get the message that the behavior is acceptable. Grooming behaviors are the precursors to the commission of sexual abuse. They are a conscious, preplanned decision to prepare a person to be sexually abused. They are never accidental.

Survey Results

The first study involved gathering data from adolescents concerning their attitudes about using force to obtain sexual contact in certain situations. Several researchers (Makepeace, 1981; Koss, 1987; Miller & Marshall, 1987) have documented the prevalence of sexual assault within the adolescent population. The beliefs of adolescents concerning date and acquaintance rape affect not only on how sex offenders justify sexual assault but also the acceptance of sexual assault by victims. This survey requested that adolescents respond to statements about the appropriateness of a male using psychological or physical coercion/force to get sexual contact from a female. The primary question that prompted the collection of this data was to learn the attitudes and beliefs of high school students involving coerced and forced sexual activity. The researcher hypothesized that more males than females justify and condone the use of psychological and physical force to attain sexual behavior from their female partners.

Surveys were collected during the 1990–1991 school year. In this study, 13 high schools were included and 1,011 males and 1,062 females between the ages of 15 and 18 were surveyed. Six schools were urban and six were suburban.

The student's answers were then scored according to whether they believed that (1) no pressure/force was appropriate to use in the given situation, (2) the use of psychological pressure/force was appropriate, and (3) the use of physical force was appropriate in the given situation.

Ninety-two percent of the males and females agreed that a woman does not owe sex as a result of a male spending "a lot of money" on a date. These results were lower than expected. However, 28% of the males and 9% of the female students felt that using psychological force in this situation was appropriate for the male and 1% of both males and females agreed that physical force was appropriate as well.

Twenty-six percent to 58% of the males and 9% to 38% of the females endorsed the use of psychological force in certain situations. One percent to 4% of the males and 1% to 2% of the females endorsed the use of physical force in certain situations. Both males and females supported the use of psychological force in the following situations:

- A partner changes his or her mind after previously agreeing to have sex.
- A male feels that they are teasing him
- A husband wishes to have sex with his wife.

Blaming the victim was a common theme in the responses. Seventy-five percent of the males and 76% of the females responded that they feel pressure from their peer groups to be sexual when they do not want to be. This appears consistent with other research results (Koss, 1987; Muehlenhard, 1988).

The second survey gathered data on the specific types of force used by sex offenders. Most perpetrators of physical and sexual violence use psychological force prior to becoming physically and sexually violent, as well as continuing to be psychologically abusive after the abusive incident(s). When working with perpetrators of physical and sexual violence in therapy, therapists should postulate that is is imperative that perpetrators identify the types of psychological force they used and that they give specific examples of how each type of psychological force was used.

This data may be used to facilitate therapist, perpetrator, and court personnel to develop specific guidelines for identifying the perpetrator's use of psychological force *before* allowing the perpetrator to have contact with his victim. Many therapists have allowed visitation between perpetrator and victim when the perpetrator no longer appears to pose a significant risk of *physically or sexually* abusing his victim, despite significant psychological force and psychological abuse occurring.

The sex offenders were involved in sex offender programs in Minnesota. A total of 115 offenders responded to this survey, and they identified a total of 530 victims. Of the 530 victims, 386 were female and 144 were male.

Approximately 48% of the sex offenders in this study engaged in begging/pressuring, 43% engaged in boundary violations, 31% in lying, 31% in game playing/manipulation, 28% in intimidation, 22% in emotional blackmail, 22% in physical force, and approximately 13% in intimidation (see Table 17.1).

The most frequently used form of psychological force was begging and/or pressuring. The most common example of this type of force involved perpetrators verbally pressuring their victims to get their own way and verbally pressuring their victims for sex.

Boundary violations were the second most commonly used force in this questionnaire. The most common forms include stealing or sneaking a kiss and misusing a position of power or authority. Game playing/manipulation and lying ranked equally as the third and fourth most commonly used types of force.

The most frequently used forms of game playing/manipulation included perpetrators playing on victims' feelings to get what they wanted; giving a back rub or massage, then moving hands to genitals; taking advantage of the victim's emotional state (depressed, lonely, or hurting); and wrestling, tickling, or other playful activities before or during sexual contact.

The most frequently used forms of lying included perpetrators telling the victim that "it (abusive behavior) will never happen again," but it does; "I'm doing this because I love you"; "come on in and we'll only talk"; and agreeing to certain sexual behaviors and then going further than agreed.

The fifth type of force used was intimidation. The most frequently used forms included perpetrators placing their hands on their victim's genitals; raising their voice; and standing in their victim's way, preventing escape.

Emotional blackmail and physical force ranked equally fifth and sixth in this study. The most frequently used examples included perpetrators giving a sob story to gain sympathy and then asking for sex to feel better and using statements such as "don't you love me?"; "if you love me, prove it"; and "this means I love you."

The sixth type of force used was physical force. The most frequently used examples included holding down, using restraint, and hitting, slapping, or punching.

The least used type of force involved the use of threats. Specific examples of this type included statements such as, "If you tell, mom(dad) and I will get divorced"; "if you tell, I'll go to jail"; and threatening to end the relationship if the victim does not do as the perpetrator says.

Interestingly, the men who participated in this study would appear not to utilize threats but would engage in other forms of force.

The results of this study indicate that most sex offenders use psychological force rather than physical force in the commission of their crimes. Clinical data and data from collateral sources such as criminal complaints and police reports appear to support this data.

The results support the premise that sex offenders use psychological force prior to and during their offense. As the data show, the majority of sex offenders have been known to be dishonest. Court materials, including victim statements, offer support that in most sex abuse offenses, psychological force, not physical force, was used during the offenses.

This appears to support the premise of this study.

Conclusion

To summarize the effects of sexual abuse, both the victim and the perpetrator experience significant trauma. It is imperative not only to address the initial concerns of the victim and the perpetrator, such as the emotional, physical, sexual, or spiritual needs, but also to focus on the psychological force that was used during the assault. Therapists should pay attention to how the victim was trapped by emotional confusion, because in most sexual abuse situations, psychological, not physical, force was used.

Therapists must help the victim, not just the perpetrator, identify the other forms of abuse that may have occurred. They must be aware that when sexual abuse occurs, physical, emotional, and psychological abuse occurred as well.

Never can a perpetrator sexually abuse someone without committing physical, psychological, and emotional abuse as well.

References

Johnson, S. (1992). *Man to man: When your partner says "no."* Brandon, VT: Safer Society Press.

Johnson, S. (1993). *When "I love you" turns violent.* Far Hills, NJ: New Horizon Press.

Johnson, S. A. (in press). The overlooked force in sexual assault. *Acta Sexologica.*

Koss, M. P. (1987). Outrageous acts and everyday seduction: Sexual aggression and victimization among college students. In B. Levy (Ed.), *Dating violence: Young women in danger* (pp. 87–96). Seattle, WA: Seal Press.

Makepeace, J. M. (1981). Courtship violence among college students. *Family Relations, 30,* 97–102.

Miller, B., & Marshall, J. (1987). Coercive sex on the university campus. *Journal of College Student Personnel, 28*(1), 38–47.

Muehlenhard, C. L. (1988). Misinterpreted dating behaviors and the risk of date rape. *Journal of Social and Clinical Psychology, 6*(1), 20–37.

Chapter 18

Assessment and Treatment of Incest Families

by Rebecca Palmer, M.S.

Overview

As society continues to struggle with the overwhelming issue of sexual abuse, treatment providers and researchers are challenged by how to diagnose and treat the problem. Much attention has been paid to the sex offender who causes the biggest threat to public safety, the offender who stalks and sexually abuses children. Although this type of sex offender is to be feared, as a society, we are still grappling with identifying and treating the sex offender who lives in the home. This is an uncomfortable issue. One way we have chosen to deal with it is by believing that it does not often happen. My clinical practice refutes that belief. Our society has become aware of the need for services for children who have been sexually abused and for women who have been victims of domestic violence. We are now paying heed to the necessity of providing intensive psychological treatment to the sex offender.

Treating the Incest Offender

It is still curious that many sex offenders are never caught and many of those who are caught are never incarcerated. Although many states have sought to incarcerate sex offenders, most are not sentenced for life. This means that unless we as a society are willing to look at the factors that contribute to and help to maintain incest, incest will continue for generations to come. Many treatment providers and victims rights organizations are not interested in assisting families in identifying and resolving the problem of interfamilial sex abuse. The question of whether to treat the incest offender within his family remains controversial. The major problem in extricating the sex offender from his family is that he will almost surely find another family with whom to reside or he will create a new family. This multiplies the number of victims to which he can have access. If the family has not been treated, the family members do not understand the factors that contributed to interfamilial sexual abuse. They may unwittingly accept that sex abuse is part of family life.

It would be fair to say that upon the disclosure of incest, many families want to know how this happened in their family. The following treatment model helps the clinician assist the family in answering this question. This model is systemic and identifies the family's vulnerabilities and the factors that have contributed to and helped to maintain the incest (Trepper & Barrett, 1989). This model helps the clinician organize his or her treatment plan and determine progress in treatment, so that order can be brought to chaos. This model aids the treatment provider and court personnel in following the offender and his family through the arduous task of healing. Because family therapy is only one aspect of treatment necessary to heal the deep wounds caused by incest, this type of treatment augments and enhances the work that is being done in group therapy, individual therapy, and couple's therapy. The inclusion of family treatment with other treatments helps heal the system that has been devastated by intrafamilial sex abuse. Often family treatment is not considered a primary part of the treatment plan for the identified sex offender because of the assumption that the family will dissolve once the incest is disclosed. Often victims of incest want to continue to have an ongoing relationship with the parent who has abused them. The child may still have warm, caring feelings for the parent and certainly has needs that can and should be met by the parent. If the family members can grow and heal through the process of family therapy, then as they mature we expect that they will not recreate their family of origin.

Clinical Assessment

Assessing the entire family gives the therapist an opportunity to witness the relationship between family members as opposed to the standard clinical interview wherein the client reports about his relationships and the clinician makes inferences regarding the relationships (Trepper & Barrett, 1989). Initially the entire family is not seen together if either parent is in denial about the facts of the abuse or if the victim is not ready to engage in a session with the offender. Denial is not an initial reason to exclude a family from treatment because denial is functional and protective to the system. The initial stages of assessment help the clinician and family understand the need for denial as well as factors that help to maintain the denial. The assessment should be seen as ongoing throughout treatment with the family. Assessment begins in the first stage of treatment. A major weakness of many treatment programs is the lack of pretreatment planning which would allow the treatment provider or professional to be aware of all the players in a particular client's case. Good pretreatment planning provides a stable foundation for ongoing treatment and positive treatment outcome. When all professionals are aware of treatment and court expectations, chances for treatment failure are minimized.

The very foundation of this family treatment model holds that all families are to greater or lesser degrees vulnerable to incest (Trepper & Barrett, 1989). Although this statement is very bold and striking, it is imperative to comprehend which factors contribute to the origin and maintenance of incestuous abuse. The assessment is very comprehensive in that it will assess the family system in its social/political contexts, familial contexts, and individual contexts. It is also very important to understand that incest cannot occur unless the family lacks coping mechanisms and precipitating events are present.

As mentioned earlier, the assessment is ongoing, but it can be conceptualized as happening in three stages.

Stage I: Creating a Context for Change

Incest families often do not believe that they are capable of change. In fact, many ask for help from the therapist to "get back to like we used to be." Many families harbor the belief that prior to the disclosure, family life was normal. Maybe there were a few things that were wrong but the family was functioning. This is an attractive invitation for the therapist, but perhaps one of the first opportunities to begin to show the family that a return to how it used to be was dysfunctional and unhealthy. During the first stage of treatment, it is very important to let the family know that the act of incest is abhorred but not the person. This concept is often difficult for our client families to accept. It is also of great importance for therapists to let the family know that they expect change, change is possible, and this journey will be difficult and painful but worth it to all family members. The time frame for the assessment lasts four to six weeks and during this time the therapist will be meeting with all family members. Using the vulnerability model, the family will be assessed to determine its vulnerabilities and resiliencies. After the assessment period the therapist meets with the family to report what he or she thinks the family will need to address in order to change.

The vulnerability model can be visualized in three steps: (1) social/political context, (2) familial context, and (3) individual context (Trepper & Barrett, 1989). All three of these areas may be assessed simultaneously while meeting with different family members. These three areas also provide therapists with an outline for the questions they will ask in the sessions as well as areas that the therapist wants to observe during each treatment session. The vulnerability model gives the clinician the opportunity to assess in what areas this particular family is vulnerable and conversely where the family's strengths lie. Many if not all families are devastated at the disclosure of incest and often do not recognize any of their strengths. When assessing the social/political contexts the therapist is searching for information about how community, gender, religion, economics, culture, and race contribute to the family's vulnerabilities. It is often thought that families of a lower socioeconomic standing are more vulnerable. Although having little income is a stressor, it is not the only factor. Gender roles contributes to a family's vulnerability by allowing for male supremacy or supporting the notion that women and children are property. It should not be overlooked that in this society, there are different standards for males and females when it comes to the expression of affection. Some communities support the availability and use of pornography that depicts families engaging in sex. Although religious beliefs can be a source of strength to families, some use their religious beliefs to support their abusive behavior. It is often believed in this society that certain cultures engage in sexual behaviors with their children and many jokes and stories continue to circulate over time about these different cultural groups.

Although it may be apparent how society contributes to the problem of incest, it may be more difficult to ascertain how the familial contexts contribute to a family's vulnerabilities. The therapist will be assessing the family's abusive style to understand the intent of the abuse. The family's hierarchy will also be assessed to determine how the family system organizes in regards to boundaries, rules, roles and communication patterns. This multiple system model sees the individual as a system unto itself, and this view requires that all individuals in the family be assessed (Trepper & Barrett, 1989). Each individual is assessed for vulnerabilities as well as resiliencies. The offending parent is assessed for levels of psychopathology, personality disorders, cognitive distortions, his sexual orientation, fantasies, and the degree to which he is a pedophile. The assessment and evaluation of the nonoffending parent involves determining emotional absence, passivity and unassertiveness, and dependency issues. A critical point to make with nonoffending parents is that they are not the ones responsible for the abuse. When assessing the child who has been victimized by the incest, it is important to address any psychological disorders. Such disorders include depression, acting-out behaviors, and social withdrawal. It is important to note that these are often symptoms of the abuse and the emotional torment this child had to endure. When assessing each family member's vulnerabilities, it is important to recognize that there are exceptions to the vulnerabilities. Each individual in the family system possesses strengths. Strengths and resiliencies should be highlighted and emphasized by the therapist so that client and therapist know that healing is possible and expected.

Interventions. After the initial assessment is completed, much information has been gathered. During the assessment phase this has provided the therapist the opportunity to join with the family. Many other parties involved with this family are monitoring the family and making sure that the children are safe from further abuse. Although this also occurs in therapy, the therapist is concerned here that all family members are committed to the treatment process. This can only occur if the therapist has joined with the family (Minuchin, 1974). Often by the end of the assessment period, the therapist will be able to recognize the family's structure. Several family structures are most vulnerable to incest. The goal of the structural session is to help the family members determine how they are structured and teach them to strive for a structure where incest will be virtually impossible. This session is useful for the family because it begins to give them a common language for describing certain family interactions and helps them know when the family's structure is out of balance. The therapist begins by giving the family a concrete visual picture of the different family structures. These different diagrams (see Tables 18.1 through 18.6) represent the possible hierarchies present for the family. This model is based on Minuchin's (1974) structural family therapy.

This visual metaphor helps the family to see how its structure contributes to the vulnerability to incest (Trepper & Barrett, 1989). Family members are given examples

Table 18.1
Functional Family Structure

Table 18.2
Father–Executive Structure

```
        F  ▲
---------------------
   C C C M
```

Table 18.3
Mother–Executive Structure

```
        M
---------------------
   C C C F
```

Table 18.4
Third-Generation Structure

a.   b.

```
        M                              F│
---------------------          ---------------------
     F│    ▲                        M ▼ ▲
-----▼----│-----------          ---------│-----------
   C    C C M                    CC      C C
```

Table 18.5
Chaotic Structure

Table 18.6
Estranged Father Structure

```
        M
--------------------- (F
   CCCC
```

Legend: F = Father; M = Mother; C = Child; ▼▲ = Up and down generational movements

about how they need to be structured to function in a healthy way. The therapist then describes the other family structures and asks family members to give examples when they are functioning in a way that is not healthy. Often family members show the therapist how they are structured by the way they seat themselves in the session. In the following example the parents have brought their oldest daughter to session for the first time. It is about two weeks before Christmas and they wanted to talk about how upset they were about not being able to celebrate the holiday together. As they enter the room, "Sue" sits between her mother and father attempting to comfort and soothe both parents as they begin to cry.

> *Mom*: We wanted you to meet our oldest daughter because you had never met.
> *Therapist*: I'm happy to meet you and get to know you, I have been working with your father for a while now and today I can see that he and your mother are both terribly upset.
> *Daughter*: My father tells me that you are helping him but this is very hard for our family not to be together for Christmas. We have many traditions that we celebrate and this year we will not be able to do that. *(Both parents are crying and Sue is distracted from our conversation so that she can attend to her parents in distress)*
> *Therapist*: Mom, what are your plans for the holidays?
> *Daughter*: We had not made many plans because it just will not be the same.
> *Therapist*: Dad, how have you planned to spend the holiday?
> Daughter: My father is so upset that we cannot all be together for this Christmas.
> *Therapist*: You know, Dad and Mom, I have asked each of you how you will spend the holiday and Sue has answered for you both. I would like for you two to have a discussion about what are some options for celebrating the holiday.
> [Both parents take this direction and attempt to have a conversation, which is difficult and painful; all the while Sue is tending to both of them but seemingly becoming more frustrated about not being included in this conversation.]
> *Therapist*: Sue, how about if you change seats with your mom so that she and dad can talk about the holiday.
> *Daughter*: Thank you for getting me out of the middle.

As the session progressed, we discussed how the family structure allowed for the daughter to have a parentified role and when she acted like a parent, what happened to the other family members. Throughout future sessions the family discovered that at times Terri (the youngest and the incest victim) had three parents or that Mom and Sue would parent Terri and Dad. Once this family was able to understand how the structure affected the balance, they were able to think of many other situations where the structure or boundaries were unhealthy or out of balance.

After all family members have an opportunity to give examples, the therapist along with the family begins the task of figuring out what they would need to do differently in each example to be functioning like a healthy family. This lesson can and is utilized throughout the treatment process. As in the previous intervention, each family believes that it is unable to behave differently from its standard operating procedure. Another useful intervention is to help the family determine when they are not behaving in a dysfunctional manner and let them see that there are exceptions or times when they can interact in a nondysfunctional manner. Upon entering treatment many, if not all, families believe that change is not possible. Therefore, one intervention the therapist can use is to help the family determine the negative consequences of change; in other words, what bad or negative things would happen if they were to change. Often for the therapist this is extremely enlightening. The intervention shows what the family "believes" will happen and how the family has become stuck in a dysfunctional pattern of interacting. The following is an example of addressing the negative consequences of change:

> *Therapist*: Joe, your wife is saying that she believes Terri when she says that you fondled her breasts and vagina. What do you say happened?
>
> *Joe*: *(crying)* I don't remember this thing happening. I am so upset that my daughter has been suffering and was hurt.
>
> *Therapist*: Would it be like your wife and daughter to make up such a story?
>
> *Joe*: No, they are both honest, they do not lie.
>
> *Therapist*: Then you are saying that they are telling the truth.
>
> *Joe*: They are honest but I just do not remember any of this happening.
>
> *Therapist*: Joe, you say that your wife and daughter are both honest and that they would never make up such a story. Well, let's pretend for a minute that you do remember what happened. If you remembered, what bad things might happen to you?
>
> *Joe*: Well, my wife would leave me.
>
> *Therapist*: Joe, she brought you here and she says that she wants to work this out. She stated here in front of both of us that she loved you and wanted to stay married to you but that she also believes Terri. It doesn't sound like she is preparing to leave you. So now what would happen if you were to remember that you had sexually abused your daughter?
>
> *Joe*: *(sobbing)* I would have to kill myself for having done such a terrible thing to my daughter. I could never live knowing I had hurt her.

We can see from this example that Joe cannot yet admit to the abuse because the consequences of doing so would mean that he would have to take his own life. Once Joe can be assured that he would not have to die and that every effort will be made to keep him safe he can begin to accept the responsibility of admitting to the abuse.

On the other hand, it is also important to identify the positive consequences of change and what good things could happen if the family were to change. Using these two interventions the therapist can begin to see what factors contribute and maintain the denial in the family system. It is not uncommon for each family member to be at different levels of denial. As stated earlier, it is imperative for the therapist not to conduct entire family sessions if either or both of the parents are in denial of the facts of the abuse. It is necessary to determine what level of denial each family member is in before conducting family sessions. Although denial is protective, it is important to recognize that several levels of denial exist (Trepper & Barrett, 1989). Following is an easy acronym to remember the different levels of denial: FAIR (*F*acts, *A*wareness, *I*mpact, *R*esponsibility).

Denial of Facts. This occurs when any or some family members say that the abuse never occurred. It is not uncommon for the offending parent to engage in the denial of facts at the beginning of treatment. Often the nonoffending parent vacillates about the occurrence of the abuse. In some judicial districts, it is common for the system to encourage the suppression of the facts. It is fairly well known that when an offender admits to the police that he is culpable, he risks being incarcerated. It is common to plea bargain in criminal cases. If the offender is successful in plea bargaining to a lesser charge, particularly from a felony to a misdemeanor, he is allowed to believe that his offense was not so serious. The system has encouraged denial. This has grave consequences for the victim and his/her family. Treatment cannot progress onto Stage II as long as there are denial of facts.

Denial of Awareness. The offender expresses denial of awareness by saying that if the abuse occurred, it happened without his awareness. However, the individual at least maintains the possibility that the abuse has occurred. Although denial of awareness is not as serious as denial of facts, it is necessary to understand that if a person had no awareness it is impossible for him to be responsible for the act.

Denial of Impact. Denial of impact occurs when the offender admits to the facts but lessens or minimizes the severity of the abuse. This is usually indicated by statements as "I only touched her once," or "She was so young she'll never remember it."

Denial of Responsibility. This is a common form of denial in which the offender admits the facts and awareness of the abuse. However, he places blame onto someone or something else. For example, "She acts so seductive and she wanted sex by the way she was looking at me," or "I just haven't been the same since I lost my job I don't know what came over me."

The most effective treatment intervention for the family in denial is to keep the offender separate from the rest of the family both in living arrangements and in treatment sessions. Often the evaluation process with the offender is a significant therapeutic intervention in beginning to address and deal with the offender's denial. Another issue that should be addressed is the impossibility of the family reuniting as long as there is denial of facts of the abuse. It has become clearer that often many families wish to solve the problem of abuse and remain intact.

Other potent interventions used in Stage I of treatment are the preacknowledgement and acknowledgement sessions. These are powerful rituals that have a great impact, and they are necessary for the family to be able to move into Stage II of treatment. Many offenders and their families state that they have already acknowledged and do not see the necessity of doing that again. What we do know as treatment providers is that it is not likely that they have apologized for the actual facts, awareness, impact, and responsibility of the abuse. Preparation for these sessions is arduous. When the offender acknowledges the abuse, he must be able to conduct himself in a manner that avoids reoffending the victim or minimizing the impact of the abuse. These sessions do not take place until the victim is ready to be present with the offender. Often the offender wishes to rush this process, thereby escaping an opportunity to fully understand his responsibility in the abusive acts. The therapist will need to exercise restraint with the client and him- or herself because of the extreme distress that results from addressing the details of the abuse. When preparing for these sessions, the therapist should be in regular contact with the victim's therapist to be apprised of the victim's readiness for the sessions. The contact with the victim's therapist is also essential in that more details are made available to the offender's therapist regarding the actual abuse. Such information prevents the offender from apologizing for what only he remembers.

The first step in preparing for this session is to ask the offender to write a letter of acknowledgement to his victim and bring that to the next session. The benefit of this concrete exercise is to have the offender put down in black and white what he has only been talking about. It takes many sessions to refine the letter, with the therapist asking for continual revisions and honesty. From this process, grist for the therapeutic mill emerges. The major goals for this session are:

- The offender takes responsibility for the abuse.
- The parents are recognized as being the caretakers of the children.
- The parents are responsible for what happens in the family

The session consolidates what the family has learned in therapy up to this point. The family therapist will have rehearsed this session with all parties so that there will be no surprises at the time of the family session. In essence, the therapist knows what all parties will say. It is important that work with the victim prepares him or her to hear the acknowledgement without letting the offender off of the hook. Once the apology session has taken place, the family is ready to move into Stage II of treatment.

Stage II: Challenging Patterns and Expanding Realities

This stage is the heart of the treatment process for the family. At times it can become wearisome, and it is easy to become bogged down in repetition. Because patterns develop over time, it is reasonable to assume that change can only take place if the old patterns are consistently challenged. While family patterns are being challenged, so are individual patterns. Family members are encouraged to make use of group treatment: a victim's group for the victim, a nonoffending parents' group, and an offender's group. Larger metropolitan areas often have support groups for the siblings who were not abused. It is essential to understand that family treatment is a substantial portion of the treatment process for the incestuous family because this is the context in which these family members live. However, it is just as important to recognize the immense necessity of having all family members in group. The group therapy context for the offender is absolutely necessary so that the offender's cognitive distortions can be addressed in a manner different from the family context. Another aspect of group treatment for the offender is that he can also receive support that will probably not occur in other therapy contexts. The use of individual therapy for offenders allows clients to address their own victimization and work toward greater victim empathy. Addressing these issues in individual therapy does not mean that these issues will not be faced in group treatment. Likewise, the use of individual therapy for the offender magnifies his need to address issues that have contributed to and maintained the incest.

Every therapist who is conducting family therapy should obtain a signed release of information forms so that he or she is able to communicate freely with the other treatment providers. The context of group and individual therapy for other family members encourages the healing process that is necessary to move on in life. Another territory of treatment that is covered in Stage II is couple's therapy. Should the couple survive the initial crisis of the disclosure of the incest without deciding on divorce, it is in Stage II that the marital patterns and dysfunctions are more directly addressed. Each person has to decide whether the relationship is worth salvaging and what changes will need to take place for the family to remain a cohesive unit. Occasionally, at this point in treatment many nonoffending partners decide that they will not try to salvage the relationship and couple's treatment needs to focus on how the family will separate and address issues of safety, custody, and a continuing relationship with both parents. Sometimes the nonoffending partner does want her spouse to continue treatment but feels that because she did not commit the abuse, she does not need to be involved in treatment. Often this is a very delicate issue to address because the offender is not yet ready to admit to total responsibility for the incest and the nonoffending spouse feels she is being blamed once the couple's vulnerabilities are brought to light.

Frequently therapists address only the dysfunctional patterns for families and individuals, but it is just as important to stress the existing patterns that are exceptions to the dysfunction. Many clients feel that they are totally dysfunctional and will be unable to change. Many times when couple identifies the exceptions to the dysfunctional pattern, another substantial gain is made in therapy whereby the client has a renewed hope that change is possible. One of the most valuable interventions in family and couple's treatment is enactment. This intervention can be very powerful in helping the system change. Unlike individual treatment, where clients are sharing only their perception of the system, family or couple's therapy allows the therapist to observe patterns of interaction. In using an enactment, the therapist shares his or her observations of a particular sequence of interacting and then directs the family members to try interacting in a healthy and functional manner. The use of enactment as an intervention allows the family members actually to see how to communicate more effectively to have their needs met. Another intervention is that of giving the client(s) tasks to complete between sessions. Out-of-session tasks can be as simple as having the client observe a particular interaction or reaction of himself or that of another family member and then report his observations at the following session. Another out-of-session task can be to have the client practice a certain behavior.

Interventions. Many variations can be tailored to meet the specific needs of the family. As the family continues to be challenged and practices new behaviors, a growing sense of accomplishment and change develops. As the family or couple recognizes that change has occurred and feels confident in the new tools for addressing the problems, there is a shift in how the family begins to use the therapy sessions. The therapist should recognize that the family has begun to report in regard to the problem and then how they were able to create and use a solution without the direct intervention of the therapist. Families find a great deal of strength and hope in their ability to continue to be a cohesive unit. When this shift occurs the client family has moved into Stage III of treatment.

Stage III: Consolidation

Stage III is shorter than the previous two stages. It usually lasts about four weeks. The work of therapy in this stage is to highlight and punctuate the changes that the family has made. Although family members know that change has occurred, often they overlook the magnitude of the change. The focus of the stage is to consolidate the positive changes that have been made. In formulating the therapy process, practitioners move through the initial stages where they are basically teaching terms, concepts, and new approaches. The next stage focuses on applying these new concepts to the family's own life and exploring how family members might apply these new concepts to their particular problems. The final stage of treatment is to have family members actually begin to apply the new skills to their life and to start doing this independently on their own.

Interventions. A helpful intervention is to pose a problem to the family and request that they handle it as they would have when they first entered therapy. Each person is asked to interact and respond as he or she would have prior to entering treatment. The strength of this intervention is that now the family can see more clearly how they have changed and how they are functioning more effectively and healthful manner. This is one method to punctuate the changes the family has made.

Predicting potential future problems is another beneficial intervention. Throughout the course of therapy the family has been in the process of healing, but reality dictates that problems will still arise and will need to be addressed in a healthful manner. In predicting future problems, it is important to choose some possible solutions. For instance, it is helpful to ask the family to determine which of the future problems are solvable and which may require a call to the therapist for help. The therapist needs to inform the family members that if they should call for help or a session they have not failed but rather they should view the call positively, as a sign of strength. Families need to be reassured that seeking help is a new habit that will help ensure the future health of the family. They are no longer living in isolation but are making appropriate choices in seeking help. There is much rejoicing in this stage of treatment and the use of some consolidation ritual is very powerful. Giving of gifts is a useful ritual in that the gift can be a metaphor for the family that will remain with them long after therapy is complete. The following exemplifies the significance of having a consolidation ritual.

> *Therapist*: Today we are here to say so long for now and discuss what the future will be like after all of the changes that you have made. In the past several sessions we have predicted what events might create stress and we have even thought of some ways to manage that stress. Let's also set a date for six months from now so that you can come in for a checkup, and this session is on me. Consider that you have earned it for all your hard work. Certainly it will be all right if you call me before that time.
>
> *Mother*: You mean we don't have to pay for that session in six months?
>
> *Therapist*: That's right, it's like you have some sessions in the bank and it's nice to know that they are there if you need them.
>
> *Therapist*: I want to change the subject a bit because I would like to focus on the many ways that you have changed over time. I have brought you a plant as a parting gift that will signify our time together. A plant is very much like a family in that it needs nourishment to live and grow as well as sunlight and rest. Please care for this plant as you would your family. You will need to talk so that not everyone feeds it too much or too little. I hope for you that you will continue to grow as does this plant.
>
> *Mother*: Well, we didn't expect a gift but we did bring one for you too.

Father: You have helped us so much to change that we will never be able to thank you. There were days I left your office and I thought to myself,"She doesn't know what she's talking about, we can never change or get better." But I'm so glad that I trusted you and you always said change was possible.

Mother: *(presenting a painted ceramic house)* This is for you to remember us.

Therapist: Thank you very much, I will keep it in a place that will remind me of how our hard work has paid off.

Sue and Terri: You have to read what we wrote on the bottom. It says, "Please, remember, every time you look at this home you'll remember what you helped to create. You've helped us create a *Hogar Feliz*—a "Happy Home."

The session then went on and tears were shed by all, but the meaning and impact of this ritual lasted for all the future sessions. In fact, at the six-month checkup session the mom reported to me that the plant was doing well and it had served as a reminder to her that if the leaves were drooping she should take a quick inventory to see what had been going on with her family.

In consolidating changes, families feel reassured by having a session that will occur six months down the road. This can be considered a right they have earned and will not have to pay for. Of course, the family can call anytime before that scheduled session should the need arise. After the six-month checkup another session is earned by the family which will take place in another six months. Scheduling these sessions can be empowering to families in that the therapist is conveying the message that whatever happens good or bad is important and deserves attention. As life proceeds change will be part of the process of living so they will need the flexibility to keep up with the necessary changes.

Conclusion

There is a continuing conflict over whether to use family therapy with incestuous families. The alternative is to insist that the family must separate forever. Even if the perpetrator is incarcerated, the nonoffending spouse can decide to remain with the perpetrator until the state has no jurisdiction over them and then to reunite the family. It may be much healthier to prepare that family for the inevitable reconciliation by openly and proactively discussing the problem. In this treatment model, three stages of treatment are discussed and interventions recommended. It is recommended that each family member simultaneously receives specialized treatment (e.g., sex-offender-specific treatment for the offender and victim's therapy for the child). The hope is that by helping the family work through denial and learn protective patterns, all the family members will contribute to an atmosphere that discourages further abuse.

References

Minuchin, S. (1974). *Families and family therapy.* Cambridge, MA: Harvard University Press.

Trepper, T., & Barrett, M. J. (1989). *Systemic treatment of incest: A therapeutic handbook.* New York: Brunner/Mazel.

Chapter 19

Developing Therapeutic Communities for Sex Offenders

by Debra Baker, M.A. and Stephen Price, B.A.

Overview

The therapeutic community (TC) is a vital part of treating sex offenders within institutions. Because sex offenders have impaired interpersonal relations, they need the type of healing environment that TCs provide. In these environments, individuals can learn to live with each other in a situation that addresses every aspect of their relationships with each other. Sex offenders are held responsible for the dysfunctional behaviors they demonstrate with each other. In this chapter we look at the history of TCs and the practical aspects of establishing and administering these living units within prisons.

An Historic View of Therapeutic Communities

For the general reader, the phrase "therapeutic community" is most likely to bring to mind either the small, intense programs for substance abusers seen on television or read about in the newspaper or reports (some very uncomplimentary) concerning Synanon, the program begun in California for alcoholics and drug addicts by Charles Dederich during the early 1960s. What many fail to realize is that the theoretical roots of the TC go back more than 125 years and the structural roots of this mode of treatment go back to the 1940s. In addition, although TCs have been very successful in assisting alcoholics and drug addicts to find and maintain recovery, some of their greatest successes have been with victims of trauma and with violent, antisocial prison inmates.

Early History. In the 1860s, Benjamin Rush wrote extensively on the concept of the "moral treatment" of the mentally disturbed. Basically, the moral therapist believed that environmental factors played a significant role in the rehabilitative process of the disturbed individual. Consequently, the emphasis of such treatment centered around humane treatment programs in which physical activity and interpersonal relationships were a hallmark.

During World War II, Dr. Maxwell Jones further developed the concept of moral treatment while treating shell-shocked members of the armed forces at a London hospital. He felt that progress and rehabilitation were more effective when attention was paid to the milieu and to the communication processes at work in the treatment process. Social systems and interpersonal relationships were viewed as providing the emotional support needed during the primary period of stress. Treatment close to friends and the implementation of daily functions would, Jones believed, reduce the length of disability. Opportunities to ventilate were also required. These beliefs demanded an open environment for communication and trust, contact with the outside communities, and strong relationships with staff.

How often do we find a psychiatric ward where a frank evaluation of the treatment aims and methods in both staff and patient groups is traditional (Jones, 1953). It was Jones's desire to have the patients in his groups work with each other toward strengthening their ability to function in the outside social system. Jones called this concept of treatment therapeutic community. Once Jones and his associates had demonstrated the benefits derived from the introduction of group psychiatric sessions and the involvement of patients in their own treatment process, these therapeutic communities became independent adjuncts to the psychiatric hospitals to which they were related. (Carr-Gregg, 1984).

In utilizing the power of one patient aiding another in overcoming their difficulties, Jones became part of a long history of practitioners who have drawn on this model. Psychiatrist J. L. Moreno, who invented psychodrama and greatly influenced the science of group therapy, wrote extensively about the major role of getting people in group therapy to help each other resolve their conflicts. In fact, Moreno judged the effectiveness of such professionals by their ability as catalysts and coordinators of the group's therapeutic energy (Yablonsky, 1989). That standard is still applied today in judging the quality of professional work within a therapeutic community.

Substance Abuse TCs. The first TC devoted to the treatment of substance abuse was founded by a recovering alcoholic, Charles E. Dederich, in 1958 in Ocean Park, California. In Synanon, recovering addicts and alcoholics lived together, supported the community, and regularly participated in seminar discussions and a form of group psychotherapy that involved encountering each other's behavior in small group sessions. By 1971, however, the goal of rehabilitation, or Jones's stress on the ability to function in the outside social system, was replaced by the goal of absorption by the community. Synanon had begun to take on cult-like qualities. This shift undermined the role of the therapeutic community in the rehabilitation process of commitment to the reintegration of community members (be they addicts, shell-shocked veterans, or criminal offenders) into wider society.

Synanon's transformation from a TC that claimed to provide a cure for substance abusers to a cult exacerbated the difficulties experienced by other therapeutic communities in endeavoring to gain acceptance from the wider society (Carr-Gregg, 1984). In addition, a number of Synanon's more punitive techniques for breaking through to residents (e.g., shaving heads and other actions felt to be humiliating to the participant) drew fire from a number of quarters, even among those friendly to the concept of therapeutic community. Still, despite its shortcomings, the TC movement owes a great deal to Synanon, and a number of ex-Synanon participants went on to form other therapeutic communities which drew from the best of their experience there.

In 1981, Naya Arbiter, a former addict and Synanon resident, formed Amity, a TC in Tucson, Arizona, which effected innovations and modifications of the original Synanon model. In speaking about developing Amity, Arbiter said:

> In developing Amity we went back to the roots of the movement and reexamined the notion and definition itself: therapeutic community. Since the phrase originated with Moreno, we began to think in terms of a therapeutic community as being an exercise in residential psychodrama. This forced a new level of detail in terms of getting intimately familiar with the details of situations in people's lives; opened doors in terms of allowing and encouraging people to act out making amends, act out their anger, and their need for family. (Yablonsky, 1989, p. 41)

Delancey Street Foundation is an outstanding example of a set of TCs. Started in

San Francisco in the 1960s, this program has a number of sites throughout the country. It serves substance abusers and offenders, both adults and juveniles. Delancey Street has developed a number of businesses which train its participants and consequently do not need to rely on outside funding which might compromise the intensity of the treatment. All the staff, with the exception of the executive director, Mimi Silbert, Ph.D., who cofounded the program with her husband, are graduates of the program. The community uses highly confrontive and intensive methods to challenge the deep-seated personality problems of its participants. Unfortunately, the program is unable to accept sex offenders.

Prison-Based TCs. One of the greatest areas of success for the TC has been prisons. Prison-based TCs grew out of a long history of corrections-based substance abuse treatment. According to Lockwood, Inciardi, and Hooper (1995), toward the close of the 1920s several members of Congress advocated the establishment of federal "narcotics farms" for the treatment of prisoners. This resulted in the Porter Narcotic Farm Act in 1929 and led to the opening of the first prison-based comprehensive drug treatment. Farms opened at Lexington, Kentucky, in 1935 and Fort Worth, Texas, in 1939. These programs had a limited effectiveness, but the limitations were attributed to the lack of community-based aftercare services.

Throughout the 1960s and into the 1970s, the most viable form of treatment for substance abuse in correctional settings appeared to be the TC. In 1962, the Nevada State Prison opened an extension of Synanon. In 1967, the Federal Bureau of Prisons opened its first TC at Danbury, Connecticut; in 1969, the New York City Addiction Services Agency opened TCs at Rikers Island and Hart Island penitentiaries (Inciardi, Lockwood, & Hooper, 1993).

One of the most effective TCs within a prison setting, however, was not limited to substance abuse treatment and had far-reaching effects beyond its own walls. From 1968 to 1974, Martin Groder worked at the maximum security federal prison at Marion, Illinois. He developed a form of therapeutic community which he called Asklepieion (after the temple for the Greek god of healing). Groder was able to get permission to work with a group of 25 volunteers who would evolve their own treatment program with the help of himself and two mental health staff. The community used Synanon confrontation groups as well as the language and understanding gained from Eric Berne's transactional analysis. Gestalt, behavior modification, and other forms of treatment also made contributions to the culture of the community as they were discussed and deemed to be relevant to the life of the group. Here, in the midst of what was reasonably considered one of the most violent, hard-core prisons in the country, a group of inmates was establishing and maintaining a community with its own unique culture—a culture that stood in radical, marked contrast to the life and culture of the prison around them. A prime example of this culture was displayed in the way in which Asklepieion modified Synanon's techniques.

> The Synanon game was modified at Marion and became less violent than at Synanon, because Marion inmates believed that confrontation without caring was unproductive. In this context a violent verbal attack on a peer was immediately reacted to by the group and the angry peer was confronted. (Jones, 1961, p. 483)

That such a modification would take place points to a level of developed empathy within the Asklepieion community which is remarkable—as was the 13% recidivism rate among inmates exposed to Asklepieion for six months or more (Jones, 1961).

Perhaps even more remarkable is the impact that Asklepieion had on other prisons through one of its ex-residents:

> Monte McKenzie, an inmate, carried the Asklepieion model with him when he was transferred to the Arizona State Prison at Fort Grant. On leaving prison McKenzie started an organization in Phoenix called "OK Community," which applies the same group support to ex-inmates that the prisoners use in their prison group. McKenzie has also started a therapeutic community like Asklepieion in the Phoenix prison, Durango. (Jones, 1961, p. 484)

Unfortunately, Asklepieion failed to win the support of prison leadership; like many TC programs around the country during the "nothing works" period of the 1970s, Asklepieion was discontinued in June 1976. Changes in power structure, changes in philosophy of treatment, prison overcrowding, and budget deficits all combined with the elimination of the Law Enforcement Assistance Act.

The late 1980s saw a rebirth in interest in TCs in the treatment of substance abuse when the National Institute of Justice Assistance (NIJA) funded a number of pilot projects throughout the country. Unfortunately, in some instances the increased funding sometimes undermined the existing programs. The Dawn Unit at Central New Mexico Correctional Center was a 45-bed TC funded within the mental health budget. Although the initial grant for $750,000 had been submitted so that there would not be a need to continue to turn to the legislature to fund the program, the NIJA had rewritten the proposal to greatly increase staff and set up a statewide bureaucracy. However, these pilot projects were only funded for a short period with the expectation on the part of the NIJA that states would pick up the programs. Indeed the funds were not picked up by the State and the program closed.

Still a number of programs such as Oregon's Cornerstone, New York's Stay'n Out, and the 12-Step program in the Connecticut Department of Corrections managed to endure. As time has gone on, these have been joined by other therapeutic community programs such as CREST in Vermont. Most of the comprehensive sex offender programs in the country, including those in Vermont, Massachusetts, Washington, Wisconsin, Minnesota, and numerous other places, utilize TCs.

As can be seen, the TC stands within a rich philosophical and methodological history. Because of the open quality of its structure, it may well be the best-suited catalyst for applying new insights and skills to the treatment of those who struggle to gain control over their lives as they shed the dysfunctional living patterns of addiction and antisocial behavior. As places where residents are intimately involved in the decisions and processes that affect their lives and treatment, TCs stand at the forefront of the movement to maintain an individual's dignity as well as his responsibility for his own future.

Creating Therapeutic Communities in Prisons

An effective TC demands the creation of a safe, secure, and therapeutic environment in which men in treatment can build relationships that will foster emotional and cognitive growth and change. A TC is a place in which a small number of men, typically no more than 50, live together and do treatment together. That is only the beginning. These men will be living in an environment like no other they have ever experienced. Their every decision will be challenged and examined for its appropriateness. Recovery will be expected and negative behavior will have a consequence. Men are held accountable for their past and present behavior to plan for future behavior without violence. The TC is a healing place, but the healing does not allow a sex offender to feel sorry for himself or excuse or lie about his behavior. Progress through treatment must be rewarded and a man must clearly understand both what is expected of him and what the consequences are for not meeting those expectations.

TCs vary greatly from one correctional setting to another. They are influenced by the attitude and support of the administration, by the quality of the treatment staff, by the acceptance of the program by correctional officers, by the layout of the facility, and by the sex offenders themselves. Other variables that influence a TC are the current politics of the state and federal government toward treatment in general and sex offenders in particular, available funding, equipment and training, and the particular treatment model used.

Progression Through Treatment

It is rare to encounter a sex offender who has truly volunteered for treatment. Typically, the offender has been caught for his criminal behavior. Then, generally, the offender is threatened with the loss of something he values—a marriage, family, his freedom, employment, parole or residence in a safer institution, and so on. Only then does he "voluntarily" come into treatment. From a treatment perspective, an offender's initial motivation for treatment does not necessarily influence the outcome of treatment (Schwartz, 1977). A man's progress through treatment can often be viewed in three stages: the beginning, the middle, and the end of treatment.

Early in treatment, generally the first three months, an offender displays some of the more common sex offender characteristics such as lying, manipulation, minimization, distorted thinking, an attitude of distrust, and self-centeredness. He may display behavior that is not conducive to treatment while speaking as if he had fully committed to working on his recovery. This is to be expected and can be understood when viewing his life during the time he was sexually acting out. During that time, he was likely to have been manipulative, secretive, angry, depressed, or stressed out. These characteristics were not obliterated after the sexual assault ended. He brings some of these same offensive behaviors into the treatment milieu and exhibits them through his daily living. They can be observed in the way he treats others, his lack of intimacy in his relationships, how he gets what he wants, and the way he communicates with others. This is to be expected. What can also be expected is that members of the TC will confront these antisocial behaviors. The treatment staff confronts through groups and classes, the custody staff through the maintenance of rules and regulations, and, most important, a group of his peers confront—that is, other sex offenders who are farther along in their treatment and will not tolerate his behavior, thus demanding he change into a more socially acceptable human being.

The middle part of treatment can best be summarized as allowing an offender to practice and integrate the new material he has learned through the program. This sounds easy but can be complicated by the manner in which institutions are traditionally operated. To allow an offender to "practice" and integrate material, he has to be allowed to lapse. An offender has to be allowed to make mistakes or refuse to change a behavior, suffer a consequence, learn from it, and incorporate the learning into new behavior. Well, consider how correctional facilities are traditionally operated. Take the example of two inmates who become verbally abusive toward one another. One attempts to "go after" the other but is stopped by a group of other inmates. Most institutions will not tolerate such behavior from their inmate population. Such behavior is usually considered a serious incident and is managed by giving both inmates disciplinary reports, moving them to a segregation unit, and never allowing them to return to the same housing unit. The "enemy situation" is frequently documented and the two men would be kept separate. In a TC, this would be viewed as a lapse with both men being held accountable for their behavior and expected to take responsibility for their actions and resolve the conflict. They may be segregated temporarily to cool off; however, both men would be assessed for their ability to continue treatment and returned to the unit.

What can we learn from this situation? First, acting out in a TC occurs and must be managed as a lapse. Second, it demonstrates the need for a supportive and flexible prison administration as changes in the way incidences are managed. The point being that in the middle part of treatment, as men begin to incorporate what they have learned, they will have lapses. A TC will provide the structure and boundaries for this behavior to occur provided it does not seriously jeopardize security.

The end of treatment for a sex offender in a TC usually occurs near the last three or four months of treatment. By this time he has taken full responsibility for his sex offenses, has demonstrated empathy for others, and has developed a comprehensive plan to avoid a reoffense. His tasks during the last part of his treatment are to provide leadership, finalize transition plans, and do closure with his community. This is not an easy time in treatment for the offender. A recovering offender is expected to use his new coping skills and demonstrate an ability to integrate all his newly acquired skills into his daily living. Add to that having to say good-bye to the men and women who have shown him a way to change his life. By this time in treatment, he has learned to trust and has developed some strong bonds with both staff and other inmates. It may well be that he has never appropriately said good-bye or left a place he felt as emotionally bound to. On the negative side, men may resist this closure and lapse into old behavior. We refer to this as short-timer's disease. On the positive side, it is not unusual for men to express love for the TC and a commitment to give back by not committing another offense.

Granted, progressing through treatment does not always follow this framework. Men often present additional behaviors on which they need to focus as they begin to develop trust. Self-disclosure (e.g., about additional victims, compulsive masturbation practices, victimization issues, and other problematic areas) may change treatment plans and progress through treatment.

The Administration of a Therapeutic Community

The critical elements of a TC are:

• Adequate funding
• Supportive correctional administrators
• A strong treatment model

- Good treatment staff
- Trained correctional staff
- Expert clinical supervision
- Adequate facility
- Clear philosophy and policy

Adequate Funding. Adequate funding is necessary for any successful treatment program. However, a TC is cost-effective. Moving the treatment program into a residential unit maximizes treatment because the participants reinforce the treatment from 18 to 24 hours a day, depending on how much time they have together. Some correctional systems still attempt to provide sex offender treatment by allowing the mental health staff to do individual therapy with sex offenders. Because they do not have a specialized treatment program for which specific funds are allocated, they may believe that they are saving money. However, they are actually spending much more money for much outcome.

Supportive Correctional Administrators. Prior to locating a site, hiring a staff, or anything else, it is critical to identify who will support sex offender treatment within a correctional facility. These people need to be committed for the long haul. Supportive prison officials and politicians are critical, and they need to understand the pros and cons of their support. For example, sex offenders will reoffend. We hope it will be in smaller numbers than those who are untreated, but it will happen. Will there be high-level support for the program even through the hard times? Is the administration committed to defending the program from critics within and outside of the department? Can the administration support the program without micromanaging it?

A Strong Treatment Model. Every TC needs to be grounded in a sound theoretical model which dictates the types of treatment provided. When a theoretical model is in place, the staff can readily refer to the underlying philosophy when making treatment decisions. From the initial evaluation to the preparation of treatment plans to deciding when an individual has completed the program, all aspects must flow from the same model.

Good Treatment Staff. Arguably, the most important element of an effective TC is its treatment staff. Factors to consider when hiring staff include professional degrees and training, meeting licensing requirements, experience in the field, personality, professional memberships, and a person's reasons for wanting to do the work. TCs vary in their selection of treatment staff depending upon budgets, philosophy, experience, and so on.

Professional degrees are a passport to the team but should not be the single most important criteria for hiring. The team should require staff who have taken the initiative to attend professional training in the field and those who have demonstrated the motivation to obtain a professional license, particularly if it is not a requirement of the job. Men and women who have involved themselves in professional organizations such as the Association for the Treatment of Sexual Abusers show at minimum an interest but more probably a dedication to the work to being done in this field. However, people new to the field should not be overlooked. Some of the best professionals are transitioning from both the fields of substance abuse and work with victims of sexual assault. In an ideal world, one world be working with a professional staff who are well educated, maintain their professional licenses, attend sex offender treatment training regularly, belong to professional organizations, and have some experience in the field. An eclectic group of people with strong, dynamic, energetic personalities who have the ability to avoid personalizing the issues seem to work out best: people who are team players and are themselves open to criticism and feedback and have the ability to support both their clients and their treatment team.

The original TCs were operated by recovering offenders and addicts. Many of the best programs still seek out such individuals as their first choice in staffing a unit. This is much less common among sex offender programs. However, some programs are able to use paraprofessional staffing to expand the types of persons who are able to work in the units. Correctional officers often make excellent group leaders. A chaplain, classification officer, or probation or parole agent may have excellent therapeutic skills coupled with a real understanding of the mind of the offender.

Finally, it is important for supervisors to examine why a person chooses to do this work. What reason could an individual possibly have for wanting to work with this population? Many of those who have been working in the field for long periods still cannot answer this question. But, individuals should explore this question in depth prior to selecting taking a position in this field; people who themselves have their own issues around sexual assault, be they victims, sexual addicts, batterers, and so on. The field of sex offender treatment is not the place to work out personal problems.

Staff should expect to spend a great deal of time doing direct service with the inmates. It is the responsibility of the supervisor to prioritize staff time so as not to overburden staff with unnecessary paperwork, meetings, or other tasks. A critical piece of therapy work is to establish rapport with clients. Only in this way will the job of confrontation and support be accepted.

Once the staff are selected, it is important to encourage them to attend professional training on a regular basis and to stay up-to-date on the current literature in the field. Supervisors must be prepared to listen to and help set boundaries around the large amount of unhealthy information staff members are subjected to on a daily basis. It is the job of the supervisor to support the staff and model appropriate behavior while on the job. This is difficult work, and it can certainly take its toll on any treatment team.

Trained Correctional Staff. The correctional staff fall into three categories.

1. The corrections officers working directly in the TC. These corrections officers (COs) should be viewed as part of the treatment team. Their input is invaluable. They see participants at times and engaged in activities that the treatment staff do not have the opportunity to observe. These officers should be adequately training in the treatment of sex offenders and should be given every opportunity to participate and observe all aspects of treatment. Officers should have the choice of working in a TC as their attitude and role modeling should be up to the same standard as that of the treatment staff.
2. Custody staff supervising sex offenders throughout the institution in jobs, education, and other daily activities. These COs should also be trained. A general

overview of treatment and a discussion of how their observation and reporting are helpful to treatment should be discussed and encouraged.

3. Correctional staff who do not appear to have direct contact with the sex offender. Team supervisors should talk to these people about what the program is doing. Their attitude and understanding of the work is important. They should have a general training about the goals and purpose of the program. Thereafter, treatment staff should make themselves available for questions and discussions.

Expert Clinical Supervision. A good TC will either contract or have on staff a clinician with expertise in the field of sex offender treatment. Regular clinical supervision time needs to be scheduled. This time should afford the treatment staff a venue for particular therapeutic concerns as well as allowing discussion of how the team is doing emotionally. Such work takes its toll of staff, and they should be afforded an opportunity to express themselves.

Adequate Facility. A therapeutic community requires an adequate facility. The unit should be separate and distinct from the rest of the facility. The men will live on this unit, study, do therapy, cry, laugh, and create a strong bond. It has to be both physically and emotionally safe. It cannot be overcrowded. The men must have a place to go to think, feel, and integrate their new selves. There must be a space large enough to accommodate gatherings of all the men at one time for community meetings and social and treatment functions. There must be a room available for small groups of men to meet to work and conduct community business. Ideally, there would be staff offices available as staff should spend a large percentage of their time in direct contact with the inmates.

Clear Philosophy and Policy. The operation of a TC can begin with the following philosophy: No more victims. This philosophy usually provides a common goal for inmates, staff, and administrators. From there, a program begins to develop that holds men responsible for their behavior and teaches them new skills to intervene on sexually deviant behavior.

The basic framework of a TC, the theoretical orientation, and staff should be firmly in place prior to the admission of inmates. The criteria for admissions, staff and inmate schedules, groups, classes, and community meeting times should all be in place.

At the initial start-up of a TC, the basic philosophy can be firmly in place without a lot of written policy and procedure. The reason for this is twofold. Working from the assumption that sex offenders have chosen not to follow the norms of our society, as evidenced by their criminal sexual behavior, a focus of treatment is to teach men to follow rules and norms. This can be done in one of two ways: (1) all the rules are firmly in place from day one, and the expectation is that the rules will be followed or a consequence such as termination from the program will occur, or (2) as the TC grows, rules and norms are established as the need for them arises. Having experienced TCs both ways, we feel that the latter is more effective. It is probably easier to have the rules established first; however, it may be less of a learning opportunity for the offender. There will already be many rules in place in a correctional facility: rules such as the times of movements, when, where meals are to be eaten, and how visits will occur. These rules would be in place with or without a TC, and sex offenders will complain about them. Then to come in and enforce another set of rules with a "Because I say so" attitude serves no purpose. However, it is purposeful to establish the rules as the need for them presents themselves (e.g., the use of pornography). Treatment providers probably consider many things pornographic that prison officials do not (e.g., pictures of children, seductive or suggestive photos, and some catalogs). A program should not begin with a rule against pornography. Instead, as the problem of possessing inappropriate sexually explicit material presents itself, and it will, the TC needs to come together as a community and make decisions about how healthy the use of such materials is and how such material feeds deviant fantasy. In doing so, the TC decides and becomes a part of making the rules. As a result, the men are far more likely to support the rules. Also, the staff will be supported by the community as a man violates the rules and consequences occur. Staff must understand this concept. This is a time-consuming process, but one that is worthwhile in the inmates owning their community.

As the community matures there will be a subtle shift from staff holding inmates accountable for their behavior to inmates holding one another accountable. This must be clearly understood as a positive development in the life of a community. Staff must always be ready to assist in this process but also must be prepared to let go of some of the control. As new men arrive and leaders leave, the community may fall back into negative ways. This is to be expected. At such times, staff should step in and guide the community back on track.

Components of a Therapeutic Community

Although TCs vary, some components are basic.

Primary Therapy Groups. Such groups are the backbone of the TC. They should not exceed 12 men in number, with 6–10 as the ideal. Groups should be lead by cotherapist, one male and one female.

Psychoeducational Classes. Such classes are an effective method of teaching men new coping skills. Classes can include victim empathy, anger management, substance abuse, communication skills, relapse prevention, and others identified as necessary.

Specialty Groups. Groups of this type are used to deal with special issues and special populations. Some TCs have a wide range of educational levels, and some participants may need a remedial or tutorial group. Other communities may have individuals with comorbid conditions such as substance abuse or mental illness. Some TCs choose to work with the participants' own victimization outside the regular primary group so that this does not become the dominant theme of the group and circumvent offender issues. Therefore, a separate group may be useful. In some TCs the participants lead the groups by themselves.

Community Meetings. At these meetings, all the community members, including staff, assemble. In the start-up of a TC, these meetings take place frequently, possibly even daily, and are usually led by staff. As norms are established, the men want to take ownership of this meeting. This is a good sign of a community coming together and it should be encouraged. Often the community will elect a chairperson and secretary on a rotating basis to conduct the meetings. As this begins to happen, staff can move out of the leadership roles. Eventually a community can meet once a week. The focus of the meeting should be to address all problems and issues that effect the community as a whole.

Tools of the Trade

Although there will be a gradual shift in power from the treatment staff to the inmates in the operation of the TC, some operational tools will be in place from day one. They are not introduced immediately but as the need for them develops.

Community Interventions. From time to time TCs need to recommit to treatment. This may be as a result of an event (discovery of pornography, watching of violent movies, the introduction of several new inmates who do not yet understand TC, or when staff feel there is a need). Community interventions are mandatory meetings in which the community is confronted with behavior that is not conducive to a TC. They generally take on a drama therapy flavor and are different from community meetings in that they are run by staff, may go on for a full day or longer, are confrontational or evoke emotion and/or tension, and do not allow for a mere discussion to explain away dysfunctional behavior. Community intervention seems to be necessary several times a year. Such interventions often include commitment rituals and focus rededication to recovery.

Intervention Committee. As a community grows in strength, the inmates should be responsible for managing their own conflicts. Clear guidelines need to be in place and followed. In our community we began to notice a lot of conflict such as arguments between roommates, inmates telling staff about others misbehaviors, and so on. One Friday we called a community intervention and presented the community with the problem and told them they would be given the weekend to come up with a resolution. When we returned to work on Monday, they had designed an intervention committee to resolve conflict. They had chosen two men from each primary group to form a committee. When conflict arose in the community, the TC had a written procedure to follow. First, men would try to work it out among themselves. If they were not successful, they would move to a meeting with members of the committee acting as mediators. If there was no resolution, the situation would be presented in primary group, where staff would hear the problem. If the situation involves violation of policy, either Department of Corrections or TC, it is mandatorily reported to staff.

Contracts. This tool is used when an inmate acts out or demonstrates a negative pattern of behavior that needs to be worked upon. Participants need to be allowed to lapse, but they must also be held accountable for their behavior by being shown what they did wrong and a way to correct the behavior and make amends, if necessary. A contract is a written document that outlines a problem area, states interventions to be taken, clearly defines a consequence for failure to comply, and is understood by the inmate. The duration of a contract can be brief, generally no less than one week, or for the length of one's treatment time. Contracts should be read by the inmate before his community. In our community, the men usually respond by asking how they can help the contractee be successful in completing his contract.

Deviant Cycles. Most sex offender TCs have a strong relapse prevention (RP) component. It is useful for the men to become aware of how they act out in the "here and now." They can then try to relate this behavior to their offending pattern. When a man acts out in the community and it does not warrant a contract, usually because it is less serious, he is often asked to "do a cycle." This is a written explanation of his behavior, broken down into the components of a deviant cycle. The participant can then begin to learn how to utilize RP to control common dysfunctional behaviors.

Terminations. TCs must have a policy for the termination of inmates. This policy must be understood and supported by the community; however, it is the responsibility of the treatment staff to initiate a termination. Reasons to terminate men from the program may include violation of Department of Corrections policy (e.g., use of drugs, sexually acting out, or fights), failure to successfully complete a contract, or other serious violations of the TC. Terminations should be done as a last resort after having tried other interventions such as work through the primary group, meetings with the intervention committee, a contract, or any other means available.

Rituals. Every community establishes its own rituals, much like families, organizations, churches, and communities do. Rituals are unique to the TC. Some of our rituals include graduation ceremonies for a man completing the program. These often include humorous skits and presentations of gag awards and certificates. Alternatively, they may be very serious and emotionally laden events. Language also becomes a part of a TC. As time goes on communities develop terms and slang unique to the community.

Social Activities. These are a necessary part of every community. They are also of the more difficult components to sell to prison administrators. Many sex offenders have poor social skills and could be better at communicating. Social activities provide valuable learning experiences for these men. Activities may include gatherings, which include food and are in celebration of an event, such as anniversaries of the program, sporting events, card or board games, or any other appropriate event in which the men come together as a community. In preparing such events, the participants learn to cooperate to plan an activity. They learn about earning funds and budgeting them. They may have to deal with the logistics of obtaining approval and coordinating with different departments in the institution. They also learn that one need not have sex, alcohol, or drugs to have fun.

Conclusion

A sex offense is a violation of interpersonal relations. Therefore, sex offenders must learn alternative ways of relating to others. When the sex offender lives in the general population and comes into a therapy once or twice a week, the program provides little opportunity to truly rebuild one's pattern of relating to others. However, living with other sex offenders 24 hours a day provides an opportunity for trying out new ways of relating to others. Sex offenders living in general population must also lie about their offenses when outside the therapy group. This perpetuates the secret which lies at the root of sexual deviancy. However, life in the TC provides a safe place for processing therapy throughout the day and evening. The treatment process expands exponentially with little additional cost. Staff also have the opportunity to observe the offender's behavior under a microscope because it is almost impossible to hide one's dysfunctional patterns of interaction from 20–200 other sex offenders whose daily lives are effecting each other. By identifying and intervening in the earliest stages of one's cycle, one learns to control one's sexual acting out, and the TC becomes the laboratory for practicing these techniques.

References

Carr-Gregg, C. (1984). *Kicking the habit.* Queensland: Queensland University Press.

Inciardi, J., Lockwood, D., & Hooper, R. M. (1993, July 14–17). *The effectiveness of the KEY-CREST continuum of treatment.* Paper presented at the 2nd annual conference of the National Institute on Drug Abuse Research and Practice: An Alliance for the 21st Century, Washington, DC.

Jones, M. (1953). *The therapeutic community.* New York: Basic Books.

Jones, M. (1961). Learning as treatment. In H. Toch (Ed.), *Psychology of crime and criminal justice* (pp. 470–487). New York: Holt, Rinehart & Winston.

Schwartz, B. K. (1977). *Factors associated with response to treatment among aggressive sex offenders.* Doctoral dissertation, University of New Mexico, Albuquerque.

Yablonsky, L. (1989). *The therapeutic community.* New York: Gardner Press.

Chapter 20

Using Drama Therapy to Do Personal Victimization Work With Sexual Aggressors— A Review of the Research

by Barbara K. Schwartz, Ph.D., L.P., C.M.H.C. and John Bergman, M.A., R.D.T.

Overview

A current issue of debate among professionals who treat sex offenders is whether to deal with their clients' personal victimization. Although some behaviorists and cognitive-behaviorists avoid dealing with past trauma and family issues, as well as affective issues in general, there is an increasing acceptance of the holistic nature of the offender as a person with issues in the physiological, cognitive-behavioral, affective, interpersonal, familial, societal, and spiritual domains. Drama therapy is a particularly effective method of confronting these issues. In this chapter we explore the theoretical foundations for using methods that evoke catharsis and abre-action and using drama therapy in that context. We also explore issues around con-frontation and touch.

History of Treating of Personal Victimization

Dealing with personal victimization issues is not anything new in the treat-ment of sex offenders. Many of the older programs such as the Massachusetts Treatment Center, the Sex Offender Treatment Program in Somers, Connecticut, the New Jersey Department of Corrections Program at Avenel, and the Transitional Sex Offender Program (TSOP) at Lino Lakes, Minnesota have for decades emphasized personal victimization work. Although many of these pro-grams have been updated with the addition of a number of behavioral and cogni-tive-behavioral techniques, the efficacy of their work in this area remains. For example, the Massachusetts Treatment Center's psychodynamic work with some of the most intractable sex offenders produced a difference of 25% and 40% between treated and untreated individuals (Prentky & Burgess, 1992). The Lino Lakes TSOP produced recidivism rates of 16% for treated sex offenders and 22% for noncompleters (Steele, 1992).

Prendergast (1978, 1991) describes the utilization of the ROARE technique at Avenel, which combined heavy confrontation, emotional exacerbation, and physical touch to relive personal victimization through regression.

> For some sexually assaultive personalities, none of the standard methods of ventilating their rage are effective. Their resistance is so great that special methods must be employed to achieve this important goal. One of the meth-ods we have used successfully involves marathon therapy and specialized badgering techniques. What occurs as a result is a regression to earlier age levels and an actual reliving of past traumatic experiences. (Prendergast, 1991, p. 40)

Dr. Prendergast reported utilizing this technique more than 2, 000 times and it was depicted in the 1980 television movie *Rage*.

Recently a number of programs have adopted a posttraumatic stress disorder (PTSD) approach to dealing with personal victimization issues. This theoretical orientation, also known as the addictions model, is advocated by individuals such as Drs. Patrick Carnes, Mark Schwartz, and William Masters. This approach is rep-resented through its own national organization, journal, and body of professional literature. Schwartz, Gilperin, and Masters (1992) summarize this approach by stating: "Serendipitously, the study of sexual abuse victims has resulted in a new understanding of paraphilia and sexual compulsivity. Frequently, men and women who are sexually abused present clinically with compulsive reenactment of early trauma in their sexual imagery" (p. 333).

Schwartz and Masters (1994) place heavy emphasis on abreactive work in reliv-ing the early trauma with sex offenders. Mark Schwartz states:

> Now the behaviorists agree that learning and conditioning theories cannot adequately account for deviant sexual behavior. Could it be that there is actu-ally the beginning of some integration in theoretical approaches—some

recognition that victimizers have experiences in their development that direct-ly contribute to their behavior? It's not "what's wrong with them, " it's "what happened to them." (1995, p. 87)

Although this model and the psychodynamic approach were once seen as rivals to behavioral and cognitive-behavioral approaches, the fields currently appear to be growing closer together. Representatives of the PTSD/addictions models routinely present at the conferences of the Association for the Treatment of Sexual Abusers (ATSA) which began as a behavioral treatment organization. Sex offender treatment pioneer Faye Honey Knopp, at the 1994 ATSA Conference, urged therapists to work on offenders' personal victimization issues when she stated:

Among many clinicians there may be a reluctance to view and treat the whole person, the victim as well as the victimizing side of the client. But these sides are inseparable. The roots of this narrower view of the offender treatment may have evolved in part from cognitive and behavioral philosophy and earlier models, but more often appear to have emanated from a fear that treating the offender as victim interferes with his or her accountability. Such apprehension may have been warranted in the early development of sex offender treatment but we now know enough about program sequencing and pretreatment educational modules to overcome those fears. (Knopp, 1994)

At the 1995 ATSA Conference, Janice Marques stated that evaluation of the Atascadero Program produced a number of recommendations for treatment including doing personal victimization work.

Pithers (1993) pointed out that "at this time, existing treatment approaches do not apply equally well to all sex offenders" (p. 181). He made a very strong statement for doing affectively-based work when he stated:

If therapy is to have long-term effects, facilitating rapists' emotional access, particularly to feelings of vulnerability, is essential. If rapists do not have access to a full range of their own emotions, it is impossible to establish empathy for victims of sexual abuse. To attach emotions to others in a real-istic fashion, rapists first must be able to accept the existence of these emotions within themselves. Rapists need to perceive their own emotions accurately in order to understand in any meaningful way, how their actions may affect others. Only then does the possibility of establishing victim empathy exist. This may be the key component of assisting change in rapists. (p. 181)

It would be very difficult to do this type of affective work, particularly around feelings of vulnerability without doing personal victimization work.

Bernard, Fuller, Robbins, and Shaw (1989), in *The Child Molester: An Integrated Approach to Evaluation and Treatment*, describe one of the components of their treat-ment program:

The experiential modules are designed to facilitate characterological under-standing and openness to change. In these modules the offender identifies and works through functioning that may result from early trauma and/or lifelong unhealthy functioning. Experiential components include cognitive/insight and peer facilitated group therapies, traumatic events modules, role play, and sen-sitivity training . . . (p. 132). During the group therapy session the resident has the opportunity to recall traumatic experiences of sexual abuse that he has experienced. Role play is used to reexperience the traumatic events and provide catharsis (p. 136).

Adele Mayer (1988), in *Sex Offenders: Approaches to Understanding and Management*, states:

> Sex offenders lack empathy for victims, partly due to unresolved early trauma, often involving physical and/or sexual abuse and resulting either in identification with aggressors or displaced anger . . . (p. 123). Through direct victim-confrontation in the here-and-now, regression therapy, bioenergetics and role plays, offenders in group therapy are able to re-experience and repeat childhood trauma in a safe atmosphere which often may result in catharsis followed by new self-understanding . . . (p. 124).

Bernard et al. (1989) discuss their approach to dealing with personal victimization issues in their Florida sex offender treatment program: "Many of the residents themselves have been sexually abused as children. For this reason, during the group therapy session the resident has the opportunity to recall traumatic experiences of sexual abuse which he has experienced" (p. 136).

There are a number of arguments for doing personal victimization work with sex offenders. For practitioners using the addictions model, it is a principle component; however, this type of work can be useful regardless of the formal model. It may allow practitioners to develop a more meaningful relapse prevention plan because the offender may have a more complete understanding of those situations that trigger emotional reactions of anger, powerlessness, or vulnerability that are related to the offense cycle. It is useful in developing victim empathy because the offender has now had an experience that directly relates to the pain of his victim. To fail to deal with personal victimization may play into the cognitive distortion that "what happened to me was not that important. Consequently what happened to my victim was really not that important either," or "If my therapist can ignore it, it really didn't do me that much harm."

Approaches to Personal Victimization Work

When a practitioner decides that treating personal victimization would be a valuable part of a sex offender treatment program, it would make sense to turn to the literature on the treatment of victims for guidance. A 1993 survey of treatment programs for victims of sexual assault identified four major models. (See Table 20.1.)

Table 20.1
Models of Treatment for Sexual Assault Victims (Safer Society, 1993)

Model	*Percentage Utilizing Model*
Insight/self-discovery	40%
PTSD	35%
Cognitive-behavioral	15%
Psychoeducational	10%

A number of authors describe the PTSD model (Brauer, 1986; Courtois, 1988; Dulton, 1990; Goulding & Schwartz, 1995; Lingley, 1985; Schwartz, Gilperin, & Masters, 1995; Semands, 1994; Steele, 1993; Walker, 1995; Cruse et al., 1990). The supposition of a number of these models is that the patient needs to abreact the trauma and the use of this technique and other related therapies is described in Table 20.2. Abreaction and other related techniques are utilized in several of these models.

Table 20.2
Utilization of Treatment Modalities (Safer Society, 1993)

Treatment Modality	Percentage of Utilization
Reliving the trauma	61.9%
Abreaction	72%
Role plays	72%
Regression	44%
Bodywork	22%
Catharsis	22%

Abreaction, according to the American Psychiatric Association (1984), is the "emotional release or discharge after recalling a painful experience that has been repressed because it was consciously intolerable. A therapeutic effect sometimes occurs through partial discharge of the painful emotions and increased insight" (p. 1).

Catharsis is a similar concept but deals with material that is factually but not emotionally remembered. These techniques date back to the early part of this century and were originally used by Pierre Janet to treat veterans of World War I (van der Hart, 1989). The value of abreaction and catharsis are described by numerous authors (Briere, 1992; Courtois, 1988; Gil, 1988; Goulding & Schwartz, 1995; Lingley, 1985; Ross, 1989; Schwartz, Gilperin, & Masters, 1990; Steele, 1993; Wegscheider-Cruse, Cruse, & Boucher, 1990). Dulton (1990) states:

> Reexperiencing the trauma as a means of integrating the experience has been described as important across a variety of trauma groups (Courtois, 1988; Horowitz, 1992; McCann & Pearlman, 1990a; Steketee & Loa, 1987). . . . Integration of trauma through re-experiencing requires a here-and-now experience, rather than a detached reporting of events . . . when avoidance of the traumatic memory is the predominant clinical presentation, strategies for intensification of emotion may be necessary. Such strategies include intensifying general level of arousal by increasing physical level of activity, physically enacting what is being described and exaggerating or repeating phrases. (Edwards, 1989; Greenberg & Safrans 1989). (p. 89)

Semands (1994) describes the process of inducing abreaction as follows:

> Retrieval of traumatic memories may be the catalyst for a powerful chain of events that leads toward integration and assimilation of the sexual abuse trauma (Courtois, 1988; Dolan, 1991; Gil, 1993; Herman, 1992; McCann &

Pearlman, 1990; Meiselman, 1990; Steele & Colrain, 1990). The major components of memory work, which often overlap, are as follows:

1. retrieving traumatic memories
2. abreaction
3. recontextualizing the meaning of the abuse
4. reassessing feelings toward family members
5. realignment of the survivor's sense of self. (p. 134)

Timms and Connors (1992) state that "remembering and reliving the trauma with the full emotion that was denied expression at the time, and with a full sense of present day safety within the therapeutic setting, gives clients a new and healing perspective on the abuse and on themselves" (p. 42). Putnam (1989) has stated:

> Revivification, the vivid reliving of past experiences, is a hallmark of abreaction. The clinical literature on abreaction, flashbacks and posttraumatic stress disorder is filled with vignettes illustrating the graphic reliving of past traumatic episodes experienced by victims. Confusion about the past and present is common during these episodes, although some patients report reliving the event on a split screen, with one half in the past and the other in the present. The vividness of these experiences is due to multisensory hallucinatory and illusory phenomenon that accompany them. The individual may see, hear, feel, smell and taste the past experience. An abreacting individual can also incorporate surrounding objects and people into the abreaction. (p. 242)

A number of other authors also discuss the importance of abreaction. (Brodsky et al., 1990; Caffaro, 1995; Dimock, Hunter, & Struve, 1995; Keane, Fairbank, Caddell, & Zimering, 1989; Lambana & Leyer, 1994; Spiegel, 1988; Van der Kolk, 1989, 1994, 1995).

Exposure Therapies

The literature has described a variety of techniques to expose the patient to traumatic material in a therapeutic setting. The entire process of psychoanalysis was originally conceived of as a way for the patient to bring unconscious traumatic material into consciousness. The technique chosen by the therapist depends on the particular training of that therapist and the level of resistance and denial manifested by the patient. Consequently, techniques that require high levels of intensive specialized training, such as hypnosis and psychodrama, are probably used less frequently than some of the behavioral techniques, such as direct therapeutic exposure, systematic desensitization, or image habituation training. Also, the descriptions of the use of the latter techniques are much more explicit than the descriptions of how to hypnotize or do psychodrama because it is assumed that professionals using the latter methods will have lengthy individualized training compared to many behavioral techniques which are meant to be used by the generic therapist.

It must also be assumed that patients come into treatment with widely varying degrees of denial and resistance. Thus a technique that would be useful for a female survivor who comes willingly and, in fact, ready to pay a substantial amount of money to an outpatient therapist for once-a-week 50-minute sessions might not be at all helpful for male survivors whose issues and basic socialization are very different. Such female groups would differ substantially from male offenders who might be much more resistant to facing the emotional reality of their own abuse as they would then risk really understanding on an affective level the harm they have done to their victims. This population has also been so cut off from their emotions that they can hurt victims without being constrained by feelings of empathy. Furthermore, incarcerated sex offenders have been socialized in their prison experience by the need to control their feelings as this is not only the "convict code" for how to "do time" but it may be vital to the emotional survival of these men who may be experiencing constant harassment by the rest of the prison population.

Survivors of sexual abuse are often emotionally numb. Numerous experts have attested to this fact. Claudia Black (1990) states, "When adult children say they feel numb, they are. They're numb from having to hold in so many feelings for so long; numb from having to build and maintain that protective wall . . ." (p. 137).

K. Louise Schmidt (1995), in *Transforming Abuse: Nonviolent Resistance and Recovery*, states:

> What becomes censored or held back eventually creates a hardening or numbing of the self to the truth of violence. And like anything frozen, our numbness prevents what is vital to life from growing. The self becomes impoverished—a form of poverty that this often manifested through low self-esteem, depression, illness or aggression. (p. 69)

Given the likelihood of widely varying amounts of numbness and denial, the therapist who wishes to evoke abreaction may need to have access to an equally wide range of techniques. Putnam (1989) points out, "The incomplete abreaction of traumatic material has been cited by many authorities as a major cause of failure of therapeutic abreaction (Kline, 1976; Kluft, 1982; Maoz & Pincus, 1979; Rosen & Myers, 1947; Shorvon & Sargeant, 1947)" (p. 249).

Consequently, a variety of psychotherapeutic interventions have been developed to induce abreaction. These range from individual or group therapy where an individual may abreact simply through talking about a traumatic experience to behavioral methods where the therapist helps the patient recreate vivid memories such as direct therapeutic exposure, imaginal exposure, image habituation training, trauma desensitization (Meichenbaum, 1994) and some types of implosive therapies and flooding techniques to more intense uses of these methods. For example, Horowitz (1992) describes the use of one approach to implosion therapy:

> The therapist would be quite forceful in the direction of imagery in the implosive technique. Harry, provided that he followed the main instructions, could not shift from fearsome ideas to guilty ideas. When the therapist talked about Harry being impaled by pipes, breathing and vomiting his own blood, it would restrict Harry to imaging his own potential harm. He must become frightened. (p. 193)

Other techniques use a variety of "external cues." Use of these cues, which could be sounds, words, props, and so on, goes back to the work of Pierre Janet with World War I soldiers and, according to Putnam (1989), he "used to provide external cues." Maoz and Pincus (1979) used sound effects such as the sound of bombs to recreate the trauma of battle with veterans suffering from PTSD. Putnam (1989) states:

> Recall of traumatic material that is wholly or partially out of conscious aware-
> ness can be facilitated and controlled by a variety of techniques. The power
> of external cues to trigger vivid recall has long been recognized by clinicians
> and has been utilized in both therapy and experimental studies of the neuro-
> physiology of abreaction (Putnam, 1989). The external cues may be sights,
> sounds, smells, behaviors or any combination thereof . . . (p. 23). External
> cues are most useful for the induction of abreaction in cases where they are
> highly situation-specific, relatively commonly experienced or associated with
> traumatic experiences. (p. 238)

Psychodrama/Drama Therapy and Experiential Therapies

Meichenbaum (1994) describes a variety of behavioral techniques for use with exposure therapy. The fourth method he describes is a "reenactment of the abusive experience":

> Use psychodrama, role playing, Gestalt empty-chair procedure (e.g. talk and
> comfort the "shamed" child). This can be conducted on a group basis as a sup-
> plement to individual guided imagery procedures. These reenactment proce-
> dures can be used to address and dramatize the victim's fears and intense
> anger towards the perpetrator. The involvement of the group helps to break
> down feelings of isolations. These reenactments are carefully structured, with
> safeguards, as other group members are called upon to play different roles and
> to provide support. (p. 325)

Psychodrama was one of the original techniques used by Janet to treat PTSD (then referred to as "shell shock"). Putnam (1989) stated that Janet used to "play roles to facilitate induction of abreaction in his patients" (p. 238). Psychodrama is routinely mentioned as one of the traditional methods for working with trauma. Meichenbaum (1994) states that psychodrama is one of the four basic techniques for working with the "distressing traumatic event" (p. 380). Baldwin (1988) states that "specific techniques for facilitating recall include hypnotic regression, voice dia-logue, dream work, Gestalt work, psychodrama and Rolfing . . ." (pp. 179-180). Faria and Belohlaviek (1984) state that "techniques from gestalt therapy and psychodrama are particularly valuable for uncovering feelings, working with dreams and integrat-ing the incest experience" (p. 470). Walker (1995) discusses role plays as one of a number of techniques used with abreaction in *Abused Women and Survivor Therapy*, as does Goodwin and Talwar (1989), Goulding and Schwartz (1995), Maoz and Pincus (1979), Walker (1995), and Brauer (1986). As previously mentioned, Bear (1993) found that 72% of the 22 treatment programs for child sexual abuse survivors treatment programs reported that they used role plays. Black (1990) states that "experiential forms of therapy such as bioenergetics, psychodrama and Gestalt are often useful" (p. 237). Courtois (1988) references work by Kearney-Cook in which "clients are then encouraged to sculpt what they remember and are further encouraged to reenact their abuse to facilitate catharsis, insight and mastery" (p. 195). Dulton (1990) states:

> Integration of trauma through re-experiencing requires a here-and-now experience, rather than a detached reporting of events . . . when avoidance of the traumatic memory is the predominant clinical presentation, strategies for intensification of emotion may be necessary. Such strategies include intensifying general level of arousal by increasing physical level of activity, physically enacting what is being described and exaggerating or repeating phrases (Edwards, 1989; Greenberg & Safrans, 1989). (p. 89)

Descriptions of the use of psychodrama or drama therapy can also be subsumed under the rubric of experiential therapy which is described by Wegscheider-Cruse et al. (1990):

> Experiential therapy blends therapies like Gestalt and family therapy with models like sculpture and role play. The purpose is to enact or reenact the emotional climate of the family of origin and/or other past and present significant relationships in an person's life. In re-experiencing these events and relationships, one is able to release the emotions that may have been blocked and repressed. (p. 69)

According to Blatner and Blatner (1988):

> Instead of allowing for the disconnection of experience, psychodrama is particularly effective because the method involves physical action and imagination, sensation and intuition, emotion and reason . . . (p. 96). Concretization allows patients to experience physically what had been experienced psychologically, and the marshaling of the multilevel resources of the body can serve as a vehicle of spontaneity and insight. (p. 155).

Chesner (1994) states:

> When we express ourselves through action we engage at a physical level. The presence of physical movement and possible physical contact within the therapy session has a powerful impact. There is profound connection between body, senses, emotional and mental states. By engaging at a physical level the client has easier access to their emotional and inner world. . . . In both dramatherapy and psychodrama the physicality of the experience brings the emotions and the unconscious into the therapeutic stage. (p. 115)

Dayton (1994) states that "by using psychodrama to bring traumatic memories to the surface, and enacting a metaphor of the situation with safe surrogates and clinical control, a context for the event can be supplied. The story can be told and the frozenness can be walked, spoken, acted, cried, raged and worked through" (p. 229).

Essential Differences Between Psychodrama and Drama Therapy. The terms "psychodrama" and "drama therapy" are often used interchangeably. However, they are not the same thing.

1. Psychodrama focuses on an individual; drama therapy focuses more on the group. The focus of the psychodrama session is on the psychodramatic jour-

ney of one group member, the protagonist, and once this person is identified, the roles taken by the other group members are largely a reflection of the protagonist's inner world. "In drama therapy the focus may come to rest on one individual for most of a session, but it is more likely that the focus will move freely around the group" (Chesner, 1994, p. 118).

2. Psychodrama stays rooted in the world of real events; drama therapy uses a much broader, fictional base. "Psychodramatic scenes tend to be deeply emotional, dealing with painful memories, childhood traumas, unresolved conflict and critical life dilemmas. . . . Drama therapy utilizes far more improvisation of fictional scenes, capitalising on the notion that to play and to pretend enables a sense of freedom and permission, and promotes expression and self-revelation, albeit obliquely" (Emunah, 1994, p. 18).

3. The psychodrama director plays a strict director's role, rarely engaging in the action of enactments. Drama therapists are much more active in their involvement: "[T]he role of the classical psychodramatist is that of director in every sense, whereas the drama therapist is generally more of a fellow player. This can range from, full participation in the drama (while simultaneously functioning as a guide) to offstage witnessing of the drama" (Emunah, 1994, p. 19).

4. Psychodrama is based on Moreno; drama therapy is based on the world of drama and theater. "A core difference of technique between dramatherapy and psychodrama stems from the historical fact that psychodrama originated in the work of one man, Moreno. . . . Dramatherapy, by contrast, has its sources directly in a variety of dramatic and theatrical traditions, such as shamanic ritual, story-telling, dramatic and creative play, and the work of a variety of theatre practitioners from Stanislavski to Grotowski" (Chesner, 1994, p. 119).

   "The techniques used in this process (dramatherapy) can be drawn from any aspect of drama or theatre. These may include working with text, performance, improvisation, storytelling, make-up mask, puppetry, movement, voice, game, sculpting and many more" (Chesner, 1994, p. 123).

5. Psychodrama is highly structured and very task focused; drama therapy is less structured, more free flowing in its direction. "Both psychodrama and dramatherapy sessions share a tripartite structure. While psychodrama involves warmth and sharing, the drama therapy session can be divided into warm-up, development, and closure . . . the central phase of the dramatherapy session does not follow the precise map which underlies the psychodrama" (Chesner, 1994, pp. 125–126).

Both Emunah and Chesner note that it is common for drama therapists to use elements of psychodrama within their work and likewise some psychodramatists use drama therapy techniques within a psychodrama. Drama therapy is the broader, more flexible of the techniques. However, when referring to the whole range of both psychodrama and drama therapy, authors tend to use the first term.

These techniques have been used specifically with offenders as described by Jeffries (1991):

> Psychodramatically this means taking the prisoner back to the primary source of his suffering: the "there-and-then" becomes the "here-and-now" so that he has access to repressed emotions. (p. 193)

The director relies on the group to use restraining and containment techniques; after group members will physically restrain the protagonist so that, against this restraint, he can verbalize his emotions. (p. 198)

A central point in explicating Ralph's extreme psycho-drama experience is to reveal that the learning-in-action on his part, combined with his private sessions, was effective. Ralph could not just talk about his anger. He required a vehicle such as psychodrama that gave him the opportunity to physically and psychologically reenact the scenarios of the early parental crimes against him in their bizarre details. In my experience with psychodrama, this seems to be the case with most people. Although most people's problems are not as extreme as Ralph's, at times we all require an action-oriented psychodramatic experience for catharsis from and insight into an emotional problem. (p. 21)

Psychodrama With Male Sexual Abuse Survivors. Drama therapy and role plays have also been used with male sexual abuse survivors. A new technique known as therapeutic trauma reenactment, developed by Peter Dimock, Mic Hunter, and Jim Struve, was the focus of the Sixth World Interdisciplinary Conference on Male Sexual Victimization. This technique involves recreating traumatic events through role plays and then facilitating a planned positive outcome which might occur either before or after the traumatic event is reenacted (Dimock et al., 1995).

Crowder (1993a) describes a treatment model developed by male adolescent sexual abuse survivors:

Various forms of emotionally expressive work are used by contributors to support their client's affective growth. The purpose of this kind of work is to recathect the original feelings that were dissociated during the abuse and to externalize them in a concrete form so that the client can increase his comfort with or reduce the fear of these emotions (pp. 66–67)

Role-plays can be a very effective way to elicit emotions. If a scene from a client's abuse is role-played, it is advisable to subsequently role play scenes which give the client nurturing and protective messages so that the client can develop a supportive and caring inner script. (p. 67)

Crowder and Avis (1993b) in a description of family role plays describe how they reenact abuse scenes: "This intervention draws on psychodrama to some degree. A group member is asked to volunteer to be the director of the role play. . . . The scene is then played out as an enactment with the director choosing whether or not to play a part depending on her own comfort level" (p. 105).

James and Nasjleti (1993) state that in working with sexually abused children, "the incident can be reenacted and various alternative methods of initiating discussion of feelings around it can be role-played" (p. 86).

"Games" and Other Intense Encounters in Therapeutic Communities

Possibly the most intense of experiential therapies was developed for use with hard-core addicts and criminals participating in therapeutic communities (TCs). These "games" are still widely utilized in substance abuse programs, particularly such TCs in prisons as the one in the Pennsylvania Department of Corrections and in the most famous program, Delancey Street.

These highly confrontational therapeutic encounters may include various rituals, role plays, and intense verbal exchanges.

According to Yablonsky (1976), a prominent psychodramatist and author of *Synanon: The Tunnel Back*:

> The synanon game is, in some respects, an emotional battlefield. Here an individual's delusions, distorted self-image, and negative behavior are attacked again and again. The verbal-attack method involves exaggerated statements, ridicule, and analogy. In some respects, this "surplus reality" is a form of psychodrama. Attack therapy in a synanon game has the effect of "toughening up" a person. It helps him to see himself as relevant others do. He gains information and insight into his problems. (p. 151)

Yablonsky (1965) also stated: "I began to learn the rules of the synanon game and that almost any kind of verbal tactic is legitimate if it helps a person to look at his behavioral soft spots" (p. 380).

Although Synanon no longer exists, the Delancey Street Foundation is alive and flourishing. Charles Hampden-Turner (1976) in *Sane Asylum* describes "haircuts," "games," and "dissipations":

> But the key to Delancey's astonishing success is the manner in which residents direct their own psychotherapy through unique group sessions called Games and Dissipations—intense and volatile meetings in which the residents deliberately provoke each other in some of the wildest, most explosive psychological confrontations yet recorded. (p. a)

> The treatment is rough and highly confrontive, but the foundation is considered by many to be the "Harvard" of rehabilitation programs for offenders. It attributes much of its success to its hard-hitting language.

> So what does Delancey Street do for its members and what can it teach us about the antidote to violent patterns? The first important lesson is as follows: The use of negative evaluation and highly critical language is essential to trimming back inflated behaviors and pretentious exaggerations. There is no permissive way of dealing with an obsessive need for mastery that has become dominant and brutal. You have to call it by its negative names. . . . (p. 228)

Using Role Plays With Sex Offenders

There is a long tradition of using role playing with the offender playing the part of the offender or the victim or both. Modified aversive behavioral rehearsal is an example of this technique. Kishner (1995) describes its use:

> The participant will reenact his sexual behavior as the other group members observe. . . . The participant is asked to reenact his behavior in as realistic a manner as possible. (p. 165)

Victim Role Play—This task is similar to the Modified Aversive Behavior Reenactment, except that the offender takes the role of and expresses the feelings and thoughts of the victim. . . . (p. 324)

A similar role-playing exercise used at Northwest Treatment Associates in Seattle is described by Knopp (1984):

The next step might be for him to become his victim in a role play. The offender may protest and start out by saying, "Well, I couldn't do that, because it creates all sorts of psychological trauma for me." Nevertheless, he is asked to become the victim, lying on the floor and simulating getting molested in front of 14 other group members. (p. 99)

Pithers (1990) described an empathy building exercise in which "during the fifth stage, each subject role-played the victimization, first from his own perspective as the abuser, while another group member took the role of his victim, then in the role of his own victim as another group member acted the role of the abuser." It is difficult to do this sort of intensive victim empathy work without doing associated work around the personal victimization issues which are evoked.

It has also been utilized specifically with sex offenders as described by Bernard et al. (1989). At a Florida-based treatment program in working with the sex offender's personal victimization issues, "role play is used to reexperience the traumatic event and provide catharsis" (p. 136). Mayer (1988), in *Sex Offenders: Approaches to Understanding and Management*, reports: "Through direct victim confrontations in the here-and-now, regression therapy, bioenergetics and role plays, offenders in group therapy are able to re-experience and repeat childhood traumas in a safe atmosphere which may result in catharsis, followed by new self-understandings" (p. 245).

Horton, Johnson, Roundy, and Williams (1990) describe how they use psychodrama to reenact the offender's personal victimization issues:

To offset the offender's sexual arousal to children, because of conditioning or modeling from earlier childhood abuse experiences, experiential techniques are used to help him reexperience a trauma and then release himself from its hold. (p. 232) The explosive emotion often released in psychodrama is used as a powerful vehicle for new learning, and as a memorable carrier for new roles. . . . Psychodrama can help people to experience intensely the subjective self and thereby recover the vitality needed for change. It helps people generate new ways of experiencing that have previously been restrained from awareness and possibility. (p. 74)

It has even been used with adolescent sex offenders. Heinz, Gargaro, and Kelly (1987), in describing the program at The Hennepin County Home School, recount how the program does anger work using psychodrama exercises.

Psychodrama aspects in anger work (methods for taking the client back to the place and time of his personal sexual victimization):

a. Have the client close his eyes and recall the event.
b. Have the client close his eyes while staff set time and place of the incident.
c. Have people role-play characters involved in the reconstructed incident. . . . (p. 37)

Physicality in Drama Therapy

Because both drama therapy and psychodrama use the total person in the therapy session, just how to work with the body is of paramount concern. The body is a remarkable source of psychological information. Yet the physical system is either sorely undervalued in the practical realm of psychological treatment or kept at arm's length as being too sensitive, a little curious, and even dangerous. For all its vaunted modernity, the United States sometimes seems more prurient in its attitudes to the body, seeming to see a temple of vice rather than a fascinating, sensitive, perceiving mechanism. Fortunately, the study of the body and its meanings, the significance of touch, the quintessential importance of proprioceptive activity, and the potency of experiential or movement based treatment is quite extensive.

Fisher and Cleveland (1958), in an essay written for the *International Encyclopaedia of the Social Sciences*, say very simply and pithily: "The individual responds to his own body with an intensity of ego involvement that can rarely be evoked by other objects" (p. 121). It is this intensity of response that ought to be part of the rationale for advanced work with sexual offenders. Traditionally, sexual offenders are affectively blighted, afraid to initiate healthy relationships for fear of emotional distress, and driven by resonances of early victimizations that leave them affectively numb and resistant to any therapy that probes too close to their core issues. Staff who work with sex offenders regularly complain that inmates learn all the moves, mouth all the answers, but still cannot dance the dance. But the exquisite sensitivity of the body, its ability to remember, its powerful sensing mechanism, and physical language for emotions embedded in a very reactive expression is ideal for bypassing resistance and establishing new cognitions and affect to combat old patterns and traumatic memories.

Touch is also becoming an area of interest in the treatment of victims of sexual abuse (Heller & Henkim, 1986; Juhan, 1987, Kepner, 1987; Kurtz, 1990; Rosenberg, Rand, & Asay, 1989; Smith, 1985). At the December 1995 Fourth Annual Conference on Advances in Treating Survivors of Abuse and Trauma, Bessel van der Kolk reported the results of recent findings that memories of early abuse may be stored in a nonverbal part of the brain. This has definite implications for how those memories will have to be retrieved.

Semands (1994) has written about the "body-felt" sense in treating victims of sexual assault. The term "body-felt sense," originated by Gendlin (1978), describes the inner sensations of the body that accompany emotional experience:

> Many survivors are disconnected from their internal body experience. This separation of body and mind protected the survivor not only from the sensations that were caused by the abuse incidents, but also from the intensity of affect that may have accompanied such experiences. (p. 22)

> Another result of the disconnection is that the survivor's bodily experience remains locked in childhood. An awareness of the body-felt sense allows the survivor to discover her adult self, giving her the means to stay grounded in the present rather than being pulled into the past. (p. 23)

Accessing this body sense may evoke bodily memories which have been buried over years. Certain physical traumas appear to be encoded or forgotten in the memory. However, these memories may be recovered through body work. Timms and Connors (1992) discuss the importance of working with these body memories. "Working with the body is a powerful means of side-stepping the conscious mind and gathering information directly from the unconscious fund of knowledge" (p. 24). Bernstein (1995), who works with female victims using movement and dance therapy, states:

> In enacting, the client recreates a significant life experience, perhaps her assault. . . . (p. 43) To deepen the process of identifying the psycho-physical impact of the past I encourage the group to generate memories of their own childhood bodies and to physicalize positions and movement that reflected their corresponding feelings. The explorations revealed movements of tension, holding, hiding, provocative showing off, sneaking, and withdrawing. To expand on this theme, I suggested that each woman recreate and physicalize a significant experience that evoked shame, or explore how this feeling manifested itself in their adult bodies. (p. 46) As the survivor remembers her history with her body, she begins to explore her kinesthetic memories and previously unexpressed emotional responses through insight-oriented improvisation. (p. 46)

The body seems to have a very special ability to convert physical messages into affective experience. Duclos and associates (1989) note that "subjects induced to adopt emotionally expressive behaviours, either facial expressions or postures, reported feeling the emotions that they were expressing. . . . A posture of anger, sadness or fear increased that emotion more strongly" (pp. 106–107).

In working with both victims and perpetrators, therapists can initiate physical actions, simple postures, and action work using whispers or sound, and recover suppressed memories. That is, the client has a tonic or physiological response to particular traumatic stimuli which he can experience in response to therapists' postural or physically interactive work. These "clinically interactive postures" (Bergman & Hewish, 1995) often use simple physical resistance such as pushing to create powerful changes in the tonus of the client as well as significant proprioceptive activity in areas that have long been numbed out by the body's self-defenses. Duclos's work substantiates Augusto Boal and other drama therapists who make great use of interactive postures to stimulate clients into accessing their body messages and images.

Arnold Mindell (Mindell & Mindell, 1972) has made significant advances in the use of different body-based techniques to stimulate affect. He says, "The more you work with your body feeling, your proprioception and your movement, the more familiar and fluid these avenues become . . ." (p. 171). Greenberg and Safran (1987) take this a step further: "Motoric and nonverbal activities that involve the body's sensory system create heightened contact with bodily reactions and promote arousal of emotion" (p. 224). This arousal of emotion signifies experiencing and therefore learning.

Their premise is that clients of all types do not significantly learn in therapy unless there is a sensation of learning. This learning appears to be action, and body oriented. The learning, they believe, occurs through experiences that generate significant affect, sometimes opening up suppressed memory and therefore creating a simultaneous confrontation with old but powerful cognitions and feelings. "Acting out certain expressions bodily by hitting, kicking, tearing or screaming, as well as paying attention to and exaggerating facial reactions, breathing, clenched fists, point-ing fingers and the like, all provide an opportunity for heightened expression" (Greenberg & Safran, 1987, p. 224). Heightened expression signifies that the experi-ence has usually been hidden, suppressed, or too painfully conflicted to access.

Psychodramatists, drama therapists, and dance therapists, as well as body work-ers and psychologists such as Arnold Mindell, have noted that the body is an impor-tant tool to use with the client. But although most action therapists are clear about the action/interaction they generate, they are often unsure of the more profound "why." The interior physiology of the body is complex and revealing. There is a "background state of the bodily musculature that is more or less relevant to the objects we are about to perceive" (Allport, 1955, p. 210). Further, there is a "general tension effect from the background excitation which maintains the body in a state of tonicity during wak-ing activity and provides a flow of returning proprioceptive action constituting the 'vigilance' of the central nervous system" (Allport, 1955, p. 222).

Allport (1955) suggests that this general tension effect or set may deeply influ-ence the content of an individual's perception. In some individuals that posture can become "fixated, especially in cases of a persistent thwarting of motivations or needs, and that 'backlash' from postural tensions thus aroused may dominate the afferent inlets so that it would be difficult for exteroceptive stimulation to break through and produce shifts in behaviour" (Christiansen, 1972, p. 176).

But people in therapy rarely sense or are aware of this internal battle. They arrest or reduce their body awareness, body image, and sensation of postural tension. Perls, Hefferline, and Goodman (1951, cited in Christiansen, 1972) gave an example of inhibiting crying, or inhibiting the expression of grief over some significant event. They noted that such a suppression could lead to a "deliberate contraction of the diaphragm" (cited in Christiansen, 1972, p. 184). In Perls' example, this then leads to the individual being neither able to breathe nor to cry. Without crying there is no catharsis, and the old trauma is eventually buried or appears as chronic diaphragmat-ic tension. But what remains is the need to sob and release the physically automatic diaphragmatic control. This is often perceived by the individual as a lack of feeling, or a much diminished body image.

Fisher and Cleveland (cited in Christiansen, 1972) made a variety of studies of body image. They focused on what type of body image people claimed, and whether people saw their bodies as either well-armored (high barrier) or easily penetrated (low barrier). These authors devised a barrier scoring which surprisingly showed first how high-barrier individuals were more sensitive to outer body issues such as arthritis but less so to interior physical problems and low-barrier individuals tended to ignore external stress and be very sensitive to problems of the heart and kidneys, and so on. High-barrier individuals were more alert, self-motivated, and more able to tolerate stress whereas low-barrier individuals were less likely to finish tasks and more prone to frustration and to using others to help control their fears of a world that can pene-trate to an individual's very core. The low-barrier child was discovered to be at greater risk for reducing relief of body tension and more likely to have experienced rigidity and family instability. In describing a similar phenomenon in the psychotic individ-ual, Christiansen's (1972) simple summary "a definite shift in body image occurs and that the shift primarily takes the form of a loss and destruction of the body image boundary" (p. 206).

Many sex offenders fit the low-barrier definitions. If early traumas have led to the inhibiting of skeletal and postural sets, and therefore to unexpressed contradictory impulses, this may also account for some of the ambient rage that many therapists see in sexual offenders. The anger may be a form of controlled aggression which acts physiologically to reduce the inability to express grief. The physical system may be vulnerable, probably stimulated by early traumas such as sexual abuse, and automatically reduces its sensitivity to external stimulus and especially to the outer skin of the body as self defense. But the interior remains highly sensitized and reactive.

The low-barrier sexual offender is extremely sensitive to all external experiences. Yet those sex offenders who have been abused are likely to have numbed most of their bodily sensations. This may produce an individual with a strong need for physical comfort but an inability to couple this with emotional intimacy. Consequently, they seek contact regardless of context. In addition, this may account for the hypochondria often seen in sex offenders.

To protect themselves, sex offenders try to slow down the degree of experience that occurs in treatment. They appear to instinctively run from anything that may jar loose fear, anxiety, or the potential for the unknown. They control situations through isolation, engaging the therapist in conversations with a "false" self that may appear quite emotionally calm but which is actually detached . As long as the offender is safe, he can maintain the life strategies that he has developed. Much talk therapy works for the offender because it relies on the use of objective, cognitive-based methods that he feels he can keep removed from his self. He feels that he can maintain his low-armored self against the probing. However, involve him physically in an unpredictable situation and the real issues may emerge. Therein lies one of the chief strengths of drama therapy.

Working with physical sensations has a long tradition in drama therapy. Chesner (1994), in *The Handbook of Dramatherapy*, discusses the theoretical foundation for physical contact.

> When we express ourselves through action we engage at a physical level. The presence of physical movement and possible physical contact within the therapy session has a powerful impact. There is profound connection between body, senses, emotional and mental states. By engaging at a physical level the client has easier access to their emotional and inner world. . . . In both dramatherapy and psychodrama the physicality of the experience brings the emotions and the unconscious into the therapeutic stage. (p. 115)

The importance of reliving events physically is stressed by Blatner and Blatner (1988): "Concretization allows patients to experience physically what had been experienced psychologically, and the marshaling of the multilevel resources of the body can serve as a vehicle of spontaneity and insight" (p. 155). Dulton (1990) has stressed the use of physically enacting events as a means of attaching the emotions connected with them. He states:

> When avoidance of the traumatic memory is the predominant clinical presentation, strategies for intensification of emotion may be necessary. Such strategies include intensifying general level of arousal by increasing physical level of activity, physically enacting what is being described and exaggerating or repeating phrases. (p. 89)

Jennings (1992) makes a similar point when she says, "The therapist uses exaggeration, dramatic presence, physicalization or staging to heighten the power of a particular scene or image in order to stimulate a greater depth of feeling in the client" (p. 123). In another book, Jennings (1973) stated in brief, "Bring in as much physical touch as possible" (p. 44). An example of this is given by Jeffries (1991) in working with inmates when she says, "The director relies on the group to use restraining and containment techniques; group members will physically restrain the protagonist so that, against this restraint, he can verbalize his emotions" (p. 198).

Drama therapy expressly uses a variety of physical stimulus, affective, and experiential learning and carefully titrated strategies. These drama-based exercises are designed to engage resistance in such a way that its conflictual nature is physically and therefore emotionally expressed. In the case of sex offenders, Geese Theatre Company uses very precise physical exercises and postural work that confronts the buried, frozen impulses of the clients and sets up a potent affective action response. If, for example, a client insists on maintaining a gregarious front that belies a sense of emptiness, he could be asked to be his most charming and outgoing but from under a table and hidden from the group. This would set up a simple dissonance that would be physically experienced.

A standard tool therefore in the arsenal of dramatherapy is the push/pull exercise. Renee Emunah (1994) uses the exercise rather paradoxically:

> As I begin the adolescent session, a rebellious 14 year old stubbornly shouts, "I'm not getting out of my chair." . . . I approach . . . and say, "Try as hard as you can to stay in the chair." Gently I take hold of his hands and attempt to pull him to a standing position as he struggles to remain seated. His aggressive and hostile stance transforms into a playful one and through the physical contact, a relationship is established between us. (p. 166)

Experience-based learning treatment often begins with warm-ups that are based on simple, common children's games—red light, green light; tag games; hiding games. These games quickly refocus the offender away from the daily need to maintain the armoring and the permanent perception of danger that permeates the proprioceptive activity. The physical system relaxes briefly, lulled by the basic nature of the games, and temporarily relieves the system of its aggressive need to battle its grieving affect. Suddenly the group is in a circle and the client has to get into the circle but it won't let him. He struggles, really physically pushes and pulls, and is also pushed away. The proprioceptive system deduces the tonic message and controls the posture that signifies rejection. He slumps his shoulders. The therapist asks him where he is now. The client's postural memory signifies a traumatic place. The affect is created instantly. The cognitions and affect are very present. Respiration has gone up. He blocks for a moment. Another member of the group holds out his hand and the client pushes back. In the skeletal change in the posture, there is a corresponding change in the affect and the focused memory is now vulnerable to real examination. The armoring is temporarily gone. The sexual offender/client can challenge the old cognition and affect.

Touch remains a controversial issue and must be used with care. It should only be used within a clear theoretical framework or socially and culturally accepted context. Except for a reassuring pat or handshake, it is recommended that touch be used only in a group setting with ample witnesses.

Advantages of Using Psychodrama/Drama Therapy With Sex Offenders

There is not a great deal of controlled research that demonstrates the efficacy of one type of treatment over another, and in programs that use a variety of techniques, it is most difficult to single out one method for study. There is one article by Pearson (1994) which reports on 11 different treatments for female victims of sexual abuse and indicates that there was little evidence to suggest that one method was better than another. Bower (1994) reports a study by Spiegel at Stanford which contrasted a trauma-focused group to a present-focused group and found that they were equally good but for different issues. Trauma-focused was better for dissociative experiences and present-focused was better for anxiety. Currently, in treating sex offenders there is a push to use a variety of techniques in a multimodal approach and eventually to begin to match combinations of treatments to specific types of offenders or offenders with specific problems. Psychodrama/drama therapy is intended to be used in a comprehensive treatment program that included other modalities including behavioral and cognitive/behavioral techniques.

Increasing numbers of sex offender programs throughout the world are moving away from single modality approaches and moving toward integrated models that acknowledge that dealing with an offender's personal victimization is an important part of treatment. This is particularly true of residential programs in which the intensity and depth of dealing sexual aggressiveness is bound to uncover victim's issues.

In dealing with victim's issues, abreaction of the memories of the abuse is recurrently stressed as is outlined in the initial portion of this chapter. Furthermore, experts in both dealing with male victims of sexual assault (Crowder, 1993; Dimock et al., 1995) and doing personal victimization work with sex offenders (Heinz et al., 1987; Mayer, 1988; Bernard et al., 1989; Horton et al., 1990, Chrowder & Avis, 1993) utilize role play to promote abreaction.

Some authors discuss specific methods for initiating abreaction. In many cases specific techniques are not outlined, but in most, psychodrama is mentioned as a common approach. Many of the techniques mentioned may not be suited to working with male sex offenders. Many of the techniques such as implosion, flooding, and direct trauma exposure are behavioral techniques meant to be done in individual sessions rather than group sessions. However, to attempt to induce abreactions using behavioral techniques in individual sessions with men who have a history of acting-out behaviors might be highly dangerous, to say nothing of the transference issues that could emerge.

Hypnosis is another recommended way of inducing abreactions. However, again this is a technique not usually done in a group. It is technique in which the patient basically loses contact with his current situation and could be difficult to manage if an abreaction does occur. Furthermore, there is currently a great deal of concern about whether therapists inadvertently can implant false memories under hypnosis.

Amytal interviews, which are another way of inducing abreactions (Putnam, 1989), require a physician who can conduct the treatment. This type of treatment is also be open to the same criticisms as hypnosis regarding false memories.

Therapists who wish to do abreactive work may need to have a variety of techniques available to them so that when one does not work, they can try another. In this respect psychodrama/drama therapy is ideally suited to this type of work because the intensity, content, and physicality of the role play can be varied instantly. It is highly frustrating to both patient and therapist to attempt abreaction work without being able to intensify the process sufficiently to induce the emotional release. It is like having a leg almost set or a tooth almost pulled.

According to Putnam (1989):

> The affects that accompany abreactions can be equally vivid and intense. They have all of the freshness of the traumatic moment and are concentrated by years of repression and dissociation . . . the affects associated with the event are what must be uncovered and abreacted before therapeutic progress can be made. The expression of these affects can be explosive and frightening for patient and therapist. (p. 242)

Therefore, there must be safeguards to keep the patient from losing control. The group in psychotherapy can be helpful, as can the fact that the patient in drama therapy is not totally tranced and the thoughts of the patient are easily monitored through the actions in the role play rather than being internal as they can be in hypnosis and drug-induced abreactions. In addition, the role play can be geared to the intensity needed to induce the abreaction.

Cautions in Doing Drama Therapy

Briere (1994) states:

> It must be remembered that abreaction can initially appear to have negative consequences. It is a common clinical experience that certain clients appear to deteriorate or "get worse" despite initial improvement- during abuse-focused therapy. As I have noted elsewhere, this process need not necessarily mean that therapy is deleterious or that, in fact, the client is experiencing a decompensation of any sort (Briere, 1989). Instead, such exacerbation can reflect avoidant defenses such as repression, numbing, denial, intellectualization, and tension reduction may decrease, leading to more direct awareness and experiencing of childhood injury. As a result of this improved ability to confront abuse-related issues and experiences, some clients experience more acute anxiety, depression, flashbacks, intrusive memories and nightmares than they did prior to (or earlier in) treatment. (p. 143)

However, this is part of the therapeutic process. Therefore it is very important to conduct this work in an environment in which plenty of support will be available to the participants.

Participants engaging in psychodrama/drama therapy should understand what in general they will be experiencing. This does not mean that every exercise must be explained. Drama therapy is a highly spontaneous activity. There is disagreement as to whether formal informed consent forms should be used, as this may imply that the activity is voluntary rather than a required portion of the program which it may be. Certainly in a traditional therapeutic community, participants are not asked to sign an informed consent prior to being confronted in a Synanon-type game. Other programs find that attendance at a drama therapy session can be required but the informed consent can be available for participants who will be the focus of intense role plays.

Drama therapy must be offered by trained professionals with formal training and supervised experience. It is not a technique that should be conducted only by one therapist, especially with individuals who have a history of acting out. A team of therapists can provide the structure and energy needed to maintain the intensity of the sessions. It should be conducted in a safe and secure environment with the proper equipment including pillows and plastic and foam bats with which to express aggression.

This powerful technique needs special precautions; however, it is important not to confuse the cautions that might be appropriate for outpatient female survivors as opposed to incarcerated male perpetrators. Many articles discussing abreactive techniques urge the therapist to have the survivor totally plan out the scene or discuss what will ensue in minute detail. Drama therapy with sex offenders may need to rely more on the element of surprise (e.g., the sudden appearance of a victim, an emotionally charged prop, or a memory-inducing physical posture or word). Sex offenders are filled with cognitive distortions that may need to be dramatically confronted. It would render the technique ineffective to request that the offender give permission to be confronted with these distortions.

Conclusion

Many comprehensive sex offender treatment programs are recognizing that many of their participants have been victimized as children and that those traumas continue to influence the behavior, thoughts, and feelings of the adult offender. Whether in developing a relapse prevention plan or attempting to develop empathy in an offender, dealing with an offender's personal victimization may assist the process. Abreaction or catharsis of the trauma are widely accepted methods of reconnecting the traumatic memories with the original emotions. Psychodrama or drama therapy may be the methods of choice for achieving these goals.

References

Allport, F. H. (1955). *Theories of perception and the concept of structure.* New York: Wiley

American Psychiatric Association. (1980). *A psychiatric glossary* (5th ed.). Washington, DC: Author.

Bear, E. (1993). *Inpatient treatment for adult survivors of sexual abuse: A summary of data from 22 programs.* Brandon, VT: Safer Society Press.

Bernard, G., Fuller, K., Robbins, L., & Shaw, T. (1989). *The child molester: An integrated approach to evaluation and treatment.* New York: Brunner/Mazel.

Black, C. (1990). *Double duty: Dual dynamics within the chemically dependent home.* New York: Ballantine Books.

Blatner, A., & Blatner, A. (1988). *Foundations of psychodrama.* New York: Springer.

Brauer, B. (1986). *Treatment of multiple personality disorder.* Washington, DC: American Psychiatric Association Press.

Caffaro, J. V. (1995). Identification and trauma: An integrative-developmental approach. *Journal of Family Violence, 10*(18), 23.

Chesner, A. (1994). Dramatherapy and psychodrama. In S. Jennings, A. Cattanach, S. Mitchell, A. Chesner, & B. Meldrum (Eds.), *The handbook of dramatherapy* (pp. 115–135). London: Routledge.

Courtois, C. (1988). *Healing the incest wound: Adult survivors in therapy.* New York: Norton.

Dayton, T. (1994). *The drama within: Psychodrama and experimental therapy.* Deerfield Beach, FL: Health Communications.

Dimock, P. T., Hunter, M., & Struve, J. (1995, October 5–7). *Survivor workshop: Therapeutic trauma reenactment.* Paper presented at the 6th World Interdisciplinary Conference on Male Sexual Victimization, Columbus, OH.

Dulton, M. A. (1990). Assessment and treatment of post-traumatic stress disorder among battered women. In K. Peterson, M. Prout, & R. Schwartz (Eds.), *Post-traumatic stress disorder: A clinician's guide* (pp. 85–104). New York: Plenum Press.

Emunah, R. (1994). *Acting for real: Drama therapy process, techniques and performance.* New York: Brunner/Mazel.

Fisher, S., & Cleveland, S. E. (1958). *Body image and personality.* Princeton, NJ: Van Nostrand.

Goodwin, J. M., & Talwar, N. (1989, June). Group psychotherapy for victims of incest. *Psychiatric Clinics of North America, 12*(2), 279–293.

Goulding, R., & Schwartz, R. (1995). *The mosaic mind: Empowering the tormented self of child abuse survivors.* New York: Norton.

Heller, J., & Henkim, W. (1986). *Bodywise.* Los Angeles: Tarcher.

Horowitz, M. J. (1992). *Stress response syndromes.* Northvale, NJ: Jason Aronson.

Jeffries, J. (1991). What we are doing here is defusing bombs: Psychodrama with hard-core offenders. In P. Holmes & M. Karp (Eds.), *Psychodrama: Inspiration and technique* (pp. 189–200). London: Tavistock/Routledge.

Jennings, S. (1973). *Remedial drama: A handbook for teachers and therapists.* London: Adam & Charles Black.

Jennings, S. (1992). *Dramatherapy: Theory and practice.* London: Tavistock/Routledge.

Joy, S. (1987). Retrospective presentations of incest: Treatment strategies for use with adult women. *Journal of Counseling and Development, 65,* 317–319.

Juhan, D. (1987). *Job's body: A handbook for body work.* Barrytown, NY: Station Hill Press.

Keane, T. M., Fairbank, J. A., Caddell, J. M., & Zimering, R. T. (1989). Implosive (flooding) therapy reduces symptoms of PTSD in Vietnam combat veterans. *Behavior Therapy, 20,* 245–260.

Kepner, J. I. (1987). *Body process.* New York: Gardner Press.

Kishner, G. R. (1995). *A path to responsibility.* Oklahoma City, OK: Wood 'n Barnes.

Kurtz, R. (1990). *Body-centered psychotherapy: The Hakomi method.* Mendocino, CA: Life Rhythm.

Lambana, J. H., & Leyer, J. B. (1994). Cognitive-systems therapy: A case excerpt. *Journal of Mental Health Counseling, 16*(4), 434–444.

Lingley, C. R. (1985). *Trauma and its wake: The study and treatment of post-traumatic stress disorder* (vol. 1). New York: Brunner/Mazel.

Mayer, A. (1988). *Sex offenders: Approaches to understanding and management.* New York: Learning Publications.

Meichenbaum, D. (1994). *A clinical handbook/practical therapist manual for assessing and treating adults with post-traumatic stress disorder.* West Ontario, Canada: Institute Press.

Pearson, Q. M. (1994). Treatment techniques for adult female survivors of childhood sexual abuse. *Journal of Counseling and Development, 73*(1), 32–37.

Prendergast, W. L. (1978). *Re-education of attitudes and repressed emotions.* Paper presented at the R.O.A.R.E. Conference, Avenel, NJ.

Prendergast, W. L. (1991). *Treating sex offenders in correctional institutions and outpatient clinics: A guide to clinical practice.* New York: Haworth.

Prentky, R., & Burgess, A. W. (1992). Rehabilitation of child molesters: A cost-benefit analyses. *American Journal of Orthopsychiatry, 60,* 108–117.

Putnam, F. W. (1989). *Diagnosis and treatment of multiple personality disorder.* New York: Guilford Press.

Rosenberg, J., Rand, M., & Asay, D. (1989). *Body, self and soul: Sustaining integration.* Atlanta: Humanics Limited.

Schwartz, M. F., Gilperin, L. D., & Masters, W. H. (1995). Dissociation and treatment of compulsive reenactment of trauma: Sexual compulsivity. In M. Hunter (Ed.), *Adult survivors of sexual abuse: Treatment innovations* (pp. 42–55). Thousand Oaks, CA: Sage.

Schwartz, M. (1995). In my opinion: Victim to victimizer. *Sexual Addiction and Compulsivity, 2*(2), 81–88.

Schwartz, M. L., & Masters, W. H. (1994). Integration of trauma-based, congnitive, behavioral systemic and addictions approaches to treatment of hypersexual pair bonding disorder. *Sexual Addictions and Compulsions, 1*(1), 52–75.

Semands, S. (1994). *Bridging the silence: Nonverbal modalities in the treatment of adult survivors of child sexual abuse.* New York: Norton.

Smith, E. W. L. (1985). *The body in psychotherapy.* Jefferson, NC: McFarland.

Spiegel, D. (1988, June). Hypnosis in the treatment of victims of sexual abuse. *Psychiatric Clinics of North America, 12*(2), 285–305.

Steele, K. (1993). Abreactive work with sexual abuse survivors: Concepts and treatments. In M. Hunter (Ed.), *The sexually abused male: Applications of treatment strategies* (vol. 2, pp. 1–55). Thousand Oaks, CA: Sage

Steele, N. M. (1992). *Return rates collected by the Minnesota Department of Corrections.* Department of Information and Analysis.

Timms, R., & Connors, P. (1992). *Embodying healing: Integrating body work and psychotherapy in recovery from childhood sexual abuse.* Orwell, VT: Safer Society Press.

Van der Kolk, B. A. (1989). Pierre Janet on post-traumatic stress. *Journal of Traumatic Stress, 2*(4), 365–378.

Van der Kolk, B. A. (1994, Spring). Childhood abuse and loss of self-regulation. *Bulletin of the Menninger Clinic, 58*(2), 145–168.

Van der Kolk, B. A. (1995). *Trauma, memory and the integration of experience.* Paper presented at the 4th Annual Conference on Advances in Treating Survivors of Abuse and Trauma: Multiple Dimensions in Healing, Philadelphia.

Walker, L. (1995). *Abused women and survivor therapy.* Washington, DC: American Psychological Association.

Wegscheider-Cruse, S., Cruse, J. R., & Boucher, G. (1990). *Experimental therapy for co-dependency.* Palo Alto, CA: Science and Behavior Books.

Chapter 21

Animal-Facilitated Sex Offender Treatment

by Emily Coleman, M.A.

Overview

The combination of sex offender treatment and animal-facilitated therapy is innovative and may well initially provoke amused skepticism. In fact, either of these endeavors alone may raise eyebrows among the general populace, who often assume there is no viable treatment for sex offenders and who have not heard of animal-facilitated therapy. Contrary to public opinion and knowledge, however, success rates in each area are impressive and the combination of therapy animals and sex offender treatment offers a powerful strategy in ultimately preventing sexual abuse.

In animal-facilitated therapy, the bond between animals and humans becomes a vehicle to enhance the effectiveness of treatment. Although this form of therapy is a new concept to many persons in and out of the mental health profession, most people in society are familiar with animals in certain helping professions. Police dogs are familiar sights. The work of rescue and tracking dogs, therapeutic riding horses, and service animals for persons who are sight-, hearing-, or mobility-impaired are also commonly recognized. There are also seizure-sensitive dogs who alert their persons to an impending seizure and so enable otherwise restricted persons to live a much more active life. Increasing media attention has been given to the work of dogs, cats, birds, rabbit, and pigs visiting the elderly, children and sick in nursing homes, hospitals, and various institutions.

Less well known is the use of animals integrated into the intricacies of psychotherapy with the chronically ill, emotionally disturbed children, abuse survivors, and so on. Here the addition of a specially chosen animal is directly related to achieving a client's specific treatment goals. Animal-facilitated therapy is directed and delivered by health/human service professionals with specialized expertise and within the scope of practice of their profession (Hurt, 1995). The focus of this chapter is on the particular therapeutic function of therapy animals employed in sex offender assessment and treatment. I examine the innovative role and practicalities of therapy animals in this unique setting. It is important to note that animal-facilitated sex offender therapy is conducted within the framework of a cognitive-behavioral and relapse prevention sex offender program. It is not being recommended as a substitute for proven techniques and approaches but is offered as a means to increase their effectiveness.

History

The first recorded use of animals to enhance therapeutic goals dates back to 1792 at the York Retreat in York, England (Cusack, 1988). Founded by William Tuke, a Quaker merchant, the York Retreat offered a striking contrast to the practices of punishment and restraint frequently used in the abusive lunatic asylums of that time. At the York Retreat patients were treated respectfully. For example, they were allowed to wear their own clothing. In this early effort at normalization, patients were also encouraged to focus on activities such as gardening and caring for rabbits and poultry. The rationale was that patients would benefit from activities that were outwardly focused.

In 1867, Bethel in West Germany began as a residential center for epileptics and was later expanded to treat persons with multiple physical and mental disabilities. As at the York Retreat, animals were central to the treatment process from the beginning. Farm animals and a wild game park were incorporated into the setting while dogs, cats, and birds lived in the treatment milieu. In the United States, organized efforts at animal-facilitated therapy started in 1942 at the Paling Army Air Force Convalescent Hospital in Paling, New York. Veterans recovering from physical or emotional trauma could work on a farm with livestock or enjoy animals in the nearby forests. Patients organized turtle races and frog jumping contests. Unfortunately, there is no quantifiable data to assess the contribution of animal-facilitated therapy in these early endeavors (McCulloch, 1983).

Boris Levinson, a psychiatrist in the 1950s, and his shaggy dog, Jingles, were pioneers in this field and formally introduced the concept of animal-facilitated therapy. When Jingles happened to be in the office before a session, Levinson noticed that a withdrawn and noncommunicative child, who had arrived early with his mother, responded very positively to Jingles and then subsequently made significant progress in therapy in the dog's presence. Levinson (1962) believed that pets can act as transitional objects and so aid in forming relationships with the therapist and then others. He wrote extensively on the application of animal-facilitated therapy initially to children and later to many other populations.

One of the first attempts at more formalized research was conducted by the Corsons. During the 1970s, Sam and Elizabeth O'Leary Corson began to research the effects of animal-facilitated therapy first with emotionally disturbed adolescents and subsequently with the elderly and adults. Their work began at Ohio State University Hospital and later extended to the Castle Nursing Home in Millersburg, Ohio. The Corsons attempted to match residents with appropriate dog companions and videotaped their interactions (Corson, Corson, Gwynne, & Arnold, 1977). The results were very encouraging and in some cases dramatic. For example, an elderly man who had not spoken for 20 years said his first words after seeing a dog.

Several national and international organizations have developed to encourage and support the therapeutic bond between animals and people. One such organization is the Delta Society, founded in 1977. Its mission is to increase recognition of the mutually nurturing relationship between people and animals and to establish services by animals to aid people with health difficulties and physical and emotional challenges. The Delta Society trains and supervises a national network of Pet Partner volunteers that has grown from 33 teams in 1991 to more than 1,600 teams in 1995 (Singlehurst, 1995). The Delta Society also operates as an information and referral service and holds annual national and international conferences.

Current Research

Levinson advocated strongly for research and the Corsons' early research attempts were encouraging. The implementation of more rigorous controlled studies with sufficiently large sample size has been hampered by the usual difficulty in finding funding and by some unique confounding difficulties of research with animals (e.g., therapist bias toward their animals). In spite of these obstacles, however, a significant body of research literature has evolved in the last 20 years. This progress is reflected in a review of papers presented at the 1994 Delta Conference. Serpell and Jackson (1994) presented follow-up data on an earlier longitudinal study (Serpell, 1991) that had detected beneficial changes in people's physical health, psychological well-being, and physical activity levels following the acquisition of pets. Allen (1994) presented the results of a two-year study with a control group of subjects on a waiting list which assessed quality-of-life issues among individuals with severe chronic physical disabilities. Especially striking in this study was the finding that subjects with assistance dogs reported requiring an average of 72% fewer hours of human personal assistant time. Katcher and Wilkins's (1994) work with children with attention-deficit hyperactive and conduct disorders provides an excellent example of good research illustrating the effectiveness of animal-facilitated therapy with this population.

Today animal-facilitated therapy is being carried out with many populations, including clients of all age groups and clients with Alzheimer's, schizophrenia, depression, anxiety, and low self-esteem.

Use of Animal-Facilitated Therapy With Offenders

A number of programs have used animals in rehabilitation programs with inmates. Perhaps the most famous account of the restorative experiences animals can have with those who are in prison was depicted in the movie *Birdman of Alcatraz*, starring Burt Lancaster as Robert Stroud. Schwartz (1987) reported on the Pen Pals Program at a prison in New Mexico which included residential animals and a variety of visiting animals including dogs, cats, horses, wallabies, foxes, raccoons, snakes, birds, possums, and other unusual creatures. Moneymaker and Strimple (1991) describe the program at the District of Columbia's Department of Corrections Lorton facility. This program utilized animals, including birds, to teach offenders animal care as a vocation as well as empathy and compassion. According to Moneymaker and Strimple (1991), "The evidence suggests that the participants have changed their behavior in several respects as can be seen from some of the earlier findings, particularly in terms of responsibility, altercations with others, and use of drugs" (p. 150) The Oakwood Forensic Center in Lima, Ohio used fish, deer, goats, macaws, parrots, hamsters, gerbils, ducks, and cats with individuals found to be criminally insane and found that "the medication level in the experimental group declined to half that of the control group, and the incidence of violence of suicide declined significantly as well" (Lee, 1983, p. 25). Several prisons in Colorado and New Mexico have used inmates to train wild horses for the Bureau of Land Management.

Several programs have involved inmates in training dogs. In a program in Joseph Harp Correctional Center in Oklahoma, the presence of two golden retriever puppies was associated with a 43% decrease in incidents of aggression (Haynes, 1991). The HEALO (Human-Environment-Animal-Love-Organization) sponsored a program to teach female offenders at the California Institution for Women at Frontera to train dogs ("Matthew Margolis Goes to Prison," 1984; Siegel, 1985; Gindick, 1985).

Probably the most famous project involving inmates and animals is the Prison Pet Partnership Program at the women's prison in Purdy, Washington. This program started with several dog trainers bringing their dogs to visit with the women and expanded to a boarding, dog grooming, and dog training program with its own kennel. Their work in training dogs for the handicapped, including the first seizure alert dogs, has been particularly impressive ("Miracle Worker," 1984/1985; Beard, 1984; Green, 1985).

Therapeutic Functions

Although researchers have sometimes had difficulty capturing and quantifying the therapeutic functions of animals, clinicians who work with therapy animals frequently describe their powerful impact on their clients. The therapeutic functions for clients with sex offending problems described here are important and relevant. At times, the impact of the therapy animal occurs rather automatically. For example, a dog sleeping on the client's feet can center, ground, and focus him. On other occasions, an obvious effort or intervention by the therapist, such as storytelling or teaching the animal a trick, is required.

Normalizing the Setting. In observing an animal-assisted therapy session, one may be struck by the relaxed posture of the canine therapist. After greeting each person individually, the therapy dog may curl up on the floor in the middle of group until she is asked or chooses to be otherwise involved. Group members consistently report that the dog's presence alone contributes to a sense of being in a safe and familiar place.

A client entering the therapist's office for the first time knowing he is expected to speak to an unfamiliar person about actions he finds humiliating and shameful is understandably uncomfortable. If the client is intellectually disabled, any change may be threatening, and the prospect dims further. Similarly, a client who has been institutionalized for many years and deprived of any setting resembling normalcy can feel anxious meeting the sex offender therapist. Seeing a friendly, well-cared-for animal in the office can be particularly reassuring in such circumstances. The effect is similar to the difference between talking to someone in a cold sterile office and talking to someone in an office with sunny windows, growing plants, and a rug on the floor. Generally, more information is obtained and more work accomplished when the client is in a comfortable setting.

Engaging the Client. A therapy animal offers an excellent vehicle to engage clients and is particularly effective at engaging children and adolescents. Most children are relieved and happy to see a dog in the office. Often, cool and disdainful adolescents unabashedly rush to talk to an adult who has a dog. One could experiment walking down a street with and without an approachable animal and count the frequency of social initiation from others. Clinicians often gain status with otherwise judgmental adolescents because they have a dog in the office. The dog acts as a reference, vouching for the therapist's caretaking abilities.

When the client enters the office, the therapy dog can act as a friendly greeter, walking up to him, wagging her tail, and sometimes licking his hand. As the client takes a seat, the therapy dog may situate herself next to the client, calmly and gently leaning against his side. If he stops talking, she may look up at him, as if to inquire, "And what happened next?" Once the client feels more relaxed, she will sometimes lay curled on the client's feet or simply go to a corner of the office and lie down. The dog is attentive and responsive to the client's needs, not the therapist's, making clear that the dog is there for the client's benefit. Sex offenders may initially perceive the reason for the dog's presence as protection for the therapist, but this misunderstanding is usually alleviated through observation of the dog's behavior.

Building Rapport and Trust. Research indicates that persons seen with an animal are more likely to be perceived in a positive light (Lockwood, 1983). This perception is often beneficial in sex offender work, when clients can experience sex offender therapists as quite intimidating. Certainly, the questions sex offender therapists have to ask are often threatening. Initially, sex offenders may look upon their sex offender therapist with suspicion, if not hostility, seeing the therapist as the enemy and an extension of the court, a part of his punishment. The sex offender may try to shift blame to the therapist, resent the therapist's personal and probing questions, and dislike being constantly reminded of his sexual offending problem. A sex offender therapist can do relatively little to make the process less painful for the client. Avenues open in other therapeutic situations are not appropriate here. Waiting until the client feels ready, easing up to the subject gradually, and accepting the clients' cognitive distortions, even temporarily, are all inappropriate. However, having a dog in the office takes no extra time, adds no financial burden, and does not interfere with questioning or in other ways avoid the stressful work required. Yet the client is more apt to look favorably on the therapist whose dog is in the office. Trust is increased and the client may be somewhat more likely to believe that the therapist is acting in his best interests even if it does not feel good.

Decreasing Anxiety and Blood Pressure. Addressing a sex offending problem directly is often very stressful. Whether disclosing specifics of sex offending behavior for the first time, developing a sex abuse cycle, or writing an apology letter to the victim, looking clearly at the harm one has done is a difficult process. Katcher (1981) has demonstrated that a person's blood pressure increases when speaking to another person but decreases when speaking to an animal. In fact, simply the presence of a dog in the room decreases blood pressure (Friedmann, Katcher, Thomas, Lynch, & Messent, 1983). A recent report even indicated the anxiety reducing benefits of dogs in a dentist's office ("Dental Dogs," 1995).

An intellectually disabled 13-year-old boy with a significant history of sexual perpetration was very anxious entering the therapist's office. In this situation, the therapy dog was particularly able to soothe the client and so aid the therapist in gathering information. When questioned about his problem behavior, the boy began to bite his hand, hit his head, and engage in other self-abusive behavior. At the therapist's suggestion, the boy and therapist sat on the floor. The therapy dog immediately sat partly in his lap, pushing her head at his hands. He could not simultaneously hit himself and pet her. As he stroked her and enjoyed her attention, he gradually relaxed. He was able to disclose the facts of his perpetration without hurting himself. By both offering a behavior incompatible with self-abuse and a means to relax, the therapy dog facilitated the interview process.

Providing a Metaphor. Throughout the assessment and treatment process, there are usually many opportunities to use the animal as a metaphor for the client, enabling him to understand a concept without becoming defensive. For example, a 37-year-old client with diagnoses of borderline personality, schizophrenia, and pedophilia was having difficulty understanding the need for him not be alone with children. He saw the therapist's admonitions not as concern for his welfare and that of potential victims but as distrust and dislike of him. He was very defensive and adamant that he could control his impulses toward children though he had not yet begun treatment and was unaware of his risk factors. The therapist noted that her therapy dog had an impulse control problem as well. Being part husky, the therapy dog held predatory urges toward fowl, in particular ducklings. On farms with many ducks and chickens about, it was important to have the therapy dog on a leash. Understanding lighted the client's face as he observed the therapy dog and understood that a well-loved creature with many positive attributes could still have a significant problem requiring external structure.

Sometimes, clients attempt to act out their power and control issues with the therapy animal in the session. Although the animal's safety always needs to be ensured, this provides an excellent opportunity for learning for the client. For example, clients may try to play with the therapy animal in a teasing manner, holding a ball just out of reach. In group therapy, a client may co-opt the therapy animal, attempting to keep her at his side and not allowing interaction with other group members. In each instance, the therapist points out what is happening and suggests alternatives. The client may learn mutually rewarding ways to play with the dog. The group member's new task may be encouraging the therapy animal to visit each group member sometime during the group.

Increasing Perceptual, Empathy, and Communication Skills. Interpersonal skills training is accepted as a significant component of most sex offender treatment programs. Sex offenders are frequently lacking in perceptive, empathy, and communication skills. Initially, interactions with other people can be too intimidating for a client to try. The client may be too anxious to learn or sometimes not concerned enough to try. However, clients can usually imagine how a cat feels as she lies in the sun or interpret correctly a dog's request for a treat. Observing the relationships in a herd of horses is fun and instructive. Social skills learned successfully first in a nonthreatening and interesting manner with animals can then be generalized to persons.

Teaching How to Learn. The principles of learning, such as shaping, reinforcement and stimulus control, are always in both humans or animals, whether addressing controlling deviant sexual behavior or controlling barking. Karen Pryor (1984) illustrates this clearly in her book, Don't Shoot the Dog. She describes eight methods of untraining a problem behavior and provides samples of each approach for problems as varied as kids too noisy in the car, a faulty tennis swing, spouse habitually in a bad mood, and cats on the kitchen table. The sex offender client who understands learning principles, such as shaping the absence of undesirable behavior, changing motivation, and learning an incompatible behavior, then has significant problem-solving skills and is less likely to relapse. However, assimilating this information can be boring if taught by textbook or threatening if immediately applied to oneself. In contrast, teaching a dog a trick is a fun, engaging way for a person to learn the same principles he needs to keep himself safe.

Providing an Opportunity for Nurturance. Research indicates that sex offenders often hold rigid, conservative attitudes and traditional stereotyped ideas of masculinity. Men who are burdened by a need to appear always self-possessed, macho, and in control sometimes forget to uphold that image when they see a dog. Otherwise "hardened criminals" pet and talk lovingly to a dog. Men who think of themselves as "the Terminator" get down on the floor and gently cuddle and talk "baby talk" to a therapy dog. Therapy animals provide the opportunity to enjoy giving nurturance, an experience alien to some sex offenders.

Increasing Sense of Self-Esteem and Mastery. All people like to be liked and feel better about themselves when acknowledged and appreciated. A therapy animal can provide this feeling naturally. For the sexual offender, low self-esteem is often an issue. Adolescent sex offenders and sex offenders who are intellectually disabled may experience even lower levels of self-esteem than other sex offenders. An animal's positive response to a person cannot be faked and the client often feels better about himself accordingly. A client, particularly a youngster who has taught the therapy animal a trick or knows how to instruct the therapy dog to heel and sit, may experience appropriate feelings of mastery, all too often a rare experience for sex offenders. A 14-year-old boy with a sex offending problem was the youngest in a family with five older brothers who frequently teased him. His brothers were present on one occasion when his mother came to pick him up. He took the therapy dog out in the heel position, asked her to sit in front of each brother and shake paws and then instructed the therapy dog to go back to the office. He impressed his brothers, gained status, and felt better about himself.

Providing Acceptable Physical Contact. Sometimes children or adolescents who are hypersexualized are temporarily restricted from any human touch because it is overstimulating. Similarly, persons who are institutionalized or isolated may not often have the opportunity to touch. Even in cases not as extreme, the importance of acceptable physical contact cannot be overemphasized. One crucial goal for sex offenders is knowing the difference between acceptable and unacceptable touches. Petting or holding a therapy animal can provide the opportunity for this.

Providing Humor. Sex offender treatment is a serious business, yet there is a place for humor. Haaven, Little, and Petre-Miller (1990) wrote of the need for humor, fun, and the bizarre in working with sex offenders who are intellectually disabled. Animals definitely provide humor although the therapist cannot always control when or where it occurs. In the midst of a tense sex offender group session, after a group member had insisted once again on a particularly outrageous cognitive distortion, the therapy dog raised her head and burped loudly. After a moment's silence, everyone including the group member laughed. The tension dissolved and the client got a little closer to accepting his thinking as an error.

Acknowledging Each Animal's Unique Contribution

Animals are not simply analogous to a toy in play therapy but offer a unique presence all their own. They are our colleagues, not our tools in this regard. Each animal has its own particular contribution which is not always obvious ahead of time. Each also offers its own story: the huge Shire who gives way to the little pony, the greyhound saved from the track, the orphaned duckling adopted by another duck mother. There is no one particular species or breed that has a corner on the market. It is important to be open and alert to all the possibilities and gifts animals offer.

When Animal-Facilitated Therapy Is Not Advisable

It is crucial to recognize clients and situations in which therapy animals are inappropriate or even counterproductive. First, the clinician must always verify that the client is not allergic, phobic, or simply dislikes animals. This should be determined before introducing the client and the animal. Much less frequent but certainly possible is the sex offender client who has a significant history of bestiality. In his case the animal may have a distracting influence. Furthermore, in working with sex offenders, there are times when the therapist does not want the client to be comfortable. If, for example, a session is anticipated in which significant confrontation of a client is required, the relaxing presence of a therapy animal is counterproductive. Finally, if the therapeutic goal involves the client's appropriate expression of anger and the client needs to express appropriate anger toward the therapist, the use of a therapy animal is not suggested. The client may be reluctant to voice his anger, however assertively, if he feels the animal may be protective of the therapist. Each client and therapeutic encounter must be evaluated individually to decide the usefulness or detriment of a therapy animal.

Choosing and Training a Therapy Animal

Although the emphasis here has been on therapy dogs, many other animals may be incorporated as well. Cats, fish, rabbits, and birds may all serve as therapy animals. Rebecca Reynolds (1995) has written eloquently of the powerful benefits of bringing animals within their whole natural environments into institutional settings. For example, she might simulate a field meadow in the fall by bringing in rabbits, a gopher snake, and an owl and placing them in a room redecorated with marsh grasses and a hollow log. However, animal-facilitated therapy need not involve this level of production. In fact, using stuffed animals or figurines with children rather than live animals may also serve some of the same functions. If a therapist has decided to incorporate a therapy dog, the choice and training of the dog is important. First, the dog needs to be well groomed and free of external and internal parasites. His toenails should be clipped and his shots up-to-date. Basic obedience training is important. Passing the American Kennel Club (AKC) Canine Good Citizen test (the only AKC certificate open to all breeds, including mixed breeds) is a good marker that the dog has basic social skills. In terms of personality, a dog who is secure, confident, friendly, and outgoing but neither dominant nor submissive is needed. The Monks of New Skete (1991) in their book, How to Raise a Puppy, offer information on personality testing for puppies and provide The Puppy Aptitude Test developed by Joachim and Wendy Volhard in an appendix. Prospective therapy dogs should probably earn mostly threes on this test, indicating an outgoing dog at ease with people or noise. In addition, Davis (1992) in her book, *Therapy Dogs*, suggests that therapy dogs be neutered and have a strong bond with the handler. Therapy dogs can become licensed through the Delta Society, Therapy Dogs International, and other organizations. There are advantages to having the therapy dog licensed, including insurance and increased credibility. A final practical suggestion is having a collar, particularly for office use, that includes the dog's name and office number but not the owner's home address and number. This both protects the confidentiality of the therapist and provides a cue to the therapy dog that he or she is going to work.

Burnout

Just as sex offender therapists need to monitor their own stress level at work, it is necessary to look carefully for potential signs of stress in animal colleagues. Animals as well as people may become burned out. Therapists should be alert for any unusual behavior by the therapy animal. Trembling, clinginess, the beginnings of aggressive behavior, and/or simply a lack of the usual enthusiasm for the job may all indicate that the therapy animal needs a break. All work and no play is not good for anyone, including therapy animals. If possible, the therapist should intersperse playdays with workdays. Therapist/owners should learn dog massage, rotate interesting toys for the dog, and provide exercise. They must ensure that the therapy animal has time to rest in a peaceful environment as well as time in stimulating environments. I recommend that the dog be crate trained and that his or her crate be available as a refuge. Most important, the therapist/owner must provide for the safety of the therapy animal at all times.

Additional Benefits

Although the purpose of animal-facilitated therapy is to enhance the therapeutic process for the client, it often also enhances the process for the therapist and other agency staff. Work is usually much more enjoyable for the therapist with his or her animal present. Therapy animals may be in demand by other agency therapists, administrators, and receptionists who benefit by dropping by for a animal hug or taking the dog a walk. The quality of life at an institution or agency may be improved; the atmosphere may become more relaxed and warm.

Conclusion

My clinical experience indicates that the bond between animals and humans can significantly enhance sex offender work. Therapists may well find it fulfilling for themselves as well as for their clients. With training and care, a therapy dog can become an important member of the sex offender therapy team.

References

Allen, K. (1994). *Physical disability and assistance dogs: Quality of life issues.* Paper presented at 13th Annual Conference of the Delta Society, New York, NY.

Beard, W. (1984). Of people, pooches and prisons: Inmates train handi-dogs. *Dog World, 3,* 14–15.

Corson, S. A., Corson, E. O., Gwynne, P. H., & Arnold, E. L. (1977). Pet dogs as nonverbal communication links in hospital psychiatry. *Comprehensive Psychiatry, 18*(1), 61–72.

Cusack, O. (1988). *Pets and mental health.* New York: Haworth Press.

Davis, K. D.(1992). *Therapy dogs: Training your dog to reach others.* New York: Macmillan.

Dental dogs. (1995, July). *Your Dog, 1*(12), 8.

Friedmann, E., Katcher, A. H., Thomas, S. A., Lynch, J. J., & Messent, P. R. (1983). Social interactions and blood pressure: Influence of animal companions. *Journal of Nervous and Mental Disease, 171,* 461–465.

Gindick, T. (1985, March 7). Pet therapy helps inmates relate to people. *Los Angeles Times*, pp. 21–22.

Green, R. (1985, October 20). Women inmates train dogs in prize-winning program. *The Seattle Times*, p. B3.

Haaven, J., Little, R., & Petre-Miller, D. (1990). *Treating intellectually disabled sex offenders: A model residential program.* Orwell, VT: Safer Society Press.

Haynes, M. (1991, August). Program lifts spirits, reduces violence in institution's mental health unit. *Corrections Today*, pp. 122–123.

Hurt, A. (Ed.). (1995). *Pet partners home study course.* Renton, WA: Delta Society.

Katcher, A. H. (1981). Interrelations between people and their pets: Form and function. In B. Fogle (Ed.), *Interrelations between people and pets* (pp. 156–178). Springfield, IL: Charles C. Thomas.

Katcher, A. H., & Wilkins, G. G. (1994). Helping children with Attention-deficit hyperactive and conduct disorders through animal-assisted therapy and education. *Interactions, 12*(4), 5–9.

Lee, D. R. (1983). Pet therapy: Helping patients through troubled times. *California Veterinarian, 5*, 24–25.

Levinson, B. M. (1962). The dog as co-therapist. *Mental Hygiene, 46*, 59–65.

Lockwood, R. (1983). The influence of animals on social perception. In A. H. Katcher & A. M. Beck (Eds.), *New perspectives on our lives with companions animals* (pp. 64–71). Philadelphia: University of Pennsylvania Press.

Matthew Margolis goes to prison. (1984). *National Institute of Dog Training Newsletter, 2*(1), 1–2.

McCulloch, M. J. (1983). Animal-facilitated therapy: Overview and future direction. In A. H. Katcher & A. M. Beck (Eds.), *New perspectives on our lives with companion animals* (pp. 410–426). Philadelphia: University of Pennsylvania Press.

Miracle worker: Very smart, very loving. (1984/1985). *Holistic Animal News*, pp. 3–6.

Moneymaker, J. M., & Strimple, E. O. (1991). Animals and inmates: A sharing companionship behind bars. *Journal of Offender Rehabilitation, 16*(3/4), 133–152.

Monks of New Skete. (1991). *The art of raising a puppy.* New York: Little, Brown.

Pryor, K. (1984). *Don't shoot the dog.* New York: Bantam Books.

Reynolds, R. (1995). *Bring me the ocean.* Acton, MA: VanderWyk & Burnham.

Schwartz, B. K. (1987). Pen pals pairs animals and inmates. *The Latham Letter, 3*(3), 6.

Serpell, J. A. (1991). Beneficial effects of pet ownership on some aspects of human health and behavior. *Journal of the Royal Society of Medicine, 840*, 717–720.

Serpell, J., & Jackson, E. (1994). *Effects of previous life stresses on the outcome of studies of the health benefits of pet ownership.* Paper presented at the 13th Annual Conference of the Delta Society, New York, NY.

Siegel, M. (1985, June). If the dogs think I'm okay,I must not be too bad. *The Gazette*, pp. 48–55.

Singlehurst, D. (1995). From the president. *Interactions, 13*(2), 4.

Part 5

Legal Issues in the Treatment of Sex Offenders

Over the past few years, legislatures, in an effort to respond to the growing concern about sexual assault, have passed a variety of laws applying to sex offenders. Statutes have ranged from laws mandating treatment to laws establishing sex offender registries and mandating public reporting of the presence of a sex offender in the community to laws mandating chemical or physical castration.

In *The Sex Offender: Corrections,Treatment and Legal Practice,* Fred Cohen discussed the history and the reemergence of the sexual psychopath statutes. Over the past several years the trend toward the reestablishment of these laws has continued despite contradictory findings by several courts. As he discusses in Chapter 22 of this volume, the federal district court in Washington State and the Supreme Court of Kansas found their sexually violent predator laws to be unconstitutional, whereas the Minnesota psychopathic personality statute and the Wisconsin sexually violent persons law have been upheld. The Kansas case has been accepted for review by the United States Supreme Court. Depending on the final ruling, the decision will have a major impact on the field of sex offender treatment. If the court rules against these laws, sex offenders who have been judged dangerous enough for involuntary commitment will be released, probably in a precipitous fashion, which may make them even more likely to reoffend. If the law is upheld, we can expect other states to quickly pass similar laws and open centers for the confinement and treatment of these individuals.

In Chapter 23, Fred Cohen discusses several issues of particular interest to clinicians. For example, in performing a pre-sentence evaluation on an offender, does the clinician have to warn the individual that information may be used against him and that he may remain silent? Many states are requiring that sex offenders complete a treatment program as either a condition of probation or a qualification for parole. Can such requirements be mandated, particularly if the treatment program requires that an offender admit his guilt and perhaps even admit to additional crimes. Can a court make treatment a condition of release even if the offender cannot afford it or even if the treatment program does not exist? New technologies used with sex offenders have raised legal issues. Can an offender be compelled to submit to a penile plethysmograph or a polygraph or be forced to submit a blood sample for a DNA data bank?

Chapter 24, by Elizabeth R. Walsh, is devoted to analysis of sex offender registration and public notification. All states now have some sort of registry for sex offenders. This registry is usually reserved for use by law enforcement officials. However, the federal government has just passed a law mandating that communities and individual citizens be informed of the presence of a sex offender in their midst. Thus, states have had to rush to adopt these laws or lose federal funding. This situation will undoubtedly have a variety of consequences — not only for the offender but for the community as well. Will these laws instigate vigilante activities? Will citizens feel safer or will an atmosphere of paranoia result? Will sex offenders attempting to amend their lives find themselves without work or housing and will their families be equally victimized? As no category of citizen in the United States has been stigmatized in any similar way, there is little precedent for predicting the ramifications.

Laws in the area of forensic mental health rarely have an impact on the lives of the typical citizen. However, laws related to sex offenders may have a real influence on the population. Not only may they be used as precedents to apply to other groups, but their efficacy or lack thereof may truly affect the safety of thousands of adults and children.

Chapter 22

Sexually Dangerous Persons/Predators Legislation

by Fred Cohen

Overview

In *In re Blodgett*,[1] the author of the Minnesota Supreme Court's recent opinion upholding the state's frequently litigated psychopathic personality statute asks: "Is it better for a person with an uncontrollable sex drive to be given an enhanced prison sentence or to be committed civilly?"[2] Ultimately the justice finds that there are no easy policy answers, but that a legislature is constitutionally free to choose either or both alternatives for dealing with the sexual predator.[3]

In asking "is it better" and answering that the legislature may choose, the court not only evades a substantive answer but fails to confront what factors go into the "better or worse" decision.

Before reviewing the recent spate of judicial activity stimulated by the resurgence of civil commitment-type legislation in this area, I will spell out my own policy preferences. These preferences clearly affect one's analysis of the cases and the legislation on point.

The litany of horrors described in the cases dealing with many of the offenders of concern to us here is almost unimaginable. A pedophile who confessed to molesting 200 young girls; a rape leaving a teenager paralyzed for life; sodomizing and dismembering young boys; raping and killing a babysitter; and doing these things repeatedly[4]: doing them three hours after being paroled; doing them year after year; again and again.

There can be no reasonable argument about the need for a response that, at a minimum, disables such offenders—a response that places barriers between them and their potential victims. The issue is a choice of means and the various civil commitment laws enacted, or reaffirmed, in the wake of Washington State's sexually violent predator law (SVPL) appear to be dubious, politically motivated, publicity generating and, most important, practically needless choices.[5]

The author's choice is to use the traditional criminal law and to subject the most recidivistic of offenders or the most serious offenders (based essentially on the harm principle) to long terms of imprisonment.

Everything legally acceptable that can be accomplished using the civil commitment processes can also be done within the criminal process. Ironically, it is the civil commitment process that raises questions of additional, constitutionally driven procedural protection: a right to treatment whether psychopathic antisocial personality is or is not a mental illness; mandates for periodic review; and more.

Of course, the one option unavailable to the criminal law is to retroactively criminalize conduct (i.e., one cannot prosecute an individual for a behavior that has later become a crime, for example, "marital rape"). One of the key motivations in the Washington SVPL was to confine certain sex offenders about to leave prison, or already out, who had not committed new crimes and who might not have been civilly committable as mentally ill and dangerous. As one writer puts it, "These new statutes . . . represent little more than an effort to retroactively extend criminal sentences for previously convicted offenders. . . ."[6]

The only significant limitation on the government's power as to the nature and duration of criminal punishment is the Eighth Amendment. In *Harmelin v. Michigan*,[7] the Court upheld a sentence of life without parole when the defendant had no prior felony convictions and the conviction was for possession of 650 grams of cocaine (with no proof of possession *for* sale).

The constitutionality of habitual offender laws has never been in doubt even when the prior offenses are relatively innocuous but are cumulated to permit sentences as long as life.[8]

Thus, from the constitutional standpoint, the Eighth Amendment is no barrier to an extremely long term of imprisonment for a first offense that is serious or for habitual criminal conduct that separately may not be so serious.[9]

A long prison term, including life, accomplishes incapacitation and it need be based only on a just desserts proportionality principle. The advantage of doing so is the avoidance of a promise of (or a premise for) treatment while reserving the right to do so. The latter point is so compelling (i.e., the right to offer treatment without undertaking the mandate) that I am mystified as to why the various states ignore it.

The Eighth Amendment does create a constitutional obligation to treat prisoners with serious mental illness.[10] To the extent that the various civil commitment laws focus on psychopaths, sexual predators, or antisocial personalities, they are focusing on offender group members who are exempt from constitutionally mandated treatment in prison or jail. Penal confinement of such persons would seem to be an attractive policy alternative in that it would allow prison and jail officials to offer treatment (or not) to those offenders it deems most worthy or likely to succeed. Participation and completion of available treatment in these settings may be, and quite often is, linked to favorable parole consideration.

Once again, nothing cannot be done in the future within the criminal process that can be done in the civil process and the criminal process offers government officials greater flexibility, including prison-to-hospital transfers, and offers the public at least as much security. The allure of doing something dramatic, of gaining headlines in the war against sexual predators, however, is irresistible for some executives and legislatures.

Washington's Sexually Violent Predator Act

In Chapter 23 of *The Sex Offender* (Cohen, 1995) the author discussed the Sexually Violent Predator Act (SVPA) and the Washington Supreme Court's decision, In In re Young, which is reproduced in full at Appendix H in that same volume.[11] Young's upholding of the law, however, was not the end of the matter for Washington's SVPA. In *Young v. Weston*,[12] the same Andre Brigham Young sought a writ of habeas corpus in federal court arguing now that his confinement was unconstitutional.

Federal District Court Judge Coughenour so completely agreed with Young that he found the SVPA unconstitutional on its face, thus obviating the need to review any possible trial errors or factual material.

The federal district court focused on three constitutional arguments:

1. That the SVPA is unconstitutional as a violation of substantive due process in that the deprivation of liberty it permits is not grounded on any rationale articulated by the Supreme Court.
2. That the SVPA violates the ex post facto clause of the Constitution in that it is penal, retroactive, and disadvantageous to the individual.
3. That the SVPA constitutes double jeopardy in that it imposes a second punishment (declaring someone to be a sexually violent predator and confining him for life) for the commission of a violent sexual offense.

Young actually prevails on all these points and although the opinion contains many complex factors, it rests on two basic premises:

1. The SVPA does not require a finding of mental illness and dangerousness. Rather, its invocation and application rest on a finding of "mental abnormality" or "personality disorder," conditions I find outside the pale of traditional, psychiatrically recognized mental illnesses.
2. Once the SVPA is removed from the area of permissible civil commitment, it becomes characterized as penal. Having reached this point, then, it is easy to find that a person in Young's position is being punished for conduct—more accurately, a condition—that was not so punishable when initially engaged in or demonstrated. The same rationale controls the virtually automatic finding of double jeopardy.

Let me now briefly return to the key points in the decision and elaborate somewhat. First, I turn to the substantive due process/mental illness point.

Substantive due process is a judicially created concept that is used sparingly and as a way to prevent certain arbitrary or shocking behavior by government. This legal concept is not concerned with how something is done—as is the case with procedural due process—its focus is on what is done. Here, the what is the deprivation of liberty as a sexual predator absent a finding that a traditional mental illness exists.

Ultimately this court finds that Washington law resembles the Louisiana commitment and retention law and practice rejected in *Foucha v. Louisiana*,[13] which is described as permitting indefinite incarceration based on little more than a prediction of dangerousness. That, of course, is not quite accurate as Louisiana itself conceded that Foucha was not mentally ill; that the evidence of antisocial personality did not fit clinically accepted views on mental illness.

We need not resolve that issue here and will return to it in the context of discussing other leading decisions on point.

Thus, Judge Coughenour invalidates the SVPA at its core, at the point at which the original sexual psychopath laws staked out their new territory; that somewhere between mental illness (as in mainline psychosis) and dangerousness for commitment and mentally ill as available within the insanity defense, the sexual compulsion of a psychopath may serve as a basis for indefinite commitment. Once psychopathy, dressed now as either sociopathy or antisocial personality, is deemed a constitutionally inadequate basis for commitment under *Foucha*, the SVPA must fall. And it does.

Once fallen, as noted, the confinement thereunder is illegal and those confined under the law are entitled to release. The confinement also may be characterized as unlawful punishment and found also to violate double jeopardy and ex post facto concepts.

Minnesota's Psychopathic Personality Statute

Phillip Jay Blodgett has a long history of misconduct in sexual matters, including sexual abuse of a brother, a sexual assault on his ex-girlfriend just three hours after release from jail, raping a 16-year-old girl while on supervised release, death threats, and other misconduct.

Blodgett challenged the lower courts' finding that he was committable as a psychopathic personality and he, like Young, claimed a violation of substantive due process. *In re Blodgett*[14] rejected the challenge and, with three dissents, upheld the Minnesota law.

Minnesota's sex psychopath law is patterned after the original legislation on point adopted by Michigan in 1937.[15] Minnesota's law was reviewed and upheld as constitutional by the Supreme Court in 1940.[16] In so ruling, the court accepted the Minnesota Supreme Court's narrowing interpretation of the SVPA. Taken together, the original legislation and the limiting language reads as follows:

> The term "psychopathic personality" is defined in the original statute as the existence in any person of such conditions of emotional instability, or impulsiveness of behavior, or lack of customary standards of good judgment, or failure to appreciate the consequences of personal acts, or a combination of any such conditions, as to render such person irresponsible for personal conduct with respect to sexual matters and thereby dangerous to other persons.

> The Minnesota court limited the statute to "those persons who, by a habitual course of misconduct in sexual matters, have evidenced an utter lack of power to control their sexual impulses and who, as a result, are likely to attack or otherwise inflict injury, loss, pain or other evil on the objects of their uncontrolled and uncontrollable desire."[17]

The core of Blodgett's argument is that although he may be socially maladjusted, he is not mentally ill. If he is not mentally ill, he argues, *Foucha* prohibits his confinement unless and until he is convicted of a crime. In effect, the argument is that *Foucha* basically overrules *Pearson*[18] even though the Supreme Court has not explicitly said so.

The *Blodgett* majority reaffirms earlier views that a psychopathic personality identifies a volitional dysfunction which seriously impairs judgment and sexual behavior. Whether the term used is "predator," "antisocial personality disorder," or "psychopath," the term is found to identify a documentable, violent, sexually deviant condition or disorder.

The majority does not read *Foucha* as undermining the Minnesota law as it was upheld much earlier by the Supreme Court in *Pearson*. Although that may be so, it is not for the reasons offered by the *Blodgett* majority. The court states, "In *Foucha* the confinement was for insanity and, when the insanity was shown to be in remission . . . Foucha had to be released."[19]

Foucha was committed after being found not guilty by reason of insanity (n.g.r.i.). Such a verdict rests on a finding of mental disease or defect which, in turn, has some functional impact (e.g., unable to control one's conduct). Insanity as used in this context is a legal conclusion of nonresponsibility; it is not the equivalent of a mental condition although plainly this is more often misunderstood than grasped.

Thus, it was Foucha's mental illness, which was either nonexistent or in remission, that required his release. The only aspect of *Foucha* that should have engaged the Minnesota court is whether antisocial (or psychopathic) personality may now serve as a constitutional basis for civil confinement or detention.

Foucha can be read, as did Judge Coughenour, as falling outside the realm of commitable mental illness or, as do others, not directly answered because Louisiana conceded that mental illness was required for retention and was not present.

After upholding the continued constitutionality of committing one with a psychopathic personality, the majority next takes on the question whether the law is unconstitutional if the condition is untreatable and commitment becomes, in effect, lifetime preventive detention. Relying heavily on the work of Dr. Barbara K. Schwartz, the court finds that it is not clear that treatment never works.[20] However, it also holds that "so long as civil commitment is programmed to provide treatment and periodic review, due process is provided."[21] Justice Wahl, writing for two other justices in dissent, finds that the psychopathic personality statute "is creating a system of wholesale preventive detention, a concept foreign to our jurisprudence."[22] He notes that persons have been committed under this law for window peeping, masturbation, sexual contact with cows, and homosexuality.

A deprivation of liberty, it is urged, requires proof of a compelling governmental interest supportive of confinement and that there be no alternative means available that involve a lesser deprivation. Here, there are no verifiable, well-defined, medically recognized and clinically valid conditions and the state has not met its burden of showing how its police power interest cannot be adequately vindicated through the criminal process.

In other words, the dissent finds *Foucha* compelling and this is consonant with my earlier expressed views on policy. Once again, the debate on what are clinically valid psychiatric conditions or finding some middle ground between "mad" and "bad" is needless and no illuminating insights are gleaned concerning how to deal with the most destructive of the sexual misconduct encounters.

Wisconsin's Sexually Violent Persons Act

The Minnesota law upheld in *Blodgett* traces its roots to the earliest sexual psychopath laws. These laws required a finding of some mental defect or psychopathy creating a lack of control as to sexual matters and as evidenced by an overt act. The most striking feature of the newer laws, including Wisconsin's, modeled after Washington's SVPA is that the laws provide for detention in addition to, not in lieu of, a criminal sentence.[23]

Section 980.02 of the Wisconsin SVPA applies when:

(a) The person satisfies any of the following criteria:

1. The person has been convicted of a sexually violent offense.

2. The person has been found delinquent for a sexually violent offense.

3. The person has been found not guilty of a sexually violent offense by reason of mental disease or defect.

The person is within 90 days of discharge or release, on parole or otherwise, from a sentence that was imposed for a conviction for a sexually violent offense, from a secured correctional facility as defined in §48.02,(15m), if the person was placed in the facility for being adjudicated delinquent under §48.34 on the basis of a sexually violent offense or from a commitment order that was entered as a result of a sexually violent offense.

(b) The person has a mental disorder.

(c) The person is dangerous to others because the person's mental disorder creates a substantial probability that he or she will engage in acts of sexual violence.[24]

Mental disorder is statutorily defined as a congenital or acquired condition affecting the emotional or volitional capacity that predisposes a person to engage in acts of sexual violence.

Two persons committed under Wisconsin's SVPA launched a broad based, constitutional attack on its most basic provisions. In *State v. Carpenter*,[25] the Wisconsin Supreme Court previously upheld the Act in the face of double jeopardy and ex post facto challenges. In *Post*, the decision reviewed here, the law is upheld in relation to the due process and equal protection challenges.

The substantive due process challenge follows what are becoming increasingly familiar lines of attack: The statutory term "mental disorder" sweeps too broadly; it is not the equivalent of mental illness and, thus, allegedly deprives a person of liberty on an arbitrary and unconstitutional basis.

Curiously, the majority rebuffs this argument with barely a reference to Foucha. The majority concludes that the key to the constitutionality of the definition is its nexus to a predisposition to commit acts of sexual violence. Not all those who commit such offenses will have a mental disorder, we are sagely told, and not all persons who are mentally disordered commit violent sexual offenses.

Of course, all of that is painfully obvious, as the dissent observes, but the *Foucha* question—is mental disorder the equivalent of mental illness for commitment—remains.

It seems reasonable to surmise that chronic sexual misconduct will drive the diagnosis of mental disorder. To the extent this is so, we actually have an habitual offender law dressed in civil clothing and begging for judicial attention.

The challengers also question what they term the seriousness of Wisconsin's commitment to providing treatment. They argue that there is no requirement for an individualized finding of amenability to treatment; they question the failure to seek commitment until completion of a sentence and urge recognition that sex offender treatment is largely ineffective. The majority, again, rebuffs the challengers, and on all their points.

The majority does hold that the state is obliged to provide treatment but that obligation does not require a prior showing of treatability.[26] Again, there really is no rationale employed and although the majority is probably correct as a matter of legal precedent, it seems content to simply string out a series of questions and respond with naked conclusions.

On the timing of treatment, the court notes that sexually violent predator (SVP) status is reserved for those for whom previous efforts have been ineffective. In focusing on those said to be most in need, the majority is not inclined to view the state as not serious about treatment.

On treatment ineffectiveness, the court finds there is by no means a consensus within the community of experts on this issue. New techniques are being used and with some claims to success.[27] The legislature is free to "vote" on the side of effectiveness or ineffectiveness and having opted to try treatment with possible effectiveness, it is a decision it constitutionally may make.

The SVPA's use of dangerousness also is upheld with reference to an accurate statement that the Supreme Court has not prescribed strict boundaries for dangerousness. Deference to legislative decisions, and presumably clinical experts, is required and the SVPA also survives this challenge.

Foucha is relied on in the context of a challenge to the nature and duration of the permissible confinement. "We do not read Foucha to prohibit the commitment of dangerous mentally disordered persons."[28] Thus, the indefiniteness of the Wisconsin law also is upheld.

Summing up this aspect of the opinion, the majority states:

> [T]here is medical justification for the commitment of person whose mental disorders predispose them to engage in sexually violent acts. Disorders such as paraphilias, which often form the diagnostic basis for chapter 980, commitments, are characterized by recurrent urges and behaviors.
>
> Treatment that is specifically geared toward helping a committed person recognize and control these patterns of behavior certainly serves the goals of individualized treatment and community protection.
>
> Finally, we point out that substantive due process analysis necessarily involves the balancing of individual liberties against the "demands of an organized society."

The balance can favor danger-preempting confinement under proper circumstances, including the necessity of detaining "mentally unstable individuals who present a danger to the public." We find that chapter 980 permissibly balances the individual's liberty interest with the public's right to be protected from the dangers posed by persons who have already demonstrated their propensity and willingness to commit sexually violent acts.[29]

The challengers prevail on one aspect of their equal protection challenge; that is, their winning argument is that there is no rational justification for granting a jury trial in traditional civil commitment and not also to SVPs.[30] Thus, in addition to the considerable procedural protection explicitly granted (e.g., criminal trial procedures, proof beyond a reasonable doubt, and regular opportunities for reviewing) SVPs are now given the right to a jury trial.

Justice Shirley Abrahamson's dissent is a likely model for those jurists inclined to find SVP-type laws unconstitutional.[31] She begins by pointing out that one-half of the lower court judges in Wisconsin and a fair number of judges in dissent in other jurisdictions, along with Federal District Court Judge Coughenour, have found similar legislation to be unconstitutional. Thus, she is alone here but not without supporters elsewhere.

The Justice's essential point is that when one studies legislative history and intent, the SVPA is unquestionably penal. Using the language of treatment or rehabilitation does not by itself make it so. The purpose is to achieve "the ongoing incarceration of convicted sex offenders who might otherwise be released."[32]

By allowing the commitment of persons who are not simultaneously mentally ill and dangerous, she concludes that substantive due process, as provided for in Foucha, is violated. As noted earlier, she views the Wisconsin effort to define mental disorder as circular and virtually meaningless.

Kansas's Sexually Violent Predator Act

Whereas the Wisconsin high court upheld that state's SVPA, the Supreme Court of Kansas goes quickly to the heart of the matter and states: "We hold that the Kansas Sexually Violent Predator Act, K.S.A. 59-29 a01 et seq., violates the due process clause of the Fourteenth Amendment to the United States Constitution."[33]

Hendricks is the most recent of the several important decisions on sexual psychopathy or sexual predator-type laws and whether the result here is a harbinger of how the Supreme Court ultimately might rule, certainly is not clear. Indeed, were I to guess, I believe the Court would uphold such laws with Justice O'Connor joining the Chief Justice and Justices Kennedy, Thomas, and Scalia to form a majority.[34]

Leroy Hendricks was 60 years of age and nearing completion of a prison sentence of 5 to 20 years. This sentence resulted from a plea agreement entered into in 1984 whereby the defendant pled guilty to two counts of indecent liberties with a child. The state then opted not to invoke the habitual criminal act, which could have tripled the sentence. The state, of course, could have sought the maximum or even consecutive sentences. It opted to plea bargain and now seemingly reconsiders, seeking a potential life sentence in the form of a SVP commitment.

Hendricks' unsettling history shows sexual involvement with children beginning in 1966. There was testimony that he is a pedophile and remains uncured.[35]

The characteristically confused expert testimony ranged from pedophilia not being a personality disorder although it is a mental abnormality to the viewpoint that Hendricks' past conduct is the best predictor of the future.[36] The jury found Hendricks to be a sexually violent predator. He appealed and now prevails on his substantive due process claim.

The Kansas SVPA is virtually identical to Washington's prototype and thus the majority ruling here puts it at odds with the Washington Supreme Court[37] while in agreement with the Federal District Court in Washington.[38] The majority, of course, rests its position squarely on Foucha in that the Kansas law focuses on a mental abnormality or personality disorder and those conditions are not accepted as the formal or functional equivalents of mental illness. Thus, the SVPA is found to be a penal law disguised as civil commitment; it allows indefinite commitment essentially on predictions of dangerousness and is therefore violative of substantive due process.

The three dissenting Justices simply read *Foucha* differently, reading it much as the majority did in *Post*,[39] the Wisconsin decision. Turning to the case at hand, the dissent finds:

> Our Act requires an ailment of the mind rising to either the level of a personality disorder or a "mental abnormality." The evidence in this case establishes that Hendricks did not have a personality disorder. The basis for commitment the State did use, that Hendricks has a mental abnormality, requires considerably more than evidence of idiosyncratic behavior which is within a range that is generally acceptable. It requires "a congenital or acquired condition affecting the emotional or volitional capacity which predisposes the person to commit sexually violent offenses in a degree constituting such person a menace to the health and safety of others." K.S.A. 59-29a02(b).
>
> Contrary to the majority opinion, this definition is not rendered meaningless by circularity. It clearly requires something more than a transitory inclination toward sexual violence generally. A person does not meet this standard for suffering from an ailment of the mind unless the person has both an ongoing mental pathology and that pathology is so severe as to prompt sexually violent behavior. The nature of the mental abnormality required before confinement is available is further limited by the fact that the mental abnormality must be of a type that makes the person likely to engage in a specific and limited type of sexual violence—predatory acts—in a specific setting—outside a secure facility. See K.S.A. 59-29a02(a).[40]

Conclusion

The Minnesota law upheld in the legislatures in states such as Washington, Wisconsin, and Kansas have given the courts an extremely difficult set of problems—problems that the judiciary must handle but invariably does so in a clumsy fashion. The political appeal of sex predator legislation is almost irresistible. What legislator would vote against it? What governor would veto it as unconstitutional?

If we may take a step back from some of the detail previously discussed, consider the following thoughts: Mental disorder, however phrased for the moment, is the predicate for the insanity defense, the trial delay of incompetence, the right to treatment under the Fourteenth and Eighth Amendments for detainees and prisoners, and for "straight" civil commitment. I think it is fair to say that the meaning and uses of the terms "mental disorder" and "mental illness" will likely vary with the context in which the term is invoked.

A psychiatrist may contract with a patient to provide mental health care but may find that only certain diagnoses will qualify under the patient's insurance plan. Sex offenders, whether denominated psychopaths or not, are not eligible for mandatory mental health care while in prison because they do not typically meet the "serious mental illness" requirement.[41]

The essence of the insanity defense is the lack of culpability when a person causes harm but is so cognitively or volitionally impaired as to lack judgment or control. On the other hand, the sex psychopath or predator laws focus on an inability to control one's sexual behavior due to a mental disorder which, in turn, is not the right type or degree to excuse the conduct.

Civil commitment laws requiring mental illness and dangerousness, in one form or another, live right next to the sex psychopath and predator laws. The eligibility distinctions between the two are often too subtle to discern save for the sexual misconduct focus of the laws under discussion here.

Curiously, the conduct involved in the cases we discussed hardly invoke a spirited defense. This is not *Bowers v. Hardwick*,[42] where the question is the propriety of punishing consensual, private homosexual conduct between adults. The conduct we review in this area is often so atrocious that the actor appears to be a monster among us.[43] At times, the conduct is perhaps only annoying and the actor an alienated, friendless outcast.

Thus, the problem is not one of acceptance or tolerance of certain types of deviance. It is one of finding the most effective and efficient means to identify, isolate, and offer treatment and surely these commitment laws are not the answer. Professor Steven J. Morse has an interesting proposal that should be given further consideration.[44]

He argues for a "new crime of reckless endangerment which requires one prior conviction of a crime of violence or one prior civil commitment for actual serious violent conduct," awareness of a very high risk of reoffending, and the failure to seek recommitment or to take other steps to avoid harm doing.

A conviction of reckless endangerment would be relatively short, and, consonant with the relapse prevention approach to sex offenders, this approach imposes responsibility on the person.

Absent something dramatically new, then, the writer simply reaffirms his preference for the criminal law as expressed in the introduction.[45]

Footnotes

[1] 510 N.W.2d 910, 917 (Minn. 1994).

[2] Ibid. at 5.

[3] Minnesota has done just that. State v. Christie, 506 N.W.2d 293 (Minn. 1993), upheld a statute where criminal sentences are increased solely because the sex offender is dangerous and likely to reoffend sexually.

[4] See Blakey, "The Indefinite Civil Commitment of Dangerous Sex Offenders Is an Appropriate Legal Compromise Between 'Mad' and 'Bad'—A Study of Minnesota's Sexual Psychopathic Personality Statute," 10 *Notre Dame J. of Law, Ethics and Pub. Pol'y* 227, 228 (1996).

5 See Cohen, "Washington's Sexually Violent Predator Act," in B. K. Schwartz & H. R. Cellini, *The Sex Offender: Corrections, Treatment and Legal Practice* Ch. 23 (1995) (hereafter *The Sex Offender*).

6 Horwitz, "Sexual Psychopath Legislation: Is There Anywhere to Go But Backwards?" 57 *U. Pitt. L. Rev.* 35, 37 (1995). The author also is convinced that the Supreme Court will likely uphold such laws, and so am I. An answer will be forthcoming in 1997. See infra note 34.

7 111 S. Ct. 2680 (1991). The Court reversed an earlier holding that allowed for more expansive judicial oversight when confronted with very long sentences. Under *Harmelin*, once a decision is made that an offense is "serious" there is no comparative-type analysis as was done previously.

8 See Rummel v. Estelle, 445 U.S. 263 (1980), arguably overruled by Solem v. Helm, 463 U.S. 277 (1983), which clearly is overruled by *Harmelin*.

9 I realize that the terms "serious" and "not so serious" are hardly precise. However, a single rape clearly qualifies as serious and virtually any sexual misconduct with minors also would qualify. Coker v. Georgia, 433 U.S. 584 (1977), prohibits the death sentence for even an aggravated rape but would seem to allow any term of years or life.

10 See Cohen, "Right to Treatment," in *The Sex Offender*, supra note 5, Ch. 24.

11 See *The Sex Offender*, supra note 5, at A-31.

12 898 F. Supp. 744 (W.D. Wash. 1995).

13 504 U.S. 71 (1992). *Foucha* dealt specifically with a person committed after being found not guilty by reason of insanity (n.g.y.i.). Despite testimony of Foucha's dangerousness, the Court required his release absent a finding of mental illness and dangerousness.

14 510 N.W.2d 910 (Minn. 1994). *Blodgett* also raised questions concerning equal protection which need not be addressed in this work.

15 See discussion in *The Sex Offender,* supra note 5, Ch. 22.

16 Minnesota *ex rel.* Pearson v. Probate Court, 309 U.S. 270 (1940).

17 See 510 N.W.2d at 913 for a complete history and detailed citations. Interestingly, only after the court's suggestion in *Blodgett*, ibid. at 917, did the Minnesota legislature incorporate the judicially imposed words of limitation first announced in 1940.

18 See supra note 16.

19 510 N.W. 2d at 916. See State v. Post, 541 N.W.2d 115, 127 (Wis. 1995), where the court correctly points out that Louisiana conceded that Foucha was not mentally ill and his condition was not treatable.

20 See, e.g., "Effective Treatment Techniques for Sex Offenders," 22 *Psychiatric Annual* 5319 (1992).

21 510 N.W.2d at 916.

22 Ibid. at 918.

23 State v. Post, 541 N.W.2d 115 (Wis. 1995). See Horwitz, supra note 6, at 52. In re Hendricks, 912 P.2d 129, 136 (Kan. 1996), discussed infra, finds that the primary objective of such laws is incarceration, not treatment.

24 Wis. Stat. § 980.01(2). Dissenting in the principal case, Justice Abrahamson points out that as every condition is either acquired or congenital and that emotional or volitional processes simply describes peoples' decision-making processes, mental disorder means no more than a predisposition to engage in acts of sexual violence. That is, she argues, entirely circular. 541 N.W.2d at 143.

25 541 N.W.2d 105 (Wis. 1995). The *Carpenter* decision will not be analyzed in this work because the double jeopardy and ex post facto issues have been discussed in the context of the *Blodgett* decision and those issues are far more legalistic—or perhaps of less interest to this readership—than the substantive due process and equal protection claims.

26 Ibid. at 125.

27 Ibid.

28 Ibid. at 127.

29 Ibid. at 128.

30 Ibid. at 132.

[31] Ibid. at 135-147.

[32] Ibid. at 140. The dissent believes the law violates double jeopardy and ex post facto prohibitions as well as due process.

[33] In re Hendricks, 912 P.2d at 138. The writer has resisted the urge to somehow work in "we're home Aunt Emma." However, one's stereotype of the Kansas Supreme Court would not have predicted this outcome. For a review of the Kansas law, see Note, "The Civil Commitment of Violent Predators in Kansas: A Modern Law for Modern Times," 42 *Kans. L. Rev.* 887 (1994).

[34] I base this prediction on nothing more sophisticated than the voting by the Justices in *Foucha.* Justice O'Connor's typically murky concurrence suggest that some narrowing of the categories of "mental illness" and dangerousness tailored to public safety concerns might persuade her to uphold a law confining an n.g.r.i. "who has regained his sanity." Shortly after this was written, the Supreme Court accepted certiorari in this case and, thus, we should have a definitive answer to the constitutionality of these types of laws sometime in 1997. Kansas v. Hendricks, 1996 WESTLAW 206058 (June 17, 1995).

[35] 912 P.2d at 137.

[36] Ibid.

[37] In re Personal Restraint of Young, 857 P.2d (Wash. 1993).

[38] Young v. Weston, 898 F. Supp. 744 (W.D. Wash. 1995).

[39] See 912 P.2d at 148 for the core of the dissents' views on *Foucha.*

[40] 912 P.2d at 148.

[41] See Bailey v. Gartebring, 940 F.2d 1150, 1155 (8th Cir. 1991), finding no deliberate indifference in the failure to treat the inmate although the inmate was also under a valid commitment order as a psychopathic personality.

[42] 478 U.S. 186 (1986).

[43] Severe homosexual pedophilia is not evidence of mental disease or defect, according to one decision. See State v. Dodd, 838 P.2d 86, 90 (Wash. 1992). Wesley Allan Dodd surely committed some of the most appalling sex offenses described in the literature.

[44] Morse, "Blame and Danger: An Essay on Preventive Detention," 76 *Bost. U.L. Rev.* 113, 152-155 (1996).

[45] There are, as you might imagine, any number of other legal decisions dealing with various aspects of laws on sexual psychopaths and predators. Some of the more interesting issues include proof of utter lack of control and planning (In re Schweninger, 520 N.W.2d 444 (Minn. Ct. App. 1994)); criteria for deciding on lack of control (In re Lineham, 518 N.W.2d 609 (Minn. 1994)); relationship between a pedophile's "grooming" activities and the requisite impulsivity (In re Bieganowski, 520 N.W.2d 525 (Minn. Ct. App. 1994)); and failure of counsel to advise defendant prior to pleading guilty of creating eligibility for later sex predator status (In re Personal Restraint of Paschke, 909 P.2d 1328 (Wash. Ct. App. 1996)). This chapter dealt with the basic legal issues attached to the legality of these laws.

Chapter 23

The Treatment and Supervised Release Relationship

by Fred Cohen

Overview

In Chapter 26 of *The Sex Offender*[1] I discussed issues of confidentiality and the privilege against self-incrimination. Three important decisions were analyzed, one of which was accepted for review by the Supreme Court of the United States but was then dismissed as improvidently granted.[2] In the relatively brief period since the earlier material was prepared, a large number of decisions have encompassed the same territory.

In addition, some new issues have become more prominent and I discuss them too in this chapter. For example, some jurisdictions are collecting blood samples from certain sex offenders with which to create a DNA bank. This has invited Fourth Amendment search and seizure challenges. Another new issue asks whether the refusal to submit to the administration of a plethysmograph is a proper basis for parole revocation? Does a prisoner have a First Amendment right to retain sexually explicit material he authored and which now may violate his sex offender treatment program contract? Is Alcoholics Anonymous or Narcotics Anonymous so religiously oriented that it may violate the First Amendment if an AA-type approach is used in a prison's only available sex offender program which, in turn, is mandated for parole consideration?

These are examples of some of the more exotic issues reaching the courts in this area. The more basic issues relate to possible coercion in obtaining pre-sentence information, the ambiguity or unconstitutionality of certain probation (or parole) conditions, and whether a defendant must be informed of the collateral consequences (e.g., eligibility for commitment as a sexual predator) of a guilty plea.

Once an offender is incarcerated, there are a host of legal issues involving the requirement of programming as a de facto or de jure basis for parole eligibility: the recurrent problem of insisting on admissions of guilt as a program prerequisite and then using these admissions either for denial or discretionary release or, in community settings, for revocation, or even as the basis for a new crime charge.

These issues, in turn, blend into the general area of revocation and the persistent problems related to the Fifth Amendment privilege against self-incrimination. A crucial element in the newer, especially cognitive-behavioral, treatments is the admission of guilt. Thus, denial is the treatment hurdle for the individual and confused and inconsistent case law on silence and the legal consequences of admissions is the dilemma for the law.[3]

Pre-Sentence and Sentencing Issues

In *State v. Tinkham*[4] an intermediate court of appeals in Washington confronted this question: Did the trial court err in prohibiting defense counsel from advising his client with regard to the Fifth Amendment privilege as that privilege might apply during a court-ordered, pre-sentence mental evaluation on the issue of future dangerousness?

The sole purpose of this postconviction order was to determine whether this convicted child rapist should be given an "exceptional sentence." The trial court ruled that the Fifth Amendment applied only to jeopardy concerning guilt or innocence and not to sentencing.

Relying on an extension of the United States Supreme Court's reasoning in *Estelle v. Smith*,[5] a capital case, the appellate court ruled here that when the state is asking for an increased penalty based on a compelled evaluation, *Miranda*-like warnings are required. That is, at a minimum the defendant must know that he has a right to remain silent.[6] In addition, the defendant's right to counsel was violated because this became a "critical stage" in the proceeding and surely counsel could at least advise his client.[7]

Parenthetically, the term "critical stage" was developed by the courts to describe points in the criminal process when an accused required the assistance of counsel. In *Coleman v. Alabama*,[8] for example, Justice Brennan stated that the constitutional principle of providing the guiding hand of counsel in a criminal proceeding is not limited to providing counsel at trial and includes a preliminary hearing. Thus, in *Tinkham* the "critical stage" right-to-counsel issue is moved from an early part of the pretrial stage to a specific aspect of the posttrial (or plea) sentencing process.

This is an unusual situation because the Fifth Amendment typically would not be available as part of the sentence information-gathering process. However, when either sentence enhancement or an admission of additional criminal activity is explicitly sought, the privilege against self-incrimination may come into play.[9] Where the privilege exists, the right to counsel to protect the privilege also will likely exist.

In a somewhat different situation, and without the trial court actually prohibiting advice on the right to remain silent, a Minnesota court reached a different conclusion.[10] The appellant claimed that using his admission of sexually abusing his niece, which he made to a licensed psychologist during a court-ordered examination, violated the Fifth Amendment. This admission was used for evidentiary purposes and the court ruled that "unless the defendant asserted the Fifth Amendment privilege, any incriminating statements made during the pre-sentence interview could be used against the defendant without violating constitutional protections."[11]

The court ruled there was no coercion or overreaching by the psychologist and this is not a "critical stage" which would invoke the right to counsel. In *Tinkham*, we should recall, the examination was designed exclusively to enhance the criminal sentence and counsel was, in effect, muzzled by the court. Here, there is no mention of counsel's role and the purpose of the examination may be viewed as different.

However, this is a problem that will not go away simply by attempting nice distinctions in the case law. That is, when there is a court-ordered, or -sanctioned, examination by an agent of government and the purpose of that examination is to effect a criminal sentence, should the defendant be told of the agency of the examiner, the purpose of the examination, the uses to which the examination results will be put, and that the defendant may remain silent in the face of a credible claim of possible self-incrimination?

I should add that any defendant undoubtedly has the power to remain fully or partially silent. The question is whether it is a right and, if so, should information be provided as to the right? Although the two cases discussed obviously involve different facts, the Washington decision (*Tinkham*) seems to be more consonant with elementary notions of fairness and more consistent with the professional and ethical obligations of a clinician or examiner.[12]

Waiver of the Fifth as Probation or Parole Condition. The Arizona Supreme Court recently faced the question whether a trial judge might condition a sex offender's probation with a requirement that he simply waive all Fifth Amendment rights in connection with a sex offender treatment program. That is, the probationer would be required to answer questions truthfully as to the current offense and any other offenses and the answers could be used as part of treatment, to revoke probation, or to file new charges.[13]

Going right to the point, the court held that the state is prohibited from making waiver of the privilege a condition of probation. The state may not force a defendant to elect between incriminating himself and losing probation by remaining silent.

Finding the condition unconstitutional, the court itself sanitizes the probation terms by substituting a requirement of answering truthfully.[14] Parenthetically, the court brushed off the argument that acceptance of the waiver condition is a voluntary waiver.[15]

That is, the mere acceptance of a condition — like saying yes with a gun to your temple — does not establish a legally acceptable waiver of the right or privilege under discussion. Indeed, as a general proposition the acceptance of probation or parole with a condition (e.g., do not register as a Democrat) that is unconstitutional does not mean the individual has forfeited the right to subsequently challenge the offending condition.

The Arizona Supreme Court was influenced by the Supreme Court's decision in *Minnesota v. Murphy*[16]: *Murphy* is essentially a *Miranda* problem — a case dealing with a probationer who was asked to meet with his probation officer who, in turn, questioned the probationer based on previously received new crime information. The session resulted in a confession to rape and murder. The probationer then argued that this was custodial interrogation conducted without proper warnings and that it violated his Fifth Amendment (or *Miranda*) rights.

In a decision that has always been puzzling to me, the Court held that although there was interrogation, this "voluntary" meeting at the probation office did not equate with custody for *Miranda* purposes.[17]

Had this been characterized as custodial interrogation, Murphy's unwarned statement would have been inadmissible. Murphy, however, may still claim that he is protected by the Fifth Amendment even though he did not invoke it because he was put in what is termed the "classic penalty" situation; that is, showing he was threatened with revocation if he did not forgo his right to silence.[18]

The Court found that the state merely required that Murphy be truthful and not that he had to choose between making incriminating statements and jeopardizing his probation. Thus, the privilege is found not to be self-executing: that Murphy had to claim it and the state did not have to inform him of the right to remain silent.[19]

Parenthetically, if Murphy had not accepted the invitation to visit the probation office then his supervised release status could have been revoked. It seems that only if the threat of revocation is made explicit is there a duty to give a *Miranda* warning.[20]

Thus, an order (or condition) to speak truthfully is now viewed by the courts as noncoercive and as not being the functional equivalent of "confess or face certain revocation!"

In *Eccles*, then, the Arizona court merely follows the somewhat tortured logic of the Supreme Court and distinguishes a command to be truthful from one that explicitly requires self-incrimination. I suspect that only lawyers will be persuaded by this and that nonlawyer readers will be shaking their heads by now.

Vagueness May Void Condition. Whereas *Eccles* dealt with a specific, albeit unenforceable, condition the North Dakota Supreme Court recently dealt with an "admission of guilt" condition characterized as unenforceable due to vagueness."[21] The trial court knew that the defendant was not admitting guilt and, on the record, the judge was sympathetic to the defendant's dilemma. In discussing the mandated treatment program the judge said, "Nobody should make you change your mind if you believe what you said. . . ."[22]

However, a probation condition was imposed by this judge which required that the defendant "attend, participate in, cooperate with and successfully complete" a program. A different judge revoked probation in the face of the probationer's steadfast refusal to admit sexually assaulting his daughter. This, of course, is what he insisted on to the sentencing judge. The defendant attempted suicide then was severely injured in prison before his release.

Construing the ambiguity in defendant's favor, the Idaho court reinstated probation. Thus, no large principle emerges here, only a decision on the facts in a particular case and a reviewing court's application of basic fairness considerations.

Guilty Pleas. As a general proposition, before a court may accept a guilty plea, the court must satisfy itself that the plea is knowing and voluntary.[23]

The question for us is, What may be included in the "knowing" requirement? Does one who pleads to first-degree sexual assault of a child have to be informed of his potential eligibility for later commitment as a sexual predator?

The cases on point are rather uniform: The prospect of civil commitment is termed a "collateral consequence," one that has no definite, immediate, or largely automatic effect and thus the voluntariness of the plea is not in doubt.[24]

As a general proposition, before a plea is accepted the court must make known to the defendant the maximum possible penalty provided by law and, in some jurisdictions, the effect of a special parole term.[25] On the other hand, "knowing" does not include a discussion of parole possibilities, the place of confinement, various civil disabilities, or the potential for being committed as mentally ill or as a sexual predator or psychopath.

Conditional Freedom and Sex Offender Programs

As sex offender programs proliferate in prisons, as well as the community, probation and parole often are conditioned on gaining access to and completing a program. The vagaries of admission to a program and successfully completing it have created a host of legal problems.

Suppose a judge, after careful evaluation and analysis, concludes that a sex offender be given a 15-year probationary term conditioned on his entering and completing treatment at a particular residential treatment facility? The offender, however, cannot pay the $34,500 (or $63 per day) for the 18 months of residential care; he has no insurance, and the county refuses to fund this treatment. In *State v. Morrow*,[26] the reviewing court found no constitutional violation when the trial court revoked probation and imprisoned the defendant.

The reviewing court actually gave this constitutional case detailed consideration. Under Minnesota law, a finding of an intentional and unexcused violation is the required norm for revocation, but probation also may be revoked, for example, when a probationer is found "unwilling to work with the treatment program" or even when a mandated program ceases to exist.

This case was analyzed within the framework of *Bearden v. Georgia*,[27] which basically held that if a probationer made bona fide efforts to pay a fine but still could not, only if alternative measures are not adequate may the impoverished probationer be imprisoned.

The point, however, is that although poverty per se does not bar the revocation, it does constitutionally require an analysis of alternative measures. In *Morrow*, the trial court was convinced that without some confinement the defendant would reoffend and when community residential care was unavailable — regardless of why — the only alternative seemed to be prison.

The judge did inquire about, and appear to arrange for, treatment at Stillwater Prison. Thus, the court found that there was no denial of due process or equal protection.

From the defendant's standpoint, of course, it was his relative poverty that led to confinement, whereas from the court's vantage point it was program unavailability and an overriding need to provide community protection in the form of residential care that led to this result.

Parole Release and Program Completion. If a state prisoner is given a parole release date contingent upon the completion of a sex offender treatment program, does the inmate have an enforceable constitutional claim of access to such a program? No, says a federal appeals court in *Jones v. Moore*.[28]

Inmate Jones received a 15-year sentence in 1982 for offenses that included forcible rape. An attempted escape in 1984 led to his transfer to a maximum security prison lacking a sex offender program. Because of his prior escape attempt, Jones was denied transfer to a prison where a program was available. After his parole date was rescinded, Jones — not unreasonably — claimed legal injury due to a discretionary release being made contingent upon a program not available to him but available to others.

However ostensibly reasonable the claim, Jones' task is formidable: He must show that he was denied a constitutionally recognized and protected liberty interest. His strongest argument in 1993 seemed to be located in Missouri statutes that require the director to establish a program of treatment, education, and rehabilitation for all imprisoned sex offenders. In addition, state law required that all such offenders must complete such a program prior to parole.

The court states that to find a liberty interest it must locate relevant mandatory language which, in effect, conditions the discretion of officials. The court cannot find such language in this Missouri law and refuses to recognize a practice — here, placing inmates in sex treatment programs 18 to 24 months prior to a presumptive release date — as creating a liberty interest.

The upshot: no right of access to the program and no right to parole release.

If *Jones v. Moore* has even a faint ring of unfairness about it as of 1993, there would not even be a reasonable argument about the correctness of the result — or certainly the analysis used — today in the wake of *Sandin v. Connor*.[29] Sandin dramatically alters what are referred to as state-created liberty interests. Jones' argument that Missouri law mandated the creation of programs and his access thereto is a form of liberty interest analysis which *Sandin* now obliterates.

That is, under Sandin the fact that a particular jurisdiction may use mandatory language as to the creation of particular programs or even access thereto is not enough to create a constitutionally based, enforceable right to an inmate. In our context, *Sandin* provides that an enforceable claim — or liberty interest — exists only if the "State's action will inevitably affect the duration of his sentence."[30]

To date, this language is taken to mean that there is a right to a hearing when earned good time credits are taken, but research has uncovered no claim of an enforceable right to the existence of a sex offender treatment (or substance abuse) program, to access thereto, or to remain within a program once admitted.[31]

A New Hampshire prisoner raised legal claims related to parole release that parallel a number of recent decisions. The inmate was convicted of aggravated felonious sexual assault and given two lengthy prison terms. When the offender was denied parole, the board informed him it was because he had not completed the prison's sexual offender program. He subsequently sought admission but was denied because he refused to admit responsibility for the crimes for which he had been convicted.

In *Knowles v. Warden*,[32] the New Hampshire Supreme Court rejected the inmate's claims that either his state or federal rights against compelled self-incrimination were violated. The court reasons from the predicate that there is no federal or state right to release on parole. Indeed, in *Greenholtz v. Nebraska Penal Inmates*,[33] the Supreme

Court held that there is no federal constitutional right to a parole release hearing although a state might create such a right if it used certain verbal combinations — as in "shall be released unless . . ." — in which case a hearing was required.[34]

Knowles was not asking for a hearing; he asked to be relieved of the obligation to admit to the crimes of conviction as a precondition for gaining admission to the treatment program. Admission to, and program completion, merely created parole release eligibility and is not related to the question whether a hearing is required.

In any event, the court finds there is no compulsion in that the inmate is free to remain out of the program. Because there is no right to release short of full term, there is no right of which he is deprived due to the requirement of a culpable admission.

The court does take note of *State v. Imlay*[35] and decided that even if viewed as persuasive authority, *Imlay* deals with revocation while *Knowles* deals with a granting decision and there is a crucial distinction between a deprivation of liberty, however conditional, and a liberty one desires.[36]

Program Completion and Release: Self-Incrimination Revisited. We turn now to a leading decision dealing with self-incrimination and the revocation of a sex offender's probation. In *State v. Fuller*,[37] the Montana Supreme Court held that as "the State improperly compelled Fuller to disclose past criminal acts in violation of his Fifth Amendment privilege against compelled self-incrimination and his constitutionally guaranteed right to remain silent, it is now prohibited from using any of the information elicited as the basis for a later, separate criminal prosecution."[38]

The facts in *Fuller* must be reviewed to grasp the significance of the holding. Fuller was convicted of three counts of sexual assault and placed on probation on condition that he enroll in a treatment program and follow all its policies. Thereafter, the Montana Supreme Court reversed these convictions for lack of evidence and ordered Fuller's acquittal.

Between the conviction and the subsequent acquittal, Fuller disclosed to his treatment group an offense history which contained admissions of at least three sexual contacts with prepubescent girls. Police were unaware of these offenses and when they did investigate, criminal charges were brought which are the basis of the decision under discussion.

Unlike so many other courts, the Montana court views Fuller's situation as the "classic penalty" situation; that is, the threat to punish him was implicit in the insistence that he speak freely in therapy. The fact that Fuller did not claim a right to remain silent is of no moment here because in the classic penalty situation — essentially, talk or else — the right to remain silent is self-executing and what is said is viewed essentially as compelled.

The court concludes by emphasizing that although the state may compel a defendant to speak truthfully in a treatment environment, what it cannot do is use those answers in a later criminal proceeding. And I must emphasize that the loss of probation is the threat, but *Fuller* involves using these compelled statements in a new criminal proceeding.[39]

In *State v. Tenbusch*,[40] the defendant was charged with sexual abuse based on statements he made during a polygraph examination administered by a therapist. The therapist urged honesty and disclosure and told the defendant that although he would not likely go to prison, the disclosure of new crimes could result in tougher probation conditions.

The defendant not only disclosed the new offenses, he was made to confront his victims and advised that the therapist would inform police or he could do so. The defendant elected to confess directly to the police.

The trial court, not surprisingly, found these statements involuntary; that the defendant's will was overborne. The Oregon appellate court then reversed.

The reviewing court seems plainly confused as to the difference between a *Miranda*-violated confession and an involuntary confession. The *Miranda* rules require that when public officials engage in custodial interrogation, the suspect must be made aware of his or her right to silence, to counsel, the consequences of speaking, and so on.

Miranda warnings are more accurately characterized as awareness of rights. *Miranda*, of course, was decided in the context of police coercion but it is not directly concerned with a finding of coercion. An involuntary confession, on the other hand, is only concerned with whether the will is overborne whether by threats or irresistible promises (e.g., talk and we'll let your pregnant wife go home).

Thus, police or correctional officials could give *Miranda* warnings in the most complete and soothing fashion possible but if threats or promises follow and they are of such a magnitude as to "overcome the will" the confession is involuntary and inadmissible.

In *Tenbusch*, the court finds it was incumbent on the offender to assert the privilege unless he could show he would have suffered a penalty for doing so.[41] I respectfully suggest that the therapist's insistence on disclosure and promises of no imprisonment create coercion and invocation of the right to silence is simply not at issue. The trial court, in my view, was correct.

In *Gyles v. State*,[42] the defendant refused to respond to a polygraph examiner's questions about either the crime of conviction or new crimes. The defendant relied on his Fifth Amendment rights. The Alaska court finds that there is no right to remain silent as to the crime of conviction. There is such a right as to new offenses although the threat of prosecution must be apparent and not simply be speculative or relate to a threat of revocation.[43]

A Wisconsin court has produced a fair summary of the confusing state of the law in this area:

> Thus, if a probationer is forced to answer questions relating to pending charges or face revocation of probation, the probationer must answer the questions as long as he or she is informed that such answers may not be used against the probationer in a subsequent criminal proceeding except for purposes of impeachment or rebuttal. However, incriminating statements may be used against a parolee in a revocation proceeding because such hearings are fundamentally different from a criminal proceeding and thus no Fifth Amendment right attaches. [Citations omitted.][44]

Requiring Submission to Plethysmograph. From the use of the polygraph we turn now to resistance to the use of a plethysmograph. John Walrath challenged the revocation of his federal parole arguing that it was revoked because he protested the administration of a plethysmograph. Walrath was convicted of a sex offense involving a young boy some 25 years earlier, released on parole in 1983, and revoked in 1990 for nonsexual offenses. When he was reparoled in 1992, there was concern about his potential as a pedophile who might again endanger young boys. Consequently, he was required to submit to studies of sexual arousal with the aid of a plethysmograph, which is a device used to measure arousal in response to various stimuli. The test was imposed as a condition of his continued freedom on parole.

Walrath's refusal to take the test led to another revocation, then another parole, with the same condition required. Shortly before the scheduled test, Walrath sued for injunctive relief and damages, leading the clinic to refuse to administer the test. The Parole Commission then put aside this test and ordered a psychiatric examination which concluded that Walrath was in a special category of high-risk sex offenders and that, without more information, the center could not gauge his tendencies toward recidivism.

Some interesting maneuvering ensued, but ultimately the commission said "submit," and Walrath said "no." The court held that Walrath had not complied with a reasonable condition of parole and revocation was proper.[45] Neither the question of the constitutionality of requiring submission to this concededly intrusive test nor that of the condition's appropriateness (i.e., its relationship to the offense or offender) was before this court.

The court viewed Walrath's legal maneuvering as a refusal to sign the consent form. This refusal was found to be inconsistent with the voluntary consent envisioned by the parole condition. With veiled threats of litigation hanging over them, the treatment center refused to proceed, so the condition could not be observed. According to the court, this was a proper basis for revocation.

The Seventh Circuit repeatedly referred to the testing as requiring a voluntary consent. The revocation itself seems grounded on Walrath's failure to consent. It does seem a bit odd to speak of voluntary consent when the court states that the parolee must agree or face revocation. The case, then, is actually about the right to force participation in this program or face prison.

DNA Banks. Oregon inmates unsuccessfully challenged a state law requiring that persons convicted of murder and certain sex offenses submit blood samples for DNA testing. Oregon prison officials usually obtained the sample shortly before release from prison, and this, of course, undermined any claims to prison security as an objective.

The inmates raised some complex issues related to Fourth Amendment protection and some more easily handled issues involving ex post facto laws and due process. In *Rise v. Oregon*,[46] the law, and practices under it, was upheld over the vigorous dissent of Judge D.W. Nelson.

The creation of a DNA data bank is based on the premise that certain murders and sex offenders have high rates of recidivism and that in the commission of these types of offenses there is often saliva, blood, or semen obtained as evidence which makes access to DNA data a valuable prosecution tool.

The law here is limited to one lifetime extraction and some specific limitations on access (e.g., prosecutors) and use (e.g., cannot be used to determine genetic predispositions).

The majority opinion does recognize that the blood extraction implicates Fourth Amendment privacy rights. However, in the face of the combination of the prisoner's impaired legal status — the relatively limited intrusion, the strong law enforcement/prosecutorial interest — the law survives the Fourth Amendment challenge. There is no requirement of a warrant or even of reasonable suspicion: This is viewed as a preventive measure, then, and not one with a primary law enforcement goal of solving a new crime.

The ex post facto claim fails on its face because nothing is made criminal retroactively nor is punishment enhanced. The due process claim founders on the basic fact that there is simply nothing to contest at a due process-driven hearing.

Judge Nelson, in dissent, writes a compelling opinion on the Fourth Amendment issues. He reviews all the Supreme Court precedent relied on by the majority and finds that nothing in the past is precedent for this undertaking. Even *Bell v. Wolfish*,[47] upholding a body cavity inspection after a detainee's contact visit, is arguably not on point because it permits this invasiveness in the name of institutional security. The DNA data bank, of course, is not concerned with such security.

The majority views fingerprinting and blood samples as closely analogous — and fingerprinting is routine — whereas the dissent argues that rolling an inked finger on paper and puncturing the skin are fundamentally different. Judge Nelson concludes that the majority has sacrificed a precious constitutional protection in the name of police efficiency and in so doing disregards basic precedents.[48]

AA, "12 Steps," and Religion. The New York Court of Appeals recently decided a case involving the religious foundations of Alcoholics Anonymous (AA), which may well have important implications for the sex offender treatment community. In *Griffin v. Coughlin*,[49] a 5 to 2 majority of this distinguished state court determined, first, that the dominant theme of AA as expressed in AA's basic writings is unequivocally religious in "manifesting faithful devotion to an acknowledged ultimate reality or deity." The court found it violates the Establishment Clause of the First Amendment to deprive an atheistic inmate of eligibility for a family visit program because of his refusal to participate in this religiously oriented, albeit apparently successful, program.[50]

The majority emphasizes the authenticity of the inmate's atheistic beliefs and the fact that there were no other substance abuse programs — that is, reasonable alternatives — available. What is very interesting is the fact that, like parole release and sex offender programs on the issue of self-incrimination, no inmate is forced to participate and no claim of a right to the program is recognized.

The court makes it plain that AA may continue in New York's prisons as long as it is voluntary and New York might also offer a secular alternative using the 12-step model.

To the extent that some sex offender programs use an approach similar to AA's, it is worthwhile to review the content in light of this opinion.

Conclusion

The material presented in this chapter is varied and complex. It certainly does not lend itself to a sharply defined conclusion. "Caution," indeed, may be a better term than "conclusion."

As sex offender programming becomes virtually mandatory for any correctional system and as it becomes the ticket to staying out, or getting out, of prison, numerous pressure points are created. As treatment providers insist on admissions as the ticket to getting in, and staying in, a program, other pressure points are created.

One overriding message here is to clearly distinguish federal constitutional rulings from state law rulings. When the United States Supreme Court announced a constitutional rule it is, of course, binding in all jurisdictions. Lower federal court rulings are authoritative within the scope of their territorial jurisdiction while state court rulings are similarly limited.

The Court of Appeals for the Seventh Circuit may persuade the Eleventh Circuit whereas the California Supreme Court may persuade the Montana Supreme Court. They may persuade but not bind.

The material in this chapter deals with some important federal constitutional concepts — self-incrimination, search and seizure, due process — and I hope the reader has learned enough to be sensitive to the issues and then obtain legal advice, when in doubt, from one familiar with local law.

The material on admissions, truth telling, and incrimination is confusing and not just to you. The courts have made ungainly decisions and left the practice arena clouded. The ground is surest when the required admission as part of treatment relates to the crime of conviction. The ground is less certain when new crimes are admitted under pressure and then used to seek a conviction.

The practitioner should seek truth but perhaps without detail as to names, places, and dates. If admission to sexual misconduct with enough detail to assure credibility is the goal, a practitioner can walk this line.

Admission and retention in a treatment program basically remain within the discretion of the authorities. Clearly, there is no constitutional mandate to have programs or treatment and when the programs exist, they exist with enormous discretion lodged in the providers.

What the law mandates and what may be fair or ethical may be two different things. Certainly there is a case for upfront clarity on confidentiality, on exactly what is expected in the treatment relationship, on ways to at least challenge decisions that may have a grave impact on obtaining or retaining one's freedom.

Footnotes

[1] Cohen, "Confidentiality, Privilege, and Self-Incrimination," in B. Schwartz & H. Cellini, *The Sex Offender: Corrections, Treatment and Legal Practice* Ch. 26 (1995) (hereafter *The Sex Offender*).

[2] The decisions are Mace v. Amstoy, 765 F. Supp. 847 (D. Vt. 1991); State v. Imlay, 813 P.2d 97 (Mont. 1991); *dismissed at* 113 S. Ct. 444 (1991); Asherman v. Meachum, 957 F.2d 978 (2d Cir. 1992) (en banc).

[3] See Solkoff, "Judicial Use Immunity Against Self-Incrimination in Court Mandated Therapy Programs," 17 *Nova L. Rev.* 1442, 1450-1457 (1993). Also, there are professional ethics at stake including termination of treatment when it seems unavailing. See American Psychological Association, *Ethical Principles of Psychologists* § 6(e) (1990).

[4] 871 P.2d 1127 (Wash. App. 1994).

[5] 101 S. Ct. 1866 (1981). We should note that Smith had no illusions that there was a treatment relationship. He did, however, have reason to believe that only competency, not death penalty eligibility, was involved.

[6] *Tinkham*, 871 P.2d at 1130.

[7] The court indicated that it was not holding that counsel had a right to be present during any such examination. Ibid. at 1131 n. 4.

[8] 399 U.S. 1 (1970).

[9] See Jones v. Cardwell, 686 F.2d 754 (9th Cir. 1982), to the same effect.

[10] State v. Barber, 494 N.W.2d 497 (Minn. App. 1993).

[11] Ibid. at 501.

[12] Because these examinations do not occur as an aspect of treatment, "doctor-patient" privileges or ordinary confidentiality is inapplicable.

On June 13, 1996, in Jaffee v. Redmond, 1996 WESTLAW 315841 (U.S.), the United States Supreme Court decided that Rule 501 of the Federal Rules of Evidence must be interpreted to include a psychotherapist privilege that extends to psychiatrists, psychologists, and certified social workers. This brings the federal courts into line with all 50 states and the District of Columbia, which all have some version of this privilege.

This was not a constitutional ruling and, of course, has direct effect only in the federal courts.

[13] State v. Eccles, 877 P.2d 799 (Ariz. 1994).

[14] Ibid. at 801.

[15] Ibid. at 802.

[16] 104 S. Ct. 1136 (1984).

[17] Ibid. at 1145-1146. That is, the inherent coercion of the police station and the inherent adversariness of the police were not present.

[18] Ibid. at 1147. There is always less concern about using these types of admissions for revocation as opposed to a new crime charge, as in *Murphy*.

[19] Ibid. at 1146.

[20] The dissenters in *Murphy* had no doubt that Murphy was threatened with a penalty if he had refused to answer the probation officer's questions. "The majority's interpretation is simply incredible. A reasonable layman would interpret the imperative, 'be truthful . . . in all matters,' as a command to answer honestly all questions presented." Ibid. at 1152-1153. Thus, a command to "answer or else" can hardly be viewed as free of coercion; as free of a threat of penalty.

[21] Morstad v. State, 518 N.W.2d 191 (N.D. 1994).

[22] Ibid. at 194.

[23] See, e.g., Brady v. United States, 397 U.S. 742 (1970).

[24] See e.g., State v. Myers, 544 N.W.2d 609 (Wis. App. 1996).

[25] See Fed. Rules of Crim. Pro., R. 11.

[26] 492 N.W.2d 539 (Minn. App. 1992).

[27] 461 U.S. 660 (1983).

[28] 996 F.2d 943 (8th Cir. 1993). Even more plainly, there is no enforceable right to the existence or continuity of sex offender treatment programs since there is no constitutional requirement to treat such offenders. See Riddle v. Mondragon, 1996 LEXIS 9911 (10th Cir., Apr. 29, 1996), rejecting such claims made by New Mexico inmates.

[29] 115 S. Ct. 2293 (1995).

[30] Ibid. at 2295.

[31] The author has read some 400 post-*Sandin* decisions as the basis for making the negative assertion in the text.

[32] 666 A.2d 972 (N.H. 1995).

[33] 99 S. Ct. 2100 (1979).

[34] I *believe* that *Sandin* overrules that aspect of *Greenholtz*, although I am not certain the Court realizes it yet.

[35] 813 P.2d 979 (1991), cert. granted and dismissed, 113 S. Ct. 444 (1992). *Imlay* is discussed in *The Sex Offender*, Ch. 26, pp. 26-9–26-11, and viewed there as incorrectly decided.

[36] 666 A.2d at 976.

[37] 915 P.2d 809 (Mont. 1996).

[38] Ibid.

[39] The lone dissenter takes the position that Fuller should have been aware of *Imlay*, which holds that

disclosure of uncharged sex crimes cannot serve as the basis for even revocation. Thus, there was no "Hobson's choice" and Fuller spoke voluntarily.

The majority found it ludicrous to insist on knowledge of *Imlay*.

See Berg, "Give Me Liberty or Give Me Silence: Taking a Stand on Fifth Amendment Implications for Court-Ordered Therapy Programs," 79 *Cornell L. Rev.* 700 (1994), which points out the inconsistency in the law of this area and argues for upholding a condition that requires admissions, at least outside the coercive atmosphere of the prison.

[40] 886 P.2d 1077 (Ore. App. 1995). The examination under discussion was, in effect, a pre-sentencing proceeding.

[41] Ibid. at 1082.

[42] 901 P.2d 1143 (Alaska App. 1995).

[43] Ibid. at 1148. Referring to *Murphy*, the court explicitly finds that because revocation of probation or parole is not criminal, the threat of revocation alone is not enough to allow invocation of the right to silence.

[44] See State v. Carrizales, 528 N.W.2d 29, 32 (Wis. App. 1995), to the same effect.

[45] Walrath v. Getty, 71 F.3d 679 (7th Cir. 1995).

[46] 59 F.3d 1556 (9th Cir. 1995).

[47] 441 U.S. 520 (1979).

[48] The Fourth Circuit, in Jones v. Murray, 962 F.2d 302 (4th Cir.) *cert. denied*, 113 S. Ct. 472 (1992), reached a result similar to that reached here by the majority. In addition, there are three lower federal court decisions and three state court (Illinois, Oregon, and Washington) decisions reaching similar results.

[49] No. 73 (N.Y. Ct. App., June 11, 1996).

[50] Two federal court decisions reach a similar result: Warner v. Orange County Department of Probation, 870 F. Supp. 69 (S.D.N.Y. 1994); O'Connor v. California, 855 F. Supp. 303 (D. Cal. 1994).

Chapter 24

Megan's Laws—Sex Offender Registration and Notification Statutes and Constitutional Challenges

by Elizabeth Rahmberg Walsh

Overview

The rape and murder of seven-year-old Megan Kanka, in July 1994, had a devastating effect on her family and friends. It was also pivotal to the development of federal and state laws regarding the collection and dissemination of information about sex offenders: who they are and where they are. Prior to Megan's death, only five states had sex offender registration laws as of 1985.[1] Since her death, and, clearly in response to it, *all* other states and the federal government have enacted their own versions of "Megan's Law," most enacted within just the last few years.[2] The Jacob Wetterling Crimes Against Children and Sexually Violent Registration Program,[3] the federal law, requires that states enact a registry for sex offenders or risk the loss of 10% of federal funding for local and state law enforcement.[4] No state is likely to suffer this loss of funds. On August 5, 1996, the Massachusetts Legislature, following closely on the heels of Vermont and Nebraska,[5] enacted its version of Megan's Law.[6] It was the last of the 50 states to do so.

A number of state legislatures have either explicitly or implicitly recognized that sex offenders present a high risk for repeating their offenses. In an effort to protect the community and assist law enforcement in conducting investigations and apprehending sex offenders, they have enacted laws requiring that offenders convicted of certain sex crimes register with a local law enforcement agency following conviction, release from a state facility, or when placed on probation. The premise appears to be that if law enforcement knows where the sex offenders may be found, the task of investigating sex offenses and apprehending perpetrators will be less complicated, and a sex offender may be less likely to commit an offense if he knows that his name appears on a list at the police department. Registration laws and community notification laws are touted as the "one-two punch" to sex offender recidivism in the community.

Community notification laws either allow or mandate a designated law enforcement agency, or an offender himself, to notify the public of the presence of the sex offender in their community. The method of notification can be designated by provisions in the statute or a set of adopted guidelines,[7] simply opening the registry for public inspection,[8] or by listing a toll-free number for the public to call and obtain information about a suspected offender in their neighborhood.[9] This, it is argued, will put members of the community on notice that there is a sex offender in their midst and they can take steps to protect themselves and their families. However, some researchers claim that the registration laws are ineffective at best, and that notifications laws may have the opposite-than-intended effect. Indeed, they are the subject of much criticism.[10]

Some of this criticism is that these laws promote a false sense of security because the system, although it does not guarantee security, may be perceived as offering such a guarantee.[11] In addition, there is no proof that the laws actually reduce recidivism.[12] In fact, some claim that rather than reducing recidivism and protecting the public, the law may actually be driving child molesters and other sexually motivated criminals to leave one community for another, less restrictive one[13] or to choose not to register at all.[14] Studies have shown that the compliance rate of sex offenders is very low and there is little funding provided for law enforcement to verify compliance, resulting in a database that is incomplete, inaccurate, and less than helpful.[15] Others have demonstrated that the threat of registration may inhibit offenders from seeking treatment, or that the effects of public harassment might keep the offender from resuming a normal life, either of which could increase an offender's chances of reoffending.[16]

In addition, the threat of community ostracism or vigilantism is not an idle one. There are numerous accounts of communities banding together to force a sex offender out of the community by threatening him, attacking him, or even burning down his home. Surely, this is not what any state legislature envisioned.[17] Moreover, offenders who might have pled guilty in the past now may wish to avoid the threat of registration and all that it entails and may be more willing to take their chances at trial.[18] Finally, there is the consideration of the cost and effort of collecting and maintaining a registry that may be less than effective.[19]

Some state statutes address the sexually violent predator (SVP), which in most states, is a distinctly different designation than that of a "simple" sex offender. SVPs may be encompassed within the same statutory section as sex offender registration, or by themselves in a distinctly separate provision. SVPs may be subject to a more restrictive requirement of registration, which allows for more widespread community notification than the simple sex offender.[20] In addition, some state statutes subject the SVP to civil commitment after serving the criminal sentence.[21] SVPs are discussed more fully in Chapters 22 and 23.

The individual characteristics of a registration or notification act must be analyzed separately because the laws affect the offender in such disparate ways as to raise different constitutional issues. It is important to know not only what the laws allow or require but also the effect that the provisions have on the offender. Nearly every provision in these statutes has been challenged by offenders subject to them.[22] Although legislatures, law enforcement agencies, and most members of the public believe Megan's Laws to be highly effective in accomplishing their purpose, a law's effectiveness and its constitutionality are very different concerns. Registration and notification laws have been challenged under the provisions of ex post facto, due process, Eighth Amendment cruel and unusual punishment, equal protection, Fourth Amendment search and seizure, and other arguments with varying degrees of success.[23] Most of the challenges to the registration statutes have not been upheld[24] because registering has been found not to be an onerous burden. However, when the offender was subjected to the registration statute erroneously, clearly in contravention of its terms, offender challenges have been successful.[25] Challenges to notification provisions have met with greater success because notification is perceived as a more onerous burden upon individual rights.[26]

This chapter details the various types of provisions in the 51 federal and state registration and community notification laws, reviews challenges that have been made thus far, and, finally, speculates where these laws will take us in the future.

Registration

Registration laws require the offender to provide certain information to law enforcement. Under the sex offender registration laws, offenders convicted or adjudicated[27] of a sex-related offense are required to report, within a certain time after their release, to a designated law enforcement agency and provide at least a name and current address. This information is then forwarded to the state agency charged with maintaining the central registry, and eventually, to the FBI, for inclusion in the nationwide sex offender registry. The formation of the nationwide registry was announced by President Clinton on August 24, 1996, during his weekly radio broadcast. Clinton said that the registry was meant to "keep track of these criminals [sex offenders] — not just in a single state, but wherever they go, wherever they move, so that parents and police have the warning they need to protect our children. . . . Deadly criminals don't stay within state lines, so neither should law enforcement's tools to stop them."[28]

A reading of the various state and federal registration statutes reveals that there are certain provisions common to many or most of the registration statutory schemes. All 50 state statutes and the federal law require, at the very least, that the sex offender register with a law enforcement agency.[29] Most require that the registering agency be the local police chief or county sheriff; some require that the offender register with their probation or parole officer, the state police, the state bureau of investigation, the department of correction, or the state board. Usually, the local law enforcement agency and a statewide agency, such as the state bureau of investigation or the state department of public safety, is charged with maintaining the central registry of sex offenders.[30]

The requirement is usually triggered by conviction of an offense specified by statute. In most cases the specific offenses triggering registration are listed,[31] but in some cases general terms are used, such as "if convicted of . . . any act of sexual perversion . . ."[32] or "any offenses in violation of this chapter."[33] In some states, only conviction of a crime when the victim is a child, or when the crime is a subsequent sex-related offense,[34] places the offender under the provisions of the Act.[35] In most states, attempts to commit the crime trigger the requirement, as does a conviction in any other jurisdiction, which, if committed within the respective state, would constitute a crime under the act.[36] In many states, the requirement to register is prompted by adjudication of delinquency or commitment to the state youth authority.[37]

Most statutes dictate that prior to release on parole or from a state mental health facility, the offender be registered or that the supervising facility notify him of the duty to register, in writing, and that the offender sign and return the notice.[38] If the offender is incarcerated, there is usually a specified period after release within which he must register with the designated law enforcement agency. If not incarcerated, he must register within the specified time after conviction or entering the jurisdiction. The periods range from "immediately" upon conviction or release from incarceration[39] to 48 hours from entering the county[40] to 30 days from the date of conviction or release, entering the county, or establishing residence,[41] to 60 days from entering into the jurisdiction if convicted in another state.[42] Most of the registration acts require that the convicted sex offender register again within so many days of a change of address,[43] and some unequivocally require the offender register annually, although many simply state that the offender is "subject to the registration requirement" for a period of so many years.[44]

The offender is asked to provide at least his name and address; in addition, some states require a date of birth, social security number, fingerprints, photograph, date of conviction, crime committed, place where convicted, place and address of employment, descriptive information about the offender, any aliases used, and the name under which convicted, and four jurisdictions require that the sex offender provide a blood sample.[45] In many states, there is a catch-all provision that requires the offender to provide "any information necessary."[46]

Some of the statutes do not say for what period the sex offender is subject to registration, but when a statute is silent, in most cases it can be presumed that the period is for life. Others specifically say that the offender must register for life or must register for 10, 15, or 20 years.[47] In 10 states, the offender must register for a set period but during this period may petition the court for relief from the requirement. In most cases in which the offender petitions for relief, if the court finds that the offender has not committed an offense since his release and the offender can demonstrate by clear and convincing evidence that he is no longer a threat, or that the purpose of the statute would not be served by continuing to register, or both, he will be relieved of the duty to register.[48]

Relief from having to register and clearing the registry of a record are two separate propositions. Eleven states have some mechanism for expungement of the record, but most will expunge the record only if the offender's conviction is reversed or set aside. The record is rarely erased on the completion of probation or parole except in one state, and one other expunges juvenile records only.[49]

In most instances the offender is entitled to notice of the duty to register, either by the court at sentencing or the department of corrections or other facility where he is incarcerated or by the parole or probation officer charged with supervising him. In several states, all persons are notified of the registration requirements when they apply for a driver's license.[50]

Every state except Alaska provides a penalty for knowing failure to register or knowingly providing false information, with offense categories ranging from a violation to a felony.[51] In addition, if the offender is on probation or parole, failure to register can be a basis for revocation.[52] Louisiana's statute is by far the most onerous on the sex offender, mandating that the offender provide notice not only to law enforcement but also to the superintendent of schools and to neighbors within a one-mile radius. He must also give notice, within 30 days, by mail, to all who reside within a designated area, and he must publish the information in the newspaper twice within the 30-day period (without cost to the state). It also allows the court to institute other forms of notice, within its discretion, "including but not limited to signs, handbills, bumper stickers, or clothing labeled to that effect."[53] In Iowa, the sex offender is assessed a $10 registration fee, which may be waived if he is indigent, and, in addition to any criminal penalty, a $200 civil penalty, payable in the same manner as a fine, is also levied against him at the time of the conviction.[54]

Finally, a few states impose a penalty for misuse of the information contained in the registry or used to commit a criminal act, such as harassment of the offender.[55] However, many statutes provide that the law enforcement officer or the agency that releases the information or fails to release the information is immune from civil liability unless he is grossly negligent or acts in bad faith.[56]

Community Notification

Community notification statutes provide that the information collected for the central registry may be disseminated in a prescribed manner to a designated person or agency. These provisions are as varied among the 50 states and the federal government as are the registration statutes. Some states have merged the registration and notification provisions within one section, while others have dedicated a separate statutory provision to notification.

The notification provisions are intended to provide members of the community with sufficient knowledge of the sexual offender's presence in their community to take steps to protect themselves and their children from harm. However, as discussed earlier, there are concerns that the laws allowing or requiring community notification not only do not achieve their purpose but may actually exacerbate the problem. Other questions asked are: Do these provision work? If they do, at what cost to individual rights?

Not all states provide for community notification but dictate instead that all information collected for the sexual offender registry is confidential or is restricted for law enforcement or other state agencies' use only.[57] Many states allow dissemination of the information to the public only if it is deemed necessary for public safety by the law enforcement agency,[58] or to specific individuals, such as victims or those the offender "may encounter."[59] A few states provide a toll-free number that individuals may call to obtain information about specific offenders,[60] while others simply direct that the information be "made available to the public."[61] A few states require the law enforcement agency to notify the public directly,[62] and others require offenders personally to notify the public of their presence in the neighborhood.[63] Many states allow notification to agencies and organizations that deal with children, such as schools, child-care agencies, and other entities that provide children's services.[64] Several states provide notification on the request of a member of the community,[65] or in accordance with state guidelines.[66] One state does not mention community notification at all.[67] These distinctions, however, seem superseded by the 1996 amendment to the Violent Crime Control Bill, which provides that the law enforcement agency "shall release relevant information that is necessary to protect the public concerning a specific person required to register under [the sex offender registration] section, except that the identity of the victim of an offense that requires registration under this section shall not be released."[68]

The New Jersey Supreme Court has given its imprimatur to the three-tier-level notification, with judicial review.[69] The procedure under such a scheme is for the designated board or person, such as a prosecutor, to determine the level of risk for reoffending pursuant to established guidelines. The offender is then notified of the probable assigned risk level. If he has been assigned level II or III, he may file a petition to challenge the risk designation. He has a right to appear and be heard, and in most cases the statute specifies that, at this hearing, the rules of evidence do not apply. In addition, the guidelines will specify, or the court will determine, what evidence it may consider at the hearing. The offender is entitled to appointed counsel if he cannot afford counsel.

The court, however, will only modify the risk designation if the decision is arbitrary or capricious, an abuse of discretion, or not in accordance with the law.[70] The designation of the level of risk is critical, because the level of risk determines the level and manner of notification to the community. For example, in Massachusetts, a level II risk designation, for moderate risk offenders, allows the board to release the name; address; work address; offense and date of conviction; descriptive information such as weight, height, and so on; and a photograph of the offender. This information may be sent to police departments in those areas in which the offender intends to live or work, which then transmits it to organizations in the community that are likely to encounter the offender, such as schools, day-care centers, religious or youth organizations, and sports leagues.[71] A level III designation, for high-risk offenders, allows the police to disseminate the information more broadly, to organizations and individual members of the public who are likely to encounter the individual.[72]

What are the results of notification? Some, such as vigilantism, are unintended and raise a genuine concern.[73] Reports from various communities say that once the neighborhood was notified of the sex offender's return to the neighborhood, the community sought to deter the sex offender from returning. For example, when a community was notified that a sex offender was to return to their neighborhood in Washington State, his future "neighbors" burned down his home.[74] In addition, in New Jersey, a father and son team broke into the home and beat a man whom they mistakenly believed was a sex offender.[75] Also in New Jersey, the Guardian Angels took it upon themselves to notify the community of the presence of a sex offender, forcing the offender to flee the area.[76] In one case in California, the community protested to the release of a notorious sex offender so vehemently that the state was forced to parole him to an outlying area; in a second case, the police were forced to provide protection to an offender as he moved his belongings out of his apartment.[77]

Notification is no doubt a more onerous provision than registration alone. Notification may intrude on an individual's federally protected rights (e.g., privacy) and may actually constitute additional punishment. For these reasons, such laws have been challenged more frequently and more successfully than the registration provisions.

Challenges to Registration and Notification

Registration and community notification provisions for convicted sex offenders have generated a fairly large body of case law within the last few years. The most common challenges are based on ex post facto, bill of attainder, double jeopardy, Eighth Amendment cruel and unusual punishment, invasion of privacy, due process, equal protection, Fourth Amendment search and seizure, and void-for-vagueness arguments. Other challenges have been brought on grounds that the state failed to notify the offender of his duty to register, that the offense for which he was convicted was not one that should have triggered registration under the statute (e.g., a juvenile offense), that the offender did not knowingly violate the registration law, that failure to register was not a continuing offense, that the tier risk level assigned was improper, and lack of jurisdiction.[78]

Punishment-Related Challenges. Ex Post Facto, Bill of Attainder, Double Jeopardy, and Cruel and Unusual Punishment are bases for challenges to registration and notification laws that I discuss together because success under each is based on a single determination: whether the imposition of the requirement to register or notification of the community constitutes "punishment." Courts generally have held that if a particular sanction constitutes punishment for one of these claims, it is punishment for them all, at least in the sex offender registration and community notification context.

Where does punishment fit within the contours of ex post facto, bill of attainder, double jeopardy, and the Eighth Amendment? The Ex Post Facto Clause prohibits the government from applying a law retroactively that "inflicts a greater punishment than the law annexed to the crime when committed."[79] The Bill of Attainder Clause forbids legislatures from engaging in "[l]egislative acts, no matter what their form, that apply either to named individuals or to easily ascertainable members of a group in such a way as to inflict punishment on them without judicial trial."[80] The Double Jeopardy Clause bans, among other things, "a second prosecution for the same offense after conviction...and multiple punishments for the same offense."[81] Finally, the Eighth Amendment prohibits the infliction of cruel and unusual punishments, which include sentences that are disproportionate to the crime committed.[82]

Ex Post Facto.[83] The foundational cases in this area are *Calder v. Bull*[84] and *Collins v. Youngblood.*[85] *Calder* identified the legislative acts that raise ex post facto concerns:

> 1st. Every law that makes an action done before the passing of the law, and which was innocent when done, criminal; and punishes such action. 2d. Every law that aggravates a crime, or makes it greater than it was, when committed. *3d. Every law that changes the punishment, and inflicts a greater punishment, than the law annexed to the crime, when committed.* 4th. Every law that alters the legal rules of evidence, and receives less, or different, testimony, than the law required at the commission of the offense, in order to convict the offender.[86]

Some 200 years later, *Collins* confirmed the holding in *Calder*, limiting the ex post facto law to "any statute which punishes as a crime an act previously committed, which was innocent when done; *which makes more burdensome the punishment for a crime, after its commission*, or which deprives one charged with a crime of any defense available according to law at the time when the act was committed."[87]

The purposes served by the clause are twofold: (1) to ensure that legislative acts give fair warning of their effect and allow individuals to rely on the holding until it is explicitly changed; and (2) to prevent legislatures from imposing legislation that is arbitrary or vindictive.[88] The third part of the *Calder* rule is relevant to sex offender registration and notification laws, as it prohibits the legislature from enacting a statute that retroactively increases the punishment for a crime. When a legislature increases punishment beyond that which was prescribed when the crime was consummated, the penal provision must be both retrospective and more onerous than the law was when the offender committed the criminal act to violate the ex post facto provisions.[89] Naturally, not all statutory changes that work some hardship on individuals will violate the clause.[90]

To determine whether a particular statute violates the Ex Post Facto Clause (and, therefore, other punishment-related provisions), the courts have drawn a distinction between laws that are "criminal and punitive, or civil and remedial."[91] If the statute is not penal, there is no ex post facto violation.[92] The threshold question is then, whether the statute is penal.

A statute's punitiveness can be determined in a number of ways, using myriad definitions. The Massachusetts Supreme Judicial Court[93] stated that to determine a statute's punitiveness, some courts have made the remedial/punitive distinction based on statutory purpose alone,[94] some have looked at the effect,[95] and some have looked at "the congruency of a law's regulatory goals to its punitive effect."[96] The United States Supreme Court has said that whether a statute is penal is not based solely on what the legislative intended but, rather, on whether the "questioned statute's design and effect evidence a purpose to regulate rather than to punish."[97] *United States v. Halper*[98] and *Austin v. United States*,[99] two other Supreme Court cases, found a civil sanction to be punitive if it could not "fairly be said solely to serve a remedial purpose."[100] These two cases were distinctly repudiated by the Court in *United States v. Ursery*,[101] where the Court concluded that when a legislature intends a statute to be remedial, it is penal only if "the statutory scheme is so punitive either in purpose or effect as to negate [its] intention to establish a civil remedial mechanism."[102] In other words, once the court finds that the intent is remedial, it must also consider whether the effect of the statute is so onerous as to overcome the nonpunitive intent.[103]

To determine legislative intent courts have looked first at the expressed language of the statute.[104] If the act does not include a statement of purpose[105] or if the purpose is unclear, courts turn next to the legislative history to ascertain the purpose. If the purpose of the statute is determined to be punitive, the examination ends there and if enacted retroactively, it would constitute an ex post facto violation. If at this point the statutory purpose is deemed remedial, the analysis may, but does not necessarily, end there.

In some cases, the courts have looked for legislative intent, performed a cursory review of the effect of the registration or community notification statute, and determined that the statute was remedial.[106] Other courts have found it necessary to conduct a more thorough examination of the "punitiveness" of the effect.

Numerous courts have utilized the *Mendoza-Martinez*[107] test to determine whether their state's sex offender registration/notification statute raised ex post facto concerns.[108] It lists seven factors to determine whether, in a given situation, the "full panoply of due process rights accorded in criminal procedures is required." However, the court provided no guidance as to how each factor should be weighed or prioritized, so the test is fairly difficult to apply with any degree of precision.[109]

In 1995, the New Jersey Supreme Court reviewed Megan's Law and found that, as it pertained to both registration and notification, it was not punishment and therefore did not violate ex post facto. It did, however, require judicial review of the prosecutor's designation of risk. It found that the intent of the statute was remedial, the provisions were aimed solely at achieving its purpose, and any deterrent effect it may have was simply a "by-product" of the remedial purpose.[110]

The Court of Appeals for the Third Circuit, in *Artway v. Attorney General of New Jersey*,[111] conducted an extremely thorough examination in determining whether New Jersey's sex offender registration and community notification statute withstood constitutional challenges before it reversed the district court's decision, which had found the law remedial and not violative of ex post facto. Before reaching its decision in *Artway*, the court considered numerous tests for punitiveness: the subjective purpose,[112] the objective purpose through proportionality,[113] history,[114] and deterrence,[115] the effect,[116] and the nature of the proceedings.[117] It then "synthesized" elements from these cases to come up with its own framework for analysis of the registration/notification statute. The court developed a three-prong analysis that looked at the actual purpose, the objective purpose, and the effect of the statute. The second part, the objective purpose, has three subparts: whether the law can be explained solely by a remedial purpose; whether it has been traditionally been regarded as punishment over time; and whether the legislature intended it to serve a mixture of deterrent and salutary purposes. The third subpart also has two subparts: whether the deterrent purpose is necessary to complement its salutary purpose and whether the measure operates in its "usual" manner. The third part, the effect, looks at the repercussions, which, if great enough, are considered punishment regardless of the legislature's intent.[118]

Using this analysis, *Artway* determined that, with regard to the registration portion of Megan's Law and the notification provision under tier I, the actual purpose, based on the legislative findings, was to promote public safety and assist law enforcement, and the intent was clearly not to punish. The court also found that it was remedial under the objective test in that, historically, it was regulatory; it had a salutary purpose; and although it may have some incidental deterrent effect, that effect was not sufficient to raise it to the level of punitiveness. Finally, the court found that the "sting" of registration is nonexistent. *Artway* refused to decide whether the notification part of the statute constituted punishment, stating that the plaintiff's claims were not ready for judicial review. However, it did suggest that if the issues had been reviewable,[119] notification would fail under the second and third prongs of the test.[120]

In an interesting twist, in July 1996, a New Jersey district court decided *W.P. v. Poritz*[121] and held that in light of *Ursery*,[122] *Artway* was no longer valid law. In support, the court in *W.P.* stated that *Artway* had found that the issues were unready for judicial review; it had itself recognized the limitations of its decision; and *Ursery* had destroyed the basis for the decision in *Artway*, its synthesized "universal rule of punishment." It argued that *Artway*'s precedential value should be limited only to those cases closely resembling its facts, issues, and constitutional provisions.[123] Then it granted the motion for summary judgment of the defendant, New Jersey Attorney General Poritz, and found that the registration and notifications were not punishment and were therefore not violative of the ex post facto law.

Several cases looked first to the legislative intent and found either that it was not discernible or that it was remedial. They next turned to the effects of the statute to determine whether the effects were so onerous as to overcome the remedial intent. A federal district court in New York considered the retroactive application of a similar registration/notification provision and found that retroactive application of the notification provision was a violation of the ex post facto law, as it constituted punishment. The court used a *Mendoza-Martinez*-like test and found that although the intent was remedial, the effects were onerous enough to convert it to a punitive statute. Thus, retroactive application of the statute was violative of ex post facto.[124]

Bill of Attainder. This issue was dealt with in summary fashion by the courts. If the registration and/or notification section did not constitute punishment for ex post fact purposes, the court that considered this issue ruled that it could not then inflict punishment on an individual or specific group for bill of attainder purposes.[125]

Double Jeopardy. The Double Jeopardy Clause prohibits governments from punishing citizens a second time for the same offense. Courts that have considered whether the registration and/or notification segment of the law violates double jeopardy concerns have decided that because it does not impose punishment under the Ex Post Facto Clause, it therefore is not punishment for purposes of double jeopardy. If it is not punishment at all, it cannot be considered to inflict "multiple punishments."[126]

Eighth Amendment Cruel and Unusual Punishment. As stated earlier, the Eighth Amendment prohibits, among other things, punishment that is disproportionate to the offense committed. The cases that have addressed cruel and unusual punishment issues have considered two factors: (1) whether the sanction is punishment at all (if it is not punishment, it cannot be cruel and unusual punishment),[127] but (2) if it is punishment, whether the punishment is disproportionate to the crime.[128]

This analysis deals with whether the statute, as applied to the particular offender, is disproportionate to the offense he has committed. *State v. Douglas*[129] relied on the three-prong test[130] in conducting a proportionality analysis: (1) the gravity of the offense and the harshness of the penalty, (2) the sentences imposed on other criminals in the same jurisdiction, and (3) the sentences imposed for commission of the same crime in other jurisdictions. Douglas was convicted of failing to register as a habitual sex offender and ordered to register under the sex offender registration act. The court found that although he had been convicted of a misdemeanor, it was a second offense and registration was required only of those offenders with at least two convictions for sex offenses. It also found that registration was a "modest burden upon a twice-convicted defendant." Further, the court found that although such a requirement was not required for more serious crimes, the legislature may have been understandably concerned about recidivism of sex offenders. Finally, it found that although California was the only other state that allowed imposition of the registration requirement for a misdemeanor conviction, the Eighth Amendment was not violated every time a state reached a different conclusion than all other states. It held that the order to register as a sex offender for someone twice convicted of sex offenses did not violate the Eighth Amendment.[131]

There is an entire body of cases from California, all of which seem to follow the same line of reasoning.[132] These cases rely on the holding in *In re Lynch*,[133] which applied a three-part test, similar, but with some differences, to the *Solem*[134] test to determine proportionality:

> (1) an examination of the nature of the offense and/or the offender, *with particular regard to the degree of danger both present to society*; (2) a comparison of the challenged penalty with those imposed in the same jurisdiction *for more serious crimes*; and (3) a comparison of the challenged penalty with those imposed for the same offense in different jurisdictions.[135]

Two California cases, using this analysis, have found that the imposition of the penalty of registering under the sex offender act based on a misdemeanor conviction was cruel and unusual punishment.[136] *Reed* not only utilized the *Lynch* test but also considered the seven-factor *Mendoza-Martinez* test to determine that the imposition of the registration requirement for the offense of disorderly conduct was disproportionate. The court held that "insofar as section 290 [the registration statute] requires conviction of such persons convicted under section 647(a), it is void under article I, section 17 of the California Constitution."[137] *King* followed *Reed* and found that imposition of the requirement to register for a conviction of misdemeanor indecent exposure, or any crime under section 314.1 was disproportionate and therefore violative of the Eighth Amendment.[138]

The remainder of the California cases have found that, regardless of the holdings in *Reed* and *King*, imposition of registration pursuant to the registration statute for misdemeanor convictions was not disproportionate to the offense. The courts have found that *Reed* and *King* did not prohibit registration for all offenses under the respective statutory provisions, but the courts must look at the particular facts and circumstances of the offense, the record of the offender, and the danger to the community under the first prong in *Lynch*. When employing that analysis, courts have found that regardless of the fact that these crimes are misdemeanors, they are serious offenses and represent a danger to the community, a danger which registration may remedy.[139]

Nonpunishment Challenges. The remining challenges have looked at the nature of the individual interest involved, the intrusiveness of the state's action, the knowledge of the offender, or the jurisdiction over the offender.

Fourteenth Amendment Procedural Due Process. Cases that have considered whether registration or notification under the state version of Megan's Law triggers procedural due process have utilized a traditional due process analysis. First, is the right affected a state or federally recognized right to life, liberty, or the pursuit of happiness? If yes, the second question is, How much process is due? The *Matthews v. Eldridge*[140] test resolved this question by saying that "the process due in a particular case is a function of the severity of the deprivation."[141] *Matthews* required that the hearing must consider four factors: (1) the importance of the private interest; (2) the length or finality of the deprivation; (3) the risk of government error; and (4) the magnitude of the government interest involved.[142] A procedural due process challenge requires the court to review the degree of punishment imposed on the offender and the level of process due in light of the degree of punishment. If a protected right is affected, the minimum process due is notice and an opportunity to be heard.[143]

Most of the cases in which Megan's Laws and the allotted procedural process have been challenged, or at least questioned, come from states where the registration statute establishes a "tiered" risk level for notification, states such as New Jersey, New York, Oregon, Nevada, Minnesota, and Massachusetts.[144] The protected right in these cases is the right to privacy or reputation, or "stigma plus" (reputation damage plus either the right to privacy or the loss of employment), affected when the community is notified of the offender's presence.[145] With the exception of *Artway*,[146] all have held that the enactment of guidelines, a hearing, judicial review of the prosecutor's or parole board's decision as to the level of risk, the fact that the rules of evidence do not apply, and appointment of counsel if indigent meet due process requirements in tier-level cases.[147]

The Oregon Supreme Court, however, decided a case that did not involve a tiered-risk-level challenge. The court decided that due process did not compel a hearing for a convicted sex offender who was required to submit a sample of blood: "Because the only criterion under [the registration chapter] for extracting blood is a conviction for a predicate offense, there would be little of substance to contest at the hearing."[148] The court held that whether the offender had or had not committed the predicate offense had already been decided at the trial, so there was nothing to determine at a hearing.

Procedural Due Process — The Tier-Level Challenges. Challenges to the assignment of risk level or the extent of notification by the prosecutor or parole board to the community have been based on a variety of claims: conduct without conviction used in the assessment of risk[149]; geographical scope of notification[150]; failure to appear at the hearing to make a determination of risk[151]; lack of clarity in the letter of notice to offender failed, it was urged, to provide notice[152]; the court's departure from the guidelines in assessing a risk 2 level when the calculation suggested a risk 1 level[153]; and a determination by the Board of Parole and Post-Prison Supervision the offender was a predatory sex offender and basing such determination on the finding that the offender was a high risk level, using the Department of Corrections sex offender assessment.[154] All the cases were decided using due process analysis, with nearly all the decisions going against the offender.

The New Jersey law[155] has been used as a prototype for tier-risk-level assessment. It requires that the offender be granted a hearing prior to any notification on a tier II or tier III level of risk. At the hearing, the rules of evidence do not apply, the court may rely on documentary evidence for all issues, and the offender is entitled to an attorney if he is indigent. The prosecutor must make a prima facie case for the level of risk and the extent of notification. Once the prima facie case is established, the offender has the burden of production of evidence.[156] If there is an issue of material fact, the court must have a fact-finding hearing and permit live testimony. The state may rely on admissible hearsay unless the offender contests such hearsay, and then the state may have to provide live testimony. Neither side, however, can compel the testimony of the victim without leave of the court.[157]

The New Jersey Attorney General has developed guidelines for the determination of the risk of reoffense and the appropriate tier level of notification. All offenders subject to registration and notification under Megan's Law are rated by the local prosecutor using the guidelines and the Registrant Risk Assessment Scale (RRAS), which was developed by the Attorney General's office after consultation with a committee composed of mental health and law enforcement experts. The RRAS identified 13 factors, which taken together ascertain the projected seriousness of the offense if the offender should recidivate and the likelihood that the offender will recidivate. The Attorney General also determined that historical factors, such as the seriousness of the offense and offense history, are more powerful predictors of recidivism than such other factors as offender characteristics and thus must be a part of the determination of risk.

In *In re Registrant C.A.*,[158] the court determined that the contested hearing provided the requisite level of due process in accordance with the *Matthews v. Eldridge* test.[159] It held that a nonconviction offense[160] was part of the statutory factors of "criminal history" and "other criminal history,"[161] which could be considered by the parole board. The court held that regardless of the statutory source of authority, powers were delegated to the Attorney General to identify factors relevant to risk of reoffense, and that such delegation was proper.[162] It also held that the state could prove the offense solely by reliable documentary hearsay evidence. However, in this case, the court ruled that genuine issues of material fact existed regarding the nonconvicted offense—whether appellant used a knife and whether the sex that took place was consensual—and the court remanded the case for rehearing and ordered that appellant be allowed to present evidence. At the rehearing, if appellant is able to show by a preponderance of the evidence that he did not commit the crime or that he did not possess a knife, the court stated that the parole board must recalculate its original RRAS designation.[163]

The *C.A.* court, on its own motion, requested that the parties and amici address the validity of the RRAS. The briefs raised two categories of issues: whether the quality and nature of the reoffense was an appropriate consideration of risk of reoffense and whether the authors of the RRSA assigned the proper weight to each of the four basic categories: seriousness of offense, offense history, characteristics of the offender, and community support. The court held:

> [The RRSA was] a reliable and useful tool that the State can use to establish its prima facie case concerning a registrant's tier classification and manner of notification. The procedures provided in a civil hearing concerning a registrant's tier classification and manner of notification together with the requirement for judicial review of those decisions adequately protect the registrant's right to procedural due process and to fundamental fairness.[164]

Fourth Amendment Substantive Due Process. Black's Law Dictionary broadly defines substance due process "as the constitutional guarantee that no person shall be arbitrarily deprived of his life, liberty or property; the essence of substantive due process is protection from arbitrary and unreasonable action."[165]

There is very little sex offender registration and/or notification case law in this area, but two cases are of interest. *Snyder v. State*[166] and *People v. Adams*[167] have decided that if there is a liberty interest involved — another way of describing substantive due process — the registration act is a "reasonable and appropriate means for achieving the state's legitimate purpose—assistance to law enforcement to protect its citizenry."[168]

Equal Protection. The Equal Protection Clause provides that no state shall "deny to any person within its jurisdiction the equal protection of the laws."[169] This does not mean, however, that "all persons must be treated alike, but, rather, that those similarly situated should be treated alike."[170] The court will look more closely at a designated class, depending on the reason for the designation. Unless the designation of a class is arbitrary,"[171] or affects a "suspect" class, such as a class designated on the basis of its race, or affects a fundamental right, such as liberty, the court will look to see whether the classification bears a rational relation to the state's purpose. If the classification or distinction is rationally related to the proper or legitimate governmental purpose, it will be upheld.[172]

In cases regarding registration and notification, courts confronted with an equal protection violation have invariably found no violation. They have held that first, sex offenders are not a suspect class, and second, no fundamental right is affected by registration or notification. Therefore, the rational basis test is applied. The state's interest in protecting its citizens is legitimate, and the requirement to register and notify the community of the registrant's whereabouts is rationally related to that purpose. There is no violation of the Equal Protection Clause.[173]

Right to Privacy/Travel. "Grounded in the Fourteenth Amendment's concept of personal liberty, the right of privacy safeguards at least two different kinds of interests: the individual interests in avoiding disclosure of personal matters, and the interest in independence in making certain kinds of important decisions."[174] In general, courts confronted with a right to privacy[175] claim in a challenge to registration or notification requirements for sex offenders have held that there is no protected privacy right to information that is a matter of public record, within the public domain, or exposed to the public, because there is no *reasonable* expectation of privacy.[176] One court found that the right to privacy was not absolute, but was "qualified by the rights of others."[177] In addition, courts have held that regardless, in sex offender cases, the interest of the government, either in public safety or in assisting law enforcement efforts, outweighs the private interest, or that the offender has waived the right by committing his crime.[178]

In the few cases in which the issue of a violation of the right to travel has been raised, courts also have been as unwilling to find that registration and/or notification statutes violate the right to travel. The Massachusetts Supreme Judicial Court found that a sex offender's right to travel actually may be impaired because it may be difficult for him to find employment and housing and he may be humiliated by notification to his new neighbors that he is a sex offender. However, the inhibition to travel comes not from government actions but from actions of individuals, and because there is no government action involved, there is no violation. The guidelines in Massachusetts have not as yet been drafted, but the court found that they most likely will be drafted carefully to correlate the danger presented by the sex offender with the plan of notification. Any potential harm to the right to travel can be cured by such correlation.[179]

Void for Vagueness. "Due process requires only that a penal statute give persons of 'common intelligence' fair notice about 'what the State commands or forbids.'"[180] In

Artway v. Attorney General of New Jersey,[181] the court denied the offender's challenge to the registration requirement on a void for vagueness claim. The offender stated that the language of the statute did not specify the predicate crimes which would subject him to the requirement. The statute subjected anyone convicted of a sex offense to registration. It stated that an offender must register if convicted and that a conviction included "a sentence on the basis of criteria similar to the criteria set forth in paragraph (1) . . . entered or imposed under the laws of the United States, this state or another state," and a finding by the court that his conduct was "characterized by a pattern of repetitive and compulsive behavior."[182] The court found that Artway knew the crime for which he had been convicted, and that he also knew he had been convicted under the prior sex offender law which specifically required a finding of violent and repetitive and compulsive behavior. At sentencing the judge made specific findings that Artway had engaged in repetitive and compulsive behavior — there was simply no valid void-for-vagueness claim.[183]

In *State v. Zichko*,[184] the offender challenged the requirement to register using a void-for-vagueness argument, claiming that the terms "resides" and "temporarily domiciled" were not defined. The court applied a three-part test[185]: the court looked to see whether the regulated conduct was constitutionally protected, whether a significant amount of the protected conduct was precluded, and whether the law gave "notice to those who are subject to the law of its requirements or limitations and sets forth guidelines for those who must enforce the law so they may distinguish between what is prohibited and what is allowed."[186]

The court found that the regulated conduct was not constitutionally protected; it did not preclude a significant amount of constitutionally conduct, and the statute gave notice to those subject to it and law enforcement who must enforce it; enough information was given to distinguish between what was lawful and what was not. The terms in question, when read with the remainder of the statute, were not found to be ambiguous and provided persons of ordinary intelligence sufficient information to understand what the state forbade or required of them.[187]

State v. Lammie[188] also involved a void-for-vagueness challenge on the basis that the statute was unclear that a conviction for an "attempt" would trigger the registration requirement. The court held that it was uncontroverted "in case law and statutory law" that an attempt to commit an offense was a "lesser-included offense within the completed offense, be it a sexual offense or otherwise."[189] Thus, any specific offense inherently — and clearly — includes an attempt. In addition, the court held that a case factually similar to the case at bar[190] had been published previous to Lammie committing his crimes, and that the previous holding there had provided adequate notice to Lammie, foiling his argument for vagueness.[191]

Fourth Amendment. The Fourth Amendment guarantees "people the right to be secure in their homes and property against unreasonable searches and seizures and providing that no warrants shall issue except upon probable cause and then only as to specific places to be searched and persons and things to be seized."[192] A Fourth Amendment challenge has arisen in the context of Megan's Laws where the statute required that a blood sample be drawn from the offender for inclusion in a DNA databank. The databank was then maintained to identify offenders in future cases of sexual assault, because DNA is perhaps the most precise form of identification currently available.

As the court in *Rise v. Oregon*[193] pointed out, the nonconsensual extraction of blood, without benefit of a warrant or probable cause, affected Fourth Amendment privacy rights because it was a physical intrusion into the skin and impinged on a reasonable expectation of privacy.[194] However, the court also pronounced that whether a privacy right was involved was only the beginning of the inquiry, because the Fourth Amendment does not proscribe all searches and seizures, but only those that are unreasonable. The court then looked to the purpose of the statute and found that the extraction of blood would be constitutional if its objective was law enforcement, and as long as the intrusion was minimal. Next, there was an inquiry into the interest in privacy and bodily integrity retained by a person convicted of a sex-related felony and found that the "gathering of genetic information for identification purposes from a convicted murderer's or sexual offender's blood once the blood has been drawn does not constitute more than a minimal intrusion upon the plaintiff's Fourth Amendment interests."[195]

The opinion went on to compare the drawing of blood with the taking of fingerprints from "free persons." Taking fingerprints from free persons would require probable cause or articulable suspicion that the person was involved in a crime. However, all persons when arrested are subject to an identification procedure of which fingerprinting is an integral part. A line was drawn between requiring persons convicted of murder or a sexual offense to supply a blood sample and one who has not been similarly convicted. Once convicted, the court held, there was no "legitimate expectation of privacy in the identifying information derived from the blood sampling."[196] The gravity of the public interest served by the creation of the databank was balanced with the severity of the interference into the private interest, and it was determined that the drawing of the blood was regulated, the use of the information was limited to law enforcement purposes, and the imposition of the blood sampling was not arbitrary (prison officials did not retain discretion as to who should provide a sample). The requirement to provide the sample, therefore, was reasonable and not violative of the Fourth Amendment.[197]

Other courts, although not conducting such an extensive analysis, have found that similar provisions that require an inmate convicted of a sexual offense to furnish a blood sample for purposes of establishing a genetic databank for use by the state police do not violate the Fourth Amendment. An "incarcerated felon possesses no privacy right in his identity that would require an individual finding of suspicion before blood could be drawn. In addition, such a search was reasonable, being only negligibly greater than taking a fingerprint, while the government interest in the identification obtained from the test was high, in that DNA cannot be altered or hidden."[198]

In *Rowe v. Burton*,[199] the offender challenged the taking of photographs and fingerprints as a Fourth Amendment violation. The court, relying on the landmark decision in *Katz v. United States*,[200] stated that "the Fourth Amendment does not protect what a person knowingly exposes to the public" and held that nontestimonial evidence such as photographs and fingerprints were not subject to Fourth Amendment protection.[201]

Administrative Procedure Act.[202] Only one case thus far has raised the Administrative Procedure Act (APA) as part of its defense to the registration or notification requirement, and the court quickly dispatched this argument. In *Doe v. Poritz*,[203] the New Jersey

Supreme Court held that the APA was not applicable in a challenge to the registration/notification of sex offenders, as the guidelines established by the Attorney General were not administrative rules which must conform to the requirements of the APA.[204]

Notice to Offender.[205] Several cases have been brought by offenders who either challenged the basis for their arrest for failing to register or simply challenged the manner in which they were notified of their duty to register. With few exceptions, courts have found that a court has *no duty* to inform the offender of his duty to register prior to taking a plea or to certify the offender as a sex offender at the time of sentencing. The requirement to register as a sex offender is not the imposition of punishment but is, rather, simply a statutory,[206] administrative,[207] or "collateral consequence" of the conviction for a sex-related crime, and not a direct consequence or a part of the sentence.[208] *State v. Skroch*,[209] however, held that there was no requirement to inform the defendant until the sentencing hearing that his plea would trigger the registration requirement.

A few of these cases have held that failure of the court to notify neither violates due process nor negates the plea agreement. The requirement to register was statutorily mandatory, it was not negotiable, and was therefore not a permissible subject for a plea bargain.[210] In addition, for success on these claims, an offender must show that, had he been notified of the duty to register as a sex offender, he would have acted differently at the plea hearing.[211]

Two California cases have held that the offender *must* be notified by the court of his duty to register prior to taking a plea. *In re Birch*[212] and *People v. Buford*[213] both held that the court must advise the offender of his duty to register prior to taking a plea. Notice to the offender was mandatory, as the statute required not only that the court notify the offender of his duty to register but that the offender sign and return to the court a written form stating that he had been so notified. According to these opinions, an offender in California cannot be charged with failure to register if he is not given proper notice that he has to do so, and there is no form in his file demonstrating that he has been so informed.[214]

Triggering Offense. In all statutes, there is a list of offenses or some recitation of the offenses that will subject the offender to registration.[215] "Triggering" offense challenges to registration primarily have claimed that the statute did not encompass the offense for which they were convicted, or that the statute was ambiguous.[216]

If the registration statute listed a specific offense, such as the "attempt" to commit a sexual offense, and the offender was convicted of such an offense, he must register.[217] Where the statute required that the juvenile offender be committed to the youth authority to be subject to registration and the juvenile was not committed, the court's order to register as a sex offender was stricken.[218] Similarly, when the jury specifically found the defendant not guilty of the predicate offense requiring registration, a sex offense, but found him guilty of a lesser-included offense, simple battery, the offender was not required to register under the statute.[219]

Sometimes the wording of the statute has been less than clear. If possible, the court may look to the legislative intent to determine whether the registration act was properly applied to the offender. For example, in *People v. Doyle*, the offender claimed that he should not have been subjected to registration because the statute required a "second or subsequent conviction," but excluded from coverage those convictions "which result from or are connected with the same act."[220] The court held that because the defendant had committed two separate offenses against two different victims, at different times, he was properly brought under the habitual offender statute, and subject to registration. The court found that the legislature clearly intended that after a second conviction, the offender would have to register, and chose not to exclude from the statute convictions simultaneously entered.[221]

Sometimes the statute is ambiguous and the court must determine whether the duty to register can be upheld. In *People v. Saunders*,[222] the court found that the statute had been inadvertently amended, omitting from the list of offenses one offense which had previously triggered registration, and of which Saunders was convicted. The court held that legislative intent governed interpretation of an ambiguous statute, and that a material change in the wording of the statute ordinarily was viewed as an intent to change the meaning. In an odd interpretation, however, the court found that regardless of the fact that the result would be incongruous, the statutory amendment must be followed and because the defendant's offense was no longer listed as requiring registration, he was not subject to it.[223]

Conversely, the court in *People v. Tate*[224] found that although there was an error in drafting the statute, it was clear from the legislative history what the legislature meant. The statute erroneously referred to a conviction under "subdivision 1" of section 647(a), which required registration as a sex offender. There was no subdivision 1 in that statutory section, and the offender argued that because there was no subdivision 1, he did not have to register as a sex offender after having been found guilty of an offense under section 647(a). The court, however, determined that it could discern the legislative intent, that the error was simply an oversight, and the defendant had to register as a sex offender.[225]

Juvenile Cases. In a number of Megan's Laws, juveniles are specifically subjected to registration as a sex offender under the statute.[226] The cases discussed here include many of the same claims that adults have made to obtain relief from the duty to register. For example, if the statute requires a specific conviction, and the juvenile has not committed such an offense, he is not subject to registration[227]; if the statute is ambiguous, the court will not uphold the statute if it is an absurd and unreasonable result and will reach a result that is reasonable and in accordance with legislative intent[228]; a juvenile offender who is less than 15 years of age must wait for two years after adjudication before petitioning to waive the registration requirement, but the burden of proof at the hearing is lessened to "a preponderance of the evidence" from the "clear and convincing" level of proof required for juveniles 15 years of age or older who may petition immediately. The two-year waiting period is the "quid pro quo" for the lesser burden of proof at the hearing and does not violate equal protection concerns.[229]

In one case, the court determined that once the registration is applied to a juvenile, however, it is the registration statute that has jurisdiction over him and not the Juvenile Court or the Juvenile Code.[230]

Failure to Register: Knowingly.[231] In an Arizona case where a person was charged with a failure to act (i.e., failing to register as a sex offender), the court held that the factual basis for a guilty plea must show that the offender had actual knowledge of the duty to register as a sex offender. Where there was no such evidence in the record, the plea could not stand.[232] In a federal case, the court held that the failure to register must be knowingly, and unless the record could be improved to show that the defendant had knowledge of the requirement to report a change of address, his failure to register cannot support the revocation of supervised release.[233]

Failure to Register: As a Continuing Offense. In some instances, when a convicted sex offender is charged with failure to register, it is a continuing offense and not subject to the statute of limitations.[234] Statutory interpretation suggests that only in exceptional circumstances is a statute considered a continuing offense. "These considerations do not mean that a particular offense should never be construed as a continuing one. They do, however, require that such a result should not be reached unless the explicit language of the substantive criminal statute compels such a conclusion, or the nature of the crime involved is such that the Congress must assuredly have intended that it be treated as a continuing one."[235]

Petitioner had a duty to register within 30 days (now 14) after each move. His duty to register did not expire at the end of the 30-day period. The purpose of the statute was to make offenders readily available to police. If the offense was considered instantaneous and not continuing, offenders would be encouraged to simply hide for the applicable statute of limitation.[236] Conversely, the court in *Wright v. Superior Court*[237] found that the offense of failing to notify of a change of address was not a continuing one, and, therefore, the offender who failed to notify the authorities of a change of address could not be charged with a felony under the statute. The court held that failing to register initially and failing to notify an agency of a change of address were different in that the only time a person would have to notify of a change of address was when he moved, which would be an "instantaneous" offense.[238]

Failure to Register: When Underlying Charge Is Dismissed. When the underlying charge has been dismissed, the offender is not required to register as a sex offender. When the state fails to make appropriate and mandatory record entries, after proper notification that the underlying charge has been dismissed, thus subjecting the purported offender to a charge of failure to register, such omission is negligent. If the employee was not entirely immune for his actions, the state was not entirely immune either under section 815.2 (a) of the California State Tort Claims Act of 1963.[239]

Jurisdiction. In *In re E.D.*,[240] the defendant lived in New Jersey and was convicted of a sex offense in New Jersey. Under Megan's Law, he was ordered to register in New Jersey. He then moved to Pennsylvania but continued to work in New Jersey. The New Jersey Superior Court found that when he was still a continuing threat to those near where he worked, his duty to register continued even though he no longer lived in the state. The court found that jurisdiction over the offender did not end even after he had moved from the jurisdiction but still worked there. The purpose of the statute was community protection, and that purpose was served by the continuing duty to register for this offender.[241]

Conclusion

Sex offender registration and community notification statutes, as they currently exist, raise critical legal issues. Although courts have held that the registration requirements are fairly benign, because the intrusion on personal privacy is minimal, notification statutes seem to expose more serious intrusions on individual liberty.

The future of sex offender law and litigation promises to be volatile. In states where there are classifications or tier levels of risk, judicial hearings will soon become a regular part of the court calendar because every sex offender who is classified as a Tier II or Tier III offender is entitled to some type of judicial review. Appellate courts will no doubt be asked to determine whether the type of hearing held, the evidence admitted, and the determination of arbitrariness meets constitutional muster.[242]

The punishment of sex offenders continues its upward climb. As this chapter was being written, California passed a statute to chemically castrate repeat child molesters.[243] Offenders would have the option of surgical castration, perhaps the ultimate in Hobson's choices. Similar efforts are under way in Massachusetts, Texas, and Wisconsin. The American Civil Liberties Union has vowed to challenge these statutes.[244] This is clearly an area in which the public is clamoring for more protection and more serious punishment, but the former does not necessarily result from the latter.

State and federal governments continue to pass legislation at a swift pace in this area. In fact, most registration and notification statutes have not been in effect for a long enough period to have reached the courts for review, as a natural time lag occurs between enactment and actual effect on an offender. But when they have had the time to mature, there will no doubt be, if not an explosion of cases, at least some fireworks.

One point is certain: We have not seen the end of this type of legislation and therefore, we can count on additional challenges to those registration and notification statutes already in effect, the proposed chemical castration statutes, and whatever other measures legislators may think are necessary to calm their constituencies' fears, as well.

Footnotes

[1] Earl-Hubbard, "The Child Offender Registration Laws: The Punishment, Liberty Deprivation, and Unintended Results Associated with the Scarlet Letter Laws of the 1990s," 90(2) *Nw. U. L. Rev.* 788, 790 n.7 (1996).

[2] Ala. Code §§13A-11-200 et seq.(1994); Alaska Stat. §§12.63.010 et seq., 18.65.087 (1995); Ariz. Rev. Stat. Ann. §§13-3821 et seq., 41-1750(B) (1989 & West Supp. 1995); Ark. Code Ann. §§12-12-901 et seq. (1995); Cal. Penal Code §290 (West Supp. 1996); Colo. Rev. Stat. Ann. §18-3-412.5 (1995 Supp.); Conn. Gen. Stat. §54-102r (Supp. 1995); Del. Code Ann. tit. 11, §4120 (1995); Fla. Stat. Ann. §§775.21 et seq. (West Supp. 1996); Ga. Code Ann. 42-9-44.1 (Michie Supp. 1996); Hawaii Penal Code §707-743 (Supp. 1995); Idaho Code §§ 18-8301 et seq., 9-340(11)(f) (Michie Supp. 1996); Ill. Comp. Stat. Ann. §150 (1992 & Smith-Hurd Supp. 1996); Burns Ind. Stat. §5-2-12-1 (Michie Supp. 1996); Iowa Code Ann. §709C (West Supp. 1996); Kan. Stat. Ann. §§22-4901 et seq., 45-215 et seq. (1995); Ky. Rev. Stat. Ann. §§17.500 et seq. (Michie Supp. 1994); La. Rev. Stat. Ann. §§15-540 et seq. (West Supp. 1996); Me. Rev. Stat. Ann. tit. 34-A, §§11001 et seq. (West Supp. 1995); Md. Code Ann. art. 27, §692B (Michie Supp. 1995); 1996 Mass. Acts, ch. 239, §§178C to 178O (H.5949, approved Aug. 5, 1996, eff. Oct. 1, 1996); Mich. Stat. Ann. §4.475 (Supp. 1996); Minn. Stat. Ann. §243.166 (West Supp. 1996); Miss. Code Ann. §§45-33-1 et seq. (Lawyer's Coop. Supp. 1995); Mo. Rev. Stat. Ann. §§566.600 et seq. (West Supp. 1996); Mont. Code Ann. §§46-23-501 et seq.(1995); 1996 Neb. Sess. Laws L.B. 645 (approved Apr. 3, 1996);

Nev. Rev. Stat. §§207.080, 207.151 et seq. (1992 & Michie Supp. 1995); N.H. Rev. Stat. Ann. §§632-A:11 et seq. (1996), 1996 N.H. Laws ch. 174 (H.B. 1543); N.J. Stat. Ann. §§2C:7-1 et seq. (West Supp. 1996); N.M. Stat. Ann. §§29-11A-1 et seq. (Michie Supp. 1996); N.Y. Corr. Law art. 6-C, §§168 et seq. (McKinney Supp. 1996); N.C. Gen. Stat. art. 27A, §§14-208.5 et seq. (Michie Supp 1995); N.D. Cent. Code §12.1-32-15 (Michie Supp. 1995); Ohio Rev. Code Ann. §§2950.01 et seq. (1993 & Supp. 1995); Okla. Stat. Ann. tit. 57, §§581 et seq. (West Supp. 1996); Or. Rev. Stat. §§181.585 et seq., 181.594, et seq. (1995); Pa. Cons. Stat. Ann. tit. 42, §§9791 et seq. (West Supp. 1996); R.I. Gen. Laws Ann. §11-37-16 (1995); S.C. Code of Laws Ann. §§23-3-400 et seq. (Lawyer's Coop. Supp. 1995); S.D. Cod. Laws Ann. §§22-22-30 to 2222-41 (Michie Supp. 1996); Tenn. Code Ann. §§38-6-110, 40-39-101 et seq. (1994 & Michie Supp. 1995); Tex. Rev. Civil Stat. Ann. art. 6262-13c.1 (West Supp. 1996); Utah Code Cr. Proc. Ann. §§77-18-9 to 77-18-14, 77-27-21.5 (Supp. 1995); Vt. Sess. Laws Act 124, to amend §1, 13 Vt. Stat. Ann. ch. 167, subch. 3, §§5401 et seq. (S.217, approved Apr. 25, 1996, eff. Sept. 1, 1996); Va. Code Ann. §§53.1-116.1, 19.2-298.1, §19.2-390.1 (1996); Wash. Rev. Code Ann. §§4.24.550, 9A.44.130 et seq., 10.01.170, 10.01.200, 43.43.745, 46.20.187, 70.48.470, 72.09.330 (1990 & West Supp. 1996); W. Va. Code Ann. §§61-11A-8, 61-8F-1 et seq. (1992 & Michie Supp. 1996); Wis. Stat. Ann. §175.45 (West Supp. 1995); Wy.Stat.Ann. §7-19-301, et seq. (1995); Jacob Wetterling Crimes Against Children and Sexually Violent Offender Act, 42 U.S.C.A. §§14072 et seq. (1995), Pub. L. No. 104-145, 110 Stat. 1345, to amend Violent Crime Control and Law Enforcement Act of 1994 ("Megan's Law") (May 17, 1996).

[3] 42 U.S.C. §§14071 et seq.

[4] Earl-Hubbard, supra note 1, at 796 n. 41.

[5] §1, 13 Vt. Stat. Ann. ch. 167, subch. 3 (approved by the Vermont Legislature, Apr. 25, 1996); 1996 Neb. Laws L.B. 645 (approved by the Governor, Apr. 3, 1996).

[6] Ch. 239, §§178C et seq. (eff. Oct. 1, 1996).

[7] See, e.g., Ariz. Rev. Stat. Ann. §13-3825 (1989 & West Supp. 1995).

[8] See, e.g., Ga. Code Ann. §42-9-44.1(e) (Michie Supp. 1996), for sex offenders released on parole.

[9] See, e.g., N.Y. Corr. Law art. 6-C, §168(p) (McKinney Supp. 1996).

[10] See Earl-Hubbard, supra note 1, at 850–855; Cierzniak, "There Goes the Neighborhood: Notifying the Public When a Convicted Child Molester Is Released Into the Community," 28 *Ind. L. Rev.* 715, 719, 721 (1995); Bedarf, "Examining Sex Offender Notification Laws," 83 *Calif. L. Rev.* 885 (1995); Silva, "Dial '1-900-Pervert' and Other Statutory Measures That Provide Public Notification of Sex Offenders," 48 *S.M.U. L. Rev.* 1961, 1979–1987 (1995).

[11] Silva, supra note 10, at 1979.

[12] Ibid. at n. 162, which quotes Robert Sheley, a Tulane University criminologist, as saying that "there is no solid research on whether the notification laws in either Washington or Louisiana prevent recidivism or protect the public." However, because the notification laws in Washington were enacted as recently as the early 1990s, it may not be possible, as yet, to detect the recidivism effects of the statutes.

[13] With the adoption of the federal law and the nationwide registry, this may become less of an issue. See supra notes 2 and 3; McGrory, infra note 28, at 8.

[14] Cierzniak, supra note 10, at 719; Earl-Hubbard, supra note 1, at 855.

[15] See Bedarf, supra note 10, at 900–901.

[16] See Earl-Hubbard, supra note 1, at 855.

[17] See Boland, "Sex Offender Registration and Community Notification: Protection, Not Punishment," 30 *New Engl. L. Rev.* 183, 185–186 (1995).

[18] See Silva, supra note 10, at 1980.

[19] Houston, "Sex Offender Registration Acts: An Added Dimension to the War on Crime," *Ga. L. Rev.* 729 (1994).

[20] See, e.g., Ga. Code Ann. §§42-1-12 et seq.

[21] SVPs will only be discussed in this chapter to the extent that they are addressed within the same statutory section as sex offenders. See Fred Cohen, Ch. 22, this volume, and Wash. Rev. Code §71.09 (1990), for involuntary commitment of SVPs after they have served their prison sentences; Or. Rev.

Stat. §§181.585 (SVPs) and 181.594 (sexual offenders); Pa. Cons. Stat. Ann. Title 42, §9791, et seq. (West Supp. 1996) (imposes requirements for both sex offender and SVPs within the same statutory section).

22 For example, in Artway v. Attorney General of New Jersey, 81 F.3d 1235 (3d Cir. 1996), *petition for reh'g denied*, 83 F.3d 594 (3d Cir. 1996), the offender challenged the statute's registration and notification provisions on ex post facto, double jeopardy, bill of attainder, equal protection, due process, and void-for-vagueness grounds. The Third Circuit drew a distinction between the claims under the registration and notification provisions, respectively. It did not reach the constitutional claims under the notification provisions for moderate and high-risk offenders, as it held that the appellant's claims were unripe. However, in addressing the constitutional challenges to the registration provisions and notification provisions for low-risk offenders, the court suggested that although registration did not violate the ex post facto laws, for example, the notifications might, as they are more onerous than registration and may be considered "punishment" for that purpose.

23 In a landmark case, the United States Supreme Court decided that a municipal statute that required all convicted felons to register with the police upon their entry to Los Angeles failed because the ordinance failed to provide adequate notice and therefore violated due process considerations. Lambert v. California, 355 U.S. 225 (1957). The petitioner did not challenge the duty of a felon to register.

24 See generally Artway v. Attorney General of New Jersey, 81 F.3d 1235 (3d Cir. 1996).

25 See generally State v. Ward, 20 Kan. App. 238, 886 P.2d 886 (1994) (where the court held that when the registration statute required a conviction to come under the statute, and Juvenile Offenders Code says that an act committed under it is civil, a juvenile violation under the Juvenile Offenders Code cannot be used to support a requirement to register); State v. Thibodeaux, slip op. 96-308 (La. App. 3d Cir. May 31, 1996) (which held that the crime for which the defendant was convicted was not a violation of 15:542, which would require registration, and therefore defendant was not subject to registration requirements).

26 See section "Challenges to Registration and Notification," at page 24-7.

27 See infra note 37. Approximately 17 states provide that juveniles adjudicated a delinquent on the basis of commission of a sexual offense must register under the statute.

28 McGrory, "Clinton Sets Tracking of Sex Offenders," *Boston Globe*, 25 Aug. 1996, pp. A1, A8.

29 See supra note 2.

30 Ibid.

31 Virtually all the states provide a list of offenses for which conviction would mandate registration under the act. See, e.g., Ky. Stat. Rev. Stat. Ann. §17.500 (Michie Supp. 1994).

32 See, e.g., Ala. Code §13-A-11-200 (1994).

33 See, e.g., R.I. Ann. Stat. §11-37-16 (1995).

34 About one-fifth of the jurisdictions provide that the offender must register if the victim was under a specified age at the time of the offense. See, e.g., Ark. Code Ann. §12-12-902 (1995), where the victim is a child; see Ohio Rev. Code Ann. §2950.01(A) ("Habitual Sex Offender)"; Ark. Code Ann. §12-12-902(1) ("Habitual Child Sex Offender").

35 Only Arkansas and Ohio require that the offender be convicted two or more times of an offense under the act before he must register. See Ark. Code Ann. §12-12-902(1) (1995); Ohio Rev. Code Ann. §2950.01(A) (1993 & Supp. 1995).

36 See, e.g., Mo. Rev. Stat. Ann. §§566.600(1), 566.600(3) (West Supp. 1996).

37 Approximately one-third of the states register as sex offenders. See, e.g., 1996 Mass. Acts, ch. 239, §178C (H.5949, approved Aug. 5, 1996; eff. Oct. 1, 1996), which provides that a sex offender is a "person convicted of a sex offense or has been adjudicated as a youthful offender or as a juvenile delinquent by reason of a sex offense."

38 Thirty-three of the 50 states require that the offender sign a form notifying him of his duty to register and return it to either the court, the department of corrections, or other supervising agency.

39 E.g., N.H. Rev. Stat. Ann. §632-A:13, "Upon release of any sex offender after conviction. . . ."

40 See, e.g., Fla. Stat. Ann. §775.22(3).

41 See, e.g., Ala. Code §13A-11-200; Ark. Code Ann. §12-12-904; Ill. Comp. Stat. Ann. ch. 730,

§150/3(1); La. Rev. Stat. Ann. §542(B) (30 days if the sex offender is a current resident and 45 days if he is not); Ohio Rev. Code Ann. §2950.02; Code of Va. §19.2-298.1(c).

42 See, e.g., Code of Laws of S.C. §23-3-460.

43 All but Pennsylvania have requirement for sex offenders to register each time they change their address. See, e.g., Code of Va. §19.2-298.1(A).

44 Twenty-one states specifically require that the sex offender reregister on an annual basis. See, e.g., Alaska Stat. §12-63.010(d).

45 The registration provisions of four states state that a blood sample must be provided by the sex offender: Cal. Penal Code §290.2(a) (blood and saliva); Fla. Stat. Ann. §775.22(3)(a)(2) ("if necessary"); Miss. Code Ann. §45-33-1(3); Okla. Stat. Ann. §584(A)(2). Other provisions, dictating terms of parole or probation, may require furnishing a blood sample as a condition of release. See Earl-Hubbard, supra note 1, at 792 n. 18. Earl-Hubbard cites 730 Ill. Comp. Stat. Ann. §515-4-3 (blood sample); Mo. Rev. Stat. §217.695 (1995) (hair sample if offender is on probation or parole); Utah Code Ann. §53-5-212.2 (blood sample).

46 See, e.g., Fla. Stat. Ann., §775.22(3)(a)(2); Burns Ind. Stat. §5-2-12-6(3); Ky. Rev. Stat. Ann. §17.500(3).

47 Alabama does not state what the period of registration is, so it is presumed to be for life (Code of Ala. §§13A-11-200 et seq.). The registration period usually differs for sex offenders and SVPs. For example, the federal statute requires the sex offender to register for a 10-year period, but the SVP is subject to registration for life. 42 U.S.C.A. §§14071(b)(6)(A), 14071(b)(6)(B). Also, whether the offender is subject to registration for a first or subsequent offense will affect the period of registration. In Kansas, first-time sex offenders must register for 10 years, but those convicted of a subsequent offense must register for life (Kan. Stat. Ann. §22-4906). In Maryland, the offender must register for 10 years (Md. Ann. Code §692B(I)); in Maine for 15 (Me. Rev. Stat. Ann. §11003(I)), and in Massachusetts, the required period is 20 years (1996 Mass. Acts ch. 239, §178G).

48 The following states allow the offender to petition for relief from the registration requirement: Ark. Code Ann. §12-12-908; Colo. Rev. Stat. §18-3-412.5(7); Hawaii Penal Code §707-743(6); Kan. Stat. Ann. §22-4908; Me. Rev. Stat. Ann. §11003(4); Miss. Code Ann. §45-33-13; Nev. Rev. Stat. §207.156; N.Y. Corr. Law art. 6-C, §168-o; N.C. Gen. Stat. §14.208.12; Rev. Civil Stat. Tex. art. 6252-13c.1(8); Wyo. Stat. Ann. §7-19-304(b). New Jersey, New York, and Massachusetts also allow the offender to petition for a hearing on the level of risk, but that is discussed in the next section, "Community Notification."

49 The following statutes allow the offender to petition for expungement of his record: Conn. Gen. Stat. §54-102r(f) (expunged automatically); Idaho Code §18-8310; 1996 Neb. Laws L.B. §645(10)(3); N.J. Stat. Ann. §2C:52-2; Or. Rev. Stat. §419A.260; R.I. Gen. Laws §11-37-16(k); S.D. Cod. Laws §22-22-31; Tenn. Code Ann. §40-39-107(c); Utah Code Cr. Proc. §§77-18-9 to 77-18-14; 13 Vt. Stat. Ann. §19.2-390.1; Wis. Stat. Ann. §175.45(7)(c). Delaware (§4120(d)) automatically expunges the record of a juvenile sex offender when he reaches 25 years of age.

50 Idaho Code §18-8307(3); La. Stat. Ann. §543(E); Md. Ann. Code §692B(c)(2)(ii); 1996 Mass. Acts ch.239, §178E(9); 1996 Neb. Sess. Laws L.B. 645 §7(3); Okla. Stat. Ann. §585(B); and Wash. Rev. Code Ann. §46.20.187 all notify all persons who apply for a driver's license of the duty of sex offenders to register. This is one mechanism for ensuring that those persons convicted out of state to receive notice.

51 Or. Rev. Stat. §181.599(2) provides that if the offender fails to register annually, he can be charged with a violation; one example of a misdemeanor violation is Code of Va. §19.2-298.1(E). Pa. Cons. Stat. Ann. §9796(d) considers failure to register a felony. In some states, as in California's Penal Code §290(g), the penalty matches the crime, so if the offender's underlying crime is a misdemeanor (there is some controversy whether requiring registration for a misdemeanor conviction violates the Eighth Amendment, see section "Challenges to Registration and Notification," at page 24-7), and if the underlying offense is a felony, failure to register is a felony. Other states (see Iowa Code Ann. §692A.7) provide that the offender is penalized for a misdemeanor on a first offense and he is punished for a felony on a second or subsequent offense.

52 Del. Code Ann. §4120(h).

53 La. Rev. Stat. Ann. §15-542 (West Supp. 1996).

[54] Iowa Code Ann. §692A.6 (West Supp. 1996).

[55] For example, in California, if the information is misused to commit a felony, the penalty is up to five years' incarceration and if used to commit a misdemeanor, the penalty can be a fine between $500 and $1,000 and civil penalties; in Connecticut it is a misdemeanor (Conn. Gen. Stat. §54-102r(g)); in New York, the person who misuses the information is subject to civil penalties (N.Y. Corr. Law art. 6-C, §168-u).

[56] 42 U.S.C.A. §42071(e); Ga. Code Ann. §42-1-12(j); Ill. Comp. Stat. Ann. §152/130; Iowa Code Ann. §692A.15; La. Rev. Stat. Ann. §15:546; 1996 Mass. Act ch. 239, §178(o); Miss. Code Ann. §45-33-17(2); Neb. Sess. Laws L.B. 645 §12; Nev. Rev. Stat. Ann. §§207.155(3), 213.1257; N.J. Stat. Ann. §2C:7-9; N.M. Stat. Ann. §29-11A-8; N.Y. Corr. Law art. 6-C, §168(r); Pa. Cons. STat. Ann. §9799; Rev. Civil Stat.Tex. Art. 6252-13c.1(5A); Vt. Stat. Ann. ch. 167, subchap. 3, §5412; and Wash. Rev. Code Ann. §4.24.550(3) all provide for immunity from prosecution if the law enforcement officer or agency acted in good faith, or for performing a discretionary function for disclosing or failing to disclose registry information.

[57] Ala. Code §13A-11-202; Ky. Rev. Stat. Ann. §17.530; Mich. Stat. Ann. §4.475(10); Mo. Rev. Stat. Ann. §566.617; 1996 Neb. Sess. Laws L.B. 645 §9; N.M. Stat. Ann. §29-11A-6, Ohio Rev. Code Ann. 2950.08; R.I. Gen. Laws Ann. §11-37-16(I); Code of Laws of S.C. §23-3-490; Wis. Stat. Ann. §175.45(7); Wyo. Stat. Ann. §7-19-303.

[58] Ariz. Rev. Stat. Ann. §13-3825; Colo. Rev. Stat. §18-3-412.5(6.5); Conn. Gen. Stat. §54-102r(g); Fla. Stat. Ann. §§775.225, 944.606; Ga. Code Ann. §§42-1-12(I)(3), 42-9-44.1; Iowa Code Ann. §692A.13; Miss. Code Ann. §45-33-17; Mont. Code Ann. §46-23-508 (must petition court first); N.D. Cent. Code §12.1-32-15(10); Tenn. Code Ann. §40-39-106(c); Wash. Rev. Code Ann. §4.24.550.

[59] Notice to victims is provided in Vt. Sess. Laws Act 124, §5410 and W. Va. Code Ann. §61-11A-8. Ill. Comp. Stat. Ann. §152/120 and many of the three-tier classification systems provide that the notification of a tier II or tier III offender may be limited to listed organizations and those that the offender is "likely to encounter." See supra note 149.

[60] See, e.g., Cal. Penal Code §290.4; N.Y. Corr. Law art. 6-C, §168(p); Or. Rev. Stat. §181.601.

[61] Some states designate all information gathered under the sex offender registration statute to be "public information." Kan. Stat. Ann. §45.215.223; S.D. Cod. Laws Ann. §22-22-40; Rev. Civil Code Tex. art. 6252.13c.1(3) to 6252.13c.1(5).

[62] E.g., Pa. Cons. Stat. Ann. tit. 42, §§9797, 9798.

[63] La. Rev. Stat. Ann. §542(B).

[64] Del. Code Ann. §4120(I); Ill. Comp. Stat. Ann. ch. 730, §152/120; Burns Ind. Stat. §5-2-12-11; Md.Ann. Code art. 27, §692B(d); 1996 N.H. Laws ch. 174 (H.B. 1543); Okla. Stat. Ann. tit. 57, §584(E); Code of Va. §19.2-390.1(B).

[65] Alaska Stat. §18.65.087; Idaho Code §9-340(11)(f); 16 Me. Rev. Stat. Ann. §611; N.C. Gen. Stat. §14-208.10; Utah Code Cr. Proc. §§77-27-21.5(1), 77-27-21.5(17)–77-27-21.5(18).

[66] Per guidelines, Ariz. Rev. Stat. Ann. §13-3825; per guidelines established to determine a three-tiered risk classification system, 1996 Mass. Acts ch. 239, §178I-N; Minn. Stat. Ann. §243.166; Nev. Rev. Stat. §§213.1247, 1253; N.J. Stat. Ann. §§2C:7-6 to 7-11; N.Y. Corr. Law art. 6-C, §§168(i), 168(p); Or. Rev. Stat. §181.585.

[67] Hawaii Penal Code §707-743 (Supp. 1995).

[68] *Amending* 42 U.S.C. §14071(d), Pub. L. No. 104-145, 110 Stat. 1345.

[69] Doe v. Poritz, 662 A.2d 367 (N.J. 1995).

[70] See, e.g., 1996 Mass. Acts ch. 239, §178M.

[71] 1996 Mass. Acts ch. 239, §178K(2)(b).

[72] 1996 Mass. Acts ch. 239, §178K(2)(c).

[73] Cierzniak, supra note 10, at 719 n. 31, discussing the extent of safety problems for the offender or family members.

[74] See Bedarf, supra note 10, at 907–908 n. 135.

[75] See ibid. at 908 n. 139.

[76] Ibid. at n. 140.

[77] Ibid. at nn. 141-143.

[78] Some of these challenges may fall generally under due process, for example, but the challenge when raised and addressed by the court was not framed in those terms.

[79] Calder v. Bull, 3 U.S. (3 Dall.) 386, 390 (1798).

[80] United States v. Brown, 381 U.S. 437, 448-449 (1965).

[81] United States v. Halper, 490 U.S. 435, 440 (1989).

[82] Solem v. Helm, 463 U.S. 277, 284 (1983).

[83] In the several cases, all or many of the punishment-related issues were raised, and the courts dealt with them almost as one. For the most part, the issue was whether the retroactive application of the registration and/or notification law was determined to be remedial or punitive for all purposes. The ex post facto discussion details the cases and the following punishment-related arguments address these issues summarily, as a full discussion would be redundant. If an additional test for punishment is particularly applicable to the clause, it is included.

[84] Supra note 79.

[85] 497 U.S. 37 (1990).

[86] *Calder,* 3 U.S. at 390 (emphasis added).

[87] *Collins,* 497 U.S. at 42 (emphasis added).

[88] Doe v. Pataki, 919 F. Supp. 691 (S.D.N.Y. 1996).

[89] Ibid.

[90] Williford v. Board of Parole, 137 Or. App. 254, 904 P.2d 1074 (1995).

[91] United States v. One Assortment of 89 Firearms, 465 U.S. 354, 362 (1984).

[92] Sequoia Books, Inc. v. Ingemunson, 901 F.2d 630 (7th Cir.), *cert. denied,* 498 U.S. 959 (1990); Jones v. Murray, 962 F.2d 302, 309 (4th Cir.), *cert. denied,* 113 S. Ct. 471 (1992); State v. Ward, 869 P.2d 1062 (Wash. 1994).

[93] Opinion of the Justices to the Senate, 423 Mass. 1201, 1221, 668 N.E.2d 738, 749 (1996).

[94] DeVeau v. Braisted, 363 U.S. 144, 160 (1960); Rise v. Oregon, 59 F.3d 1556 (9th Cir. 1995); People v. Adams, 144 Ill. 2d 381, 163 Ill. Dec. 483, 581 N.E.2d 637 (1991) (in an Eighth Amendment context).

[95] Artway v. Attorney General of New Jersey, 81 F.3d 1235, 1263 (9th Cir. 1996).

[96] See *Opinion of the Justices to the Senate,* 423 Mass. at 1221, 668 N.E.2d at 749, which cites Doe v. Poritz, 662 A.2d 367 (N.J. 1995), as an example.

[97] United States v. Huss, 7 F.3d 1444, 1447-1448 (9th Cir. 1993). See also DeVeau v. Braisted, 363 U.S. 144, 160 (1960), which held that "the question in each case where unpleasant consequences are brought to bear upon an individual for prior conduct, is whether the legislative aim was to punish that individual for past activity, or whether the restriction of the individual comes about as a relevant *incident to a regulation* of a present situation" (emphasis added).

[98] 490 U.S. 435, 448 (1989).

[99] 509 U.S. 602, 610 (1993).

[101] United States v. Ursery, 64 U.S.L.W. 4565 (June 25, 1996).

[101] Ibid. at 4571 (citations omitted).

[102] Ibid. at 4568.

[103] Artway v. Attorney General of New Jersey, 81 F.3d 1235 (3d Cir. 1996), in its discussion of Department of Corrections v. Morales, 115 S. Ct. 1597 (1995), held that "while even a substantial 'sting' will not render a measure a 'punishment,' at some level the 'sting' will be so sharp that it can only be considered punishment regardless of the legislators' subjective thoughts." 81 F.3d at 1261.

[104] Snyder v. State, 912 P.2d 1127 (Wyo. 1996), held that because there was no statement of legislative purpose or any legislative history, the "plain reading of the statutory scheme . . . indicates that the legislature intended to facilitate law enforcement and protect children. There was no intent to inflict greater punishment." Ibid. at 1131.

[105] See, e.g., Colo. Rev. Stat. Ann. §18-3-412.4(6.5)' Fla. Stat. Ann. §775.21(2) (West Supp. 1995): Idaho Code §18-8302 (Michie Supp. 1996); La. Rev. Stat. Ann. §15-540 (West Supp. 1996); N.M.

Stat. Ann. §29-11A-2 (Michie Supp. 1996); N.C. Gen. Stat. art. 27A, §14-208.5 (Michie Supp. 1995); Or. Rev. Stat. §181.602 (1995); Pa. Cons. Stat. Ann. tit. 42, §9791 (West Supp. 1996); Code of Laws of S.C. §23-3-400 (Lawyer's Coop. Supp. 1995) all of which have a provision stating that the legislature finds that sex offenders are violent, the recidivism rate among them is very high, they have a high number of victims, they are prosecuted for a fraction of their crimes, and they represent a high-risk level of threat to public safety.

[106] Williford v. Board of Parole, 137 Or. App. 254, 904 P.2d 1074 (1995), and Hall v. Board of Parole, 138 Or. App. 177, 906 309 (Or. App. 1995) (community notification not penal and retroactive application not an ex post facto violation); Petition of Estavillo, 69 Wash. App. 401, 848 P.2d 1335 (Wash. App. Div. 1 1993) (registration statute not penal); Rise v. Oregon, 59 F.3d 1556 (1995) (collection of blood sample from convicted sex offender not penal); State v. Costello, 643 A.2d 531 (N.H. 1994) (punitive effect of registration requirement de minimis).

[107] See Kennedy v. Mendoza-Martinez, 372 U.S. 144, 169 (1972).

[108] The Massachusetts Supreme Court, in its *Opinion of the Justices to the Senate*, explained that *Ursery* seemed to be repudiating the *Mendoza-Martinez* test in the ex post facto arena, but the following courts have utilized it to deem whether a particular sanction was punishment: State v. Noble and State v. McCuin, 171 Ariz. 171, 829 P.2d 1217, 1221 (Ariz. 1992); State v. Taylor, 67 Wash. App. 350, 835 P.2d 245, 248 (Wash. App. Div. 1 1992); Rowe v. Burton, 884 F. Supp. 1372, 1377 (D. Alaska 1994); Doe v. Pataki, 919 F. Supp. 691, 700 (S.D.N.Y. 1996); 123 Wash. 2d 488, 869 P.2d 1062, 1068 (1994); State v. Manning, 532 N.W.2d 244, 247 (1995).

[109] *Mendoza-Martinez*'s seven factors, weighing for and against the statute's punitiveness, are (1) whether it is an affirmative disability or restraint; (2) whether it is historically regarded as punishment; (3) whether it comes into play on a finding of scienter; (4) whether it promotes the traditional aims of punishment, such as deterrent or retribution; (5) whether the burden to which it applies is already a crime; (6) whether an alternative purpose to which it may rationally be connected is assignable for it; and (7) whether the statute is excessive in relation to its nonpunitive purpose.

[110] See *Doe v. Poritz*, supra note 69.

[111] 81 F.3d 1235 (3d Cir. 1996).

[112] DeVeau v. Braisted, 363 U.S. 144 (1990), *cited in Artway*, 81 F.3d at 1254.

[113] United States v. Halper, 490 U.S. 435 (1989), *cited in Artway*, 81 F.3d at 1254.

[114] Austin v. United States, 509 U.S. 602 (1993), *cited in Artway*, 81 F.3d at 1256.

[115] Department of Revenue v. Kurth Ranch, 511 U.S. 767 (1994), *cited in Artway*, 81 F.3d at 1258.

[116] Department of Corrections v. Morales, 115 S. Ct. 1597 (1995), *cited in Artway*, 81 F.3d at 1260.

[117] Kennedy v Mendoza-Martinez, 372 U.S. 144 (1963), *cited in Artway*, 81 F.3d at 1261.

[118] *Artway*, 81 F.3d at 1264–1267.

[119] The community notification scheme in New Jersey operates on a three-tier level system, with the prosecutor decision about the sex offender's risk of reoffense subject to judicial review. If the offender is rated a moderate (level II) risk, community organizations may be notified, and if he is rated a high (level III) risk, community organizations and individuals may be notified of his presence in the community. The court found that Megan's Law was applied retroactively to Artway. The issue whether such application of the notification provision constituted an ex post facto violation was unripe as it pertained to Artway because he had neither registered as yet as a sex offender, nor had the prosecutor designated a level of risk for Artway.

[120] "Artway's argument has considerable force, but the notification issue is not before us," in response to Artway's claim that the notification provision resembled the Scarlet Letter punishment under the second prong; in response to Artway's arguments about the effects of community notification, the court said, "Artway marshals strong reasons that notification would have devastating effects." 81 F.3d at 1266.

[121] W.P. v. Poritz, 931 F. Supp. 1199 (D.N.J. 1996).

[122] See *Ursery*, supra note 100, which limited *Halper* to a narrower scope, applicable only when the facts and circumstances were the same; limited *Austin* to Excessive Fines Clause application; and limited *Kurth Ranch* cases involving imposition of a tax.

[123] See *W.P. v. Poritz*, 931 F. Supp. at 1208–1209.

[124] Doe v. Pataki, 919 F. Supp. 691 (S.D.N.Y. 1996).

[125] See *Doe v. Poritz*, 662 A.2d at 406; *Artway*, 81 F.3d at 1267 (registration and tier I notification only).

[126] *Doe v. Poritz*, 662 A.2d at 406; *W.P. Poritz*, 931 F. Supp. at 1219; and *Artway*, 81 F.3d at 1267; *Opinion of the Justices to the Senate*, 423 Mass. at 1240, 668 N.E.2d at 760, where the Massachusetts court found that notification was a civil sanction and it was not imposed as part of the sentence of the court. Again, if it was not punishment, therefore it was not "multiple punishments." Ibid. Double jeopardy defense to sex offender registration and/or notification has always been raised as one of several "punishment-related issues and never on its own.

[127] People v. Adams, 144 Ill. 2d 381, 163 Ill. Dec. 483, 581 N.E.2d 637, 641 (1967); *Opinion of the Justices to the Senate*, 423 Mass. at 1236–1239, 668 N.E.2d at 758–759; *Doe v. Poritz*, 662 A.2d at 406; Snyder v. State, 912 P.2d 1127 (Wyo. 1996), which held that "our determination that registration is not punishment is dispositive of Snyder's claim that it is cruel and unusual punishment in violation of the United States Constitution's Eighth Amendment." Ibid. at 1131.

[128] In re Lynch, 8 Cal. 3d 410, 425-429, 105 Cal. Rptr. 217, 503 P.2d 921 (1972); People v. Rodrigues, 63 Cal. 3d Supp. 1, 133 Cal. Rptr. 765 (1976); People v. Mills, 81 Cal. App. 3d 171, 177–179, 146 Cal. Rptr. 411 (1978); In re Reed, 33 Cal. 3d 914, 191 Cal. Rptr. 658, 663 P.2d 216 (1983); In re King, 157 Cal. App. 3d 554, 558, 204 Cal. Rptr. 39 (1984); People v. Monroe, 168 Cal. App. 3d 1205, 215 Cal. Rptr. 51 (1985); In re Debeque, 212 Cal. App. 3d 241; 260 Cal. Rptr. 441 (1989); State v. Ohio, 66 Ohio App. 3d 788, 586 N.E.2d 1096 (1989); People v. King, 16 Cal. App. 4th 567, 20 Cal. Rptr. 220 (1993); State v. Cameron, 916 P.2d 1183 (Ariz. App. Div. 1 1996).

[129] 66 Ohio App. 3d 788, 586 N.E. 1096, 1098–1099 (1989).

[130] Solem v. Helm, 463 U.S. 277, 284 (1983).

[131] *Douglas*, 586 N.E. at 1099. See also State v. Lammie, 164 Ariz. 377, 793 P.2d 134 (Ariz. App. 1990).

[132] People v. Mills, 81 Cal. App. 3d 171, 146 Cal. Rptr. 411 (Dist. 4 1978); In re Reed, 33 Cal. 3d 914, 191 Cal. Rptr. 658, 663 P.2d 216 (1983); In re King, 157 Cal. App. 3d 554, 204 Cal. Rptr. 39 (Dist. 4 1984); People v. Rodrigues, 63 Cal. 3d Supp. 1, 133 Cal. Rptr. 765 (1976); People v. King, 16 Cal. App. 4th 567, 20 Cal. Rptr. 2d 220 (Dist. 1 1993); In re Debeque, 212 Cal. App. 3d 241, 260 Cal. Rptr. 441 (Dist. 4 1989); People v. Monroe, 168 Cal. App. 3d 1205, 215 Cal. Rptr. 51 (Dist. 5 1985).

[133] 8 Cal. 3d 410, 423, 105 Cal. Rptr. 217, 503 P.2d 921 (1972).

[134] See *Solem v. Helm*, supra note 130.

[135] *In re Reed*, supra note 132, at 220, which summarizes the test applied in *In re Lynch*, supra note 128 (emphasis added).

[136] In re Reed, 33 Cal. Rptr. 914, 191 Cal. Rptr. 658, 663 P.2d 216 (Cal. 1983); In re King, 157 Cal. App. 3d 554, 204 Cal. Rptr 39 (1984).

[137] *Reed*, 663 P.2d at 222.

[138] *King*, 157 Cal. App. 3d at 558.

[139] See People v. Rodrigues, 63 Cal. 3d Supp. 1, 133 Cal. Rptr. 765 (1976); People v. King, 16 Cal. App. 4th 567, 20 Cal. Rptr. 2d 220 (Dist. 1 1993); In re Debeque, 212 Cal. App. 3d 241, 260 Cal. Rptr. 441 (Dist. 4 1989); People v. Monroe, 168 Cal. App. 3d 1205, 215 Cal. Rptr. 51 (Dist. 5 1985). These courts have not stated that the rulings in *Reed* and *King* were incorrect in holding that registration based upon conviction of a misdemeanor, such as indecent exposure, was disproportionate, but they have clarified the holdings, stating that there are certain misdemeanors which are sufficiently serious to warrant registration and are an imposition of the registration based on such a crime is not disproportionate under the Eighth Amendment.

[140] 424 U.S. 319 , 335 (1976), which looks at the private interest that will be affected by the official action; the risk of an erroneous deprivation of such interest through the procedures used, and the probable value, if any, of additional or substitute procedural safeguards; and finally, the Government's interest, including the function involved and the fiscal and administrative burdens that the additional or substitute procedural requirement would entail.

[141] Ibid. at 334–335.

[142] Ibid.

[143] *Doe v. Poritz*, 662 A.2d at 406, which held that considerations of due process and fundamental fairness required at least a hearing prior to classification of a tier II or II risk level.

[144] See statutes in Massachusetts, Minnesota, Nevada, New Jersey, New York, and Oregon, supra note 66. The Massachusetts court reviewed the risk assessment portion of the statute on its face and not as applied, and found that the procedures developed in §174B, the development of guidelines, the right to judicial review of the risk assessment when the rules of evidence do not apply, and the appointment of counsel for indigent offenders satisfied due process constraints, and it was constitutional due process.

[145] See *W.P. v. Poritz*, 931 F. Supp. at 1219, which held that the offender had a federally recognized liberty interest in the stigma of being labeled a sex offender and the "incursion on his right to privacy, or the stigma and the loss of employment, where some due process was warranted." After conducting a *Matthews* analysis, the court determined that the requirements for the offender under the statute were deemed not criminal by this court and resulted in a lower level of due process applied — because it was not punishment, only minimum safeguards are required.

[146] See Artway v. Attorney General of New Jersey, 81 F.3d 1235, 1263 (9th Cir. 1996), which held that, although registration did not affect a liberty interest requiring due process, the offender may have a "liberty interest in notification under state law triggering federal due process protections." Ibid. at 1268-1269.

[147] See *Opinion of the Justices to the Senate*, 423 Mass. at 1229, 668 N.E.2d at 753; *W.P. v. Poritz*, 931 F. Supp. at 1219–1220; *Doe v. Poritz*, 662 A.2d at 420–422, finding that at least with regard to tier II and tier III, a hearing is required.

[148] See *Rise v. Oregon*, 59 F.3d at 1563.

[149] In re Registrant C.A., 146 N.J. 71, 679 A.2d 1153 (1996).

[150] In re Registrant G.B., 286 N.J. Super. 396, 669 A.2d 303 (N.J. Super. App. Div. 1996), where the court held that the offender's admissions, along with the victim's statements, were sufficient to classify him as a tier II offender, but that there was insufficient evidence in the record to justify the prosecutor's proposed two-mile radius notification and that the offender was entitled to retain an expert to show that the factors related to the specifics of the offender and his crime justified less than a tier II classification; In re Registrant E.A., 285 N.J. Super. 554, 667 A.2d 1077 (N.J. Super. App. Div. 1996), where the court held that evidence in the record showing that the prosecutor had based his two-mile radius of notification on such factors as population concentration or density, adult and child mobility in such population density, proof of advanced age or debilitating illness, and distances of schools and/or day-care centers affected the offender's range of contact with members of the public, or whom offender was "likely to encounter." The court directed the prosecutor to prepare a gridded map in the future showing population densities, and so on. It also held that the prosecutor could not give notification to community organizations that were not registered pursuant to the guidelines.

[151] People v. Brasier, 646 N.Y.S.2d 442 (N.Y. Sup. Ct. 1996), held that where the defendant was notified of the hearing on the risk-level assessment and failed to appear for the hearing, he had forfeited his right to be present at the hearing. The court says that the language of N.Y. Corr. Law §168-n (McKinney) is permissive and not mandatory: The court "shall allow the offender to appear and be heard," but the offender's appearance is not required. Ibid. at 443.

[152] In In re Registrant A.B., 285 N.J. Super. 399, 667 A.2d 200 (1995), the court stated that the offender had shown good cause for the permission of a late filing for judicial review. Offender demonstrated that the letter notifying him of the deadline for application of judicial review of his tier II classification was abbreviated and in a "form not universally utilized in this country." The court found it would be in the "interests of justice to permit a late filing." Ibid. at 203.

[153] People v. Lombardo, 640 N.Y.S.2d 995 (N.Y. County Ct. 1996), where the court held that in a case when there was no incarceration ordered, it was within the court's discretion to depart up or down from the "presumptive" risk level of a "65" score on the scale, where the numbers were obtained by assigning numerical values to the risk factors in the guidelines. The court may "depart from it, up or down, if 'special circumstances' warrant such a departure. 'The ability to depart is premised on a recognition that an objective instrument, no matter how well designed, will not fully capture the nuances of every case . . .' a court is therefore permitted to bring its sound judgment and expertise to bear on an otherwise coldly objective exercise which seeks to

quantify that which may prove to be highly subjective." Ibid. at 943–944, quoting from the Sex Offender Registration Act, "Risk Assessment Guidelines and Commentary," January 1996, at 4.

[154] Schuch v. Board of Parole, 139 Or. App. 327, 912 P.2d 403 (1996), where the court held that "the Board's determination that petitioner is a predatory sex offender was not outside the range of the discretion delegated to it by law. ORS 183.482(8)." Ibid. at 404.

[155] See *Doe v. Poritz*, supra note 69.

[156] People v. Ross, 646 N.Y.S.2d 249 (N.Y. Sup. Ct. 1996), where the court held that the offender had challenged his classification as a level three sex offender. The state introduced sufficient evidence for its prima facie case, but the offender failed to produce sufficient evidence to rebut the Board's findings and recommendations.

[157] See *In re Registrant C.A.*, supra note 149.

[158] Ibid.

[159] See Matthews v. Eldridge, 424 U.S. 319 (1976).

[160] A nonconviction offense is criminal conduct for which the defendant was never convicted.

[161] N.J. Stat. Ann. §2C:7-8b(3), which lists criminal history and other criminal history factors indicative of high risk of reoffense, which looks at repetitive and compulsive behavior; the term served prior; whether the offenses were committed against a child; the relationship between the offender and the victim; the use of a weapon violence of infliction of injury during the offense; and the number, date, and nature of prior offenses.

[162] See *In re Registrant C.A.*, 679 A.2d at 1162.

[163] Ibid. at 1164–1167.

[164] Ibid. at 1172, finding constitutional due process and fundamental fairness under the state constitution.

[165] *Black's Law Dictionary* 1281 (5th ed., 1979).

[166] 912 P.2d 1127, 1132 (Wyo. 1996).

[167] 144 Ill. 2d 381, 581 N.E.2d 637, 642 (1991).

[168] See *Snyder v. State*, 912 P.2d at 1132 (Snyder neglected to specify what liberty interest was affected by the registration statute); *People v. Adams*, 581 N.E.2d at 642.

[169] United States Constitution amend. XIV, sec. 1.

[170] City of Cleburne, Texas v. Cleburne Living Center, 473 U.S. 432, 439 (1985).

[171] State v. Mortimer, 135 N.J. 517, 536, 641 A.2d 257, *cert. denied*, 115 S. Ct. 440 (1994).

[172] *Opinion of the Justices to the Senate*, 423 Mass. at 1232, 668 N.E.2d at 755; *Doe v. Poritz*, 662 A.2d at 413; *Artway* , 81 F.3d at 1267-1268.

[173] People v. Mills, 81 Cal. App. 3d 171, 180 (1978); People v. Adams, 581 N.E.2d at 642; *State v. Ward*, 869 P.2d at 1076-1077; *Snyder v. State*, 912 P.2d at 1131; Gilbert v. Peters, 1994 WESTLAW 369643 (W.D. Ill.), which dealt with the collection of blood sample from those convicted of sex offenses. There, the court found that the collection and maintenance of genetic records was rationally related to law enforcement purposes. *Opinion of the Justices to the Senate*, 423 Mass. at 1232–1234, 668 N.E.2d at 755–756; *Doe v. Poritz*, 662 A.2d at 413–415; *Artway* , 81 F.3d at 1267–1268.

[174] *Doe v. Poritz*, 662 A.2d at 406 (citations omitted).

[175] See *Opinion of the Justices to the Senate*, 423 Mass. at 1234, 668 N.E.2d at 756, which found that the constitutional right to privacy was recognized for the first time in Griswold v. Connecticut, 381 U.S. 479 (1965), and Roe v. Wade, 410 U.S. 113 (1973), where the focus of these cases and the ones following them was on the "intrusion by government regulation and prohibition into the especially intimate aspects of a person's life implicated in procreation and childbearing." *Opinion of the Justice to the Senate*, 423 Mass. at 1234, 668 N.E.2d at 756.

[176] See *Opinion of the Justices to the Senate,* 423 Mass. at 1234–1236, 668 N.E.2d at 756–758; *Doe v. Poritz*, 662 A.2d at 413; *Rowe v. Burton*, 884 F. Supp. at 1384.

[177] State v. Calhoun, 669 So. 2d 1351, 1357-1359, where the court held that the state has a compelling interest in protecting the public from sex offenders, registration furthers this legitimate state interest, and convicted sex offenders have a reduced expectancy of privacy, to uphold the statute.

[178] Ibid.; People v. Mills, 81 Cal. App. 3d 171 (1978), which held that any person who "physically molests a seven-year-old child has waived any right to privacy and may absolutely forfeit for a considerable time . . . his right to travel." Ibid. at 181-182. In addition, state statutes have specifically provided that sex offenders released into the community have a reduced expectation of privacy. See, e.g., Ariz. Rev. Stat. Ann. §13-4601; Colo. Rev. Stat. §18-3-412.5 (6.5); Fla. Stat. Ann. §944.606.

[179] *Opinion of the Justices to the Senate*, 423 Mass. at 1234, 668 N.E.2d at 756.

[180] Lanzetta v. New Jersey, 306 U.S. 451, 453 (1939).

[181] 81 F.3d at 1269.

[182] Ibid., *quoting* N.J. Stat. Ann. §2c:7-1b.

[183] Ibid. at 1269–1270.

[184] 1996 WESTLAW 420385 (Idaho July 29, 1996).

[185] State v. Bitt, 118 Idaho 584, 585-586, 798 P.2d 43, 44–45 (1990).

[186] State v. Zichko, supra note 184, at 2.

[187] Ibid. at 2–3.

[188] 793 P.2d at 138–139.

[189] Id. at 138.

[190] State v. Cory, 156 Ariz. 346, 767 P.2d 233 (Ariz.App. 1988).

[191] *State v. Lammie*, 793 P.2d at 138.

[192] *Black's Law Dictionary*, supra note 165, at 591.

[193] 59 F.3d 1556 (9th Cir. 1995).

[194] Ibid. at 1558-1559.

[195] Ibid. at 1559, finding support in several U.S. Supreme Court cases, such as Skinner v. Railway Labor Executives' Association, 489 U.S. 602, 625 (1989); Winston v. Lee, 470 U.S. 753, 762 (1985); Schmerber v. California, 384 U.S. 757, 771 (1966); Breithaupt v. Abram, 352 U.S. 432, 436 (1957).

[196] *Rise v. Oregon*, 59 F.3d at 1560.

[197] Ibid. at 1560–1562.

[198] *Gilbert v. Peters*, supra note 173, at 3; People v. Calahan, 272 Ill. App. 3d 293, 208 Ill. Dec. 532, 649 N.E. 2d 588, 591 (1995), *citing* Jones v. Murray, 962 F.2d 302, 306-307 (4th Cir.), *cert. denied*, 113 S. Ct. 471 (1992).

[199] 884 F. Supp. at 1381.

[200] 389 U.S. 347, 351 (1967).

[201] See *Rowe v. Burton*, 884 F. Supp. at 1381.

[202] The Administrative Procedure Act is a federal law that was enacted in 1946. It governs practice and proceeding before federal administrative agencies. *Black's Law Dictionary*, supra note 165, at 43.

[203] 662 A.2d at 415–417.

[204] Ibid.

[205] The requirement that the court notify the offender prior to taking a pleas should not be confused with whether the offender knowingly failed to register as a sex offender. State statutes may designate that the court, the probation or parole officer, or the registry of motor vehicles notify the offender of his duty to register. As such, the court may have no statutory responsibility to notify the offender.

[206] State v. Calhoun, 669 So. 2d 1351, 1355-1356 (La. App. 1st Cir. 1996); State v. Boros, 646 So. 2d 1183, 1186–1187 (La. App. 5th Cir. 1994).

[207] *People v. Adams*, 581 N.E.2d at 643–644, which held that not including the certification (of the offender as a sex offender for purposes of registration) in the order of commitment was harmless error, as the defendant had signed the habitual child abuse offender form at the time of sentencing, all the requisite findings were made by the court, and the inclusion of the certification in the order of commitment required no discretion but was simply an administrative function. The omission was simply administrative oversight, not affecting any of the offender's substantive rights. The certification order signed later and included in the offender's file was nunc pro tunc; that is, it allowed "the record to reflect that which was already done previously, but which was omitted from the record." Ibid. at 643 (citations omitted).

[208] State v. Young, 112 Ariz. 361, 542 P.2d 20 (1975); People v. McClellan, 6 Cal. 4th 367, 24 Cal. Rptr. 2d 739, 862 P.2d 739 (Cal. 1993); People v. Taylor, 203 Ill. App. 3d 636, 149 Ill. Dec. 115, 561 N.E.2d 393 (Ill. App. 4th Dist. 1990); People v. Murphy, 207 Ill. App. 3d 539, 152 Ill. Dec. 441, 565 N.E.2d 1359 (Ill. App. 4th Dist. 1991); State v. Perkins, 108 Wash. 2d 212, 737 P.2d 250 (1987); State v. Ward, 123 Wash. 488, 869 P.2d 1062 (Wash. 1994). See also Chapter 22, this volume.

[209] 883 P.2d 1256 (Mont. 1994), referring to Mont. Code Ann. §46-18-254, and holding that the plea was therefore voluntary.

[210] *State v. Boros*, 646 So. 2d at 1187.

[211] *People v. McClellan*, 862 P.2d at 746–747, which also found that defendant had failed to object at the time of the omission by the court at the sentencing hearing; State v. Calhoun, 669 So. 2d at 1355–1356; State v. Boros, 646 So. 2d at 1186–1187.

[212] 110 Cal. Rptr. 212, 515 P.2d 12 (1973), where the defendant was also not advised of his right to counsel, and so made his plea without benefit of counsel and without benefit of the notice that by pleading guilty to a misdemeanor, he would have to register as a sex offender.

[213] 42 Cal. App. 3d 975, 117 Cal. Rptr. 333 (1974).

[214] Ibid. at 986.

[215] See supra note 2.

[216] A statute is found to be ambiguous when it can be said to have several meanings, or can be understood to have more than one connection. A statute which is vague is uncertain or does not inform the person of what is prohibited by the government.

[217] *State v. Lammie*, 793 P.2d at 135–136; State v. Cory, 156 Ariz. 27, 749 P.2d 936 (1987); State v. Boucher, 159 Ariz. App. 346, 767 P.2d 233 (Ariz. App. 1989); *State v. Thibodeaux*, slip op. at 96-308, 1996 WESTLAW 304689 (La. App. 3d Cir. May 31, 1996), Murphy v. Wood, 545 N.W.2d 52 (1996), which held that although the defendant was not convicted of a sex offense, but the statute allowed registration where the conviction arose "out of the same circumstances" as a sex offense, the defendant may be subject to registration. However, whether the conviction arose out of the same facts is a question of fact, and where a material fact exists, there can be no summary judgment for either party. Ibid. at 53–54.

[218] In re Bernardino S., 4 Cal. App. 4th 613, 5 Cal. Rptr. 2d 746 (1992).

[219] People v. Tye, 160 Cal. App. 3d 796, 206 Cal. Rptr. 813 (1984).

[220] 217 Ill. App. 3d 770, 160 Ill. Dec. 836, 578 N.E.2d 15, 17–19. (Ill. App. 2d Dist. 1991).

[221] Ibid. at 17. The statute no longer requires a second or subsequent offense to trigger registration.

[222] 232 Cal. App. 3d 1592, 284 Cal. Rptr. 212 (1991).

[223] Ibid. at 1597-1598; People v. Rogers, 197 Ill. App. 3d 722, 144 Ill. Dec. 156, 555 N.E.2d 53 (Ill. App. 2d Dist. 1990), where the offense of contributing to the sexual delinquency of a minor, a misdemeanor criminal sexual abuse charge, could not serve as a basis for certification as a habitual sex offender a second or subsequent offense, but where there was an error in drafting the statute, but which both parties knew was erroneous (modifying language, "when the offense was a felony," was placed incorrectly to modify aggravated criminal sexual abuse, which is always a felony, instead of in place to modify "criminal sexual abuse," which can be a misdemeanor or a felony.

[224] 164 Cal. App. 3d 133, 210 Cal. Rptr. 117 (1985).

[225] Ibid. at 136-140. See also In re Welfare of J.L.M. and D.R.O., infra note 226.

[226] Alabama, California, Colorado, Delaware, Indiana, Iowa, Massachusetts, Michigan, Minnesota, Mississippi, Oregon, Rhode Island, South Carolina, Texas, Virginia, Washington, and Wisconsin all provide specifically that juvenile sex offenders come under the registration statute.

[227] State v. Ward, 20 Kan. App. 2d 238, 886 P.2d 890 (Kan. App. 1994); State v. S.M.H., 76 Wash. App. 550, 887 P.2d 903 (Wash. App. Div. 1 1995).

[228] In re Welfare of J.L.M. and D.R.O., 1996 WESTLAW 380664 (Minn. App. July 9, 1996), where the statute stated that the offender must register if "charged or petitioned for a felony violation . . . and convicted of or adjudicated delinquent of that offense or of another offense arising out of the same circumstances." The juveniles were petitioned for a felony offense but adjudicated of a misdemeanor offense and held responsible to register as sex offenders. The court held, however, that although "[o]n its face, the statute provides that juveniles who are charged with criminal sexual

conduct can be forced to register as sex offenders even if they are not adjudicated delinquent of a sex offense, which is exactly what happened in this case," requiring them to register as sex offenders is both unreasonable and unnecessary to restore law-abiding conduct." Ibid. at 1–2.

[229] State v. Heiskell, 129 Wash. 2d 113, 916 P.2d 366 (Wash. 1996).

[230] In In re Interest of B.G., 289 N.J. Super. 361, 674 A.2d 178 (1996), the court found that registration was not contrary to the Juvenile Code, and the Juvenile Code does not apply in determining when the registration period ends. The more specific statute is the registration statute, and that does not require that the registration end at age 18. State v. Acheson, 75 Wash. App. 151, 877 P.2d 217 (Wash. App. Div 2 1994), held that the registration specifically provided that juveniles adjudicated for sex offenses must register for life, unless they petitioned and obtained relief from the court, and because the Juvenile Court did not have jurisdiction over him, the duty to register did not automatically end at age 21.

[231] See supra note 205. Whether the defendant knew of his duty to register is a separate determination than whether the court has an obligation to notify the offender of his duty.

[232] State v. Garcia, 156 Ariz. 381, 752 P.2d 34 (Ariz. App. 1987).

[233] United States v. Williams, 53 F.3d 341 (Table) (9th Cir. 1995).

[234] In re Parks, 184 Cal. App. 3d 476, 229 Cal. Rptr. 202 (1986).

[235] Toussie v. United States, 397 U.S. 112, 114–115 (1970).

[236] In re Parks, 184 Cal. App. 3d at 480–481.

[237] 44 Cal. App. 4th 859, 52 Cal. Rptr. 2d 194 (1996).

[238] Ibid. at 864.

[239] Bradford v. California, 36 Cal. App. 3d 16, 111 Cal. Rptr. 852 (1973).

[240] 288 N.J. Super. 166, 672 A.2d 183 (App. Div. 1966).

[241] Ibid.

[242] One judge in Orange County, New York said that he had just had his first request for a judicial hearing on the tier-level classification. The issue before him was whether the Legal Aid Society (LAS) was responsible for providing representation in this case. The LAS attorney interpreted the hearing as a "civil" proceeding and argued that he was therefore not responsible to provide representation. The judge said that the statute was ambiguous on that issue and in many other areas. He stated that New York's Megan's Law would have escalated the number of cases in his county.

[243] A.B. 3339, an act to repeal and add Cal. Penal Code §645, signed by Governor Wilson on September 17, 1996.

[244] The Associated Press, Worcester Telegram and Gazette, 30 August 1996, p. A6.

Appendices

Appendix A

Bibliography

Aarens, M., Cameron, T., Roizen, J., Roizen, R., Room, R., Schneberk, D., & Wingard, D. (1978). *Alcohol, casualties and crime*. Berkeley, CA: Social Research Group.

Abbey, A. (1991). Acquaintance rape and alcohol consumption on college campuses: How are they linked? *Journal of American College Health, 39*, 165–169.

Abel, G. G., Becker, J. V., & Cunningham-Rathner, J. (1984). Complications, consent and cognitions in sex between children and adults. *International Journal of Law and Psychiatry, 7*, 89–103.

Abel, G. G., Becker, J. V., Cunningham-Rathner, J. Mittelman, M., & Rouleau, J. L. (1988). Multiple paraphilic diagnoses among sex offenders. *Bulletin of the American Academy of Psychiatry and the Law, 16*(2), 153–168.

Abel, G. G., Becker, J. V. Mittelman, M., Cunningham-Rathner, J., & Murphy, W. D. (1987). Self-reported sex crimes of incarcerated paraphilics. *Journal of Interpersonal Violence, 2*(1), 3–25.

Abel, G. G., Becker, J. V., Murphy, W. D., & Flanagan, B. (1981). Identifying dangerous child molesters. In R. B. Short (Ed.), *Violent behavior: Social learning approaches to prediction, management and treatment* (pp. 116–137). New York: Brunner/Mazel.

Abel, G. G., & Blanchard, E. E. (1974). The role of fantasy in the treatment of sexual deviation. *Archives of General Psychiatry, 30*, 467–475.

Abel, G. G., Blanchard, E. B., & Becker, J. V. (1978). An integrated treatment program for rapists. In R. Rada (Ed.), *Clinical aspects of the rapist*. New York: Grune & Stratton.

Abel, G. G., Gore, D. K., Holland, C. L., Camp, N., Becker, J. V., & Rathner, J. (1989). The measurement of cognitive distortions in child molesters. *Annals of Sex Research, 2*, 135–153.

Abel, G. G., Mittelman, M. S., & Becker, J. V. (1985). Sexual offenders: Results of assessment and recommendations for treatment. In M. H. Ben-Aron, S. J. Hucker, & C. D. Webster (Eds.), *Clinical criminology: The assessment and treatment of criminal behavior* (pp. 191–205). Toronto: University of Toronto.

Abel, G. G., Mittelman, M. S., Becker, J. V., Rathner, J., & Rouleau, J. L. (1988). Predicting child molesters' response to treatment. *Annals of the New York Academy of Sciences, 528*, 223–234.

Abel, G., Osborn C., Anthony, D., & Gardos, P. (Eds.). (1982). Current treatment of paraphiliacs. *Annual Review of Sex offender Research: An Integrative and Interdisciplinary Review, 3*.

Abrams, S. A., Hoyt, D., & Jewell, C. (1991). The effectiveness of the disclosure test with sex abusers of children. *Polygraph, 20*, 197–203.

Abramson, L. Y., Seligman, M. E. P., & Teasdale, J. D. (1978). *Learned helplessness in humans: Critique and reformulation*. *Journal of Abnormal Psychology, 87*, 49–74.

Aday, R. H. (1994a). Aging in prison: A case study of new elderly offenders. *International Journal of Offender Therapy and Comparative Criminology, 38*(1), 79–91.

Aday, R. H. (1994b). Golden years behind bars: Special programs and facilities for elderly inmates. *Federal Probation, 58*(2), 47–54.

Agnew, R. (1991). The interactive effects of peer variables on delinquency. *Criminology, 29*, 47–72.

Ainsworth, M. D. S. (1989). Attachments beyond infancy. *American Psychologist, 44*, 709–716.

Ainsworth, M. D. S., Blehar, M. C., Waters, E., & Walls, S. (1978). *Patterns of attachment: A psychological study of the strange situation*. Hillsdale, NJ: Erlbaum.

Ainsworth, M. D. S., & Bowlby, J. (1991). An ethological approach to personality development. *American Psychologist, 46,* 333–341.

Alberti, R. I., & Emmons, M. L. (1982). *Your perfect right: A guide to assertive living.* San Luis Obispo, CA: Impact.

Alexander. P. C. (1992). Application of attachment theory to the study of sexual abuse. *Journal of Consulting and Clinical Psychology, 60,* 185–195.

Allen, C. M. (1991). Women as perpetrators of child sexual abuse: Recognition barriers. In A. L. Horton, B. L. Johnson, L. M. Roundy, & D. Williams (Eds.), *The incest perpetrator: A family member no one wants to treat* (pp. 108–125). Newbury Park, CA: Sage.

Allen, K. (1994). *Physical disability and assistance dogs: Quality of life issues.* Paper presented at 13th Annual Conference of the Delta Society, New York City.

Allport, F. H. (1955). *Theories of perception and the concept of structure.* New York: Wiley.

Allport, G. (1954). *The nature of prejudice.* Cambridge: Addison-Wesley.

Allport, G. W. (1985). The historical background of social psychology. In G. Lindzey & E. Aronson (Eds.), *Handbook of social psychology* (3rd. ed., pp. 1–46). New York: Random House.

American Psychiatric Association. (1980). *A psychiatric glossary* (5th ed.). Washington, DC: Author.

American Psychiatric Association. (1980). *Diagnostic and statistical manual for mental disorders* (3rd ed.). Washington, DC: Author.

American Psychiatric Association. (1987). *Diagnostic and statistical manual for mental disorders* (3rd ed., rev.). Washington, DC: Author.

American Psychiatric Association. (1994). *Diagnostic and statistical manual for mental disorders* (4th ed.). Washington, DC: Author.

American Psychological Association. (1992). Ethical principles of psychologists and code of conduct. *American Psychologist, 47*(12), 1597–1611.

Amir, M. (1967). Alcohol and forcible rape. *British Journal of Addictions, 62,* 219–232.

Anderson, A., & Goolishian, H., (1988). Human systems as linguistic systems: Preliminary and evolving ideas about the implications of clinical theory. *Family Process, 27,* 371–394.

Anderson, J. (1973). "Aqualung." On *Jethro Tull: Aqualung.* New York: Chrysalis Records.

Anson, R. H., & Hancock, B. W. (1992). Crowding, proximity, inmate violence, and the eighth amendment. *Journal of Offender Rehabilitation, 17*(3/4), 123-132.

Arbogast, D. (1995). *Wounded warriors—A time for healing.* Omaha, NE: Little Turtle.

Arriessohn, R. M. (1981). Recidivism revisited. *Juvenile and Family Court Journal, 32*(4), 59–68.

Awad, G. A., & Saunders, E. B. (1989). Adolescent child molesters: Clinical observations. *Child Psychiatry and Human Development, 19,* 195–206.

Awad, G. A., & Saunders, E. B. (1991). Male adolescent sexual assaulters: Clinical observations. *Journal of Interpersonal Violence, 6,* 446–460.

Awad, G., Saunders, E., & Levene, J. (1984). A clinical study of male sex offenders, *International Journal of Offender Therapy and Comparative Criminology, 28,* 105–115.

Ballard, D. T., Blair, G. D., Devereaux, S., Valentine, L. K., Horton, A. L., & Johnson, B. L. (1990). A comparative profile of the incest perpetrator: Background characteristics, abuse history, and use of social skills. In A. L. Horton, B. L. Johnson, L. M. Roundy, & D. Williams (Eds.), *The incest perpetrator: A family member no one wants to treat* (pp. 43–64). Newbury Park, CA: Sage.

Bandura, A. (1986). *Social foundations of thought and action: A social cognitive theory.* Englewood Cliffs, NJ: Prentice Hall.

Bannister, A. (1991). Learning to live again: Psychodrama techniques with sexually abused young people. In P. Holmes & M. Karp (Eds.), *Psychodrama: Inspiration and technique* (pp. 77–86) London: Tavistock/Routledge.

Barbaree, H. E. (1991). Denial and minimization among sex offenders: Assessment and treatment outcome. *Forum on Corrections Research, 3*, 30–33.

Barbaree, H. E., & Cortoni, F. A. (1993). Treatment of the juvenile sex offender within the criminal justice and mental health systems. In H. E. Barbaree (Ed.), *The juvenile sex offender.* New York: Guilford Press.

Barbaree, H. E., & Marshall, W. L. (1989). Erectile responses among heterosexual child molesters, father-daughter incest offenders, and matched non-offenders: Five distinct age preference profiles. *Canadian Journal of Behavioral Science, 21*(1), 70-82.

Barbaree, H., Marshall, W., & Lanthier, R. (1979). Deviant sexual arousal in rapists. *Behavior Research and Therapy, 17*, 215-222.

Barbaree, H. E., Seto, M. C., Serin, R. C., Amos, N. L., & Preston, D. L. (1994). Comparisons between sexual and nonsexual rapist subtypes: Sexual arousal to rape, offense precursors, and offense characteristics. *Criminal Justice and Behavior, 21*, 95–114.

Barnard, G. W., Fuller, A. K., Robbins, L., & Shaw, T. (1989). *The child molester: An integrated approach to evaluation and treatment.* New York: Brunner/Mazel.

Barrett, M. J., Sykes, C., & Byrnes, W. (1986). A systemic model for the treatment of intra-family child sexual abuse. In T. Trepper & M. J. Barrett (Eds.), *Treating incest: A multiple systems perspective* (pp. 67–82). New York: Haworth Press.

Bartholomew, K. (1990). Avoidance of intimacy: An attachment perspective. *Journal of Social and Personal Relationships, 7*, 147–178.

Bartholomew, K., & Horowitz, L. M. (1991). Attachment styles among adults: A test of a four category model. *Journal of Personality and Social Psychology, 61*, 226–244.

Baruk, H. (1945). *Psychiatrie morale expérimentale, individuelle et sociale: Haines et réactions de culpabilité* [*Moral experimental, individual and social psychiatry: Hatred and guilt reactions*]. Paris: Presses Universitaires de France.

Bass, E., & Davis, L. (1988). *The courage to heal.* New York: Harper & Row.

Baumeister, R. F., & Leary, M. R. (1995). The need to belong: Desire for interpersonal attachments as a fundamental human motivation. *Psychological Bulletin, 117*, 497–529.

Bear, E. (1993). *Inpatient treatment for adult survivors of sexual abuse: A summary of data from 22 programs.* Brandan, VT: Safer Society Press.

Beard, W. (1984). Of people, pooches and prisons: Inmates train handi-dogs. *Dog World, 3*, 14–15.

Becker, J. V. (1990). Treating adolescent sexual offenders. *Professional Psychology: Research and Practice, 21*, 362–365.

Becker, J. V., Cunningham-Rathner, J., & Kaplan, M. S. (1986). Adolescent sexual offenders: Demographics, criminal and sexual histories, and recommendations for reducing future offenses. *Journal of Interpersonal Violence, 1*, 431–445.

Becker, J. V., Harris, C. D., & Sales, B. D. (1993). Juveniles who commit sexual offenses: A critical review of research. In G. C. N. Hall & R. Hirschman (Eds.), *Sexual aggression: Issues in etiology and assessment, treatment and policy* (pp. 215–228). Washington, DC: Taylor & Francis.

Becker, J. V., Kaplan, M. S., Cunningham-Rathner, J., & Kavoussi, R. (1986). Characteristics of adolescent incest perpetrators: Preliminary findings. *Journal of Family Violence, 1*, 85–97.

Becker, J. V., Kaplan, M. S., & Tenke, C. E. (1992). The relationship of abuse history, denial, and erectile response profiles of adolescent sexual perpetrators. *Behavior Therapy, 23*, 87–97.

Becker, J. V., Kaplan, M. S., Tenke, C. E., & Tartaglini, A. (1991). The incidence of depressive symptomology in juvenile sex offenders with a history of abuse. *Child Abuse and Neglect, 15*, 531–536.

Beckett, R., Beech, A., Fisher, D., & Fordham, A. S. (1994). *Community-based treatment for sex offenders: An evaluation of seven treatment programmes* [Home Office Occasional Paper]. London: Home Office.

Beckett, R., & Fisher, D. (1994, November). *Assessing victim empathy: A new measure*. Paper presented at the 13th Annual Conference of the Association for the Treatment of Sexual Abusers, San Francisco.

Bell, A. P., & Hall, C. S. (1971). *The personality of a child molester*. Chicago: Aldine-Atherton.

Bemm, S. L. (1985). Androgyny and gender schema theory: A conceptual and empirical integration. In T. B. Sonderegger (Ed.), *Psychology and gender* (pp. 179–226). Lincoln: University of Nebraska Press.

Bennett, T., & Wright, R. (1984). The relationship between alcohol use and burglary. *British Journal of Addiction, 79*, 431–437.

Benoit, J. L., & Kennedy, W. A. (1992). The abuse history of male adolescent sex offenders. *Journal of Interpersonal Violence, 7*, 543–548.

Bergman, J., (1985). *Fishing for barracuda: Pragmatics of brief systemic therapy* (pp. 116–150). New York: Norton.

Bernard, G., Fuller, K., Robbins, L., & Shaw, T. (1989). *The child molester: An integrated approach to evaluation and treatment*. New York: Brunner/Mazel.

Black, C. (1990). *Double duty: Dual dynamics within the chemically dependent home*. New York: Ballantine Books.

Blakey, "The Indefinite Civil Commitment of Dangerous Sex Offenders Is an Appropriate Legal Compromise Between 'Mad' and 'Bad'—A Study of Minnesota's Sexual Psychopathic Personality Statute," 10 *Notre Dame J. of Law, Ethics and Pub. Pol'y* 227 (1996).

Blanchard, G. T. (1995). *The difficult connection: The therapeutic relationship in sex offender treatment*. Brandon, VT: Safer Society Press.

Blaske, D. M., Borduin, C. M., Henggeler, S., & Mann, B. (1989). Individual, family and peer characteristics of adolescent sexual offenders and assaultive offenders. *Developmental Psychology, 25*, 846-855.

Blatner, A., & Blatner, A. (1988). *Foundations of psychodrama*. New York: Springer.

Blatt, S. J., Hart, B., Quinlan, D. M., Leadbeater, B., & Auerbach, J. (1993). Interpersonal and self-critical dysphoria and behavioral problems in adolescents. *Journal of Youth and Adolescence, 22*, 253–267.

Boone Jr., H. N. (1994). An examination of recidivism and other outcome measures: A review of literature. *Perspectives, American Probation and Parole Association*, 12–18.

Borduin, C. M., Henggeler, S. W., Blaske, D. M., & Stein, R. J. (1990). Multisystemic treatment of adolescent sexual offenders. *International Journal of Offender Therapy and Comparative Criminology, 34*, 105–113.

Bowlby, J. (1969). *Attachment and loss: Attachment* (vol. 1). New York: Basic Books.

Bowlby, J. (1973). *Attachment and loss: Separation* (vol. 2). New York: Basic Books.

Bowlby, J. (1980). *Attachment and loss: Loss, sadness and depression* (vol. 3). New York: Basic Books.

Bowling, A. P., Edelmann, R. J., Leaver, J., & Hoekel, T. (1989). Loneliness, mobility, well-being and social support in a sample of over 85 year olds. *Personality and Individual Differences, 10*(11), 1189-1192.

Brannon, J. M., & Troyer, R. (1991). Peer group counseling: A normalized residential alternative to the specialized treatment of adolescent sexual offenders. *International Journal of Offender Therapy and Comparative Criminology, 35*, 225-234.

Brauer, B. (1986). *Treatment of multiple personality disorder*. Washington, DC: American Psychiatric Association Press.

Breunlin, D., Schwartz, R., & MacKune Karrer, B. (1992). A blueprint for family therapy. In D. Breunlin, R. Schwartz, & B. MacKune Karrer (Eds.), *Metaworks: A new blueprint for family therapy*. San Francisco: Jossey-Bass.

Briddell, D. W., Rimm, D. C., Caddy, G. R., Krawitz, G., Sholis, D., & Wunderlin, R. (1978). Effects of alcohol and cognitive set on sexual arousal to deviant stimuli. *Journal of Abnormal Psychology, 87*, 418–430.

Briere, F., & Malamuth, N. M. (1993). Predicting self reported likelihood of sexually abusive behavior:Attitude versus sexual explanations. *Journal of Research in Personality, 17,* 315–323.

Brown, R. G., Jahanshahi, M., Quinn, N., & Marsden, C. D. (1990). Sexual function in patients with Parkinson's disease and their partners. *Journal of Neurological and Neurosurgical Psychiatry, 53,* 480-486.

Brown, S. A., Christiansen, B. A., & Goldman, M. S. (1987). The Alcohol Expectancy Questionnaire: An instrument for the assessment of adolescent and adult alcohol expectancies. *Journal of Studies on Alcohol, 48,* 483–491.

Brown, S. A., Goldman, M. S., Inn, A., & Anderson, L. R. (1980). Expectations of reinforcement from alcohol: Their domain and relation to drinking patterns. *Journal of Clinical and Consulting Psychology, 48,* 419–426.

Brownfield, D., & Sorenson, A. M. (1993). Self-control and juvenile delinquency: Theoretical issues and an empirical assessment of selected elements of a general theory of crime. *Deviant Behavior, 14,* 243–264.

Brownfield, D., & Thompson, K. (1991). Attachment to peers and delinquent behavior. *Canadian Journal of Criminology, 33,* 45-60.

Bryant, S., & Rakowski, W. (1992). Predictors of mortality among elderly African-Americans. *Research on Aging, 14*(1), 50-67.

Bumby, K. M. (1996). Assessing the cognitive distortions of child molesters and rapists: Development and validation of the MOLEST and RAPE scales. *Sexual Abuse: A Journal of Research and Treatment, 8,* 37-54.

Bumby, K. M., & Bumby, N. H. (1993, November). *Adolescent females who sexually perpetrate: Preliminary findings.* Paper presented at the 12th annual Research and Treatment Conference of the Association for the Treatment of Sexual Abusers, Boston.

Bumby, K. M., & Bumby, N. H. (1995, October). *Emotional, behavioral, and developmental comparisons between juvenile female sexual offenders and nonoffenders.* Paper presented at the 14th annual Research and Treatment Conference of the Association for the Treatment of Sexual Abusers, New Orleans.

Bumby, K. M., Bumby, N. H., Burgess, A. W., & Hartman, C. R. (1996). *From victims to victimizers: Sexually aggressive post-traumatic responses of sexually abused adolescent females.* Manuscript in preparation.

Bumby, K. M., Burgess, A. W., Hartman, C. R., Bumby, N. H., Raney, T. J., & McAuliff, B. D. (1994, July). *The information processing of trauma model and adolescent aggressive response patterns to physical and sexual abuse.* Paper presented at the 1994 National Conference on Family Violence: Research and Practice, Omaha, NE.

Bumby, K. M., & Marshall, W. L. (1994, October). *Loneliness and intimacy deficits among incarcerated rapists and child molesters.* Paper presented at the 13th annual research and treatment conference of the Association for the Treatment of Sexual Abusers, San Francisco.

Bunk, P. D. (1994). *Influence of parental coping on the psychological development of children following severe traumatization.* Paper presented at the 13th International Congress of the International Association for Child and Adolescent Psychiatry and Allied Professionals, San Francisco.

Burditt, T. (1995, October). *Treating sex offenders who deny their guilt: The application of motivational interviewing to the denier's pilot study.* Paper presented at the annual research and treatment conference of the Association for the Treatment of Sexual Abusers, New Orleans.

Bureau of Justice Statistics. (1994). *Sourcebook of criminal justice statistics.* Washington, DC: U.S. Department of Justice, Office of Justice Programs.

Burgess, A. W., Hartman, C. R., McCausland, M. P., & Powers, P. (1984). Response patterns in children and adolescents exploited through sex rings and pornography. *American Journal of Psychiatry, 141,* 656-662.

Burgess, A. W., Hartman, C. R., & McCormack, A. (1987). Abused to abuser: Antecedents of socially deviant behaviors. *American Journal of Psychiatry, 144,* 1431–1436.

Burgess, A. W., Johnson, T. C., & van der Kolk, B. (1993, November). *Childhood trauma and aggressive outcome.* Paper presented at the 12th annual Research and Treatment Conference of the Association for the Treatment of Sexual Abusers, Boston.

Burns, A., Jacoby, R., & Levy, R. (1990). Psychiatric phenomena in Alzheimer's disease. IV: Disorders of behaviour. *British Journal of Psychiatry, 157,* 86-94.

Byles, J. A. (1981). Evaluation of an attendance center program for male juvenile probationers. *Canadian Journal of Criminology, 23*(3), 343-355.

Cadigan, T. P. (1991). Electronic monitoring in Federal Pretrial Release. *Federal Probation, 55*(1), 26-30.

Caffaro, J. V. (1995). Identification and trauma: An integrative-developmental approach. *Journal of Family Violence, 10*(18), 23.

Camp, B. H., & Thyer, B. A. (1993). Treatment of adolescent sex offenders: A review of empirical research. *Journal of Applied Social Sciences, 17,* 191–206.

Cantwell, H. B. (1988). Child sexual abuse: Very young perpetrators. *Child Abuse and Neglect, 12,* 579–582.

Carnes, P. J. (1983). *The sexual addiction.* Minneapolis, MN: CompCare Press.

Carpenter, J., & Armenti, N. (1972). Some effects of ethanol on human sexual and aggressive behavior. In B. Kissin & H. Begleiter (Eds.), *The biology of alcoholism: Physiology and behavior* (vol. 2, pp. 509-543). New York: Plenum Press.

Carr-Gregg, C. (1984). *Kicking the habit.* Queensland: Queensland University Press.

Carrasco, N. (1990). *The relationship between parental support and control and adolescent self-esteem in Mexican, Mexican-American and Anglo-American families.* Doctoral dissertation. University of Texas, Austin.

Carrasco, N., King, R., & Garza-Louis, D. (1996). The Hispanic sex offender: Machismo and cultural values. *Forum.*

Cattell, R. B., Cattell, M. D. L., & Johns, E. P. (1984). *Manual and norms for the High School Personality Questionnaire.* Champaign, IL: Institute for Personality and Ability Testing.

Chasnoff, I. J., Burns, W. J., Schnoll, S. H., Burns, K., Chisum, G., Kyle-Sproe, L. (1986). Maternal-neonatal incest. American *Journal of Orthopsychiatry, 56,* 577–580.

Chavaria, F.R. (1992). Successful drug treatment in a criminal justice setting: A case study. *Federal Probation, 56*(1), 48-52.

Check, J. V. P., Perlman, D., & Malamuth, N.M. (1985). Loneliness and aggressive behavior. *Journal of Social and Personal Relationships, 2,* 243-252.

Chesner, A. (1994). Dramatherapy and psychodrama. In S. Jennings, A. Cattanach, S. Mitchell, A. Chesner, & B. Meldrum (Eds.), *The handbook of dramatherapy.* London: Routledge.

Cogen, R., & Steinman, W. (1990). Sexual function and practice in elderly men of lower socioeconomic status. *Journal of Family Practice, 31*(2), 162-166.

Cohen, F. (1995). Right to treatment. In B. K. Schwartz & H. R. Cellini (Eds.), *The sex offender: Corrections, treatment, and legal practice.* Kingston, NJ: Civic Research Institute.

Cohen, F. (1995). Washington's Sexually Violent Predator Act. In B. K. Schwartz & H. R. Cellini, *The sex offender: Corrections, treatment and legal practice.* Kingston, NJ: Civic Research Institute.

Collins, N. L., & Read, S. J. (1990). Adult attachment, working models and relationship quality in dating couples. *Journal of Personality and Social Psychology, 58,* 644-663.

Committee on Government Policy, Group for the Advancement of Psychiatry. (1994). *Forced into treatment: The role of coercion in clinical practice.* Washington, DC: American Psychiatric Press.

Commonwealth of Virginia. (1991). *Drugs in Virginia: A criminal justice perspective.* Richmond: Commonwealth of Virginia, Department of Justice Services.

Connors, G. J., Tarbox, A. R., & Faillace, L. A. (1993). Changes in alcohol expectancies and drinking behavior among treated problem drinkers. *Journal of Studies on Alcohol, 53,* 676–683.

Cooper, M. L., Russell, M., & George, W. H. (1988). Coping, expectancies, and alcohol abuse: A test of social learning formulations. *Journal of Abnormal Psychology, 97,* 218–230.

Conte, J. R. (1988).The effects of sexual abuse on children: Results of a research project. In R. A. Prentky & V. I. Quinsey (Eds.), *Human sexual aggression: Current perspectives.* New York: New York Academy of Sciences.

Corbo, C. A. (1988). *Release outcome in New Jersey 1982 release cohort: A 36-month follow-up study.* Trenton: New Jersey Department of Corrections. (NCJRS Document No. 117207)

Corson, S. A., Corson, E. O., Gwynne, P. H., & Arnold, E. L.(1977). Pet dogs as nonverbal communication links in hospital psychiatry. *Comprehensive Psychiatry, 18*(1), 61–72.

Cotten-Hustan, A. L. (1984). Comparisons of sex offenders with non-offenders on attitudes toward masturbation and female fantasy as related to participation in human sexuality sessions. *Journal of Offender Counseling, Services, and Rehabilitation, 8,* 13–26.

Courtois, C. (1988). Healing the incest wound: *Adult survivors in therapy.* New York: Norton.

Cowden, J. E., Peterson, W. M., & Pacht, A. R. (1969). The MCI vs. the Jesness Inventory as a screening and classification instrument at a juvenile correctional institution. *Journal of Clinical Psychology, 25,* 57–60.

Crawford, D. A. (1981). Treatment approaches with pedophiles. In M. Cook & K. Howells (Eds.), *Adult sexual interest in children* (pp. 181–217). New York: Academic Press.

Critchlow, B. (1983). Blaming the booze: The attribution of responsibility for drunken behavior. *Personality and Social Psychology Bulletin, 9,* 451–473.

Crowe, L. C., & George, W. H. (1989). Alcohol and human sexuality: Review and integration. *Psychological Bulletin, 105,* 374–386.

Curry, J. F. (1991). Outcome research on residential treatment: Implications and suggested directions. *American Journal of Orthopsychiatry, 61*(3), 348–357.

Cusack, O. (1988). *Pets and mental health.* New York: Haworth Press.

Dahms, A. M. (1972). *Emotional intimacy: Overlooked requirement for survival.* Boulder, CO: Pruett.

Davis, G. E., & Leitenberg, H. (1987). Adolescent sex offenders. *Psychological Bulletin, 101*(3), 417–427.

Davis, K. D.(1992). *Therapy dogs: Training your dog to reach others.* New York: Macmillan.

Davis, M. H. (1980). A multidimensional approach to individual differences in empathy. *JSAS Catalog of Selected Documents in Psychology, 10*(4), 85.

Davis, M. H. (1983). Measuring individual differences in empathy: Evidence for a multidimensional approach. *Journal of Personality and Social Psychology, 44,* 113-126.

Dayton, T. (1994). *The drama within: Psychodrama and experimental therapy.* Deerfield Beach, FL: Health Communications.

De La Cancela, V. (1986). A critical analysis of Puerto Rico machismo: Implications for clinical practice. *Psychotherapy, 23*(2), 291-296.

Dental dogs. (1995, July). *Your dog, 1*(12), 8.

de Shazer, S. (1985). *Keys to solution in brief therapy* (pp. 65–80). New York: Norton.

DeYoung, Y., & Zigler, E. F. (1994). Machismo in two cultures: Relation to punitive child-rearing practices. American *Journal of Orthopsychiatry, 64*(3), 386-394.

Diamant, L., & Windholz, G. (1981). Loneliness in college students: Some theoretical, empirical and therapeutic considerations. *Journal of College Students Personality, 22*, 515–252.

Diaz-Guerrero, R. (1975). *Psychology of the Mexican: Culture and personality.* Austin: University of Texas Press.

DiClemente, C. C., & Hughes, S. O. (1990). Stages of change profiles in outpatient alcoholism treatment. *Journal of Substance Abuse, 2*, 217–235.

Dimock, P. T., Hunter, M., & Struve, J. (1995, October 5–7). *Survivor workshop: Therapeutic trauma reenactment.* Paper presented at the Sixth World Interdisciplinary Conference on Male Sexual Victimization. Columbus, OH.

Dougher, M. J. (1988). Clinical assessment of sex offenders. In B. K. Schwartz (Ed.), *A practitioner's guide to treating the incarcerated male sex offender: Breaking the cycle of sexual abuse* (pp. 77–84). Washington, DC: Department of Justice, National Institute of Corrections.

Dulton, M. A. (1990). Assessment and treatment of post-traumatic stress disorder among battered women. In K. Peterson, M. Prout, & R. Schwartz (Eds.), *Post-traumatic stress disorder: A clinicians guide.* New York: Plenum Press.

Durkin, R. P., & Durkin, A. B. (1975). Evaluating residential programs for disturbed children. In M. Guttentag & E. Strevening (Eds.), *Handbook of evaluation research* (vol. 2, pp. 275–339). Newbury Park, CA: Sage.

Dweck, C. S., & Elliott, E. S. (1983). Achievement motivation. In P. H. Mussen (Gen. Ed.) & E. M. Hetherington (Vol. Ed.), *Handbook of child psychology: Social and personality development* (vol. 4, pp. 643–691). New York: Wiley.

Dweck, C. S., & Leggett. E. L. (1988). A social-cognitive approach to motivation and personality. *Psychological Review, 95*, 256–273.

Effective treatment techniques for sex offenders. 22 *Psychiatric Annual* 5319 (1992).

Eisenberg, N., & Miller, P. A. (1987). Empathy, sympathy, and altruism: Empirical and conceptual links. In N. Eisenberg & J. Strayer (Eds.), *Empathy and its development* (pp. 292–316). Cambridge, MA: Cambridge University Press.

Eisenberg, N., & Strayer, J. (Eds.). (1987). *Empathy and its development.* Cambridge, MA: Cambridge University Press.

Elliott, D. S. (1994). *National Youth Survey: Wave III, 1978.* Ann Arbor, MI: Inter-university Consortium of Political and Social Research.

Elliott, D. S., & Huizinga, D. (1987, March). *Scales from the National Youth Survey: Progress report* (Project report no. 38). Boulder, CO: Institute for Behavioral Science.

Elliott, D. S., Huizinga, D., & Ageton, S. S. (1985). *Explaining delinquency and drug use.* Beverly Hills, CA: Sage.

Ellis, K. (1991). Overcrowding, inmate violence and cruel and unusual punishment. *Criminal Justice Journal, 13*(1), 81–99.

Ellsworth, T., & Helle, K. A. (1994). Older offenders on probation. *Federal Probation, 58*(4), 43–50.

Emerick, R. L., & Dutton, W. A. (1993). The effect of polygraphy on the self report of adolescent sex offenders: Implications for risk assessment. *Annals of Sex Research, 6*, 83–103.

Emunah, R. (1994). *Acting for real: Drama therapy process, techniques and performance.* New York: Brunner/Mazel.

English, K., Colling-Chadwick, S., Pullen, S., & Jones, L. (1996). *How are sex offenders managed on probation and parole? A national survey.* Washington, DC: National Institute of Justice and Colorado Division of Criminal Justice.

English, K., Pullen, S., & Jones, L. (1996). *Managing adult sex offenders: A containment approach.* Colorado Division of Criminal Justice & American Probation and Parole Association.

Erickson, E. H. (1950). *Childhood and society.* New York: Norton.

Erwin, B. S., & Bennett, L. A. (1987). *New dimensions in probation: Georgia's experience with intensive probation supervision.* Washington, DC: U.S. Department of Justice, National Institute of Justice.

Evans, C. M. (1980). Alcohol, violence, and aggression. *British Journal on Alcohol and Alcoholism, 15*(3), 104–117.

Fagan, J. & Wexler, S. (1988). Explanations of sexual assault among violent delinquents. *Journal of Adolescent Research, 3*, 363–385.

Faller, K. (1987). Women who sexually abuse children. *Violence and Victims, 2*, 263–276.

Faller, K. C. (1988). *Child sexual abuse: An interdisciplinary manual for diagnosis, case management, and treatment.* New York: Columbia University Press.

Federal Bureau of Investigation. (1991). *Uniform crime reports for the United States, 1990.* Washington, DC: Author.

Fehr, B., & Perlman, D. (1985). The family as a social network and support system. In L. L'Abate (Ed.), *Handbook of family psychology and therapy* (vol. 1, pp. 323-356). Champaign, IL: Dow.

Fehrenbach, P. A., & Monastersky, C. (1988). Characteristics of female sexual offenders. *American Journal of Orthopsychiatry, 58*, 148-151.

Fehrenbach, P. A., Smith, W., Monastersky, C., & Deisher, R. W. (1986). Adolescent sexual offenders: Offender and offense characteristics. *American Journal of Orthopsychiatry, 56*, 225-233.

Fenichel, D. (1945). *The psychoanalytic theory of neurosis.* New York: Norton.

Finkelhor, D. (1984). *Child sexual abuse: New theory and research.* New York: Free Press.

Finkelhor, D. (1986). *A sourcebook on child sexual abuse.* Thousand Oaks, CA: Sage.

Finkelhor, D., & Araji, S. (1986). Explanations of pedophilia: A four factor model. *Journal of Sex Research, 22*, 145–161.

Finkelhor, D., & Russell, D. (1984). Women as perpetrators: Review of the evidence. In D. Finkelhor (Ed.), *Child sexual abuse: New theory and research* (pp. 171–187). New York: Free Press.

Finkelhor, D., Williams, L. M., & Burns, N. (1988). *Nursery crimes: Sexual abuse in day care.* Newbury Park, CA: Sage.

Fisch, R., Weaklund, J. H., & Spiegel, L. (1982). *The tactics of change: Doing therapy briefly.* San Francisco: Jossey-Bass.

Fisher, S., & Cleveland, S. E. (1958). *Body image and personality.* Princeton, NJ: Van Nostrand.

Fox, J. W. (1980). *Development of predictive factors for recidivism risk levels (Kentucky, 1979).* Richmond, KY: Eastern Kentucky University Department of Corrections. (NCJRS Document No. 076179).

Freeman-Longo, R. E., & Knopp, F. H. (1992). *State-of-the-art sex offender treatment: Outcome and issues.* Orwell, VT: Safer Society Press.

Freud, S. (1962). *Three essays on the theory of sexuality* (J. Strachey, Trans.). New York: Basic Books. (Original work published 1905)

Friedmann, E., Katcher, A. H., Thomas, S. A., Lynch, J. J., & Messent, P. R. (1983). Social interactions and blood pressure: Influence of animal companions. *Journal of Nervous and Mental Disease, 171*, 461-465.

Friedrich, W. N., & Luecke, W. J. (1988). Young school-age sexually aggressive children. *Professional Psychology: Research and Practice, 19*, 155-164.

Fromuth, M. E., & Burkhart, B. R. (1987). Childhood sexual victimization among college men: Definitional and methodological issues. *Violence and Victims, 2*, 241-253.

Furby, L., Weinrott, M. R., & Blackshaw, L. (1989). Sex offender recidivism: A review. *Psychological Bulletin, 105*, 3-30.

Garbarino, J., Dubrow, N., Kostelny, K., & Pardo, C. (1992). *Children in danger: Coping with the consequences of community violence.* San Francisco: Jossey-Bass.

Garbarino, J., Kostelny, K., & Dubrow, N. (1991). What children can tell us about living in danger. *American Psychologist, 46*, 376-383.

Garrison Jr., J. E. (1989). Sexual dysfunction in the elderly: Causes and effects. Journal of *Psychotherapy and the Family, 5*(1-2), 149–162.

Garza-Louis, D., & Peralta, F. (1993). *The macho syndrome: Myths and and realities of the Hispanic sex offender*. Paper presented at the 1993 Annual Conference of Sex Offender Treatment, Huntsville, TX.

Gebhard, P., Gagnon, J., Pomeroy, W., & Christensen, C. (1965). *Sex offenders: An analysis of types*. New York: Harper & Row.

Gelman, D., Springen, K., Elam, R., Joseph, N., Robins, K., & Hager, M. (1990, July 23). The mind of the rapist. *Newsweek*, pp. 46-52.

George, W., Dermen, K. H., & Nochajski, T. H. (1989). Expectancy set, self-reported expectancies, and predispositional traits: Predicting interest in violence and erotica. *Journal of Studies on Alcohol, 50*, 541–551.

George, W., & Marlatt, G. A. (1986). The effects of alcohol and anger on interest in violence, erotica, and deviance. Journal of *Abnormal Psychology, 95*, 150–158.

George, W., & Norris, J. (1991). Alcohol, disinhibition, sexual arousal, and deviant sexual behavior. *Alcohol Health and Research World, 15*, 133–138.

Giarretto, H. (1982). *Integrated treatment of child sexual abuse: A treatment and training manual*. Palo Alto, CA: Science and Behavior Books.

Giarretto, H., Giarretto, A., & Sgroi, S. M. (1978). Coordinated community treatment of incest. In A. W. Burgess, A. N. Groth, L. L. Holmstrom, & S. M. Sgroi (Eds.), *Sexual assault of children and adolescents*. Lexington, MA: Lexington Books.

Gindick, T. (1985, March 7). Pet therapy helps inmates relate to people. *Los Angeles Times*, pp. 21–22.

Glaser, D., & Gordon, M. A. (1991). Profitable penalties for lower level courts. *Judicature, 73*(5), 248-252.

Goldman, E. E., & Morrison, D. S. (1984). *Psychodrama: Experience and process*. Dubuque, IA: Kendall/Hunt.

Goldman, M. S., Brown, S. A., & Christiansen, B. A. (1987). Expectancy theory: Thinking about drinking. In H. T. Blane & K. E. Leonard (Eds.), *Psychological theories about drinking and alcoholism* (pp. 181–226). New York: Guilford Press.

Goldman, M. S., & Roehrich, L. (1991). Alcohol expectancies and sexuality. *Alcohol Health and Research World, 15*, 126–132.

Goodwin, J. M., & Talwar, N. (1989, June). Group psychotherapy for victims of incest. *Psychiatric Clinics of North America, 12*(2), 279–293.

Gottfredson, S. D., & Gottfredson, D. M. (1979) *Screening for risk, a comparison of methods*. Washington, DC: U.S. Department of Justice National Institute of Corrections.

Gould, M. A. (1986, February). *Treatment of incest offenders in a correctional facility*. Paper presented at the New Mexico Association for Counseling and Development, Annual Meeting, Las Cruces, NM.

Goulding, R., & Schwartz, R. (1995). *The mosaic mind: Empowering the tormented self of child abuse survivors*. New York: Norton.

Gove, W. R., & Crutchfield, R. D. (1982). The family and juvenile delinquency. *Sociological Quarterly, 23*, 301-319.

Graham, S. A. (1981). Predictive and concurrent validity of the Jesness Inventory Asocial Index: When does a offender become a offender? *Journal of Consulting and Clinical Psychology, 49*(5), 740–742.

Green, A., & Kaplan, M. (1994). Psychiatric impairment and childhood victimization experiences in female child molesters. *Journal of the American Academy of Child and Adolescent Psychiatry, 33*, 954–961.

Green, R. (1985, October 20). Women inmates train dogs in prize-winning program. *The Seattle Times*, p. B3.

Green, R. (1995). Comprehensive treatment planning for sex offenders. In B. K. Schwartz & H. R. Cellini (Eds.), *The sexual offender: Corrections, treatment, and legal practice.* Kingston, NJ: Civic Research Institute.

Greenwood, P. W., & Turner, S. (1987). *The VisionQuest Program: An evaluation.* California: RAND Corporation.

Gregory, W. L., Cialdini, R. B., & Carpenter, K. M. (1982). Self-relevant scenarios as mediators of likelihood estimates and compliance: Does imagining make it so? *Journal of Personality and Social Psychology, 43,* 89–99.

Griffen, D. W., & Bartholomew, K. (1991). *The metaphysics of measurement: The case of adult attachment.* In K. Bartholomew & D. Perlman (Eds.), Attachment processes in adulthood (pp. 17–52). London: Jessica Kingsley.

Grinder, R., & Bandler, R., (1976). *The structure of magic II: A book about communication and change.* Palo Alto, CA: Science and Behavior Books.

Groth, N. A. (1982). The incest offender. In S. M. Sgroi (Ed.), *Handbook of clinical intervention in child sexual abuse.* Lexington, MA: Lexington Books.

Groth, N. A. (1992). *Understanding sexual assault: The offense and the offender.* Paper presented at Restorative Justice for Juvenile Sex Offenders, Lake Tahoe, NV.

Groth, N. A., & Burgess, A. W. (1979). Sexual trauma in the life histories of rapists and child molesters. *Victimology, 4,* 10–16.

Groth, A. N., Hobson, W. F., & Gary, T. S. (1982). *The child molester: Clinical observations. In Social work and child sexual abuse* (pp. 129–144). New York: Haworth Press.

Groth, A. N., & Loredo, C. M. (1981). Juvenile sexual offenders: Guidelines for assessment. *International Journal of Offender Therapy and Comparative Criminology, 25,* 31–39.

Haaven,J., Little, R., & Petre-Miller, D. (1990). *Treating intellectually disabled sex offenders: A model residential program.* Orwell, VT: Safer Society.

Haddad, P. M., & Benbow, S. M. (1993). Sexual problems associated with dementia: Part 1. Problems and their consequences. *International Journal of Geriatric Psychiatry, 8,* 547-551.

Hairston, C. F. (1988). Family ties during imprisonment: Do the influence criminal activity? *Federal Probation, 52*(1), 48-52.

Haley, J. (1973). *Uncommon therapy: The psychiatric techniques of Milton Erickson, M.D.* New York: Norton.

Haley J. (1976). *Problem solving therapy: New strategies for effective family therapy.* San Francisco: Jossey-Bass.

Haley, J. (1984). *Ordeal therapy* (pp. 175-185) San Francisco: Jossey-Bass.

Hall, G. C. (1995). Sexual offender recidivism revisited: A meta-analysis of recent treatment studies. *Journal of Consulting and Clinical Psychology, 63*(5), 802-809.

Hanson, R. K. (1996). *Assessing sexual offenders perspective taking ability: The Empathy for Women Test — Revised version.* Manuscript submitted for publication.

Hanson, R. K. (in press). Assessing sexual offenders capacity for empathy. *Psychology, Crime and Law.*

Hanson, R. K. (1991). *Assessing risk for sexual offending: A review of questionnaire measures.* Paper presented at the 10th Annual Research and Treatment Conference of the Association for the Treatment of Sexual Abusers.

Hanson, R. K., Cox, B., & Woszczyna, C. (1991a). *Sexuality, personality and attitude questionnaires for sexual offenders: A review* (User Report No. 1991-13). Ottawa: Corrections Branch, Ministry of the Solicitor General of Canada.

Hanson, R. K., Cox, B., & Woszczyna, C. (1991b). Assessing treatment outcome for sexual offenders. *Annals of Sex Research, 4,* 177–208.

Hanson, R. K., Gizzarelli, R., & Scott, H. (1994). The attitudes of incest offenders; Sexual entitlement and acceptance of sex with children. *Criminal Justice and Behavior, 21,* 187-202.

Hanson, R. K., & Scott, H. (1995). Assessing perspective taking among sexual offenders, nonsexual criminals and nonoffenders. *Sexual Abuse: A Journal of Research and Treatment, 7*, 259-277.

Hanson, R. K., Scott, H., & Steffy, R. A. (1995). A comparison of child molesters and nonsexual criminals: Risk predictors and long-term recidivism. *Journal of Research in Crime and Delinquency, 32*, 325–337.

Hanson, R. K., & Slater, S. (1993). Reactions to motivational accounts of child molesters. *Journal of Child Sexual Abuse, 2*(4), 43–59.

Hanson, R. K., & Tangney, J. P. (1996). The Test of Self-Conscious Affect—Social Deviance (TOSCA-SD) version. [Unpublished test]. (Available from R. K. Hanson, Department of the Solicitor General of Canada, 340 Laurier Ave., West, Ottawa, K1A 0P8)

Happel, R. M. & Auffrey, J. J. (1995). Sex offender assessment: Interrupting the dance of denial. *American Journal of Forensic Psychology, 13*(2), 5-22.

Hare, R. D. (1991). *Manual for the revised Psychopathy Checklist*. Toronto: Multi-Health Systems.

Hare, R. D., Harpur, T. J., Hakstian, A. R., Forth, A. E., Hart, S. D., & Newman, J. P. (1990). The Revised Psychopathy Checklist: Reliability and factor structure. *Psychological Assessment, 2*, 338-341.

Harris, M. J. (1991). Controversy and culmination: Meta-analysis and research on interpersonal expectancy effects. *Personality & Social Psychology Bulletin, 17*, 316–322.

Hartman, C. R., & Burgess, A. W. (1988). Information processing of trauma: Case application of a model. *Journal of Interpersonal Violence, 3*, 443–457.

Hartman, C. R., & Burgess, A. W. (1993). Information processing of trauma. *Child Abuse and Neglect, 17*, 47–58.

Hartup, W. W. (1986). On relationships and development. In W. W. Hartup & Z. Zubin (Eds.), *Relationships and development* (pp. 1–26). Hillsdale, NJ: Erlbaum.

Haynes, M. (1991, August). Program lifts spirits,reduces violence in institution's mental health unit. *Corrections Today*, pp. 122–123.

Haywood, T. W., & Grossman, L. S. (1994). Denial of deviant sexual arousal and psychopathology in child molesters. *Behavior Therapy. 25*, 327–340.

Hazan, C., & Shaver, P. (1987). Romantic love conceptualised as an attachment process. *Journal of Personality and Social Psychology, 52*, 511–524.

Hazan, C., & Shaver, P. (1994). Attachment as an organisational framework for research on close relationships. *Psychological Inquiry, 5*, 1–22.

Hazelwood, R. R., & Warren, J. (1989). The serial rapist: His characteristics and victims (conclusion). *FBI Law Enforcement Bulletin, 58*, 18–25.

Heller, J., & Henkim, W. (1986). *Bodywise*. Los Angeles: Tarcher.

Henderson, M., & Hewstone, M. (1984). Prison inmates' explanations for interpersonal violence: Accounts and attributions. *Journal of Consulting and Clinical Psychology, 52*, 789–794.

Henn, F. A., Herjanic, M., & Vanderpearl, R. H. (1976). Forensic psychiatry: Profiles of two types of sex offenders. *American Journal of Psychiatry, 133*, 694–696.

Herman, J. L. (1990). Sex offenders: A feminist perspective. In W. L. Marshall, D. R. Laws, & H. E. Barbaree (Eds.), *Handbook of sexual assault: Issues, theories and the treatment of the offender* (pp. 177–190). New York: Plenum Press.

Herring, R. D. (1994). Substance use among Native American Indian youth: A selected review of causality. *Journal of Counseling and Development, 72*, 578–584.

Higgs, D. C., Canavan, M. M., & Meyer, W. J. (1992). Moving from defense to offense: The development of an adolescent female sex offender. *Journal of Sex Research, 29*, 131–139.

Hildebran, D., & Pithers, W. D. (1989). Enhancing offender empathy for sexual-abuse victims. In D. R. Laws (Ed.), *Relapse prevention with sex offenders* (pp. 236–243). New York: Guilford Press.

Hindman, J. (1990). *Just before dawn*. Ontario, OR: Alexandria.

Hirschi, T. (1969). *Causes of delinquency*. Berkeley: University of California Press.

Hodgins, D. C., & Lightfoot, L. O. (1989). The use of the Alcohol Dependence Scale with incarcerated male offenders. *International Journal of Offender Therapy and Comparative Criminology, 33,* 59–67.

Hogan, R. (1969). Development of an empathy scale. *Journal of Consulting and Clinical Psychology, 33,* 307–316.

Hoke, S. L., Sykes, C., & Winn, M. (1989). Systemic/strategic interventions targeting denial in the incestuous family. *Journal of Strategic and Systemic Therapies, 8*(4), 44–51.

Holmes, T. H. (1981). *Schedule of Recent Experience (SRE).* Seattle: University of Washington Press.

Horowitz, M. J. (1992). *Stress response syndromes.* Northvale, NJ: Jason Aronson.

Horwitz, "Sexual Psychopath Legislation: Is There Anywhere to Go But Backwards?" 57 *U. Pitt. L. Rev.* 35, 37 (1995).

Howard, K. I., Lueger, R. J., Maling, M. S., & Martinovich, Z.(1993). A phase model of psychotherapy outcome: Causal mediation of change. *Journal of Consulting and Clinical Psychology, 61*(4), 678–685.

Howells, K. (1978). Some meanings of children for pedophiles. In Cook, M., & Wilson, G. (Eds.), *Love and attraction* (pp. 57–82). London: Pergamon Press.

Howells, K. (1981). Adult sexual interest in children: Considerations relevant to theories of aetiology. In M. Cook, & K. Howells (Eds.), *Adult sexual interest in children.* (pp. 55–94). New York: Academic Press.

Hoyt, M. F. (1994). Constructive therapies: Introduction. In M. F. Hoyt (Ed.), *Constructive therapies* (pp. 2–10). New York: Guilford Press.

Hucker, S. J. (1984). Psychiatric aspects of crime in old age. In E. S. Newman, D. J. Newman, & M. L. Gewirtz (Eds.), *Elderly criminals.* Cambridge, MA: Oelgeschlager, Gunn & Hain.

Hucker, S., Langevin, G., Wortzman, G., Bain, J., Handy, L., Chambers, J., & Wright, S. (1986). Neuropsychological impairment in pedophiles. *Canadian Journal of Behavioral Science, 18,* 440–448.

Hudson, S. M., Marshall, W. L., Wales, D., McDonald, E., Bakker, L. W., & McLean, A. (1993). Emotional recognition skills of sex offenders. *Annals of Sex Research, 6,* 199–211.

Hudson, S. M., & Ward, T. (in press-a). Attachment, anger, and intimacy in sexual offenders. *Journal of Interpersonal Violence.*

Hudson, S. M., & Ward, T. (in press-b). Rape: Psychopathology and theory. In D. R. Laws & W. T. O'Donohue (Eds.), *Handbook of sexual deviance: Theory and application.* New York: Guilford Press.

Hunter, J. A. Jr., & Becker, J. V. (1994). The role of deviant sexual arousal in juvenile sexual offending. *Criminal Justice and Behavior, 21,* 132–149.

Hunter, J. A., Lexier, L. J., Goodwin, D. W., Browne, P. A., & Dennis, C. (1993). Psychosexual, attitudinal, and developmental characteristics of juvenile female sexual perpetrators in a residential treatment setting. *Journal of Child and Family Studies, 2,* 317–326.

Hurt, A. (Ed.). (1995). Pet partners home study course. Renton, WA: Delta Society.

Iannotti, L. A. (1978). Effect of role taking experiences on role taking, empathy, altruism and aggression. *Developmental Psychology, 41,* 119–124.

Imber-Black, E. (1989). Creating rituals in therapy. *Family Therapy Network, 13*(4), 38–44.

Inciardi, J., Lockwood, D., & Hooper, R. M. (1993, July 14–17). *The effectiveness of the KEY-CREST continuum of treatment.* Paper presented at the 2nd annual conference of the National Institute on Drug Abuse Research and Practice: An Alliance for the 21st Century, Washington, DC.

Ingersoll, S. L., & Patton, S. O. (1990). *Treating perpetrators of sexual abuse.* Lexington, MA: Lexington Books.

Irish, J. F. (1989). Probation and recidivism: *A study of probation adjustment and its relationship to pst-probation outcome for adult criminal offenders in Nassau County, New York.* Mineola, NY: Nassau County Probation Department. (NCJRS Document No. 124663).

Jamison, M. (1981). *Serious 602 offender project of the Contra Costa probation department—Final Evaluation report.*San Francisco, CA: Urban and Rural Systems Associates. (NCJRS Document No. 085006).

Janes, M. S. (1993, June). Polygraph: A current perspective. Interchange—Cooperative *Newsletter of the National Adolescent Perpetrator Network*, p. 1.

Janoff-Bulman, R. (1979). Characterological versus behavioral self- blame: Inquiries into depression and rape. *Journal of Personality and Social Psychology, 37*, 1798-1809.

Jeffries, J. (1976). What we are doing here is defusing bombs: Psychodrama with hardcore offenders. In P. Holmes & M. Karp (Eds.), *Psychodrama: Inspiration and technique* (pp. 189-200). London: Tavistock/Routledge.

Jenkins, A. J. (1990). *Invitations to responsibility:The therapeutic engagement of men who are violent and abusive.* Adelaide, South Australia: Dulwich Centre Publications.

Jenkins-Hall, K. D., & Marlatt, G. A. (1989). Apparently irrelevant decisions in the relapse process. In D. R. Laws (Ed.), *Relapse prevention with sex offenders* (pp. 47–55). New York: Guilford Press.

Jennings, S. (1973). *Remedial drama: A handbook for teachers and therapists.* London: Adam & Charles Black.

Jennings, S. (1992). *Dramatherapy: Theory and practice.* London: Tavistock/Routledge.

Jesness, C. F. (1966). *The Jesness Inventory* (rev. ed.). North Tonawanda, NY: Multi-Health Systems.

Jesness, C. F. (1991). *Classifying juvenile offenders.* North Tonawanda, NY: Multi-Health Systems.

Jessor, R., & Jessor, S. L. (1977). *Problem behavior and psychological development.* New York: Academic Press.

Johnson, D. R. (1981). The theory and technique of transformations in drama therapy. *Arts in Psychotherapy, 10*(4), 285-300.

Johnson, S. A. (in press). The overlooked force in sexual assault. *Acta Sexologica.*

Johnson, S. D., Gibson, L., & Linden, R. (1978). Alcohol and rape in Winnipeg: 1966-1975. *Journal of Studies of Alcohol, 39*, 1887-1894.

Johnson, T. C. (1988). Child perpetrators: Children who molest other children: Preliminary findings. *Child Abuse and Neglect, 12*, 219-229.

Johnson, T. C. (1989). Female child perpetrators: Children who molest other children. *Child Abuse and Neglect, 13*, 571-585.

Jones, M. (1953). *The therapeutic community.* New York: Basic Books.

Jones, M. (1979). Learning as treatment. In Hans Toch (Ed.), *Psychology of crime and criminal justice* (pp. 470–487). New York: Holt, Rinehart & Winston.

Jones P. R. (1991). The risk of recidivism: Evaluating the public-safety implications of a community corrections program. *Journal of Criminal Justice, 19*, 49–66.

Josephs, R. A., & Steele, C. M. (1990). The two faces of alcohol myopia: Attentional mediation of psychological stress. *Journal of Abnormal Psychology, 99*, 115–126.

Joy, S. (1987). Retrospective presentations of incest: Treatment strategies for use with adult women. *Journal of Counseling and Development, 65*, 317-319.

Juhan, D. (1987). *Jobs body: A handbook for body work.* Barrytown, NY: Station Hill Press.

Junger-Tas, J. (1992). An empirical test of social control theory [Special issue]. *Journal of Quantitative Criminology, 8*, 9–28.

Justice, B., & Justice R. (1976). *The abusing family.* New York: Human Science Press.

Justice, B., & Justice, R. (1979). *The broken taboo: Sex in the family.* New York: Human Sciences Press.

Kahn, T. J. (1990). *Pathways: A guided workbook for youth beginning treatment.* Brandon, VT: Safer Society Press.

Kahn, T. J., & Chambers, H. J. (1991). Assessing reoffense risk with juvenile sexual Offenders. *Child Welfare, 70*, 333–345.

Kahneman, D., & Tversky, A. (1982). The simulation heuristic. In D. Kahneman, P. Slovic, & A. Tversky, (Eds.), *Judgment under uncertainty: Heuristics and biases* (pp. 201–208). New York: Cambridge University Press.

Kaplan, H. S. (1990). Sex, intimacy and the aging process. *Journal of the American Academy of Psychoanalysis, 18*(2), 185–205.

Kaplan, M. S., & Green, A. (1995). Incarcerated female sexual offenders: A comparison of sexual histories with eleven female nonsexual offenders. *Sexual Abuse: A Journal of Research and Treatment, 7*, 287-300.

Katcher, A. H. (1981). Interrelations between people and their pets: Form and function. In B. Fogle (Ed.), *Interrelations between people and pets.* Springfield, IL: Charles C. Thomas.

Katcher, A. H., & Wilkins, G. G. (1994). Helping children with Attention-deficit hyperactive and conduct disorders through animal-assisted therapy and education. *Interactions, 12*(4), 5-9.

Katz, R. C. (1990). Psychological adjustment in adolescent child molesters. *Child Abuse and Neglect, 14*, 567-575.

Keane, T. M., Fairbank, J. A., Caddell, J. M., & Zimering, R. T. (1989). Implosive (flooding) therapy reduces symptoms of PTSD in Vietnam combat veterans. *Behavior Therapy, 20*, 245-260.

Kellett, J. M. (1993). Sexuality in later life. *Reviews in Clinical Gerontology, 3*, 309-314.

Kempton, T., & Forehand, R. (1992). Juvenile sex offenders: Similar to, or different from, other incarcerated delinquent offenders? *Behavior Research and Therapy, 30*, 533-536.

Kepner, J. I. (1987). *Body process.* New York: Gardner Press.

Kishner, G. R. (1995). *A path to responsibility* . Oklahoma City, OK: Wood 'n Barnes.

Kivela, S., & Pahkala, K. (1989). The prognosis of depression in old age. *International Psychogeriatrics, 1*(2), 119-133.

Klayman, J., & Ha, Y-W. (1989). Confirmation, disconfirmation, and information on hypothesis testing. *Psychological Review, 94*, 211–228.

Knight, R. A., & Prentky, R. A. (1987). The developmental antecedents and adult adaptations of rapist subtypes. *Criminal Justice and Behavior, 14*, 403-426.

Knight, R. A., & Prentky, R. A. (1990). Classifying sexual offenders: The development and corroboration of taxonomic models. In W. L. Marshall, D. R. Laws, & H. E. Barbaree (Eds.), *Handbook of sexual assault: Issues, theories, and treatment of the offender* (pp. 23–52). New York: Plenum Press.

Knight, R. A., & Prentky, R. A. (1993). Exploring characteristics for classifying juvenile sex offenders. In H. E. Barbaree, W. L. Marshall, & S. M. Hudson (Eds.), *The juvenile sex offender* (pp. 45–78). New York: Guilford Press.

Knopp, F. H., Freeman-Longo, R. E., & Stevenson, W. (1992). *Nationwide survey of juvenile and adult sex-offender treatment programs.* Orwell, VT: Safer Society Press.

Knopp, F., & Lackey, L. (1989). *Female sexual abusers: A summary of data from 44 treatment providers.* Orwell, VT: Safer Society Press.

Koehler, D. J. (1991). Explanation, imagination, and confidence in judgment. *Psychological Bulletin, 110*, 499–519.

Koss, M. P. (1987). Outrageous acts and everyday seduction: Sexual aggression and victimization among college students. In B. Levy (Ed.), *Dating violence: Young women in danger.* Seattle, WA: Seal Press.

Krafft-Ebing, R. (1965). *Psychopathia sexualis with especial reference to the antipathic sexual instinct: A medico-forensic study* (F. S. Klaf, Trans.). New York: Stein & Day, Scarborough Books Edition. (Original work published 1882)

Kramer, S. P., Bench, L. L., Erickson, S. (1996). *A study of twelve different measures of recidivism on 450 sex offenders released since 1980.* Manuscript in preparation.

Kunce, J. T., & Hemphill, H. (1983). Delinquency and Jesness Inventory scores. *Journal of Personality Assessment, 47*, 632-634.

Kurtz, R. (1990). *Body-centered psychotherapy: The Hakomi method.* Mendocino, CA: Life Rhythm.

Laflen, B., & Sturm, W. R. (1993). *Understanding and working with denial in sexual offenders and their families.* Paper presented at the 12th annual meeting of the Association for the Treatment of Sexual Abusers, Boston.

Lakey, J. F. (1994). The profile and treatment of male adolescent sex offenders. *Adolescence, 29*, 755-761.

Lambana, J. H., & Leyer, J.B. (1994) Cognitive-systems therapy: A case excerpt. *Journal of Mental Health Counseling, 16*(4), 434-444. Lehne, G. K. (1991). Sexual trauma and masochism. In C. Silverstein (Ed.), *Gays, lesbians and their therapists: Studies in psychotherapy.* New York: Norton.

Lang, A. R., Searles, J., Lauerman, R., & Adesso, V. (1980). Expectancy, alcohol, and sex guilt as determinants of interest in and reaction to sexual stimuli. *Journal of Abnormal Psychology, 89*, 644–653.

Langevin, R. (1983). *Sexual strands: Understanding and treating sexual anomalies in men.* Hillsdale, NJ: Erlbaum.

Lansky, D., & Wilson, G. T. (1981). Alcohol, expectations, and sexual arousal in males: An information processing analysis. Journal of *Abnormal Psychology, 90*, 35–45.

Lara-Cantu, M. A. (1989). A sex-role inventory with scales for "machismo" and "self-sacrificing women." *Journal of Cross-Cultural Psychology, 20*(4), 386-398.

Laws, D. R., & Marshall, W. L. (1990). A conditioning theory of the etiology and maintenance of deviant sexual preference and behavior. In W. L. Marshall, D. R. Laws, & H. E. Barbaree, (Eds.), *Handbook of sexual assault* (pp. 209–229). New York: Plenum Press.

Lee, D. R. (1983). Pet therapy: Helping patients through troubled times. *California Veterinarian, 5*, 24–25.

Leigh, B. C. (1987). Evaluation of alcohol expectancies: Do they add to the predictability of drinking patterns? *Psychology of Addictive Behavior, 1*, 135–139.

Leitenberg, H., & Henning, K. (1995). Sexual fantasy. *Psychological Bulletin, 117*, 469–496.

Levant, M. D., & Bass, B. A. (1991). Parental identification of rapists and pedophiles. *Psychological Reports, 69*, 463–466.

Levinson, B. M. (1962). The dog as co-therapist. *Mental Hygiene, 46*, 59–65.

Lewis, D. O., Shankok, S. S., & Pincus, J. H. (1979). Juvenile male sexual assaulters. *American Journal of Psychiatry, 136*, 1194–1196.

Lewis, H. B. (1971). *Shame and guilt in neurosis.* New York: International Universities Press.

Lewis, O. (1959). *Five families.* New York: Basic Books.

Libman, E., Creti, L., Amsel, R., Fichten, C. S., Weinstein, N., & Brender, W. (1989). Sleeping and waking-state measurement of erectile function in an aging male population. *Psychological Assessment, 1*(4), 284–291.

Lichtman, C. M., & Smock, S. M. (1982). Effects of social services on probationer recidivism—A field experiment. Journal of *Research in Crime and Delinquency, 19*(2), 277–298.

Lindman, R. (1982). Social and solitary drinking: Effects on consumption and mood in male social drinkers. *Physiology and Behavior, 28*, 1093–1095.

Lingley, C. R. (1985). *Trauma and its wake: The study and treatment of post-traumatic stress disorder* (vol. 1). New York: Brunner/Mazel.

Lipton, D. N., McDonel, E. C., & McFall, R. M. (1987). Heterosocial perception in rapists. *Journal of Consulting and Clinical Psychology, 55*, 17–21.

Lisak, D., & Ivan, C. (1995). Deficits in intimacy and empathy in sexually aggressive men. *Journal of Interpersonal Violence, 10*(3), 296–308.

Lisak, D., & Roth, S. (1990). Motives and psychodynamics of self-reported, unincarcerated rapists. *American Journal of Orthopsychiatry, 60*, 268–280.

Lockwood, R. (1983). The influence of animals on social perception. In A. H. Katcher & A. M. Beck (Eds.), *New perspectives on our lives with companions animals* (pp. 64–71). Philadelphia: University of Pennsylvania Press.

Loeber, R., & Stouthamer-Loeber, M. (1986). Family factors and correlates and predictors of juvenile conduct problems and delinquency. In M. Tonry & N. Morris (Eds.), *Crime and justice: An annual review of research* (vol. 7, pp. 29–149). Chicago: University of Chicago Press.

Longo, R. E. (1982). Sexual learning and experience among adolescent sexual offenders. *International Journal of Offender Therapy and Comparative Criminology, 26*, 235–241.

LoPiccolo, J. (1992). *Handbook for assessment and treatment of sexual deviance.* St. Louis, MO: Author.

Loss, P., & Glancy, E. (1983). Men who sexually abuse their children. *Medical Aspects of Human Sexuality, 17*, 328–329.

Loza, W., & Clements, P. (1991). Incarcerated alcoholics' and rapists' attributions of blame for criminal acts. *Canadian Journal of Behavioural Science, 23*, 76–83.

Madanes, C. (1990). *Sex, love, and violence: Strategies for transformation.* New York: Norton.

Madsen, W. (1964). *The Mexican American in south Texas.* New York: Holt, Rinehart & Winston.

Maisto, S. A., Connors, G. J., & Sachs, P. R. (1981). Expectation as a mediator in alcohol intoxication: A reference level model. *Cognitive Therapy and Research, 5*, 1–18.

Mak, A. S. (1990). Testing a psychosocial control theory of delinquency. *Criminal Justice and Behavior, 17*, 215–230.

Makepeace, J. M. (1981). Courtship violence among college students. *Family Relations, 30*, 97–102.

Makepeace, J. M. (1986). Gender differences in courtship violence victimization. *Family Relations, 35*, 383–388.

Malamuth, N. M. (1981). Rape proclivity among males. *Journal of Social Issues, 37*(4), 138–157.

Malamuth, N. M. (1986). Predictors of naturalistic sexual aggression. *Journal of Personality and Social Psychology, 50*, 953–962.

Malamuth, N. M., & Brown, L. M. (1994). Sexually aggressive men's perception of women's communications: Testing three explanations. *Journal of Personality and Social Psychology, 67*, 699–712.

Malamuth, N. M., Heavey, C. L., & Linz, D. (1993). Predicting men's antisocial behavior against women: The interaction model of sexual aggression. In G. N. Hall, R. Hirschman, J. Graham, & M. Zaragosa (Eds.), *Sexual aggression: Issues in etiology, assessment, and treatment* (pp. 63–97). Washington, DC: Hemisphere.

Malamuth, N. M., Sockloski, R. J., Koss, M. P., & Tanaka, J. S. (1991). Characteristics of aggressors against women: Testing a model using a national sample of college students. *Journal of Consulting and Clinical Psychology, 59*, 670–681.

Maletzky, B .M. (1991). *Treating the sexual offender.* Newbury Park, CA: Sage.

Maletzky, B. M. (1993). Factors associated with success and failure in the behavior and cognitive treatment of sexual offenders. *Annals of Sex Research, 6*, 241–258.

Maletzky, B. M. (1996). Denial of treatment or treatment of denial? Sexual Abuse: A *Journal of Research and Treatment, 8*(1), 1–5.

Maletzky, B. M., & McFarland, B. (1995). *Treatment results in offenders who deny their crimes.* Manuscript submitted for publication.

Mann, L. M., Chassin, L., & Sher, K. J. (1987). Alcohol expectancies and the risk for alcoholism. *Journal of Consulting and Clinical Psychology, 55*, 411–417.

Margolin, L. (1984). A treatment model for the adolescent sex offender. *Journal of Offender Counseling, Services and Rehabilitation, 8*, 1–11.

Margolin, L. (1991). Child sexual abuse by nonrelated caregivers. *Child Abuse and Neglect, 15*, 213–221.

Marlatt, G.A. (1989). Feeding the pig: The problem of immediate gratification. In D. R. Laws (Ed.), *Relapse prevention with sex offenders* (pp. 56–62). New York: Guilford Press.

Marlatt, G. A., & Rohsenow, D. J. (1980). Cognitive processes in alcohol use: Expectancy and balanced placebo design. *Advances in Substance Use, 1*, 159–199.

Marques, J. (1995). *Long-term effects of relapse prevention: Recidivism data from California's SOTEP study.* Paper presented at the NOTA/ATSA Joint International Conference, Cambridge, England.

Marques, J. K., Day, D. M., Nelson, C., Minor, M. H. (1990). The sex offender treatment and evaluation project: California's relapse prevention program. In D. R. Laws (Eds.), *Relapse prevention with sex offenders.* New York: Guilford Press.

Marshall, W. L. (1989). Invited essay: Intimacy, loneliness & sexual offenders. *Behavior Research and Therapy, 27*, 491-503.

Marshall, W. L. (1993). The role of attachment, intimacy, and loneliness in the etiology and maintenance of sexual offending. *Sexual and Marital Therapy, 8*, 109–121.

Marshall, W. L. (1994). Treatment effects on denial and minimization in incarcerated sex offenders. *Behavior Research and Therapy, 32*(5), 559–564.

Marshall, W. L., & Barbaree, H. E. (1990). An integrated theory of the etiology of sexual offending. In W. L. Marshall, D. R. Laws, & H. E. Barbaree (Eds.), *Handbook of sexual assault: Issues, theories, and treatment of the offender* (pp. 257–275). New York: Plenum Press.

Marshall, W. L., & Barbaree, H. E. (1990). Outcome of comprehensive cognitive-behavioral treatment programs. In W. L. Marshall, D. R. Laws, & H. E. Barbaree (Eds.), *Handbook of sexual assault.* New York: Plenum Press.

Marshall, W. L., Barbaree, H. E., & Eccles, A. (1989). *Long-term outcome in the treatment of exhibitionists.* Paper presented at the 5th Annual Conference of the Association for the Behavioral Treatment of Sexual Abusers, Seattle, WA.

Marshall, W. L., Barbaree, H. E., & Eccles, A. (1991). Early onset and deviant sexuality in child molesters. *Journal of Interpersonal Violence, 6*, 323–336.

Marshall, W. L., Barbaree, H. E., & Fernandez, Y. M. (1995). Some aspects of social competence in sexual offenders. *Sexual Abuse: A Journal of Research and Treatment, 7*, 113–127.

Marshall, W. L., Hudson, S. M., Jones, R., & Fernandez, Y. M. (1995). Empathy in sex offenders. *Clinical Psychology Review, 15*(2), 99–113.

Marshall, W. L., Jones, R., Ward, T., Johnston, P., & Barbaree, H. E. (1991). Treatment outcome with sex offenders, *Clinical Psychology Review, 11*, 465–485.

Martin, R. D. (1981). Cross-validation of the Jesness Inventory with offenders and nonoffenders. *Journal of Consulting and Clinical Psychology, 49*(1), 10–14.

Matthew Margolis goes to prison. (1984). *National Institute of Dog Training Newsletter, 2*(1), 1-2.

Matthews, J. K., Mathews, R., & Speltz, K. (1991). Female sexual offenders: A typology. In M. K. Patton (Ed.), *Family Sexual Abuse: Frontline research and evaluation* (pp. 199–219). Newbury Park, CA: Sage.

May, P. A. (1989). Alcohol abuse and alcoholism among American Indians: An overview. In T. D. Watts & R. Wright (Eds.), *Alcoholism in minority populations* (pp. 96–119). Springfield, IL: Charles C. Thomas.

May, P. A., Hymbaugh, K. J., Aase, J. M., & Samet, J. M. (1983). Epidemiology of Fetal Alcohol Syndrome among American Indians of the southwest. *Social Biology, 30*, 374–387.

Mayer, A. (1988). *Sex offenders: Approaches to understanding and management.* New York: Learning Publications.

Mayfield, D. (1976). Alcoholism, alcohol, intoxication and assaultive behavior. Diseases of the Nervous System, 37, 228-231. Medina, E. L. (1970). The role of alcohol in accidents and violence. In R. Popham (Ed.), *Alcohol and alcoholism* (pp. 351–355).Toronto: University of Toronto Press.

McAdams, D. P. (1982). Intimacy motivation. In A. J. Stewart (Ed.), *Motivation and society* (pp. 133–171). San Francisco: Jossey-Bass.

McCarty, L. (1986). Mother-child incest: Characteristics of the offender. *Child Welfare, 65*, 447–458.

McCleary, R., Chew, K. S. Y., Hellsten, J. J., & Flynn-Bransford, M. (1991). Age- and sex- specific cycles in United States suicides, 1973-1985. *American Journal of Public Health, 81*, 1494–1497.

McClelland, D. C. (1981). Is personality consistent? In A. I. Rabin, J. Aronoff, A. M. Barclay, & R. A. Zucker (Eds.), *Further explorations in personality* (pp. 87–113). New York: Wiley.

McCulloch, M. J. (1983). Animal-facilitated therapy: Overview and future direction. In A. H. Katcher & A. M. Beck (Eds.), *New perspectives on our lives with companion animals* (pp. 410–426). Philadelphia: University of Pennsylvania Press.

McDonel, E. C., & McFall, R. M. (1991). Construct validity of two heterosocial perception skill measures for assessing rape proclivity. *Violence and Victims, 6,* 17–30.

McFall, R. M. (1990). The enhancement of social skills: An information-processing analysis. In W. L. Marshall, D. R. Laws, & H. E. Barbaree (Eds.), *Handbook of sexual assault* (pp. 311–330). New York: Plenum Press.

McGrath, R. (1991). Sex offender risk assessment and disposition planning: A review of empirical and clinical findings. *International Journal of Offender Therapy and Comparative Criminology, 35,* 329-351.

McGrath, R. J. (1992). Assessing sex offender risk. *American Probation and Parole Association: Perspectives, 16*(3),

McGrath, R. J. (1991). Sex offender risk assessment and disposition planning: A review of empirical and clinical findings. *International Journal of Offender Therapy and Comparative Criminology, 35*(4).

Meichenbaum, D. (1994). *A clinical handbook/practical therapist manual for assessing and treating adults with post-traumatic stress disorder.* West Ontario: Institute Press.

Meining, M., & Bonner, B. (1990, October). Returning the treated sex offender to the family. *Violence Update,* pp. 3–11.

Menard, S., Elliott, D. S., & Wofford, S. (1993). Social control theories in developmental perspective. Studies on Crime and *Crime Prevention, 2,* 69–87.

Menard, S., & Huizinga, D. (1994). Changes in conventional attitudes and delinquent behavior in adolescence. *Youth and Society, 26,* 23–53.

Miller, B. (1988). Date rape: Time for a new look at prevention. *Journal of College Student Development, 29,* 553–555.

Miller, B., & Marshall, J. (1987). Coercive sex on the university campus. *Journal of College Student Personnel, 28*(1), 38–47.

Miller, W. R., Benefield, R. G., & Tonigan, J. S. (1993). Enhancing motivation for change in problem drinking: A controlled comparison of two therapist styles. *Journal of Consulting and Clinical Psychology, 63*(1), 455–461.

Miller, W. R., & Marlatt, G. A. (1984). *Manual for the comprehensive drinker profile.* Odessa, FL: Psychological Assessment Resources.

Miller, W. R., & Rollnick, S. (1991). *Motivational interviewing: Preparing people to change addictive behavior.* New York: Guilford Press.

Millon, T. (1996). *Disorders of personality: DSM-IV and beyond.* New York: Wiley.

Milner, & Robertson, (1990). Comparison of physical child abusers, intrafamilial sexual child abusers and child neglecters. *Journal of Interpersonal Violence, 5,* 37-48.

Minuchin, S. (1974). *Families and family therapy.* Cambridge, MA: Harvard University Press.

Minuchin, S. (1981). *Family therapy techniques* (pp. 11–27, 29–31). Cambridge, MA: Harvard University Press.

Miracle worker: Very smart, very loving. (1984/1985). *Holistic Animal News,* pp. 3–6.

Mishra, D. N., & Shulka, G. D. (1988). Sexual disturbances in male diabetics: Phenomenological and clinical aspects. *Indian Journal of Psychiatry, 30*(2), 135-143.

Mohr, I. W., Turner, R. E., & Jerry, M. B. (1964). *Pedophilia and exhibitionism.* Toronto: University of Toronto Press.

Moneymaker, J. M., & Strimple, E. O. (1991). Animals and inmates: A sharing companionship behind bars. *Journal of Offender Rehabilitation, 16*(3/4), 133–152.

Monks of New Skete. (1991). *The art of raising a puppy.* New York: Little, Brown.

Moody, E. E., Brissie, J., & Kim, J. (1994). Personality and background characteristics of adolescent sexual offenders. *Journal of Addictions and Offender Counseling, 14,* 30–48.

Morley, J. E., Korenman, S. G., Mooradian, A. D., & Kaiser, F. E. (1987). UCLA geriatric grand rounds: Sexual dysfunction in the elderly male. *Journal of the American Geriatrics Society, 35,* 1014–1022.

Morrison, T., Erooga, M., & Beckett, R. C. (1994). Sexual offending against children. London: Routledge.

Morse, "Blame and Danger: An Essay on Preventive Detention," 76 *Bost. U.L. Rev.* 113, 152–155 (1996).

Moskowitz, D. S., & Schwartzman, A. E. (1989). Life paths of aggressive and withdrawn children. In D. M. Boss, & N. Cantor (Eds.), *Personality psychology: Recent trends and emerging direction*s (pp. 99–114). New York: Springer-Verlag.

Muehlenhard, C. L. (1988). Misinterpreted dating behaviors and the risk of date rape. *Journal of Social and Clinical Psychology, 6*(1), 20–37.

Mulligan, T., & Moss, C. R. (1991). Sexuality and aging in male veterans: A cross-sectional study of interest, ability and activity. *Archives of Sexual Behavior, 20*(1), 17–25.

Munson, R. F., & Blincoe, M. M. (1984). Evaluation of a residential treatment center for emotionally disturbed adolescents. *Adolescence, 14*(74), 253-261.

Munson, R. F., & LaPaille, K. (1984). Personality tests as a predictor of success in a residential treatment center. *Adolescence, 19*(75), 697–701.

Murphy, G. (1949). *Historical introduction to modern psychology.* New York: Harcourt, Brace.

Murphy, J. J., & Barry, D. J. (1995). *A six-month adapted version of the denier's pilot study.* Paper presented at the 14th annual meeting of the Association for the Treatment of Sexual Abusers, New Orleans.

Murphy, J. J., & Barry, D. J. (1995, October). *Treating sex offenders who deny their guilt: A six month adapted version of the denier's pilot study.* Paper presented at the annual research and treatment conference of the Association for the Treatment of Sexual Abusers. New Orleans.

Murphy, T. H. (1981). *Michigan risk prediction—A replication study—Final report.* Lansing, MI: Michigan Department of Corrections. (NCJRS Document No. 079872)

Murphy, W. D. (1990). Assessment and modification of cognitive distortions in sex offenders. In W. L. Marshall, D. R. Laws, & H. E. Barbaree, (Eds.), *Handbook of sexual assault* (pp. 331–342). New York: Plenum Press.

Murphy, W. D., Coleman, E. M., & Haynes, M. R. (1983). Treatment and evaluation issues with the mentally retarded sex offender. In J. G. Greer & I. R. Stuart (Eds.), *The sexual aggressor: Current perspectives on treatment.* New York: Van Nostrand Reinhold.

Murphy, W. D., Coleman, E. M., & Haynes, M. R. (1986). Factors related to coercive sexual behavior in a nonclinical sample of males. *Violence and Victims, 1,* 255–278.

Neff, J. A., Prihoda, T. J., Hoppe, S. (1991). "Machismo," self-esteem, education and high maximum drinking among Anglo, black and Mexican-American male drinkers. *Journal of Studies on Alcohol, 52,* 458–463.

Neubeck, G. (1974). The myriad of motives for sex. In L. Gross (Ed.), *Sexual aggression: Current issues.* Flushing, NY: Spectrum.

Nichols, H. R., & Molinder, I. (1984). *Multiphasic sex inventory manual.* Tacoma, WA: Authors.

Norris, C. (1993). *An approach to treating incarcerated sex offenders who are resistant to treatment involvement.* Paper presented at the 12th annual meeting of the Association for the Treatment of Sexual Abusers, Boston.

Note, "The Civil Commitment of Violent Predators in Kansas: A Modern Law for Modern Times," 42 *Kans. L. Rev.* 887 (1994).

O'Connor, A. A. (1987). Female sex offenders. *British Journal of Psychiatry, 150,* 615–620.

O'Donohue, W., & Letourneau, E. (1993). A brief group treatment for the modification of denial in child sexual abusers: outcome and follow-up. *Child Abuse & Neglect, 17,* 299–304.

Oei, T. P. S., Hokin, D., & Young, R. (1990). Differences between personal and general alcohol-related beliefs. *International Journal of Addictions, 25,* 641–651.

Office of Juvenile Justice and Prevention. (1992). *Juvenile offending and victimization: A national report.* Washington, DC: Author.

Oliver, L., Nagayama Hall, G. C., & Neuhaus, S. M. (1993). A comparison of the personality and background characteristics of adolescent sex offenders and other adolescent offenders. *Criminal Justice and Behavior, 20*(4), 359–370.

Overholser, C., & Beck, S. (1986). Multimethod assessment of rapists, child molesters, and three control groups on behavioral and psychological measures. *Journal of Consulting and Clinical Psychology, 53*, 55–63.

Owen, G., & Steele, N. (1991). Incest offenders after treatment. In M. Q. Patton (Ed.) *Family sexual abuse: Frontline research and evaluation* (pp. 178–198. Newbury Park, CA: Sage.

Paterson, R. J., & Moran, G. (1988). Attachment theory, personality development, and psychotherapy. *Clinical Psychology Review, 8*, 611–636.

Pearson, Q. M. (1994). Treatment techniques for adult female survivors of childhood sexual abuse. *Journal of Counseling and Development, 73*(1), 32–37.

Pernanen, K. (1976). Alcohol and crimes of violence. In B. Kissin & H. Begleiter (Eds.), *Social aspects of alcoholism* (pp. 351–443). New York: Plenum Press.

Peters, J. J. (1976). Children who are victims of sexual assault and the psychology of offenders. *American Journal of Psychotherapy, 30*, 398–421.

Petersilia, J., & Turner, S. (1993). *Evaluating intensive supervision probation/parole: Results of a nationwide experiment.* Washington DC: U.S. Department of Justice, National Institute of Justice.

Pithers, W. D. (1987). *Estimated cost savings of sex offender treatment in Vermont in 1987.* Waterbury, Vt: Vermont Center for the Prevention and Treatment of Sexual Abuse.

Pithers, W. D. (1988). Relapse prevention. In B. K. Schwartz (Ed.), *A practitioner's guide to treating the incarcerated male sex offender: Breaking the cycle of sexual abuse* (pp. 123–140). Washington, DC: Department of Justice, National Institute of Corrections.

Pithers, W. D. (1990). Relapse prevention with sexual aggressors: A method for maintaining therapeutic gain and enhancing external supervision. In W. L. Marshall, D. R. Laws, & H. E. Barbaree (Eds.), *Handbook of sexual assault* (pp. 343–362). New York: Plenum Press.

Pithers, W. D. (1994). Process evaluation of a group therapy component designed to enhance sex offenders' empathy for sexual abuse survivors. *Behavior Research and Therapy, 32*, 565–570.

Pithers, W. D., Buell, M. M., Kashima, K. M., Cumming, G. F., & Beal, L. S. (1987). *Precursors to sexual offenses.* Paper presented at the first annual meeting of the Association for the Behavioral Treatment of Sexual Aggressors. Newport, OR.

Pithers, W. D., & Cumming, G. F. (1995). Relapse prevention: A method for enhancing behavioral self-management and external supervision of the sexual aggressor. In B. K. Schwartz & H. R. Cellini (Eds.), *The sex offender: Corrections, treatment, and legal practice.* Kingston, NJ: Civic Research Institute.

Pithers, W. D., Kashima, K. M., Cumming, G. F., & Beal, L. S. (1988). Relapse prevention: A method of enhancing maintenance of change in sex offenders. In A. C. Salter (Ed.), *Treating child sex offenders and victims: A practical guide* (pp. 131–170). Newbury Park, CA: Sage.

Pithers, W. D., Kashima, K., Cumming, G. F., Beal L. S., & Buell, M. (1988). Relapse prevention of sexual aggression. In R. Prentky & V. Quinsey (Eds.), *Human sexual aggression: Current perspectives* (pp. 67–87). New York: New York Academy of Sciences.

Pollock, N. L., & Hashmall, J. M. (1991). The excuses of child molesters. Behavioral Sciences and the Law, 9, 53-59.

Prendergast, W. L. (1978). *Re-education of attitudes and repressed emotions.* Paper presented at the R.O.A.R.E. Conference, Avenel, NJ.

Prendergast, W. L. (1991). *Treating sex offenders in correctional institutions and outpatient clinics: A guide to clinical practice.* New York: Haworth.

Prentky, R. A., & Burgess, A. W. (1991). Hypothetical biological substrates of a fantasy-based drive mechanism for repetitive sexual aggression. In A. W. Burgess (Ed.), *Rape and sexual assault III: A research handbook* (pp. 235–256). New York: Garland.

Prentky, R., & Burgess, A. W. (1992). Rehabilitation of child molesters: A cost-benefit analysis. *American Journal of Orthopsychiatry, 60*, 108–117.

Prentky, R. A., Knight, R. A., Rosenberg, R., & Lee, A. (1989). A path analytic approach to the validation of a taxonomic system for child molesters. *Journal of Quantitative Criminology, 6*, 231–259.

Prentky, R. A., Knight, R. A., Sims-Knight, J. E., Strauss, H., Rokous, F., & Cerce, D. (1989). Developmental antecedents of sexual aggression. *Development and Psychopathology, 1*, 153–169.

Pritchard, C. (1992). Changes in elderly suicides in the USA and the developed world 1974-87: Comparison with current homicide. *International Journal of Geriatric Psychiatry, 7*, 125–134.

Prochaska, J. O., & DiClemente, C. C. (1992). Stages of change in the modification of problem behaviors. In M. Hersen, R. M. Eisler, & P. M. Miller (Eds.), *Progress in behavior modification.* Sycamore, IL: Sycamore Publishing.

Prochaska, J. O., DiClemente, C. C., & Norcross, J. C. (1992). In search of how people change: Applications to addictive behaviors. *American Psychologist, 47*(9), 1102–1114.

Pryor, K. (1984). *Don't shoot the dog.* New York: Bantam Books.

Puffer, P., & Sawyer, S. (1993). *Treatment model for treating the resistant client.* Paper presented at the 12th annual meeting of the Association for the Treatment of Sexual Abusers, Boston.

Putnam, F. W. (1989). *Diagnosis and treatment of multiple personality disorder.* New York: Guilford Press.

Quinsey, V. L. (1977). The assessment and treatment of child molesters: A review. *Canadian Psychological Review, 18*(3), 204–220.

Quinsey, V. L., Chaplin, T. C., & Carrigan, W. F. (1979). Sexual preferences among incestuous and non-incestuous child molestors. *Behavior Therapy, 10*, 562–565.

Quinsey, V. L., Harris, G. R., Rice, M. E., & LaLumiere, M. L. (1995). Predicting sexual offenses. In J. C. Campbell (Ed.), *Assessing dangerousness: Violence by sexual offenders, batterers, and child abusers.* Thousand Oaks, CA: Sage.

Rabins, P. V., Mace, N. L., & Lucas, M. J. (1982). The impact of dementia on the family. *Journal of the American Medical Association, 248*(3), 333–335.

Rada, R. T. (1976). Alcoholism and the child molester. *Annals of New York Academy of Sciences, 273*, 492–496.

Rada, R. T. (1975). Alcoholism and forcible rape. *American Journal of Psychiatry, 132*, 444–446.

Rada, R. T. (1976). Alcoholism and the child molester. *Annals of the New York Academy of Sciences, 273*, 492–496.

Ramirez III, M. (1967). Identification with Mexican family values and authoritarianism in Mexican-American. *Journal of Social Psychology, 73*, 3–11.

Reynolds, R. (1995). *Bring me the ocean.* Acton, MA: VanderWyk & Burnham.

Reynolds, W. M. (1989). *Reynolds Child Depression Scale.* Odessa, FL: Psychological Assessment Resources.

Rice, M., Quinsey, V. L., & Harris, G. T. (1991). Sexual recidivism among child molesters released from a maximum security psychiatric institution. *Journal of Consulting and Clinical Psychology, 59*(3), 381–386.

Richardson, D., & Campbell, J. L. (1982). Alcohol and rape: The effect of alcohol on attributions of blame for rape. *Personality and Social Psychology Bulletin, 8*, 468–476.

Risin, L. I., & Koss, M. P. (1987). The sexual abuse of boys: Prevalence and descriptive characteristics of childhood victimizations. *Journal of Interpersonal Violence, 2*, 309–323.

Roehrich, L., & Kinder, B. N. (1991). Alcohol expectancies and male sexuality: Review and implications for sex therapy. *Journal of Sex and Marital Therapy, 17*(1), 45–54.

Rohrbaugh, M., Tennen, H., Press, S., & White, L. (1981). Compliance, defiance, and therapeutic paradox: Guidelines for strategic use of therapeutic interventions. *American Journal of Orthopsychiatry, 51*, 581–599.

Rohsenow, D. J. & Bachorowski, J. (1984). Effects of alcohol and expectancies on verbal aggression in men and women. *Journal of Abnormal Psychology, 93*, 418–432.

Rosenberg, J., Rand, M., & Asay, D. (1989). *Body, self and soul: Sustaining integration.* Atlanta: Humanics Limited.

Ross, L., Greene, D., & House, P. (1977). The "false consensus effect": An egocentric bias in social perception and attribution processes. *Journal of Experimental Social Psychology, 13*, 279–301.

Ross, L., Lepper, M. R., & Hubbard, M. (1975). Perseverance in self-perception and social perception: Biased attributional processes in the debriefing paradigm. *Journal of Personality and Social Psychology, 32*, 880–892.

Rowan, E. L., Rowan, J. B., & Langelier, P. (1990). Women who molest children. *Bulletin of the American Academy of Psychiatry and Law, 18*, 79–83.

Rubenstein, J. R. (1992). *Neuropsychological and personality differences between controls and pedophiles.* Doctoral dissertation, University of New Mexico, Albuquerque.

Rubin, K. H., LeMare, L. J., & Lollis, S. (1990). Social withdrawal in childhood: Developmental pathways to peer rejection. In S. R. Asher & J. D. Coie (Eds.), *Rejection in childhood* (pp. 17–59). Cambridge, England: Cambridge University Press.

Ruckert, J. (1987). The four-footed therapist. Berkeley, CA: Ten Speed Press.

Rusbult, C. E., & Iwaniszek, J. (1986). *Problem-solving in male and female homosexual and heterosexual relationships.* Unpublished manuscript, University of Kentucky, Lexington.

Ryan, G., & Lane, S. (1991). *Juvenile sexual offending: Causes, consequences and correction.* Lexington, MA: Lexington Books.

Ryan, G., Lane, S., Davis, J., & Isaac, C. (1987). Juvenile sex offenders: Development and correction. *Child Abuse and Neglect, 11*, 385–395.

Salter, A. C. (1988). *Treating child sex offenders and victims: A practical guide.* Newbury Park, CA: Sage.

Sapp, A. D., & Vaughn, M. S. (1990). Juvenile sex offender treatment at state-operated correctional institutions. *International Journal of Offender Therapy and Comparative Criminology, 21*, 131–143.

Satir, V. (1964). *Conjoint family therapy.* Palo Alto, CA: Science and Behavior Books.

Saunders, E. B., & Awad, G. A. (1988). Assessment, management, and treatment for male adolescent sexual offenders. *American Journal of Orthopsychiatry, 58*, 571–579.

Saunders, E., Awad, G. A., & White, G. (1986). Male adolescent sexual offenders: The offender and the offence. *Canadian Journal of Psychiatry, 31*, 542–549.

Saunders, G. R., & Davies, M. B. (1976). The validity of the Jesness Inventory with British offenders. *British Journal of Social and Clinical Psychology, 15*, 33–39.

Sayette, M. A., Contrada, R. J., & Wilson, G. T. (1990). Alcohol and correspondence between self-report and physiological measures of anxiety. *Behavior Research and Therapy, 28*, 351–354.

Scalia, J. (1994). Psychoanalytic insights and prevention of pseudosuccess in the cognitive-behavioral treatment of batterers. *Journal of Interpersonal Violence, 9*(4), 548–555.

Scharfe, E., & Bartholomew, K. (1994). Reliability and stability of adult attachment patterns. *Personal Relationships, 1*, 23–43.

Schiavi, R. C., Mandeli, J., & Schreiner-Engel, P. (1994). Sexual satisfaction in healthy aging men. *Journal of Sex and Marital Therapy, 20*(1), 3–13.

Schiavi, R. C., Schreiner-Engel, P., Mandeli, J., Schanzer, H., & Cohen, E. (1990). Healthy aging and male sexual function. *American Journal of Psychiatry, 147*(6), 766–771.

Schichor, D. (1988). An exploratory study of elderly probationers. *International Journal of Offender Therapy and Comparative Criminology, 32*(2), 163–174.

Schlank, A. M., & Shaw, T. (1996). Treating sexual offenders who deny their guilt: A pilot study. *Sexual Abuse: A Journal of Research and Treatment, 8*(1), 17–23.

Schumacker, R. E., Anderson, D. B., & Anderson, S. L. (1990). Vocational and academic indicators of parole success. *Journal of Correctional Education, 41*(1), 8–13.

Schwartz, B. K. (1987). Pen pals pairs animals and inmates. *The Latham Letter, 3*(3), 6.

Schwartz, B. K. (1988). *A practitioner's guide to treating the incarcerated male sex offender: Breaking the cycle of sexual abuse.* Washington, DC: Department of Justice, National Institute of Corrections.

Schwartz, B. K. (1995). Group therapy. In B. K. Schwartz & H. R. Cellini (Eds.), *The sex offender: Corrections, treatment, and legal practice.* Kingston, NJ: Civic Research Institute.

Schwartz, B. K. (1995). Theories of sex offenders. In B. K. Schwartz & H. R. Cellini (Eds.), *The sex offender: Corrections, treatment, and legal practice* (pp. 2-1 to 2-32). Kingston, NJ: Civic Research Institute.

Schwartz, M. (1995). In my opinion: Victim to victimizer. *Sexual Addiction and Compulsivity, 2*(2), 81–88.

Schwartz, M. F., Gilperin, L. D., & Masters, W. H. (1995). Dissociation and treatment of compulsive reenactment of trauma: Sexual compulsivity. In M. Hunter (Ed.), *Adult survivors of sexual abuse: Treatment innovations* (pp. 42–55). Thousand Oaks, CA: Sage.

Schwartz, M. F., & Masters, W. H. (1993). Investigation of trauma-based, cognitive behavioral, systematic and addiction approaches for treatment of hypersexual pair-bonding disorder. In P. J. Carnes (Ed.), *Sexual addiction and compulsivity* (vol. 1). New York: Brunner/Mazel.

Scott, L. (1994). *An overview of sex offenders who failed on probation.* Paper presented at the Association for the Behavioral Treatment of Sexual Abusers. San Francisco.

Scott, W. (1993). Group psychotherapy for male sex offenders: Strategic interventions. *Journal of Family Psychotherapy, 5*, 1–20.

Sefarbi, R. (1990). Admitters and deniers among adolescent sex offenders and their families: A preliminary study. American *Journal of Orthopsychiatry, 60*(3), 460–465.

Segal, Z. V., & Stermac, L. E. (1990). The role of cognition in sexual assault. In Marshall, W. L., Laws, D. R., & Barbaree, H. E. (Eds.), *Handbook of sexual assault* (pp. 161–174). New York: Plenum Press.

Seghorn, T. K. Prentky, R. A., & Boucher, R. J. (1987). Child abuse in the lives of sexually aggressive offenders, *Journal of the American Academy of Child and Adolescent Psychiatry, 26*, 262–267.

Seidman, B., Marshall, W. L., Hudson, S. M., & Robertson, P. J. (1994). An examination of intimacy and loneliness in sex offenders. *Journal of Interpersonal Violence, 9*, 518–534.

Seltzer, M. L. (1971). The Michigan Alcoholism Screening Test: The quest for a new diagnostic instrument. *American Journal of Psychiatry, 127*, 89–94.

Selvini-Palazzoli, M., Boscolo, L., Cecchin, G., & Prata, G. (1978). *Paradox and counterparadox.* New York: Jason Aronson.

Semands, S. (1994). *Bridging the silence: Nonverbal modalities in the treatment of adult survivors of child sexual abuse.* New York: Norton.

Serpell, J. A. (1991). Beneficial effects of pet ownership on some aspects of human health and behavior. *Journal of the Royal Society of Medicine, 840*, 717–720.

Serpell, J., & Jackson, E. (1994). *Effects of previous life stresses on the outcome of studies of the health benefits of pet ownership.* Paper presented at the 13th Annual Conference of the Delta Society, New York City.

Sgroi, S. (1982). *Handbook of clinical intervention in child sexual abuse*. Lexington, MA: Lexington Books.

Shaken, D. (1939). 100 sex offenders. American *Journal of Orthopsychiatry, 9*, 565–569.

Shaver, K. G. (1970). Defensive attribution: Effects of severity and relevance on the responsibility assigned for an accident. *Journal of Personality and Social Psychology, 14*, 101–113.

Shaver, P. R., Collins, N., & Clark, C. L. (1996). Attachment styles and internal working models of self and relationship partners. In G. O. Fletcher & J. Fitness (Eds.), *Knowledge structures in close relationships: A social psychological approach* (pp. 25–61). Hillsdale, NJ: Erlbaum.

Shaver, P. R., & Hazen, C. (1988). A biased overview of the study of love. *Journal of Social and Personal Relationships, 5*, 473–501.

Shaw, J. A., Campo-Bowen, A. E., Applegate, B., Perez, D., Antoine, L. B., Hart, E. L., Lahey, B. B., Testa, R. J., & Devaney, A. (1993). Young boys who commit serious sexual offenses: Demographics, psychometrics, and phenomenology. *Bulletin of the American Academy of Psychiatry and Law, 21*, 399–408.

Shaw, T., & Schlank, A. M. (1992, October). *Treating sexual offenders who deny their guilt*. Paper presented at the annual research and treatment conference of the Association for the Treatment of Sexual Abusers, Portland, OR.

Shaw, T., & Schlank, A. M. (1993, November). *Update: Treating sex offenders who deny their guilt*. Paper presented at the annual research and treatment conference of the Association for the Treatment of Sexual Abusers, Boston.

Shaw, T., & Schlank, A. M. (1995). *An update on a denier's pilot study*. Paper presented at the 14th annual meeting of the Association for the Treatment of Sexual Abusers, New Orleans.

Shoor, M., Speed, H. H., & Bartlett, C. (1986). Syndrome of the adolescent child molester. *American Journal of Psychiatry, 122*, 783–798.

Short, J. F. Jr. (1985). Differential association as a hypothesis: Problems of empirical testing. *Social Problems, 8*, 14-25.

Siegel, M. (1985, June). If the dogs think I'm okay,I must not be too bad. *The Gazette*, pp. 48-55.

Singlehurst, D. (1995). From the president. *Interactions, 13*(2), 4.

Skinner, H. A. (1979). Multivariate evaluation of MAST. *Journal of Studies on Alcohol, 40*, 831–844.

Skinner, L. J., Carroll, K. A., & Berry, K. K. (1995). A typology for sexually aggressive males in dating relationships. *Journal of Offender Rehabilitation, 22*, 29–45.

Slosson, R. L. (1991). *Slosson Intelligence Test SIT-R* (rev. ed.). East Aurora, NY: Slosson Educational Publications.

Smets, A. C., & Cebula, C. M. (1987). A group treatment program for adolescent sex offenders: Five steps toward resolution. *Child Abuse and Neglect, 11*, 247–254.

Smith, E. W. L. (1985). *The body in psychotherapy*. Jefferson, NC: McFarland.

Smith, H., & Israel, E. (1987). Sibling incest: A study of dynamics of 25 cases. *Child Abuse and Neglect, 11*, 101–108.

Smith, W. R., & Monastersky, C. (1986). Assessing juvenile sexual offenders' risk for reoffending. *Criminal Justice and Behavior, 13*, 115–140.

Smith, W. R., Monastersky, C., & Deisher, R. M. (1987). MMPI-based personality types among juvenile sexual offenders. *Journal of Clinical Psychology, 43*, 422–430.

Snell, T. L. (1991). *Correctional populations in the United States. Bureau of Justice Statistics, 1993* (NCJ-142729). Washington, DC: Bureau of Justice.

Southwick, L., Steele, C., Marlatt, A., & Lindell, M. (1981). Alcohol-related expectancies: Defined by phase of intoxication and drinking experience. *Journal of Consulting and Clinical Psychology, 49*, 713–721.

Spence, S. H. (1992). Psychosexual dysfunction in the elderly. *Behavior Change, 9*(2), 55–64.

A-28 THE SEX OFFENDER

Spence, J. T., & Helmreich, R. L. (1978). *Masculinity and femininity: Their psychological dimensions, correlates and antecedents.* Austin. University of Texas Press.

Spiegel, D. (1988, June). Hypnosis in the treatment of victims of sexual abuse. *Psychiatric Clinics of North America, 12*(2), 285–305.

Spitzer, R. L., Williams, J. B. W., & Gibbon, M. (1985, July 1). *Instruction manual for the Structural Clinical Interview for DSM-III-R (SCID)* (rev.). New York: Research Department, New York State Psychiatric Institute.

Stangor, C., & Ford, T. E. (1992). Accuracy and expectancy-confirming processing orientations and the development of stereotypes and prejudice. *European Review of Social Psychology, 3*, 57–89.

Stattin, H., & Magnusson, D. (1989). The role of early aggressive behavior in the frequency, seriousness, and types of later crime. *Journal of Consulting and Clinical Psychology, 57*(6), 710–718.

Steele, C. M., & Josephs, R. A. (1988). Drinking your troubles away II: An attention-allocation model of alcohol's effect on psychological stress. *Journal of Abnormal Psychology, 97*, 196–205.

Steele, C. M., & Josephs, R. A. (1990). Alcohol myopia: Its prized and dangerous effects. *American Psychologist, 45*, 921–933.

Steele, K. (1993). Abreactive work with sexual abuse survivors: Concepts and treatments. In M. Hunter (Ed.), *The sexually abused male: Applications of treatment strategies* (vol. 2, pp. 1–55). Thousand Oaks, CA: Sage

Steele, N. M. (1991). *Return rates collected by the Minnesota Department of Corrections.* Department of Information and Analysis.

Steele, N. (1995). Cost effectiveness of treatment. In B. K. Schwartz & H. R. Cellini (Eds.), *The sex offender: Corrections, treatment, and legal practice.* Kingston, NJ: Civic Research Institute.

Steele, C. M., & Southwick, L. (1985). Alcohol and social behavior I: The psychology of drunken excess. *Journal of Personality and Social Psychology, 48*, 18–34.

Steele, C. M., Southwick, L., & Pagano, R. (1986). Drinking your troubles away: The role of activity in mediating alcohol's reduction of psychological stress. *Journal of Abnormal Psychology, 95*, 173–180.

Steen, C. (1992). *Treating the denying juvenile sex offender.* Paper presented at Restorative Justice for Juvenile Sex Offenders, Lake Tahoe, NV.

Steen, C. (1992, October). *Treating sexual offenders who deny their guilt.* Paper presented at the annual research and treatment conference of the Association for the Treatment of Sexual Abusers, Portland, OR.

Steen, C. (1995). Treating denying sex offenders. *California Coalition on Sexual Offending Newsletter*, pp. 2, 2–3.

Stenson, P., & Anderson, C. (1987). Treating juvenile sex offenders and preventing the cycle of abuse. *Journal of Child Care, 3*, 91–102.

Stermac, L. E., & Quinsey, V. L. (1986). Social competence among rapists. *Behavioral Assessment, 8*, 171–185.

Stokes, R. E. (1964). A research approach to sexual offenses involving children. Canadian *Journal of Corrections, 6*, 87–94.

Stoller, R. J. (1975). *Perversion: The erotic form of hatred.* New York: Random House.

Strauss, M. A. (1991). Discipline and deviance: physical punishment of children and violence and other crime in adulthood. *Social Problems, 38*, 133–154.

Strayer, J. (1993). Children's concordant emotions and cognitions in response to observed emotions. *Child Development, 64*, 188–201.

Sutherland, E. H., & Cressey, D. R. (1978). *Criminology.* Philadelphia: J.B. Lippincott.

Sutker, P. B., Allain, A. N., Brantley, P. J., & Randall, C. L. (1982). Acute alcohol intoxication, negative affect, and autonomic arousal in women and men. *Addictive Behaviors, 7*, 17–25.

Swinomish Tribal Community. (1993). *A gathering of wisdoms.* LaConner, WA: Swinomish Tribal Mental Health Project.

Swonger, A. K., & Constantine, L. L. (1983). *Drugs and therapy: A handbook of psychotropic drugs.* Boston: Little, Brown.

Tangney, J. P. (1991). Moral affect: The good, the bad, and the ugly. *Journal of Personality and Social Psychology, 61,* 598–607.

Tangney, J. P., Wagner, P., Fletcher, C., & Gramzow, R. (1992). Shamed into anger? The relation of shame and guilt to anger and self-reported aggression. *Journal of Personality and Social Psychology, 62,* 669–675.

Tangney, J. P., Wagner, P., & Gramzow, R. (1989). *The Test of Self- Conscious Affect.* Fairfax, VA: George Mason University Press.

Tarragona, M., & Orlinsky, D. E. (1988). *Beyond the therapeutic hour: An exploration of the relationship between patients' experiences of therapy within and between sessions.* Paper presented at the annual meeting of the Society of Psychotherapy Research, Santa Fe, NM.

Tarter, R. E., Hegedus, A. M., Alterman, A. I., & Katz-Garris, L. (1983). Cognitive capacities of juvenile, violent, nonviolent, and sexual offenders. *Journal of Nervous and Mental Disease, 171,* 564–567.

Taylor, P. J., & Parrott, J. M. (1988). Elderly offenders: A study of age-related factors among custodially remanded prisoners. *British Journal of Psychiatry, 152,* 340–346.

Taylor, S. E., & Brown, J. D. (1988). Illusion and well-being: A social psychological perspective on mental health. *Psychological Bulletin, 103,* 193–210.

Thomas, A., & Lieb, R. (1995). *Sex offender registration: A review of state laws.* Olympia, WA: Washington State Institute for Public Policy.

Thornton, B. (1984). Defensive attribution of responsibility: Evidence for an arousal-based motivational bias. *Journal of Personality and Social Psychology, 46,* 721–734.

Timms, R., & Connors, P. (1992). *Embodying healing: Integrating body work and psychotherapy in recovery from childhood sexual abuse.* Orwell, VT: Safer Society Press.

Tingle, D., Barnard, G. W., Robbin, L., Newman., G., & Hutchinson, D. (1986). Childhood and adolescent characteristics of pedophiles and rapists. *International Journal of Law and Psychiatry, 9,* 103–116.

Tomm, K. (1986). Interventive interviewing: Part I, strategizing as a fourth guideline for the therapist. *Family Process, 26,* 3–13.

Travin, S., & Cullin, K., & Protter, B. (1990). Female sex offenders: Severe victims and victimizers. *Journal of Forensic Sciences, 35,* 140–150.

Tremblay, R. E., Pihl, R. O., Vitaro, F., & Dobkin, P. L. (1994). Predicting early onset of male antisocial behavior from preschool behavior. *Archives of General Psychiatry, 51*(9), 732–739.

Trepper, T., & Barrett, M.J., (1989). *Systemic treatment of incest: A therapeutic handbook.* New York: Brunner/Mazel.

Turner, G. S., & Champion, D. J. (1989). The elderly offender and sentencing leniency. *Journal of Offender Counseling Services and Rehabilitation, 13*(2), 125–140

Udry, J. R. (1988). Biological predispositions and social control in adolescent sexual behavior. *American Sociological Review, 53,* 709–722.

Valdez, L. F., Baron, A., & Ponce F. Q. (1987). Counseling Hispanic men. In M. Scher, M. Stevens, G. Good, & G. A. Eichenfield (Eds.), *Handbook of counseling and psychotherapy.* Newbury Park, CA: Sage.

Van der Kolk, B. A. (1989). Pierre Janet on post-traumatic stress. *Journal of Traumatic Stress, 2*(4), 365–378.

Van der Kolk, B. A. (1994, Spring). Childhood abuse and loss of self-regulation. *Bulletin of the Menninger Clinic, 58*(2), 145–168.

Van der Kolk, B. A. (1995). *Trauma, memory and the integration of experience.* Paper presented to the Fourth Annual Conference on Advances in Treating Survivors of Abuse and Trauma: Multiply Dimensions in Healing. Philadelphia.

Van Ness, S. R. (1984). Rape and instrumental violence: A study of youth offenders. *Journal of Offender Counseling Services and Rehabilitation, 9,* 161–170.

Vega, M., & Silverman, M. (1988). Stress and the elderly convict. *International Journal of Offender Therapy and Comparative Criminology, 32*(2), 153–162.

Vigil, J. D. (1980). *From Indian to Chicanos: A sociocultural history.* St. Louis, MO: Mosby.

Villemez, W. J., & Touhey, J. C. (1977). A measure of individual differences in sex stereotyping and sex discrimination: The macho scale. *Psychological Reports, 41,* 411-415.

Vito, G. F. (1986). *Felony probation and recidivism in Kentucky.* Frankfort, KY: Kentucky Criminal Justice Statistical Analysis Center. (NCJRS Document No. 112566)

Wakefield, H., & Underwager, R. (1991). Female child sexual abusers: A critical review of the literature. *American Journal of Forensic Psychology, 9,* 43–69.

Walker, L. (1995). *Abused women and survivor therapy.* Washington, DC: American Psychological Association.

Walsh, A. (1985). An evaluation of the effects of adult basic education on rearrest rates among probationers. *Journal of Offender Counseling, Services, and Rehabilitation, 9*(4), 53–61.

Walters, G. D., & Chlumsky, M. L. (1993). The Lifestyle Criminality Screening Form and antisocial personality disorder: Predicting release outcome in a state prison sample. *Behavioral Sciences and the Law, 11,* 111–115.

Ward, T., Hudson, S. M., & France, K. G. (1993). Self-reported reasons for offending behavior in child molesters. *Annals of Sex Research, 6,* 139–148.

Ward, T., Hudson, S. M., & Marshall, W. (1995). Cognitive distortions and affective deficits in sex offenders: A cognitive deconstructionist interpretation. Sexual Abuse: A *Journal of Research and Treatment, 7,* 67–83.

Ward, T., Hudson, S. M., & Marshall, W. L. (in press). Attachment style in sex offenders: A preliminary study. *Journal of Sex Research.*

Ward, T., Hudson, S. M., Marshall, W. L., & Siegert, R. (1995). Attachment style and intimacy deficits in sex offenders: A theoretical framework. *Sexual Abuse: A Journal of Research and Treatment, 7,* 317–335.

Ward, T., Louden, K., Hudson, S. M., & Marshall, W. L. (1995). A descriptive model of the offense chain for child molesters. *Journal of Interpersonal Violence, 10,* 453–473.

Ward, T., McCormack, J., & Hudson, S. M. (in press). Sexual offenders perceptions' of their intimate relationships. *Sexual Abuse: A Journal of Research and Treatment.*

Waring, E. M. (1984). The measurement of marital intimacy. *Journal of Marital and Family Therapy, 10,* 185–192.

Waring, E. M., & Chelene, G. J. (1983). Marital intimacy and self disclosure. *Journal of Clinical Psychology, 39,* 183–190.

Watson, J. M. (1989). Legal and social alternatives in treating older child sexual offenders. *Journal of Offender Counseling Services and Rehabilitation, 13*(2), 141–147.

Watzlawick, P., Weaklund, J., & Fisch, R. (1974). *Change: Principles of problem formation and problem resolution.* New York: Norton.

Weeks, G., & L'Abate, L., (1982). *Paradoxical psychotherapy: Theory and*

Appendix B

Table of Tables

Appendix C

Table of Cases

Index

[References are to pages.]

[References are to pages.]

[References are to pages.]

[References are to pages.]

role plays, 20-11
structure, incest vulnerability and, 18-4–18-7
therapeutic discussions about, 5-11
Family Attitude Scale (FAS), 13-4
Family therapy, 18-2
  interventions
    for consolidation, 18-11–18-12
    for incest family, 18-4–18-7
  pretreatment for, 18-2–18-3
Family values, 13-4
FAS. *See* Family Attitude Scale
Father, relationship with
  child molesters and, 2-8
  rapists and, 2-9
  of sex offenders, 2-8–2-9
Fear of rejection, 2-6–2-7
Female adolescent sex offenders
  age of, 10-5
  characteristics of, 10-2
  comparison study, 10-7–10-9
  descriptive studies of, 10-3–10-5
  findings, current, 10-13–10-14
  information processing of trauma model of, 10-12–10-13
  inpatients, findings from, 10-5–10-7
  questions, for future research, 10-7
  research
    findings of, 10-9
    review of, 10-2–10-3
  risk factors, 10-9
Field Trials for Disruptive Behavior Disorders, 9-6
Fifth Amendment, 23-2, 23-3–23-4, 23-10
Filial obedience, 13-7–13-8
Fingerprinting, 23-10, 24-16
First Amendment, 23-1
Floodgates of inhibition
  characterological factors, 4-4
  distribution of, 4-8–4-12
  factors in, 4-4
  impairment of, 4-4
  neurological factors, 4-4
  in sexual assault, 4-3
Flooding, 20-19
Force
  physical, 17-1–17-2
  psychological, 17-2–17-4
Fourteenth Amendment, 22-9, 24-11–24-12
Fourth Amendment, 23-9, 24-3, 24-15–24-16
Funding, for therapeutic community, 19-7

G
Game playing, 17-3
Games, in therapeutic communities, 20-11–20-12
Games and Dissipations sessions, in psychotherapy, 20-12
Gender roles, in family vulnerability, 18-3–18-4
General tension effect, 20-16
Geriatric sex offenders, 12-1–12-2
  definition of, 12-2
  emotional health of, 12-4–12-5
  incarcerated, 12-3

legal issues, 12-2–12-3
  as mentors, 12-8
  prevalence, 12-2
  social support issues for, 12-3–12-4
  treatment interventions for, 12-6–12-9
Gestalt empty-chair technique, 20-8
Gift giving rituals, 18-11
Grooming patterns, evaluation of, 17-8
Group therapy, 19-3
  for incest family, 18-9–18-10
  membership in, 7-11
Guilt, vs. shame, 1-7–1-8

H
Habitual offender laws, constitutionality of, 22-2
Healing rituals, 7-11–7-12
HEALO. *See* Human-Environment-Animal-Love-Organization
Hispanic culture, 13-8–13-9
  family values and, 13-4
  macho vs. machismo, 13-1, 13-2–13-3
  sex offenders, 13-8–13-9
    machismo and, 13-2–13-4
    stepdaughters and, 13-7
    treatment implications for, 13-6–13-8
    treatment selection for, 13-1–13-2
Hitchhikers, 17-9
Hope, for sex offender, 5-8–5-9
Horizontal violence, 14-4
Hostile masculinity, 9-7
Human-Environment-Animal-Love-Organization (HEALO), 21-4
Humor, provision in animal-facilitated therapy, 21-8
Hypnosis, 20-19
Hypnotherapy, 7-4

I
Identity definition, rituals of, 7-12
Ideomotor signaling, 7-4
IFS. *See* Internal family system
I-level theory, 11-3
Impact, denial of, 18-8
Implosion therapy, 20-7, 20-19
Impotence
  alcohol and, 3-4
  drug-related, 12-6
Impulse control, for American Indian sex offenders, 14-8
Impulsivity, in treatment outcome prediction, 11-8
Incarceration
  convict code and, 20-7
  programming for, 23-1–23-2
Incest family
  clinical assessment of, 18-2–18-3
  denial by, 18-7–18-9
  extrication of offender from, 18-2
  future problems, prediction of, 18-11
  interventions for, 18-4–18-7
  therapy
    challenging patterns in, 18-9–18-10

[References are to pages.]

[References are to pages.]

[References are to pages.]

[References are to pages.]

[References are to pages.]

[References are to pages.]